한국의 토익 수험자 여러분께,

토익 시험은 세계적인 직무 영어능력 평가 시험으로, 지난 40여 년간 비즈니스 현장에서 필요한 영어능력 평가의 기준을 제시해 왔습니다. 토익 시험 및 토익스피킹, 토익라이팅 시험은 세계에서 가장 널리 통용되는 영어능력 검증 시험으로, 160여 개국 14,000여 기관이 토익 성적을 의사결정에 활용하고 있습니다.

YBM은 한국의 토익 시험을 주관하는 ETS 독점 계약사입니다.

ETS는 한국 수험자들의 효과적인 토익 학습을 돕고자 YBM을 통하여 'ETS 토익 공식 교재'를 독점 출간하고 있습니다. 또한 'ETS 토익 공식 교재' 시리즈에 기출문항을 제공해 한국의 다른 교재들에 수록된 기출을 복제하거나 변형한 문항으로 인하여 발생할 수 있는 수험자들의 혼동을 방지하고 있습니다.

복제 및 변형 문항들은 토익 시험의 출제의도를 벗어날 수 있기 때문에 기출문항을 수록한 'ETS 토익 공식 교재'만큼 시험에 잘 대비할 수 없습니다.

'ETS 토익 공식 교재'를 통하여 수험자 여러분의 영어 소통을 위한 노력에 큰 성취가 있기를 바랍니다.

감사합니다.

Dear TOEIC Test Takers in Korea,

The TOEIC program is the global leader in English-language assessment for the workplace. It has set the standard for assessing English-language skills needed in the workplace for more than 40 years. The TOEIC tests are the most widely used English language assessments around the world, with 14,000+ organizations across more than 160 countries trusting TOEIC scores to make decisions.

YBM is the ETS Country Master Distributor for the TOEIC program in Korea and so is the exclusive distributor for TOEIC Korea.

To support effective learning for TOEIC test-takers in Korea, ETS has authorized YBM to publish the only Official TOEIC prep books in Korea. These books contain actual TOEIC items to help prevent confusion among Korean test-takers that might be caused by other prep book publishers' use of reproduced or paraphrased items.

Reproduced or paraphrased items may fail to reflect the intent of actual TOEIC items and so will not prepare test-takers as well as the actual items contained in the ETS TOEIC Official prep books published by YBM.

We hope that these ETS TOEIC Official prep books enable you, as test-takers, to achieve great success in your efforts to communicate effectively in English.

Thank you.

LC

All New

토익
정기시험
실전 1

1000

토익 정기시험
실전❶ 1000
LC

발행인	허문호
발행처	YBM

편집	이태경, 박효민, 오유진
디자인	강상문, 이미화, 이현숙
마케팅	정연철, 박천산, 고영노, 김동진, 박찬경, 김윤하

초판인쇄	2023년 6월 12일
3쇄발행	2024년 1월 2일

신고일자	1964년 3월 28일
신고번호	제 300-1964-3호
주소	서울시 종로구 종로 104
전화	(02) 2000-0515 [구입문의] / (02) 2000-0383 [내용문의]
팩스	(02) 2285-1523
홈페이지	www.ybmbooks.com

ISBN   978-89-17-23931-7

LC

All New
토익®
정기시험
실전 1

1000

PREFACE

Dear test taker,

Welcome to the new ETS® TOEIC® 정기시험 실전 1000 Vol.1. Now more than ever, English proficiency is a key to success in our increasingly globalized world. Whether you want to clearly communicate with friends and work colleagues, efficiently interpret business documents, or easily navigate international travel, this test preparation book has been designed to help you meet your English-language goals through the TOEIC test.

The ETS® TOEIC® 정기시험 실전 1000 Vol.1 is unique among test preparation materials. This book contains TOEIC practice tests created by the same team of English-language experts at ETS who develop the actual TOEIC Tests. These practice tests go through the same rigorous review process as the ones you will encounter on test day. There is no better resource to use as you prepare to take the TOEIC test.

The ETS® TOEIC® 정기시험 실전 1000 Vol.1 includes the following key features:

- Nine complete practice test forms and one actual test
- New TOEIC questions of the same quality and difficulty level as those in actual TOEIC test forms
- Specific explanations to help learners prepare for the test
- The same voice actors that you will hear in an ETS test administration

By using this test preparation book, you can be confident that you will be studying authentic materials that will help you to build both your English skills and your familiarity with the test structure and question types. It is one of the best resources available to help you maximize your TOEIC test score and demonstrate to the world what you can do.

Thank you for choosing to use the ETS® TOEIC® 정기시험 실전 1000 Vol.1 for your test-preparation needs. We wish you all the best in your language-learning journey.

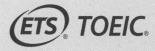

최신 실전문제
전격 공개!

'출제기관이 독점 제공한' 실전문제가 담긴 유일한 교재!

이 책에는 정기시험 실전문제 9세트와 기출문제 1세트가 수록되어 있다.
최신 ETS 실전문제로 실전 감각을 키워 시험에 확실하게 대비하자!

'정기시험 성우 음성'으로 실전 대비!

이 책에 수록된 10세트의 LC 음원은 모두 실제 시험에서 나온
정기시험 성우의 음원이다.
시험장에서 듣게 될 음성으로 공부하면 까다로운 영국·호주식 발음도 걱정 없다!

'ETS가 제공하는' 표준 점수 환산표!

출제기관 ETS가 독점 제공하는 표준 점수 환산표를 수록했다.
채점 후 환산표를 통해 자신의 실력이 어느 정도인지 가늠해 보자!

TOEIC 소개

TOEIC Test of English for International Communication(국제적 의사소통을 위한 영어 시험)의 약자로, 영어가 모국어가 아닌 사람들이 일상생활 또는 비즈니스 현장에서 꼭 필요한 실용적 영어 구사 능력을 갖추었는가를 평가하는 시험이다.

시험 구성

구성	PART	유형		문항 수	시간	배점
Listening	Part 1	사진 묘사		6	45분	495점
	Part 2	질의응답		25		
	Part 3	짧은 대화		39		
	Part 4	짧은 담화		30		
Reading	Part 5	단문 빈칸 채우기		30	75분	495점
	Part 6	장문 빈칸 채우기		16		
	Part 7	독해	단일 지문	29		
			이중 지문	10		
			삼중 지문	15		
Total	7 Parts			200문항	120분	990점

평가 항목

LC	RC
단문을 듣고 이해하는 능력	읽은 글을 통해 추론해 생각할 수 있는 능력
짧은 대화체 문장을 듣고 이해하는 능력	장문에서 특정한 정보를 찾을 수 있는 능력
비교적 긴 대화체에서 주고받은 내용을 파악할 수 있는 능력	글의 목적, 주제, 의도 등을 파악하는 능력
장문에서 핵심이 되는 정보를 파악할 수 있는 능력	뜻이 유사한 단어들의 정확한 용례를 파악하는 능력
구나 문장에서 화자의 목적이나 함축된 의미를 이해하는 능력	문장 구조를 제대로 파악하는지, 문장에서 필요한 품사, 어구 등을 찾는 능력

※ 성적표에는 전체 수험자의 평균과 해당 수험자가 받은 성적이 백분율로 표기되어 있다.

수험 정보

시험 접수 방법

한국 토익 위원회 사이트(www.toeic.co.kr)에서 시험일 약 2개월 전부터
온라인으로 접수 가능

시험장 준비물

신분증	규정 신분증만 가능 (주민등록증, 운전면허증, 기간 만료 전의 여권, 공무원증)
필기구	연필, 지우개 (볼펜이나 사인펜은 사용 금지)

시험 진행 시간

09:20	입실 (9:50 이후 입실 불가)
09:30 ~ 09:45	답안지 작성에 관한 오리엔테이션
09:45 ~ 09:50	휴식
09:50 ~ 10:05	신분증 확인
10:05 ~ 10:10	문제지 배부 및 파본 확인
10:10 ~ 10:55	듣기 평가 (LISTENING TEST)
10:55 ~ 12:10	독해 평가 (READING TEST)

**TOEIC
성적 확인**

시험일로부터 약 10-11일 후, 인터넷과 ARS(060-800-0515)로 성적을 확인할 수 있다.
TOEIC 성적표는 우편이나 온라인으로 발급받을 수 있다(시험 접수 시 양자택일).
우편으로 발급받을 경우는 성적 발표 후 대략 일주일이 소요되며, 온라인 발급을 선택하면
유효기간 내에 홈페이지에서 본인이 직접 1회에 한해 무료 출력할 수 있다. TOEIC 성적은
시험일로부터 2년간 유효하다.

토익 점수

TOEIC 점수는 듣기 영역(LC)과 읽기 영역(RC)을 합계한 점수로 5점 단위로 구성되며 총점은
990점이다. TOEIC 성적은 각 문제 유형의 난이도에 따른 점수 환산표에 의해 결정된다.

토익 경향 분석

PART 1 사진 묘사 Photographs

총 6문제

1인 등장 사진

주어는 He/She, A man/woman 등이며 주로 앞부분에 나온다.

2인 이상 등장 사진

주어는 They, Some men/women/people, One of the men/women 등이며 주로 중간 부분에 나온다.

사물/배경 사진

주어는 A car, Some chairs 등이며 주로 뒷부분에 나온다.

사람 또는 사물 중심 사진

주어가 일부는 사람, 일부는 사물이며 주로 뒷부분에 나온다.

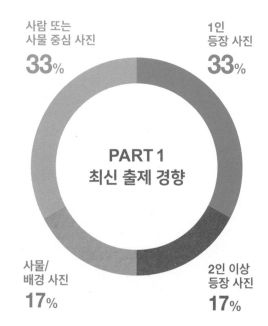

사람 또는 사물 중심 사진 **33%**

1인 등장 사진 **33%**

PART 1 최신 출제 경향

사물/배경 사진 **17%**

2인 이상 등장 사진 **17%**

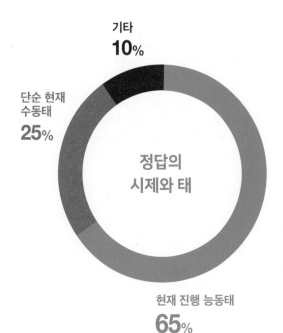

기타 **10%**

단순 현재 수동태 **25%**

정답의 시제와 태

현재 진행 능동태 **65%**

현재 진행 능동태

<is/are + 현재분사> 형태이며 주로 사람이 주어이다.

단순 현재 수동태

<is/are + 과거분사> 형태이며 주로 사물이 주어이다.

기타

<is/are + being + 과거분사> 형태의 현재 진행 수동태, <has/have + been + 과거분사> 형태의 현재 완료 수동태, '타동사 + 목적어' 형태의 단순 현재 능동태, There is/are와 같은 단순 현재도 나온다.

평서문
질문이 아니라 객관적인 사실이나 화자의 의견 등을 나타내는 문장이다.

의문사 의문문
각 의문사마다 1~2개씩 나온다. 의문사가 단독으로 나오기도 하지만 What time ~?, How long ~?, Which room ~? 등에서처럼 다른 명사나 형용사와 같이 나오기도 한다.

명령문
동사원형이나 Please 등으로 시작한다.

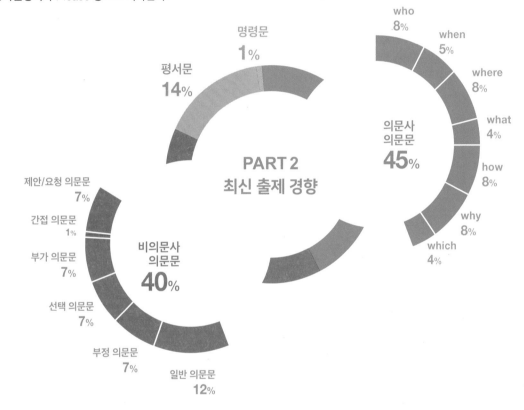

비의문사 의문문
일반(Yes/No) 의문문 적게 나올 때는 한두 개, 많이 나올 때는 서너 개씩 나오는 편이다.
부정 의문문 Don't you ~?, Isn't he ~? 등으로 시작하는 문장이며 일반 긍정 의문문보다는 약간 더 적게 나온다.
선택 의문문 A or B 형태로 나오며 A와 B의 형태가 단어, 구, 절일 수 있다. 구나 절일 경우 문장이 길어져서 어려워진다.
부가 의문문 ~ don't you?, ~ isn't he? 등으로 끝나는 문장이며, 일반 부정 의문문과 비슷하다고 볼 수 있다.
간접 의문문 의문사가 문장 처음 부분이 아니라 문장 중간에 들어 있다.
제안/요청 의문문 정보를 얻기보다는 상대방의 도움이나 동의 등을 얻기 위한 목적이 일반적이다.

PART 3 짧은 대화 Short Conversations

- 3인 대화의 경우 남자 화자 두 명과 여자 화자 한 명 또는 남자 화자 한 명과 여자 화자 두 명이 나온다. 따라서 문제에서는 2인 대화에서와 달리 the man이나 the woman이 아니라 the men이나 the women 또는 특정한 이름이 언급될 수 있다.

- 대화 & 시각 정보는 항상 파트의 뒷부분에 나온다.

- 시각 정보의 유형으로 chart, map, floor plan, schedule, table, weather forecast, directory, list, invoice, receipt, sign, packing slip 등 다양한 자료가 골고루 나온다.

2인 대화 & 시각 정보 23%
2인 대화 63%
3인 대화 14%

PART 3 대화의 유형

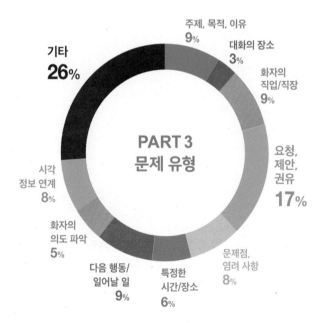

기타 26%
주제, 목적, 이유 9%
대화의 장소 3%
화자의 직업/직장 9%
요청, 제안, 권유 17%
문제점, 염려 사항 8%
특정한 시간/장소 6%
다음 행동/일어날 일 9%
화자의 의도 파악 5%
시각 정보 연계 8%

PART 3 문제 유형

- 주제, 목적, 이유, 대화의 장소, 화자의 직업/직장 등과 관련된 문제는 주로 대화의 첫 번째 문제로 나오며 다음 행동/일어날 일 등과 관련된 문제는 주로 대화의 세 번째 문제로 나온다.

- 화자의 의도 파악 문제는 주로 2인 대화에 나오지만, 가끔 3인 대화에 나오기도 한다. 시각 정보 연계 대화에는 나오지 않고 있다.

- Part 3에서 화자의 의도 파악 문제는 2개가 나오고 시각 정보 연계 문제는 3개가 나온다.

PART 4 짧은 담화 Short Talks

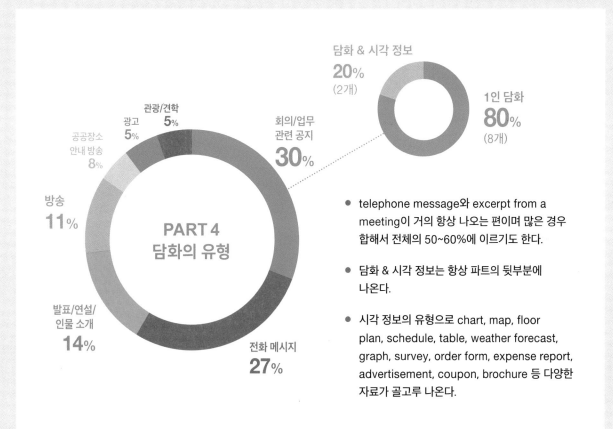

PART 4 담화의 유형

- 담화 & 시각 정보 20% (2개)
- 1인 담화 80% (8개)
- 회의/업무 관련 공지 30%
- 관광/견학 5%
- 광고 5%
- 공공장소 안내 방송 8%
- 방송 11%
- 발표/연설/인물 소개 14%
- 전화 메시지 27%

- telephone message와 excerpt from a meeting이 거의 항상 나오는 편이며 많은 경우 합해서 전체의 50~60%에 이르기도 한다.

- 담화 & 시각 정보는 항상 파트의 뒷부분에 나온다.

- 시각 정보의 유형으로 chart, map, floor plan, schedule, table, weather forecast, graph, survey, order form, expense report, advertisement, coupon, brochure 등 다양한 자료가 골고루 나온다.

- 문제 유형은 기본적으로 Part 3과 거의 비슷하다.

- 주제, 목적, 이유, 담화의 장소, 화자의 직업/직장 등과 관련된 문제는 주로 담화의 첫 번째 문제로 나오며 다음 행동/일어날 일 등과 관련된 문제는 주로 담화의 세 번째 문제로 나온다.

- Part 4에서 화자의 의도 파악 문제는 3개가 나오고 시각 정보 연계 문제는 2개가 나온다.

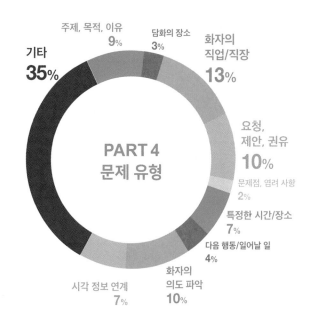

PART 4 문제 유형

- 주제, 목적, 이유 9%
- 담화의 장소 3%
- 화자의 직업/직장 13%
- 기타 35%
- 요청, 제안, 권유 10%
- 문제점, 염려 사항 2%
- 특정한 시간/장소 7%
- 다음 행동/일어날 일 4%
- 화자의 의도 파악 10%
- 시각 정보 연계 7%

문법 문제

시제와 대명사와 관련된 문법 문제가 2개씩,
한정사와 분사와 관련된 문법 문제가 1개씩
나온다. 시제 문제의 경우 능동태/수동태나
수의 일치와 연계되기도 한다. 그 밖에 한정사,
능동태/수동태, 부정사, 동명사 등과 관련된
문법 문제가 나온다.

어휘 문제

동사, 명사, 형용사, 부사와 관련된 어휘
문제가 각각 2~3개씩 골고루 나온다.
전치사 어휘 문제는 3개씩 꾸준히
나오지만, 접속사나 어구와 관련된 어휘
문제는 나오지 않을 때도 있고 3개가
나올 때도 있다.

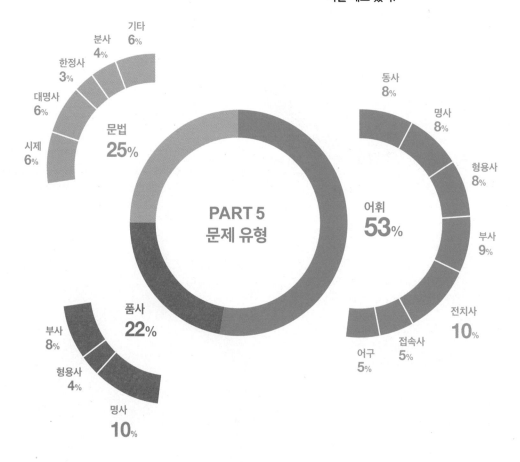

품사 문제

명사와 부사와 관련된 품사 문제가
2~3개씩 나오며, 형용사와 관련된 품사
문제가 상대적으로 적은 편이다.

PART 6 장문 빈칸 채우기 Text Completion

한 지문에 4문제가 나오며 평균적으로 어휘 문제가 2개, 품사나 문법 문제가 1개, 문맥에 맞는 문장 고르기 문제가 1개 들어간다. 문맥에 맞는 문장 고르기 문제를 제외하면 문제 유형은 기본적으로 파트 5와 거의 비슷하다.

어휘 문제

동사, 명사, 부사, 어구와 관련된 어휘 문제는 매번 1~2개씩 나온다. 부사 어휘 문제의 경우 therefore(그러므로)나 however(하지만)처럼 문맥의 흐름을 자연스럽게 연결해 주는 부사가 자주 나온다.

문맥에 맞는 문장 고르기

문맥에 맞는 문장 고르기 문제는 지문당 한 문제씩 나오는데, 나오는 위치의 확률은 4문제 중 두 번째 문제, 세 번째 문제, 네 번째 문제, 첫 번째 문제 순으로 높다.

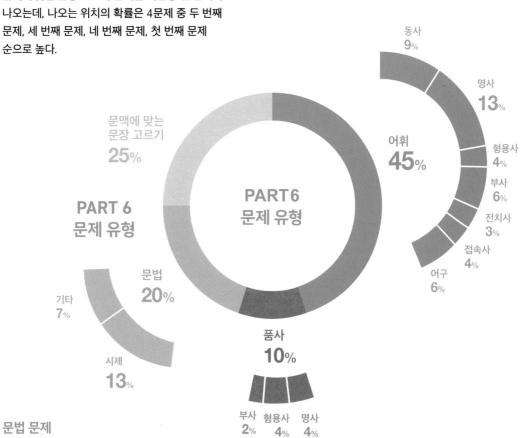

PART 6 문제 유형

- 문맥에 맞는 문장 고르기 **25%**
- 문법 **20%**
- 기타 **7%**
- 시제 **13%**
- 어휘 **45%**
  - 동사 9%
  - 명사 13%
  - 형용사 4%
  - 부사 6%
  - 전치사 3%
  - 접속사 4%
  - 어구 6%
- 품사 **10%**
  - 부사 2%
  - 형용사 4%
  - 명사 4%

문법 문제

문맥의 흐름과 밀접하게 관련이 있는 시제 문제가 2개 정도 나오며, 능동태/수동태나 수의 일치와 연계되기도 한다. 그 밖에 대명사, 능동태/수동태, 부정사, 접속사/전치사 등과 관련된 문법 문제가 나온다.

품사 문제

명사나 형용사 문제가 부사 문제보다 좀 더 자주 나온다.

PART 7 독해 Reading Comprehension

지문 유형	지문당 문제 수	지문 개수	비중 %
단일 지문	2문항	4개	약 15%
	3문항	3개	약 16%
	4문항	3개	약 22%
이중 지문	5문항	2개	약 19%
삼중 지문	5문항	3개	약 28%

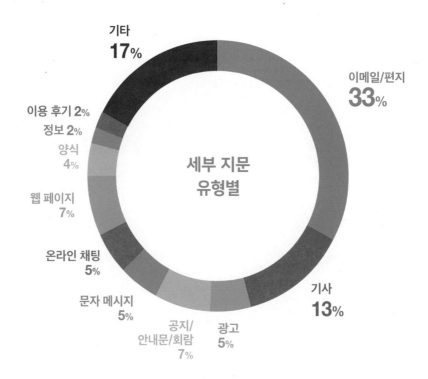

세부 지문
유형별

- 이메일/편지 **33%**
- 기사 **13%**
- 광고 5%
- 공지/안내문/회람 7%
- 문자 메시지 5%
- 온라인 채팅 5%
- 웹 페이지 7%
- 양식 4%
- 정보 2%
- 이용 후기 2%
- 기타 **17%**

- 이메일/편지, 기사 유형 지문은 거의 항상 나오는 편이며 많은 경우 합해서 전체의 50~60%에 이르기도 한다.

- 기타 지문 유형으로 agenda, brochure, comment card, coupon, flyer, instructions, invitation, invoice, list, menu, page from a catalog, policy statement, report, schedule, survey, voucher 등 다양한 자료가 골고루 나온다.

(이중 지문과 삼중 지문 속의 지문들을 모두 낱개로 계산함 - 총 23지문)

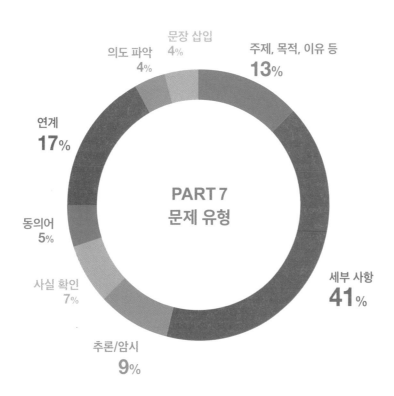

PART 7
문제 유형

문장 삽입 4%

의도 파악 4%

주제, 목적, 이유 등 13%

연계 17%

동의어 5%

사실 확인 7%

추론/암시 9%

세부 사항 41%

- 동의어 문제는 주로 이중 지문이나 삼중 지문에 나온다.
- 연계 문제는 일반적으로 이중 지문에서 한 문제, 삼중 지문에서 두 문제가 나온다.
- 의도 파악 문제는 문자 메시지(text-message chain)나 온라인 채팅(online chat discussion) 지문에서
  출제되며 두 문제가 나온다.
- 문장 삽입 문제는 주로 기사, 이메일, 편지, 회람 지문에서 출제되며 두 문제가 나온다.

점수 환산표 및 산출법

점수 환산표 이 책에 수록된 각 Test를 풀고 난 후, 맞은 개수를 세어 점수를 환산해 보세요.

LISTENING Raw Score (맞은 개수)	LISTENING Scaled Score (환산 점수)	READING Raw Score (맞은 개수)	READING Scaled Score (환산 점수)
96-100	475-495	96-100	460-495
91-95	435-495	91-95	425-490
86-90	405-470	86-90	400-465
81-85	370-450	81-85	375-440
76-80	345-420	76-80	340-415
71-75	320-390	71-75	310-390
66-70	290-360	66-70	285-370
61-65	265-335	61-65	255-340
56-60	240-310	56-60	230-310
51-55	215-280	51-55	200-275
46-50	190-255	46-50	170-245
41-45	160-230	41-45	140-215
36-40	130-205	36-40	115-180
31-35	105-175	31-35	95-150
26-30	85-145	26-30	75-120
21-25	60-115	21-25	60-95
16-20	30-90	16-20	45-75
11-15	5-70	11-15	30-55
6-10	5-60	6-10	10-40
1-5	5-50	1-5	5-30
0	5-35	0	5-15

점수 산출 방법 아래의 방식으로 점수를 산출할 수 있다.

STEP 1

자신의 답안을 수록된 정답과 대조하여 채점한다. 각 Section의 맞은 개수가 본인의 Section별 '실제 점수(통계 처리하기 전의 점수, raw score)'이다. Listening Test와 Reading Test의 정답 수를 세어, 자신의 실제 점수를 아래의 해당란에 기록한다.

	맞은 개수	환산 점수대
LISTENING		
READING		
총점		

Section별 실제 점수가 그대로 Section별 TOEIC 점수가 되는 것은 아니다. TOEIC은 시행할 때마다 별도로 특정한 통계 처리 방법을 사용하며 이러한 실제 점수를 환산 점수(converted[scaled] score)로 전환하게 된다. 이렇게 전환함으로써, 매번 시행될 때마다 문제는 달라지지만 그 점수가 갖는 의미는 같아지게 된다. 예를 들어 어느 한 시험에서 총점 550점의 성적을 받는 실력이라면 다른 시험에서도 거의 550점대의 성적을 받게 되는 것이다.

STEP 2

실제 점수를 위 표에 기록한 후 왼쪽 페이지의 점수 환산표를 보도록 한다. TOEIC이 시행될 때마다 대개 이와 비슷한 형태의 표가 작성되는데, 여기 제시된 환산표는 본 교재에 수록된 Test용으로 개발된 것이다. 이 표를 사용하여 자신의 실제 점수를 환산 점수로 전환하도록 한다. 즉, 예를 들어 Listening Test의 실제 정답 수가 61~65개이면 환산 점수는 265점에서 335점 사이가 된다. 여기서 실제 정답 수가 61개이면 환산 점수가 265점이고, 65개이면 환산 점수가 335점 임을 의미하는 것은 아니다. 본 책의 Test를 위해 작성된 이 점수 환산표가 자신의 영어 실력이 어느 정도인지 대략적으로 파악하는 데 도움이 되긴 하지만, 이 표가 실제 TOEIC 성적 산출에 그대로 사용된 적은 없다는 사실을 밝혀 둔다.

토익 정기시험
실전 ❶ 1000
LC

토익 정기시험
실전 ❶ 1000
LC

실전 TEST

01

LISTENING TEST

In the Listening test, you will be asked to demonstrate how well you understand spoken English. The entire Listening test will last approximately 45 minutes. There are four parts, and directions are given for each part. You must mark your answers on the separate answer sheet. Do not write your answers in your test book.

PART 1

Directions: For each question in this part, you will hear four statements about a picture in your test book. When you hear the statements, you must select the one statement that best describes what you see in the picture. Then find the number of the question on your answer sheet and mark your answer. The statements will not be printed in your test book and will be spoken only one time.

Statement (C), "They're sitting at a table," is the best description of the picture, so you should select answer (C) and mark it on your answer sheet.

1.

2.

GO ON TO THE NEXT PAGE ➤

3.

4.

5.

6.

GO ON TO THE NEXT PAGE

PART 2

Directions: You will hear a question or statement and three responses spoken in English. They will not be printed in your test book and will be spoken only one time. Select the best response to the question or statement and mark the letter (A), (B), or (C) on your answer sheet.

7. Mark your answer on your answer sheet.

8. Mark your answer on your answer sheet.

9. Mark your answer on your answer sheet.

10. Mark your answer on your answer sheet.

11. Mark your answer on your answer sheet.

12. Mark your answer on your answer sheet.

13. Mark your answer on your answer sheet.

14. Mark your answer on your answer sheet.

15. Mark your answer on your answer sheet.

16. Mark your answer on your answer sheet.

17. Mark your answer on your answer sheet.

18. Mark your answer on your answer sheet.

19. Mark your answer on your answer sheet.

20. Mark your answer on your answer sheet.

21. Mark your answer on your answer sheet.

22. Mark your answer on your answer sheet.

23. Mark your answer on your answer sheet.

24. Mark your answer on your answer sheet.

25. Mark your answer on your answer sheet.

26. Mark your answer on your answer sheet.

27. Mark your answer on your answer sheet.

28. Mark your answer on your answer sheet.

29. Mark your answer on your answer sheet.

30. Mark your answer on your answer sheet.

31. Mark your answer on your answer sheet.

PART 3

Directions: You will hear some conversations between two or more people. You will be asked to answer three questions about what the speakers say in each conversation. Select the best response to each question and mark the letter (A), (B), (C), or (D) on your answer sheet. The conversations will not be printed in your test book and will be spoken only one time.

32. Why is the woman calling?

(A) To request a ticket change
(B) To make a dinner reservation
(C) To order merchandise
(D) To plan a vacation

33. Why does the man apologize?

(A) An event was canceled.
(B) A line is very long.
(C) A payment option is unavailable.
(D) A computer program is not working.

34. What does the man remind the woman about?

(A) A meal voucher
(B) Some free souvenirs
(C) An increase in price
(D) A refund policy

35. What event will the speakers be attending later today?

(A) A job fair
(B) A film screening
(C) A lunch
(D) A conference

36. Why does the man say, "she has a van"?

(A) To suggest inquiring about a ride
(B) To express surprise at a coworker's choice of vehicle
(C) To explain why a coworker was late
(D) To clarify that a coworker helped him move

37. What will the woman most likely do next?

(A) Reschedule an event
(B) Talk to another coworker
(C) Request time off
(D) Make a phone call

38. Where do the speakers work?

(A) At a grocery store
(B) At a shipping facility
(C) At a restaurant
(D) At a doctor's office

39. What does the woman say she is concerned about?

(A) Fuel prices
(B) Her work hours
(C) A staff shortage
(D) An inventory process

40. What does the man suggest that the woman do?

(A) Complete a training program
(B) Order extra equipment
(C) Hire a consultant
(D) Take time to make a decision

41. Why is the woman calling?

(A) Her taxi never arrived.
(B) Her luggage is missing.
(C) Her train was canceled.
(D) Her ticket is lost.

42. What event is the woman planning to attend?

(A) An awards ceremony
(B) A trade show
(C) An art exhibit opening
(D) A building inspection

43. What does the man give the woman as an apology?

(A) A partial discount
(B) Vouchers for future travel
(C) A full refund
(D) A better seat

GO ON TO THE NEXT PAGE

44. Where does the woman work?

(A) At a distribution center
(B) At a conference center
(C) At a car dealership
(D) At a real estate agency

45. What problem with some e-mails does the man mention?

(A) Confusion about the intended recipients
(B) A delay in message delivery
(C) An incorrectly typed word
(D) Lack of information

46. What will the woman most likely do next?

(A) Arrange a meeting
(B) Make a phone call
(C) Speak to her employees
(D) Review an invoice

47. What is the conversation mainly about?

(A) A policy change
(B) A product launch
(C) Some customer feedback
(D) A scheduled maintenance visit

48. What does the woman say people at the company are currently working on?

(A) Exploring publicity options
(B) Finding a new vendor
(C) Assembling a sales team
(D) Negotiating a monthly fee

49. Why is the man concerned?

(A) Customers have complained.
(B) Price estimates are high.
(C) Some changes require approval.
(D) A plan may be delayed.

50. What are the speakers preparing for?

(A) An interview
(B) A food delivery
(C) A special event
(D) An inspection

51. What does the woman say will be delivered in an hour?

(A) Some flower arrangements
(B) Some gifts for attendees
(C) Some audio equipment
(D) Some tables and chairs

52. What will the speakers most likely do next?

(A) Review a guest list
(B) Meet with a photographer
(C) Take a break
(D) Taste some food

53. What event are the speakers discussing?

(A) A bank opening
(B) A contest
(C) A business conference
(D) A company anniversary

54. What does the man mean when he says, "there's a lot of damage"?

(A) He finally fully understands a problem.
(B) The woman should expect a bill in the mail.
(C) The woman's assumption is incorrect.
(D) A schedule needs to be adjusted.

55. What does the woman recommend?

(A) Using an outdoor area
(B) Arranging technical support
(C) Confirming a catering menu
(D) Interviewing some job applicants

56. What industry do the speakers most likely work in?

(A) Medicine
(B) Music
(C) Publishing
(D) Finance

57. According to the man, why has a software program become popular?

(A) It is less expensive than similar products.
(B) It makes information more accessible.
(C) It reduces environmental impact.
(D) It comes with customer support.

58. What might Marion still need to do?

(A) Contact some service providers
(B) Sign a release form
(C) Check some financial information
(D) Repair some equipment

59. What are the speakers discussing?

(A) Proposing a business merger
(B) Relocating a company's headquarters
(C) Developing additional products
(D) Hiring more employees

60. What challenge does Stan mention?

(A) A profit margin will decrease.
(B) Additional equipment will be needed.
(C) There are not enough job applicants.
(D) There are delays in production.

61. What does Pedro say he will do?

(A) Contact a facility manager
(B) Adjust a budget
(C) Change a work schedule
(D) Research a product

Time	Tour
9 A.M.	Fishing Expedition
10 A.M.	Whale Watching
11 A.M.	Sea-Ride Special
12 P.M.	Island Exploration

62. According to the man, why is today's Sea-Ride Special tour popular?

(A) It offers a chance to see migrating birds.
(B) Water conditions are likely to be favorable.
(C) A guest chef is preparing lunch.
(D) Someone special will be guiding the tour.

63. Look at the graphic. What time will the woman depart on a tour?

(A) At 9 A.M.
(B) At 10 A.M.
(C) At 11 A.M.
(D) At 12 P.M.

64. What will the woman most likely do next?

(A) Return to her hotel
(B) Visit a café
(C) Call a friend
(D) Store her bags in a locker

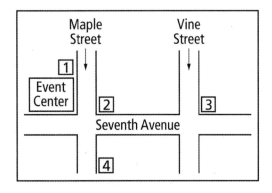

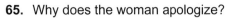

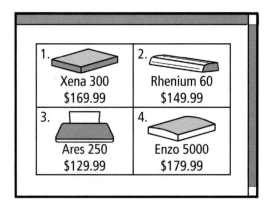

65. Why does the woman apologize?

    (A) A conference session is full.
    (B) An elevator is not working.
    (C) A workshop has changed locations.
    (D) Parking is not free.

66. Look at the graphic. Which location does the woman recommend?

    (A) Area 1
    (B) Area 2
    (C) Area 3
    (D) Area 4

67. Why is the man in a hurry?

    (A) A workshop is starting soon.
    (B) A parking pass is about to expire.
    (C) A shuttle is running late.
    (D) A friend is waiting outside.

68. Why does the woman call?

    (A) She wants to request a refund.
    (B) She is unable to place an order online.
    (C) She wants to extend a deadline.
    (D) She is unhappy with a product purchased recently.

69. Look at the graphic. What is the price of the item the woman wants to buy?

    (A) $169.99
    (B) $149.99
    (C) $129.99
    (D) $179.99

70. What will the man most likely do tomorrow?

    (A) Update a Web site
    (B) Search a storage area
    (C) Contact another store location
    (D) Check an incoming shipment

PART 4

Directions: You will hear some talks given by a single speaker. You will be asked to answer three questions about what the speaker says in each talk. Select the best response to each question and mark the letter (A), (B), (C), or (D) on your answer sheet. The talks will not be printed in your test book and will be spoken only one time.

71. What feature of a business does the speaker emphasize?

    (A) The quality of its food
    (B) The extended hours it is open
    (C) The style of its decor
    (D) The affordable prices it offers

72. What can attendees do at the grand opening event?

    (A) Go on a tour
    (B) Get a free gift
    (C) Talk to an actor
    (D) Watch some movies

73. What does the speaker advise event attendees to do?

    (A) Arrive early
    (B) Use public transportation
    (C) Order tickets in advance
    (D) Purchase a membership

74. What does the listener want to do?

    (A) Request shuttle service
    (B) Extend a hotel stay
    (C) Change a room assignment
    (D) Cancel a reservation

75. Why does the speaker say, "those rooms are always booked far in advance"?

    (A) To express approval for a room design
    (B) To explain why a hotel is successful
    (C) To indicate his disbelief
    (D) To deny the listener's request

76. According to the speaker, what should the listener bring?

    (A) Some warm clothes
    (B) Some swimwear
    (C) A credit card
    (D) A copy of a key

77. Who most likely is the speaker?

    (A) An archaeologist
    (B) A marine biologist
    (C) A conservation expert
    (D) An athletic trainer

78. What does the speaker advise the listeners to do?

    (A) Take a water bottle
    (B) Consult a site map
    (C) Apply sunscreen regularly
    (D) Write careful notes

79. What does the speaker say she is going to do next?

    (A) Answer some questions
    (B) Demonstrate a process
    (C) Introduce a colleague
    (D) Take the listeners to lunch

80. Why will the speaker be traveling?

    (A) To inspect a factory
    (B) To repair a product
    (C) To perform in a concert
    (D) To attend a workshop

81. Why is the speaker concerned?

    (A) A seating arrangement is wrong.
    (B) A company credit card was not charged.
    (C) Some meal tickets were not sent.
    (D) Her taxi driver is unable to find a hotel.

82. What does the speaker ask the listener to do?

    (A) Send an e-mail
    (B) Meet at an office
    (C) Confirm a schedule
    (D) Look up an account number

GO ON TO THE NEXT PAGE

83. What does the speaker remind the listeners to do?

(A) Keep a gate closed
(B) Return equipment to a shed
(C) Check a list of supplies
(D) Select a free gift

84. According to the speaker, what can the listeners apply for?

(A) A garden plot
(B) A volunteer opportunity
(C) A gardening workshop
(D) A farmers market table

85. How can the listeners get information about future events?

(A) By signing up for a newsletter
(B) By joining a membership program
(C) By looking at a Web site
(D) By attending weekly meetings

86. What service does the business offer?

(A) Financial planning
(B) Digital marketing
(C) Real estate sales
(D) International shipping

87. According to the speaker, how is the business different from its competitors?

(A) It has several local offices.
(B) It offers a money-back guarantee.
(C) Its employees have industry certification.
(D) Its employees work one-on-one with clients.

88. How can the listeners make an appointment?

(A) By sending an e-mail
(B) By calling customer service
(C) By filling out a questionnaire
(D) By sending a text message

89. Who most likely are the listeners?

(A) Marine biologists
(B) Museum directors
(C) Rare-book librarians
(D) Agricultural engineers

90. What does the speaker mean when he says, "they received over 200 applications"?

(A) An opportunity is unlikely to occur.
(B) An award is impressive.
(C) A decision will take longer than usual.
(D) A competitor has been very successful.

91. Why does the speaker say that work cannot begin right away?

(A) Additional funds are needed.
(B) Some special training is required.
(C) An application has to be approved.
(D) Some equipment needs to be ordered.

92. What is the purpose of the talk?

(A) To recognize outstanding achievements
(B) To introduce new products to the public
(C) To announce a manager's retirement
(D) To provide new employees with information

93. Where is the talk taking place?

(A) At a banquet hall
(B) At a government building
(C) At a factory
(D) At a construction site

94. What does the speaker mean when she says, "I have a consultation with a client"?

(A) She needs to reschedule a meeting.
(B) She will not be with the listeners in the afternoon.
(C) A customer has just placed a large order.
(D) A marketing campaign will begin soon.

Refrigerator Options

Model	Extra Large	Stainless Steel	Ice Maker
SG-200			✓
SG-250		✓	
XG-300	✓		✓
XG-350	✓	✓	

95. What is the main purpose of the call?

(A) To place an order
(B) To dispute a charge
(C) To arrange a meeting
(D) To check a store's inventory

96. Look at the graphic. Which model does the speaker prefer?

(A) SG-200
(B) SG-250
(C) XG-300
(D) XG-350

97. What does the speaker ask about?

(A) A warranty
(B) A return process
(C) A delivery fee
(D) Product availability

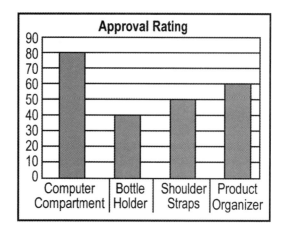

98. Who most likely are the listeners?

(A) Marketing experts
(B) Product testers
(C) Product designers
(D) Audio engineers

99. Look at the graphic. What was the approval rating of the feature that will be improved?

(A) 40 percent
(B) 50 percent
(C) 60 percent
(D) 80 percent

100. According to the speaker, why is a revision urgent?

(A) A competitor is making a similar product.
(B) A product will be offered for sale soon.
(C) A product will be introduced at a trade show.
(D) The cost of a product's materials will rise soon.

This is the end of the Listening test.

토익 정기시험
실전 ❶ 1000
LC

실전 TEST

02

LISTENING TEST

In the Listening test, you will be asked to demonstrate how well you understand spoken English. The entire Listening test will last approximately 45 minutes. There are four parts, and directions are given for each part. You must mark your answers on the separate answer sheet. Do not write your answers in your test book.

PART 1

Directions: For each question in this part, you will hear four statements about a picture in your test book. When you hear the statements, you must select the one statement that best describes what you see in the picture. Then find the number of the question on your answer sheet and mark your answer. The statements will not be printed in your test book and will be spoken only one time.

Statement (C), "They're sitting at a table," is the best description of the picture, so you should select answer (C) and mark it on your answer sheet.

1.

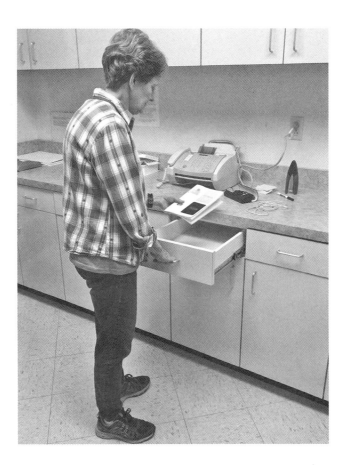

2.

GO ON TO THE NEXT PAGE ➤

TEST 2

3.

4.

5.

6.

GO ON TO THE NEXT PAGE ▶

PART 2

Directions: You will hear a question or statement and three responses spoken in English. They will not be printed in your test book and will be spoken only one time. Select the best response to the question or statement and mark the letter (A), (B), or (C) on your answer sheet.

7. Mark your answer on your answer sheet.

8. Mark your answer on your answer sheet.

9. Mark your answer on your answer sheet.

10. Mark your answer on your answer sheet.

11. Mark your answer on your answer sheet.

12. Mark your answer on your answer sheet.

13. Mark your answer on your answer sheet.

14. Mark your answer on your answer sheet.

15. Mark your answer on your answer sheet.

16. Mark your answer on your answer sheet.

17. Mark your answer on your answer sheet.

18. Mark your answer on your answer sheet.

19. Mark your answer on your answer sheet.

20. Mark your answer on your answer sheet.

21. Mark your answer on your answer sheet.

22. Mark your answer on your answer sheet.

23. Mark your answer on your answer sheet.

24. Mark your answer on your answer sheet.

25. Mark your answer on your answer sheet.

26. Mark your answer on your answer sheet.

27. Mark your answer on your answer sheet.

28. Mark your answer on your answer sheet.

29. Mark your answer on your answer sheet.

30. Mark your answer on your answer sheet.

31. Mark your answer on your answer sheet.

PART 3

Directions: You will hear some conversations between two or more people. You will be asked to answer three questions about what the speakers say in each conversation. Select the best response to each question and mark the letter (A), (B), (C), or (D) on your answer sheet. The conversations will not be printed in your test book and will be spoken only one time.

32. Why is the man calling?

(A) To rent a facility
(B) To hire a photographer
(C) To request a price list
(D) To schedule a repair

33. What problem does the woman mention?

(A) Her employee does not have transportation.
(B) Her service does not cover sports events.
(C) The weather will be bad on Tuesday.
(D) The time the man requested is too late.

34. What does the woman say she will do?

(A) Issue a refund
(B) Cancel an order
(C) Talk to an employee
(D) E-mail her manager

35. Where most likely are the speakers?

(A) In a restaurant
(B) In a school
(C) In a warehouse
(D) In a library

36. Why do the speakers mention Maria Jeong?

(A) She placed a very large order.
(B) She wants to replace a product.
(C) She is unable to work today.
(D) She may be able to help with a task.

37. What will the man probably do next?

(A) Pack an order
(B) Call a colleague
(C) Process a refund
(D) Write to a customer

38. What do the speakers need to choose?

(A) An introductory activity for a retreat
(B) A residential site for a retreat
(C) Decorations for a party
(D) A location for a dinner

39. What do the speakers like about McNally's?

(A) It is nearby.
(B) It is open late.
(C) It is highly recommended.
(D) It has been remodeled.

40. What does the woman offer to do?

(A) See what the retreat attendees prefer
(B) Find an alternative site
(C) Discuss pricing options
(D) Contact a hotel

41. What does the speakers' company produce?

(A) Computers
(B) Software
(C) Web sites
(D) Medical equipment

42. What does the man say has been helpful?

(A) Focus group data
(B) An engineering consultant
(C) A search engine
(D) Customer feedback

43. What is the next step in the project that the speakers are discussing?

(A) Giving a presentation to the client
(B) Sending a product to another group in the company
(C) Creating a schedule for the next phase of development
(D) Determining the price of a product

GO ON TO THE NEXT PAGE

44. What is the purpose of the phone call?

   (A) To help a customer choose a product
   (B) To check on a customer's satisfaction
   (C) To inform a customer of a price estimate
   (D) To advertise a special offer

45. What does the man say about replacing kitchen cabinets?

   (A) He guarantees his company will do a good job.
   (B) His company is too busy to do the work.
   (C) His company does not do that type of work.
   (D) He thinks it will be an expensive job.

46. What will the man most likely do next?

   (A) Send workers to the woman's house
   (B) Find a telephone number for the woman
   (C) Check kitchen cabinet prices
   (D) Discuss a new product with some workers

47. Where is the conversation taking place?

   (A) At a travel agency
   (B) At a pharmacy
   (C) At a mobile phone store
   (D) At a hotel

48. What does the woman say she will do at lunch today?

   (A) Go to the airport
   (B) Print out a ticket
   (C) Register for a giveaway
   (D) Call a doctor

49. What does the man offer to do?

   (A) Arrange a delivery
   (B) Postpone an appointment
   (C) Check a discount rate
   (D) Download an application

50. Where does the woman work?

   (A) At a baseball stadium
   (B) At a fitness center
   (C) At a shipping warehouse
   (D) At a school

51. What is the woman concerned about?

   (A) A store's closing time
   (B) Overall costs
   (C) When an order will be received
   (D) The color of some uniforms

52. What will the man do next?

   (A) Look up some prices
   (B) Package an order
   (C) Call a manager
   (D) Check the store's inventory

53. What problem does the woman mention?

   (A) There is no time to create centerpieces.
   (B) The shop never received the man's order.
   (C) A supplier cannot fulfill an order.
   (D) The wrong date is on the order form.

54. What does the man say about his company's logo?

   (A) It was designed many years ago.
   (B) It contains the color pink.
   (C) It won an award.
   (D) It features a drawing of flowers.

55. What does the man mean when he says, "I suppose no one will really be disappointed"?

   (A) He will postpone the luncheon.
   (B) He will accept the woman's offer.
   (C) He will find a replacement award.
   (D) He will modify the company's logo.

56. What kind of company do the speakers most likely work for?

(A) Manufacturing
(B) Financial
(C) Publishing
(D) Educational

57. What problem are the speakers discussing?

(A) A pause while more funding is obtained
(B) A delay in making a delivery
(C) A need for the company to relocate
(D) The loss of some experienced staff

58. What does the man request?

(A) A report from the client
(B) A faster pace of work
(C) Additional employees
(D) Daily updates from the team

59. What does the woman say about Central Airport?

(A) The airport operates two shuttles.
(B) There are not enough people working there.
(C) It is not far from the Legend Hotel.
(D) It is more modern than the local airport.

60. Why does the man say, "That's good news"?

(A) He will be able to take a shuttle to the hotel.
(B) His flight was rescheduled.
(C) Central Airport will reopen soon.
(D) He will be able to change his hotel reservation.

61. What will the woman do for the man?

(A) Give him the shuttle company's phone number
(B) Find information about Central Airport
(C) Give him a discount on his reservation
(D) Make sure that his room has been prepared

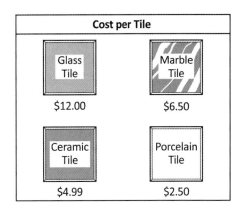

Cost per Tile

Glass Tile	Marble Tile
$12.00	$6.50

Ceramic Tile	Porcelain Tile
$4.99	$2.50

62. What did the man do yesterday?

(A) He visited a property.
(B) He contacted a supplier.
(C) He sent a plan.
(D) He took some measurements.

63. What does the woman say she likes?

(A) The cost the man has estimated
(B) The open-space design
(C) The colors the man has selected
(D) The remodeling timeline

64. Look at the graphic. How much will the woman pay for each tile?

(A) $12.00
(B) $6.50
(C) $4.99
(D) $2.50

GO ON TO THE NEXT PAGE

Room Types	Price
Executive suite	€ 120
Deluxe double	€ 115
Standard king	€ 99
Single basic	€ 89

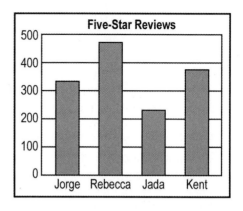

65. Why is the man calling?

(A) To request a room change
(B) To make a group reservation
(C) To order room service
(D) To complain about noise

66. Look at the graphic. Which room type does the woman mention?

(A) Executive suite
(B) Deluxe double
(C) Standard king
(D) Single basic

67. Who is Pablo Gonzales?

(A) An accountant
(B) A client
(C) A bus driver
(D) An event planner

68. What is the conversation mainly about?

(A) A sales strategy
(B) An improvement in customer service
(C) A new manager
(D) An award

69. Who does the woman say she will send a reminder to?

(A) The management team
(B) The customer service representatives
(C) A magazine editor
(D) A repair technician

70. Look at the graphic. Which representative is the man most likely talking about?

(A) Jorge
(B) Rebecca
(C) Jada
(D) Kent

PART 4

Directions: You will hear some talks given by a single speaker. You will be asked to answer three questions about what the speaker says in each talk. Select the best response to each question and mark the letter (A), (B), (C), or (D) on your answer sheet. The talks will not be printed in your test book and will be spoken only one time.

71. What is being advertised?

(A) A trip to Mexico
(B) A city tour
(C) A farm visit
(D) A botanical garden

72. What event is happening this weekend?

(A) A competition will be held.
(B) Special plants will be on display.
(C) Crops will be planted.
(D) A special sale will take place.

73. What does the speaker say about a café building?

(A) It will soon be repainted.
(B) It was once a greenhouse.
(C) It is located near public transportation.
(D) It is closed this spring.

74. Who most likely is the speaker?

(A) A salesperson
(B) A manager
(C) A safety inspector
(D) A software developer

75. What is the main topic of the talk?

(A) A delivery route
(B) A corporate merger
(C) Performance reviews
(D) Hiring procedures

76. What does the speaker ask the listeners to do?

(A) Pass along some information to workers
(B) Sign up for a training course
(C) Get some information from customers
(D) Talk with employees about their goals for the year

77. Who is the speaker most likely calling?

(A) A real estate firm
(B) A moving company
(C) A travel agency
(D) A furniture store

78. Why does the speaker say, "my apartment is on a very high floor"?

(A) To correct a misunderstanding
(B) To negotiate a price
(C) To ask about a property's value
(D) To warn about a situation

79. What will the speaker do next week?

(A) Host an event
(B) Make a payment
(C) Travel abroad
(D) Begin a new job

80. Why might the listeners be disappointed?

(A) A performance has been canceled.
(B) A performer will not be appearing.
(C) A new production will be delayed.
(D) A production is not new.

81. What does the speaker indicate about Rita Marks?

(A) She has flown in from Toronto.
(B) She taught the speaker.
(C) She has experience with a role.
(D) She is a good friend of the speaker's.

82. What does the speaker imply when he says, "I saw the reviews from Toronto"?

(A) He attended the opera in Toronto.
(B) An audience disliked Lisa Gornicka.
(C) Critics disagree about Rita Marks's performance.
(D) Rita Marks has been praised for her singing.

GO ON TO THE NEXT PAGE

83. Where does the speaker most likely work?

(A) At an automobile company
(B) At a data analysis company
(C) At a toy manufacturer
(D) At a department store

84. What does the speaker mean when she says, "It's been a mixed bag"?

(A) The product she is discussing cannot be returned for a refund.
(B) Customers often purchase more than one of the product.
(C) A competitor has developed a similar product.
(D) A product has had both positive and negative reviews.

85. What does the speaker ask the listeners to do?

(A) Try using the product she is discussing
(B) Improve one part of the product
(C) Get more information from customers
(D) Collaborate with the marketing team

86. Where is the announcement most likely being made?

(A) At a supermarket
(B) At a community center
(C) At a restaurant
(D) At a shopping mall

87. What is the main topic of the announcement?

(A) A discount offer
(B) A new product
(C) A giveaway
(D) A volunteer opportunity

88. What does the speaker say about some Shopsmart products?

(A) They are not available at all Shopsmart locations.
(B) They are acquired from overseas distributors.
(C) They are currently on sale.
(D) They are the only products that qualify for an event.

89. What work was the speaker hired to do?

(A) Deliver firewood
(B) Repair a roof
(C) Install flooring
(D) Complete a landscaping job

90. What does the speaker say about the distributor?

(A) It lowered a price.
(B) It is no longer in business.
(C) It expects a delay.
(D) It has not responded to his request.

91. Why did the speaker wait to place an order?

(A) He is not sure what quantity is needed.
(B) He wants a customer to reconsider a decision.
(C) He forgot what the customer requested.
(D) He learned that a product is no longer available.

92. Who most likely is the speaker?

(A) A teacher in a classroom
(B) A worker at an environmental center
(C) A salesperson in a sporting goods store
(D) A guide in a natural history museum

93. What is the purpose of the project?

(A) To recruit volunteers
(B) To release bluebirds into the wild
(C) To provide shelter for bluebirds
(D) To educate people about bluebirds

94. What is marked on some maps?

(A) Locations where work can be done
(B) Flight patterns of bluebirds
(C) The location of nearby attractions
(D) Directions to the environmental center

44

Pattern	Wholesale Orders (Number of complete sets)
Everyday	7,000
Dawn	5,000
Café	2,000
Holiday	6,200
New Year	6,000
Harvest Festival	200

Package Name	Number of Games Included
Holiday package	6
Sunday package	16
Friday night package	19
Discount package	36

95. What product does the speaker's company sell?

(A) Bath towels
(B) Dishware
(C) Tablecloths
(D) Drinking glasses

96. Why will the CEO be pleased?

(A) The company bought a new warehouse.
(B) Customer reviews have been positive.
(C) Shipping costs have gone down.
(D) An investment was successful.

97. Look at the graphic. What number of orders does the speaker say the Harvest Festival pattern must reach?

(A) 5,000
(B) 2,000
(C) 6,000
(D) 200

98. Who most likely is the speaker?

(A) A baseball player
(B) A travel agent
(C) A new job applicant
(D) A customer service trainer

99. Why are ticket sales expected to be good?

(A) The prices have been reduced.
(B) The team's previous season was successful.
(C) There is a new advertising campaign.
(D) The team has many new players.

100. Look at the graphic. How many games are included in the new ticket package that the speaker describes?

(A) 6
(B) 16
(C) 19
(D) 36

This is the end of the Listening test.

토익 정기시험
실전❶1000
LC

실전 TEST

03

LISTENING TEST

In the Listening test, you will be asked to demonstrate how well you understand spoken English. The entire Listening test will last approximately 45 minutes. There are four parts, and directions are given for each part. You must mark your answers on the separate answer sheet. Do not write your answers in your test book.

PART 1

Directions: For each question in this part, you will hear four statements about a picture in your test book. When you hear the statements, you must select the one statement that best describes what you see in the picture. Then find the number of the question on your answer sheet and mark your answer. The statements will not be printed in your test book and will be spoken only one time.

Statement (C), "They're sitting at a table," is the best description of the picture, so you should select answer (C) and mark it on your answer sheet.

1.

2.

GO ON TO THE NEXT PAGE

3.

4.

5.

6.

GO ON TO THE NEXT PAGE

PART 2

Directions: You will hear a question or statement and three responses spoken in English. They will not be printed in your test book and will be spoken only one time. Select the best response to the question or statement and mark the letter (A), (B), or (C) on your answer sheet.

7. Mark your answer on your answer sheet.

8. Mark your answer on your answer sheet.

9. Mark your answer on your answer sheet.

10. Mark your answer on your answer sheet.

11. Mark your answer on your answer sheet.

12. Mark your answer on your answer sheet.

13. Mark your answer on your answer sheet.

14. Mark your answer on your answer sheet.

15. Mark your answer on your answer sheet.

16. Mark your answer on your answer sheet.

17. Mark your answer on your answer sheet.

18. Mark your answer on your answer sheet.

19. Mark your answer on your answer sheet.

20. Mark your answer on your answer sheet.

21. Mark your answer on your answer sheet.

22. Mark your answer on your answer sheet.

23. Mark your answer on your answer sheet.

24. Mark your answer on your answer sheet.

25. Mark your answer on your answer sheet.

26. Mark your answer on your answer sheet.

27. Mark your answer on your answer sheet.

28. Mark your answer on your answer sheet.

29. Mark your answer on your answer sheet.

30. Mark your answer on your answer sheet.

31. Mark your answer on your answer sheet.

PART 3

Directions: You will hear some conversations between two or more people. You will be asked to answer three questions about what the speakers say in each conversation. Select the best response to each question and mark the letter (A), (B), (C), or (D) on your answer sheet. The conversations will not be printed in your test book and will be spoken only one time.

32. Why is the woman talking to the man?

(A) She wants to cancel a reservation.
(B) She wants to watch a demonstration.
(C) She wants to rent some equipment.
(D) She wants to hire a gardener.

33. What problem does the man mention?

(A) A garden show has been canceled.
(B) A radio program was discontinued.
(C) A presenter is not available.
(D) Some equipment is late arriving.

34. What does the man advise the woman to do?

(A) Talk to the manager on Saturday
(B) Sign up for a class online
(C) Place an order for some tools
(D) Arrive early for an event

35. What does the woman need advice about?

(A) Which company to hire
(B) Which materials to use
(C) When to begin some repair work
(D) Where to lay down some paths

36. According to the woman, why is some repair work complicated?

(A) It will take place during the winter.
(B) It is part of a larger job.
(C) It has been postponed.
(D) It requires a special permit.

37. Why does the man tell the woman to talk to Mr. Lukich?

(A) He can perform some construction work.
(B) His sales record is excellent.
(C) His background is relevant to the woman's needs.
(D) He was assigned to the woman's project.

38. Who is the man?

(A) A marketing agent
(B) A musician
(C) An event organizer
(D) A journalist

39. What does the woman want to do?

(A) Host an international fair
(B) Create a new parking area
(C) Organize a concert
(D) Give an interview

40. What does the woman suggest the man do?

(A) View a map
(B) Schedule a meeting
(C) Provide references
(D) Decorate a space

41. Where most likely are the speakers?

(A) At a café
(B) At an art gallery
(C) At a school
(D) At an art supply store

42. What does the man say he might do?

(A) Buy a painting
(B) Speak to Jose
(C) Invite friends to a show
(D) Go home

43. What plan do the speakers make?

(A) To visit some artists
(B) To organize a show
(C) To meet some sponsors
(D) To go out to lunch

GO ON TO THE NEXT PAGE

44. Where do the speakers most likely work?

(A) At a hospital
(B) At a law firm
(C) At a university
(D) At a manufacturing company

45. Why does the man object to Mr. Smith?

(A) He does not have an extensive work history.
(B) He was late for the interview.
(C) He did not answer questions clearly.
(D) He did not dress appropriately.

46. What will the woman do next?

(A) Double-check Ms. Wong's references
(B) Answer Ms. Wong's question
(C) Review Ms. Wong's employment history
(D) Bring Ms. Wong in for another interview

47. Where most likely is the conversation taking place?

(A) In an office building
(B) In a hotel
(C) In an apartment complex
(D) In a hospital

48. What does the woman imply when she says, "I have a conference call at 8 A.M."?

(A) She will not be able to meet the man.
(B) She would like a faster Internet connection.
(C) She would like to check out early.
(D) She cannot work because of some noise.

49. What does the man say he will do?

(A) Try to find the woman another room
(B) Give the woman a refund
(C) Bring the notice to the woman's room
(D) Ask that the drilling be stopped

50. What are the speakers mainly discussing?

(A) Employee responsibilities
(B) An advertising campaign
(C) Developing a new product
(D) A type of phone

51. What do the women imply about hiring a new consultant?

(A) It would be expensive.
(B) It might not solve their problem.
(C) It will be challenging to find someone with the right skills.
(D) It has already happened.

52. What does the man suggest they do?

(A) Stop production
(B) Hire temporary employees
(C) Review costs
(D) Spend less on advertising

53. Where most likely are the speakers?

(A) In a medical office
(B) At a repair shop
(C) At a department store
(D) In a warehouse

54. Who most likely is Barbara?

(A) A technician
(B) A manager
(C) A salesperson
(D) A fitness instructor

55. What does the man ask the woman to do?

(A) Order some supplies
(B) Call Barbara
(C) Reserve an exercise room
(D) Help a patient tomorrow

56. What does the woman imply when she says, "they maintain the parking area and outdoor lighting"?

(A) Items were mistakenly added to a bill.
(B) Some costs might be reasonable.
(C) New rates went into effect.
(D) A billing period is longer than one month.

57. What does the man think a medical clinic should do?

(A) Hire more employees
(B) Use fewer parking spaces
(C) Pay a larger share of a bill
(D) Move to a new building

58. What will the woman most likely do at the monthly meeting?

(A) Choose a new landscaping company
(B) Discuss a payment arrangement
(C) Suggest enlarging the parking lot
(D) Review a plan for new outdoor lighting

---

59. Why are the speakers celebrating?

(A) A new restaurant is opening.
(B) Their companies will be working together.
(C) They have received an important loan.
(D) They have received an award.

60. What does the man say he liked about a meeting today?

(A) Some unexpected news
(B) Some photos from a presentation
(C) A speech that was given
(D) A change to the agenda

61. What will the women do tomorrow morning?

(A) Finalize some paperwork
(B) Meet at the airport
(C) Make sure the office is locked up
(D) Compare some reports

Time	Task
5:00	Arrive
5:00–6:00	Set up
7:00–10:00	Reception
10:00–10:30	Entertainment
10:30–midnight	Clean up

62. What industry do the speakers most likely work in?

(A) Shipping
(B) Music recording
(C) Catering
(D) Tourism

63. Look at the graphic. What task in the schedule does the woman express concern about?

(A) Arrive
(B) Set up
(C) Entertainment
(D) Clean up

64. What does the woman ask the man to do?

(A) Check on a hotel delivery
(B) Help to prepare some food
(C) Help to load some supplies
(D) Arrange for the truck to arrive early

GO ON TO THE NEXT PAGE

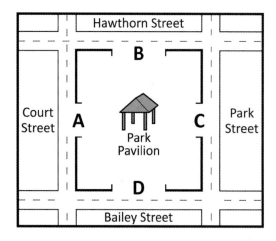

Stage 1	Framing
Stage 2	Plumbing
Stage 3	Insulation
Stage 4	Drywall Installation
Stage 5	Finish Interior

65. What event will the speakers attend at the park this weekend?

(A) A picnic
(B) An athletic event
(C) An environmental fair
(D) A volunteer trash cleanup

66. What does the woman ask the man to do the day of the event?

(A) Hand out prizes
(B) Direct people where to go
(C) Decorate the park pavilion
(D) Hang up signs

67. Look at the graphic. Which entrance will participants use for the event?

(A) Entrance A
(B) Entrance B
(C) Entrance C
(D) Entrance D

68. What did the man do yesterday?

(A) Communicated with the woman about the schedule
(B) Contacted an electrician
(C) Changed an aspect of the house's design
(D) Ordered some supplies

69. Look at the graphic. What stage has recently been completed?

(A) Framing
(B) Plumbing
(C) Insulation
(D) Drywall installation

70. What does the man suggest the woman do?

(A) Cancel an order
(B) Make some design decisions
(C) Pay a bill in advance
(D) Change suppliers

PART 4

Directions: You will hear some talks given by a single speaker. You will be asked to answer three questions about what the speaker says in each talk. Select the best response to each question and mark the letter (A), (B), (C), or (D) on your answer sheet. The talks will not be printed in your test book and will be spoken only one time.

71. What is being advertised?

    (A) An online supermarket
    (B) A travel guide
    (C) A beverage product
    (D) A hotel chain

72. What does the speaker emphasize?

    (A) The eco-friendly policy of a business
    (B) The superior flavor of a product
    (C) The extensive selection on a Web site
    (D) The positive reviews of a brand

73. What is a benefit of membership?

    (A) It provides a discount.
    (B) It makes ordering more efficient.
    (C) It includes access to an online chat room.
    (D) It comes with a gift.

74. Who is Sarah Levinson?

    (A) A university professor
    (B) A coach
    (C) A computer scientist
    (D) A book author

75. What is the main topic of the broadcast?

    (A) Digital trends in publishing
    (B) Qualities of a good bank
    (C) How to save for retirement
    (D) Best jobs in finance

76. What kind of company sponsors the broadcast?

    (A) A local store
    (B) A publishing company
    (C) A technology firm
    (D) A health supplement manufacturer

77. Why did the company hire temporary workers?

    (A) It has opened a new office.
    (B) It is selling a wider variety of products.
    (C) It is very busy this time of year.
    (D) It is installing a new computer system.

78. What will Margaret Malin discuss?

    (A) How to take customers' orders
    (B) How to open a bank account
    (C) How to close the store each night
    (D) How to handle customer complaints

79. Why does the speaker say, "There's a white folder on the table in front of you"?

    (A) To review a gardening supplies price list
    (B) To share some company history
    (C) To introduce some job duties
    (D) To ask for some banking information

80. What is the speaker discussing?

    (A) A supermarket sale
    (B) An agricultural show
    (C) An educational program
    (D) An outdoor festival

81. Who is the announcement intended for?

    (A) Cattle farmers
    (B) Foresters
    (C) College students
    (D) Restaurant cooks

82. How can a person get more information?

    (A) By going to a farm
    (B) By sending an e-mail
    (C) By going to a Web site
    (D) By calling a phone number

GO ON TO THE NEXT PAGE

83. Who is the speaker?

  (A) A plumber
  (B) A shop owner
  (C) A reporter
  (D) A city employee

84. What problem does the speaker identify?

  (A) A broken water pipe
  (B) A heavy rainstorm
  (C) A change to an insurance policy
  (D) A misleading phone call

85. What will the listener most likely do after listening to the message?

  (A) Cancel his insurance policy
  (B) Move his bakery
  (C) Open his store for business
  (D) Arrange for a repair

---

86. What type of event is taking place?

  (A) A writers' workshop
  (B) A debate competition
  (C) A sports awards ceremony
  (D) A book signing

87. What does the speaker mean when he says, "This moment is such a thrill for me"?

  (A) He admires a guest speaker.
  (B) He likes speaking to audiences.
  (C) He is enjoying a meal.
  (D) He is pleased to win an award.

88. What are the listeners reminded to do?

  (A) Hold their applause until the end
  (B) Finish their meals
  (C) Turn off their phones
  (D) Avoid taking pictures

---

89. What is causing heavy traffic in the city center?

  (A) Road construction
  (B) Preparation for an event
  (C) Bad weather conditions
  (D) A disabled vehicle

90. Why should the listeners visit the radio station's Web site?

  (A) To enter a contest
  (B) To request some music
  (C) To ask some questions about city planning
  (D) To learn about the progress of a sporting event

91. What does the speaker recommend the listeners do?

  (A) Work from home
  (B) Avoid driving into the city center
  (C) Wait for another traffic report
  (D) Take a different exit

---

92. Where does the speaker work?

  (A) At a jewelry store
  (B) At a dental office
  (C) At a medical supply store
  (D) At a hotel chain

93. What did the speaker forget to do?

  (A) Give back a necklace
  (B) Write down a phone number
  (C) Send some X-ray results
  (D) Call a receptionist

94. Why does the speaker say, "our office is open until seven tonight"?

  (A) To remind the listener about a delivery
  (B) To recommend that a contract be signed quickly
  (C) To ask the listener to return to an office
  (D) To indicate that a sale is ending

ROCKNOSE HANDCARTS	
Models	**Cost**
Classic Handcart	$ 50
Superior Handcart	$ 80
Deluxe Handcart	$110
Super Duty Handcart	$150

95. Where does the speaker most likely work?

(A) At a hardware store
(B) At a tool manufacturer
(C) At a landscaping service
(D) At a construction company

96. What is the speaker's highest priority?

(A) Buying a long-lasting product
(B) Spending as little money as possible
(C) Having the order delivered quickly
(D) Getting the largest product available

97. Look at the graphic. Which handcart does the speaker want to buy?

(A) Classic Handcart
(B) Superior Handcart
(C) Deluxe Handcart
(D) Super Duty Handcart

TRAINING MODULES	DURATION
Plan and Organize Your Work	25 min.
From Opportunities to Deals	30 min.
Work as a Team	20 min.
Visualize Success	10 min.

98. Who is the training intended for?

(A) Sales personnel
(B) Executive officers
(C) Human Resource employees
(D) Product developers

99. Look at the graphic. How long will the training be?

(A) 25 minutes
(B) 30 minutes
(C) 20 minutes
(D) 10 minutes

100. What does the speaker tell the listeners to do?

(A) Turn off their phones
(B) Get some refreshments
(C) Ask questions often
(D) Role-play a situation

This is the end of the Listening test.

토익 정기시험
실전❶1000
LC

실전 TEST

04

LISTENING TEST

In the Listening test, you will be asked to demonstrate how well you understand spoken English. The entire Listening test will last approximately 45 minutes. There are four parts, and directions are given for each part. You must mark your answers on the separate answer sheet. Do not write your answers in your test book.

PART 1

Directions: For each question in this part, you will hear four statements about a picture in your test book. When you hear the statements, you must select the one statement that best describes what you see in the picture. Then find the number of the question on your answer sheet and mark your answer. The statements will not be printed in your test book and will be spoken only one time.

Statement (C), "They're sitting at a table," is the best description of the picture, so you should select answer (C) and mark it on your answer sheet.

1.

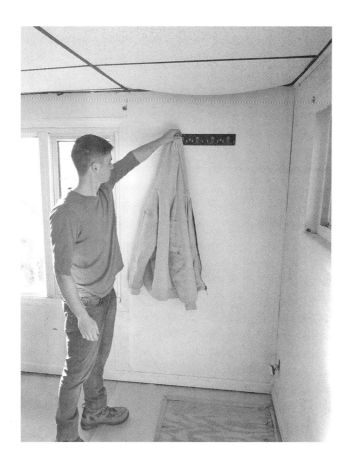

2.

GO ON TO THE NEXT PAGE

3.

4.

5.

6.

GO ON TO THE NEXT PAGE

PART 2

Directions: You will hear a question or statement and three responses spoken in English. They will not be printed in your test book and will be spoken only one time. Select the best response to the question or statement and mark the letter (A), (B), or (C) on your answer sheet.

7. Mark your answer on your answer sheet.

8. Mark your answer on your answer sheet.

9. Mark your answer on your answer sheet.

10. Mark your answer on your answer sheet.

11. Mark your answer on your answer sheet.

12. Mark your answer on your answer sheet.

13. Mark your answer on your answer sheet.

14. Mark your answer on your answer sheet.

15. Mark your answer on your answer sheet.

16. Mark your answer on your answer sheet.

17. Mark your answer on your answer sheet.

18. Mark your answer on your answer sheet.

19. Mark your answer on your answer sheet.

20. Mark your answer on your answer sheet.

21. Mark your answer on your answer sheet.

22. Mark your answer on your answer sheet.

23. Mark your answer on your answer sheet.

24. Mark your answer on your answer sheet.

25. Mark your answer on your answer sheet.

26. Mark your answer on your answer sheet.

27. Mark your answer on your answer sheet.

28. Mark your answer on your answer sheet.

29. Mark your answer on your answer sheet.

30. Mark your answer on your answer sheet.

31. Mark your answer on your answer sheet.

PART 3

Directions: You will hear some conversations between two or more people. You will be asked to answer three questions about what the speakers say in each conversation. Select the best response to each question and mark the letter (A), (B), (C), or (D) on your answer sheet. The conversations will not be printed in your test book and will be spoken only one time.

32. Who most likely is the man?
    (A) A delivery person
    (B) A contractor
    (C) A salesperson
    (D) A house cleaner

33. What will the man most likely bring when he returns?
    (A) An updated invoice
    (B) A product recommended to him
    (C) A new tool
    (D) A replacement tile

34. When will the man most likely return to the woman's house?
    (A) On Thursday morning
    (B) On Thursday afternoon
    (C) On Friday morning
    (D) On Friday afternoon

35. What are the speakers mainly discussing?
    (A) The condition of forest paths
    (B) Hiking options
    (C) A recycling program
    (D) Vending machines

36. What is the woman concerned about?
    (A) The condition of the visitor center
    (B) Materials being disposed of properly
    (C) The need for new plastic bins
    (D) Her work schedule

37. What does the man suggest?
    (A) Showing a video
    (B) Purchasing a television
    (C) Recording some instructions
    (D) Hiring additional workers

38. Who most likely is the woman?
    (A) A manager
    (B) A consultant
    (C) A salesperson
    (D) A trainer

39. What did Takeshi tell the man?
    (A) The training session will increase sales.
    (B) The training session was not useful.
    (C) Some people prefer independent work.
    (D) More salespeople will be hired.

40. What will the man most likely do next?
    (A) Meet with the salespeople face-to-face
    (B) Ask Takeshi to talk to his teams
    (C) Cancel this week's sales meeting
    (D) Discuss future training sessions

41. Where do the speakers most likely work?
    (A) At an accounting firm
    (B) At a warehouse
    (C) At a university bookstore
    (D) At a book-publishing company

42. What is the woman's assignment?
    (A) To prepare a sales report
    (B) To train recently hired employees
    (C) To take notes during staff meetings
    (D) To proofread reports

43. Why will the woman be unable to help the man?
    (A) She lacks the technical training.
    (B) She is too busy.
    (C) She is unsure of what Anna really wants.
    (D) She sent her laptop to be serviced.

GO ON TO THE NEXT PAGE

44. Who most likely are the speakers?

(A) School teachers
(B) Employees of a nature area
(C) Members of a bird-watching club
(D) Construction workers

45. What problem are the speakers discussing?

(A) The proposed location of a building
(B) The schedule of a community event
(C) Some recently completed construction
(D) Damage caused by animals

46. What does the man suggest the speakers do?

(A) Contact some builders
(B) Conduct a tour of a nature preserve
(C) Hold a meeting at their workplace
(D) Post an announcement at the community center

47. What does the man say about hiring a new employee?

(A) The hiring process is already finished.
(B) Hiring may not be necessary.
(C) There are no qualified applicants.
(D) There is no money in the budget.

48. What does the woman suggest?

(A) Contracting some advertising work
(B) Discussing the problem at the next meeting
(C) Training new factory team workers
(D) Hiring a temporary employee

49. Why will the speakers talk to Janet Olsen?

(A) To get her opinion about an issue
(B) To ask how a problem was solved previously
(C) To learn whether they can use her office
(D) To ask about a recently hired team member

50. What may prevent the woman from seeing the exhibit?

(A) The exhibit will close early.
(B) A parade will be held.
(C) The buses are not running.
(D) She has a work commitment.

51. What does the man tell the woman she can do?

(A) Get a full refund
(B) Donate the cost of her tickets
(C) Exchange her tickets for another date
(D) Give her tickets to family members

52. What does the woman imply when she says, "Oh, I have too many financial commitments at the moment"?

(A) She will call the man back later.
(B) She will not visit the gift shop.
(C) She will not attend a special event.
(D) She will not purchase a membership.

53. What did Petra do on her way to the office?

(A) She dropped a brochure off at a local store.
(B) She stopped at a printing shop.
(C) She shopped at an office store for some supplies.
(D) She contacted a repair technician.

54. What does the man say about the brochure the speakers are discussing?

(A) He likes the bright colors.
(B) He already approved it.
(C) It contains too much information.
(D) It was redesigned several times.

55. Why will Petra make a phone call?

(A) To order copies
(B) To change a deadline
(C) To get a mistake corrected
(D) To try to get a price reduced

56. What does the woman imply when she says, "I haven't had a chance to look at it"?

(A) She is not interested in the price list.
(B) She likes the old furniture in the meeting room.
(C) The furniture prices are very high.
(D) The office furniture has not been ordered.

57. What is most likely true about the travel arrangements that the woman is working on?

(A) They are taking more time than expected.
(B) They will be finished tomorrow.
(C) There are only two people working on them.
(D) The man is responsible for managing them.

58. What does the man suggest that the woman do?

(A) Train a coworker to order furniture
(B) Ask whether a responsibility can be removed
(C) Find somebody to help with travel planning
(D) Apply for a management position

59. Who most likely is the woman?

(A) A consulting company employee
(B) A Web developer
(C) A supervisor
(D) A certified trainer

60. What does the woman tell Felix' supervisor?

(A) She can provide some paperwork.
(B) She is paid hourly.
(C) She is not familiar with a feature.
(D) She has employees who can complete a task.

61. When will a Web site be launched?

(A) Once a feature is added
(B) Later that day
(C) After two companies merge
(D) In the coming week

Monarch Pottery	
Weekly Schedule	
Monday	Hand Building (adults)
Tuesday	Wheel Throwing (adults)
Wednesday	Hand Building (children)
Thursday	Wheel Throwing (children)
Friday	No classes

62. What problem does the woman mention?

(A) Her order arrived late.
(B) Her order is missing an item.
(C) She did not order enough of an item.
(D) She did not receive an invoice.

63. What does the man say about some buckets of glaze?

(A) They contain the wrong color glaze.
(B) They are on the delivery truck now.
(C) They were left behind.
(D) They are heavier than they look.

64. Look at the graphic. On which day is the conversation taking place?

(A) Tuesday
(B) Wednesday
(C) Thursday
(D) Friday

GO ON TO THE NEXT PAGE

Monaco Hotel

Host your business event
with us!

❧ Package	Number of guests ❧
Bronze	125
Silver	150
Gold	175
Platinum	200

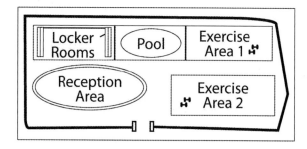

65. What are the speakers mainly discussing?

(A) A conference hosted by another
company
(B) A location for an upcoming conference
(C) The purpose of an annual conference
(D) A conference speaker they both admire

66. What does the man imply about conference
participants?

(A) They will choose food options from a
menu.
(B) They will eat breakfast together.
(C) They will not be provided with meals.
(D) They must buy snacks from a nearby
store.

67. Look at the graphic. Which package will the
speakers most likely purchase?

(A) Bronze
(B) Silver
(C) Gold
(D) Platinum

68. Where most likely does the woman work?

(A) At a delivery company
(B) At a fitness center
(C) At a truck repair facility
(D) At an exercise equipment manufacturer

69. Look at the graphic. Where will the five
heavy boxes be put?

(A) In the reception area
(B) In the locker rooms
(C) In exercise area 1
(D) In exercise area 2

70. What equipment was delivered yesterday?

(A) Rowing machines
(B) Furniture
(C) Pool supplies
(D) Weight-lifting equipment

PART 4

Directions: You will hear some talks given by a single speaker. You will be asked to answer three questions about what the speaker says in each talk. Select the best response to each question and mark the letter (A), (B), (C), or (D) on your answer sheet. The talks will not be printed in your test book and will be spoken only one time.

71. Who is the speaker?

(A) A book author
(B) A park ranger
(C) A tour guide
(D) A painter

72. What will the listeners mostly see during their visit?

(A) Rare plants
(B) Works of art
(C) Antique furnishing
(D) A nineteenth-century library

73. What does the speaker invite the listeners to do?

(A) Use a map
(B) Make a purchase
(C) Stay with the group
(D) Take pictures

74. What does the speaker recommend doing?

(A) Creating more charging stations
(B) Buying an electric pickup truck
(C) Getting new tires
(D) Shopping for a sports car

75. What disadvantage of electric pickup trucks does the speaker mention?

(A) Their high cost
(B) Their engine noise
(C) Their slow speed
(D) Their small size

76. What alternative use for electric pickup trucks does the speaker mention?

(A) Sheltering animals
(B) Generating radio signals
(C) Supporting building structures
(D) Powering homes

77. Who most likely is the speaker?

(A) A store cashier
(B) A produce supplier
(C) A restaurant owner
(D) A supermarket manager

78. What are the owners doing?

(A) Increasing staff pay
(B) Introducing new products
(C) Hosting a dinner
(D) Hiring more employees

79. What does the speaker imply when she says, "There's a sign-up sheet in the staff room"?

(A) The new work hours are voluntary.
(B) People who sign up get a reward.
(C) All employees must sign up for a shift.
(D) The meeting will continue in the staff room.

80. What is being advertised?

(A) A solar heating system for homes
(B) A contest for a new heating system
(C) A home cleaning service
(D) A service for home heating systems

81. What does the advertisement emphasize about the company?

(A) Its 24-hour service
(B) Its special cameras
(C) Its low prices
(D) Its customer service

82. How can the listeners get a discount?

(A) By presenting a coupon
(B) By scheduling an appointment online
(C) By mentioning a radio advertisement
(D) By joining a mailing list

GO ON TO THE NEXT PAGE

83. What is the purpose of the meeting?

    (A) To welcome new managers
    (B) To fix a problem with a training program
    (C) To provide an update
    (D) To announce a change in strategy

84. What does the speaker imply when he says, "But we hope to be a strong partner with Regent during this construction boom"?

    (A) Regent is a new construction company.
    (B) The plant may earn profits soon.
    (C) The plant needs to create new products.
    (D) The company needs to build more plants.

85. What did new employees do?

    (A) They inspected local mines.
    (B) They delivered raw materials.
    (C) They constructed a building.
    (D) They acquired certification.

86. What will happen at Coleman's Downtown Theater this weekend?

    (A) Movies of a special type will be shown.
    (B) An actor will sign autographs.
    (C) Collectors will gather for a trade show.
    (D) An outdoor seating area will be opened.

87. What might people learn this weekend?

    (A) How to prepare to run a marathon
    (B) How the city has grown in 100 years
    (C) The history of space exploration
    (D) The history of an art form

88. Who will be in the lobby on Sunday?

    (A) A professional who works in the movies
    (B) A writer who has released a new book
    (C) A historian from a nearby university
    (D) An astronaut who has been to space

89. What work do the listeners do?

    (A) Train security guards
    (B) Make advertisements
    (C) Create security software
    (D) Provide financial advice

90. What will happen tonight?

    (A) Security systems will be updated.
    (B) More security guards will be on duty.
    (C) Financial data will be revised.
    (D) New computers will be purchased.

91. Why does the speaker say, "We are the most trusted company in the industry, and we want to stay that way"?

    (A) To congratulate a colleague
    (B) To show appreciation to clients
    (C) To motivate the listeners to act
    (D) To introduce the next speaker

92. What is the purpose of the broadcast?

    (A) To promote healthy eating habits
    (B) To describe new recipes
    (C) To review local restaurants
    (D) To promote Italian culture

93. What does the speaker criticize about Maria's Kitchen?

    (A) The cost
    (B) The service
    (C) The parking
    (D) The view

94. What does the speaker recommend that the listeners do?

    (A) Try the Italian food at Maria's Kitchen
    (B) Cook Italian food at home
    (C) Order the chicken at Arno's Bistro
    (D) Travel outside the area for the best Italian food

Save Our Date

Sophia and Randy

June 2
Newfield Hotel
5:00 P.M. reception in the Rose Garden
Music by Moderne Heart

95. Who most likely is the listener?

    (A) A band leader
    (B) A wedding planner
    (C) A restaurant worker
    (D) A professional printer

96. What problem does the speaker mention?

    (A) A delayed flight
    (B) An unavailable musician
    (C) Additional guests
    (D) A change in weather

97. Look at the graphic. What information will most likely be changed?

    (A) Newfield Hotel
    (B) 5:00 P.M.
    (C) Rose Garden
    (D) Moderne Heart

Car Production Stages

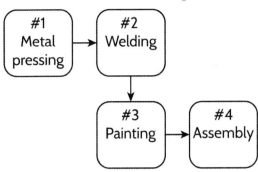

98. Who is Sayan Mitra?

    (A) A customer service representative
    (B) An accountant
    (C) A car dealer
    (D) A consultant

99. Look at the graphic. Which stage of car production is the speaker discussing?

    (A) Stage 1
    (B) Stage 2
    (C) Stage 3
    (D) Stage 4

100. What will the listeners most likely do next?

    (A) View a presentation
    (B) Ask some questions
    (C) Review some specifications
    (D) Return to their desks

TEST 4

This is the end of the Listening test.

토익 정기시험
실전 ❶ 1000
LC

실전 TEST

05

LISTENING TEST

In the Listening test, you will be asked to demonstrate how well you understand spoken English. The entire Listening test will last approximately 45 minutes. There are four parts, and directions are given for each part. You must mark your answers on the separate answer sheet. Do not write your answers in your test book.

PART 1

Directions: For each question in this part, you will hear four statements about a picture in your test book. When you hear the statements, you must select the one statement that best describes what you see in the picture. Then find the number of the question on your answer sheet and mark your answer. The statements will not be printed in your test book and will be spoken only one time.

Statement (C), "They're sitting at a table," is the best description of the picture, so you should select answer (C) and mark it on your answer sheet.

1.

2.

GO ON TO THE NEXT PAGE ➡

3.

4.

5.

6.

GO ON TO THE NEXT PAGE

PART 2

Directions: You will hear a question or statement and three responses spoken in English. They will not be printed in your test book and will be spoken only one time. Select the best response to the question or statement and mark the letter (A), (B), or (C) on your answer sheet.

7. Mark your answer on your answer sheet.

8. Mark your answer on your answer sheet.

9. Mark your answer on your answer sheet.

10. Mark your answer on your answer sheet.

11. Mark your answer on your answer sheet.

12. Mark your answer on your answer sheet.

13. Mark your answer on your answer sheet.

14. Mark your answer on your answer sheet.

15. Mark your answer on your answer sheet.

16. Mark your answer on your answer sheet.

17. Mark your answer on your answer sheet.

18. Mark your answer on your answer sheet.

19. Mark your answer on your answer sheet.

20. Mark your answer on your answer sheet.

21. Mark your answer on your answer sheet.

22. Mark your answer on your answer sheet.

23. Mark your answer on your answer sheet.

24. Mark your answer on your answer sheet.

25. Mark your answer on your answer sheet.

26. Mark your answer on your answer sheet.

27. Mark your answer on your answer sheet.

28. Mark your answer on your answer sheet.

29. Mark your answer on your answer sheet.

30. Mark your answer on your answer sheet.

31. Mark your answer on your answer sheet.

Directions: You will hear some conversations between two or more people. You will be asked to answer three questions about what the speakers say in each conversation. Select the best response to each question and mark the letter (A), (B), (C), or (D) on your answer sheet. The conversations will not be printed in your test book and will be spoken only one time.

32. What are the speakers discussing?

 (A) Plans for an upcoming event
 (B) The quality of the man's poems
 (C) The publishing company they work for
 (D) A problem with the woman's phone

33. What does the man need?

 (A) Permission from his company
 (B) Contact information
 (C) An extra table
 (D) The location of a park

34. What will the woman do next?

 (A) Call the man's manager
 (B) Send a text message
 (C) Talk with an editor
 (D) Check a schedule

35. Why does the woman call the man?

 (A) To discuss renewing a contract
 (B) To discuss a transportation issue
 (C) To announce a change in price
 (D) To announce a personnel change

36. What does the man say about the current advertising?

 (A) It is a good low-cost option.
 (B) It has not led to a significant increase in sales.
 (C) His colleagues have decided to cancel it.
 (D) His colleagues do not have time to discuss it.

37. What will the speakers discuss in their next meeting?

 (A) Hiring a celebrity
 (B) Advertising on the Internet
 (C) Expanding an advertising budget
 (D) Changing advertising companies

38. Where does the conversation most likely take place?

 (A) At a farmers market
 (B) In a restaurant kitchen
 (C) In a grocery store
 (D) At a shipping company

39. Why is Miho concerned about the delivery?

 (A) It seems too small.
 (B) It arrived late.
 (C) It contains a large quantity of one item.
 (D) One type of item is missing from it.

40. What does Miho offer to do?

 (A) Help the man with his task
 (B) Contact Mr. Okamura
 (C) Sign for a delivery
 (D) Find a replacement worker

41. What will the man do tomorrow morning?

 (A) Meet with a client
 (B) Visit a doctor's office
 (C) Relocate to a different office
 (D) Attend a presentation

42. What does the woman tell the man to do?

 (A) Fill in some forms
 (B) Update a contact number
 (C) Make a payment
 (D) Choose a menu item

43. What reminder does the woman give the man?

 (A) A colleague is out of town.
 (B) A price has changed.
 (C) Some software must be updated.
 (D) A parking area is closed.

GO ON TO THE NEXT PAGE

44. Where is the conversation most likely taking place?

(A) At a bus terminal
(B) At an airport
(C) In a hotel lobby
(D) In a conference hall

45. What does the woman ask for?

(A) A different seat
(B) A name badge
(C) A room upgrade
(D) A special menu

46. Why does the woman say, "I'm the guest speaker at a conference"?

(A) To confirm her conference attendance
(B) To introduce herself
(C) To refuse an offer
(D) To clarify a misunderstanding

47. What issue does the man discuss with the woman?

(A) His employees need access to the roof.
(B) Part of his plan needs to be rescheduled.
(C) A shipment of steel was incomplete.
(D) A renovation project is over budget.

48. Who most likely is the woman?

(A) An architect
(B) A financial analyst
(C) A construction worker
(D) A building manager

49. What will the man do next?

(A) Close the building temporarily
(B) Get approval from his supervisor
(C) Reach out to city officials
(D) Arrange a new payment schedule

50. What does Mr. Jones announce?

(A) A change of plans
(B) A book-signing event
(C) New store hours
(D) A price change

51. What is the woman concerned about?

(A) The accuracy of some software
(B) An increased workload
(C) Customer complaints
(D) Running out of supplies

52. What does Marc emphasize?

(A) Reduced operating expenses
(B) Greater inventory availability
(C) The efficiency of a new system
(D) The need for extra training

53. What will begin next month?

(A) A television show
(B) A musical
(C) A photo exhibition
(D) A rehearsal for a music video

54. What does the woman say about the e-mail?

(A) She is not happy with the attached photos.
(B) She expected it to contain a video.
(C) She thought it would arrive earlier.
(D) She has not had time to read it.

55. What does the woman suggest that Michael Byrne do on Friday?

(A) Talk with her on the phone about a video
(B) Share some ideas for a new musical
(C) Help her with a problem at the studio
(D) Allow extra time to get to his appointment

56. What are the speakers mainly discussing?

(A) A musician who has become successful
(B) A company decision to stop offering a service
(C) A licensing agreement with a popular singer
(D) A possible change to a product

57. What problem was identified in a customer survey about video games?

(A) Some video games are too difficult.
(B) Customers do not like the music.
(C) Some games only work with expensive equipment.
(D) Some games are completely defective.

58. Why does the woman say, "So, let's not rush this decision"?

(A) To request more funding from the division leaders
(B) To reject the man's suggestion
(C) To obtain a replacement product
(D) To recommend a different musician

59. What does the man say he will do today?

(A) Greet patients
(B) Train a new employee
(C) Transfer medical records
(D) Make appointments

60. What is the woman concerned about?

(A) The cost of hiring a new office assistant
(B) Maintaining the security of electronic files
(C) The privacy of patients in the office
(D) Using a scheduling system

61. Why does the man feel confident in the temporary office assistant?

(A) He will be able to help the assistant if the office gets busy.
(B) He has worked with the assistant on other projects.
(C) The doctor recommended that he hire the assistant.
(D) The assistant comes from an agency that specializes in medical work.

Invoice	
From: Prebble Flower Distributors	
To: Michelle's Flower Shop	
Roses (125)	$155
Tulips (100)	$130
Calla lilies (75)	$180
Carnations (50)	$85

62. Why is the woman calling?

(A) To report that an order is incomplete
(B) To report that some flowers are damaged
(C) To ask for a discount
(D) To check on a client

63. What did the man forget to do?

(A) To provide a discount
(B) To meet with some clients
(C) To report a delay
(D) To correct an invoice

64. Look at the graphic. Which price will change on the invoice?

(A) $155
(B) $130
(C) $180
(D) $85

GO ON TO THE NEXT PAGE

Handimax Coffee Maker

On — Light 1

Keep Warm — Light 2

Light 4 — Add Water

Off — Light 3

65. What is the problem with the coffee maker?

(A) It often needs to be refilled with water.
(B) It turns off unexpectedly.
(C) Its display panel causes confusion.
(D) The lights are not bright enough.

66. What was different about previous models?

(A) They had more lights.
(B) They had larger lights.
(C) They had multicolor lights.
(D) They had flashing lights.

67. Look at the graphic. Which light does the man suggest moving?

(A) Light 1
(B) Light 2
(C) Light 3
(D) Light 4

Langenfeld Bakery, Inc. Multiphase Schedule Product: oatmeal raisin cookies		
Phase 1	Final internal taste test (corporate–level only)	March 1
Phase 2	Shipping to local stores	March 2–4
Phase 3	Free sample distribution and 10% discount	March 5–6
Phase 4	Resumption of full–price sales	March 7

68. What does the woman say about the bakery's customers?

(A) They are dissatisfied with the quality of a product.
(B) They think the bakery's products are overpriced.
(C) They are now aware of the bakery's social media accounts.
(D) They sometimes arrive before the bakery opens.

69. Look at the graphic. Which phase is being extended?

(A) Phase 1
(B) Phase 2
(C) Phase 3
(D) Phase 4

70. What does the woman say the bakery should do?

(A) Ship a product early
(B) Sell a wider range of products
(C) Hold a contest
(D) Advertise a discount

PART 4

Directions: You will hear some talks given by a single speaker. You will be asked to answer three questions about what the speaker says in each talk. Select the best response to each question and mark the letter (A), (B), (C), or (D) on your answer sheet. The talks will not be printed in your test book and will be spoken only one time.

71. Who is the speaker?

   (A) An investment banker
   (B) An attorney
   (C) A real estate agent
   (D) An architect

72. What does the speaker reassure the listener about?

   (A) A price is negotiable.
   (B) Some supplies have arrived.
   (C) A job applicant is qualified.
   (D) Clients are satisfied.

73. What is an advantage of Peckham?

   (A) It has beautiful scenery.
   (B) It has several parks.
   (C) It is a safe neighborhood.
   (D) It is popular.

74. Where does the talk most likely take place?

   (A) At a physical therapy office
   (B) At a primary school
   (C) At a gym
   (D) At a hospital

75. What does the speaker imply when she says, "I always double-check that the steam is working OK"?

   (A) She deserves a promotion.
   (B) She does not enjoy doing extra work.
   (C) Some complaints are unreasonable.
   (D) A task is important.

76. What will the listeners do after opening the facility?

   (A) Rent lockers to guests
   (B) Check membership identification cards
   (C) Fold towels
   (D) Answer phones

77. What is the topic of today's broadcast?

   (A) Weather
   (B) Astronomy
   (C) Gardening
   (D) Sports

78. What can the listeners do this weekend?

   (A) Learn to improve their vision
   (B) Watch a meteor shower
   (C) Go to a musical event
   (D) Listen to a special program

79. What does the speaker say some listeners can do?

   (A) Win a prize
   (B) Request advice
   (C) Ask questions
   (D) Call again later

80. What is the purpose of the luncheon?

   (A) To announce a merger
   (B) To introduce a new company president
   (C) To launch a new product
   (D) To celebrate a company's anniversary

81. What does the speaker say about the Panecks Corporation?

   (A) It opened an office in Japan.
   (B) It designed a new type of car.
   (C) It sold a large number of car radios.
   (D) It made a video of the company's history.

82. Why does the speaker say, "We have three monitors here in the front of the room"?

   (A) To introduce new staff
   (B) To remind the listeners to be careful
   (C) To emphasize technology improvements
   (D) To direct the listeners to watch a video

GO ON TO THE NEXT PAGE

83. What is Faster Now?

    (A) Job-recruiting software
    (B) An online Web site builder
    (C) A self-paced training program
    (D) A reservation app for restaurants

84. What type of business do the listeners work for?

    (A) A catering service
    (B) A technology company
    (C) A law firm
    (D) A supermarket

85. What will happen next in the meeting?

    (A) A product demonstration
    (B) A brainstorming session
    (C) A job interview
    (D) A client introduction

86. What project is the speaker discussing?

    (A) The grand opening of a shopping center
    (B) The maintenance of a city park
    (C) The repair of a highway
    (D) The construction of a building

87. What problem does the speaker mention?

    (A) Some heavy machinery is broken.
    (B) A price has changed.
    (C) There is a labor shortage.
    (D) Some supplies are late.

88. Why does the speaker say, "I know this is a last-minute request"?

    (A) To refuse an upgrade deal
    (B) To apologize for an inconvenience
    (C) To cancel a merchandise order
    (D) To express her surprise

89. According to the speaker, what will happen next week?

    (A) Some laundry rooms will be updated.
    (B) The main office of the apartment complex will be closed.
    (C) Some new tenants will move into a vacant apartment.
    (D) A parking area will become unavailable.

90. What does the speaker say about the Maple building?

    (A) It has more tenants than the other buildings.
    (B) It is the only building with a laundry room.
    (C) It is first in the project schedule.
    (D) It is where the main office is located.

91. Why should tenants stop at the main office?

    (A) To pay a laundry fee
    (B) To pick up a questionnaire
    (C) To sign a permission form
    (D) To receive a new key

92. Who most likely is the listener?

    (A) A city inspector
    (B) An electrician
    (C) A business owner
    (D) A lawyer

93. What does the speaker say about a storage room?

    (A) It will be used for electrical equipment.
    (B) It is available for rent.
    (C) It has not been built yet.
    (D) It was recently repaired.

94. What does the speaker believe will happen on the first of October?

    (A) The store will open.
    (B) The contract will be signed.
    (C) The inspection will take place.
    (D) Construction work will start.

Carsin's Food Shop

10% Off Your Total Order

Rewards Coupon

Rules of Use

1. Coupon must be presented at time of purchase.
2. Stamps, milk, and gift cards excluded.
3. May not be used with other discounts.
4. Only one coupon per customer.

95. What is the purpose of the announcement?

(A) To describe a new customer discount
(B) To introduce new employees to the team
(C) To announce the end of a rewards program
(D) To review customer-complaint policies

96. What does the speaker say about Gilroy's?

(A) It does not offer discounts.
(B) It operates outside the local area.
(C) It is a competitor.
(D) It has strict rules for employees.

97. Look at the graphic. Which rule might be changed?

(A) Rule 1
(B) Rule 2
(C) Rule 3
(D) Rule 4

Team-Building Activities

Activity 1	Quiz Game
Activity 2	Volleyball
Activity 3	Paint a Picture
Activity 4	Problem-Solving Activity

98. Who most likely is the speaker?

(A) An office manager
(B) A sports coach
(C) An accountant
(D) A computer technician

99. When will the group have a team-building activity?

(A) This afternoon
(B) Tomorrow morning
(C) Next Friday
(D) Next Saturday

100. Look at the graphic. Which activity does the speaker most likely prefer?

(A) Activity 1
(B) Activity 2
(C) Activity 3
(D) Activity 4

This is the end of the Listening test.

토익 정기시험
실전❶1000
LC

실전 TEST

06

LISTENING TEST

In the Listening test, you will be asked to demonstrate how well you understand spoken English. The entire Listening test will last approximately 45 minutes. There are four parts, and directions are given for each part. You must mark your answers on the separate answer sheet. Do not write your answers in your test book.

PART 1

Directions: For each question in this part, you will hear four statements about a picture in your test book. When you hear the statements, you must select the one statement that best describes what you see in the picture. Then find the number of the question on your answer sheet and mark your answer. The statements will not be printed in your test book and will be spoken only one time.

Statement (C), "They're sitting at a table," is the best description of the picture, so you should select answer (C) and mark it on your answer sheet.

1.

2.

GO ON TO THE NEXT PAGE

3.

4.

5.

6.

GO ON TO THE NEXT PAGE

PART 2

Directions: You will hear a question or statement and three responses spoken in English. They will not be printed in your test book and will be spoken only one time. Select the best response to the question or statement and mark the letter (A), (B), or (C) on your answer sheet.

7. Mark your answer on your answer sheet.

8. Mark your answer on your answer sheet.

9. Mark your answer on your answer sheet.

10. Mark your answer on your answer sheet.

11. Mark your answer on your answer sheet.

12. Mark your answer on your answer sheet.

13. Mark your answer on your answer sheet.

14. Mark your answer on your answer sheet.

15. Mark your answer on your answer sheet.

16. Mark your answer on your answer sheet.

17. Mark your answer on your answer sheet.

18. Mark your answer on your answer sheet.

19. Mark your answer on your answer sheet.

20. Mark your answer on your answer sheet.

21. Mark your answer on your answer sheet.

22. Mark your answer on your answer sheet.

23. Mark your answer on your answer sheet.

24. Mark your answer on your answer sheet.

25. Mark your answer on your answer sheet.

26. Mark your answer on your answer sheet.

27. Mark your answer on your answer sheet.

28. Mark your answer on your answer sheet.

29. Mark your answer on your answer sheet.

30. Mark your answer on your answer sheet.

31. Mark your answer on your answer sheet.

Directions: You will hear some conversations between two or more people. You will be asked to answer three questions about what the speakers say in each conversation. Select the best response to each question and mark the letter (A), (B), (C), or (D) on your answer sheet. The conversations will not be printed in your test book and will be spoken only one time.

32. What does the man want to do at the bank?

   (A) Close an account
   (B) Make a deposit
   (C) Apply for a loan
   (D) Interview for a job

33. What new policy are the speakers discussing?

   (A) Extending business hours
   (B) Charging a maintenance fee
   (C) Increasing online security
   (D) Offering membership benefits

34. What will the woman do next?

   (A) Go to lunch
   (B) Speak to her manager
   (C) Provide a document
   (D) Schedule an appointment

35. What event is taking place?

   (A) A retirement dinner
   (B) A client meeting
   (C) An industry conference
   (D) An award ceremony

36. What problem does the man have?

   (A) His car broke down.
   (B) He is at the wrong location.
   (C) He forgot some tickets.
   (D) He has a schedule conflict.

37. Why will the man go to his office?

   (A) To sign for a delivery
   (B) To meet a colleague
   (C) To print out a document
   (D) To pick up a gift

38. What type of business is Kelfern Limited?

   (A) A furniture company
   (B) An automobile manufacturer
   (C) A restaurant supply store
   (D) An architectural design firm

39. According to the man, what was the cause of a problem?

   (A) A delivery was late.
   (B) A part was missing.
   (C) A product was damaged.
   (D) A code was entered incorrectly.

40. What will the woman offer Kelfern Limited?

   (A) Free installation
   (B) Next-day delivery
   (C) A discount
   (D) A full refund

41. What industry do the speakers work in?

   (A) Transportation
   (B) Tourism
   (C) Food service
   (D) Journalism

42. According to the woman, what event will be held on Saturday?

   (A) A farmers market
   (B) A theater performance
   (C) A sports competition
   (D) A community festival

43. What is the man concerned about?

   (A) Getting enough tickets
   (B) Having the appropriate permit
   (C) Publicizing an event
   (D) Preparing for rain

GO ON TO THE NEXT PAGE

TEST 6

44. Who most likely is the woman?

    (A) An antiques appraiser
    (B) An interior decorator
    (C) A graphic artist
    (D) A repair technician

45. What does the man say he plans to do with an item?

    (A) Give it to a family member
    (B) Donate it to a museum
    (C) Display it in his home
    (D) Sell it at an auction

46. What will the woman give the man?

    (A) A brochure
    (B) A list of contacts
    (C) A bill
    (D) An event schedule

47. What problem are the speakers discussing?

    (A) An office space is too small.
    (B) Some medical forms are incomplete.
    (C) Some patients are missing appointments.
    (D) The wrong supplies were delivered.

48. What does the man suggest doing?

    (A) Purchasing some software
    (B) Hiring an additional staff member
    (C) Contacting an equipment vendor
    (D) Locating a confirmation number

49. What does the woman say she will do next?

    (A) Get recommendations
    (B) Confirm a budget
    (C) Call in a prescription order
    (D) Update patient contact details

50. What industry do the men work in?

    (A) Fishing
    (B) Tourism
    (C) Trucking
    (D) Manufacturing

51. What problem are the speakers discussing?

    (A) The weather is unpredictable.
    (B) A machine is broken.
    (C) An employee is absent.
    (D) Operating costs have risen.

52. What will the woman most likely do next?

    (A) Lead a group outing
    (B) Open a weather application
    (C) Check a schedule
    (D) Negotiate a discount

53. Why is the man going to a conference?

    (A) To promote his products
    (B) To earn a certification
    (C) To facilitate a workshop
    (D) To learn about new technology

54. Why does the woman say, "there are no presentations in the evenings"?

    (A) To decline an invitation
    (B) To express surprise
    (C) To make a suggestion
    (D) To complain about an event

55. What does the woman remind the man to do?

    (A) Keep some receipts
    (B) Confirm a reservation
    (C) Make a phone call
    (D) Check a map

56. Where do the women work?

(A) At a research laboratory
(B) At a wildlife park
(C) At a newspaper
(D) At an event venue

57. What will the women most likely purchase from the man?

(A) Outdoor cameras
(B) Construction supplies
(C) Printing materials
(D) Safety equipment

58. What advantage do the women mention?

(A) Training opportunities
(B) Cost savings
(C) Increased publicity
(D) Efficient staff scheduling

59. Where do the speakers most likely work?

(A) At an electronics store
(B) At a bank
(C) At a medical clinic
(D) At a radio station

60. What will the woman do on Tuesday?

(A) Take inventory
(B) Speak at a convention
(C) Conduct an interview
(D) Respond to e-mails

61. What does the woman mean when she says, "but the program isn't completely accurate"?

(A) Some software needs to be upgraded.
(B) Some transcripts should be checked.
(C) There was a mistake in the budget.
(D) A schedule will need to be confirmed.

Model	Power Source
10G	Gas-powered
15EW	Electric (wired)
20AB	Battery (traditional)
50SP	Solar (rechargeable)

62. What is the woman preparing?

(A) An owner's manual
(B) A media release
(C) A financial report
(D) A questionnaire

63. Look at the graphic. According to the woman, which is the most successful model?

(A) 10G
(B) 15EW
(C) 20AB
(D) 50SP

64. What does the man think consumers like about a product?

(A) It has an extended warranty.
(B) It is widely available.
(C) It is easy to install.
(D) It is reasonably priced.

GO ON TO THE NEXT PAGE

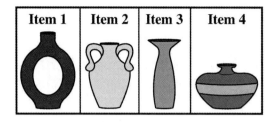

Item 1	Item 2	Item 3	Item 4

65. What has the man been hired to decorate?

(A) A museum entrance
(B) A client's office
(C) A hotel lobby
(D) A rooftop garden

66. Look at the graphic. Which item does the man choose?

(A) Item 1
(B) Item 2
(C) Item 3
(D) Item 4

67. What will the woman talk to a colleague about?

(A) A delivery date
(B) An employee discount
(C) A payment method
(D) A product substitution

Somerville Tours	Time	Length
Downtown West	9 A.M.	1 hour
Downtown East	10 A.M.	1 hour
Riverside	11 A.M.	1 ½ hours
Combination tour	12 P.M.	2 hours

68. Why is the man interested in taking a tour?

(A) To do research for a book
(B) To choose an area to live in
(C) To evaluate a company's service
(D) To take photographs for a Web site

69. Look at the graphic. What time does the most popular tour begin?

(A) At 9 A.M.
(B) At 10 A.M.
(C) At 11 A.M.
(D) At 12 P.M.

70. What will the man most likely do?

(A) Book tickets in advance
(B) Rent an audio device
(C) Visit the library
(D) Wait for cooler weather

Directions: You will hear some talks given by a single speaker. You will be asked to answer three questions about what the speaker says in each talk. Select the best response to each question and mark the letter (A), (B), (C), or (D) on your answer sheet. The talks will not be printed in your test book and will be spoken only one time.

71. What product is being advertised?

(A) A refrigerator
(B) An automobile
(C) A blender
(D) A fan

72. Why is the company proud of the product?

(A) It is available worldwide.
(B) It is quiet.
(C) It is affordable.
(D) It won an award.

73. How can the listeners receive a discount?

(A) By creating an online profile
(B) By purchasing multiple products
(C) By using a special code
(D) By writing a product review

74. Where does the talk most likely take place?

(A) At a restaurant
(B) At a print shop
(C) At a computer store
(D) At a manufacturing plant

75. According to the speaker, why is a change being made?

(A) To save storage space
(B) To address customer feedback
(C) To be environmentally responsible
(D) To improve employee satisfaction

76. What does the speaker ask the listeners to do?

(A) Review a safety manual
(B) Record time accurately
(C) Wear appropriate clothing
(D) Assist customers with a process

77. What does the speaker's company sell?

(A) Children's clothing
(B) Office furniture
(C) Bottled drinks
(D) Sports equipment

78. What did Claudia suggest doing?

(A) Holding a contest for customers
(B) Placing advertisements on social media
(C) Hiring a celebrity spokesperson
(D) Sponsoring a music festival

79. What will the listeners receive on June 3 ?

(A) A salary bonus
(B) A day off
(C) A new ID card
(D) A product sample

80. Why do the listeners have to follow a protocol?

(A) To secure the building
(B) To ensure accurate data
(C) To protect delicate items
(D) To obtain certification

81. Where should the listeners place their belongings?

(A) On a shelf
(B) In lockers
(C) On study tables
(D) In a filing cabinet

82. What information does the speaker provide about the cafeteria?

(A) Its menu
(B) Its seating capacity
(C) Its hours of operation
(D) Its location

TEST 6

GO ON TO THE NEXT PAGE

83. What type of business does the speaker work for?

(A) An accounting firm
(B) A law firm
(C) A graphic design service
(D) An editing service

84. According to the speaker, what will the listener receive by e-mail?

(A) An updated price list
(B) A system notification
(C) A calendar invitation
(D) A revised agenda

85. What does the speaker imply when she says, "We guarantee a turnaround time of ten days"?

(A) A request may not be met.
(B) A refund will be issued soon.
(C) Additional staff is needed.
(D) High rates are justified.

86. What is the podcast about?

(A) Real estate
(B) Forestry
(C) Sports management
(D) Solar energy

87. What job benefit does Jessica Williams mention?

(A) Meeting new people
(B) Having flexible hours
(C) Being outdoors
(D) Working remotely

88. What will the speaker ask Jessica Williams about?

(A) Her teaching experience
(B) Her publications
(C) Her travels
(D) Her education

89. Where is the announcement taking place?

(A) On a boat
(B) On a bus
(C) On a train
(D) On an airplane

90. What information does the speaker say he will provide?

(A) Historical facts
(B) Sightseeing suggestions
(C) Details about special events
(D) Safety instructions

91. Why does the speaker say, "the path is too wet from last night's rain"?

(A) To request directions
(B) To make a recommendation
(C) To announce a change of plans
(D) To decline an invitation

92. What industry does the speaker most likely work in?

(A) Aviation
(B) Construction
(C) Automotive
(D) Shipping

93. Why does the speaker say, "But we'll always need workers here"?

(A) To complain about a staff shortage
(B) To address a concern
(C) To suggest a schedule change
(D) To disagree with a proposal

94. What will the speaker do next?

(A) Distribute a document
(B) Begin a slideshow
(C) Demonstrate a product
(D) Hand out awards

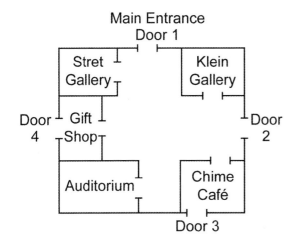

Main Entrance
Door 1

Stret Gallery

Klein Gallery

Door 4

Gift Shop

Door 2

Auditorium

Chime Café

Door 3

Daily Schedule	
Appointment Time	Doctor
9:30 A.M.	Dr. Sugiyama
11:00 A.M.	Dr. Stewart
12:00 P.M.	Dr. Kim
12:30 P.M.	Dr. Alabi

95. Who most likely is the speaker?

(A) A tour guide
(B) An artist
(C) A security guard
(D) An exhibit curator

96. What does the speaker recommend?

(A) Eating outside on a terrace
(B) Becoming museum members
(C) Purchasing souvenirs
(D) Viewing a film

97. Look at the graphic. Where will the listeners meet in one hour?

(A) At Door 1
(B) At Door 2
(C) At Door 3
(D) At Door 4

98. Look at the graphic. Which dentist will the listener see?

(A) Dr. Sugiyama
(B) Dr. Stewart
(C) Dr. Kim
(D) Dr. Alabi

99. Why is the speaker calling?

(A) To explain a procedure
(B) To reschedule an appointment
(C) To ask about a payment
(D) To confirm insurance information

100. What does the speaker recommend that the listener do?

(A) Review the dentist's instructions
(B) Park on the street
(C) Fill out some paperwork
(D) Use a different credit card

This is the end of the Listening test.

토익 정기시험
실전❶1000
LC

실전 TEST

07

LISTENING TEST

In the Listening test, you will be asked to demonstrate how well you understand spoken English. The entire Listening test will last approximately 45 minutes. There are four parts, and directions are given for each part. You must mark your answers on the separate answer sheet. Do not write your answers in your test book.

PART 1

Directions: For each question in this part, you will hear four statements about a picture in your test book. When you hear the statements, you must select the one statement that best describes what you see in the picture. Then find the number of the question on your answer sheet and mark your answer. The statements will not be printed in your test book and will be spoken only one time.

Statement (C), "They're sitting at a table," is the best description of the picture, so you should select answer (C) and mark it on your answer sheet.

1.

2.

GO ON TO THE NEXT PAGE

3.

4.

5.

6.

GO ON TO THE NEXT PAGE ➡

PART 2

7. Mark your answer on your answer sheet.

8. Mark your answer on your answer sheet.

9. Mark your answer on your answer sheet.

10. Mark your answer on your answer sheet.

11. Mark your answer on your answer sheet.

12. Mark your answer on your answer sheet.

13. Mark your answer on your answer sheet.

14. Mark your answer on your answer sheet.

15. Mark your answer on your answer sheet.

16. Mark your answer on your answer sheet.

17. Mark your answer on your answer sheet.

18. Mark your answer on your answer sheet.

19. Mark your answer on your answer sheet.

20. Mark your answer on your answer sheet.

21. Mark your answer on your answer sheet.

22. Mark your answer on your answer sheet.

23. Mark your answer on your answer sheet.

24. Mark your answer on your answer sheet.

25. Mark your answer on your answer sheet.

26. Mark your answer on your answer sheet.

27. Mark your answer on your answer sheet.

28. Mark your answer on your answer sheet.

29. Mark your answer on your answer sheet.

30. Mark your answer on your answer sheet.

31. Mark your answer on your answer sheet.

PART 3

Directions: You will hear some conversations between two or more people. You will be asked to answer three questions about what the speakers say in each conversation. Select the best response to each question and mark the letter (A), (B), (C), or (D) on your answer sheet. The conversations will not be printed in your test book and will be spoken only one time.

32. What are the speakers discussing?

    (A) Moving to a new office
    (B) Painting some walls
    (C) Purchasing some furniture
    (D) Raising employee salaries

33. What did the woman ask a team about?

    (A) Group assignments
    (B) Vacation schedules
    (C) Software preferences
    (D) Work-from-home dates

34. What does the man offer to do?

    (A) Contact some businesses
    (B) Get a manager's approval
    (C) Calculate some costs
    (D) Send a notification e-mail

35. Where do the speakers most likely work?

    (A) At an appliance store
    (B) At a restaurant
    (C) At a food-manufacturing plant
    (D) At a cooking school

36. What problem does the man mention?

    (A) Some uniforms have not been delivered.
    (B) Some paperwork was misfiled.
    (C) A business will be understaffed.
    (D) A permit has not been approved.

37. What does the woman say she will do?

    (A) Schedule an upcoming training session
    (B) Inform customers of a potential delay
    (C) Work an extra shift
    (D) Contact a vendor

38. What was the woman hired to do for a video game?

    (A) Provide feedback
    (B) Create some animations
    (C) Compose a musical score
    (D) Write a script

39. According to the man, who has a video game been designed for?

    (A) Medical personnel
    (B) Human resource specialists
    (C) Delivery drivers
    (D) Assembly-line workers

40. What does the man invite the woman to do?

    (A) Store her items in a locker
    (B) Tour a building
    (C) Choose a place to work
    (D) Get some food

41. Why did the man come to the woman's office?

    (A) To discuss a report
    (B) To deliver some tools
    (C) To review job applications
    (D) To make a repair

42. What does the man ask the woman to do?

    (A) Provide a signature
    (B) Confirm a budget
    (C) Print a document
    (D) Clear a work space

43. What does the man notice?

    (A) An item is not a standard size.
    (B) Some information is missing.
    (C) A cord is unplugged.
    (D) A manual is not accurate.

GO ON TO THE NEXT PAGE

44. Why is the woman calling?

   (A) To report a power outage
   (B) To inquire about a bill
   (C) To get advice about energy savings
   (D) To transfer a service to a new location

45. What did the woman do a month ago?

   (A) She had solar panels installed.
   (B) She changed banks.
   (C) She took a vacation.
   (D) She opened a business.

46. What does the man say the woman needs to do?

   (A) Schedule an inspection
   (B) Talk to a building manager
   (C) Complete an online form
   (D) Pay an extra fee

47. Who most likely is the woman?

   (A) A research scientist
   (B) An advertising executive
   (C) A software engineer
   (D) A dentist

48. What does the woman say she has decided to do?

   (A) Accept a job offer
   (B) Purchase some equipment
   (C) Move to a new office
   (D) Take a training course

49. What do the men say are available?

   (A) Some preliminary sketches
   (B) Some consultation services
   (C) Payment plans
   (D) User manuals

50. Who most likely is the man?

   (A) A sales representative
   (B) A restaurant chef
   (C) A repair technician
   (D) A health inspector

51. What does the man offer to do?

   (A) Reduce a price
   (B) Expedite an order
   (C) Post an online notice
   (D) Photograph some items

52. Why does the woman say she is concerned?

   (A) Profits have decreased.
   (B) A competitor has recently opened.
   (C) Some supplies may run out.
   (D) Her business Web site is down.

53. Where does the woman most likely work?

   (A) At an elementary school
   (B) At a pet store
   (C) At a medical clinic
   (D) At a department store

54. What do the men suggest doing?

   (A) Upgrading a sound system
   (B) Installing a fish tank
   (C) Changing a color scheme
   (D) Replacing some flooring

55. How will some measurements be used?

   (A) To draft a cost estimate
   (B) To purchase some bookshelves
   (C) To decide what materials to use
   (D) To apply for a building permit

56. Where most likely are the speakers?

(A) At a car show
(B) At a job fair
(C) At a training workshop
(D) At a product launch

57. What does the man imply when he says, "I'm very interested in learning"?

(A) He met a deadline earlier than expected.
(B) He requires more product information.
(C) He has many hobbies.
(D) He lacks experience.

58. What does the woman give the man?

(A) A brochure
(B) A business card
(C) A company T-shirt
(D) An event schedule

---

59. What is the man organizing?

(A) A client meeting
(B) A trade show
(C) An awards banquet
(D) A company outing

60. What factor influenced the man's selection?

(A) Affordability
(B) Proximity
(C) Positive reviews
(D) Catering options

61. What does the woman imply when she says, "We book at least six months in advance"?

(A) A colleague is mistaken about a date.
(B) A request might not be accommodated.
(C) A decision needs to be made soon.
(D) A cancellation will not be possible.

Professional Cleaning!

Cost by size of business

100 square meters	$70
200 square meters	$140
300 square meters	$200
400 square meters	$300

62. What was the woman uncertain about?

(A) Transportation costs
(B) Weekend availability
(C) A company's reputation
(D) Membership fees

63. Look at the graphic. How much will the woman be charged?

(A) $70
(B) $140
(C) $200
(D) $300

64. What does the man recommend Star Services to do?

(A) Manage payroll
(B) Install mirrors
(C) Shampoo the carpets
(D) Clean the windows

GO ON TO THE NEXT PAGE

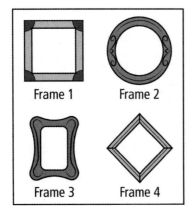

Frame 1 Frame 2

Frame 3 Frame 4

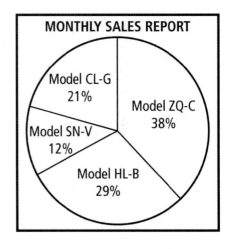

MONTHLY SALES REPORT

Model CL-G 21%
Model ZQ-C 38%
Model SN-V 12%
Model HL-B 29%

65. What is the man having framed?

(A) An invitation
(B) A photograph
(C) A diploma
(D) A painting

66. Look at the graphic. Which frame will the man most likely select?

(A) Frame 1
(B) Frame 2
(C) Frame 3
(D) Frame 4

67. What is included in the price?

(A) Delivery
(B) Labor
(C) Gift wrapping
(D) UV glass

68. Why did the woman miss an update?

(A) She was on vacation.
(B) She was meeting with clients.
(C) She was training new employees.
(D) She was at a medical appointment.

69. Look at the graphic. Which model are the speakers discussing?

(A) Model ZQ-C
(B) Model HL-B
(C) Model SN-V
(D) Model CL-G

70. According to the woman, what do customers like about an air-conditioner model?

(A) It is quiet.
(B) It is easy to install.
(C) It is energy efficient.
(D) It is inexpensive.

PART 4

Directions: You will hear some talks given by a single speaker. You will be asked to answer three questions about what the speaker says in each talk. Select the best response to each question and mark the letter (A), (B), (C), or (D) on your answer sheet. The talks will not be printed in your test book and will be spoken only one time.

71. What type of company does the speaker work for?
    - (A) A technology consulting firm
    - (B) A landscaping company
    - (C) A construction company
    - (D) A law firm

72. What good news does the speaker share about the company?
    - (A) It won a city contract.
    - (B) It will expand its headquarters.
    - (C) It has won an industry award.
    - (D) Its profits have increased.

73. What does the speaker say he will do later this week?
    - (A) Purchase new equipment
    - (B) Update some software
    - (C) Contact an advertising agency
    - (D) Post some job openings

74. Where does the talk most likely take place?
    - (A) At a press conference
    - (B) At a trade show
    - (C) At an award ceremony
    - (D) At a sports competition

75. What aspect of a product does the speaker mention?
    - (A) Its improved graphics
    - (B) Its fast download speeds
    - (C) Its high-quality audio
    - (D) Its smartphone compatibility

76. What does the speaker say the listeners can do after the talk?
    - (A) Start a free trial
    - (B) Speak to a representative
    - (C) Enjoy some refreshments
    - (D) Enter a contest

77. Where is the meeting most likely taking place?
    - (A) At a farm
    - (B) At a cafeteria
    - (C) At a warehouse
    - (D) At a grocery store

78. What does the speaker say is required?
    - (A) Requesting vacation time in advance
    - (B) Updating employee contact information
    - (C) Wearing the appropriate clothing
    - (D) Completing some employee training

79. What did the speaker find out about this week?
    - (A) Business has been slower than usual.
    - (B) Inventory has been running low.
    - (C) Employees have been missing meetings.
    - (D) Workers have been taking extended breaks.

80. What type of business is coming to an area?
    - (A) A research facility
    - (B) A delivery service
    - (C) A computer repair company
    - (D) An electronics manufacturer

81. Why was a specific location chosen?
    - (A) It is near public transportation.
    - (B) It is affordable.
    - (C) It is near an educational institution.
    - (D) It will attract a lot of customers.

82. How can the listeners find out more information?
    - (A) By attending an event
    - (B) By visiting a Web site
    - (C) By contacting a city official
    - (D) By subscribing to a newsletter

GO ON TO THE NEXT PAGE

83. What is the broadcast mainly about?

    (A) The announcement of a sporting competition
    (B) The completion of a construction project
    (C) The closing of a local business
    (D) The election of a city official

84. According to the speaker, which industry will benefit from an event?

    (A) Technology
    (B) Manufacturing
    (C) Fishing
    (D) Tourism

85. Why does the speaker say, "that's less than taking the ferry"?

    (A) To show surprise
    (B) To stress a disadvantage
    (C) To acknowledge a mistake
    (D) To offer a counterargument

86. What kind of business does the speaker work for?

    (A) A publicity agency
    (B) A plastic bag manufacturer
    (C) An accounting firm
    (D) A grocery store

87. What does the speaker mainly discuss?

    (A) Upgrading the bookkeeping system
    (B) Preparing for a new regulation
    (C) Revising a company logo
    (D) Increasing online advertising

88. What does the speaker expect one of the listeners to do?

    (A) Contact another department
    (B) Draft a timeline
    (C) Find a new supplier
    (D) Design a showroom layout

89. Who most likely is the speaker?

    (A) A journalist
    (B) An accountant
    (C) A restaurant owner
    (D) A customer service representative

90. What does the speaker say she needs the listener to do?

    (A) Contact some clients
    (B) Check an inventory list
    (C) Create a marketing campaign
    (D) Scan some information

91. Why does the speaker say, "we're offering a workshop on that topic next month"?

    (A) To reject an invitation
    (B) To explain a delay
    (C) To make a recommendation
    (D) To ask for help

92. What is the speaker discussing?

    (A) Updating a database
    (B) Hiring more staff
    (C) Revising safety guidelines
    (D) Purchasing supplies

93. Where does the speaker most likely work?

    (A) At a warehouse
    (B) At a fitness center
    (C) At a home-improvement store
    (D) At a cleaning service

94. What does the speaker imply when he says, "Tunji, I think you have a free hour tomorrow morning"?

    (A) Tunji should complete the task.
    (B) Tunji can attend the client meeting.
    (C) Tunji's schedule needs to be corrected.
    (D) Tunji can leave work early.

Item Name	Color	Price per Box
Toy cars	Red	$15
Toy cars	Mixed colors	$17
Plastic jewelry	Mixed colors	$18
Key chains	Bluc	$14

95. Where does the speaker work?

(A) At a community center
(B) At a car repair shop
(C) At a supermarket
(D) At a department store

96. Look at the graphic. How much will the speaker pay for today's order?

(A) $15
(B) $17
(C) $18
(D) $14

97. What does the speaker want to install?

(A) A beverage vending machine
(B) An air-conditioning unit
(C) Some security cameras
(D) Some carpeting

Inbox		
✉ **Takanori Kimura** Discuss new account		11:45
✉ **Ozan Demir** Retirement lunch		11:21
✉ **Robert Wilson** Sales tips		10:09
✉ **Ivan Stepanov** Create your fitness plan		9:52

98. Look at the graphic. Who is the speaker?

(A) Takanori Kimura
(B) Ozan Demir
(C) Robert Wilson
(D) Ivan Stepanov

99. How is the company trying to increase participation in a program?

(A) By offering free snacks
(B) By providing paid time off
(C) By awarding a salary increase
(D) By giving away a free trip

100. What will the speaker do next?

(A) Introduce some committee members
(B) Review some sales figures
(C) Pass out tickets to an upcoming event
(D) Give examples of employee goals

TEST 7

This is the end of the Listening test.

토익 정기시험
실전❶1000
LC

토익 정기시험
실전❶1000
LC

실전 TEST

08

LISTENING TEST

In the Listening test, you will be asked to demonstrate how well you understand spoken English. The entire Listening test will last approximately 45 minutes. There are four parts, and directions are given for each part. You must mark your answers on the separate answer sheet. Do not write your answers in your test book.

PART 1

Directions: For each question in this part, you will hear four statements about a picture in your test book. When you hear the statements, you must select the one statement that best describes what you see in the picture. Then find the number of the question on your answer sheet and mark your answer. The statements will not be printed in your test book and will be spoken only one time.

Statement (C), "They're sitting at a table," is the best description of the picture, so you should select answer (C) and mark it on your answer sheet.

1.

2.

GO ON TO THE NEXT PAGE ➤

3.

4.

5.

6.

GO ON TO THE NEXT PAGE ➤

TEST 8

PART 2

Directions: You will hear a question or statement and three responses spoken in English. They will not be printed in your test book and will be spoken only one time. Select the best response to the question or statement and mark the letter (A), (B), or (C) on your answer sheet.

7. Mark your answer on your answer sheet.

8. Mark your answer on your answer sheet.

9. Mark your answer on your answer sheet.

10. Mark your answer on your answer sheet.

11. Mark your answer on your answer sheet.

12. Mark your answer on your answer sheet.

13. Mark your answer on your answer sheet.

14. Mark your answer on your answer sheet.

15. Mark your answer on your answer sheet.

16. Mark your answer on your answer sheet.

17. Mark your answer on your answer sheet.

18. Mark your answer on your answer sheet.

19. Mark your answer on your answer sheet.

20. Mark your answer on your answer sheet.

21. Mark your answer on your answer sheet.

22. Mark your answer on your answer sheet.

23. Mark your answer on your answer sheet.

24. Mark your answer on your answer sheet.

25. Mark your answer on your answer sheet.

26. Mark your answer on your answer sheet.

27. Mark your answer on your answer sheet.

28. Mark your answer on your answer sheet.

29. Mark your answer on your answer sheet.

30. Mark your answer on your answer sheet.

31. Mark your answer on your answer sheet.

PART 3

Directions: You will hear some conversations between two or more people. You will be asked to answer three questions about what the speakers say in each conversation. Select the best response to each question and mark the letter (A), (B), (C), or (D) on your answer sheet. The conversations will not be printed in your test book and will be spoken only one time.

32. Who most likely is the woman?
   (A) An architect
   (B) A building manager
   (C) An interior decorator
   (D) A real estate agent

33. Which feature is most important to the man?
   (A) Location
   (B) Size
   (C) Appearance
   (D) Room layout

34. What will the woman most likely do next?
   (A) Process a payment
   (B) Measure a room
   (C) Schedule an appointment
   (D) Order some furniture

35. Where is the conversation most likely taking place?
   (A) At a fitness center
   (B) At a warehouse
   (C) At a hotel
   (D) At an eye clinic

36. What does the man offer to do?
   (A) Unpack a shipment
   (B) Cancel some appointments
   (C) Take inventory
   (D) Process a payment

37. What will take place at 6 P.M. tomorrow?
   (A) A safety inspection
   (B) A training session
   (C) A package delivery
   (D) A job interview

38. What does the man ask the woman about?
   (A) Safety regulations
   (B) Security procedures
   (C) Working weekend shifts
   (D) Changing jobs

39. What does the woman say she will do next month?
   (A) Take a vacation
   (B) Celebrate a work anniversary
   (C) Retire from a job
   (D) Transfer to another facility

40. What will the man most likely do next?
   (A) Check a work schedule
   (B) Review an operator's manual
   (C) Speak with a supervisor
   (D) Register for a course

41. Why is the man calling?
   (A) To dispute a charge
   (B) To inquire about a loan
   (C) To register a business
   (D) To place an advertisement

42. What does the woman say the man must provide?
   (A) An inspection certificate
   (B) A form of identification
   (C) Financial records
   (D) Product descriptions

43. What does the woman tell the man he can do online?
   (A) Fill out an application
   (B) Create an account
   (C) View pricing options
   (D) Print a mailing label

GO ON TO THE NEXT PAGE

44. Which industry does the woman most likely work in?

(A) Journalism
(B) Marketing
(C) Entertainment
(D) Technology

45. What does the man say is beneficial about a farming technique?

(A) It is easy to learn.
(B) It improves air quality.
(C) It reduces food waste.
(D) It requires less water.

46. What does the woman ask permission to do?

(A) Review some financial documents
(B) Taste some food samples
(C) Take some photographs
(D) Return on another day

47. What are the speakers discussing?

(A) A satellite television subscription
(B) A solar panel installation
(C) A security system upgrade
(D) An electric-car charging station

48. What will the woman ask her neighbors about?

(A) Caring for some indoor plants
(B) Borrowing some garden tools
(C) Using a parking space
(D) Cutting some tree branches

49. What will the man most likely do next?

(A) Move a vehicle
(B) Recharge a battery
(C) Check the size of a space
(D) Write down a price estimate

50. Where do the speakers most likely work?

(A) At a supermarket
(B) At a restaurant
(C) At a hardware store
(D) At a manufacturing plant

51. What problem does the man mention?

(A) The door of an appliance was left open.
(B) The sign outside the business is broken.
(C) A power cord cannot be located.
(D) A training session was not provided.

52. What does the man ask the women to do?

(A) Clean a work area
(B) Reschedule some shifts
(C) Assist a repair person
(D) Make a telephone call

53. What field do the speakers work in?

(A) Market research
(B) Art restoration
(C) Entertainment
(D) Publishing

54. Why does the man say, "Fabrice is exceptionally good with graphics"?

(A) To express surprise
(B) To recommend a promotion
(C) To confirm that training is unnecessary
(D) To decline a request

55. What does the man plan to do after lunch?

(A) Submit a report
(B) Pack for a trip
(C) Share some ideas
(D) Read through an agenda

56. What is the woman concerned about?

(A) Having enough workers for a project
(B) Staying within budget
(C) Passing an inspection
(D) Completing work on time

57. What does Gregor say about Route 37 North?

(A) Its toll prices have increased.
(B) It was closed for repairs.
(C) Traffic was really heavy.
(D) Oversized vehicles are not permitted.

58. What does the woman say she will do?

(A) Sign an invoice
(B) Open a garage door
(C) Guide a truck
(D) Contact a homeowner

59. Where is the conversation most likely taking place?

(A) At a medical clinic
(B) At a fitness center
(C) At a sporting goods store
(D) At a pottery studio

60. Why does the woman say, "I signed up only yesterday"?

(A) To explain why she was not notified
(B) To confirm that she made a payment
(C) To request some needed materials
(D) To justify some class absences

61. What does the man most likely show to the woman?

(A) A price list
(B) A floor plan
(C) An invoice
(D) A schedule

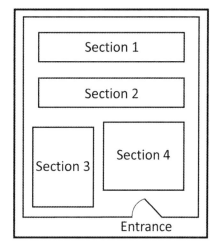

62. Where does the conversation take place?

(A) In a supermarket
(B) In an appliance store
(C) In an automotive store
(D) In a department store

63. Look at the graphic. Where will the man find a product?

(A) In Section 1
(B) In Section 2
(C) In Section 3
(D) In Section 4

64. What does the woman hand to the man?

(A) A catalog
(B) A flyer
(C) A floor map
(D) A receipt

GO ON TO THE NEXT PAGE

TEST 8

Morning Tasks

1. Organize books — Sarai
2. Wash windows — Astrid
3. Paint chairs — Camille
4. Clear shelves — Eun-Mi
5. Mop floor — Abdel

Today's Cakes

Strawberry Shortcake $20.00	Chocolate Sponge Cake $22.00
Red Velvet Cupcakes $17.00	Coffee Butter Cake $25.00

65. Where are the speakers?

(A) At a bookstore
(B) At a community center
(C) At an art studio
(D) At a warehouse

66. Look at the graphic. Who most likely is the woman?

(A) Sarai
(B) Astrid
(C) Camille
(D) Eun-Mi

67. According to the man, what happened yesterday?

(A) Furniture was donated.
(B) Cleaning supplies were delivered.
(C) Signs were ordered.
(D) Books were purchased.

68. What event does the woman mention?

(A) A client luncheon
(B) A store opening
(C) A holiday party
(D) A retirement celebration

69. Look at the graphic. How much will the woman pay for the cake?

(A) $20.00
(B) $22.00
(C) $17.00
(D) $25.00

70. What does the man offer to do?

(A) Reduce a price
(B) Supply plastic utensils
(C) Provide free delivery
(D) Customize an item

PART 4

Directions: You will hear some talks given by a single speaker. You will be asked to answer three questions about what the speaker says in each talk. Select the best response to each question and mark the letter (A), (B), (C), or (D) on your answer sheet. The talks will not be printed in your test book and will be spoken only one time.

71. Who is Olga Popova?
    (A) A video game designer
    (B) A chess player
    (C) A swimmer
    (D) An actor

72. What does the speaker say is especially impressive about Olga Popova?
    (A) Her young age
    (B) Her communication skills
    (C) Her educational background
    (D) Her volunteer activities

73. What will be discussed next?
    (A) Training strategies
    (B) A sponsorship agreement
    (C) Equipment recommendations
    (D) A recent trip

74. What does the speaker appreciate about the company?
    (A) It offers paid vacations.
    (B) It offers promotion opportunities.
    (C) It offers career development workshops.
    (D) It offers flexible work hours.

75. What qualification does the speaker mention?
    (A) Five years of experience
    (B) Attention to detail
    (C) Interpersonal skills
    (D) Professional certification

76. What does the speaker encourage the listeners to do?
    (A) Leave their business cards
    (B) Pick up a brochure
    (C) Sign up for an interview
    (D) Submit questions

77. Where is the announcement taking place?
    (A) At a theater
    (B) At an amusement park
    (C) At a convention center
    (D) At an art gallery

78. Why does the speaker apologize?
    (A) There will be a long wait time.
    (B) Some supplies have run out.
    (C) An entrance is under construction.
    (D) A replacement has been made.

79. What does the speaker remind the listeners to do?
    (A) Pick up their parking vouchers
    (B) Silence their electronic devices
    (C) Purchase souvenir merchandise
    (D) Download a program

80. According to the speaker, why is Trent Avenue closed?
    (A) It is blocked by fallen branches.
    (B) A traffic light has stopped working.
    (C) A parade is scheduled.
    (D) A water pipe has burst.

81. What does the speaker imply when she says, "that's the main route into the city center"?
    (A) She will take a different route.
    (B) She will work from home.
    (C) Funding will be made available soon.
    (D) A task should be given priority.

82. According to the speaker, what is scheduled for three o'clock?
    (A) A sales presentation
    (B) An analysis of survey results
    (C) A job interview
    (D) A meeting with a supervisor

GO ON TO THE NEXT PAGE

83. Where are the instructions being given?

   (A) In a laboratory
   (B) At a swimming pool
   (C) At a national park
   (D) At a sporting goods store

84. According to the speaker, why is a task important?

   (A) It prevents wasting chemicals.
   (B) It promotes visitor satisfaction.
   (C) It keeps equipment in good condition.
   (D) It ensures accurate inventory records.

85. What will the listeners do next?

   (A) Watch a training video
   (B) See where some supplies are stored
   (C) Learn how to operate a machine
   (D) Review a list of safety regulations

86. Who is the speaker?

   (A) A filmmaker
   (B) An actor
   (C) A costume designer
   (D) A sound engineer

87. What is the movie about?

   (A) A historical expedition
   (B) An important invention
   (C) An athletic competition
   (D) A medical discovery

88. What does the speaker mean when he says, "we have no way of knowing everything that happened"?

   (A) A criticism is unfair.
   (B) A story is not entirely factual.
   (C) A movie reviewer is mistaken.
   (D) More research is necessary.

89. What event is being held?

   (A) A community fund-raiser
   (B) A retirement party
   (C) An anniversary celebration
   (D) A project launch ceremony

90. Who is Asako Tamura?

   (A) A news reporter
   (B) A professional athlete
   (C) An architect
   (D) A professor

91. What does the speaker invite Asako Tamura to do?

   (A) Sign her name
   (B) Give a speech
   (C) Take some photographs
   (D) Answer some questions

92. What does the speaker point out about Kiftaynee State Park?

   (A) It is the largest in the region.
   (B) It has some unusual wildlife.
   (C) It is maintained entirely by volunteers.
   (D) It has unique archaeological sites.

93. Why does the speaker say, "our park closes at four"?

   (A) To encourage a faster hiking pace
   (B) To announce a change in park hours
   (C) To indicate why a trail is not an option
   (D) To emphasize that camping is not permitted

94. What does the speaker encourage the listeners to buy?

   (A) A park map
   (B) Some hiking poles
   (C) An annual pass
   (D) A bird-watching guide

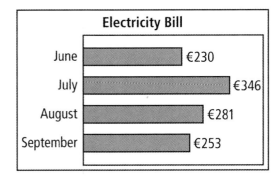

Electricity Bill

Month	Amount
June	€230
July	€346
August	€281
September	€253

Food	Cook Time
Brussels sprouts	4 minutes
Broccoli	5 minutes
Asparagus	6 minutes
Carrots	7 minutes

95. What is the speaker mainly discussing?

(A) When to collect data
(B) Reasons for a miscalculation
(C) Ways to reduce expenses
(D) How to be more environmentally friendly

96. Look at the graphic. Which month does the speaker refer to?

(A) June
(B) July
(C) August
(D) September

97. What will the speaker do this afternoon?

(A) Take inventory
(B) Conduct some research
(C) Update a spreadsheet
(D) Pay a bill

98. What type of product is the speaker demonstrating?

(A) A toaster oven
(B) An electric grill
(C) An air fryer
(D) A food steamer

99. Look at the graphic. How long will the ingredient be cooked?

(A) 4 minutes
(B) 5 minutes
(C) 6 minutes
(D) 7 minutes

100. What does the speaker offer the listeners?

(A) A discount coupon
(B) A free sample
(C) An extended warranty
(D) A recipe book

This is the end of the Listening test.

토익 정기시험
실전① 1000
LC

실전 TEST

09

LISTENING TEST

In the Listening test, you will be asked to demonstrate how well you understand spoken English. The entire Listening test will last approximately 45 minutes. There are four parts, and directions are given for each part. You must mark your answers on the separate answer sheet. Do not write your answers in your test book.

PART 1

Directions: For each question in this part, you will hear four statements about a picture in your test book. When you hear the statements, you must select the one statement that best describes what you see in the picture. Then find the number of the question on your answer sheet and mark your answer. The statements will not be printed in your test book and will be spoken only one time.

Statement (C), "They're sitting at a table," is the best description of the picture, so you should select answer (C) and mark it on your answer sheet.

1.

2.

GO ON TO THE NEXT PAGE ▶

3.

4.

5.

6.

GO ON TO THE NEXT PAGE

TEST 9

PART 2

Directions: You will hear a question or statement and three responses spoken in English. They will not be printed in your test book and will be spoken only one time. Select the best response to the question or statement and mark the letter (A), (B), or (C) on your answer sheet.

7. Mark your answer on your answer sheet.

8. Mark your answer on your answer sheet.

9. Mark your answer on your answer sheet.

10. Mark your answer on your answer sheet.

11. Mark your answer on your answer sheet.

12. Mark your answer on your answer sheet.

13. Mark your answer on your answer sheet.

14. Mark your answer on your answer sheet.

15. Mark your answer on your answer sheet.

16. Mark your answer on your answer sheet.

17. Mark your answer on your answer sheet.

18. Mark your answer on your answer sheet.

19. Mark your answer on your answer sheet.

20. Mark your answer on your answer sheet.

21. Mark your answer on your answer sheet.

22. Mark your answer on your answer sheet.

23. Mark your answer on your answer sheet.

24. Mark your answer on your answer sheet.

25. Mark your answer on your answer sheet.

26. Mark your answer on your answer sheet.

27. Mark your answer on your answer sheet.

28. Mark your answer on your answer sheet.

29. Mark your answer on your answer sheet.

30. Mark your answer on your answer sheet.

31. Mark your answer on your answer sheet.

PART 3

Directions: You will hear some conversations between two or more people. You will be asked to answer three questions about what the speakers say in each conversation. Select the best response to each question and mark the letter (A), (B), (C), or (D) on your answer sheet. The conversations will not be printed in your test book and will be spoken only one time.

32. Where do the speakers most likely work?

    (A) At a bank
    (B) At a hotel
    (C) At an electronics store
    (D) At a medical clinic

33. What most likely is the man's job?

    (A) Receptionist
    (B) Security guard
    (C) Cleaning staff member
    (D) Computer technician

34. What will the woman give the man?

    (A) A schedule
    (B) A key
    (C) A manual
    (D) A cup of coffee

35. Who most likely is the woman?

    (A) A receptionist
    (B) A florist
    (C) A repair technician
    (D) A woodworker

36. Why is the man calling?

    (A) To clarify a process
    (B) To ask about a delivery
    (C) To request a service
    (D) To complain about an invoice

37. What does the woman ask the man for?

    (A) A photograph
    (B) An address
    (C) A telephone number
    (D) A passcode

38. What does the man ask the woman about?

    (A) A shirt size
    (B) A shirt price
    (C) A warehouse location
    (D) Store hours

39. What does the woman offer to do?

    (A) Unlock a fitting room
    (B) Look for a different color shirt
    (C) Send a shirt to the man's home
    (D) Put a shirt back on a shelf

40. What will the man most likely do?

    (A) Contact a manufacturer
    (B) Come back tomorrow
    (C) Look through a catalog
    (D) Visit a different store

41. Who is Sofia?

    (A) A teacher
    (B) An artist
    (C) A real estate agent
    (D) A gallery owner

42. What are the men curious about?

    (A) The creator of some artwork
    (B) The lighting in a room
    (C) The number of people at an event
    (D) How long a business has been open

43. What will the speakers most likely do next?

    (A) Purchase a painting
    (B) Eat a meal together
    (C) Review some floor plans
    (D) Look at some artwork

GO ON TO THE NEXT PAGE

44. What kind of product are the speakers discussing?

(A) A laptop
(B) A mobile phone
(C) A fitness tracker
(D) A navigation device

45. What does the woman say she is currently working on?

(A) A marketing campaign
(B) A transportation contract
(C) A fee negotiation
(D) A design feature

46. What is the man concerned about?

(A) Staff shortages
(B) Supply chain disruptions
(C) Budget constraints
(D) Increased competition

47. What does the woman hope to do this year?

(A) Earn a promotion
(B) Win an award
(C) Give a presentation
(D) Move to a different city

48. What does the woman mean when she says, "some of the numbers in my presentation came from you"?

(A) She is grateful for the man's help.
(B) She thinks someone else got credit by mistake.
(C) The man should check the accuracy of some numbers.
(D) The man should also give a presentation.

49. What does the man remind the woman about?

(A) A team meeting has been canceled.
(B) A product will be released soon.
(C) A report will not be distributed.
(D) A task needs to be done.

50. What does the man say will happen tomorrow?

(A) New equipment will be installed.
(B) An inspection will take place.
(C) A delivery will be late.
(D) The water will be shut off.

51. Where do the speakers most likely work?

(A) At a factory
(B) At a grocery store
(C) At a restaurant
(D) At a shipping company

52. What does the man say he will do?

(A) Conduct an interview
(B) Reschedule a training session
(C) Contact staff members
(D) Clean some filters

53. What did the man just do?

(A) He purchased a computer.
(B) He installed some software.
(C) He returned from a doctor's appointment.
(D) He created a training video.

54. According to the man, why has a product become popular?

(A) It is less expensive than similar products.
(B) It is energy efficient.
(C) It provides easy access to information.
(D) It has 24-hour customer support.

55. Why does Francesca interrupt the conversation?

(A) She needs assistance.
(B) She is taking lunch orders.
(C) Some forms require a signature.
(D) A client has arrived.

56. Who most likely are the speakers?

(A) News reporters
(B) Construction workers
(C) Travel agents
(D) City officials

57. Why does the woman say, "summer is the region's busiest season"?

(A) To express surprise
(B) To explain a price increase
(C) To agree with an opinion
(D) To request assistance with a project

58. What does the woman offer to do?

(A) Make a list
(B) Confirm a meeting time
(C) Inspect some equipment
(D) Adjust a budget

---

59. What is the man making a payment for?

(A) An automobile
(B) A house
(C) A credit card
(D) A medical bill

60. What problem does the woman describe?

(A) An online system is not working.
(B) There are not enough customer service agents.
(C) A manager is not available.
(D) A password needs to be updated.

61. What does the woman promise the man?

(A) He will be able to pay later in the day.
(B) He will receive a refund.
(C) He will not have to wait a long time.
(D) He will not be charged a late fee.

Marcel Breton's Schedule	
Monday March 14	Ms. Smith (10–11 A.M.) Training (1–3 P.M.)
Tuesday March 15	Restaurant client (9–10 A.M.)
Wednesday March 16	Staff meeting (9–11 A.M.)
Thursday March 17	Vacation

62. Where does the man work?

(A) At an advertising agency
(B) At an accounting firm
(C) At a publishing company
(D) At a real estate agency

63. Look at the graphic. Which day will the woman meet with Marcel Breton?

(A) On Monday
(B) On Tuesday
(C) On Wednesday
(D) On Thursday

64. What does the woman ask for?

(A) An e-mail address
(B) A receipt
(C) A cost estimate
(D) A résumé

GO ON TO THE NEXT PAGE

TEST 9

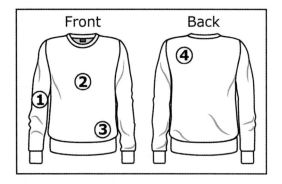

Front   Back

Song	Songwriter
"Roses on a Hill"	Marta Ruiz
"Time Again Blues"	Oliver Hughes
"Lake Charon"	Brandon Toprak
"Ice at Dawn"	Zaina Feras

65. What type of business does the woman work for?

(A) A fashion design company
(B) A custom clothing store
(C) A sporting equipment shop
(D) A secondhand clothing store

66. Look at the graphic. Where does the man want a logo to appear?

(A) Location 1
(B) Location 2
(C) Location 3
(D) Location 4

67. What is the man willing to pay extra for?

(A) High-quality material
(B) An unusual color
(C) A variety of sizes
(D) A rush order

68. Who most likely are the speakers?

(A) Stage managers
(B) Musicians
(C) Radio show hosts
(D) Recording executives

69. What is the woman concerned about?

(A) A sound equipment failure
(B) Some song lyrics
(C) A band member's inexperience
(D) A rehearsal space conflict

70. Look at the graphic. Which song does the man suggest replacing?

(A) "Roses on a Hill"
(B) "Time Again Blues"
(C) "Lake Charon"
(D) "Ice at Dawn"

Directions: You will hear some talks given by a single speaker. You will be asked to answer three questions about what the speaker says in each talk. Select the best response to each question and mark the letter (A), (B), (C), or (D) on your answer sheet. The talks will not be printed in your test book and will be spoken only one time.

71. Who most likely is the listener?

(A) A school secretary
(B) A farmer
(C) A delivery driver
(D) A restaurant manager

72. What problem does the speaker mention?

(A) An employee is on vacation.
(B) An item is not available.
(C) The cost of an item has changed.
(D) An order was processed incorrectly.

73. What does the speaker ask the listener to do?

(A) Confirm a flower choice
(B) Approve a new delivery time
(C) Submit a receipt
(D) Call a different store

74. What service does Prospective provide?

(A) Employee recruiting
(B) Technology support
(C) Digital marketing
(D) Customized printing

75. What recent improvement did Prospective make?

(A) It matches competitor prices.
(B) It sends updates regularly.
(C) It offers personalized consultations.
(D) It provides international service.

76. How can the listeners try Prospective for free?

(A) By entering a contest
(B) By calling a radio station
(C) By visiting a business
(D) By completing a survey

77. Who most likely is the speaker?

(A) A property inspector
(B) A real estate agent
(C) An electrician
(D) An architect

78. What is the problem with a property?

(A) A roof is leaking.
(B) A wall needs to be reinforced.
(C) Some wiring needs to be updated.
(D) Some windows need to be replaced.

79. What does the speaker imply when she says, "the process normally takes a long time"?

(A) This case may be an exception.
(B) Hiring more workers is advisable.
(C) A store opening may be delayed.
(D) The listener should submit a form soon.

80. What type of work are the listeners training for?

(A) Construction
(B) Real estate
(C) Manufacturing
(D) Truck driving

81. What recent change does the speaker mention?

(A) Inspections are taking place more frequently.
(B) Information must be entered electronically.
(C) A training course has been shortened.
(D) Membership fees have decreased.

82. According to the speaker, why is it a good time to enter a profession?

(A) Pay is high.
(B) Schedules are flexible.
(C) Certification requirements are not strict.
(D) Technological innovations are expected.

GO ON TO THE NEXT PAGE

TEST 9

83. What event is the speaker reporting on?

    (A) A holiday parade
    (B) A speech by the city mayor
    (C) An opening ceremony
    (D) A building demolition

84. What news did officials share earlier in the year?

    (A) Traffic was lighter than projected.
    (B) Work was being done faster than expected.
    (C) Additional workers would be hired.
    (D) A project budget was being revised.

85. Who did the speaker interview?

    (A) Some construction engineers
    (B) A local store owner
    (C) A government official
    (D) Some delivery drivers

86. What industry does the speaker most likely work in?

    (A) Finance
    (B) Advertising
    (C) Architecture
    (D) Technology

87. What did the speaker learn yesterday?

    (A) He will be promoted to a management position.
    (B) The funding for a project has increased.
    (C) A client asked for work to be completed early.
    (D) A client complained about a company's service.

88. What does the speaker imply when he says, "you usually do excellent work"?

    (A) He wants the listener to work on his team.
    (B) He is surprised that the listener made an error.
    (C) The listener is likely to receive a raise.
    (D) The listener should replace him as project manager.

89. What news does the speaker report?

    (A) The company is planning to expand.
    (B) The company exceeded its sales target.
    (C) New computers will be distributed.
    (D) A business trip has been organized.

90. What department do the listeners work in?

    (A) Quality Control
    (B) Human Resources
    (C) Data Analytics
    (D) Customer Service

91. What does the speaker say he will do?

    (A) Order some supplies
    (B) E-mail an agenda
    (C) Fix some software
    (D) Upload some files

92. What is being reported on?

    (A) The purchase of a baseball team
    (B) The signing of a baseball player
    (C) The construction of a baseball stadium
    (D) The retirement of a baseball coach

93. What does the speaker say Mr. Abalora is passionate about?

    (A) Job creation
    (B) Community building
    (C) Local news reporting
    (D) Innovative thinking

94. Why does the speaker say, "we've been told that before"?

    (A) To express doubt
    (B) To support a decision
    (C) To correct a colleague
    (D) To reinforce an instruction

Kolee Exercise Equipment Sales

- Exercise Bicycles 20%
- Rowing Machines 15%
- Weight Lifting Benches 35%
- Treadmills 30%

Education Office Staff Directory	
Online Activities	Sabine Klein
Camp Director	Ji-Soo Jeong
School Liaison	Carmen Ruiz
Adult Education	Brian Hughes

95. Who are the listeners?

(A) Investors
(B) Sales staff
(C) Fitness trainers
(D) Manufacturing executives

96. What does the speaker hope will happen?

(A) The assembly process will be completed more efficiently.
(B) Customers will be told about Kolee's high-quality products.
(C) Customers will use exercise bicycles rather than treadmills.
(D) Kolee's manufacturing will be done at a different plant.

97. Look at the graphic. What type of exercise equipment does the speaker say is new for the company?

(A) Rowing machines
(B) Exercise bicycles
(C) Treadmills
(D) Weight lifting benches

98. What is the speaker pleased to announce?

(A) A special exhibit
(B) A new education director
(C) Learning activities for teens
(D) Discounted museum tickets

99. What does the speaker say about science camps?

(A) A registration deadline has changed.
(B) No more spaces are available.
(C) A payment plan has been added.
(D) Some classes will be held in a different location.

100. Look at the graphic. Who can the listeners speak to by pressing seven?

(A) Sabine Klein
(B) Ji-Soo Jeong
(C) Carmen Ruiz
(D) Brian Hughes

This is the end of the Listening test.

토익 정기시험
실전❶1000
LC

LISTENING TEST

In the Listening test, you will be asked to demonstrate how well you understand spoken English. The entire Listening test will last approximately 45 minutes. There are four parts, and directions are given for each part. You must mark your answers on the separate answer sheet. Do not write your answers in your test book.

PART 1

Directions: For each question in this part, you will hear four statements about a picture in your test book. When you hear the statements, you must select the one statement that best describes what you see in the picture. Then find the number of the question on your answer sheet and mark your answer. The statements will not be printed in your test book and will be spoken only one time.

Statement (C), "They're sitting at a table," is the best description of the picture, so you should select answer (C) and mark it on your answer sheet.

1.

2.

GO ON TO THE NEXT PAGE

TEST 10

3.

4.

5.

6.

GO ON TO THE NEXT PAGE

PART 2

Directions: You will hear a question or statement and three responses spoken in English. They will not be printed in your test book and will be spoken only one time. Select the best response to the question or statement and mark the letter (A), (B), or (C) on your answer sheet.

7. Mark your answer on your answer sheet.

8. Mark your answer on your answer sheet.

9. Mark your answer on your answer sheet.

10. Mark your answer on your answer sheet.

11. Mark your answer on your answer sheet.

12. Mark your answer on your answer sheet.

13. Mark your answer on your answer sheet.

14. Mark your answer on your answer sheet.

15. Mark your answer on your answer sheet.

16. Mark your answer on your answer sheet.

17. Mark your answer on your answer sheet.

18. Mark your answer on your answer sheet.

19. Mark your answer on your answer sheet.

20. Mark your answer on your answer sheet.

21. Mark your answer on your answer sheet.

22. Mark your answer on your answer sheet.

23. Mark your answer on your answer sheet.

24. Mark your answer on your answer sheet.

25. Mark your answer on your answer sheet.

26. Mark your answer on your answer sheet.

27. Mark your answer on your answer sheet.

28. Mark your answer on your answer sheet.

29. Mark your answer on your answer sheet.

30. Mark your answer on your answer sheet.

31. Mark your answer on your answer sheet.

PART 3

Directions: You will hear some conversations between two or more people. You will be asked to answer three questions about what the speakers say in each conversation. Select the best response to each question and mark the letter (A), (B), (C), or (D) on your answer sheet. The conversations will not be printed in your test book and will be spoken only one time.

32. Who most likely are the speakers?

(A) Chefs
(B) Florists
(C) Bank tellers
(D) Fashion designers

33. What does the man say he will do?

(A) Send a payment
(B) Arrange a meeting
(C) Find another supplier
(D) Review a checklist

34. Why does the woman say she will need to leave early?

(A) She is going on vacation.
(B) She is having her car repaired.
(C) She has a family event.
(D) She has a medical appointment.

35. Who most likely is the woman?

(A) A receptionist
(B) A security guard
(C) A laboratory assistant
(D) A cashier

36. What problem does the man report?

(A) He has lost his identification card.
(B) Some mail was not delivered.
(C) He is going to arrive late.
(D) Some equipment is broken.

37. What does the woman remind the man about?

(A) A payment option
(B) A change in location
(C) Some required paperwork
(D) An online directory

38. What are the speakers mainly discussing?

(A) Hiring an actor
(B) Recreating a scene
(C) Replacing some cameras
(D) Purchasing some costumes

39. How does the man intend to resolve a problem?

(A) By changing a start date
(B) By doing some research
(C) By revising a film script
(D) By negotiating a salary

40. What does the woman ask the man to look at?

(A) A catering contract
(B) Some flight arrangements
(C) An employment law
(D) Some lodging possibilities

41. Who is the man?

(A) A farmer
(B) A banker
(C) A restaurant owner
(D) A city official

42. Why does the man call the woman?

(A) To ask her to volunteer
(B) To hire her as a consultant
(C) To inform her about an award
(D) To collect some data

43. What strategy does the woman's company use?

(A) It keeps inventory low.
(B) It plants native species.
(C) It reduces paper waste.
(D) It maintains strong customer relations.

GO ON TO THE NEXT PAGE

44. What is causing a change in the speakers' plans?

(A) A scheduling conflict
(B) A last-minute business trip
(C) Budget reductions
(D) Upcoming weather conditions

45. Which group is an event intended for?

(A) City officials
(B) Valued customers
(C) Potential investors
(D) Company employees

46. What will the woman do next?

(A) Make a room reservation
(B) Compose an e-mail
(C) Book a music group
(D) Request a refund

47. What field does the woman most likely work in?

(A) Health care
(B) Finance
(C) Hospitality
(D) Transportation

48. What most likely is the man's job?

(A) Data analyst
(B) Athlete
(C) Journalist
(D) Delivery driver

49. What does the woman say is necessary?

(A) A revised report
(B) A bill payment
(C) A return visit
(D) A confidentiality agreement

50. What is being celebrated next Tuesday?

(A) A birthday
(B) A retirement
(C) A work promotion
(D) A grand opening

51. Why does the man say, "our budget is limited"?

(A) To request more funding
(B) To question a decision
(C) To complain about a price
(D) To decline an offer

52. What does the man ask the woman about?

(A) Some decorations
(B) Some ingredients
(C) A pickup location
(D) The time a store opens

53. Where do the speakers most likely work?

(A) At a bank
(B) At an advertising firm
(C) At an employment agency
(D) At a printing company

54. Why does the woman say, "Four of our people are on vacation"?

(A) To apologize for an error
(B) To express concern about an order
(C) To suggest that a meeting be canceled
(D) To explain a company policy

55. What does the man suggest offering to motivate employees?

(A) Increased time off
(B) Free meals
(C) Renovated work spaces
(D) Extra pay

56. What is the main topic of the conversation?

(A) A leadership reorganization plan
(B) An office relocation project
(C) An energy efficiency initiative
(D) An employee retirement plan

57. According to the woman, what are employees responding positively to?

(A) An office relocation
(B) A revised vacation policy
(C) A monthly contest
(D) An employee survey

58. What does the woman plan to do?

(A) Lease some equipment
(B) Hire a contractor
(C) Pause item production
(D) Research some competitors

59. Where is the conversation most likely taking place?

(A) At a zoo
(B) At a beach
(C) At a park
(D) At a farm

60. What are the women going to do today?

(A) Take some measurements
(B) Pour some concrete
(C) Calculate a price estimate
(D) Clear some trees

61. What does Adriana point out about some land?

(A) It is dry.
(B) It is flat.
(C) It is sandy.
(D) It is surrounded by a fence.

Flight	Status
Flight 105	Delayed
Flight 451	On time
Flight 57	Canceled
Flight 23	Boarding

62. Why is the man traveling?

(A) To view a property
(B) To participate in an interview
(C) To give a talk
(D) To visit family

63. Look at the graphic. Which flight did the man book?

(A) Flight 105
(B) Flight 451
(C) Flight 57
(D) Flight 23

64. Why is the man surprised?

(A) A refund will be issued.
(B) A departure gate has changed.
(C) A meal will not be served on a flight.
(D) A voucher will be provided.

GO ON TO THE NEXT PAGE

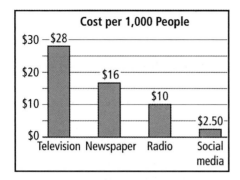

65. Why does the woman want to change an advertising strategy?

(A) A competitor has revised a prototype.
(B) Some costs are too high.
(C) A project was delayed.
(D) A product is not selling well.

66. Look at the graphic. What type of media do the speakers decide to use for advertising?

(A) Television
(B) Newspaper
(C) Radio
(D) Social media

67. What will the man most likely do?

(A) Hire an extra employee
(B) Conduct a customer survey
(C) Prepare a slideshow
(D) Contact a colleague

68. Where do the speakers most likely work?

(A) At a television studio
(B) At a cooking school
(C) At a train station
(D) At a tourism office

69. According to the man, what happened last year?

(A) A television show premiered.
(B) An advertising campaign was launched.
(C) A community garden was started.
(D) A local festival was canceled.

70. Look at the graphic. Which business will be removed from the map?

(A) Tokyo Café
(B) Diaz Family Restaurant
(C) Yang Bistro
(D) Fontana's Desserts

PART 4

Directions: You will hear some talks given by a single speaker. You will be asked to answer three questions about what the speaker says in each talk. Select the best response to each question and mark the letter (A), (B), (C), or (D) on your answer sheet. The talks will not be printed in your test book and will be spoken only one time.

71. Where does the tour take place?

(A) At an art museum
(B) At an amusement park
(C) At a zoo
(D) At a nature park

72. What activity does the speaker recommend?

(A) Renting a bicycle
(B) Taking photographs
(C) Watching birds
(D) Buying souvenirs

73. Why should the listeners meet the speaker at noon?

(A) To eat lunch
(B) To return some equipment
(C) To take a group photo
(D) To see a performance

74. Who is the speaker?

(A) A real estate agent
(B) A construction worker
(C) An interior decorator
(D) A building inspector

75. Why does the speaker say, "we did have a cleaning crew come yesterday"?

(A) To emphasize an accomplishment
(B) To disagree with a decision
(C) To suggest an explanation
(D) To complain about a cost

76. What does the speaker tell the listener to do?

(A) Choose some photos
(B) Check a schedule
(C) Submit a payment
(D) Apply for a permit

77. What are the listeners preparing for?

(A) A sports competition
(B) A music festival
(C) A company picnic
(D) A harvest fair

78. What will Maria be responsible for?

(A) Setting out extra chairs
(B) Collecting event tickets
(C) Putting up some decorations
(D) Showing vendors where they need to be

79. What does the speaker mean when she says, "we haven't had a day this nice in a while"?

(A) Some tests may not be necessary.
(B) She is excited about an outing with friends.
(C) An event will probably not need to be moved.
(D) The weather has been unusually cold recently.

80. Where does the speech most likely take place?

(A) At a wellness fair
(B) At an employee luncheon
(C) At a training seminar
(D) At a press conference

81. What industry does the speaker work in?

(A) Fishing
(B) Tourism
(C) Shipping
(D) Health care

82. What does the speaker say he is proud of?

(A) A hiring process
(B) An environmental initiative
(C) Funding innovative research
(D) Supporting local businesses

GO ON TO THE NEXT PAGE

83. What industry does the speaker most likely work in?

(A) Publishing
(B) Advertising
(C) Film
(D) Hospitality

84. What does the speaker say recently happened?

(A) A book was made into a film.
(B) A new executive was hired.
(C) A manuscript was found.
(D) An anniversary celebration was held.

85. Why does the speaker want the listener to call her back?

(A) To finalize a design
(B) To confirm a guest list
(C) To discuss a contract
(D) To develop a timeline

86. What is the speaker currently working on?

(A) Listing some job duties
(B) Correcting errors in a report
(C) Updating an equipment manual
(D) Designing a new company logo

87. What did the board talk about in October?

(A) Purchasing some software
(B) Changing a meeting time
(C) Keeping some documents online
(D) Opening a new branch location

88. What will the speaker be available to do?

(A) Issue a press release
(B) Assist a colleague
(C) Create a progress report
(D) Revise a client contract

89. What did the listener buy?

(A) A software program
(B) A tablet computer
(C) An advertising service
(D) A video camera

90. According to the speaker, how will the product improve a business?

(A) It will make sharing information easier.
(B) It will ensure security.
(C) It will help attract more clients.
(D) It will collect customer data.

91. What does the speaker recommend?

(A) Writing down a serial number
(B) Using a second device
(C) Restarting a machine
(D) Conducting a quality test

92. Where does the speaker most likely work?

(A) At a television station
(B) At a publishing company
(C) At an advertising agency
(D) At a tour company

93. Why does the speaker say, "a comedy club just opened up in the arts district"?

(A) To express surprise about a timeline
(B) To complain about a location
(C) To suggest a solution to a problem
(D) To apologize for a mistake

94. What will the speaker do next?

(A) Announce award winners
(B) Distribute invitations
(C) Play a video
(D) Ask for volunteers

Subscription Options	
1 month $10.00	2 months $18.00
3 months $25.00	6 months $45.00

95. What is being advertised for monthly delivery?

(A) Office supplies
(B) Potted plants
(C) Best-selling books
(D) International snacks

96. What does the speaker say will be available in January?

(A) Weekend delivery
(B) Free gift wrapping
(C) Refrigerated shipping
(D) Online tracking

97. Look at the graphic. What is the smallest subscription amount needed to receive an extra box?

(A) $10.00
(B) $18.00
(C) $25.00
(D) $45.00

1 Share Screen	2 Captions
3 Breakout Rooms	4 Chat

98. What is the topic of the workshop?

(A) Arranging flowers
(B) Making candles
(C) Painting pictures
(D) Decorating cakes

99. Look at the graphic. Which button represents a new feature of the software program?

(A) Button 1
(B) Button 2
(C) Button 3
(D) Button 4

100. What does the speaker say is a benefit of subscribing?

(A) Additional video content
(B) Individual instruction
(C) Discounted supplies
(D) Networking opportunities

This is the end of the Listening test.

ANSWER SHEET

ETS® TOEIC® 토익® 정기시험 실전 1000

수험번호						

응시일자 : 20 년 월 일

성명	한 글	
	한 자	
	영 자	

Test 01 (Part 1~4)

1	ⓐ ⓑ ⓒ ⓓ	21	ⓐ ⓑ ⓒ	41	ⓐ ⓑ ⓒ ⓓ	61	ⓐ ⓑ ⓒ ⓓ	81	ⓐ ⓑ ⓒ ⓓ
2	ⓐ ⓑ ⓒ ⓓ	22	ⓐ ⓑ ⓒ	42	ⓐ ⓑ ⓒ ⓓ	62	ⓐ ⓑ ⓒ ⓓ	82	ⓐ ⓑ ⓒ ⓓ
3	ⓐ ⓑ ⓒ ⓓ	23	ⓐ ⓑ ⓒ	43	ⓐ ⓑ ⓒ ⓓ	63	ⓐ ⓑ ⓒ ⓓ	83	ⓐ ⓑ ⓒ ⓓ
4	ⓐ ⓑ ⓒ ⓓ	24	ⓐ ⓑ ⓒ	44	ⓐ ⓑ ⓒ ⓓ	64	ⓐ ⓑ ⓒ ⓓ	84	ⓐ ⓑ ⓒ ⓓ
5	ⓐ ⓑ ⓒ ⓓ	25	ⓐ ⓑ ⓒ	45	ⓐ ⓑ ⓒ ⓓ	65	ⓐ ⓑ ⓒ ⓓ	85	ⓐ ⓑ ⓒ ⓓ
6	ⓐ ⓑ ⓒ ⓓ	26	ⓐ ⓑ ⓒ	46	ⓐ ⓑ ⓒ ⓓ	66	ⓐ ⓑ ⓒ ⓓ	86	ⓐ ⓑ ⓒ ⓓ
7	ⓐ ⓑ ⓒ	27	ⓐ ⓑ ⓒ	47	ⓐ ⓑ ⓒ ⓓ	67	ⓐ ⓑ ⓒ ⓓ	87	ⓐ ⓑ ⓒ ⓓ
8	ⓐ ⓑ ⓒ	28	ⓐ ⓑ ⓒ	48	ⓐ ⓑ ⓒ ⓓ	68	ⓐ ⓑ ⓒ ⓓ	88	ⓐ ⓑ ⓒ ⓓ
9	ⓐ ⓑ ⓒ	29	ⓐ ⓑ ⓒ	49	ⓐ ⓑ ⓒ ⓓ	69	ⓐ ⓑ ⓒ ⓓ	89	ⓐ ⓑ ⓒ ⓓ
10	ⓐ ⓑ ⓒ	30	ⓐ ⓑ ⓒ	50	ⓐ ⓑ ⓒ ⓓ	70	ⓐ ⓑ ⓒ ⓓ	90	ⓐ ⓑ ⓒ ⓓ
11	ⓐ ⓑ ⓒ	31	ⓐ ⓑ ⓒ	51	ⓐ ⓑ ⓒ ⓓ	71	ⓐ ⓑ ⓒ ⓓ	91	ⓐ ⓑ ⓒ ⓓ
12	ⓐ ⓑ ⓒ	32	ⓐ ⓑ ⓒ ⓓ	52	ⓐ ⓑ ⓒ ⓓ	72	ⓐ ⓑ ⓒ ⓓ	92	ⓐ ⓑ ⓒ ⓓ
13	ⓐ ⓑ ⓒ	33	ⓐ ⓑ ⓒ ⓓ	53	ⓐ ⓑ ⓒ ⓓ	73	ⓐ ⓑ ⓒ ⓓ	93	ⓐ ⓑ ⓒ ⓓ
14	ⓐ ⓑ ⓒ	34	ⓐ ⓑ ⓒ ⓓ	54	ⓐ ⓑ ⓒ ⓓ	74	ⓐ ⓑ ⓒ ⓓ	94	ⓐ ⓑ ⓒ ⓓ
15	ⓐ ⓑ ⓒ	35	ⓐ ⓑ ⓒ ⓓ	55	ⓐ ⓑ ⓒ ⓓ	75	ⓐ ⓑ ⓒ ⓓ	95	ⓐ ⓑ ⓒ ⓓ
16	ⓐ ⓑ ⓒ	36	ⓐ ⓑ ⓒ ⓓ	56	ⓐ ⓑ ⓒ ⓓ	76	ⓐ ⓑ ⓒ ⓓ	96	ⓐ ⓑ ⓒ ⓓ
17	ⓐ ⓑ ⓒ	37	ⓐ ⓑ ⓒ ⓓ	57	ⓐ ⓑ ⓒ ⓓ	77	ⓐ ⓑ ⓒ ⓓ	97	ⓐ ⓑ ⓒ ⓓ
18	ⓐ ⓑ ⓒ	38	ⓐ ⓑ ⓒ ⓓ	58	ⓐ ⓑ ⓒ ⓓ	78	ⓐ ⓑ ⓒ ⓓ	98	ⓐ ⓑ ⓒ ⓓ
19	ⓐ ⓑ ⓒ	39	ⓐ ⓑ ⓒ ⓓ	59	ⓐ ⓑ ⓒ ⓓ	79	ⓐ ⓑ ⓒ ⓓ	99	ⓐ ⓑ ⓒ ⓓ
20	ⓐ ⓑ ⓒ	40	ⓐ ⓑ ⓒ ⓓ	60	ⓐ ⓑ ⓒ ⓓ	80	ⓐ ⓑ ⓒ ⓓ	100	ⓐ ⓑ ⓒ ⓓ

Test 02 (Part 1~4)

1	ⓐ ⓑ ⓒ ⓓ	21	ⓐ ⓑ ⓒ	41	ⓐ ⓑ ⓒ ⓓ	61	ⓐ ⓑ ⓒ ⓓ	81	ⓐ ⓑ ⓒ ⓓ
2	ⓐ ⓑ ⓒ ⓓ	22	ⓐ ⓑ ⓒ	42	ⓐ ⓑ ⓒ ⓓ	62	ⓐ ⓑ ⓒ ⓓ	82	ⓐ ⓑ ⓒ ⓓ
3	ⓐ ⓑ ⓒ ⓓ	23	ⓐ ⓑ ⓒ	43	ⓐ ⓑ ⓒ ⓓ	63	ⓐ ⓑ ⓒ ⓓ	83	ⓐ ⓑ ⓒ ⓓ
4	ⓐ ⓑ ⓒ ⓓ	24	ⓐ ⓑ ⓒ	44	ⓐ ⓑ ⓒ ⓓ	64	ⓐ ⓑ ⓒ ⓓ	84	ⓐ ⓑ ⓒ ⓓ
5	ⓐ ⓑ ⓒ ⓓ	25	ⓐ ⓑ ⓒ	45	ⓐ ⓑ ⓒ ⓓ	65	ⓐ ⓑ ⓒ ⓓ	85	ⓐ ⓑ ⓒ ⓓ
6	ⓐ ⓑ ⓒ ⓓ	26	ⓐ ⓑ ⓒ	46	ⓐ ⓑ ⓒ ⓓ	66	ⓐ ⓑ ⓒ ⓓ	86	ⓐ ⓑ ⓒ ⓓ
7	ⓐ ⓑ ⓒ	27	ⓐ ⓑ ⓒ	47	ⓐ ⓑ ⓒ ⓓ	67	ⓐ ⓑ ⓒ ⓓ	87	ⓐ ⓑ ⓒ ⓓ
8	ⓐ ⓑ ⓒ	28	ⓐ ⓑ ⓒ	48	ⓐ ⓑ ⓒ ⓓ	68	ⓐ ⓑ ⓒ ⓓ	88	ⓐ ⓑ ⓒ ⓓ
9	ⓐ ⓑ ⓒ	29	ⓐ ⓑ ⓒ	49	ⓐ ⓑ ⓒ ⓓ	69	ⓐ ⓑ ⓒ ⓓ	89	ⓐ ⓑ ⓒ ⓓ
10	ⓐ ⓑ ⓒ	30	ⓐ ⓑ ⓒ	50	ⓐ ⓑ ⓒ ⓓ	70	ⓐ ⓑ ⓒ ⓓ	90	ⓐ ⓑ ⓒ ⓓ
11	ⓐ ⓑ ⓒ	31	ⓐ ⓑ ⓒ	51	ⓐ ⓑ ⓒ ⓓ	71	ⓐ ⓑ ⓒ ⓓ	91	ⓐ ⓑ ⓒ ⓓ
12	ⓐ ⓑ ⓒ	32	ⓐ ⓑ ⓒ ⓓ	52	ⓐ ⓑ ⓒ ⓓ	72	ⓐ ⓑ ⓒ ⓓ	92	ⓐ ⓑ ⓒ ⓓ
13	ⓐ ⓑ ⓒ	33	ⓐ ⓑ ⓒ ⓓ	53	ⓐ ⓑ ⓒ ⓓ	73	ⓐ ⓑ ⓒ ⓓ	93	ⓐ ⓑ ⓒ ⓓ
14	ⓐ ⓑ ⓒ	34	ⓐ ⓑ ⓒ ⓓ	54	ⓐ ⓑ ⓒ ⓓ	74	ⓐ ⓑ ⓒ ⓓ	94	ⓐ ⓑ ⓒ ⓓ
15	ⓐ ⓑ ⓒ	35	ⓐ ⓑ ⓒ ⓓ	55	ⓐ ⓑ ⓒ ⓓ	75	ⓐ ⓑ ⓒ ⓓ	95	ⓐ ⓑ ⓒ ⓓ
16	ⓐ ⓑ ⓒ	36	ⓐ ⓑ ⓒ ⓓ	56	ⓐ ⓑ ⓒ ⓓ	76	ⓐ ⓑ ⓒ ⓓ	96	ⓐ ⓑ ⓒ ⓓ
17	ⓐ ⓑ ⓒ	37	ⓐ ⓑ ⓒ ⓓ	57	ⓐ ⓑ ⓒ ⓓ	77	ⓐ ⓑ ⓒ ⓓ	97	ⓐ ⓑ ⓒ ⓓ
18	ⓐ ⓑ ⓒ	38	ⓐ ⓑ ⓒ ⓓ	58	ⓐ ⓑ ⓒ ⓓ	78	ⓐ ⓑ ⓒ ⓓ	98	ⓐ ⓑ ⓒ ⓓ
19	ⓐ ⓑ ⓒ	39	ⓐ ⓑ ⓒ ⓓ	59	ⓐ ⓑ ⓒ ⓓ	79	ⓐ ⓑ ⓒ ⓓ	99	ⓐ ⓑ ⓒ ⓓ
20	ⓐ ⓑ ⓒ	40	ⓐ ⓑ ⓒ ⓓ	60	ⓐ ⓑ ⓒ ⓓ	80	ⓐ ⓑ ⓒ ⓓ	100	ⓐ ⓑ ⓒ ⓓ

ANSWER SHEET

ETS® TOEIC® 토익® 정기시험 실전 1000

성명
한글
한자
영자

Test 03 (Part 1~4)

Test 04 (Part 1~4)

ANSWER SHEET

ETS TOEIC® 토익 정기시험 실전 1000

수험번호

응시일자 : 20   년   월   일

성명 한글 / 한자 / 영자

Test 05 (Part 1~4)

(answer bubble grid for questions 1–100)

Test 06 (Part 1~4)

(answer bubble grid for questions 1–100)

ANSWER SHEET

ETS® TOEIC® 토익® 정기시험 실전 1000

수험번호						

응시일자 : 20 년 월 일

성명		
	한 글	
	한 자	
	영 자	

Test 07 (Part 1~4)

1	ⓐ ⓑ ⓒ ⓓ	21	ⓐ ⓑ ⓒ	41	ⓐ ⓑ ⓒ ⓓ	61	ⓐ ⓑ ⓒ ⓓ	81	ⓐ ⓑ ⓒ ⓓ
2	ⓐ ⓑ ⓒ ⓓ	22	ⓐ ⓑ ⓒ	42	ⓐ ⓑ ⓒ ⓓ	62	ⓐ ⓑ ⓒ ⓓ	82	ⓐ ⓑ ⓒ ⓓ
3	ⓐ ⓑ ⓒ ⓓ	23	ⓐ ⓑ ⓒ	43	ⓐ ⓑ ⓒ ⓓ	63	ⓐ ⓑ ⓒ ⓓ	83	ⓐ ⓑ ⓒ ⓓ
4	ⓐ ⓑ ⓒ ⓓ	24	ⓐ ⓑ ⓒ	44	ⓐ ⓑ ⓒ ⓓ	64	ⓐ ⓑ ⓒ ⓓ	84	ⓐ ⓑ ⓒ ⓓ
5	ⓐ ⓑ ⓒ ⓓ	25	ⓐ ⓑ ⓒ	45	ⓐ ⓑ ⓒ ⓓ	65	ⓐ ⓑ ⓒ ⓓ	85	ⓐ ⓑ ⓒ ⓓ
6	ⓐ ⓑ ⓒ ⓓ	26	ⓐ ⓑ ⓒ	46	ⓐ ⓑ ⓒ ⓓ	66	ⓐ ⓑ ⓒ ⓓ	86	ⓐ ⓑ ⓒ ⓓ
7	ⓐ ⓑ ⓒ	27	ⓐ ⓑ ⓒ	47	ⓐ ⓑ ⓒ ⓓ	67	ⓐ ⓑ ⓒ ⓓ	87	ⓐ ⓑ ⓒ ⓓ
8	ⓐ ⓑ ⓒ	28	ⓐ ⓑ ⓒ	48	ⓐ ⓑ ⓒ ⓓ	68	ⓐ ⓑ ⓒ ⓓ	88	ⓐ ⓑ ⓒ ⓓ
9	ⓐ ⓑ ⓒ	29	ⓐ ⓑ ⓒ	49	ⓐ ⓑ ⓒ ⓓ	69	ⓐ ⓑ ⓒ ⓓ	89	ⓐ ⓑ ⓒ ⓓ
10	ⓐ ⓑ ⓒ	30	ⓐ ⓑ ⓒ	50	ⓐ ⓑ ⓒ ⓓ	70	ⓐ ⓑ ⓒ ⓓ	90	ⓐ ⓑ ⓒ ⓓ
11	ⓐ ⓑ ⓒ	31	ⓐ ⓑ ⓒ	51	ⓐ ⓑ ⓒ ⓓ	71	ⓐ ⓑ ⓒ ⓓ	91	ⓐ ⓑ ⓒ ⓓ
12	ⓐ ⓑ ⓒ	32	ⓐ ⓑ ⓒ ⓓ	52	ⓐ ⓑ ⓒ ⓓ	72	ⓐ ⓑ ⓒ ⓓ	92	ⓐ ⓑ ⓒ ⓓ
13	ⓐ ⓑ ⓒ	33	ⓐ ⓑ ⓒ ⓓ	53	ⓐ ⓑ ⓒ ⓓ	73	ⓐ ⓑ ⓒ ⓓ	93	ⓐ ⓑ ⓒ ⓓ
14	ⓐ ⓑ ⓒ	34	ⓐ ⓑ ⓒ ⓓ	54	ⓐ ⓑ ⓒ ⓓ	74	ⓐ ⓑ ⓒ ⓓ	94	ⓐ ⓑ ⓒ ⓓ
15	ⓐ ⓑ ⓒ	35	ⓐ ⓑ ⓒ ⓓ	55	ⓐ ⓑ ⓒ ⓓ	75	ⓐ ⓑ ⓒ ⓓ	95	ⓐ ⓑ ⓒ ⓓ
16	ⓐ ⓑ ⓒ	36	ⓐ ⓑ ⓒ ⓓ	56	ⓐ ⓑ ⓒ ⓓ	76	ⓐ ⓑ ⓒ ⓓ	96	ⓐ ⓑ ⓒ ⓓ
17	ⓐ ⓑ ⓒ	37	ⓐ ⓑ ⓒ ⓓ	57	ⓐ ⓑ ⓒ ⓓ	77	ⓐ ⓑ ⓒ ⓓ	97	ⓐ ⓑ ⓒ ⓓ
18	ⓐ ⓑ ⓒ	38	ⓐ ⓑ ⓒ ⓓ	58	ⓐ ⓑ ⓒ ⓓ	78	ⓐ ⓑ ⓒ ⓓ	98	ⓐ ⓑ ⓒ ⓓ
19	ⓐ ⓑ ⓒ	39	ⓐ ⓑ ⓒ ⓓ	59	ⓐ ⓑ ⓒ ⓓ	79	ⓐ ⓑ ⓒ ⓓ	99	ⓐ ⓑ ⓒ ⓓ
20	ⓐ ⓑ ⓒ	40	ⓐ ⓑ ⓒ ⓓ	60	ⓐ ⓑ ⓒ ⓓ	80	ⓐ ⓑ ⓒ ⓓ	100	ⓐ ⓑ ⓒ ⓓ

Test 08 (Part 1~4)

1	ⓐ ⓑ ⓒ ⓓ	21	ⓐ ⓑ ⓒ	41	ⓐ ⓑ ⓒ ⓓ	61	ⓐ ⓑ ⓒ ⓓ	81	ⓐ ⓑ ⓒ ⓓ
2	ⓐ ⓑ ⓒ ⓓ	22	ⓐ ⓑ ⓒ	42	ⓐ ⓑ ⓒ ⓓ	62	ⓐ ⓑ ⓒ ⓓ	82	ⓐ ⓑ ⓒ ⓓ
3	ⓐ ⓑ ⓒ ⓓ	23	ⓐ ⓑ ⓒ	43	ⓐ ⓑ ⓒ ⓓ	63	ⓐ ⓑ ⓒ ⓓ	83	ⓐ ⓑ ⓒ ⓓ
4	ⓐ ⓑ ⓒ ⓓ	24	ⓐ ⓑ ⓒ	44	ⓐ ⓑ ⓒ ⓓ	64	ⓐ ⓑ ⓒ ⓓ	84	ⓐ ⓑ ⓒ ⓓ
5	ⓐ ⓑ ⓒ ⓓ	25	ⓐ ⓑ ⓒ	45	ⓐ ⓑ ⓒ ⓓ	65	ⓐ ⓑ ⓒ ⓓ	85	ⓐ ⓑ ⓒ ⓓ
6	ⓐ ⓑ ⓒ ⓓ	26	ⓐ ⓑ ⓒ	46	ⓐ ⓑ ⓒ ⓓ	66	ⓐ ⓑ ⓒ ⓓ	86	ⓐ ⓑ ⓒ ⓓ
7	ⓐ ⓑ ⓒ	27	ⓐ ⓑ ⓒ	47	ⓐ ⓑ ⓒ ⓓ	67	ⓐ ⓑ ⓒ ⓓ	87	ⓐ ⓑ ⓒ ⓓ
8	ⓐ ⓑ ⓒ	28	ⓐ ⓑ ⓒ	48	ⓐ ⓑ ⓒ ⓓ	68	ⓐ ⓑ ⓒ ⓓ	88	ⓐ ⓑ ⓒ ⓓ
9	ⓐ ⓑ ⓒ	29	ⓐ ⓑ ⓒ	49	ⓐ ⓑ ⓒ ⓓ	69	ⓐ ⓑ ⓒ ⓓ	89	ⓐ ⓑ ⓒ ⓓ
10	ⓐ ⓑ ⓒ	30	ⓐ ⓑ ⓒ	50	ⓐ ⓑ ⓒ ⓓ	70	ⓐ ⓑ ⓒ ⓓ	90	ⓐ ⓑ ⓒ ⓓ
11	ⓐ ⓑ ⓒ	31	ⓐ ⓑ ⓒ	51	ⓐ ⓑ ⓒ ⓓ	71	ⓐ ⓑ ⓒ ⓓ	91	ⓐ ⓑ ⓒ ⓓ
12	ⓐ ⓑ ⓒ	32	ⓐ ⓑ ⓒ ⓓ	52	ⓐ ⓑ ⓒ ⓓ	72	ⓐ ⓑ ⓒ ⓓ	92	ⓐ ⓑ ⓒ ⓓ
13	ⓐ ⓑ ⓒ	33	ⓐ ⓑ ⓒ ⓓ	53	ⓐ ⓑ ⓒ ⓓ	73	ⓐ ⓑ ⓒ ⓓ	93	ⓐ ⓑ ⓒ ⓓ
14	ⓐ ⓑ ⓒ	34	ⓐ ⓑ ⓒ ⓓ	54	ⓐ ⓑ ⓒ ⓓ	74	ⓐ ⓑ ⓒ ⓓ	94	ⓐ ⓑ ⓒ ⓓ
15	ⓐ ⓑ ⓒ	35	ⓐ ⓑ ⓒ ⓓ	55	ⓐ ⓑ ⓒ ⓓ	75	ⓐ ⓑ ⓒ ⓓ	95	ⓐ ⓑ ⓒ ⓓ
16	ⓐ ⓑ ⓒ	36	ⓐ ⓑ ⓒ ⓓ	56	ⓐ ⓑ ⓒ ⓓ	76	ⓐ ⓑ ⓒ ⓓ	96	ⓐ ⓑ ⓒ ⓓ
17	ⓐ ⓑ ⓒ	37	ⓐ ⓑ ⓒ ⓓ	57	ⓐ ⓑ ⓒ ⓓ	77	ⓐ ⓑ ⓒ ⓓ	97	ⓐ ⓑ ⓒ ⓓ
18	ⓐ ⓑ ⓒ	38	ⓐ ⓑ ⓒ ⓓ	58	ⓐ ⓑ ⓒ ⓓ	78	ⓐ ⓑ ⓒ ⓓ	98	ⓐ ⓑ ⓒ ⓓ
19	ⓐ ⓑ ⓒ	39	ⓐ ⓑ ⓒ ⓓ	59	ⓐ ⓑ ⓒ ⓓ	79	ⓐ ⓑ ⓒ ⓓ	99	ⓐ ⓑ ⓒ ⓓ
20	ⓐ ⓑ ⓒ	40	ⓐ ⓑ ⓒ ⓓ	60	ⓐ ⓑ ⓒ ⓓ	80	ⓐ ⓑ ⓒ ⓓ	100	ⓐ ⓑ ⓒ ⓓ

ANSWER SHEET

ETS TOEIC® 토익 정기시험 실전 1000

성명

한글	
한자	
영자	

수험번호

응시일자 : 20   년   월   일

Test 09 (Part 1~4)

Test 10 (Part 1~4)

LC

All New
토익
정기시험
실전 1

1000

정답 및 해설

1 (D)	2 (C)	3 (B)	4 (C)	5 (D)
6 (A)	7 (B)	8 (A)	9 (B)	10 (C)
11 (A)	12 (B)	13 (A)	14 (C)	15 (A)
16 (C)	17 (B)	18 (B)	19 (C)	20 (A)
21 (C)	22 (C)	23 (B)	24 (A)	25 (B)
26 (A)	27 (C)	28 (A)	29 (C)	30 (B)
31 (B)	32 (A)	33 (D)	34 (C)	35 (C)
36 (A)	37 (B)	38 (A)	39 (B)	40 (D)
41 (C)	42 (B)	43 (D)	44 (C)	45 (D)
46 (B)	47 (B)	48 (A)	49 (D)	50 (C)
51 (D)	52 (A)	53 (C)	54 (C)	55 (A)
56 (A)	57 (B)	58 (A)	59 (C)	60 (B)
61 (A)	62 (A)	63 (D)	64 (B)	65 (D)
66 (C)	67 (A)	68 (B)	69 (D)	70 (C)
71 (C)	72 (D)	73 (B)	74 (C)	75 (D)
76 (B)	77 (C)	78 (A)	79 (B)	80 (D)
81 (C)	82 (A)	83 (D)	84 (A)	85 (A)
86 (B)	87 (D)	88 (C)	89 (A)	90 (B)
91 (D)	92 (D)	93 (C)	94 (B)	95 (A)
96 (D)	97 (C)	98 (C)	99 (B)	100 (B)

PART 1

1 M-Cn

(A) A woman is standing near a desk.
(B) A woman is climbing some stairs.
(C) A woman is entering a building.
(D) A woman is looking at a map.

(A) 여자가 책상 근처에 서 있다.
(B) 여자가 계단을 오르고 있다.
(C) 여자가 건물 안으로 들어가고 있다.
(D) 여자가 지도를 보고 있다.

어휘 climb 오르다 enter 들어가다

해설 1인 등장 사진 – 사람의 동작/상태 묘사
(A) 사진에 없는 명사를 이용한 오답. 사진에 책상(a desk)이 보이지 않으므로 오답.
(B) 동사 오답. 여자가 계단을 오르고 있는(is climbing some stairs) 모습이 아니므로 오답.
(C) 동사 오답. 여자가 건물 안으로 들어가고 있는(is entering a building) 모습이 아니므로 오답.

(D) 정답. 여자가 지도를 보고 있는(is looking at a map) 모습이므로 정답.

2 W-Am

(A) She's swimming in the water.
(B) She's jogging near the ocean.
(C) Chairs are set up on the beach.
(D) A hat is lying on the sand.

(A) 여자가 물에서 수영하고 있다.
(B) 여자가 바다 근처에서 조깅하고 있다.
(C) 의자들이 해변에 설치되어 있다.
(D) 모자가 모래 위에 놓여 있다.

어휘 set up 설치하다 lie 놓여 있다

해설 혼합 사진 – 사람/사물/풍경 혼합 묘사
(A) 동사 오답. 여자가 물에서 수영하고 있는(is swimming in the water) 모습이 아니므로 오답.
(B) 동사 오답. 여자가 바다 근처에서 조깅하고 있는(is jogging near the ocean) 모습이 아니므로 오답.
(C) 정답. 의자들(Chairs)이 해변에 설치되어 있는(are set up on the beach) 모습이므로 정답.
(D) 동사 오답. 모자(A hat)가 모래 위에 놓여 있는(is lying on the sand) 모습이 아니므로 오답.

3 W-Br

(A) She's reaching for an item from a display case.
(B) She's holding on to a shopping cart.
(C) Some goods are being arranged on shelves.
(D) Some merchandise has fallen on the floor.

(A) 여자가 진열장에서 물건을 집으려고 손을 뻗고 있다.
(B) 여자가 쇼핑 카트를 붙잡고 있다.
(C) 상품들이 선반에 정리되고 있다.
(D) 상품들이 바닥에 떨어져 있다.

어휘 reach for ~을 잡으려고 손을 뻗다 arrange 정리하다 shelf 선반 merchandise 상품

해설 혼합 사진 – 사람/사물/풍경 혼합 묘사
(A) 동사 오답. 여자가 물건을 집으려고 손을 뻗고 있는(is reaching for an item) 모습이 아니므로 오답.
(B) 정답. 여자가 쇼핑 카트를 붙잡고 있는(is holding on to a shopping cart) 모습이므로 정답.

(C) 동사 오답. 상품들(Some goods)이 선반에 정리되고 있는(are being arranged on shelves) 모습이 아니므로 오답.

(D) 동사 오답. 상품들(Some merchandise)이 바닥에 떨어져 있는(has fallen on the floor) 모습이 아니므로 오답.

4 W-Am

(A) A fence is being painted in a park.
(B) One of the women is putting on a jacket.
(C) Some people are working in a garden.
(D) Some people are looking up at the trees.

(A) 공원에서 울타리를 칠하고 있다.
(B) 여자들 중 한 명이 재킷을 입고 있다.
(C) **사람들이 정원에서 일하고 있다.**
(D) 사람들이 나무들을 올려다보고 있다.

어휘 put on ~을 입다, 착용하다(입고 있는 동작)

해설 혼합 사진 – 사람/사물/풍경 혼합 묘사

(A) 동사 오답. 울타리(A fence)를 칠하고 있는(is being painted) 모습이 아니므로 오답.

(B) 동사 오답. 여자들 중 한 명(One of the women)이 재킷을 입고 있는(is putting on a jacket) 모습이 아니므로 오답.

(C) 정답. 사람들이 정원에서 일하고 있는(are working in a garden) 모습이므로 정답.

(D) 동사 오답. 사람들이 나무들을 올려다보고 있는(are looking up at the trees) 모습이 아니므로 오답.

5 M-Au

(A) A carpet is being rolled up.
(B) Some curtains have been closed.
(C) Some cushions are piled on the floor.
(D) Some reading materials have been placed in front of a sofa.

(A) 카펫을 말고 있다.
(B) 커튼 일부가 닫혀 있다.
(C) 쿠션들이 바닥에 쌓여 있다.
(D) **읽을거리들이 소파 앞에 놓여 있다.**

어휘 pile 쌓다 in front of ~ 앞에

해설 사물/풍경 사진 – 사물 묘사

(A) 동사 오답. 카펫(A carpet)을 말고 있는(is being rolled up) 모습이 아니므로 오답.

(B) 사진에 없는 명사를 이용한 오답. 사진에 커튼(Some curtains)이 보이지 않으므로 오답.

(C) 동사 오답. 쿠션들(Some cushions)이 바닥에 쌓여 있는(are piled on the floor) 모습이 아니므로 오답.

(D) 정답. 읽을거리들(Some reading materials)이 소파 앞에 놓여 있는(have been placed in front of a sofa) 모습이므로 정답.

6 W-Br

(A) Some musicians are performing on a porch.
(B) Some steps are being repaired.
(C) Some music stands are being folded up.
(D) Some instruments have been placed in their cases.

(A) **음악가들이 현관에서 연주하고 있다.**
(B) 계단이 수리되고 있다.
(C) 보면대들을 접고 있다.
(D) 악기들이 케이스 안에 놓여 있다.

어휘 perform 연주하다 porch 현관 repair 수리하다 music stand 보면대 instrument 악기

해설 혼합 사진 – 사람/사물/풍경 혼합 묘사

(A) 정답. 음악가들(Some musicians)이 현관에서 연주하고 있는(are performing on a porch) 모습이므로 정답.

(B) 동사 오답. 계단(Some steps)이 수리되고 있는(are being repaired) 모습이 아니므로 오답.

(C) 동사 오답. 보면대들(Some music stands)을 접고 있는(are being folded up) 모습이 아니므로 오답.

(D) 동사 오답. 악기들(Some instruments)이 케이스 안에 놓여 있는(have been placed in their cases) 모습이 아니므로 오답.

PART 2

7

M-Cn What type of food does that store sell?

W-Br (A) What a delicious recipe.
      (B) They have all kinds of cheese.
      (C) With a new jacket.

저 가게는 어떤 음식을 파나요?
(A) 정말 맛있는 요리법이네요.
(B) 온갖 종류의 치즈를 구비하고 있어요.
(C) 새 재킷과 함께요.

어휘 recipe 요리[조리]법

해설 음식 종류를 묻는 What 의문문

(A) 연상 단어 오답. 질문의 food에서 연상 가능한 delicious와 recipe를 이용한 오답.

(B) 정답. 어떤 음식을 파는지 묻는 질문에 모든 종류의 치즈라며 명확하게 알려 주고 있으므로 정답.

(C) 연상 단어 오답. 질문의 store와 sell에서 연상 가능한 new jacket을 이용한 오답.

8

W-Am When should we leave for the airport?

M-Au (A) This afternoon at two o'clock.
(B) I prefer an aisle seat.
(C) Mr. Choi traveled there last year.

우리는 언제 공항으로 출발해야 하나요?
(A) 오늘 오후 2시요.
(B) 저는 통로 쪽 좌석이 더 좋아요.
(C) 최 씨는 작년에 그곳을 여행했어요.

어휘 leave for ~을 향해 출발하다   prefer 선호하다   aisle 통로

해설 출발 시점을 묻는 When 의문문
(A) 정답. 언제 공항으로 출발해야 하는지를 묻는 질문에 오후 2시라고 응답하고 있으므로 정답.
(B) 연상 단어 오답. 질문의 airport에서 연상 가능한 aisle seat를 이용한 오답.
(C) 연상 단어 오답. 질문의 airport에서 연상 가능한 traveled를 이용한 오답.

9

W-Br Where's the hiring event being held?

W-Am (A) She sent it to a colleague.
(B) In the main conference room.
(C) If they open on time.

채용 행사는 어디에서 열리고 있나요?
(A) 그녀가 그것을 동료에게 보냈어요.
(B) 주 회의실에서요.
(C) 만약 제시간에 문을 연다면요.

어휘 hiring 채용   be held (행사가) 열리다   colleague 동료
on time 제시간에

해설 행사 장소를 묻는 Where 의문문
(A) 연상 단어 오답. 질문의 hiring에서 연상 가능한 colleague를 이용한 오답.
(B) 정답. 행사가 어디에서 열리고 있는지를 묻는 질문에 주 회의실이라고 개최 장소를 알려 주고 있으므로 정답.
(C) 질문과 상관없는 오답.

10

M-Cn Why is the budget being updated?

W-Br (A) When we rented the building.
(B) With the new designs.
(C) Because new sales figures came in.

예산은 왜 새로 수정되고 있나요?
(A) 우리가 건물을 임차했을 때요.
(B) 새로운 디자인과 함께요.
(C) 새로운 매출액이 보고되었기 때문이에요.

어휘 budget 예산   sales figures 매출액

해설 예산이 새로 수정되는 이유를 묻는 Why 의문문
(A) 질문과 상관없는 오답. When 의문문에 대한 응답이므로 오답.
(B) 연상 단어 오답. 질문의 updated에서 연상 가능한 new를 이용한 오답.
(C) 정답. 예산이 수정되는 이유를 묻는 질문에 새로운 매출액이 보고되었기 때문이라며 이유를 제시하고 있으므로 정답.

11

W-Am Can you cover my shift at work tomorrow?

M-Au (A) No, I'm taking the day off.
(B) Before he updated the Web site.
(C) It's on the agenda for Tuesday.

내일 제 근무 시간에 대신 일해 주실 수 있나요?
(A) 아니요, 제가 내일은 쉬어요.
(B) 그가 웹사이트를 업데이트하기 전에요.
(C) 그건 화요일 안건에 있어요.

어휘 cover (자리에 없는 사람의 일을) 대신하다   shift (교대조) 근무 시간
take a day off 연차 휴가를 내다, 하루 쉬다   agenda 안건

해설 부탁/요청의 의문문
(A) 정답. 근무 시간에 대신 일해 줄 수 있는지 요청하는 질문에 아니요(No)라고 대답한 뒤, 거절하는 이유를 알려 주고 있으므로 정답.
(B) 질문과 상관없는 오답. When 의문문에 대한 응답이므로 오답.
(C) 연상 단어 오답. 질문의 tomorrow에서 연상 가능한 Tuesday를 이용한 오답.

12

W-Br Who ordered these vegetables?

W-Am (A) All of it.
(B) I believe Luis did.
(C) It was excellent, thanks.

누가 이 채소를 주문했죠?
(A) 전부요.
(B) 루이스가 했을 거예요.
(C) 정말 좋았어요, 고마워요.

해설 채소 주문자를 묻는 Who 의문문
(A) 질문과 상관없는 오답. Which 의문문에 대한 응답이므로 오답.
(B) 정답. 채소를 주문한 사람을 묻는 질문에 Luis라는 사람 이름을 제시하고 있으므로 정답.
(C) 질문과 상관없는 오답. How 의문문에 대한 응답이므로 오답.

13

M-Au How often should I mail the notices?

W-Br (A) Once a month.
(B) After three o'clock.
(C) About half of them.

통지서를 얼마나 자주 우편으로 부쳐야 하나요?
(A) 한 달에 한 번이요.
(B) 3시 이후에요.
(C) 그것들 중 절반 정도요.

어휘 mail (우편으로) 부치다[보내다]

해설 통지서 발송의 빈도를 묻는 How often 의문문
(A) 정답. 통지서를 얼마나 자주 우편으로 부쳐야 하는지를 묻는 질문에 한 달에 한 번이라며 빈도를 제시하고 있으므로 정답.
(B) 질문과 상관없는 오답. When 의문문에 대한 응답이므로 오답.
(C) 질문과 상관없는 오답. How many 의문문에 대한 응답이므로 오답.

14

W-Am Which folder are the documents in?

M-Au (A) We agreed on the deadline.
(B) Sure, I'll take a look.
(C) Let me show you.

서류는 어느 폴더에 있나요?
(A) 우리는 마감일에 합의를 봤어요.
(B) 물론이죠, 제가 한번 볼게요.
(C) 제가 알려 드릴게요.

어휘 document 서류 take a look (한번) 보다

해설 서류가 있는 폴더를 묻는 Which 의문문
(A) 연상 단어 오답. 질문의 documents에서 연상 가능한 deadline을 이용한 오답.
(B) Yes/No 불가 오답. Which 의문문에는 Yes/No 응답이 불가능한데, Sure도 일종의 Yes 응답이라고 볼 수 있으므로 오답.
(C) 정답. 어느 폴더에 서류가 있는지를 묻는 질문에 자신이 알려 주겠다고 말하므로 정답.

15

M-Cn Did you end up going to a movie or to the concert last night?

W-Br (A) I saw the new action film.
(B) It just ended.
(C) Just a couple of my friends.

어젯밤에 결국 영화를 보러 갔나요, 아니면 콘서트를 보러 갔나요?
(A) 새로 나온 액션 영화를 봤어요.
(B) 방금 끝났어요.
(C) 제 친구 두어 명만요.

어휘 end up -ing 결국 ~하게 되다 a couple of 두서너 명[개]의

해설 어젯밤에 한 일을 묻는 선택 의문문
(A) 정답. 어젯밤에 한 일을 묻는 선택 의문문에 새로 나온 액션 영화를 봤다며 제시된 일 중 하나를 선택해 응답하고 있으므로 정답.
(B) 파생어 오답. 질문의 end와 파생어 관계인 ended를 이용한 오답.
(C) 연상 단어 오답. 질문의 going to a movie or to the concert에서 연상 가능한 a couple of my friends를 이용한 오답.

16

M-Au We'll take the company bus to the conference center.

M-Cn (A) I'm sure it's not.
(B) Maybe we did.
(C) That's a good plan.

우리는 회사 버스를 타고 회의장으로 갈 겁니다.
(A) 그건 절대 아닙니다.
(B) 우리가 그랬을지도 모르죠.
(C) 좋은 계획이에요.

어휘 conference 회의

해설 의사 전달의 평서문
(A) 평서문과 상관없는 오답.
(B) 단어 반복 오답. 평서문의 We를 반복 이용한 오답.
(C) 정답. 회사 버스를 타고 회의장으로 간다는 의사를 전달하는 평서문에 좋은 계획이라고 호응하고 있으므로 정답.

17

W-Am What should we put in the introduction to the report?

M-Au (A) After the summary.
(B) The research highlights.
(C) I met him yesterday.

보고서 서론에 무엇을 넣어야 할까요?
(A) 요약 뒤에요.
(B) 조사 연구에서 가장 중요한 부분이요.
(C) 저는 어제 그를 만났어요.

어휘 introduction 서론 summary 요약 highlight 가장 중요한[강조된] 부분

해설 보고서 서론에 넣을 내용을 묻는 What 의문문
(A) 연상 단어 오답. 질문의 report에서 연상 가능한 summary를 이용한 오답.
(B) 정답. 보고서 서론에 어떤 걸 넣어야 할지를 묻는 질문에 조사 연구에서 가장 중요한 부분을 넣으라고 알려 주고 있으므로 정답.
(C) 질문과 상관없는 오답.

18

M-Cn We should have a new logo designed.

W-Am (A) They're about five miles from here.
(B) I know a good graphic artist.
(C) An order for some new calendars.

우리는 새로운 로고 디자인을 맡겨야 해요.
(A) 여기에서 5마일 정도 떨어져 있어요.
(B) 제가 괜찮은 그래픽 아티스트를 알고 있어요.
(C) 새 달력 주문이에요.

해설 제안/권유의 평서문
(A) 평서문과 상관없는 오답. How far 의문문에 대한 응답이므로 오답.
(B) 정답. 새로운 로고 디자인을 맡겨야 한다는 제안에 대해 로고 디자인을 할 만한 괜찮은 그래픽 아티스트를 알고 있다며 호응의 뜻을 우회적으로 표현하고 있으므로 정답.
(C) 단어 반복 오답. 평서문의 new를 반복 이용한 오답.

19

M-Au   Did you select a site for the new headquarters?

W-Br   (A) Is that so?
(B) No one can attend the training.
(C) Yes, in the center of town.

새 본사를 위한 부지를 선정했나요?
(A) 그런가요?
(B) 아무도 교육에 참석할 수 없어요.
(C) 네, 시내 중심가예요.

어휘 select 선정[선택]하다   site 부지, 장소

해설 본사 부지의 선정 여부를 확인하는 조동사(Did) 의문문
(A) 질문과 상관없는 오답. 평서문에 대한 응답이므로 오답.
(B) 연상 단어 오답. 질문의 headquarters에서 연상 가능한 training을 이용한 오답.
(C) 정답. 새 본사 부지를 선정했는지 여부를 묻는 질문에 네(Yes)라고 대답한 뒤, 시내 중심가라며 긍정 답변과 일관된 내용을 덧붙이고 있으므로 정답.

20

W-Br   Who's going to cancel the meeting?

W-Am   (A) Martin is the most senior team member.
(B) Josie's chair is broken.
(C) The client signed the contract.

누가 회의를 취소할 건가요?
(A) 마틴이 팀에서 가장 고참이에요.
(B) 조시의 의자가 부러졌어요.
(C) 고객이 계약서에 서명했어요.

어휘 senior (계급 지위가) 고참의, 고위의   broken 부서진, 고장 난   contract 계약(서)

해설 회의 취소를 담당할 사람을 묻는 Who 의문문
(A) 정답. 회의를 취소할 사람을 묻는 질문에 마틴이 팀에서 가장 고참이라며 취소할 사람을 우회적으로 알리고 있으므로 정답.
(B) 연상 단어 오답. Who 의문문에 대한 답으로 연상 가능한 사람의 이름 Josie를 이용한 오답.
(C) 연상 단어 오답. Who 의문문과 the meeting에서 연상 가능한 client를 이용한 오답.

21

M-Au   How was your business trip?

M-Cn   (A) They found some just in time.
(B) I like that idea.
(C) It was very productive.

출장은 어땠나요?
(A) 그들이 때마침 몇 개 찾았어요.
(B) 아이디어가 마음에 들어요.
(C) 결실이 많았어요.

어휘 just in time 때마침   productive 결실이 있는, 생산적인

해설 출장의 결과를 묻는 How 의문문
(A) 질문과 상관없는 오답.
(B) 질문과 상관없는 오답. 제안/권유 의문문에 대한 응답이므로 오답.
(C) 정답. 출장이 어땠는지를 묻는 질문에 결실이 많았다며 결과에 대해 알려 주고 있으므로 정답.

22

M-Cn   Why did Chae-Won hire an assistant?

W-Br   (A) She will submit an estimate in September.
(B) Anyway, they thought I was late.
(C) Haven't you noticed how busy she is?

채원은 왜 보조를 고용했나요?
(A) 그녀는 9월에 견적서를 제출할 거예요.
(B) 어쨌든 그들은 내가 늦었다고 생각했어요.
(C) 그녀가 얼마나 바쁜지 모르셨어요?

어휘 submit 제출하다   estimate 견적(서)   notice 알아차리다

해설 보조를 고용한 이유를 묻는 Why 의문문
(A) 연상 단어 오답. 질문의 Chae-Won에서 연상 가능한 대명사 She를 이용한 오답.
(B) 질문과 상관없는 오답.
(C) 정답. 채원이 보조를 고용한 이유를 묻는 질문에 그녀가 얼마나 바쁜지 몰랐냐고 되물으며 우회적으로 이유를 알려 주고 있으므로 정답.

23

W-Am   Would you mind showing me the new office space?

M-Cn   (A) I think that's correct.
(B) Sure—it won't take long.
(C) Everyone available participated.

새 사무실 공간을 보여 주시겠어요?
(A) 맞는 것 같아요.
(B) 물론이죠. 오래 걸리지 않을 거예요.
(C) 시간이 되는 사람은 전부 참가했어요.

어휘 participate 참가하다

해설 부탁/요청의 의문문
(A) 질문과 상관없는 오답.
(B) 정답. 새 사무실 공간을 보여 달라고 요청하는 질문에 물론(Sure)이라

고 대답한 뒤, 오래 걸리지 않을 것이라며 긍정 답변과 일관된 내용을
덧붙이고 있으므로 정답.

(C) 질문과 상관없는 오답. Who 의문문에 대한 응답이므로 오답.

24

M-Cn　We're trying to decide where to order from for
　　　 lunch.

M-Au　(A) I loved those sandwiches from Gino's last
　　　　 week.
　　　 (B) My brother's friend was there.
　　　 (C) I remember that song very well.

우리는 점심을 어디에서 주문할지 결정하려고 해요.
(A) 지난주 지노스 샌드위치가 너무 좋았어요.
(B) 제 남동생 친구가 거기에 있었어요.
(C) 저는 그 노래를 생생하게 기억해요.

해설　정보 전달의 평서문

(A) 정답. 점심을 어디에서 주문할지 결정하려고 한다는 평서문에 대해 지
노스 샌드위치가 좋았다며 점심 주문으로 적당한 식당을 우회적으로
추천하고 있으므로 정답.
(B) 연상 단어 오답. 평서문의 where에서 연상 가능한 there를 이용한
오답.
(C) 평서문과 상관없는 오답.

25

W-Br　When do you plan to finish the advertising
　　　 campaign?

W-Am　(A) Next to Irina's office.
　　　 (B) By Monday morning at the latest.
　　　 (C) Because it didn't make sense to me.

언제 광고 캠페인을 끝낼 계획인가요?
(A) 이리나 사무실 옆이요.
(B) 아무리 늦어도 월요일 오전까지요.
(C) 저한테는 말이 안 됐으니까요.

어휘　advertising 광고　at the latest 아무리 늦어도　make sense
　　　 말이 되다[타당하다]

해설　광고 캠페인을 끝내는 시점을 묻는 When 의문문

(A) 질문과 상관없는 오답. Where 의문문에 대한 응답이므로 오답.
(B) 정답. 언제 광고 캠페인을 끝낼 계획인지 묻는 질문에 늦어도 월요일
오전이라고 시점을 언급하고 있으므로 정답.
(C) 질문과 상관없는 오답. Why 의문문에 대한 응답이므로 오답.

26

W-Br　Where will the guest speaker be joining us
　　　 from?

M-Au　(A) Nobody shared the details with me.
　　　 (B) He wasn't gone too long.
　　　 (C) First thing in the morning, I believe.

초빙 연사는 어디에서 저희와 합류하나요?
(A) 아무도 세부 내용을 저에게 알려 주지 않았어요.
(B) 그는 그리 오랫동안 자리를 비우진 않았어요.
(C) 아침에 제일 먼저 해야 할 일 같아요.

어휘　join 합류하다　share (남에게) 말하다, 공유하다　detail 세부 내용

해설　초빙 연사가 합류하는 장소를 묻는 Where 의문문

(A) 정답. 초빙 연사가 어디에서 합류하는지를 묻는 질문에 아무도 세부
내용을 알려 주지 않았다며 자신은 모른다는 것을 우회적으로 표현하
고 있으므로 정답.
(B) 연상 단어 오답. 질문의 Where에서 연상 가능한 gone을 이용한 오
답.
(C) 질문과 상관없는 오답.

27

M-Cn　Wouldn't you prefer that Mi-Sun lead the
　　　 training?

W-Br　(A) No, I filed it three months ago.
　　　 (B) I just gave them to the director.
　　　 (C) I don't think she works here anymore.

미선이 교육을 주도하는 게 낫지 않으세요?
(A) 아니요, 저는 3개월 전에 제출했어요.
(B) 제가 방금 이사님께 드렸어요.
(C) 그녀는 더 이상 여기에서 일하지 않을 걸요.

어휘　file (소송, 민원 등을) 제출[제기]하다

해설　제안/권유의 의문문

(A) 연상 단어 오답. Wouldn't you ~? 의문문에 대한 답으로 연상 가능
한 No를 이용한 오답.
(B) 연상 단어 오답. 질문의 lead the training에서 연상 가능한
director를 이용한 오답.
(C) 정답. 미선이 교육을 주도하는 게 낫지 않냐며 제안하는 질문에 그녀
는 더 이상 여기에서 일하지 않을 것이라며 반대의 의사를 우회적으로
표현하고 있으므로 정답.

28

M-Au　We should get some feedback on this book
　　　 cover design.

W-Am　(A) Ahmed has a visual arts degree.
　　　 (B) They probably skipped a week.
　　　 (C) It was really hard to hear.

우리는 이 책 표지 디자인에 대한 의견을 받아야 해요.
(A) 아흐메드가 시각 예술 학위를 가지고 있어요.
(B) 그들은 아마 일주일 건너뛰었을 거예요.
(C) 정말 듣기 힘들었어요.

어휘　feedback 의견, 피드백　visual arts 시각 예술　degree 학위
　　　 skip 건너뛰다

해설　제안/권유의 평서문

(A) 정답. 책 표지 디자인에 대한 조언을 받아야 한다는 제안에 대해 아흐
메드가 시각 예술 학위를 가지고 있다며 호응의 뜻을 우회적으로 표현
하고 있으므로 정답.

(B) 평서문과 상관없는 오답.
(C) 연상 단어 오답. 평서문의 book cover에서 연상 가능한 hard를 이용한 오답.

29

W-Am Would you be able to delay the meeting?

M-Cn (A) How much storage does it have?
(B) Most people seemed to enjoy it.
(C) Tatyana needs to leave for the airport in an hour.

회의를 연기할 수 있을까요?
(A) 저장 용량이 얼마나 되죠?
(B) 대다수 사람이 즐기는 것 같았어요.
(C) 타티야나가 한 시간 후에 공항으로 출발해야 해요.

어휘 storage 저장 (용량) leave for ~을 향해 출발하다

해설 부탁/요청의 의문문
(A) 질문과 상관없는 오답.
(B) 질문과 상관없는 오답. How 의문문에 대한 응답이므로 오답.
(C) 정답. 회의를 연기해 달라고 요청하는 질문에 타티야나가 한 시간 후에 공항으로 출발해야 한다며 회의를 연기할 수 없음을 우회적으로 알리고 있으므로 정답.

30

W-Br Will you rent a car or take the train while you're visiting?

M-Cn (A) They found some near the coast.
(B) I don't like driving in the city.
(C) Mostly some old desks.

방문하는 동안 차를 대여할 건가요, 아니면 기차를 탈 건가요?
(A) 그들이 해안 근처에서 몇 개 발견했어요.
(B) 저는 도시에서 운전하는 걸 좋아하지 않아요.
(C) 대부분 낡은 책상이에요.

어휘 rent 대여하다, 빌리다 coast 해안(가) mostly 대부분, 주로

해설 이동 수단을 묻는 선택 의문문
(A) 질문과 상관없는 오답. Where 의문문에 대한 응답이므로 오답.
(B) 정답. 방문하는 동안 이동 수단을 묻는 선택 의문문에 도시에서 운전하는 것을 좋아하지 않는다며 기차를 탈 것이라는 의사를 우회적으로 표현하고 있으므로 정답.
(C) 질문과 상관없는 오답.

31

M-Au Seven thirty at night is rather late for a meeting, isn't it?

W-Br (A) If people agree on it, I will.
(B) I promise I'll keep it short.
(C) I am not sure who he meant.

저녁 7시 30분이면 회의하기에는 좀 늦지 않아요?
(A) 사람들이 동의한다면 제가 할게요.
(B) 간략하게 하겠다고 약속할게요.
(C) 그가 누구를 의미했는지 잘 모르겠어요.

어휘 rather 좀, 약간 keep ~ short ~을 간략하게[짧게] 하다

해설 의사 전달의 부가 의문문
(A) 연상 단어 오답. 질문의 meeting에서 연상 가능한 agree를 이용한 오답.
(B) 정답. 회의하기에 늦은 시간이라는 의견에 공감하는지를 묻는 질문에 짧게 하겠다며 대안을 제시하고 있으므로 정답.
(C) 연상 단어 오답. 질문의 isn't it?에서 연상 가능한 대답인 I am not sure를 이용한 오답.

PART 3

32-34

W-Am Hello. ³²I'm calling about my tickets for tonight's baseball game. I'm hoping to upgrade my seats so we can sit closer to the field. The reservation is under my name: Joanna Reynolds.

M-Cn Let me take a look. Hmm. ³³I'm sorry, Ms. Reynolds, but our system seems to be down at the moment. I can do the exchange manually, but it'll take a little longer.

W-Am No problem. I have time.

M-Cn Thanks. Oh, and ³⁴just a reminder that better seats will cost more—you'll need to pay about 15 dollars more per seat.

여 안녕하세요. **오늘 밤 야구 경기 티켓 때문에 전화했어요. 경기장에 더 가까이 앉을 수 있도록 좌석을 업그레이드하고 싶어요.** 예약자 이름은 조안나 레이놀즈예요.

남 한번 볼게요. 흠. **죄송하지만 레이놀즈 씨, 지금 시스템이 먹통인 것 같아요.** 교환은 수동으로 할 수 있지만 시간이 좀 더 걸려요.

여 괜찮아요. 시간 있어요.

남 감사합니다. 아, 그리고 혹시나 해서 다시 말씀드리는데 더 **좋은 자리는 더 비싸요.** 한 자리당 15달러 정도 더 내셔야 합니다.

어휘 field 경기장 reservation 예약 exchange 교환하다 manually 수동으로 just a reminder 혹시나 해서 다시 이야기하는데

32

Why is the woman calling?
(A) To request a ticket change
(B) To make a dinner reservation
(C) To order merchandise
(D) To plan a vacation

여자는 왜 전화를 하고 있는가?
(A) 티켓 변경을 요청하기 위해
(B) 저녁 식사를 예약하기 위해
(C) 상품을 주문하기 위해
(D) 휴가 계획을 세우기 위해

해설 전체 내용 관련 – 여자가 전화하는 목적

여자는 첫 대사에서 야구 경기 티켓 때문에 전화한다(I'm calling about my tickets for tonight's baseball game)면서 좌석 업그레이드를 요청(I'm hoping to upgrade ~ to the field)하고 있으므로 정답은 (A)이다.

> **Paraphrasing** 대화의 upgrade my seats
> → 정답의 a ticket change

33

Why does the man apologize?
(A) An event was canceled.
(B) A line is very long.
(C) A payment option is unavailable.
(D) A computer program is not working.

남자는 왜 사과하는가?
(A) 행사가 취소됐다.
(B) 줄이 아주 길다.
(C) 결제 선택 사항을 이용할 수 없다.
(D) 컴퓨터 프로그램이 작동하지 않는다.

어휘 unavailable 이용할 수 없는

해설 세부 사항 관련 – 남자가 사과하는 이유

남자는 첫 대사에서 여자에게 사과하며, 시스템이 먹통인 것 같다(I'm sorry, Ms. Reynolds, but our system seems to be down at the moment)고 했으므로 정답은 (D)이다.

> **Paraphrasing** 대화의 our system seems to be down
> → 정답의 A computer program is not working

34

What does the man remind the woman about?
(A) A meal voucher
(B) Some free souvenirs
(C) An increase in price
(D) A refund policy

남자는 여자에게 무엇에 관해 상기시키는가?
(A) 식권
(B) 무료 기념품
(C) 가격 인상
(D) 환불 정책

어휘 souvenir 기념품 increase 인상

해설 세부 사항 관련 – 남자가 여자에게 상기시키는 것

남자는 마지막 대사에서 여자에게 더 좋은 자리는 더 비싸다(just a reminder that better seats will cost more)고 상기시키고 있으므로 정답은 (C)이다.

> **Paraphrasing** 대화의 cost more
> → 정답의 An increase in price

35-37

> W-Am Thilo, **35are you going to the company lunch later this morning at Sullivan Bistro? 36I'm not sure how to get there.**
>
> M-Au Well, **36the train stops right near it on Hanover Street, but you'd have to transfer a few times.** You know, **35, 36I'm getting a ride with Farida,** and she has a van.
>
> W-Am Oh, that would be convenient! **37Do you know where her desk is?**
>
> M-Au Yes. **37She has the cubicle closest to the stairs.**

> 여 틸로, 오늘 오전 늦게 설리번 비스트로에서 열리는 점심 회식에 가나요? 거기 가는 길을 몰라서요.
>
> 남 열차가 하노버 가 바로 근처에서 정차해요. 하지만 몇 번 갈아타야 해요. 전 파리다랑 같이 차로 가요. 그녀에게 밴이 있어요.
>
> 여 아, 그게 편하겠네요! 파리다 자리가 어딘지 아세요?
>
> 남 네. 계단에서 가장 가까운 칸막이 자리예요.

> 어휘 transfer 갈아타다, 환승하다 convenient 편리한 cubicle 칸막이로 막은 작은 근무 공간

35

What event will the speakers be attending later today?
(A) A job fair
(B) A film screening
(C) A lunch
(D) A conference

화자들은 오늘 낮에 어떤 행사에 참석할 것인가?
(A) 취업 박람회
(B) 영화 상영
(C) 점심 식사
(D) 회의

해설 세부 사항 관련 – 화자들이 참석하는 행사

여자가 첫 대사에서 남자에게 점심 회식에 가는지(are you going to the company lunch later this morning at Sullivan Bistro?) 물었고, 남자가 자신은 파리다와 같이 차로 간다(I'm getting a ride with Farida)고 대답한 것으로 보아 정답은 (C)이다.

36

Why does the man say, "she has a van"?

(A) To suggest inquiring about a ride
(B) To express surprise at a coworker's choice of vehicle
(C) To explain why a coworker was late
(D) To clarify that a coworker helped him move

남자는 왜 "그녀에게 밴이 있어요"라고 말하는가?

(A) 타고 가는 것에 관해 문의하는 것을 제안하려고
(B) 동료의 차량 선택에 놀라움을 표하려고
(C) 동료가 늦은 이유를 설명하려고
(D) 동료가 이사를 도왔다고 분명히 말하려고

어휘 inquire 묻다 express 표현하다 clarify 분명히 하다, 밝히다

해설 화자의 의도 파악 – 그녀에게 밴이 있다는 말의 의도
앞에서 여자가 장소에 가는 길을 모른다(I'm not sure how to get there)고 하자, 남자가 열차가 하노버 가 근처에서 정차하지만 몇 번 갈 아타야 한다(the train stops right near it on Hanover Street, but you'd have to transfer a few times)고 한 후, 자신은 파리다와 같이 차로 간다(I'm getting a ride with Farida)면서 인용문을 언급했으므로 여자에게 차로 갈 수 있는 방법을 알아보라고 귀띔해 주려는 의도로 볼 수 있다. 따라서 정답은 (A)이다.

37

What will the woman most likely do next?

(A) Reschedule an event
(B) Talk to another coworker
(C) Request time off
(D) Make a phone call

여자는 다음에 무엇을 할 것 같은가?

(A) 행사 일정 변경하기
(B) 다른 동료와 대화하기
(C) 휴식 요청하기
(D) 전화 걸기

해설 세부 사항 관련 – 여자가 다음에 할 일
여자가 두 번째 대사에서 파리다의 자리가 어딘지(Do you know where her desk is?) 묻자, 남자가 계단에서 가장 가까운 칸막이 자리(She has the cubicle closest to the stairs)라고 알려 주는 것으로 보아 정답은 (B)이다.

38-40

M-Au Hi, Sarika. ³⁸We need a new assistant manager here at Jeera Groceries. You've been one of our best cashiers for two years now. Are you interested in the position?

W-Br Wow. I definitely am. ³⁹My one concern is the working hours. Would my schedule change significantly?

M-Au You might have to work overtime once in a while, like when food deliveries arrive late, but that doesn't happen often. ⁴⁰Why don't you think about it for a few days? Let me know what you decide.

남 안녕하세요, 사리카. 여기 지라 식료품점에 새로운 부팀장이 필요해요. 당신은 2년 동안 최고의 계산원 중 한 명이었어요. 그 자리에 관심이 있나요?

여 와. 물론 관심 있죠. 한 가지 걱정이 있는데 근무 시간이에요. 제 일정이 많이 바뀔까요?

남 가끔 초과 근무를 해야 할 수도 있어요. 음식 배송이 늦을 때 같은 경우죠. 하지만 그런 일이 자주 있지는 않아요. 며칠 동안 생각해 보는 게 어때요? 결정하면 알려 줘요.

어휘 definitely 확실히 significantly 많이, 상당히 once in a while 가끔

38

Where do the speakers work?

(A) At a grocery store
(B) At a shipping facility
(C) At a restaurant
(D) At a doctor's office

화자들은 어디에서 일하는가?

(A) 식료품점
(B) 운송 시설
(C) 식당
(D) 병원

해설 전체 내용 관련 – 화자들의 근무지
남자가 첫 대사에서 여기 지라 식료품점에 새로운 부팀장이 필요하다(We need a new assistant manager here at Jeera Groceries)면서 여자에게 2년 동안 최고의 계산원이었다(You've been one of our best cashiers for two years now)고 한 것으로 보아 정답은 (A)이다.

39

What does the woman say she is concerned about?

(A) Fuel prices
(B) Her work hours
(C) A staff shortage
(D) An inventory process

여자는 무엇에 대해 걱정된다고 말하는가?

(A) 연료 가격
(B) 근무 시간
(C) 직원 부족
(D) 재고 관리 절차

어휘 fuel 연료 inventory 재고 (관리)

해설 세부 사항 관련 – 여자의 우려 사항
여자가 첫 대사에서 한 가지 걱정은 근무 시간(My one concern is the working hours)이라고 했으므로 정답은 (B)이다.

40

What does the man suggest that the woman do?
(A) Complete a training program
(B) Order extra equipment
(C) Hire a consultant
(D) Take time to make a decision

남자는 여자에게 무엇을 하라고 제안하는가?
(A) 교육 프로그램 이수하기
(B) 추가 장비 주문하기
(C) 컨설턴트 고용하기
(D) 시간을 두고 결정하기

어휘 equipment 장비

해설 세부 사항 관련 – 남자의 제안 사항

남자가 마지막 대사에서 며칠 동안 생각해 보는 게 어떠냐(Why don't you think about it for a few days?)고 물으며 결정하면 알려 달라(Let me know what you decide)고 했으므로 정답은 (D)이다.

> **Paraphrasing** 대화의 think about it for a few days
> → 정답의 Take time
> 대화의 decide → 정답의 make a decision

41-43

M-Cn Good morning. This is Westerly Travel's customer service. How may I help you?

W-Br Yes, **41I was supposed to take the two** P.M. **from Denver to Colorado Springs, but it was canceled. I need to book a different train. 42I'm presenting at a trade show first thing in the morning, so I'm hoping you can get me on another train today.**

M-Cn The four P.M. departure gets you in by six thirty, and there are plenty of seats available.

W-Br That sounds great.

M-Cn **43And to apologize for the inconvenience, I've upgraded you to business class at no extra charge.**

남 안녕하세요. 웨스털리 여행사 고객 서비스입니다. 무엇을 도와드릴까요?

여 네, 덴버에서 콜로라도 스프링스까지 가는 오후 2시 열차를 타기로 했는데 취소됐어요. 다른 기차를 예약해야 하는데요. 아침에 무역 박람회에서 제가 제일 먼저 발표하니까 오늘 가는 다른 기차를 구해 주셨으면 좋겠어요.

남 오후 4시에 출발하면 6시 30분까지 도착할 수 있어요. 좌석은 많이 있습니다.

여 잘됐네요.

남 그리고 불편을 끼쳐 드린 점 사과하는 의미에서 추가 요금 없이 비즈니스 클래스로 업그레이드해 드렸습니다.

어휘 be supposed to ~하기로 되어 있다   plenty of 많은   apologize 사과하다   inconvenience 불편

41

Why is the woman calling?
(A) Her taxi never arrived.
(B) Her luggage is missing.
(C) Her train was canceled.
(D) Her ticket is lost.

여자는 왜 전화를 하고 있는가?
(A) 택시가 도착하지 않았다.
(B) 짐이 없어졌다.
(C) 기차가 취소됐다.
(D) 표를 분실했다.

해설 전체 내용 관련 – 여자가 전화하는 목적

여자가 첫 대사에서 덴버에서 콜로라도 스프링스까지 가는 오후 2시 열차를 타기로 했는데 취소됐다(I was supposed to take the two P.M. from Denver to Colorado Springs, but it was canceled)면서 다른 기차를 예약해야 한다(I need to book a different train)고 했으므로 정답은 (C)이다.

42

What event is the woman planning to attend?
(A) An awards ceremony
(B) A trade show
(C) An art exhibit opening
(D) A building inspection

여자는 어떤 행사에 참석할 계획인가?
(A) 시상식
(B) 무역 박람회
(C) 미술 전람회 개막식
(D) 건축물 점검

어휘 inspection 점검

해설 세부 사항 관련 – 여자가 참석할 계획인 행사

여자가 첫 대사에서 무역 박람회에서 제일 먼저 발표하므로 오늘 가는 다른 기차를 구해주길 바란다(I'm presenting at a trade show ~ another train today)고 했으므로 정답은 (B)이다.

43

What does the man give the woman as an apology?
(A) A partial discount
(B) Vouchers for future travel
(C) A full refund
(D) A better seat

남자는 여자에게 사과의 표시로 무엇을 제공하는가?
(A) 부분 할인
(B) 향후 여행에 쓸 수 있는 쿠폰
(C) 전액 환불
(D) 더 좋은 좌석

해설 세부 사항 관련 – 남자가 여자에게 사과의 표시로 제공하는 것

남자가 마지막 대사에서 불편에 사과하는 의미로 비즈니스 클래스로 업그레이드해 주었다(And to apologize for the inconvenience, I've upgraded you to business class at no extra charge)고 했으므로 정답은 (D)이다.

> **Paraphrasing** 대화의 upgraded you to business class
> → 정답의 A better seat

44-46

> **W-Am** This is Marcy Ardmore at Sladen Motors. **44Some automotive parts we ordered from your factory haven't arrived at our dealership yet.**
>
> **M-Au** I'm sorry to hear that. We sent your order over a week ago, but the shipping company has been experiencing delays. Unfortunately, **45the tracking e-mails they sent us don't contain enough detail to determine when the parts will get to you.**
>
> **W-Am** I see. **46Do you have contact information for the shipping company? I'd like to see what I can find out.**
>
> **M-Au** **46Yes, I can give you their phone number.** But I'll also call them. Hopefully the more inquiries they get, the more seriously they'll take the issue.

> 여 슬래든 모터스의 마시 아드모어입니다. **공장에 주문한 자동차 부품들이 아직 저희 대리점에 도착하지 않았어요.**
>
> 남 죄송합니다. 주문을 일주일 전에 보냈지만 운송 회사에서 계속 지연되고 있어요. 안타깝게도 **운송 회사가 우리한테 보낸 추적 이메일에는 부품이 언제 도착할지 판단할 수 있을 정도로 세부 정보가 충분하지 않네요.**
>
> 여 그렇군요. 운송 회사 연락처를 가지고 있나요? 제가 알아낼 게 있을지 확인하고 싶어요.
>
> 남 **네, 전화번호를 알려 드릴 수 있습니다.** 하지만 저도 전화해 볼게요. 문의를 많이 받을수록 그쪽에서 문제를 더 심각하게 받아들였으면 합니다.

> 어휘 dealership (자동차) 대리점 unfortunately 안타깝게도 contact information 연락처 inquiry 문의 seriously 심각하게, 진지하게

44

Where does the woman work?
(A) At a distribution center
(B) At a conference center
(C) At a car dealership
(D) At a real estate agency

여자는 어디에서 일하는가?
(A) 물류 센터
(B) 회의장
(C) 자동차 대리점
(D) 부동산 중개소

해설 전체 내용 관련 – 여자의 근무지

여자가 첫 대사에서 공장에 주문한 자동차 부품들이 아직 우리 대리점에 도착하지 않았다(Some automotive parts we ordered from your factory haven't arrived at our dealership yet)고 한 것으로 보아 정답은 (C)이다.

45

What problem with some e-mails does the man mention?
(A) Confusion about the intended recipients
(B) A delay in message delivery
(C) An incorrectly typed word
(D) Lack of information

남자는 이메일의 어떤 문제점을 언급하는가?
(A) 대상 수신자 혼동
(B) 메시지 전송 지연
(C) 잘못 입력된 단어
(D) 정보 부족

어휘 confusion 혼동 recipient 수신자, 수령인 incorrectly 틀리게, 부정확하게 lack 부족

해설 세부 사항 관련 – 남자가 언급하는 이메일의 문제점

남자가 첫 대사에서 운송 회사가 보낸 추적 이메일에는 세부 정보가 충분하지 않다(the tracking e-mails they sent us don't contain enough detail to determine when the parts will get to you)고 했으므로 정답은 (D)이다.

> **Paraphrasing** 대화의 don't contain enough detail
> → 정답의 Lack of information

46

What will the woman most likely do next?
(A) Arrange a meeting
(B) Make a phone call
(C) Speak to her employees
(D) Review an invoice

여자는 다음에 무엇을 할 것 같은가?
(A) 회의 준비하기
(B) 전화 걸기
(C) 직원들에게 말하기
(D) 송장 검토하기

해설 세부 사항 관련 – 여자가 다음에 할 일

여자가 두 번째 대사에서 운송 회사 연락처를 가지고 있는지(Do you have contact information for the shipping company?) 물으면서 알아낼 게 있을지 확인하고 싶다(I'd like to see what I can find out)고 하자, 남자가 전화번호를 알려 주겠다(Yes, I can give you their phone number)고 한 것으로 보아 정답은 (B)이다.

47-49

M-Au	Amina, ⁴⁷how are plans progressing for the September release of our new model of mobile phone?
W-Br	⁴⁷Good. ⁴⁸Right now, the marketing department is looking at advertising options and thinking about the best way to get maximum exposure in the media.
M-Au	Great. And what's the update from our manufacturer about when they'll begin production? Last time we spoke, ⁴⁹you mentioned that the factory was at full capacity with other projects, and I'm worried that'll affect our timeline.
W-Br	I just spoke with them, and they'll free up room for us soon.

남	아미나, 9월에 출시되는 휴대폰 신모델에 대한 계획은 어떻게 진행되고 있죠?
여	잘되고 있어요. 현재 마케팅 부서에서 광고 옵션을 살펴보면서 미디어에 최대한 노출시킬 수 있는 최선의 방법을 생각하고 있어요.
남	좋아요. 그리고 언제 생산을 시작할지 제조업체에서 새로 보낸 소식은요? 지난번에 얘기했을 때 공장이 다른 프로젝트들로 최대 가동되고 있다고 언급했잖아요. 우리 일정에 영향을 미칠까 봐 걱정되네요.
여	방금 그들과 얘기했는데 곧 우리를 위해 비워 둔다고 하네요.

어휘 progress 진행되다 exposure 노출 manufacturer 제조업체 production 생산 at full capacity 최대한 가동하는 affect 영향을 미치다

47

What is the conversation mainly about?
(A) A policy change
(B) A product launch
(C) Some customer feedback
(D) A scheduled maintenance visit

대화는 주로 무엇에 관한 것인가?
(A) 정책 변경
(B) 제품 출시
(C) 고객 의견
(D) 예정된 유지 보수 방문

해설 전체 내용 관련 – 대화의 주제
남자가 첫 대사에서 여자에게 9월에 출시되는 휴대폰 신모델에 대한 계획이 어떤지(how are plans progressing ~ release of our new model of mobile phone?) 물었고, 뒤이어 여자가 잘되고 있다(Good)면서 휴대폰 출시에 대한 이야기를 이어 가고 있으므로 정답은 (B)이다.

> Paraphrasing 대화의 release of our new model of mobile phone → 정답의 A product launch

48

What does the woman say people at the company are currently working on?
(A) Exploring publicity options
(B) Finding a new vendor
(C) Assembling a sales team
(D) Negotiating a monthly fee

여자는 회사 사람들이 현재 무엇을 하고 있다고 말하는가?
(A) 홍보 옵션 탐색
(B) 새 판매업체 물색
(C) 영업팀 구성
(D) 월 비용 협상

어휘 publicity 홍보 vendor 판매업체 negotiate 협상하다

해설 세부 사항 관련 – 회사 사람들이 현재 하고 있다고 여자가 말하는 것
여자가 첫 대사에서 현재 마케팅 부서에서 광고 옵션을 살펴보면서 미디어 노출을 위한 최선의 방법을 생각하고 있다(Right now, the marketing department is looking at advertising options ~ maximum exposure in the media)고 했으므로 정답은 (A)이다.

> Paraphrasing 대화의 looking at advertising options → 정답의 Exploring publicity options

49

Why is the man concerned?
(A) Customers have complained.
(B) Price estimates are high.
(C) Some changes require approval.
(D) A plan may be delayed.

남자는 왜 걱정하는가?
(A) 고객들이 불만을 제기했다.
(B) 견적 가격이 비싸다.
(C) 변경 사항에 승인이 필요하다.
(D) 계획이 지연될 수 있다.

어휘 approval 승인

해설 세부 사항 관련 – 남자의 우려 사항
남자가 두 번째 대사에서 공장이 다른 프로젝트로 최대 가동되고 있어 일정에 영향을 미칠까 봐 걱정(you mentioned that the factory was at full capacity with other projects, and I'm worried that'll affect our timeline)이라고 한 것으로 보아 정답은 (D)이다.

> Paraphrasing 대화의 affect our timeline → 정답의 A plan may be delayed

50-52

W-Br	Hi, Luca. ⁵⁰Is the restaurant almost ready for this afternoon's awards dinner?
M-Au	⁵⁰Actually, now that the room's been set up, ⁵¹I see that we're short a few tables and chairs.

W-Br	Oh, **51I've already taken care of that. I called a rental company, and they'll be delivering the furniture we need in an hour.**
M-Au	Thanks for doing that. **52Did you also look over the final guest list?** I haven't had time to do that yet.
W-Br	**52No, I haven't. Why don't we do that together now?**
여	안녕, 루카. 식당이 오늘 오후 시상식 만찬 준비를 거의 끝냈나요?
남	실은 이제 방 배치가 끝났는데 탁자와 의자가 몇 개 부족해 보여요.
여	아, 그건 제가 이미 처리했어요. 대여 회사에 전화했는데 한 시간 뒤에 필요한 가구를 배달해 줄 거예요.
남	그렇게 해 줘서 고마워요. 최종 손님 명단도 검토했나요? 저는 그럴 겨를이 없었어요.
여	아니요, 못 했어요. 지금 같이 하는 게 어때요?
어휘	take care of ~을 처리하다 look over ~을 검토하다

50

What are the speakers preparing for?
(A) An interview
(B) A food delivery
(C) A special event
(D) An inspection

화자들은 무엇을 준비하고 있는가?
(A) 인터뷰
(B) 음식 배달
(C) 특별한 행사
(D) 점검

해설 세부 사항 관련 – 화자들이 준비하고 있는 것

여자가 첫 대사에서 식당이 오늘 오후 시상식 만찬 준비를 거의 끝냈는지(Is the restaurant almost ready for this afternoon's awards dinner?) 묻자 남자가 방 배치가 끝났다(Actually, now that the room's been set up)고 답한 것으로 보아 정답은 (C)이다.

Paraphrasing	대화의 awards dinner → 정답의 A special event

51

What does the woman say will be delivered in an hour?
(A) Some flower arrangements
(B) Some gifts for attendees
(C) Some audio equipment
(D) Some tables and chairs

여자는 한 시간 후에 무엇이 배달될 것이라고 말하는가?
(A) 꽃꽂이
(B) 참석자들을 위한 선물
(C) 오디오 장비
(D) 탁자와 의자

해설 세부 사항 관련 – 여자가 한 시간 후에 배달된다고 말하는 것

남자가 첫 대사에서 탁자와 의자가 부족하다(I see that we're short a few tables and chairs)고 하자 여자가 처리했다(I've already taken care of that)면서 대여 회사에서 한 시간 뒤에 필요한 가구를 배달해 줄 것(I called a rental company, and they'll be delivering the furniture we need in an hour)이라고 했으므로 정답은 (D)이다.

Paraphrasing	대화의 the furniture → 정답의 tables and chairs

52

What will the speakers most likely do next?
(A) Review a guest list
(B) Meet with a photographer
(C) Take a break
(D) Taste some food

화자들은 다음에 무엇을 할 것 같은가?
(A) 손님 명단 검토하기
(B) 사진작가 만나기
(C) 휴식하기
(D) 음식 맛보기

해설 세부 사항 관련 – 화자들이 다음에 할 일

남자가 두 번째 대사에서 최종 손님 명단도 검토했는지(Did you also look over the final guest list?) 물었고, 여자가 못 했다(No, I haven't)며 같이 하는 게 어떤지(Why don't we do that together now?) 제안하는 것으로 보아 정답은 (A)이다.

Paraphrasing	대화의 look over the final guest list → 정답의 Review a guest list

53-55

M-Cn	**53Marcella, we have a problem with the business conference we're hosting next week.** I just got a call from the conference center, and they said there's been water damage to three of the meeting rooms.
W-Am	Oh no! **54But the rooms will be repaired in time for our conference, right?**
M-Cn	They said there's a lot of damage.
W-Am	OK. **55Well, the weather's supposed to be nice, so we could host some of the seminars outdoors.** It's a little unconventional, but there's plenty of space surrounding the conference center.

남	마르셀라, 다음 주에 개최하는 비즈니스 회의에 문제가 **생겼어요.** 방금 회의장에서 전화가 왔는데, 회의실 3개가 수해를 입었다고 하네요.
여	저런! 하지만 회의 시간에 맞춰 방들이 복구되겠죠?
남	피해가 크다고 하더군요.
여	알겠어요. 어, 날씨가 좋다고 하니까 세미나 일부를 야외에서 **열 수 있을 거예요.** 조금 파격적이긴 하지만 회의장 주변에 공간이 넉넉하잖아요.

어휘 unconventional 파격적인

53

What event are the speakers discussing?
(A) A bank opening
(B) A contest
(C) A business conference
(D) A company anniversary

화자들은 어떤 행사를 논의하고 있는가?
(A) 은행 개점
(B) 대회
(C) 비즈니스 회의
(D) 회사 기념일

해설 전체 내용 관련 – 화자들이 논의하고 있는 행사

남자가 첫 대사에서 여자에게 다음 주에 개최하는 비즈니스 회의에 문제가 생겼다(Marcella, we have a problem with the business conference we're hosting next week)고 알리면서 관련 내용으로 대화를 이어 가고 있으므로 정답은 (C)이다.

54

What does the man mean when he says, "there's a lot of damage"?
(A) He finally fully understands a problem.
(B) The woman should expect a bill in the mail.
(C) The woman's assumption is incorrect.
(D) A schedule needs to be adjusted.

남자가 "피해가 크다"라고 말할 때 무엇을 의미하는가?
(A) 그는 마침내 문제를 완전히 파악하고 있다.
(B) 여자는 우편으로 청구서를 받을 예정이다.
(C) 여자의 짐작이 틀렸다.
(D) 일정을 조정해야 한다.

어휘 assumption 짐작   adjust 조정하다

해설 화자의 의도 파악 – 피해가 크다는 말의 의도

앞에서 여자가 회의 시간에 맞춰 방들이 복구될 것인지(But the rooms will be repaired in time for our conference, right?) 여부에 대한 의견을 묻자 인용문을 언급한 것이므로 피해가 커서 일정에 맞게 수리가 될 수 없다는 의견을 표현하려는 의도로 볼 수 있다. 따라서 정답은 (C)이다.

55

What does the woman recommend?
(A) Using an outdoor area
(B) Arranging technical support
(C) Confirming a catering menu
(D) Interviewing some job applicants

여자는 무엇을 권하는가?
(A) 야외 공간 사용
(B) 기술 지원 준비
(C) 공급 음식 메뉴 확정
(D) 구직자 면접

어휘 applicant 지원자

해설 세부 사항 관련 – 여자의 제안 사항

여자가 마지막 대사에서 날씨가 좋을 예정이라 세미나 일부를 야외에서 열 수 있을 것이다(Well, the weather's supposed to be nice, so we could host some of the seminars outdoors)고 했으므로 정답은 (A)이다.

> Paraphrasing   대화의 host some of the seminars outdoors → 정답의 Using an outdoor area

56-58 3인 대화

M-Au	OK, **[56]Marion, the new health-care software is all set up on your computer.** It should be pretty straightforward to use. But call technology support if you run into any issues.
W-Am	Great. **[56]I hear a lot of health-care providers are switching to this same software.**
M-Au	Yes. **[57]It's becoming popular because it retains all of a patient's medical records from different providers in one central system.**
W-Br	Excuse me. Sorry to interrupt.
M-Au	No problem, Francesca. What's up?
W-Br	I overheard what you said, and just to clarify, **[58]the program can only collect and retain records from providers who use the same software, [56,58]so Marion may find she still has to call around to obtain all the patient records she needs.**

남	좋아요, **마리온, 새로운 의료 서비스 소프트웨어가 컴퓨터에 전부 설치됐어요.** 사용하기에 꽤 간단할 거예요. 그래도 문제가 생기면 기술 지원부에 전화하세요.
여1	좋아요. 많은 의료 서비스 제공자들이 똑같은 소프트웨어로 **전환하고 있다고 들었어요.**
남	네. **여러 제공자들에게서 받은 환자의 모든 의료 기록을 하나의 중앙 시스템에 보관하기 때문에 인기를 얻고 있어요.**
여2	실례합니다. 방해해서 미안해요.

남 괜찮아요, 프란체스카. 무슨 일이죠?

여2 당신이 하는 말을 우연히 들어서 분명히 해 두려고요. **이 프로그램은 동일한 소프트웨어를 사용하는 제공자의 기록만 수집하고 보관할 수 있어요. 그러니까 마리온이 필요한 환자 기록을 전부 얻으려면 여전히 전화를 해야 할 수도 있어요.**

어휘	straightforward 간단한, 쉬운 run into (문제에) 부딪히다 switch 전환하다, 바꾸다 retain 보관하다 interrupt 방해하다 overhear 우연히 듣다 clarify 분명히 하다 obtain 얻다

56

What industry do the speakers most likely work in?
(A) Medicine
(B) Music
(C) Publishing
(D) Finance

화자들은 어떤 업계에서 일하는 것 같은가?
(A) 의학
(B) 음악
(C) 출판
(D) 금융

해설 전체 내용 관련 – 화자들의 근무 업계

남자가 첫 대사에서 마리온의 컴퓨터에 새 의료 서비스 소프트웨어가 설치되었다(Marion, the new health-care software is all set up on your computer)고 하자, 첫 번째 여자인 마리온이 많은 의료 서비스 제공자들이 똑같은 소프트웨어로 전환하고 있다고 들었다(I hear a lot of health-care providers ~ same software)고 했고, 두 번째 여자가 마지막 대사에서 마리온이 필요한 환자 기록을 얻으려면 여전히 전화를 해야 할 것(so Marion may find ~ she needs)이라고 한 것으로 보아 정답은 (A)이다.

57

According to the man, why has a software program become popular?
(A) It is less expensive than similar products.
(B) It makes information more accessible.
(C) It reduces environmental impact.
(D) It comes with customer support.

남자에 따르면, 소프트웨어 프로그램은 왜 인기를 끌게 되었는가?
(A) 비슷한 제품보다 저렴하다.
(B) 정보에 더 쉽게 접근할 수 있다.
(C) 환경에 미치는 영향을 줄인다.
(D) 고객 지원과 함께 제공된다.

어휘 expensive 비싼 accessible 접근[이용]할 수 있는 reduce 줄이다 environmental 환경의 impact 영향

해설 세부 사항 관련 – 남자가 말하는 소프트웨어 프로그램이 인기 있는 이유

남자가 두 번째 대사에서 여러 제공자들에게서 받은 환자의 모든 의료 기록을 하나의 중앙 시스템에 보관하기 때문에 인기가 있다(It's becoming

popular because it retains all of a patient's medical records from different providers in one central system)고 했으므로 정답은 (B)이다.

Paraphrasing	대화의 retains all of a patient's medical records from different providers in one central system → 정답의 makes information more accessible

58

What might Marion still need to do?
(A) Contact some service providers
(B) Sign a release form
(C) Check some financial information
(D) Repair some equipment

마리온은 여전히 무엇을 해야 할지도 모르는가?
(A) 서비스 공급자에게 연락하기
(B) 공개 동의서에 서명하기
(C) 재무 정보 확인하기
(D) 장비 수리하기

해설 세부 사항 관련 – 마리온이 여전히 해야 할 수도 있는 일

두 번째 여자가 마지막 대사에서 프로그램은 동일한 소프트웨어를 사용하는 (의료 서비스) 제공자의 기록만 수집하고 보관할 수 있어서 마리온이 필요한 환자 기록을 전부 얻으려면 여전히 전화를 해야 할 것(the program can only collect and retain records ~ call around to obtain all the patient records she needs)이라고 했으므로 정답은 (A)이다.

Paraphrasing	대화의 call around → 정답의 Contact

59-61 3인 대화

W-Am Let's get this product-innovation meeting started. **59Sales of our fruit-and-nut bars have been strong, so we'd like to develop some other types of snack bars. What do you recommend, Stan?**

M-Cn Well, we know that many people are allergic to nuts, so **60we should develop some snack bars without nuts. The only thing is, we'd need a separate set of equipment to avoid contamination between the two production areas.**

W-Am We don't have room at this facility for that. **61Pedro, you've been to our new production facility in Glenview, right? Is there space there for new equipment?**

M-Au I think there's extra space there. **61I'll check with the facility manager to make sure, though.**

여	제품 혁신 회의를 시작하겠습니다. **과일 견과류 바 판매가 호조를 보이고 있어서 다른 유형의 스낵바를 개발하려고 합니다.** 어떤 걸 추천하시겠어요, 스탠?
남1	흠, 많은 사람이 견과류에 알레르기가 있기 때문에 **견과류가 없는 스낵바를 개발해야 합니다. 단지 문제는, 두 생산 구역 사이에 오염을 방지하려면 별도의 장비 세트가 필요합니다.**
여	이 시설에는 그럴 공간이 없어요. **페드로, 글렌뷰에 있는 새 생산 시설에 가 보셨죠? 거기에 새 장비가 들어갈 공간이 있나요?**
남2	거기에 여분의 공간이 있는 것 같아요. 하지만 **시설 관리자에게 확실히 알아보겠습니다.**

어휘	allergic 알레르기가 있는 separate 별도의 avoid 방지하다 contamination 오염 facility 시설

59

What are the speakers discussing?
(A) Proposing a business merger
(B) Relocating a company's headquarters
(C) Developing additional products
(D) Hiring more employees

화자들은 무엇에 대해 논의하고 있는가?
(A) 업체 합병 제안
(B) 본사 이전
(C) 추가 제품 개발
(D) 직원 추가 고용

어휘 merger 합병 relocate 이전하다

해설 전체 내용 관련 – 화자들의 논의 사항

여자가 첫 대사에서 과일 견과류 바가 잘 팔리므로 다른 유형의 스낵바를 개발하려 한다(Sales of our fruit-and-nut bars have been strong, so we'd like to develop some other types of snack bars)면서 무엇을 추천할지(What do you recommend, Stan?) 물으며 다른 화자들과 제품 개발과 관련된 논의를 이어 가고 있으므로 정답은 (C)이다.

Paraphrasing	대화의 develop some other types of snack bars → 정답의 Developing additional products

60

What challenge does Stan mention?
(A) A profit margin will decrease.
(B) Additional equipment will be needed.
(C) There are not enough job applicants.
(D) There are delays in production.

스탠은 어떤 어려움을 언급하는가?
(A) 수익 폭이 감소할 것이다.
(B) 추가 장비가 필요할 것이다.
(C) 구직자가 부족하다
(D) 생산이 지연되고 있다.

어휘 profit margin 수익 폭

해설 세부 사항 관련 – 스탠이 언급하는 어려움

여자가 첫 번째 남자인 스탠에게 추천할 것을 묻자 스탠이 견과류가 없는 스낵바를 개발해야 한다(we should develop ~ without nuts)고 한 뒤, 단지 문제는 두 생산 구역 사이에 오염을 방지하려면 별도의 장비가 필요하다(The only thing is, we'd need a separate set of equipment ~ between the two production areas)고 했으므로 정답은 (B)이다.

Paraphrasing	대화의 need a separate set of equipment → 정답의 Additional equipment will be needed

61

What does Pedro say he will do?
(A) Contact a facility manager
(B) Adjust a budget
(C) Change a work schedule
(D) Research a product

페드로는 무엇을 할 것이라고 말하는가?
(A) 시설 관리자에게 문의
(B) 예산 조정
(C) 작업 일정 변경
(D) 제품 조사

해설 세부 사항 관련 – 페드로가 할 것이라고 말하는 일

여자가 두 번째 대사에서 페드로에게 글렌뷰에 있는 새 생산 시설에 가 보았는지(Pedro, you've been to our new production facility in Glenview, right?) 물은 후, 거기에 새 장비가 들어갈 공간이 있는지(Is there space there for new equipment?) 묻자, 두 번째 남자인 페드로가 시설 관리자에게 알아보겠다(I'll check with the facility manager to make sure)고 했으므로 정답은 (A)이다.

Paraphrasing	대화의 check with the facility manager → 정답의 Contact a facility manager

62-64 대화 + 일정표

M-Au	Welcome to The Boat Center. How may I help you?
W-Am	Hi. **62Do you have any tickets for the Sea-Ride Special tour today?** I was hoping to catch a last-minute tour.
M-Au	Sorry. **62We're sold out. It's a really popular tour this time of year because the penguins are migrating through the area.**
W-Am	Oh, too bad. I'm leaving tomorrow morning, and I was really hoping to take one of your tours.
M-Au	Well, **63the Island Exploration tour still has a couple of spots left.**
W-Am	**63Great! 64And that'll give me time to get something to eat before it starts.** I see there's a coffee shop just down the street.

남	보트 센터에 오신 걸 환영합니다. 무엇을 도와드릴까요?
여	안녕하세요. **오늘 해양 보트 타기 스페셜 투어 티켓이 있나요?** 막판에 투어를 하고 싶었어요.
남	죄송합니다. **매진이에요. 펭귄들이 이 지역을 지나 이동하고 있어서 연중 이 시기에는 정말 인기 있는 투어거든요.**
여	아, 아까워라. 내일 아침에 떠나는데 투어 하나는 꼭 해 보고 싶었거든요.
남	음, 섬 탐험 투어는 아직 자리가 두어 개 남아 있어요.
여	좋아요! 게다가 시작하기 전에 먹을 걸 살 시간이 생기겠어요. 길 바로 저쪽에 커피숍이 보이네요.

어휘	last-minute 막판의 migrate 이동하다 exploration 탐험 spot 자리

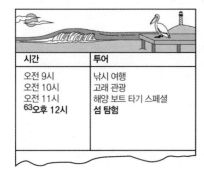

Time	Tour
9 A.M.	Fishing Expedition
10 A.M.	Whale Watching
11 A.M.	Sea-Ride Special
63 12 P.M.	Island Exploration

시간	투어
오전 9시	낚시 여행
오전 10시	고래 관광
오전 11시	해양 보트 타기 스페셜
63 오후 12시	섬 탐험

62

According to the man, why is today's Sea-Ride Special tour popular?

(A) It offers a chance to see migrating birds.
(B) Water conditions are likely to be favorable.
(C) A guest chef is preparing lunch.
(D) Someone special will be guiding the tour.

남자에 따르면, 오늘 해양 보트 타기 스페셜 투어는 왜 인기 있는가?
(A) 이동하는 새를 볼 수 있는 기회를 제공한다.
(B) 바다 여건이 양호할 것 같다.
(C) 초빙 요리사가 점심을 준비하고 있다.
(D) 특별한 누군가가 투어를 안내할 것이다.

어휘 favorable 양호한

해설 세부 사항 관련 – 남자가 말하는 해양 보트 타기 스페셜 투어가 인기 있는 이유

여자가 첫 대사에서 오늘 해양 보트 타기 스페셜 투어 티켓이 있는지(Do you have any tickets for the Sea-Ride Special tour today?) 묻자, 남자가 매진(We're sold out)이라면서 펭귄들이 이 지역을 지나 이동하고 있어서 연중 이 시기에는 인기 있는 투어(It's a really popular tour this time of year because the penguins are migrating through the area)라고 했으므로 정답은 (A)이다.

Paraphrasing	대화의 penguins are migrating → 정답의 migrating birds

63

Look at the graphic. What time will the woman depart on a tour?

(A) At 9 A.M.
(B) At 10 A.M.
(C) At 11 A.M.
(D) At 12 P.M.

시각 정보에 의하면, 여자는 몇 시에 투어를 떠날 것인가?
(A) 오전 9시
(B) 오전 10시
(C) 오전 11시
(D) 오후 12시

해설 시각 정보 연계 – 여자가 투어를 떠나는 시각

남자가 세 번째 대사에서 섬 탐험 투어는 자리가 남아 있다(the Island Exploration tour still has a couple of spots left)고 하자, 여자가 좋다(Great!)고 했고, 일정표에 섬 탐험 투어는 오후 12시라고 되어 있으므로 정답은 (D)이다.

64

What will the woman most likely do next?

(A) Return to her hotel
(B) Visit a café
(C) Call a friend
(D) Store her bags in a locker

여자는 다음에 무엇을 할 것 같은가?
(A) 호텔로 돌아가기
(B) 카페 방문하기
(C) 친구에게 전화하기
(D) 사물함에 가방 보관하기

해설 세부 사항 관련 – 여자가 다음에 할 일

여자가 마지막 대사에서 시작하기 전에 먹을 걸 살 시간이 생기겠다(And that'll give me time to get something to eat before it starts)고 한 후, 길 바로 저쪽에 커피숍이 보인다(I see there's a coffee shop just down the street)고 한 것으로 보아 정답은 (B)이다.

Paraphrasing	대화의 a coffee shop → 정답의 a café

65-67 대화 + 지도

M-Cn	Hi. I'm here for the health and wellness conference. I parked in the event center parking area. I was wondering, **65is parking free for conference attendees?**
W-Br	**65No. I'm sorry.** We don't provide any reimbursements for parking. But **66if you're willing to move your car, there's a cheaper parking area at Seventh Avenue and Vine Street.** It's about a block away.
M-Cn	Oh, unfortunately, **67I don't have time. I'm scheduled to attend the strength-training seminar that starts in fifteen minutes.** But tomorrow I'll get here earlier and park at the other lot. Seventh and Vine, you said. Right?
W-Br	That's correct.

남	안녕하세요. 건강과 웰빙에 관한 회의 참석차 왔습니다. 행사장 주차 구역에 주차했어요. 궁금한 게 있는데, **회의 참석자는 주차가 무료인가요?**
여	**아니요. 죄송해요.** 저희는 어떠한 주차비 상환도 제공하지 않습니다. 하지만 **차를 옮길 의향이 있으시면 7번가와 바인 가에 더 저렴한 주차 공간이 있어요.** 한 블록 정도 떨어져 있고요.
남	아, 안타깝게도 **시간이 없네요. 15분 후에 시작하는 근력 강화 세미나에 참석할 예정이거든요.** 하지만 내일은 더 일찍 와서 다른 구역에 주차할게요. 7번가와 바인 가, 맞죠?
여	맞습니다.

어휘	attendee 참석자 reimbursement 상환, 보상

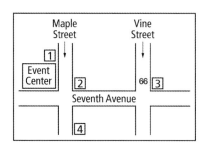

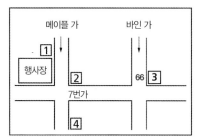

65

Why does the woman apologize?
(A) A conference session is full.
(B) An elevator is not working.
(C) A workshop has changed locations.
(D) Parking is not free.

여자는 왜 사과하는가?
(A) 회의 시간에 인원이 꽉 찼다.
(B) 엘리베이터가 작동하지 않는다.
(C) 워크숍 장소가 변경됐다.
(D) 주차가 무료가 아니다.

해설 세부 사항 관련 – 여자가 사과하는 이유
남자가 첫 대사에서 회의 참석자는 주차가 무료인지(is parking free for conference attendees?) 묻자, 여자가 아니요(No)라며 죄송하다(I'm sorry)고 사과했으므로 정답은 (D)이다.

66

Look at the graphic. Which location does the woman recommend?
(A) Area 1
(B) Area 2
(C) Area 3
(D) Area 4

시각 정보에 의하면, 여자는 어떤 장소를 추천하는가?
(A) 구역 1
(B) 구역 2
(C) 구역 3
(D) 구역 4

해설 시각 정보 연계 – 여자가 추천하는 장소
여자가 첫 대사에서 차를 옮길 의향이 있으면 7번가와 바인 가에 더 저렴한 주차 공간이 있다(if you're willing to move your car, there's a cheaper parking area at Seventh Avenue and Vine Street)고 알려주었고, 지도에 따르면 구역 3이므로 정답은 (C)이다.

67

Why is the man in a hurry?
(A) A workshop is starting soon.
(B) A parking pass is about to expire.
(C) A shuttle is running late.
(D) A friend is waiting outside.

남자는 왜 서두르는가?
(A) 워크숍이 곧 시작된다.
(B) 주차권이 곧 만료된다.
(C) 셔틀이 연착하고 있다.
(D) 친구가 밖에서 기다리고 있다.

어휘 expire 만료되다

해설 세부 사항 관련 – 남자가 서두르는 이유
남자가 두 번째 대사에서 시간이 없다(I don't have time)면서 15분 후에 시작하는 근력 강화 세미나에 참석할 것(I'm scheduled to attend the strength-training seminar that starts in fifteen minutes)이라고

한 것으로 보아 정답은 (A)이다.

68-70 대화 + 상점 카탈로그

M-Cn	Molina's Office Store. How can I help?
W-Am	Hi. **68I've been trying to order a product on your Web site, but every time I get to the checkout screen, everything freezes, and I can't place the order.**
M-Cn	**69What are you trying to buy?**
W-Am	**69The Enzo 5000 scanner.**
M-Cn	Hmm. That product's currently out of stock. Can I recommend the Rhenium 60 instead? It's a popular model.
W-Am	I really need the Enzo 5000—I'm an artist and I make my own prints, so I need a model that produces top-quality images.
M-Cn	I see. Well, **70we're expecting a shipment tomorrow. If it includes the model you're looking for, I can reserve it for you.**

남	몰리나 오피스 스토어입니다. 무엇을 도와드릴까요?
여	안녕하세요. **웹사이트에서 제품을 주문하려고 했지만 결제 화면에 도달하면 매번 전부 멈춰서 주문을 할 수가 없어요.**
남	**사려고 하시는 게 뭔가요?**
여	**엔조 5000 스캐너예요.**
남	흠. 그 제품은 현재 품절입니다. 대신 레늄 60을 추천해도 될까요? 인기 있는 모델이에요.
여	엔조 50000이 정말 필요해요. 저는 예술가라 저만의 출력물을 만들어요. 그래서 최고 품질의 이미지를 생산하는 모델이 필요해요.
남	그렇군요. 음, **내일 배송품이 올 예정이에요. 찾으시는 모델이 포함돼 있다면 고객님을 위해 물건을 따로 빼놓을 게요.**

어휘 freeze 멈추다 place an order 주문하다 currently 현재 out of stock 품절인 reserve (따로) 남겨 두다

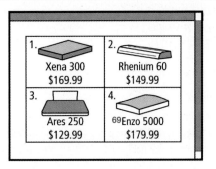

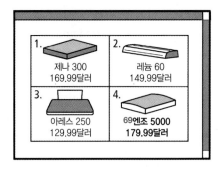

68

Why does the woman call?
(A) She wants to request a refund.
(B) She is unable to place an order online.
(C) She wants to extend a deadline.
(D) She is unhappy with a product purchased recently.

여자는 왜 전화를 하는가?
(A) 환불을 요청하고 싶다.
(B) 온라인으로 주문할 수 없다.
(C) 기한을 연장하고 싶다.
(D) 최근 구매한 제품에 불만이 있다.

어휘 extend 연장하다 purchase 구매하다 recently 최근에

해설 전체 내용 관련 – 여자가 전화하는 목적

여자가 첫 대사에서 웹사이트에서 제품을 주문하려고 했지만 주문을 할 수가 없다(I've been trying to order ~ I can't place the order)고 했으므로 정답은 (B)이다.

69

Look at the graphic. What is the price of the item the woman wants to buy?
(A) $169.99
(B) $149.99
(C) $129.99
(D) $179.99

시각 정보에 의하면, 여자가 사려는 물건의 가격은 얼마인가?
(A) 169.99달러
(B) 149.99달러
(C) 129.99달러
(D) 179.99달러

해설 시각 정보 연계 – 여자가 사려는 물건의 가격

남자가 두 번째 대사에서 사려는 것이 무엇(What are you trying to buy?)인지 묻자, 여자가 엔조 5000 스캐너(The Enzo 5000 scanner)라고 대답하므로 상점 카탈로그에서 엔조 5000을 찾으면 정답은 (D)이다.

70

What will the man most likely do tomorrow?
(A) Update a Web site
(B) Search a storage area
(C) Contact another store location
(D) Check an incoming shipment

남자는 내일 무엇을 할 것 같은가?
(A) 웹사이트 업데이트하기
(B) 집하장 탐색하기
(C) 다른 매장에 연락하기
(D) 들어오는 배송품 확인하기

해설 세부 사항 관련 – 남자가 내일 할 일
남자가 마지막 대사에서 내일 배송이 올 예정(we're expecting a shipment tomorrow)이라면서 여자가 찾는 모델이 포함돼 있다면 물건을 따로 빼놓을 것(If it includes the model you're looking for, I can reserve it for you)이라고 했으므로 정답은 (D)이다.

PART 4

71-73 광고

W-Am Attention all film lovers! **71The Braddon Cinema has just opened. Its interior is designed to resemble the classic cinemas from the 1920s.** It offers comfortable, reclining seats and individual tray tables for food and drinks. **72The grand opening is next week and will feature showings of classic films from different eras!** **73And here's good advice: to avoid traffic in the city center, the Braddon Cinema is easily reached by riding the train to Center Station.**

영화 애호가 여러분, 모두 주목하세요! **브래든 시네마가 막 문을 열었습니다. 내부는 1920년대의 고전적인 영화관을 본떠 설계됐습니다.** 편안한 리클라이닝 좌석, 음식과 음료를 놓을 개별 접이식 탁자를 제공합니다. **개관식은 다음 주이며 여러 시대의 고전 영화 상영을 특집으로 다룰 예정입니다!** 그리고 요긴한 조언을 드릴게요. 도심 교통 체증을 피하기 위해 기차를 타고 중앙역으로 오면 브래든 시네마에 쉽게 도착하실 수 있습니다.

어휘 resemble 닮다 comfortable 편안한 reclining 뒤로 넘어가는 individual 개별의 grand opening 개관식, 개장 feature ~을 특집으로 하다 showing 상영 era 시대

71

What feature of a business does the speaker emphasize?
(A) The quality of its food
(B) The extended hours it is open
(C) The style of its decor
(D) The affordable prices it offers

화자는 업체의 어떤 특징을 강조하는가?
(A) 음식의 품질
(B) 연장된 영업시간
(C) 장식 스타일
(D) 알맞은 가격

어휘 feature 특징 emphasize 강조하다 extended 연장된, 길어진 decor 장식 affordable (가격이) 알맞은

해설 세부 사항 관련 – 업체의 특징
화자가 초반부에 브래든 시네마가 문을 열었다(The Braddon Cinema has just opened)면서 내부는 1920년대의 고전적인 영화관을 본떠 설계됐다(Its interior is designed to resemble the classic cinemas from the 1920s)고 했으므로 정답은 (C)이다.

> **Paraphrasing** 담화의 interior → 정답의 decor

72

What can attendees do at the grand opening event?
(A) Go on a tour
(B) Get a free gift
(C) Talk to an actor
(D) Watch some movies

참석자들은 개관 행사에서 무엇을 할 수 있는가?
(A) 견학하기
(B) 사은품 받기
(C) 배우와 대화하기
(D) 영화 관람하기

해설 세부 사항 관련 – 참석자들이 개관 행사에서 할 수 있는 일
화자가 중반부에 개관식은 다음 주이며 여러 시대의 고전 영화 상영을 특집으로 다룰 예정(The grand opening is next week and will feature showings of classic films from different eras)이라고 알리고 있으므로 정답은 (D)이다.

> **Paraphrasing** 담화의 showings of classic films
> → 정답의 Watch some movies

73

What does the speaker advise event attendees to do?
(A) Arrive early
(B) Use public transportation
(C) Order tickets in advance
(D) Purchase a membership

화자는 행사 참석자들에게 무엇을 하라고 조언하는가?
(A) 일찍 도착하기
(B) 대중교통 이용하기
(C) 티켓 미리 주문하기
(D) 회원권 구입하기

어휘 in advance 미리, 사전에

해설 세부 사항 관련 – 화자가 행사 참석자에게 하는 조언
화자가 후반부에 조언을 준다(And here's good advice)며 도심 교통 체증을 피하기 위해 기차를 타면 브래든 시네마에 쉽게 도착할 수 있다(to

avoid traffic ~ by riding the train to Center Station)고 했으므로 정답은 (B)이다.

74-76 전화 메시지

> **M-Cn** Hi. This is Abdi calling from the Springtown Hotel reservation desk. We received your e-mail regarding your upcoming reservation. **74,75I see that you asked to move to a room facing the ocean. 75We make every effort to accommodate such requests, but** those rooms are always booked far in advance. Your current room, though, has a lovely view of our garden, which we think you will quite enjoy this time of year. **76And don't forget to bring your swimming suit!** Our new pool will be open for the first time this weekend.

> 안녕하세요. 스프링타운 호텔 예약 데스크의 아브디입니다. 다가오는 예약 건에 대한 고객님의 이메일을 받았습니다. 바다를 마주보는 객실로 옮겨 달라고 요청하셨네요. 해당 요청을 수용하기 위해 모든 노력을 다하고 있지만 그 객실들은 항상 훨씬 전에 예약됩니다. 하지만 현재 고객님 객실은 멋진 정원 전망이 있고, 연중 이 시기에는 상당히 즐기실 수 있을 거라고 생각합니다. 그리고 수영복을 잊지 말고 가져오십시오! 새 수영장이 이번 주말에 처음으로 문을 엽니다.

> **어휘** upcoming 다가오는 facing 마주 보는 make every effort to ~하는 데 온갖 노력을 다하다 accommodate 수용하다 far 훨씬 this time of year 연중 이 시기에는, 이맘때에 for the first time 처음으로

74

What does the listener want to do?
(A) Request shuttle service
(B) Extend a hotel stay
(C) Change a room assignment
(D) Cancel a reservation

청자는 무엇을 하고 싶어 하는가?
(A) 셔틀 서비스 요청
(B) 호텔 숙박 연장
(C) 객실 배정 변경
(D) 예약 취소

어휘 assignment 배정

해설 세부 사항 관련 – 청자가 하고 싶은 일
화자가 초반부에 청자가 바다를 마주보는 객실로 옮겨 달라고 요청했다(I see that you asked to move to a room facing the ocean)고 했으므로 정답은 (C)이다.

75

Why does the speaker say, "those rooms are always booked far in advance"?
(A) To express approval for a room design
(B) To explain why a hotel is successful
(C) To indicate his disbelief
(D) To deny the listener's request

화자는 왜 "그 객실들은 항상 훨씬 전에 예약됩니다"라고 말하는가?
(A) 객실 디자인 승인을 나타내려고
(B) 호텔이 성공한 이유를 설명하려고
(C) 불신을 나타내려고
(D) 청자의 요청을 거절하려고

어휘 approval 승인, 허가 indicate 나타내다 disbelief 불신 deny 거절하다

해설 화자의 의도 파악 – 그 객실들은 항상 훨씬 전에 예약된다는 말의 의도
화자가 인용문 앞 문장에서 청자가 바다를 마주보는 객실로 옮겨 달라고 요청했다(I see that you asked to move to a room facing the ocean)고 했고, 해당 요청을 수용하기 위해 모든 노력을 다하고 있지만(We make every effort to accommodate such requests, but)이라고 한 것으로 보아 청자의 요청대로 바다를 바라보는 객실로 옮기는 것이 어려워 요청을 거절하기 위한 것임을 알 수 있다. 따라서 정답은 (D)이다.

76

According to the speaker, what should the listener bring?
(A) Some warm clothes
(B) Some swimwear
(C) A credit card
(D) A copy of a key

화자에 따르면, 청자는 무엇을 가져와야 하는가?
(A) 따뜻한 옷
(B) 수영복
(C) 신용 카드
(D) 복제 열쇠

해설 세부 사항 관련 – 청자가 가져와야 하는 것
화자가 후반부에 수영복을 잊지 말고 가져오라(And don't forget to bring your swimming suit!)고 했으므로 정답은 (B)이다.

77-79 담화

> **W-Am** **77Good morning, volunteers. My name is Lisa Campbell. Thank you for coming today to help us maintain the natural habitat here at the Blue Mountain Forest Preserve.** Forest conservation is so important! Since this is your first day, I'll cover some of the basics. **78I advise you to always carry water with you.** We have refillable bottles, and

everyone is welcome to take one as a gift from us at the forest preserve. It can get hot in the afternoon, so staying hydrated is important. Now, if you'll follow me, **79I'll show you the steps for planting young tree saplings to support biodiversity.**

안녕하세요, 자원봉사자 여러분. 제 이름은 리사 캠벨입니다. 오늘 블루마운틴 산림 보호 구역에 이곳 자연 서식지를 유지할 수 있도록 도와주러 오셔서 감사드립니다. 산림 보호는 매우 중요합니다! 오늘은 첫날이므로 기본적인 사항들을 다루겠습니다. **항상 물을 가지고 다닐 것을 권고드립니다.** 보충 가능한 병이 있는데 누구나 산림 보호 구역에서 기증품으로 하나 가져가실 수 있습니다. 오후에는 더워질 수 있기 때문에 수분 섭취를 잘하는 것이 중요합니다. 이제, 저를 따라오시면 **생물 다양성을 유지하기 위해 어린 묘목을 심는 단계를 보여 드리겠습니다.**

어휘 habitat 서식지 forest preserve 산림 보호 구역 conservation (자연환경) 보호, 보존 cover 다루다 refillable 보충 가능한 hydrate 수분을 공급하다 sapling 묘목, 어린 나무 biodiversity 생물 다양성

77

Who most likely is the speaker?
(A) An archaeologist
(B) A marine biologist
(C) A conservation expert
(D) An athletic trainer

화자는 누구인 것 같은가?
(A) 고고학자
(B) 해양 생물학자
(C) 자연환경 보호 전문가
(D) 운동 트레이너

해설 전체 내용 관련 – 화자의 직업
화자가 초반부에 자원봉사자에게 인사(Good morning, volunteers)를 하고 자신을 소개(My name is Lisa Campbell)한 후, 산림 보호 구역에서 자연 서식지를 유지할 수 있도록 도와주어 고맙다(Thank you for coming ~ Blue Mountain Forest Preserve)면서 보호 구역 자원봉사자들에게 감사를 표하고 있는 것으로 보아 정답은 (C)이다.

78

What does the speaker advise the listeners to do?
(A) Take a water bottle
(B) Consult a site map
(C) Apply sunscreen regularly
(D) Write careful notes

화자는 청자들에게 무엇을 하라고 권고하는가?
(A) 물병 가져가기
(B) 현장 지도 참고하기
(C) 자외선 차단제 자주 바르기
(D) 꼼꼼하게 메모 작성하기

어휘 consult 참고하다 apply 바르다, 도포하다 careful 면밀한

해설 세부 사항 관련 – 화자의 권고 사항
화자가 중반부에 청자들에게 항상 물을 지참하라(I advise you to always carry water with you)고 권고하고 있으므로 정답은 (A)이다.

> **Paraphrasing** 담화의 carry water with you
> → 정답의 Take a water bottle

79

What does the speaker say she is going to do next?
(A) Answer some questions
(B) Demonstrate a process
(C) Introduce a colleague
(D) Take the listeners to lunch

화자는 다음에 무엇을 하겠다고 말하는가?
(A) 질문에 답하기
(B) 절차 시연하기
(C) 동료 소개하기
(D) 청자들을 점심 식사에 데려가기

해설 세부 사항 관련 – 화자가 다음에 할 일
화자가 마지막에 생물 다양성 유지를 위해 묘목을 심는 단계를 보여 주겠다(I'll show you the steps for planting young tree saplings to support biodiversity)고 했으므로 정답은 (B)이다.

> **Paraphrasing** 담화의 show → 정답의 Demonstrate
> 담화의 the steps for planting young tree saplings → 정답의 a process

80-82 전화 메시지

> W-Br Hello. **80I'm calling about the financial-management workshop that your company is hosting later this week.** I'm with the Archton Group; **80we registered for the workshop over a month ago.** **81I realized that we never received the meal vouchers that are supposed to be part of the workshop package.** We need these because we have ten people attending, and **80,81we are traveling long-distance to attend the conference.** **82Would you please send me an e-mail with the meal vouchers included as an attachment as soon as you can?** Thank you.

안녕하세요. **이번 주 후반에 귀사에서 개최하는 재무 관리 워크숍에 관련하여 전화드렸습니다.** 저는 아치턴 그룹 소속입니다. **저희가 워크숍에 등록한 지 한 달이 넘었습니다.** 워크숍 패키지에 포함되어 있어야 할 식권을 전혀 받지 못했다는 것을 알게 되었습니다. 10명이 참석하는데 회의에 참석하기 위해 장거리 여행을 하므로 식권이 필요합니다. 식권이 첨부된 이메일을 가능한 한 빨리 보내 주시겠어요? 감사합니다.

80

Why will the speaker be traveling?
(A) To inspect a factory
(B) To repair a product
(C) To perform in a concert
(D) To attend a workshop

화자는 왜 장거리 여행을 할 것인가?
(A) 공장을 점검하려고
(B) 제품을 수리하려고
(C) 콘서트 공연을 하려고
(D) 워크숍에 참석하려고

어휘 travel (장거리를) 가다[다니다], 여행하다 inspect 점검하다

해설 세부 사항 관련 – 화자가 장거리 여행을 하는 이유

화자가 초반부에 귀사에서 개최하는 재무 관리 워크숍에 관련하여 전화했다
(I'm calling about the financial-management workshop that your
company is hosting later this week)고 한 후, 워크숍에 등록한 지 한
달이 넘었다(we registered for the workshop over a month ago)고
하고, 뒤이어 워크숍 패키지에 포함된 못 받은 식권 요청을 하면서 회의에
참석하기 위해 장거리 여행을 한다(we are traveling long-distance to
attend the conference)고 언급한 것으로 보아 정답은 (D)이다.

81

Why is the speaker concerned?
(A) A seating arrangement is wrong.
(B) A company credit card was not charged.
(C) Some meal tickets were not sent.
(D) Her taxi driver is unable to find a hotel.

화자는 왜 걱정하는가?
(A) 좌석 배치가 잘못됐다.
(B) 회사 신용 카드로 청구되지 않았다.
(C) 식권이 발송되지 않았다.
(D) 택시 기사가 호텔을 찾을 수 없다.

어휘 seating arrangement 좌석 배치 charge 청구하다

해설 세부 사항 관련 – 화자가 걱정하는 이유

화자가 중반부에 워크숍 패키지에 포함되어 있어야 할 식권을 받지 못
했다(I realized that we never received the meal vouchers ~ the
workshop package)면서 회의에 참석하기 위해 장거리 여행을 하므
로 식권이 필요하다(We need these ~ traveling long-distance to
attend the conference)고 했으므로 정답은 (C)이다.

> **Paraphrasing** 담화의 we never received the meal vouchers
> → 정답의 Some meal tickets were not sent

82

What does the speaker ask the listener to do?
(A) Send an e-mail
(B) Meet at an office
(C) Confirm a schedule
(D) Look up an account number

화자는 청자에게 무엇을 하도록 요청하는가?
(A) 이메일 보내기
(B) 사무실에서 만나기
(C) 일정 확정하기
(D) 계좌 번호 조회하기

어휘 look up 조회하다, 찾아보다

해설 세부 사항 관련 – 화자가 청자에게 요청하는 일

화자가 후반부에 청자에게 식권이 첨부된 이메일을 가능한 한 빨리 보
내 주겠는지(Would you please send me an e-mail with the meal
vouchers included as an attachment as soon as you can?) 요청
하고 있으므로 정답은 (A)이다.

83-85 관광 정보

M-Au This is the end of our tour. Thank you for
coming to the Oakton Garden Collective. I hope
you've learned a lot about urban gardening. Feel
free to spend more time looking around. **83Don't
forget to pick up your free vegetable seedling
before you leave.** You can choose a cucumber plant
or a tomato plant. Also, **84if you'd like to have
your own garden plot next spring, applications
are now available.** You'll get a plot for just a small
fee. **85We have many other fun activities listed
in our monthly newsletter. Consider joining our
e-mail list to receive these monthly updates about
upcoming events.**

이것으로 투어는 끝입니다. 오크턴 가든 컬렉티브에 와 주셔서 감사합
니다. 도시 텃밭 가꾸기에 대해 많이 배우셨기를 바랍니다. 시간을 더
들여서 마음껏 주변을 둘러보세요. **떠나기 전에 잊지 말고 무료 채소 묘
목을 가져가세요.** 오이 모종이나 토마토 모종을 선택하실 수 있습니다.
또한 **내년 봄에 여러분도 텃밭 부지를 가지고 싶다면, 지금 신청하실 수
있습니다.** 적은 비용으로 부지를 소유하시게 될 겁니다. **월간 소식지에
는 재미있는 여러 다른 활동들이 많이 기재되어 있습니다. 다가오는 행
사에 대한 매월 최신 소식을 받으시려면 당사 이메일 발송 명단에 가입
하는 것을 고려해 보세요.**

어휘 collective 공동 사업(체) urban 도시의 seedling 묘목
plant 모종 plot (특정 용도의) 작은 땅[부지] application 신청
newsletter 소식지 upcoming 다가오는, 곧 있을

83

What does the speaker remind the listeners to do?
(A) Keep a gate closed
(B) Return equipment to a shed
(C) Check a list of supplies
(D) Select a free gift

화자는 청자들에게 무엇을 하라고 상기시키는가?
(A) 문 닫아 두기
(B) 창고로 장비 반환하기
(C) 비품 목록 확인하기
(D) 사은품 선택하기

어휘 shed 창고, 헛간

해설 세부 사항 관련 – 화자가 청자들에게 상기시키는 일
화자가 초반부에 청자들에게 떠나기 전에 잊지 말고 무료 채소 묘목을 가져가라(Don't forget to pick up your free vegetable seedling before you leave)고 일깨우고 있으므로 정답은 (D)이다.

> Paraphrasing 담화의 free vegetable seedling
> → 정답의 a free gift

84

According to the speaker, what can the listeners apply for?
(A) A garden plot
(B) A volunteer opportunity
(C) A gardening workshop
(D) A farmers market table

화자에 따르면, 청자들은 무엇을 신청할 수 있는가?
(A) 텃밭 부지
(B) 자원봉사 기회
(C) 원예 워크숍
(D) 농산물 시장 가판대

해설 세부 사항 관련 – 청자들이 신청할 수 있는 것
화자가 중반부에 청자들에게 내년 봄에 텃밭 부지를 갖고 싶다면, 지금 신청할 수 있다(if you'd like to have your own garden plot next spring, applications are now available)고 했으므로 정답은 (A)이다.

85

How can the listeners get information about future events?
(A) By signing up for a newsletter
(B) By joining a membership program
(C) By looking at a Web site
(D) By attending weekly meetings

청자들은 어떻게 향후 행사에 관한 정보를 얻을 수 있는가?
(A) 소식지 구독을 신청해서
(B) 회원 프로그램에 가입해서
(C) 웹사이트를 봐서
(D) 주간 회의에 참석해서

해설 세부 사항 관련 – 청자들이 향후 행사에 관한 정보를 얻을 수 있는 방법
화자가 후반부에 월간 소식지에 여러 다른 활동들이 기재되어 있다(We have many other fun activities listed in our monthly newsletter)며 다가오는 행사에 대해 매월 최신 소식을 받으려면 당사의 이메일 발송 명단에 가입하라(Consider joining our e-mail list to receive these monthly updates about upcoming events)고 권하고 있으므로 정답은 (A)이다.

> Paraphrasing 담화의 joining our e-mail list to receive these monthly updates
> → 정답의 signing up for a newsletter

86-88 광고

W-Br **86Have you developed the perfect product but are unsure how to reach more customers? At Whole Planet Marketing, our team of expert digital marketers is ready to help you reach your target audience. 87Unlike other marketing firms, we'll connect you with a digital marketer who'll work with you individually.** During your one-on-one meetings, you'll develop a marketing plan that will draw in customers. **88Just go to wholeplanetmarketing.com today to complete a brief questionnaire. Then, one of our specialists will contact you to make an appointment for a free proposal.** Let Whole Planet Marketing bring customers to you!

완벽한 제품을 개발했지만 더 많은 고객에게 다가갈 방법을 잘 모르십니까? 홀 플래닛 마케팅의 전문 디지털 마케터 팀이 목표 고객에게 다가갈 수 있도록 도와드리겠습니다. 다른 마케팅 회사들과 달리 당사는 여러분 한 사람 한 사람과 협력할 디지털 마케터를 연결해 드립니다. 일대일 회의 중에 고객을 끌어들일 마케팅 계획을 수립할 것입니다. 오늘 바로 wholeplanetmarketing.com으로 가서 간단한 질문지를 작성하세요. 그러면 저희 전문가가 연락해서 무료 제안을 위해 예약을 잡아 드립니다. 홀 플래닛 마케팅을 통해 고객을 확보하세요!

어휘 expert 전문가 target audience 목표 고객, 이용 대상 individually 개별적으로 draw 끌어들이다 complete 작성하다 brief 간단한 questionnaire 질문지 make an appointment 예약[약속]을 잡다 proposal 제안

86

What service does the business offer?
(A) Financial planning
(B) Digital marketing
(C) Real estate sales
(D) International shipping

업체는 어떤 서비스를 제공하는가?

(A) 재무 계획
(B) 디지털 마케팅
(C) 부동산 매매
(D) 국제 운송

해설 전체 내용 관련 – 업체가 제공하는 서비스

화자가 초반부에 완벽한 제품을 개발했지만 더 많은 고객에게 다가갈 방법을 모르는지(Have you developed the perfect product but are unsure how to reach more customers?) 물었고, 홀 플래닛 마케팅의 전문 디지털 마케터 팀이 목표 고객에게 다가갈 수 있도록 도와준다(At Whole Planet Marketing, our team of expert digital marketers is ready to help you reach your target audience.)고 한 것으로 보아 정답은 (B)이다.

87

According to the speaker, how is the business different from its competitors?

(A) It has several local offices.
(B) It offers a money-back guarantee.
(C) Its employees have industry certification.
(D) Its employees work one-on-one with clients.

화자에 따르면, 업체는 경쟁업체들과 어떻게 다른가?

(A) 지역 사무소가 여러 곳 있다.
(B) 환불 보증을 제공한다.
(C) 직원들이 업계 인증을 받았다.
(D) 직원들이 고객과 일대일로 일한다.

어휘 competitor 경쟁업체 money-back 환불이 가능한 guarantee 보증(서) certification 인증, 증명

해설 세부 사항 관련 – 업체가 경쟁업체들과 다른 점

화자가 중반부에 다른 마케팅 회사들과 달리 당사는 한 사람 한 사람과 협력할 디지털 마케터를 연결해 준다(Unlike other marketing firms, we'll connect you with a digital marketer who'll work with you individually)고 했으므로 정답은 (D)이다.

> Paraphrasing 담화의 a digital marketer who'll work with you individually → 정답의 Its employees work one-on-one with clients

88

How can the listeners make an appointment?

(A) By sending an e-mail
(B) By calling customer service
(C) By filling out a questionnaire
(D) By sending a text message

청자들은 어떻게 예약을 잡을 수 있는가?

(A) 이메일을 보내서
(B) 고객 서비스 부서에 전화해서
(C) 질문지를 작성해서
(D) 문자 메시지를 보내서

해설 세부 사항 관련 – 청자들이 예약을 잡을 수 있는 방법

화자가 후반부에 웹사이트에 접속해서 간단한 질문지를 작성하라(Just go to wholeplanetmarketing.com today to complete a brief questionnaire)면서 전문가가 연락해서 무료 제안을 위해 예약을 잡을 것(Then, one of our specialists will contact you to make an appointment for a free proposal)이라고 알려 주고 있으므로 정답은 (C)이다.

> Paraphrasing 담화의 complete a brief questionnaire → 정답의 filling out a questionnaire

89-91 발표

M-Au Hello, everyone. **[89]There's very exciting news for all of us here at the Ziegler Research Institute. We've just been awarded the Sugiyama Grant to support our research into aquatic ecosystems.** We can now invest in state-of-the-art equipment to study the biodiversity of coral reefs. As you may know, **[90]the Sugiyama Foundation offers a variety of substantial grants each year.** It's notable, though, that **[90]for this particular award, they received over 200 applications.** **[91]Our work at the reefs will probably not begin for several months. We still need to order the equipment.** But I want to thank you for your efforts on the application.

안녕하세요, 여러분. 여기 지글러 연구소에 있는 우리 모두에게 매우 신나는 소식이 있습니다. 방금 수중 생태계에 대한 연구에 뒷받침이 될 스기야마 보조금을 받았습니다. 이제 산호초의 생물 다양성을 연구하기 위해 최첨단 장비에 투자할 수 있습니다. 아시다시피, 스기야마 재단은 해마다 이런저런 상당한 보조금을 제공합니다. 하지만 이 특정한 지원금의 경우 그들이 200개가 넘는 신청서를 받았다는 사실은 주목할 만합니다. 아마도 몇 달 동안은 산호초에서 수행하는 작업이 시작되지 않을 수도 있습니다. 아직 장비를 주문해야 하니까요. 하지만 여러분이 보조금 신청에 기울인 노력에 감사하고 싶습니다.

어휘 institute 기관 be awarded (상을) 받다 grant 보조금, 기금 aquatic 수중[해양]의 ecosystem 생태계 invest in ~에 투자하다 state-of-the-art 최첨단의 biodiversity 생물 다양성 coral reef 산호초 substantial 상당한 notable 주목할 만한 particular 특별한

89

Who most likely are the listeners?

(A) Marine biologists
(B) Museum directors
(C) Rare-book librarians
(D) Agricultural engineers

청자들은 누구인 것 같은가?

(A) 해양 생물학자
(B) 박물관장
(C) 희귀 서적 사서
(D) 농공학자

어휘 marine 해양의 biologist 생물학자 rare 희귀한 librarian (도서관) 사서

해설 전체 내용 관련 – 청자들의 직업

화자가 초반부에 여기 지글러 연구소에 있는 우리 모두에게 매우 신나는 소식이 있다(There's very exciting news for all of us here at the Ziegler Research Institute)면서 수중 생태계에 대한 연구에 뒷받침이 될 스기야마 보조금을 받았다(We've just been awarded the Sugiyama Grant to support our research into aquatic ecosystems)고 한 것으로 보아, 청자들은 연구소에서 수중 생태계를 연구하는 사람들임을 알 수 있다. 따라서 정답은 (A)이다.

> **Paraphrasing** 담화의 aquatic ecosystems → 정답의 Marine

90

What does the speaker mean when he says, "they received over 200 applications"?
(A) An opportunity is unlikely to occur.
(B) An award is impressive.
(C) A decision will take longer than usual.
(D) A competitor has been very successful.

화자가 "그들이 200개가 넘는 신청서를 받았다"라고 말할 때 무엇을 의도하는가?

(A) 기회가 생길 것 같지 않다.
(B) 지원금을 받은 것이 대단하다.
(C) 결정이 평소보다 오래 걸릴 것이다.
(D) 경쟁업체가 크게 성공했다.

어휘 be unlikely to ~할 것 같지 않다 award 지원금, 상 impressive 인상적인

해설 화자의 의도 파악 – 그들이 200개가 넘는 신청서를 받았다는 말의 의도

앞에서 스기야마 재단은 해마다 이런저런 상당한 보조금을 제공(the Sugiyama Foundation offers a variety of substantial grants each year)하지만, 이 특정한 지원금의 경우(for this particular award) 200개가 넘는 신청서를 받았다는 인용문을 언급했으므로 지원금의 가치가 커서 신청한 단체가 많다는 것을 나타내려는 의도로 볼 수 있다. 따라서 정답은 (B)이다.

91

Why does the speaker say that work cannot begin right away?
(A) Additional funds are needed.
(B) Some special training is required.
(C) An application has to be approved.
(D) Some equipment needs to be ordered.

화자는 왜 작업이 바로 시작될 수 없다고 말하는가?

(A) 추가 자금이 필요하다.
(B) 특별한 훈련이 필요하다.
(C) 신청서가 승인을 받아야 한다.
(D) 장비가 주문되어야 한다.

해설 세부 사항 관련 – 작업이 바로 시작될 수 없다고 말하는 이유

화자가 후반부에 몇 달 동안은 작업이 시작되지 않을 수도 있다(Our work at the reefs will probably not begin for several months)고 한 후, 아직 장비를 주문해야 한다(We still need to order the equipment)며 이유를 제시하고 있으므로 정답은 (D)이다.

> **Paraphrasing** 담화의 We still need to order the equipment → 정답의 Some equipment needs to be ordered

92-94 담화

W-Am **[93]On behalf of Onetech Solar, I'd like to welcome you to our manufacturing facility** and congratulate you on your employment here. **[92]I'm Yuri Yamakawa, and today I'll be leading this orientation for new hires.** We'll start with a video that provides an overview of the production process for the solar panels we make. Then we'll tour the various areas of the factory, including the assembly line and the quality-control inspection center. **[94]After lunch, my colleague Mariko Hara will join you.** I have a consultation with a client. And now, let's get started with the video.

원테크 솔라를 대표해 저희 제조 시설에 오신 것을 환영하며 이곳에 채용되신 것을 축하합니다. **저는 오늘 신입 사원 오리엔테이션을 진행할 유리 야마카와입니다.** 우리가 만드는 태양 전지판의 생산 과정을 개괄적으로 보여 주는 동영상부터 시작하겠습니다. 그런 다음 조립 라인과 품질 관리 검사 센터를 포함해 공장 내 다양한 구역을 둘러보도록 하겠습니다. **점심 식사 후에는 동료인 마리코 하라가 여러분들과 함께하겠습니다.** 저는 고객과 상담이 있어요. 이제 동영상을 시작하겠습니다.

어휘 on behalf of ~을 대표하여 manufacturing facility 제조 시설[공장] employment 채용, 고용 new hire 신입 사원 overview 개요 production 생산 solar panel 태양 전지판 assembly 조립 quality-control 품질 관리 colleague 동료 consultation 상담

92

What is the purpose of the talk?
(A) To recognize outstanding achievements
(B) To introduce new products to the public
(C) To announce a manager's retirement
(D) To provide new employees with information

담화의 목적은 무엇인가?

(A) 탁월한 성과를 인정하려고

(B) 대중에게 신제품을 소개하려고

(C) 관리자의 은퇴를 발표하려고

(D) 신입 사원에게 정보를 제공하려고

어휘 recognize 인정하다   outstanding 탁월한   achievement 성과

해설 전체 내용 관련 – 담화의 목적

화자가 초반부에 자신을 신입 사원 오리엔테이션을 진행할 유리 야마카와 (I'm Yuri Yamakawa, and today I'll be leading this orientation for new hires)라고 소개하고 있으므로 정답은 (D)이다.

> **Paraphrasing** 담화의 orientation for new hires
> → 정답의 provide new employees with information

93

Where is the talk taking place?

(A) At a banquet hall

(B) At a government building

(C) At a factory

(D) At a construction site

담화는 어디에서 진행되고 있는가?

(A) 연회장

(B) 정부 청사

(C) 공장

(D) 건설 현장

해설 전체 내용 관련 – 담화의 장소

화자가 맨 처음에 청자들에게 원테크 솔라를 대표해 자신들의 제조 시설에 온 것을 환영한다(On behalf of Onetech Solar, I'd like to welcome you to our manufacturing facility)고 했으므로 정답은 (C)이다.

> **Paraphrasing** 담화의 our manufacturing facility
> → 정답의 a factory

94

What does the speaker mean when she says, "I have a consultation with a client"?

(A) She needs to reschedule a meeting.

(B) She will not be with the listeners in the afternoon.

(C) A customer has just placed a large order.

(D) A marketing campaign will begin soon.

화자가 "저는 고객과 상담이 있어요"라고 말할 때 무엇을 의미하는가?

(A) 회의 일정을 다시 잡아야 한다.

(B) 오후에는 청자들과 함께 있지 않을 것이다.

(C) 고객이 방금 대량 주문을 했다.

(D) 마케팅 캠페인이 곧 시작된다.

해설 화자의 의도 파악 – 고객과 상담이 있다는 말의 의도

인용문 앞에서 점심 식사 후에는 동료인 마리코 하라가 합류하겠다(After lunch, my colleague Mariko Hara will join you)고 말한 뒤, 자신은 고객과 상담이 있다고 한 것으로 보아 자신을 대신해서 동료가 일을 진행할 것임을 알리려는 의도로 볼 수 있다. 따라서 정답은 (B)이다.

M-Cn Hi. This is Vinod Singh. ⁹⁵**I was in your store on Monday looking at refrigerators for my apartment. One of your employees showed me what you have in stock.** ⁹⁵,⁹⁶**I've decided to go with the extra-large refrigerator—the one with the stainless-steel finish**, because it'll match the other appliances in my apartment. Oh, also, ⁹⁷**is there an additional charge for delivering outside of the downtown area?** Please call me at 555-0130 so we can finalize the details.

안녕하세요. 비노드 싱입니다. **월요일에 매장에서 아파트에 놓을 냉장고를 보고 있었어요. 직원 한 명이 재고로 있는 상품을 보여 주었습니다. 저는 스테인리스로 마감한 특대형 냉장고로 결정했어요.** 아파트에 있는 다른 가전제품들과 어울릴 거라서요. 아, 그리고 **시내 이외의 지역은 추가되는 배송비가 있나요?** 세부 사항을 마무리 지을 수 있게 555-0130으로 전화 주세요.

어휘 in stock 재고로   go with ~로 하다   finish 마감   appliance 가전제품   additional 추가의   finalize 마무리하다   detail 세부 사항

Refrigerator Options			
Model	**Extra Large**	**Stainless Steel**	**Ice Maker**
SG-200			✓
SG-250		✓	
XG-300	✓		✓
⁹⁶XG-350	✓	✓	

냉장고 옵션			
모델	**특대형**	**스테인리스 스틸**	**얼음 제조기**
SG-200			✓
SG-250		✓	
XG-300	✓		✓
⁹⁶XG-350	✓	✓	

95

What is the main purpose of the call?

(A) To place an order

(B) To dispute a charge

(C) To arrange a meeting

(D) To check a store's inventory

통화의 주된 목적은 무엇인가?

(A) 주문을 하려고

(B) 요금에 이의를 제기하려고

(C) 면담을 예약하려고

(D) 매장 재고를 확인하려고

어휘 place an order 주문하다 dispute 이의를 제기하다, 논쟁하다 arrange 계획하다 inventory 재고

해설 전체 내용 관련 – 통화의 주된 목적

화자가 초반부에 매장에서 아파트에 놓을 냉장고를 보고 있었다(I was in your store on Monday looking at refrigerators for my apartment)고 했고, 직원 한 명이 재고로 있는 상품을 보여 줬다(One of your employees showed me what you have in stock)면서 스테인리스로 마감한 특대형 냉장고로 결정했다(I've decided to go with the extra-large refrigerator—the one with the stainless-steel finish)고 알리는 것으로 보아 정답은 (A)이다.

96

Look at the graphic. Which model does the speaker prefer?
(A) SG-200
(B) SG-250
(C) XG-300
(D) XG-350

시각 정보에 의하면, 화자는 어떤 모델을 선호하는가?
(A) SG-200
(B) SG-250
(C) XG-300
(D) XG-350

해설 시각 정보 연계 – 화자가 선호하는 모델

화자가 중반부에 자신은 스테인리스로 마감한 특대형 냉장고로 결정했다(I've decided to go with the extra-large refrigerator—the one with the stainless-steel finish)고 했는데, 차트에서 특대형이면서 스테인리스 마감인 냉장고는 XG-350이므로 정답은 (D)이다.

97

What does the speaker ask about?
(A) A warranty
(B) A return process
(C) A delivery fee
(D) Product availability

화자는 무엇에 대해 묻는가?
(A) 보증서
(B) 반품 절차
(C) 배송비
(D) 제품 구입 가능성

어휘 warranty 보증(서) return 반품, 반납

해설 세부 사항 관련 – 화자의 문의 사항

화자가 후반부에 시내 이외의 지역은 추가되는 배송비가 있는지(is there an additional charge for delivering outside of the downtown area?) 묻고 있으므로 정답은 (C)이다.

Paraphrasing 담화의 an additional charge for delivering
→ 정답의 A delivery fee

98-100 회의 발췌 + 도표

W-Am Good afternoon, everyone. I'd like to go over the product tests for our laptop-computer backpack, because they will require some design changes. As you know, [98]**we hired a marketing firm to test the prototype you designed among consumers.** Now, we received very positive feedback overall. Consumers liked the separate computer compartment. However, [99]**many people felt that the shoulder straps were uncomfortable when the bag was full. It's important that the backpack have comfortable shoulder straps, since its purpose is to carry heavy equipment.** [98, 99, 100]**We need to revise the design as quickly as possible,** [100]**since we're scheduled to have our official product release early next year.**

안녕하세요, 여러분. 노트북 컴퓨터 백팩에 대한 제품 테스트를 검토하고 싶어요. 디자인 변경이 필요하거든요. 아시다시피 **여러분이 디자인한 시제품을 소비자들 사이에서 테스트하기 위해 마케팅 회사를 고용했습니다.** 자, 전반적으로 매우 긍정적인 의견을 받았어요. 소비자들은 별도로 있는 컴퓨터 칸을 좋아했습니다. 하지만 **많은 사람들이 가방이 가득 찼을 때 어깨 끈이 불편하다고 느꼈습니다. 무거운 장비를 휴대하는 것이 목적이므로 백팩 어깨 끈이 편안한지가 중요하죠. 내년 초에 정식 제품 출시가 있을 예정이므로 가능한 한 빨리 디자인을 수정해야 합니다.**

어휘 go over 검토하다 prototype 시제품 positive 긍정적인 overall 전반적으로 separate 별도의 compartment 칸, 구획 strap 끈 uncomfortable 불편한 revise 수정하다 official 정식의, 공식의 release 출시

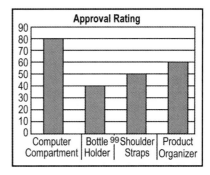

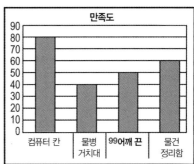

98

Who most likely are the listeners?
(A) Marketing experts
(B) Product testers
(C) Product designers
(D) Audio engineers

청자들은 누구인 것 같은가?
(A) 마케팅 전문가
(B) 제품 검사자
(C) 제품 디자이너
(D) 오디오 엔지니어

해설 전체 내용 관련 – 청자들의 직업

화자가 초반부에 청자들이 디자인한 시제품을 테스트하기 위해 마케팅 회사를 고용했다(we hired a marketing firm to test the prototype you designed among consumers)고 했고, 후반부에 가능한 한 빨리 디자인을 수정해야 한다(We need to revise the design as quickly as possible)고 다시 언급한 점을 보아 청자들은 제품 디자이너인 것을 알 수 있다. 따라서 정답은 (C)이다.

99

Look at the graphic. What was the approval rating of the feature that will be improved?
(A) 40 percent
(B) 50 percent
(C) 60 percent
(D) 80 percent

시각 정보에 의하면, 개선될 기능에 대한 만족도는 무엇이었는가?
(A) 40퍼센트
(B) 50퍼센트
(C) 60퍼센트
(D) 80퍼센트

해설 시각 정보 연계 – 개선될 기능에 대한 만족도

화자가 담화 중반부에서 많은 사람들이 가방이 가득 찼을 때 어깨 끈이 불편하다고 느꼈다(many people felt that the shoulder straps were uncomfortable when the bag was full)고 한 후, 무거운 장비를 휴대하는 것이 목적이므로 백팩 어깨 끈이 편안한 것이 중요하다(It's important ~ carry heavy equipment)면서 빨리 디자인을 수정해야 한다(We need to revise the design as quickly as possible)고 했으므로 개선될 기능은 어깨 끈임을 알 수 있다. 도표에서 어깨 끈의 만족도는 50퍼센트이므로 정답은 (B)이다.

100

According to the speaker, why is a revision urgent?
(A) A competitor is making a similar product.
(B) A product will be offered for sale soon.
(C) A product will be introduced at a trade show.
(D) The cost of a product's materials will rise soon.

화자에 따르면, 수정은 왜 시급한가?
(A) 경쟁업체가 비슷한 제품을 만들고 있다.
(B) 제품이 곧 판매될 것이다.
(C) 제품이 무역 박람회에서 선보일 것이다.
(D) 제품의 재료비가 곧 인상될 것이다.

어휘 revision 수정, 변경   urgent 시급한, 긴급한   sale 판매
　　 material 재료

해설 세부 사항 관련 – 수정이 시급한 이유

화자가 후반부에 내년 초에 정식 제품 출시가 있을 예정이므로 가능한 한 빨리 디자인을 수정해야 한다(We need to revise the design as quickly as possible, since we're scheduled to have our official product release early next year)고 했으므로 정답은 (B)이다.

> **Paraphrasing** 담화의 have our official product release early next year
> → 정답의 A product will be offered for sale soon

실전 TEST 2

1 (B)	**2** (D)	**3** (C)	**4** (A)	**5** (A)
6 (B)	**7** (C)	**8** (B)	**9** (A)	**10** (B)
11 (C)	**12** (A)	**13** (B)	**14** (A)	**15** (C)
16 (A)	**17** (C)	**18** (B)	**19** (A)	**20** (A)
21 (B)	**22** (C)	**23** (B)	**24** (A)	**25** (B)
26 (A)	**27** (B)	**28** (C)	**29** (B)	**30** (C)
31 (B)	**32** (B)	**33** (D)	**34** (C)	**35** (C)
36 (D)	**37** (A)	**38** (D)	**39** (A)	**40** (C)
41 (B)	**42** (D)	**43** (B)	**44** (B)	**45** (C)
46 (B)	**47** (B)	**48** (D)	**49** (A)	**50** (D)
51 (B)	**52** (C)	**53** (C)	**54** (B)	**55** (B)
56 (A)	**57** (B)	**58** (D)	**59** (B)	**60** (A)
61 (D)	**62** (C)	**63** (B)	**64** (B)	**65** (B)
66 (C)	**67** (D)	**68** (D)	**69** (A)	**70** (B)
71 (D)	**72** (B)	**73** (B)	**74** (B)	**75** (C)
76 (B)	**77** (B)	**78** (D)	**79** (C)	**80** (B)
81 (C)	**82** (B)	**83** (C)	**84** (D)	**85** (B)
86 (A)	**87** (C)	**88** (D)	**89** (C)	**90** (A)
91 (B)	**92** (B)	**93** (C)	**94** (A)	**95** (B)
96 (D)	**97** (B)	**98** (D)	**99** (B)	**100** (B)

PART 1

1 W-Br

(A) A woman is holding a power tool.
(B) A woman is opening a drawer.
(C) A printer is being unplugged.
(D) Office supplies are being put into a box.

(A) 여자가 전동 공구를 들고 있다.
(B) 여자가 서랍을 열고 있다.
(C) 프린터 플러그가 뽑히고 있다.
(D) 사무용품이 상자에 담기고 있다.

어휘 power tool 전동 공구   office supplies 사무용품

해설 혼합 사진 – 사람/사물/풍경 혼합 묘사

(A) 사진에 없는 명사를 이용한 오답. 전동 공구(a power tool)의 모습이 보이지 않으므로 오답.
(B) 정답. 여자가 서랍을 열고 있는(is opening a drawer) 모습이므로 정답.
(C) 동사 오답. 프린터(A printer) 플러그가 뽑히고 있는(is being unplugged) 모습이 아니므로 오답.

(D) 동사 오답. 사무용품(Office supplies)이 상자에 담기고 있는(are being put into a box) 모습이 아니므로 오답.

---

2 M-Au

(A) Plants are on top of a cart.
(B) A watering can is next to some trees.
(C) A man is digging in a garden.
(D) A man is near a display of potted plants.

(A) 식물들이 카트 위에 있다.
(B) 물뿌리개가 나무들 옆에 있다.
(C) 남자가 정원에서 땅을 파고 있다.
(D) 남자가 화분 진열대 근처에 있다.

어휘 dig 파다

해설 혼합 사진 – 사람/사물/풍경 혼합 묘사

(A) 위치 오답. 식물들(Plants)이 카트 위에 있는(are on top of a cart) 모습이 아니므로 오답.
(B) 사진에 없는 명사를 이용한 오답. 사진에 물뿌리개(A watering can)의 모습이 보이지 않으므로 오답.
(C) 동사 오답. 남자가 정원에서 땅을 파고 있는(is digging in a garden) 모습이 아니므로 오답.
(D) 정답. 남자가 화분 진열대 근처에 있는(is near a display of potted plants) 모습이므로 정답.

---

3 W-Am

(A) The man is fixing a machine.
(B) The man is buying some equipment.
(C) The man is lifting a weight.
(D) The man is looking at the ceiling.

(A) 남자가 기계를 고치고 있다.
(B) 남자가 장비를 사고 있다.
(C) 남자가 아령을 들어 올리고 있다.
(D) 남자가 천장을 쳐다보고 있다.

어휘 fix 고치다   equipment 장비   weight 아령, 역기

해설 1인 등장 사진 – 사람의 동작/상태 묘사

(A) 동사 오답. 남자가 기계를 고치고 있는(is fixing a machine) 모습이 아니므로 오답.
(B) 동사 오답. 남자가 장비를 사고 있는(is buying some equipment) 모습이 아니므로 오답.
(C) 정답. 남자가 아령을 들어 올리고 있는(is lifting a weight) 모습이므

로 정답.

(D) 사진에 없는 명사를 이용한 오답. 사진에 천장(the ceiling)의 모습이 보이지 않으므로 오답.

---

4 M-Au

(A) A wall is decorated with various items.
(B) Two chairs are blocking a doorway.
(C) A door has been propped open with a statue.
(D) A painting is hanging next to a window.

(A) 벽이 다양한 물건들로 장식되어 있다.
(B) 의자 두 개가 출입구를 막고 있다.
(C) 문이 조각상으로 받쳐져 열려 있다.
(D) 그림이 창문 옆에 걸려 있다.

어휘 prop 받치다 statue 조각상

해설 사물/풍경 사진 – 사물 묘사

(A) 정답. 벽(A wall)이 다양한 물건들로 장식되어 있는(is decorated with various items) 모습이므로 정답.
(B) 동사 오답. 의자 두 개(Two chairs)가 출입구를 막고 있는(are blocking a doorway) 모습이 아니므로 오답.
(C) 동사 오답. 문(A door)이 조각상으로 받쳐져 열려 있는(has been propped open with a statue) 모습이 아니므로 오답.
(D) 사진에 없는 명사를 이용한 오답. 사진에 창문(a window)의 모습이 보이지 않으므로 오답.

---

5 W-Br

(A) Some people are browsing in a shop.
(B) Some people are exchanging gifts.
(C) A customer is paying for some goods.
(D) Some salespeople are preparing a display.

(A) 사람들이 매장을 둘러보고 있다.
(B) 사람들이 선물을 교환하고 있다.
(C) 손님이 물건값을 지불하고 있다.
(D) 판매원들이 진열을 준비하고 있다.

어휘 browse 둘러보다

해설 2인 이상 등장 사진 – 사람의 동작/상태 묘사

(A) 정답. 사람들이 매장을 둘러보고 있는(are browsing in a shop) 모습이므로 정답.
(B) 동사 오답. 사람들이 선물을 교환하고 있는(are exchanging gifts) 모습이 아니므로 오답.

(C) 동사 오답. 손님(A customer)이 물건값을 지불하고 있는(is paying for some goods) 모습이 아니므로 오답.
(D) 사진에 없는 명사를 이용한 오답. 진열을 준비하고 있는(are preparing a display) 판매원들(salespeople)의 모습이 보이지 않으므로 오답.

---

6 M-Cn

(A) Cones are blocking access to a road.
(B) Some soil is in a pile on the ground.
(C) Some bushes have been planted in front of a building.
(D) A tree is lying in the roadway.

(A) 안전 고깔들이 도로 접근을 막고 있다.
(B) 흙이 땅 위에 쌓여 있다.
(C) 관목들이 건물 앞에 심어져 있다.
(D) 나무 한 그루가 도로에 쓰러져 있다.

어휘 access 접근 soil 흙 pile 더미 bush 관목

해설 사물/풍경 사진–풍경 묘사

(A) 동사 오답. 안전 고깔들(Cones)이 도로 접근을 막고 있는(are blocking access to a road) 모습이 아니므로 오답.
(B) 정답. 흙(Some soil)이 땅 위에 쌓여 있는(is in a pile on the ground) 모습이므로 정답.
(C) 사진에 없는 명사를 이용한 오답. 사진에 건물(a building)의 모습이 보이지 않으므로 오답.
(D) 동사 오답. 나무(A tree)가 도로에 쓰러져 있는(is lying in the roadway) 모습이 아니므로 오답.

PART 2

7

W-Br Who's responsible for hiring at our fitness center?

M-Au (A) Mr. Gonzalez is going to get a membership.
(B) I forgot to sign in at reception.
(C) Mr. Lin and Ms. Weiss are.

우리 헬스장에서 누가 채용을 담당하고 있나요?
(A) 곤잘레스 씨는 회원에 가입할 거예요.
(B) 접수처에서 서명하는 걸 깜빡했어요.
(C) 린 씨와 와이스 씨예요.

어휘 responsible for ~을 담당하는

해설 헬스장의 채용 담당자를 묻는 Who 의문문

(A) 연상 단어 오답. 질문의 fitness center에서 연상 가능한 membership을 이용한 오답.
(B) 연상 단어 오답. 질문의 fitness center에서 연상 가능한 reception을 이용한 오답.

(C) 정답. 헬스장의 채용 담당자를 묻는 질문에 Mr. Lin과 Ms. Weiss라는 사람 이름을 제시하고 있으므로 정답.

8

M-Cn Where do you usually purchase office supplies?

W-Am (A) We put them in the hallway cabinets.
　　　(B) At the store on Maple Avenue.
　　　(C) A manager's approval.

사무용품은 주로 어디에서 사시나요?
(A) 저희는 복도 캐비닛에 넣어 놓아요.
(B) 메이플 가에 있는 가게에서요.
(C) 매니저의 승인이요.

어휘 purchase 사다　hallway 복도　approval 승인

해설 사무용품 구입처를 묻는 Where 의문문
(A) 연상 단어 오답. 질문의 office supplies에서 연상 가능한 cabinets를 이용한 오답.
(B) 정답. 사무용품 구입처를 묻는 질문에 메이플 가에 있는 가게라며 가게가 위치한 장소를 제시하고 있으므로 정답.
(C) 연상 단어 오답. 질문의 office에서 연상 가능한 manager를 이용한 오답.

9

W-Br What time does Mr. Park usually leave?

M-Cn (A) Around six o'clock in the evening.
　　　(B) He left everything we need.
　　　(C) We've had many interns over the years.

박 씨는 보통 몇 시에 퇴근하나요?
(A) 저녁 6시쯤이요.
(B) 그는 우리에게 필요한 건 다 남겼어요.
(C) 몇 년 동안 인턴들이 많이 있었어요.

해설 퇴근 시간을 묻는 What 의문문
(A) 정답. 박 씨가 보통 퇴근하는 시간을 묻는 질문에 저녁 6시쯤이라며 구체적인 시간을 제시하고 있으므로 정답.
(B) 파생어 오답. 질문의 leave와 파생어 관계인 left를 이용한 오답.
(C) 질문과 상관없는 오답.

10

M-Au Do you want to present your research to the marketing team?

W-Br (A) That's what I've heard as well.
　　　(B) If we can find the time for it.
　　　(C) Yes, I received the gift.

조사 결과를 마케팅팀에게 발표하시겠어요?
(A) 저도 그렇게 들었어요.
(B) 우리가 그럴 시간을 낼 수 있다면요.
(C) 네, 선물 받았어요.

해설 조사 결과를 발표할지를 묻는 조동사(Do) 의문문
(A) 질문과 상관없는 오답.
(B) 정답. 조사 결과를 마케팅팀에게 발표할지를 묻는 질문에 그럴 시간을 낼 수 있다면 하겠다는 조건을 제시하고 있으므로 정답.
(C) 연상 단어 오답. 질문의 present를 '선물'로 해석했을 때 연상 가능한 gift를 이용한 오답.

11

W-Am Our company picnic is on Friday, isn't it?

M-Cn (A) Those times are both booked.
　　　(B) Only if you can find them easily.
　　　(C) Right—in two days.

회사 야유회가 금요일 맞죠?
(A) 그 시간들은 둘 다 예약이 찼어요.
(B) 당신이 쉽게 찾을 수만 있다면요.
(C) 맞아요—이틀 뒤예요.

해설 회사 야유회 요일을 확인하는 부가 의문문
(A) 연상 단어 오답. 질문의 Friday에서 연상 가능한 times를 이용한 오답.
(B) 질문과 상관없는 오답.
(C) 정답. 회사 야유회가 금요일인지를 묻는 질문에 맞아요(Right)라고 대답한 뒤, 이틀 뒤라며 덧붙이고 있으므로 정답.

12

M-Au Isn't the bus supposed to stop here?

W-Am (A) Yes, according to the schedule.
　　　(B) I'm on my way now.
　　　(C) It listed several potential clients.

버스가 여기에서 정차해야 하는 거 아닌가요?
(A) 네, 일정표에 따르면요.
(B) 저 지금 가는 중이에요.
(C) 거기에는 잠재 고객 몇 사람이 기재됐어요.

어휘 be supposed to ~해야 한다, ~하기로 되어 있다

해설 버스가 특정 지점에 정차하는지를 확인하는 부정 의문문
(A) 정답. 버스가 여기에서 정차하는지를 묻는 질문에 네(Yes)라고 대답한 뒤, 일정표에 따르면 그렇다는 긍정 답변에 대한 근거를 제시하고 있으므로 정답.
(B) 연상 단어 오답. 질문의 bus에서 연상 가능한 on my way를 이용한 오답.
(C) 질문과 상관없는 오답.

13

M-Cn We should fill this order quickly, shouldn't we?

W-Br (A) No, I haven't yet.
　　　(B) Yes, it's for an important client.
　　　(C) Try using this key.

이번 주문은 빨리 처리해야 하지 않을까요?
(A) 아니요, 전 아직이에요.
(B) 네, 중요한 고객을 위한 거예요.
(C) 이 열쇠를 써 보세요.

어휘 fill an order 주문을 처리하다, 주문품을 납품하다

해설 주문을 빨리 처리해야 하는지 여부를 확인하는 부가 의문문
(A) 질문과 상관없는 오답.
(B) 정답. 주문을 빨리 처리해야 하는지 여부를 확인하는 질문에 네(Yes)라고 대답한 뒤, 중요한 고객을 위한 거라며 이유를 제시하고 있으므로 정답.
(C) 단어 반복 오답. 질문의 this를 반복 이용한 오답.

14

W-Am How do you like your new job?

M-Au (A) I can work from home quite often.
　　　(B) A career in electrical engineering.
　　　(C) My sister helped me apply.

새 직장은 어때요?
(A) 꽤 자주 집에서 일할 수 있어요.
(B) 전기 공학 경력이요.
(C) 여동생이 지원하도록 도와줬어요.

해설 새 직장이 어떤지를 묻는 How 의문문
(A) 정답. 새 직장이 어떤지를 묻는 질문에 꽤 자주 집에서 일할 수 있다는 특징을 말하고 있으므로 정답.
(B) 연상 단어 오답. 질문의 job에서 연상 가능한 career와 engineering을 이용한 오답.
(C) 연상 단어 오답. 질문의 job에서 연상 가능한 apply를 이용한 오답.

15

M-Cn Let's go to the cafeteria for lunch today.

W-Br (A) There should be one in the filing cabinet.
　　　(B) Which local restaurant do you prefer?
　　　(C) I don't think I can take a break.

오늘은 구내식당에 가서 점심을 먹읍시다.
(A) 파일 캐비닛에 하나 있을 거예요.
(B) 어떤 동네 식당을 선호하세요?
(C) 저는 쉴 수 없을 것 같아요.

해설 제안/권유의 평서문
(A) 평서문과 상관없는 오답.
(B) 연상 단어 오답. 평서문의 cafeteria와 lunch에서 연상 가능한 restaurant를 이용한 오답.
(C) 정답. 오늘은 구내식당에 가서 점심을 먹자고 제안하는 평서문에 자신은 쉴 수 없을 것 같다며 우회적으로 거절하고 있으므로 정답.

16

W-Am When will we hire the new interns?

M-Cn (A) Mr. Wyeth is handling that.
　　　(B) With more time to spare than usual.
　　　(C) The highest available salary.

새 인턴은 언제 뽑나요?
(A) 그 일은 와이어스 씨가 처리하고 있어요.
(B) 평소보다 할애할 시간이 더 많아요.
(C) 가능한 가장 높은 급여예요.

어휘 than usual 평소보다

해설 새 인턴을 뽑는 시점을 묻는 When 의문문
(A) 정답. 새 인턴을 뽑는 시점을 묻는 질문에 와이어스 씨가 알고 있음을 우회적으로 알려 주고 있으므로 정답.
(B) 질문과 상관없는 오답.
(C) 연상 단어 오답. 질문의 hire에서 연상 가능한 salary를 이용한 오답.

17

M-Au How often should I mail these statements?

M-Cn (A) Yes, you can buy one online.
　　　(B) The post office on Grant Street.
　　　(C) We send them out once a month.

이 명세서들을 얼마나 자주 부쳐야 하나요?
(A) 네, 온라인으로 구매하실 수 있어요.
(B) 그랜트 가에 있는 우체국이에요.
(C) 우리는 한 달에 한 번 발송해요.

어휘 statement (청구) 명세서

해설 명세서 발송 빈도를 묻는 How often 의문문
(A) Yes/No 불가 오답. How 의문문에는 Yes/No 응답이 불가능하므로 오답.
(B) 연상 단어 오답. 질문의 mail에서 연상 가능한 post office를 이용한 오답.
(C) 정답. 명세서 발송 빈도를 묻는 질문에 한 달에 한 번 발송한다며 구체적인 횟수로 답하고 있으므로 정답.

18

W-Br Why did you put that food in the freezer?

M-Au (A) It's not working well currently.
　　　(B) I meant to put it in the refrigerator.
　　　(C) Let's start making dinner soon.

음식을 왜 냉동고에 넣었죠?
(A) 지금 제대로 작동하지 않아요.
(B) 전 냉장고에 넣는다고 넣었는데요.
(C) 곧 저녁 준비를 시작합시다.

어휘 currently 지금

해설 음식을 냉동고에 넣은 이유를 묻는 Why 의문문
(A) 연상 단어 오답. 질문의 freezer에서 연상 가능한 working well을 이용한 오답.
(B) 정답. 음식을 냉동고에 넣은 이유를 묻는 질문에 자신은 냉장고에 넣는다고 넣었다며 실수로 냉동고에 넣었음을 우회적으로 인정하고 있으므로 정답.
(C) 연상 단어 오답. 질문의 food에서 연상 가능한 dinner를 이용한 오답.

19

M-Cn Could you print the agenda for the meeting?

W-Am (A) It's already on your desk.
(B) No, the other printer.
(C) Was that a client?

회의 안건을 출력해 주시겠어요?

(A) 이미 책상 위에 있어요.
(B) 아니요, 다른 프린터요.
(C) 고객이었나요?

어휘 agenda 안건

해설 부탁/요청의 의문문
(A) 정답. 회의 안건을 출력해 달라는 요청에 이미 책상 위에 있다며 출력을 할 필요가 없음을 우회적으로 표현하고 있으므로 정답.
(B) 파생어 오답. 질문의 print와 파생어 관계인 printer를 이용한 오답.
(C) 연상 단어 오답. 질문의 meeting에서 연상 가능한 client를 이용한 오답.

20

W-Br How far are you from the clinic?

M-Au (A) I'm close enough to walk.
(B) I need to see the doctor.
(C) It's a well-known clinic.

병원에서 얼마나 떨어진 곳에 계시죠?

(A) 전 걸어갈 수 있을 만큼 가까이에 있어요.
(B) 진료를 받아야겠어요.
(C) 유명한 병원이에요.

어휘 well-known 유명한, 잘 알려진

해설 병원과의 거리를 묻는 How far 의문문
(A) 정답. 병원에서 얼마나 떨어진 곳에 있는지를 묻는 질문에 걸어갈 수 있을 만큼 가깝다고 알리고 있으므로 정답.
(B) 연상 단어 오답. 질문의 clinic에서 연상 가능한 doctor를 이용한 오답.
(C) 단어 반복 오답. 질문의 clinic을 반복 이용한 오답.

21

W-Br Didn't you get a printout of the company newsletter from Emiko?

M-Cn (A) She started working here three years ago.
(B) I was out of town last week.
(C) Yes, I do like to write.

에미코한테 회사 소식지 출력물 못 받았어요?

(A) 그녀는 3년 전부터 여기서 일하기 시작했어요.
(B) 전 지난주에 타지에 있었어요.
(C) 네, 저는 글 쓰는 일을 정말 좋아해요.

어휘 printout 출력물

해설 회사 소식지 출력물을 받았는지 여부를 확인하는 부정 의문문
(A) 연상 단어 오답. 질문의 company에서 연상 가능한 working을 이용한 오답.
(B) 정답. 에미코한테 회사 소식지 출력물을 받았는지 여부를 묻는 질문에 자신은 지난주에 타지에 있었다며 못 받았다는 것을 우회적으로 전달하고 있으므로 정답.
(C) 연상 단어 오답. 질문의 newsletter에서 연상 가능한 write를 이용한 오답.

22

M-Au When do you need to renew your passport?

W-Br (A) Be careful not to lose your tickets.
(B) A brand-new type of microchip.
(C) Soon, because it's about to expire.

언제 여권을 갱신해야 하나요?

(A) 표를 분실하지 않도록 주의하세요.
(B) 새로운 유형의 마이크로칩이에요.
(C) 곧 해야 해요. 금방 만료될 예정이거든요.

어휘 renew 갱신하다 be about to 막 ~하려고 하다 expire 만료되다

해설 여권 갱신 시점을 묻는 When 의문문
(A) 연상 단어 오답. 질문의 passport에서 연상 가능한 tickets를 이용한 오답.
(B) 유사 발음 오답. 질문의 renew와 부분적으로 발음이 유사한 new를 이용한 오답.
(C) 정답. 여권 갱신 시점을 묻는 질문에 곧 해야 한다며 금방 만료될 예정이라는 이유를 제시하고 있으므로 정답.

23

W-Am Who can help me find replacement parts for my computer?

M-Cn (A) Here are all the latest statements.
(B) I can help you look through the inventory.
(C) Put these on that shelf.

제 컴퓨터 교체 부품 찾는 일 도와주실 분 있나요?

(A) 여기 최근 명세서 전부예요.
(B) 제가 재고 찾는 일을 도와드릴게요.
(C) 이것들을 선반에 올려놓으세요.

어휘 replacement 교체 latest 최신의 inventory 재고

해설 컴퓨터 교체 부품 찾는 일을 도와줄 사람을 묻는 Who 의문문
(A) 유사 발음 오답. 질문의 replacement와 부분적으로 발음이 유사한 statements를 이용한 오답.
(B) 정답. 컴퓨터의 교체 부품을 찾는 일을 도와줄 사람을 묻는 질문에 자신이 재고 찾는 일을 도와주겠다며 응답하고 있으므로 정답.
(C) 연상 단어 오답. 질문의 replacement parts에서 연상 가능한 shelf를 이용한 오답.

24

M-Au I can't make it to the company dinner tonight.

W-Am (A) Managers expect everyone to be there.
(B) A buffet-style restaurant.
(C) A meeting once a week.

오늘 저녁 회식에 못 갈 것 같아요.

(A) 매니저들은 모두가 거기 왔으면 하는데요.
(B) 뷔페식 식당이에요.
(C) 일주일에 한 번 하는 회의예요.

어휘 expect 기대하다, 예상하다

해설 의사 전달의 평서문

(A) 정답. 오늘 저녁 회식에 못 갈 것 같다는 의사를 전달하는 평서문에 매니저들은 모두가 왔으면 한다며 회식에 참석해 주었으면 하는 뜻을 우회적으로 표현하고 있으므로 정답.
(B) 연상 단어 오답. 평서문의 dinner에서 연상 가능한 buffet-style restaurant을 이용한 오답.
(C) 연상 단어 오답. 평서문의 company에서 연상 가능한 meeting을 이용한 오답.

25

M-Cn Do you work in this neighborhood?

W-Br (A) Yes, I'd like to.
(B) No, my office isn't nearby.
(C) There aren't any of those here.

이 동네에서 일하세요?
(A) 네, 좋아요.
(B) 아니요, 제 사무실은 근처에 없어요.
(C) 여기에는 그런 게 전혀 없어요.

해설 이 동네에서 일하는지 여부를 묻는 조동사(Do) 의문문

(A) 질문과 상관없는 오답.
(B) 정답. 이 동네에서 일하는지 여부를 묻는 질문에 아니요(No)라고 대답한 뒤, 자신의 사무실은 근처에 없다며 부정 답변과 일관된 내용을 덧붙이고 있으므로 정답.
(C) 연상 단어 오답. 질문의 this neighborhood에서 연상 가능한 here를 이용한 오답.

26

W-Am It's time for our quarterly earnings report, isn't it?

M-Au (A) Was there an e-mail reminder about it?
(B) To pay for a new advertising campaign.
(C) No, a different pair of earrings.

분기 수익 보고서를 낼 때죠?
(A) 그것에 관해 이메일 알림이 있었나요?
(B) 새로운 광고 캠페인 대금을 지불하려고요.
(C) 아니요, 다른 귀걸이예요.

어휘 quarterly 분기의   earnings report 수익 보고서

해설 분기 수익 보고서 제출 시기를 확인하는 부가 의문문

(A) 정답. 분기 수익 보고서를 낼 때가 되었는지 확인하는 질문에 그것에 관해 이메일 알림이 있었는지 되물으며 이메일을 확인해 봐야 함을 우회적으로 알리고 있으므로 정답.
(B) 연상 단어 오답. 질문의 earnings에서 연상 가능한 pay를 이용한 오답.
(C) 유사 발음 오답. 질문의 earnings와 부분적으로 발음이 유사한 earrings를 이용한 오답.

27

M-Cn What did you do with the guest list that I sent you?

W-Am (A) After everyone received it.
(B) I passed it along to everyone who needed it.
(C) We're supposed to leave soon.

제가 보낸 고객 명단은 어떻게 하셨나요?
(A) 모두 받은 후에요.
(B) 필요한 사람 모두에게 나눠 줬어요.
(C) 우리는 곧 떠나야 해요.

어휘 be supposed to ~해야 한다

해설 고객 명단을 어떻게 했는지 묻는 What 의문문

(A) 연상 단어 오답. 질문의 sent에서 연상 가능한 received를 이용한 오답.
(B) 정답. 자신이 보낸 고객 명단을 어떻게 했는지 묻는 질문에 필요한 사람 모두에게 나눠 주었다고 알려 주고 있으므로 정답.
(C) 질문과 상관없는 오답.

28

W-Br Did you see the announcement about Emily's promotion?

M-Au (A) All the technology's been upgraded.
(B) Perhaps a good career counselor.
(C) I've been busy all morning.

에밀리의 승진에 관한 공고 보셨어요?
(A) 모든 기술이 향상되었어요.
(B) 훌륭한 직업 상담사 같네요.
(C) 전 오전 내내 바빴어요.

어휘 promotion 승진

해설 승진 공고를 보았는지 확인하는 조동사(Did) 의문문

(A) 질문과 상관없는 오답.
(B) 연상 단어 오답. 질문의 promotion에서 연상 가능한 career를 이용한 오답.
(C) 정답. 에밀리의 승진 공고를 보았는지를 묻는 질문에 오전 내내 바빴다며 공고를 보지 못했음을 우회적으로 응답하고 있으므로 정답.

29

W-Am Let's try our best to finish the project on time.

M-Au (A) All except the first one.
(B) We may need a few more days.
(C) I think over time it will.

프로젝트를 제시간에 끝내도록 최선을 다합시다.
(A) 첫 번째 것을 제외하고 전부요.
(B) 며칠 더 필요할지도 몰라요.
(C) 제 생각에는 시간이 지나면 그렇게 될 것 같아요.

어휘 except ~을 제외하고

해설 제안/권유의 평서문

(A) 평서문과 상관없는 오답.

(B) 정답. 프로젝트를 제시간에 끝내도록 최선을 다하자고 제안하는 평서문에 며칠 더 필요할지도 모른다며 불확실성을 우회적으로 표현하고 있으므로 정답.

(C) 단어 반복 오답. 평서문의 time을 반복 이용한 오답.

30

W-Br Where's the store manager?

M-Cn (A) A recent hiring decision.
(B) I enjoy shopping at that store.
(C) She went out for lunch.

점장은 어디 있나요?
(A) 최근 채용 결정이에요.
(B) 전 그 가게에서 쇼핑을 즐겨요.
(C) 점심 먹으러 나갔어요.

어휘 recent 최근의 decision 결정

해설 점장이 있는 장소를 묻는 Where 의문문

(A) 연상 단어 오답. 질문의 manager에서 연상 가능한 hiring을 이용한 오답.

(B) 단어 반복 오답. 질문의 store를 반복 이용한 오답.

(C) 정답. 점장이 있는 장소를 묻는 질문에 점심을 먹으러 나갔다며 지금은 점장을 만날 수 없음을 우회적으로 알려 주고 있으므로 정답.

31

M-Au The software you're using isn't very reliable.

W-Br (A) These chairs aren't very comfortable.
(B) I've been using it for years with no problems.
(C) I saw that computer at the store.

당신이 쓰고 있는 그 소프트웨어는 그다지 미덥지 않아요.
(A) 이 의자들은 그다지 편안하지 않네요.
(B) 저는 몇 년째 아무 문제 없이 쓰고 있어요.
(C) 저는 가게에서 그 컴퓨터를 봤어요.

어휘 reliable 신뢰할 수 있는 comfortable 편안한

해설 의사 전달의 평서문

(A) 유사 발음 오답. 평서문의 reliable과 부분적으로 발음이 유사한 comfortable을 이용한 오답.

(B) 정답. 상대방이 쓰고 있는 소프트웨어가 그다지 미덥지 않다는 의견의 평서문에 자신은 몇 년째 아무 문제 없이 쓰고 있다며 상반되는 의견을 전달하고 있으므로 정답.

(C) 연상 단어 오답. 평서문의 software에서 연상 가능한 computer를 이용한 오답.

PART 3

32-34

W-Am 32Hello, Forest Grove Photography Services. How can I help you?

M-Cn Hi, 32I'd like to get a photographer to cover our event. 33It's a charity basketball game next Tuesday night. I was hoping to get Thomas Zukowski. He works for you, right?

W-Am Yes, but unfortunately, 33Thomas doesn't usually work evenings.

M-Cn Oh, too bad. 34Could you recommend somebody else?

W-Am 34Before I do that, let me talk to him. He might make an exception. Tom does love basketball.

여 **안녕하세요, 포레스트 그로브 사진 서비스입니다. 무엇을 도와드릴까요?**

남 안녕하세요, **행사를 맡아 줄 사진작가를 구하고 싶은데요. 다음 주 화요일 밤 자선 농구 경기예요.** 토마스 주코스키가 했으면 하는데요. 그분 여기서 일하죠?

여 네, 그런데 아쉽게도 **토마스는 저녁에는 보통 일을 안 해요.**

남 아, 저런. **다른 사람 좀 추천해 주시겠어요?**

여 **그러기 전에 그에게 먼저 얘기해 볼게요. 예외로 할지도 모르니까요.** 톰이 농구를 정말 좋아하거든요.

어휘 cover 담당하다, 포함하다 charity 자선 unfortunately 아쉽게도 recommend 추천하다 exception 예외

32

Why is the man calling?
(A) To rent a facility
(B) To hire a photographer
(C) To request a price list
(D) To schedule a repair

남자는 왜 전화하고 있는가?
(A) 시설을 임대하려고
(B) 사진작가를 고용하려고
(C) 가격 목록을 요청하려고
(D) 수리 일정을 잡으려고

해설 전체 내용 관련 – 남자가 전화하는 목적

여자가 첫 대사에서 포레스트 그로브 사진 서비스(Hello, Forest Grove Photography Services)라고 전화를 받으며 무엇을 도와줄지(How can I help you?)를 묻자 남자가 행사를 맡아 줄 사진작가를 구하고 싶다(I'd like to get a photographer to cover our event)고 했으므로 정답은 (B)이다.

Paraphrasing 대화의 get a photographer
→ 정답의 hire a photographer

33

What problem does the woman mention?
(A) Her employee does not have transportation.
(B) Her service does not cover sports events.
(C) The weather will be bad on Tuesday.
(D) The time the man requested is too late.

여자는 어떤 문제를 언급하는가?
(A) 직원에게 교통편이 없다.
(B) 서비스는 스포츠 행사를 포함하지 않는다.
(C) 화요일에 날씨가 안 좋을 것이다.
(D) 남자가 요청한 시간이 너무 늦다.

어휘 transportation 교통(편) cover 다루다

해설 세부 사항 관련 – 여자가 언급하는 문제
남자가 첫 번째 대사에서 다음 주 화요일 밤 자선 농구 경기(It's a charity basketball game next Tuesday night)라며 토마스 주코스키가 했으면 한다(I was hoping to get Thomas Zukowski)고 하자 여자가 토마스는 저녁에는 보통 일을 안 한다(Thomas doesn't usually work evenings)고 했으므로 정답은 (D)이다.

34

What does the woman say she will do?
(A) Issue a refund
(B) Cancel an order
(C) Talk to an employee
(D) E-mail her manager

여자는 무엇을 할 것이라고 말하는가?
(A) 환불하기
(B) 주문 취소하기
(C) 직원과 대화하기
(D) 매니저에게 이메일 보내기

해설 세부 사항 관련 – 여자가 할 것이라고 말하는 일
남자가 마지막 대사에서 다른 사람 좀 추천해 주겠는지(Could you recommend somebody else?) 묻자 여자가 그러기 전에 그에게 먼저 얘기해 보겠다(Before I do that, let me talk to him)고 했고, 예외로 할지도 모른다(He might make an exception)고 한 것으로 보아 톰에게 직접 물어볼 것임을 알 수 있다. 따라서 정답은 (C)이다.

35-37

M-Cn	Good morning. ³⁵It looks like we received a lot of new orders online last night.
W-Br	Yes, ³⁵I saw that when I got in this morning. Can you package all of them by yourself?
M-Cn	Well, there are so many, I may not be able to finish everything today.
W-Br	OK. ³⁶I'll call Maria Jeong and ask if she can come in early today to help.
M-Cn	³⁶That'd be great. ³⁷We also have to pack that big shipment for the Henderson order. We finally got all of the items in.
W-Br	Oh, yes, ³⁷do that first.

남	안녕하세요. 간밤에 온라인으로 신규 주문이 많이 들어온 것 같네요.
여	네, 저도 오늘 아침에 와서 봤어요. 혼자서 전부 포장하실 수 있나요?
남	너무 많아서 오늘 다 끝내지는 못할 것 같아요.
여	네. 마리아 정에게 전화해서 오늘 일찍 와서 도와줄 수 있는지 물어볼게요.
남	그럼 좋죠. 헨더슨 주문 건 때문에 큰 배송품도 포장해야 하거든요. 드디어 물건이 전부 들어왔어요.
여	아, 네, 그것부터 하세요.

어휘 by oneself 혼자서 shipment 배송(품)

35

Where most likely are the speakers?
(A) In a restaurant
(B) In a school
(C) In a warehouse
(D) In a library

화자들은 어디에 있는 것 같은가?
(A) 식당
(B) 학교
(C) 창고
(D) 도서관

해설 전체 내용 관련 – 대화의 장소
남자가 첫 대사에서 간밤에 온라인으로 신규 주문이 많이 들어온 것 같다(It looks like we received a lot of new orders online last night)고 했고, 여자가 자신도 오늘 아침에 와서 봤다(I saw that when I got in this morning)며 혼자서 전부 포장할 수 있는지(Can you package all of them by yourself?)를 묻고 있다. 따라서 화자들은 주문품이 준비되는 창고에 있다는 것을 알 수 있으므로 정답은 (C)이다.

36

Why do the speakers mention Maria Jeong?
(A) She placed a very large order.
(B) She wants to replace a product.
(C) She is unable to work today.
(D) She may be able to help with a task.

화자들은 왜 마리아 정을 언급하는가?
(A) 그녀가 대량으로 주문했다.
(B) 그녀가 제품을 교체하고 싶어 한다.
(C) 그녀가 오늘 일할 수 없다.
(D) 그녀가 일을 도울 수 있을지도 모른다.

어휘 place an order 주문하다 be unable to ~할 수 없다

여 　동감이에요. 하지만 **일반 메뉴를 주문하는 대신에 할인된 음식 요금을 제공해 줄 수 있는지 알아볼게요.**

어휘　corporate retreat 사내 수련회, 회사 야유회 convenient 편리한　reduced 할인된　catering (요식업체가 제공하는) 음식　rate 요금

해설 세부 사항 관련 – 마리아 정을 언급하는 이유

여자가 두 번째 대사에서 마리아 정에게 전화해서 오늘 일찍 와서 도와줄 수 있는지 물어보겠다(I'll call Maria Jeong and ask if she can come in early today to help)고 하자 남자가 좋다(That'd be great)고 했으므로 정답은 (D)이다.

37

What will the man probably do next?

(A) Pack an order
(B) Call a colleague
(C) Process a refund
(D) Write to a customer

남자는 다음에 무엇을 할 것 같은가?

(A) 주문품 포장하기
(B) 동료에게 전화하기
(C) 환불 처리하기
(D) 고객에게 편지 쓰기

해설 세부 사항 관련 – 남자가 다음에 할 일

남자가 마지막 대사에서 헨더슨 주문 건 때문에 큰 배송품도 포장해야 한다(We also have to pack that big shipment for the Henderson order)고 했고, 여자가 그것부터 하라(do that first)고 했으므로 정답은 (A)이다.

> Paraphrasing　대화의 pack that big shipment
> → 정답의 Pack an order

38-40

M-Au	Haruna, we've planned most of the details for the corporate retreat, including housing and most activities, but ³⁸**we still need to decide where to go for Saturday's closing dinner.**
W-Am	³⁸**Yes, I sent you several menus. Did you like any of the places?** ³⁹**McNally's is close by.**
M-Au	³⁹**Yes, that would be convenient.** We could even walk there from the hotel. But the prices are a little high.
W-Am	I agree. But ⁴⁰**I could see if they can offer us a reduced catering rate, rather than ordering off the regular menu.**

남	하루나, 숙소와 대다수 활동을 포함해 사내 수련회 세부 사항에 관한 계획을 대부분 짰어요. 그런데 **토요일 폐회 만찬으로 어디에 갈지 결정해야 해요.**
여	네, 제가 몇 가지 메뉴를 보냈어요. 그 장소들 중 마음에 드는 곳이 있나요? 맥날리는 가까워요.
남	네, 편하겠어요. 호텔에서 거기까지 걸어갈 수도 있고요. 그런데 가격이 좀 비싸네요.

38

What do the speakers need to choose?

(A) An introductory activity for a retreat
(B) A residential site for a retreat
(C) Decorations for a party
(D) A location for a dinner

화자들은 무엇을 선택해야 하는가?

(A) 수련회 도입부 활동
(B) 수련회를 위한 기숙 부지
(C) 파티용 장식
(D) 저녁 식사 장소

어휘　residential 거주 시설을 갖춘

해설 세부 사항 관련 – 화자들이 선택해야 하는 것

남자가 첫 대사에서 토요일 폐회 만찬으로 어디에 갈지 결정해야 한다(we still need to decide where to go for Saturday's closing dinner)고 하자 여자가 자신이 몇 가지 메뉴를 보냈다(Yes, I sent you several menus)며 그 장소들 중 마음에 드는 곳이 있는지(Did you like any of the places?) 묻는 것으로 보아 화자들은 저녁 식사 장소를 선택해야 함을 알 수 있다. 따라서 정답은 (D)이다.

> Paraphrasing　대화의 where to go for Saturday's closing
> dinner → 정답의 A location for a dinner

39

What do the speakers like about McNally's?

(A) It is nearby.
(B) It is open late.
(C) It is highly recommended.
(D) It has been remodeled.

화자들은 맥날리의 어떤 점을 좋아하는가?

(A) 근처에 있다.
(B) 늦게까지 영업한다.
(C) 적극 추천된다.
(D) 개보수되었다.

해설 세부 사항 관련 – 화자들이 맥날리에 대해 좋아하는 점

여자가 첫 번째 대사에서 맥날리는 가깝다(McNally's is close by)고 했고, 남자가 편하겠다(Yes, that would be convenient)고 호응한 것으로 보아 정답은 (A)이다.

> Paraphrasing　대화의 close by → 정답의 nearby

40

What does the woman offer to do?
(A) See what the retreat attendees prefer
(B) Find an alternative site
(C) Discuss pricing options
(D) Contact a hotel

여자는 무엇을 하겠다고 제안하는가?
(A) 수련회 참석자들이 선호하는 것 알아보기
(B) 대체 장소 찾기
(C) 가격 옵션 논의하기
(D) 호텔에 연락하기

어휘 attendee 참석자   alternative 대체하는

해설 세부 사항 관련 – 여자의 제안 사항
여자가 마지막 대사에서 일반 메뉴를 주문하는 대신에 할인된 음식 요금을 제공해 줄 수 있는지 알아보겠다(I could see if they can offer us a reduced catering rate, rather than ordering off the regular menu)고 했으므로 정답은 (C)이다.

> Paraphrasing 대화의 see if they can offer us a reduced catering rate → 정답의 Discuss pricing options

41-43 3인 대화

> W-Am **41Janelle and Rico, could you give me an update on how our new medical records software is coming?**
>
> W-Br Sure. Per the customer's request, I've updated the logo and changed the font.
>
> M-Cn **42The customer has communicated with us a lot on this project. Having their feedback at every stage of the process has been helpful.**
>
> W-Am Excellent. **43It sounds like we're on schedule for completing our beta version. Then we can hand it off to our marketing team.**

> 여1 자넬과 리코, 우리의 새로운 의료 기록용 소프트웨어가 어떻게 되어 가는지 최근 상황 좀 알려 줄래요?
>
> 여2 물론이죠. 고객의 요청에 따라 로고를 업데이트하고 글꼴을 바꿨어요.
>
> 남 고객이 이 프로젝트에 대해 우리와 대화를 많이 나누었어요. 진행 단계마다 피드백을 받아서 무척 도움이 됐어요.
>
> 여1 좋아요. 일정에 맞춰 베타 버전을 완성할 수 있을 것 같군요. 이후에는 마케팅팀에 넘기면 돼요.

> 어휘 process (진행) 과정   on schedule 일정에 맞춰   hand off 넘기다

41

What does the speakers' company produce?
(A) Computers
(B) Software
(C) Web sites
(D) Medical equipment

화자들의 회사는 무엇을 생산하는가?
(A) 컴퓨터
(B) 소프트웨어
(C) 웹사이트
(D) 의료 장비

해설 세부 사항 관련 – 화자들의 회사가 생산하는 것
첫 번째 여자가 첫 대사에서 다른 화자들에게 자신들의 새로운 의료 기록용 소프트웨어가 진행되어 가는 최근 상황을 알려 줄 수 있는지(Janelle and Rico, could you give me an update on how our new medical records software is coming?) 묻는 것으로 보아 정답은 (B)이다.

42

What does the man say has been helpful?
(A) Focus group data
(B) An engineering consultant
(C) A search engine
(D) Customer feedback

남자는 무엇이 도움이 됐다고 말하는가?
(A) 표적 집단 데이터
(B) 엔지니어링 컨설턴트
(C) 검색 엔진
(D) 고객 피드백

어휘 focus group 표적 집단(시장 조사 등을 위해 뽑은 소수의 집단)

해설 세부 사항 관련 – 남자가 도움이 됐다고 말하는 것
남자가 고객이 이 프로젝트에 대해 우리와 대화를 많이 나누었다(The customer has communicated with us a lot on this project)고 했고, 진행 단계마다 피드백을 받아서 무척 도움이 됐다(Having their feedback at every stage of the process has been helpful)고 했으므로 정답은 (D)이다.

43

What is the next step in the project that the speakers are discussing?
(A) Giving a presentation to the client
(B) Sending a product to another group in the company
(C) Creating a schedule for the next phase of development
(D) Determining the price of a product

화자들이 논의하고 있는 프로젝트의 다음 단계는 무엇인가?
(A) 고객에게 발표하기
(B) 사내 다른 집단에게 제품 보내기
(C) 다음 개발 단계를 위한 일정 짜기
(D) 제품 가격 결정하기

어휘 phase 단계   determine 결정하다

해설 세부 사항 관련 – 프로젝트의 다음 단계
첫 번째 여자가 마지막 대사에서 일정에 맞춰 베타 버전을 완성할 수 있을 것 같다(It sounds like we're on schedule for completing our beta version)면서 이후에는 마케팅팀에 넘기면 된다(Then we can hand it off to our marketing team)고 했으므로 정답은 (B)이다.

Paraphrasing	대화의 hand it off to our marketing team
	→ 정답의 Sending a product to another
	group in the company

44-46

M-Cn	Hello, this is Ian Nelson from Regal Bathrooms. **⁴⁴I'm following up to make sure that you're pleased with the job our workers did in your house.**
W-Am	Thank you for calling. Yes. They did a great job. The bathroom floor was replaced, and the new tile looks great. I'm very happy with the job.
M-Cn	That's good to hear. If there are other jobs you need done, I hope you'll reach out to us again.
W-Am	That reminds me. **⁴⁵I was thinking of replacing my kitchen cabinets. Is that something you'd possibly do?**
M-Cn	**⁴⁵We don't,** but **⁴⁶I can recommend a company I often work with.** Their customers have been very satisfied. **⁴⁶Let me get their phone number.** One second.
W-Am	Thanks.

남	안녕하세요, 리걸 욕실의 이안 넬슨입니다. **저희 직원들이 고객님 댁에서 한 작업에 만족하시는지 확인하기 위해 후속 연락을 드리고 있습니다.**
여	전화 주셔서 감사합니다. 네. 정말 훌륭했어요. 욕실 바닥이 교체되었고, 새 타일은 멋지네요. 작업에 아주 만족해요.
남	다행이네요. 필요한 다른 작업이 있으면 저희에게 다시 연락 주시기 바랍니다.
여	그러고 보니 생각나네요. **부엌 찬장을 교체할까 생각 중이었어요. 혹시 거기에서 하는 일인가요?**
남	**아니요,** 하지만 **제가 자주 협업하는 회사를 추천해 드릴 수 있습니다.** 고객들이 무척 만족하더군요. **거기 전화번호를 찾아볼게요.** 잠깐만요.
여	감사합니다.

어휘	follow up 후속 조치를 취하다 replace 교체하다
	reach out 연락하다

44

What is the purpose of the phone call?
(A) To help a customer choose a product
(B) To check on a customer's satisfaction
(C) To inform a customer of a price estimate
(D) To advertise a special offer

전화의 목적은 무엇인가?
(A) 고객이 제품 선택하는 것을 도우려고
(B) 고객의 만족도를 확인하려고
(C) 고객에게 가격 견적을 알려 주려고
(D) 특가품을 광고하려고

어휘 satisfaction 만족(도)   estimate 견적   special offer 특가품

해설 전체 내용 관련 – 전화의 목적
남자가 첫 대사에서 우리 직원들이 고객의 집에서 한 작업에 만족하는지 확인하기 위해 후속 연락을 하고 있다(I'm following up to make sure that you're pleased with the job our workers did in your house)고 한 것으로 보아 정답은 (B)이다.

Paraphrasing	대화의 following up to make sure that
	you're pleased with the job
	→ 정답의 check on a customer's
	satisfaction

45

What does the man say about replacing kitchen cabinets?
(A) He guarantees his company will do a good job.
(B) His company is too busy to do the work.
(C) His company does not do that type of work.
(D) He thinks it will be an expensive job.

남자는 부엌 찬장 교체에 관해 무엇이라고 말하는가?
(A) 자신의 회사가 잘한다고 장담한다.
(B) 자신의 회사는 너무 바빠서 그 일을 할 수 없다.
(C) 자신의 회사는 그 일을 하지 않는다.
(D) 돈이 많이 드는 일이라고 생각한다.

어휘 guarantee 장담하다, 보장하다   expensive 돈이 많이 드는

해설 세부 사항 관련 – 남자가 부엌 찬장 교체에 관해 말하는 것
여자가 두 번째 대사에서 부엌 찬장을 교체할까 생각 중(I was thinking of replacing my kitchen cabinets)이라면서 혹시 거기에서 하는 일인지(Is that something you'd possibly do?) 묻자 남자가 아니요(We don't)라고 했으므로 정답은 (C)이다.

46

What will the man most likely do next?
(A) Send workers to the woman's house
(B) Find a telephone number for the woman
(C) Check kitchen cabinet prices
(D) Discuss a new product with some workers

남자는 다음에 무엇을 할 것 같은가?
(A) 여자의 집으로 작업자들 보내기
(B) 여자를 위해 전화번호 찾기
(C) 주방 찬장 가격 확인하기
(D) 작업자들과 신제품에 관해 논의하기

해설 세부 사항 관련 – 남자가 다음에 할 일

남자가 마지막 대사에서 자신이 자주 협업하는 회사를 추천해 줄 수 있다(I can recommend a company I often work with)며 거기 전화번호를 찾아보겠다(Let me get their phone number)고 했으므로 여자에게 추천할 회사의 전화번호를 찾을 것임을 알 수 있다. 따라서 정답은 (B)이다.

> **Paraphrasing** 대화의 get their phone number
> → 정답의 Find a telephone number

47-49

> W-Br My name is Laura. **47I refill my medication here at this pharmacy once a month.** But on Monday I'm going to travel abroad for work for two months, and I wonder if I can get a two-month refill this time.
>
> M-Cn It shouldn't be a problem. However, your doctor must send us the two-month prescription, so you need to contact her first.
>
> W-Br Oh, I see. **48I'll give her a call during my lunch break today.** When are you open until today?
>
> M-Cn Until nine P.M. But once we receive your doctor's prescription, **49we can deliver the medication directly to your home.**

> 여 제 이름은 로라입니다. **저는 한 달에 한 번 여기 약국에서 약을 다시 타 갑니다.** 그런데 월요일에 업무차 두 달 동안 해외로 나가거든요. 그래서 이번에는 두 달 치를 타 갈 수 있는지 궁금해서요.
>
> 남 문제없어요. 하지만 의사가 우리에게 두 달 치 처방전을 보내야 합니다. 그러니 의사에게 먼저 문의하셔야 해요.
>
> 여 아, 그렇군요. **오늘 점심시간에 의사에게 전화할게요.** 오늘 몇 시까지 영업하세요?
>
> 남 오후 9시까지예요. 하지만 의사의 처방전을 받는 대로 **댁으로 바로 약을 배달해 드릴 수도 있습니다.**

> 어휘 medication 약 pharmacy 약국 prescription 처방(전), 처방 약

47

Where is the conversation taking place?
(A) At a travel agency
(B) At a pharmacy
(C) At a mobile phone store
(D) At a hotel

대화는 어디에서 이루어지고 있는가?
(A) 여행사
(B) 약국
(C) 휴대폰 판매점
(D) 호텔

해설 전체 내용 관련 – 대화의 장소

여자가 첫 대사에서 자신은 한 달에 한 번 여기 약국에서 약을 다시 타 간다(I refill my medication here at this pharmacy once a month)고 밝히고 있으므로 정답은 (B)이다.

48

What does the woman say she will do at lunch today?
(A) Go to the airport
(B) Print out a ticket
(C) Register for a giveaway
(D) Call a doctor

여자는 오늘 점심에 무엇을 할 것이라고 말하는가?
(A) 공항 가기
(B) 티켓 출력하기
(C) 경품 신청하기
(D) 의사에게 전화하기

어휘 giveaway 경품, 무료 증정품

해설 세부 사항 관련 – 여자가 오늘 점심에 할 것이라고 말하는 일

여자가 두 번째 대사에서 오늘 점심시간에 의사에게 전화하겠다(I'll give her a call during my lunch break today)고 했으므로 정답은 (D)이다.

> **Paraphrasing** 대화의 give her a call → 정답의 Call a doctor

49

What does the man offer to do?
(A) Arrange a delivery
(B) Postpone an appointment
(C) Check a discount rate
(D) Download an application

남자는 무엇을 해 주겠다고 제안하는가?
(A) 배달 조치하기
(B) 예약 연기하기
(C) 할인율 확인하기
(D) 애플리케이션 내려받기

어휘 postpone 연기하다

해설 세부 사항 관련 – 남자의 제안 사항

남자가 마지막 대사에서 여자의 집으로 바로 약을 배달해 줄 수 있다(we can deliver the medication directly to your home)고 제안하고 있으므로 정답은 (A)이다.

> **Paraphrasing** 대화의 deliver → 정답의 Arrange a delivery

50-52

M-Au	Miller's Sporting Goods. Joey speaking.
W-Am	Hello, **50I'm calling from West End High School. 51We're looking to make a big purchase for our student baseball teams.** Our equipment is getting old, and we would like to get new uniforms too. **51We have budget restrictions, though.**
M-Au	Well, we do offer discounts for bulk purchases. And we have a number of price ranges for uniforms; many are very reasonable. **52Let me get the manager on the phone, and you can discuss the specifics.**

남	밀러 스포츠 용품입니다. 저는 조이입니다.
여	안녕하세요. **웨스트 엔드 고등학교에서 전화드립니다. 학생 야구팀을 위해 대량 구매를 하려고 합니다.** 장비도 낡았고 유니폼도 새로 구하고 싶어요. **그런데 예산에 제한이 있어요.**
남	대량 구매 시 할인해 드립니다. 그리고 유니폼은 가격대가 다양하고요. 아주 저렴한 것들이 많아요. **점장에게 전화를 연결할 테니 자세한 사항은 상담해 보세요.**

어휘	purchase 구매 restriction 제한, 한정 reasonable 저렴한

50

Where does the woman work?
(A) At a baseball stadium
(B) At a fitness center
(C) At a shipping warehouse
(D) At a school

여자는 어디에서 일하는가?
(A) 야구장
(B) 헬스장
(C) 배송 창고
(D) 학교

해설 전체 내용 관련 – 여자의 근무지
여자가 첫 번째 대사에서 웨스트 엔드 고등학교에서 전화한다(I'm calling from West End High School)고 한 것으로 보아 정답은 (D)이다.

51

What is the woman concerned about?
(A) A store's closing time
(B) Overall costs
(C) When an order will be received
(D) The color of some uniforms

여자는 무엇을 걱정하는가?
(A) 가게 폐점 시간
(B) 총비용
(C) 주문품 수령 시기
(D) 유니폼 색상

해설 세부 사항 관련 – 여자의 우려 사항
여자가 첫 대사에서 학생 야구팀을 위해 대량 구매를 하려고 한다(We're looking to make a big purchase for our student baseball teams)고 한 후, 그런데 예산에 제한이 있다(We have budget restrictions, though)고 했으므로 정답은 (B)이다.

52

What will the man do next?
(A) Look up some prices
(B) Package an order
(C) Call a manager
(D) Check the store's inventory

남자는 다음에 무엇을 할 것인가?
(A) 가격 찾아보기
(B) 주문품 포장하기
(C) 점장에게 전화하기
(D) 가게 재고 확인하기

해설 세부 사항 관련 – 남자가 다음에 할 일
남자가 마지막 대사에서 점장에게 전화를 연결할 테니 자세한 사항은 상담해 보라(Let me get the manager on the phone, and you can discuss the specifics)고 했으므로 정답은 (C)이다.

> **Paraphrasing** 대화의 get the manager on the phone
> → 정답의 Call a manager

53-55

W-Br	Hi, this is Gemini Flowers. **53I'm calling about the order you placed for your award luncheon on July twelfth. Unfortunately, our supplier is out of pink roses.**
M-Cn	Oh, no! **54Pink matches our corporate logo!** I ordered them especially for this occasion!
W-Br	I understand your disappointment, sir. **55I can offer a ten percent discount on the total cost of your order and replace the pink roses with yellow ones.**
M-Cn	Well, **55I didn't tell anyone about the roses.** I suppose no one will really be disappointed.

여	안녕하세요. 제미니 플라워스입니다. **7월 12일 시상식 오찬을 위해 주문하신 건 때문에 전화드립니다.** 아쉽게도 공급업체에 분홍색 장미가 품절이에요.

남 맙소사! **분홍색이 우리 회사 로고와 어울리는데요!** 이번 행사를 위해 특별히 주문했거든요!

여 실망하신 점 이해합니다. 주문하신 총금액에서 **10퍼센트를 할인해 드리고 분홍색 장미를 노란색 장미로 교체해 드리겠습니다.**

남 흠, 아무에게도 장미 이야기는 하지 않았어요. 정말로 실망하는 사람은 아무도 없을 거예요.

어휘 luncheon 오찬 supplier 공급업체 occasion 행사, 기회 disappointment 실망

53

What problem does the woman mention?
(A) There is no time to create centerpieces.
(B) The shop never received the man's order.
(C) A supplier cannot fulfill an order.
(D) The wrong date is on the order form.

여자는 어떤 문제를 언급하는가?
(A) 중앙부 장식을 만들 시간이 없다.
(B) 가게는 남자의 주문을 받지 못했다.
(C) 공급업체가 주문품을 납품할 수 없다.
(D) 주문서에 엉뚱한 날짜가 기재되었다.

어휘 centerpiece 중앙부 장식 fulfill an order 주문품을 납품하다

해설 세부 사항 관련 – 여자가 언급하는 문제
여자가 첫 대사에서 7월 12일 시상식 오찬을 위해 주문한 건 때문에 전화한다(I'm calling about the order you placed for your award luncheon on July twelfth)며 아쉽게도 공급업체에서 분홍색 장미가 품절이다(Unfortunately, our supplier is out of pink roses)라고 문제점을 언급하고 있으므로 정답은 (C)이다.

> Paraphrasing 대화의 is out of pink roses
> → 정답의 cannot fulfill an order

54

What does the man say about his company's logo?
(A) It was designed many years ago.
(B) It contains the color pink.
(C) It won an award.
(D) It features a drawing of flowers.

남자는 회사 로고에 관해 무엇이라고 말하는가?
(A) 몇 년 전에 디자인되었다.
(B) 분홍색이 들어 있다.
(C) 상을 탔다.
(D) 꽃 그림이 특징이다.

해설 세부 사항 관련 – 남자가 회사 로고에 관해 말하는 것
남자가 첫 번째 대사에서 분홍색이 우리 회사 로고와 어울린다(Pink matches our corporate logo)라고 한 것으로 보아 정답은 (B)이다.

> Paraphrasing 대화의 Pink matches our corporate logo
> → 정답의 It contains the color pink

55

What does the man mean when he says, "I suppose no one will really be disappointed"?
(A) He will postpone the luncheon.
(B) He will accept the woman's offer.
(C) He will find a replacement award.
(D) He will modify the company's logo.

남자가 "정말로 실망하는 사람은 아무도 없을 거예요"라고 말할 때 무엇을 의미하는가?
(A) 오찬을 연기할 것이다.
(B) 여자의 제안을 받아들일 것이다.
(C) 대체 상을 찾을 것이다.
(D) 회사 로고를 수정할 것이다.

어휘 replacement 대체, 교체 modify 수정하다

해설 화자의 의도 파악 – 정말로 실망하는 사람은 아무도 없을 것이라는 말의 의도
앞에서 여자가 주문하신 총금액에서 10퍼센트를 할인해 주고 분홍색 장미를 노란색 장미로 교체해 주겠다(I can offer a ten percent discount on the total cost of your order and replace the pink roses with yellow ones)고 제안하자 아무에게도 장미 이야기는 하지 않았다(I didn't tell anyone about the roses)며 인용문을 언급했으므로, 노란색 장미로 교체하는 제안을 받아들일 생각이라는 의도로 볼 수 있다. 따라서 정답은 (B)이다.

56-58 3인 대화

W-Br Unfortunately, our development team has some bad news. It turns out **56,57we'll need to push back the shipment of the prototype motor we've been developing for our client.**

M-Cn Uh-oh. **57Why will there be a delay?**

W-Br Well, some of the components we received to build the prototype are failing initial tests, so we won't be able to make the delivery deadline. Janet, could you let the client know?

W-Am Yes, I'll contact them right away.

M-Cn And **58I'd like the development team to start giving me daily briefings about progress on this issue.**

여1 안타깝게도 개발팀에 안 좋은 소식이 있습니다. 결론을 말씀드리면 **우리가 고객을 위해 개발해 온 시제품 모터의 선적을 미뤄야 합니다.**

남 저런. **지연되는 이유가 뭐죠?**

여1 어, 시제품을 제작하기 위해 받은 부품 일부가 1차 테스트를 통과하지 못해서 배송 기한을 맞출 수 없게 됐어요. 재닛, 고객에게 통보하시겠어요?

여2 네, 바로 연락하겠습니다.

남　그리고 **개발팀은 이 문제의 진행 상황에 대해 제게 일일 브리핑을 시작해 주세요.**

| 어휘 | it turns out (that) ~로 결론이 나다, 알고 보니 ~이다 push back (날짜를) 미루다　prototype 시제품 component 부품　initial 처음의　progress 진행 (과정) |

56

What kind of company do the speakers most likely work for?
(A) Manufacturing
(B) Financial
(C) Publishing
(D) Educational

화자들은 어떤 업종에서 일하는 것 같은가?
(A) 제조
(B) 금융
(C) 출판
(D) 교육

해설　전체 내용 관련 – 화자들의 근무 업종

첫 번째 여자가 첫 대사에서 자신들이 고객을 위해 개발해 온 시제품 모터의 선적을 미뤄야 한다(we'll need to push back the shipment of the prototype motor we've been developing for our client)고 한 것으로 보아 정답은 (A)이다.

57

What problem are the speakers discussing?
(A) A pause while more funding is obtained
(B) A delay in making a delivery
(C) A need for the company to relocate
(D) The loss of some experienced staff

화자들은 어떤 문제에 대해 논의하고 있는가?
(A) 자금을 더 확보하는 동안 일시 중단
(B) 배송 지연
(C) 회사 이전의 필요성
(D) 경험 많은 직원의 퇴사

어휘　obtain 확보하다, 얻다　relocate 이전하다

해설　전체 내용 관련 – 대화의 주제

첫 번째 여자가 첫 대사에서 자신들이 고객을 위해 개발해 온 시제품 모터의 선적을 미뤄야 한다(we'll need to push back the shipment of the prototype motor we've been developing for our client)고 했고, 남자가 지연되는 이유가 무엇인지(Why will there be a delay?) 물으며 이후 이 지연에 대한 이야기를 이어 가고 있으므로 정답은 (B)이다.

> **Paraphrasing**　대화의 push back the shipment → 정답의 A delay in making a delivery

58

What does the man request?
(A) A report from the client
(B) A faster pace of work
(C) Additional employees
(D) Daily updates from the team

남자는 무엇을 요청하는가?
(A) 고객으로부터 온 보고서
(B) 더 빠른 작업 속도
(C) 추가 직원
(D) 팀의 일일 최신 정보 보고

해설　세부 사항 관련 – 남자의 요청 사항

남자가 마지막 대사에서 개발팀은 이 문제의 진행 상황에 대해 일일 브리핑을 해 달라(I'd like the development team to start giving me daily briefings ~ on this issue)고 요청하고 있으므로 정답은 (D)이다.

> **Paraphrasing**　대화의 daily briefings → 정답의 Daily updates

59-61

W-Br	Good evening. Legend Hotel. How may I help you?
M-Au	Hello. I'm at the local airport. Does the hotel run shuttle buses to here?
W-Br	We usually don't, but... was your flight originally scheduled for Central Airport?
M-Au	It was, but apparently [59]**there's a problem at Central.**
W-Br	Yes, [59]**there's a personnel shortage,** but several flights have been rerouted to the local airport. [60]**We have started running an airport shuttle this morning.**
M-Au	OK. That's good news. When is the next shuttle?
W-Br	Buses run every half hour. What's your reservation number? [61]**I'll ensure that your room is ready for you when you arrive.**

여　안녕하세요. 레전드 호텔입니다. 무엇을 도와드릴까요?
남　안녕하세요. 저는 지역 공항에 있는데요. 호텔에서 여기까지 셔틀버스를 운행하나요?
여　보통은 운행을 안 해요, 그런데… 비행기가 원래 센트럴 공항에 내리기로 되어 있었나요?
남　그랬죠, 그런데 보아하니 **센트럴에 문제가 생긴 것 같아요.**
여　네, **인력이 부족해서** 여러 항공편이 지역 공항으로 노선을 변경했어요. **저희는 오늘 아침부터 공항 셔틀을 운행하기 시작했어요.**
남　그렇군요. 반가운 소식이네요. 다음 셔틀이 언제인가요?
여　버스는 30분마다 운행합니다. 예약 번호가 어떻게 되나요? **도착하시면 객실이 준비되도록 조치해 놓겠습니다.**

59

What does the woman say about Central Airport?
(A) The airport operates two shuttles.
(B) There are not enough people working there.
(C) It is not far from the Legend Hotel.
(D) It is more modern than the local airport.

여자는 센트럴 공항에 관해 무엇이라고 말하는가?
(A) 공항에서 셔틀 두 대를 운행한다.
(B) 그곳에서 일하는 사람이 충분하지 않다.
(C) 레전드 호텔에서 멀지 않다.
(D) 지역 공항보다 더 현대적이다.

해설 세부 사항 관련 – 여자가 센트럴 공항에 관해 말하는 것
남자가 두 번째 대사에서 센트럴에 문제가 생긴 것 같다(there's a
problem at Central)고 하자 여자가 인력이 부족하다(there's a
personnel shortage)며 문제점을 특정하고 있으므로 정답은 (B)이다.

> Paraphrasing 대화의 a personnel shortage
> →정답의 not enough people working

60

Why does the man say, "That's good news"?
(A) He will be able to take a shuttle to the hotel.
(B) His flight was rescheduled.
(C) Central Airport will reopen soon.
(D) He will be able to change his hotel reservation.

남자는 왜 "반가운 소식이네요"라고 말하는가?
(A) 그는 호텔로 가는 셔틀을 탈 수 있을 것이다.
(B) 그의 항공편 일정이 바뀌었다.
(C) 센트럴 공항이 곧 재개장할 것이다.
(D) 그는 호텔 예약을 변경할 수 있을 것이다.

해설 화자의 의도 파악 – 반가운 소식이라는 말의 의도
앞에서 여자가 자신들이 오늘 아침부터 공항 셔틀을 운행하기 시작했다
(We have started running an airport shuttle this morning)고 알
리자 남자가 인용문을 언급한 것이므로, 셔틀을 이용할 수 있는 것에 대한
반가움의 표현으로 볼 수 있다. 따라서 정답은 (A)이다.

61

What will the woman do for the man?
(A) Give him the shuttle company's phone number
(B) Find information about Central Airport
(C) Give him a discount on his reservation
(D) Make sure that his room has been prepared

여자는 남자를 위해 무엇을 할 것인가?
(A) 남자에게 셔틀 회사 전화번호 주기
(B) 센트럴 공항에 관한 정보 찾기
(C) 남자에게 예약 할인해 주기
(D) 남자의 객실 준비 확인하기

해설 세부 사항 관련 – 여자가 남자를 위해 할 일
여자가 마지막 대사에서 남자에게 도착하면 객실이 준비되도록 조치해 놓
겠다(I'll ensure that your room is ready for you when you arrive)
고 했으므로 정답은 (D)이다.

> Paraphrasing 대화의 ensure that your room is ready
> for you → 정답의 Make sure that his room
> has been prepared

62-64 대화 + 이미지

M-Au Hi, Marla. **62I'm calling to check whether
you received my outline of the design
project for your apartment remodeling. I
e-mailed it to you yesterday.**

W-Am Yes. Thank you for doing such a great job.
**63I really liked your idea of opening up the
kitchen and creating an open space with
the living room.**

M-Au Great. If everything looks good to you, I
can start ordering the supplies tomorrow.

W-Am Actually, **64I don't like the ceramic tiles you
picked for the kitchen. I like the marble
ones much better. I know they are more
expensive, but it's a small space.**

남 안녕하세요, 말라. **아파트 리모델링을 위한 설계 프로젝트의
개요를 받으셨는지 확인차 전화드립니다.** 어제 이메일로
보냈습니다.

여 네. 정말 훌륭하게 해 주셔서 감사합니다. **부엌을 터서
거실과 함께 개방된 공간을 만들자는 아이디어가 정말 마음에
들었어요.**

남 잘됐네요. 모두 마음에 드신다면, 내일부터 물품 주문을
시작할 수 있습니다.

여 사실, **주방용으로 고르신 세라믹 타일이 마음에 안 들어요.
전 대리석 타일이 훨씬 더 좋거든요. 그게 더 비싸다는 건
알지만, 좁은 공간이니까요.**

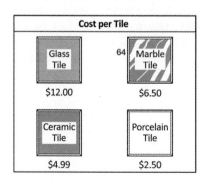

Cost per Tile

Glass Tile	Marble Tile 64
$12.00	$6.50
Ceramic Tile	Porcelain Tile
$4.99	$2.50

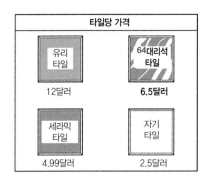

타일당 가격	
유리 타일	⁶⁴대리석 타일
12달러	6.5달러
세라믹 타일	자기 타일
4.99달러	2.5달러

62

What did the man do yesterday?
(A) He visited a property.
(B) He contacted a supplier.
(C) He sent a plan.
(D) He took some measurements.

남자는 어제 무엇을 했는가?
(A) 건물에 방문했다.
(B) 공급업체에게 연락했다.
(C) 계획안을 보냈다.
(D) 치수를 쟀다.

어휘 property 건물, 부동산   measurement 측정

해설 세부 사항 관련 – 남자가 어제 한 일
남자가 첫 대사에서 아파트 리모델링을 위한 설계 프로젝트의 개요를 받았는지 확인차 전화한다(I'm calling to check whether you received my outline ~ remodeling)며, 어제 이메일로 보냈다(I e-mailed it to you yesterday)고 한 것으로 보아 프로젝트 계획안을 어제 이메일로 보냈음을 알 수 있다. 따라서 정답은 (C)이다.

> **Paraphrasing** 대화의 my outline → 정답의 a plan

63

What does the woman say she likes?
(A) The cost the man has estimated
(B) The open-space design
(C) The colors the man has selected
(D) The remodeling timeline

여자는 무엇이 마음에 든다고 말하는가?
(A) 남자가 견적을 낸 비용
(B) 개방 공간 설계
(C) 남자가 고른 색깔
(D) 개보수 일정

어휘 estimate 견적을 내다, 추정하다

해설 세부 사항 관련 – 여자가 마음에 든다고 말하는 것
여자가 첫 번째 대사에서 부엌을 터서 거실과 함께 개방된 공간을 만들자는 아이디어가 정말 마음에 들었다(I really liked your idea of opening up the kitchen and creating an open space with the living room)고 했으므로 정답은 (B)이다.

> **Paraphrasing** 대화의 creating an open space
> → 정답의 The open-space design

64

Look at the graphic. How much will the woman pay for each tile?
(A) $12.00
(B) $6.50
(C) $4.99
(D) $2.50

시각 정보에 의하면, 여자는 타일 한 장에 얼마를 지불할 것인가?
(A) 12달러
(B) 6.5달러
(C) 4.99달러
(D) 2.5달러

해설 시각 정보 연계 – 여자가 타일 한 장에 지불할 금액
여자가 마지막 대사에서 주방용으로 고른 세라믹 타일이 마음에 안 든다(I don't like the ceramic tiles you picked for the kitchen)고 했고, 대리석 타일이 훨씬 더 좋다(I like the marble ones much better)면서 그게 더 비싸다는 건 알지만, 좁은 공간이다(I know they are more expensive, but it's a small space)이라고 한 것으로 보아 대리석 타일을 선택할 것임을 알 수 있다. 이미지에 따르면 대리석 타일은 6.5달러이므로 정답은 (B)이다.

65-67 대화 + 가격표

> **M-Cn** Hi. ⁶⁵**I'd like to make a reservation for a group of clients that will be visiting our company from the first to the sixth of June.** I need eight rooms.
>
> **W-Br** We do have availability for that period. ⁶⁶**The type of room I recommend for you is normally 99 euros per night,** but we can offer a group discount.
>
> **M-Cn** That'll work. Also, on June fifth, we want to take our clients on a tour of the local attractions. Could you help arrange that?
>
> **W-Br** ⁶⁷**We have an event planner here who'll be able to help you. His name is Pablo Gonzales.** I'll connect you to his office once I've completed your reservation.

> 남 안녕하세요. **6월 1일부터 6일까지 회사에 방문할 단체 고객을 위해 예약하려고 합니다.** 방이 8개 필요합니다.
>
> 여 그 기간에는 빈 객실이 있습니다. **제가 추천하는 객실 타입은 보통 1박에 99유로인데** 단체 할인이 가능합니다.
>
> 남 그러면 되겠네요. 또 6월 5일에는 고객들을 데리고 지역 명소 관광을 하고 싶은데요. 준비를 도와주실 수 있나요?
>
> 여 **여기에 도와줄 행사 기획자가 있습니다. 이름은 파블로 곤잘레스예요.** 예약을 마무리하는 대로 그분 사무실로 연결해 드리겠습니다.

> 어휘 make a reservation 예약하다   normally 보통   attraction (관광) 명소   complete 마무리하다

Room Types	Price
Executive suite	€ 120
Deluxe double	€ 115
[66]Standard king	€ 99
Single basic	€ 89

객실 유형	가격
고급 특실	120유로
디럭스 더블	115유로
[66]스탠다드 킹	99유로
싱글 베이식	89유로

65

Why is the man calling?
(A) To request a room change
(B) To make a group reservation
(C) To order room service
(D) To complain about noise

남자는 왜 전화를 하고 있는가?
(A) 객실 변경을 요청하려고
(B) 단체 예약을 하려고
(C) 룸서비스를 주문하려고
(D) 소음 때문에 항의하려고

해설 전체 내용 관련 – 남자가 전화하는 목적
남자가 첫 대사에서 6월 1일부터 6일까지 회사에 방문할 단체 고객을 위해 예약하려 한다(I'd like to make a reservation for a group of clients that will be visiting our company from the first to the sixth of June)고 했으므로 정답은 (B)이다.

> **Paraphrasing** 대화의 a reservation for a group of clients
> → 정답의 a group reservation

66

Look at the graphic. Which room type does the woman mention?
(A) Executive suite
(B) Deluxe double
(C) Standard king
(D) Single basic

시각 정보에 의하면, 여자는 어떤 객실 유형을 언급하는가?
(A) 고급 특실
(B) 디럭스 더블
(C) 스탠다드 킹
(D) 싱글 베이식

해설 시각 정보 연계 – 여자가 언급하는 객실 유형
여자가 첫 번째 대사에서 자신이 추천하는 객실 타입은 보통 1박에 99유로(The type of room I recommend for you is normally 99 euros per night)라고 했으므로, 가격표에서 99유로를 찾으면 정답은 (C)이다.

67

Who is Pablo Gonzales?
(A) An accountant
(B) A client
(C) A bus driver
(D) An event planner

파블로 곤잘레스는 누구인가?
(A) 회계사
(B) 고객
(C) 버스 운전기사
(D) 행사 기획자

해설 세부 사항 관련 – 파블로 곤잘레스의 직업
여자가 마지막 대사에서 여기에 도와줄 행사 기획자가 있다(We have an event planner here who'll be able to help you)며 이름은 파블로 곤잘레스(His name is Pablo Gonzales)라고 했으므로 정답은 (D)이다.

68-70 대화 + 막대그래프

M-Au	Hi, Joanna. [68]**The management group needs to submit nominees for this year's award for outstanding employee. My supervisor wants to know if any managers have nominated anyone yet.**
W-Br	Not yet, Charles. I e-mailed everyone about it a week ago, but I haven't heard anything yet. [69]**I'll have to follow up with the managers and let them know the deadline is coming up.**
M-Au	OK, well, [70]**I printed out a breakdown of the customer service representatives with the most five-star reviews from customers last year.** We had someone who was really outstanding.
W-Br	Those are excellent numbers. Could you go ahead and submit a nomination?

남	안녕하세요, 조애나. **관리자들은 올해 우수 사원 수상 후보자를 제출해야 해요. 관리자 중에 누구라도 추천한 사람이 있는지 상사가 알고 싶어 해요.**
여	아직 없어요, 찰스. 일주일 전에 모두에게 이메일을 보냈는데, 아직 감감무소식이네요. **관리자들에게 후속 연락을 해서 마감일이 다가오고 있다고 알려야겠어요.**
남	그렇군요, 음, 제가 지난해 고객 후기에서 별 다섯 개를 가장 많이 받은 고객 서비스 담당자들을 분류해서 출력했어요. 우리 부서에 정말 뛰어난 분이 있었어요.

여 숫자가 월등하네요. 진행해서 후보 추천을 제출해
주시겠어요?

어휘 nominee 후보자, 지명[추천]된 사람 outstanding
뛰어난 supervisor 상사 nominate 후보자로 추천하다,
지명하다 breakdown 분류, 명세 representative
담당자, 직원

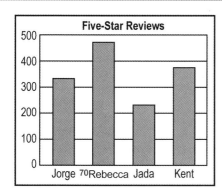

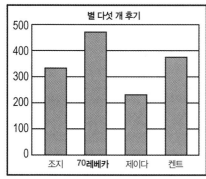

68

What is the conversation mainly about?
(A) A sales strategy
(B) An improvement in customer service
(C) A new manager
(D) An award

대화는 주로 무엇에 관한 것인가?
(A) 판매 전략
(B) 고객 서비스 개선
(C) 신임 매니저
(D) 상

어휘 improvement 개선

해설 전체 내용 관련 – 대화의 주제

남자가 첫 대사에서 관리자들은 올해 우수 사원 수상 후보자를 제출해
야 한다(The management group needs to submit nominees for
this year's award for outstanding employee)고 했고, 관리자 중에
누구라도 추천한 사람이 있는지 상사가 알고 싶어 한다(My supervisor
wants to know if any managers have nominated anyone yet)고
여자에게 알리며 수상과 관련된 이야기를 이어 가고 있으므로 정답은 (D)
이다.

69

Who does the woman say she will send a reminder to?
(A) The management team
(B) The customer service representatives
(C) A magazine editor
(D) A repair technician

여자는 누구에게 알림 메일을 보내겠다고 말하는가?
(A) 관리팀
(B) 고객 서비스 담당자
(C) 잡지 편집자
(D) 수리 기술자

어휘 editor 편집자 repair 수리

해설 세부 사항 관련 – 여자가 알림 메일을 보낼 사람

여자가 첫 번째 대사에서 관리자들에게 후속 연락을 해서 마감일이 다가
오고 있다고 알리겠다(I'll have to follow up with the managers and
let them know the deadline is coming up)고 한 것으로 보아 정답은
(A)이다.

> Paraphrasing 대화의 the managers
> → 정답의 The management team

70

Look at the graphic. Which representative is the man
most likely talking about?
(A) Jorge
(B) Rebecca
(C) Jada
(D) Kent

시각 정보에 의하면, 남자가 말하고 있는 직원은 누구인 것 같은가?
(A) 조지
(B) 레베카
(C) 제이다
(D) 켄트

해설 시각 정보 연계 – 남자가 말하는 직원

남자가 마지막 대사에서 자신이 지난해 고객 후기에서 별 다섯 개를 가
장 많이 받은 고객 서비스 담당자들을 분류해서 출력했다(I printed out
a breakdown of the customer service representatives with the
most five-star reviews from customers last year)면서, 자신의
부서에 정말 뛰어난 분이 있었다(We had someone who was really
outstanding)고 했다. 막대그래프에서 남자가 언급하는 가장 뛰어난 사람
은 레베카이므로 정답은 (B)이다.

PART 4

71-73 광고

> W-Br Looking for an interesting activity to
> celebrate the coming of spring? **71Winford Gardens
> offers an escape filled with calm, peace, and quiet
> just a few miles from the downtown area. Winford**

Gardens has acres of outdoor gardens filled with plants you won't typically find anywhere near here. 72This weekend we will have an exhibition of Mexican blue palms. If you have never seen these striking and unique plants, now is your chance! 73Winford's café is a converted building that used to be a greenhouse. The surrounding tropical plants and flowers help make dining there a pleasure.

봄이 온 것을 기념하기 위해 흥미진진한 활동을 찾고 있나요? **윈포드 가든**은 시내에서 불과 몇 마일 떨어진 곳에서 평온, 평화, 고요함이 가득한 도피처를 제공합니다. 윈포드 가든에는 이 근처 어디에서도 흔히 볼 수 없는 식물들로 가득한 넓은 야외 정원이 있습니다. 이번 주말에 저희는 멕시코블루야자 전시회를 열 예정입니다. 만약 이 인상적이고 독특한 식물을 본 적이 없다면, 지금이 기회입니다! 윈포드 카페는 한때 온실이던 곳을 개조한 건물입니다. 주변의 열대 식물과 꽃들은 그곳에서 하는 식사를 한층 즐겁게 해 줍니다.

어휘 escape 도피 (수단) acres of 넓은, 많은 typically 흔히, 보통 exhibition 전시(회) convert 개조하다

71

What is being advertised?
(A) A trip to Mexico
(B) A city tour
(C) A farm visit
(D) A botanical garden

무엇이 광고되고 있는가?
(A) 멕시코 여행
(B) 시티 투어
(C) 농장 방문
(D) 식물원

해설 전체 내용 관련 – 광고되고 있는 것
화자가 중반부에 윈포드 가든은 시내에서 불과 몇 마일 떨어진 곳에서 평온, 평화, 고요함이 가득한 도피처를 제공한다(Winford Gardens offers an escape filled with calm, peace, and quiet just a few miles from the downtown area)며 윈포드 가든에는 이 근처 어디에서도 흔히 볼 수 없는 식물들로 가득한 넓은 야외 정원이 있다(Winford Gardens has acres of outdoor gardens filled with plants you won't typically find anywhere near here)고 한 것으로 보아 정답은 (D)이다.

72

What event is happening this weekend?
(A) A competition will be held.
(B) Special plants will be on display.
(C) Crops will be planted.
(D) A special sale will take place.

이번 주말에 어떤 행사가 열릴 것인가?
(A) 대회가 열릴 것이다.
(B) 특별한 식물이 전시될 것이다.
(C) 농작물을 심을 것이다.
(D) 특별 할인이 있을 것이다.

어휘 crop 농작물

해설 세부 사항 관련 – 이번 주말에 열릴 행사
화자가 중반부에 이번 주말에 자신들은 멕시코블루야자 전시회를 열 예정(This weekend we will have an exhibition of Mexican blue palms)이라며 이 인상적이고 독특한 식물을 본 적이 없다면, 지금이 기회(If you have never seen these striking and unique plants, now is your chance!)라고 했으므로 정답은 (B)이다.

Paraphrasing	담화의 We will have an exhibition of Mexican blue palms → 정답의 Special plants will be on display 담화의 these striking and unique plants → 정답의 Special plants

73

What does the speaker say about a café building?
(A) It will soon be repainted.
(B) It was once a greenhouse.
(C) It is located near public transportation.
(D) It is closed this spring.

화자는 카페 건물에 관해 무엇이라고 말하는가?
(A) 곧 다시 페인트가 칠해질 것이다.
(B) 한때 온실이었다.
(C) 대중교통 근처에 위치해 있다.
(D) 올봄에 문을 닫았다.

해설 세부 사항 관련 – 화자가 카페 건물에 관해 말하는 것
화자가 후반부에 윈포드 카페는 한때 온실이던 곳을 개조한 건물(Winford's cafe is a converted building that used to be a greenhouse)이라고 했으므로 정답은 (B)이다.

74-76 회의 발췌

M-Au Good afternoon. **74Welcome to this week's managers' meeting here at South Truck Deliveries.** As you know, we've always written performance evaluations for our drivers and other employees on paper. I am pleased to announce some important changes. **75Beginning this year, we will use a software application called Personnel Profile to enter performance appraisals.** Let me introduce Ms. Hwa Young Lee, the head of our IT department. **76She will walk you through how to enroll in a training course on using Personnel Profile, and you will complete your enrollment by the end of this meeting.**

안녕하세요. **여기 사우스 트럭 배송에서 열리는 이번 주 매니저 회의에 오신 것을 환영합니다.** 알다시피, 저희는 항상 운전기사와 다른 직원들의 업무 평가를 종이에 작성해 왔습니다. 저는 몇 가지 중요한 변화들을 발표하게 되어 기쁩니다. **올해부터 퍼스널 프로파일이라는 소프트웨어 애플리케이션을 사용해 업무 평가를 입력할 예정입니다.** 우리 IT 부서의 책임자인 이화영 씨를 소개합니다. **그녀가 퍼스널 프로파일 사용에 관한 교육 과정에 등록하는 방법을 여러분에게 안내할 겁니다. 그러면 여러분은 이 회의가 끝날 때까지 등록을 완료해야 합니다.**

어휘 performance evaluation 업무 평가 appraisal 평가 walk A through B A에게 B를 안내하다 enroll 등록하다

74

Who most likely is the speaker?
(A) A salesperson
(B) A manager
(C) A safety inspector
(D) A software developer

화자는 누구인 것 같은가?
(A) 판매원
(B) 매니저
(C) 안전 검사원
(D) 소프트웨어 개발자

어휘 inspector 검사원

해설 전체 내용 관련 – 화자의 직업
화자가 회의 발체 도입부에서 여기 사우스 트럭 배송에서 열리는 이번 주 매니저 회의에 오신 것을 환영한다(Welcome to this week's managers' meeting here ~ Deliveries)고 한 것으로 보아 정답은 (B)이다.

75

What is the main topic of the talk?
(A) A delivery route
(B) A corporate merger
(C) Performance reviews
(D) Hiring procedures

담화의 주제는 무엇인가?
(A) 배송 경로
(B) 기업 합병
(C) 성과 평가
(D) 채용 절차

어휘 merger 합병 procedure 절차

해설 전체 내용 관련 – 담화의 주제
화자가 중반부에 올해부터 퍼스널 프로파일이라는 소프트웨어 애플리케이션을 사용해 업무 평가를 입력할 예정(Beginning this year, we will use a software application called Personnel Profile to enter performance appraisals)이라며 업무 평가를 위한 새로운 방법에 대해 설명을 이어 가고 있으므로 정답은 (C)이다.

> Paraphrasing 담화의 performance appraisals
> → 정답의 Performance reviews

76

What does the speaker ask the listeners to do?
(A) Pass along some information to workers
(B) Sign up for a training course
(C) Get some information from customers
(D) Talk with employees about their goals for the year

화자는 청자들에게 무엇을 하라고 요청하는가?
(A) 작업자들에게 정보 전달하기
(B) 교육 과정에 등록하기
(C) 고객으로부터 정보 얻기
(D) 직원들과 올해 목표에 관해 대화하기

어휘 sign up for ~에 등록하다

해설 세부 사항 관련 – 화자의 요청 사항
화자가 마지막에 앞에서 소개한 책임자가 퍼스널 프로파일 사용에 관한 교육 과정에 등록하는 방법을 여러분에게 안내할 것이고 여러분은 이 회의가 끝날 때까지 등록을 완료해야 한다(She will walk you through how to enroll in a training course on using Personnel Profile, and you will complete your enrollment by the end of this meeting)고 했으므로 정답은 (B)이다.

> Paraphrasing 담화의 enroll in → 정답의 Sign up for

77-79 전화 메시지

W-Br Hi. This is Ms. Mitra. **⁷⁷You're scheduled to move my furniture to my new apartment tomorrow morning at eight.** **⁷⁸I'm calling because I just learned that the freight elevator in my building is broken,** and my apartment is on a very high floor. I will check first thing tomorrow morning to see what the situation is. But please give me a call as soon as you can. **⁷⁹I have an overseas trip coming up next week,** so this work will have to happen soon.

안녕하세요. 미트라입니다. **내일 아침 8시에 가구를 제 새 아파트로 옮기기로 되어 있는데요.** **방금 건물에 있는 화물용 엘리베이터가 고장 났다는 것을 알고 전화드립니다.** 제 아파트는 꽤 높은 층에 있습니다. 내일 아침에 제가 상황이 어떤지 먼저 확인하겠습니다. 하지만 가능한 한 빨리 전화 주세요. **다음 주에 해외여행이 있어서** 이 일을 빨리 해야 합니다.

어휘 freight 화물 floor 층 situation 상황

77

Who is the speaker most likely calling?
(A) A real estate firm
(B) A moving company
(C) A travel agency
(D) A furniture store

화자는 누구에게 전화하고 있는 것 같은가?
(A) 부동산 회사
(B) 이삿짐 회사
(C) 여행사
(D) 가구점

해설 세부 사항 관련 – 화자가 전화를 거는 대상
화자가 초반부에 청자가 내일 아침 8시에 가구를 자신의 새 아파트로 옮기기로 되어 있다(You're scheduled to move my furniture to my new apartment tomorrow morning at eight)고 말하는 것으로 보아 정답은 (B)이다.

78

Why does the speaker say, "my apartment is on a very high floor"?
(A) To correct a misunderstanding
(B) To negotiate a price
(C) To ask about a property's value
(D) To warn about a situation

화자는 왜 "제 아파트는 꽤 높은 층에 있습니다"라고 말하는가?
(A) 오해를 바로잡으려고
(B) 가격을 협상하려고
(C) 부동산 가치에 대해 문의하려고
(D) 상황에 대해 경고하려고

해설 화자의 의도 파악 – 제 아파트는 꽤 높은 층에 있다는 말의 의도
앞에서 방금 건물에 있는 화물용 엘리베이터가 고장 났다는 것을 알고 전화한다(I'm calling because I just learned that the freight elevator in my building is broken)고 말한 뒤 인용문을 언급했으므로, 고장으로 상황이 힘들 수 있다는 점을 미리 알리려는 의도로 볼 수 있다. 따라서 정답은 (D)이다.

79

What will the speaker do next week?
(A) Host an event
(B) Make a payment
(C) Travel abroad
(D) Begin a new job

화자는 다음 주에 무엇을 할 것인가?
(A) 행사 주최
(B) 대금 납부
(C) 해외여행
(D) 새로운 일 시작

해설 세부 사항 관련 – 화자가 다음 주에 할 일
화자가 마지막에 다음 주에 해외여행이 있다(I have an overseas trip coming up next week)고 했으므로 정답은 (C)이다.

> **Paraphrasing** 담화의 have an overseas trip
> → 정답의 Travel abroad

80-82 안내 방송

M-Cn Good evening, everyone! Welcome to a new season of City Opera. I bring some bad news, I'm afraid. **80Soprano Lisa Gornicka informed me earlier today that she will not be able to perform tonight. I know how disappointing this is.** But I also have good news! Soprano Rita Marks is in town and has agreed to step in for Ms. Gornicka. **81Not only is Ms. Marks familiar with the role of Laura, but she also knows the choreography, since she worked with our director when this production premiered in Toronto.** **82Wondering what her voice is like?** Well, judge for yourself, but I saw the reviews from Toronto. **82I can guarantee that we are in for a treat!**

안녕하세요, 여러분! 시티 오페라의 새로운 시즌에 오신 것을 환영합니다. 죄송하지만 안타까운 소식을 가져왔어요. **소프라노 리사 고르닉카 씨가 오늘 일찍 저한테 오늘 밤 공연을 할 수 없다고 알렸습니다. 얼마나 실망스러우실지 압니다.** 하지만 좋은 소식도 있어요! 소프라노 리타 막스 씨가 시내에 있는데 고르니카 씨를 대신하기로 했습니다. 막스 씨는 로라 역을 잘 알고 있을 뿐만 아니라, 이 작품이 토론토에서 처음 공연되었을 때 감독님과 함께 작업했기 때문에 안무도 잘 알고 있습니다. 그녀의 목소리가 어떤지 궁금하신가요? 음, 스스로 판단해 보세요. 하지만 전 토론토 지역의 비평을 봤어요. 제가 장담하는데, 기대해도 좋습니다!

어휘 disappointing 실망스러운 step in for ~을 대신해서 일하다 choreography 안무 production 작품 premiere 처음 공연[공개]되다 in for a treat 기대해도 좋은

80

Why might the listeners be disappointed?
(A) A performance has been canceled.
(B) A performer will not be appearing.
(C) A new production will be delayed.
(D) A production is not new.

청자들은 왜 실망할 수도 있는가?
(A) 공연이 취소되었다.
(B) 공연자가 출연하지 않을 것이다.
(C) 신작이 지연될 것이다.
(D) 작품이 새롭지 않다.

어휘 appear 출연하다

해설 세부 사항 관련 – 청자들이 실망하는 이유
화자가 초반부에 소프라노 리사 고르닉카 씨가 오늘 밤 공연을 할 수 없다고 알렸다(Soprano Lisa Gornicka informed me earlier today that she will not be able to perform tonight)며, 얼마나 실망스러울지 안다(I know how disappointing this is)고 한 것으로 보아 정답은 (B)이다.

> **Paraphrasing** 담화의 she will not be able to perform
> → 정답의 A performer will not be appearing

81

What does the speaker indicate about Rita Marks?
(A) She has flown in from Toronto.
(B) She taught the speaker.
(C) She has experience with a role.
(D) She is a good friend of the speaker's.

화자는 리타 막스에 관해 무엇을 명시하는가?
(A) 토론토에서 비행기를 타고 왔다.
(B) 화자를 가르쳤다.
(C) 역할을 해 본 경험이 있다.
(D) 화자의 막역한 친구다.

해설 세부 사항 관련 – 화자가 리타 막스에 관해 명시하는 것
화자가 중반부에 막스 씨는 로라 역을 잘 알고 있을 뿐만 아니라, 이 작품이 토론토에서 처음 공연되었을 때 감독님과 함께 작업했기 때문에 안무도 잘 알고 있다(Not only is Ms. Marks familiar with the role of Laura, but she also knows the choreography, since she worked with our director when this production premiered in Toronto)고 했으므로 정답은 (C)이다.

82

What does the speaker imply when he says, "I saw the reviews from Toronto"?
(A) He attended the opera in Toronto.
(B) An audience disliked Lisa Gornicka.
(C) Critics disagree about Rita Marks's performance.
(D) Rita Marks has been praised for her singing.

화자가 "전 토론토 지역의 비평을 봤어요"라고 말할 때 무엇을 의도하는가?
(A) 그는 토론토에서 열린 오페라에 참석했다.
(B) 관객들은 리사 고르닉카를 싫어했다.
(C) 비평가들은 리타 막스의 공연에 대해 의견이 일치하지 않는다.
(D) 리타 막스는 노래로 찬사를 받았다.

어휘 critic 비평가 disagree 의견이 다르다 praise 칭찬하다

해설 화자의 의도 파악 – 토론토 지역의 비평을 봤다는 말의 의도
앞에서 그녀의 목소리가 어떤지 궁금한지(Wondering what her voice is like?) 물었고, 인용문에 이어 장담하는데 기대해도 좋다(I can guarantee that we are in for a treat!)고 한 것으로 보아 목소리, 즉 노래가 기대해도 좋을 만큼 평가가 좋았음을 나타내려는 의도로 볼 수 있다. 따라서 정답은 (D)이다.

83-85 회의 발췌

W-Am Thank you for inviting me and other members of the marketing department to this meeting of the research and development team. **83We always welcome the opportunity to share customer information about our toys with you.** I'd like to start off with some information about the remote-control car that we launched in department stores and toy stores one month ago. It's been a mixed bag. **84Customers love the smooth action**

of the car and the high speed it can achieve. However, they are somewhat disappointed with the rechargeable battery the car comes with. **85I encourage your team to find ways to make the battery charge faster and last longer.**

이번 연구개발팀 회의에 저와 마케팅 부서 직원들을 초대해 주셔서 감사합니다. 저희는 당사 장난감에 대한 고객 정보를 여러분과 나눌 수 있는 기회를 언제나 환영합니다. 한 달 전 백화점과 완구점에서 출시한 리모컨 자동차에 대한 정보부터 시작하려고 합니다. 평가는 갈렸습니다. 고객들은 자동차의 부드러운 움직임과 도달할 수 있는 빠른 속도를 무척 좋아합니다. 하지만 자동차에 딸려 있는 충전식 배터리에는 다소 실망하고 있어요. 배터리 충전이 더 빠르고 더 오래가도록 만들 방법을 그쪽 팀에서 찾아 주시길 바랍니다.

어휘 launch 출시하다 mixed bag (평가나 반응이) 엇갈림
achieve 달성하다 be disappointed with ~에 실망하다
rechargeable 충전이 가능한

83

Where does the speaker most likely work?
(A) At an automobile company
(B) At a data analysis company
(C) At a toy manufacturer
(D) At a department store

화자는 어디에서 일하는 것 같은가?
(A) 자동차 회사
(B) 데이터 분석 회사
(C) 장난감 제조업체
(D) 백화점

해설 전체 내용 관련 – 화자의 근무지
화자가 초반부에 자신들은 당사 장난감에 대한 고객 정보를 청자들과 나눌 수 있는 기회를 언제나 환영한다(We always welcome the opportunity to share customer information about our toys with you)고 한 것으로 보아 정답은 (C)이다.

84

What does the speaker mean when she says, "It's been a mixed bag"?
(A) The product she is discussing cannot be returned for a refund.
(B) Customers often purchase more than one of the product.
(C) A competitor has developed a similar product.
(D) A product has had both positive and negative reviews.

화자가 "평가는 갈렸습니다"라고 말할 때 무엇을 의미하는가?
(A) 그녀가 거론하고 있는 제품은 반품해서 환불받을 수 없다.
(B) 고객들은 종종 제품을 두 개 이상 구매한다.
(C) 경쟁업체에서 비슷한 제품을 개발했다.
(D) 제품은 긍정적인 평가와 부정적인 평가를 모두 받았다.

어휘 competitor 경쟁업체 positive 긍정적인 negative 부정적인

해설 화자의 의도 파악 – 평가는 갈렸다는 말의 의도

인용문 바로 뒤 문장에서 고객들은 자동차의 부드러운 움직임과 도달할 수 있는 빠른 속도를 무척 좋아한다(Customers love the smooth action of the car and the high speed it can achieve)면서 하지만 자동차에 딸려 있는 충전식 배터리에는 다소 실망하고 있다(However, they are somewhat disappointed with the rechargeable battery the car comes with)고 했으므로, 인용문은 제품에 대해 좋은 평가와 나쁜 평가가 둘 다 있음을 알리려는 의도로 볼 수 있다. 따라서 정답은 (D)이다.

85

What does the speaker ask the listeners to do?
(A) Try using the product she is discussing
(B) Improve one part of the product
(C) Get more information from customers
(D) Collaborate with the marketing team

화자는 청자들에게 무엇을 하라고 요청하는가?
(A) 그녀가 거론하고 있는 제품 써 보기
(B) 제품의 부품 개선하기
(C) 고객으로부터 추가 정보 얻기
(D) 마케팅팀과 협업하기

어휘 improve 개선하다

해설 세부 사항 관련 – 화자의 요청 사항

화자가 마지막에 배터리 충전이 더 빠르고 더 오래가도록 만들 방법을 그쪽 팀에서 찾아 주길 바란다(I encourage your team to find ways to make the battery charge faster and last longer)고 요청한 것으로 보아 정답은 (B)이다.

> Paraphrasing 담화의 make the battery charge faster and last longer → 정답의 Improve one part of the product

86-88 안내 방송

> W-Br ⁸⁶Attention, Shopsmart shoppers! ⁸⁷In case you didn't pick up our flyer, we are kicking off a Shopsmart giveaway event. ⁸⁶For every two cans of Shopsmart soup or vegetables that you buy, you will be entered in a drawing to win a gift certificate that can be used at any Shopsmart location. ⁸⁸Gift certificates worth $100 each will be awarded to three lucky shoppers on May first. This offer is good only for Shopsmart-brand canned goods. Act now! Stock up and join the giveaway! The more you buy, the more chances you have to win!

> 숍스마트 고객 여러분, 주목하세요! 전단을 챙기지 못하신 경우를 대비해 저희가 숍스마트 무료 증정품 행사를 시작합니다. 숍스마트 수프나 채소 통조림 2통을 구매할 때마다 숍스마트 어느 지점에서나 사용할 수 있는 상품권을 타는 추첨에 참여하게 됩니다. 5월 1일에 각 100달

러 상당의 상품권이 행운의 고객 세 분에게 증정됩니다. 이번 제안은 숍스마트 브랜드 통조림에만 적용됩니다. 당장 행동하세요! 물건을 쟁이고 경품 행사에 참여하세요! 많이 살수록 경품을 탈 확률은 커집니다!

> 어휘 flyer 전단 kick off 시작하다 giveaway 무료 증정품 drawing 추첨 gift certificate 상품권 stock up 쟁이다, 사재다

86

Where is the announcement most likely being made?
(A) At a supermarket
(B) At a community center
(C) At a restaurant
(D) At a shopping mall

안내 방송은 어디에서 나오고 있는 것 같은가?
(A) 슈퍼마켓
(B) 주민 센터
(C) 식당
(D) 쇼핑몰

해설 전체 내용 관련 – 안내 방송의 장소

화자가 안내 방송 도입부에 숍스마트 고객 여러분은 주목해 달라(Attention, Shopsmart shoppers!)고 하면서 숍스마트 수프나 채소 통조림 2통을 구매할 때마다(For every two cans of Shopsmart soup or vegetables that you buy)라고 한 것으로 보아 정답은 (A)이다.

87

What is the main topic of the announcement?
(A) A discount offer
(B) A new product
(C) A giveaway
(D) A volunteer opportunity

안내 방송의 주제는 무엇인가?
(A) 할인 제공
(B) 신제품
(C) 무료 증정품
(D) 자원봉사 기회

해설 전체 내용 관련 – 안내 방송의 주제

화자가 초반부에 전단을 챙기지 못한 경우를 대비해 숍스마트 무료 증정품 행사를 시작한다(In case you didn't pick up our flyer, we are kicking off a Shopsmart giveaway event)고 한 후, 이 무료 증정품 행사에 대한 안내를 이어 가고 있으므로 정답은 (C)이다.

88

What does the speaker say about some Shopsmart products?
(A) They are not available at all Shopsmart locations.
(B) They are acquired from overseas distributors.
(C) They are currently on sale.
(D) They are the only products that qualify for an event.

화자는 숍스마트 일부 제품에 관해 무엇이라고 말하는가?
(A) 일부 숍스마트 지점에서는 구할 수 없다.
(B) 해외 유통업체에서 구입한다.
(C) 현재 할인 중이다.
(D) 행사에 부합하는 유일한 제품이다.

어휘 acquire 구입하다, 얻다   distributor 유통업체   qualify 부합하다

해설 세부 사항 관련 – 화자가 숍스마트 일부 제품에 관해 말하는 것
화자가 후반부에 5월 1일에 각 100달러 상당의 상품권이 행운의 고객 세 분에게 증정된다(Gift certificates worth $100 each will be awarded to three lucky shoppers on May first)고 하면서 이번 제안은 숍스마트 브랜드 통조림에만 적용된다(This offer is good only for Shopsmart-brand canned goods)고 했으므로 정답은 (D)이다.

> **Paraphrasing**   담화의 good only for Shopsmart-brand canned goods → 정답의 the only products that qualify for an event

89-91 전화 메시지

M-Au Hi, Mr. Collins. I'm calling from Silva's Flooring. **89I was about to place your order for the maple floors that you wanted me to put in, but I decided to call you first. 90,91I just found out that the hardwood distributor has lowered the price of the oak flooring. 91I think you originally preferred oak but decided it was too expensive. The reduction looks to be about fifteen percent.** Please call me back and let me know if I should still order the maple for you or if you would prefer that I order the oak.

안녕하세요, 콜린스 씨. 실바 마루에서 전화드립니다. **설치해 달라고 하신 단풍나무 마루를 막 주문하려던 참인데 먼저 선생님께 전화부터 하기로 했어요. 방금 알았는데 목재 유통업체가 참나무 바닥재 가격을 낮췄다고 합니다. 제가 알기로 원래 참나무를 선호하셨는데 너무 비싸다고 판단하셨죠. 할인율은 15퍼센트 정도 되는 듯합니다.** 제가 고객님을 위해 그대로 단풍나무를 주문해야 하는지 아니면 참나무를 주문하길 원하시는지 다시 전화해서 알려 주세요.

어휘 lower 낮추다   reduction 할인(율)

89
What work was the speaker hired to do?
(A) Deliver firewood
(B) Repair a roof
(C) Install flooring
(D) Complete a landscaping job

화자는 어떤 일을 하기 위해 고용되었는가?
(A) 땔나무 배달
(B) 지붕 수리
(C) 바닥 설치
(D) 조경 작업 완료

어휘 firewood 땔나무

해설 세부 사항 관련 – 화자가 고용된 이유
화자가 초반부에 설치해 달라고 한 단풍나무 마루를 막 주문하려던 참인데 먼저 청자에게 전화부터 하기로 했다(I was about to place your order for the maple floors that you wanted me to put in, but I decided to call you first)고 했으므로 정답은 (C)이다.

90
What does the speaker say about the distributor?
(A) It lowered a price.
(B) It is no longer in business.
(C) It expects a delay.
(D) It has not responded to his request.

화자는 유통업체에 관해 무엇이라고 말하는가?
(A) 가격을 낮췄다.
(B) 더 이상 영업하지 않는다.
(C) 지연을 예상한다.
(D) 요청에 응하지 않았다.

해설 세부 사항 관련 – 화자가 유통업체에 관해 말하는 것
화자가 중반부에 방금 알았는데 목재 유통업체가 참나무 바닥재 가격을 낮췄다고 한다(I just found out that the hardwood distributor has lowered the price of the oak flooring)고 했으므로 정답은 (A)이다.

91
Why did the speaker wait to place an order?
(A) He is not sure what quantity is needed.
(B) He wants a customer to reconsider a decision.
(C) He forgot what the customer requested.
(D) He learned that a product is no longer available.

화자는 왜 주문하려고 기다렸는가?
(A) 수량이 얼마나 필요한지 확신할 수 없다.
(B) 고객이 결정을 재고했으면 한다.
(C) 고객이 요청한 사항을 깜박했다.
(D) 더 이상 제품을 구할 수 없다는 사실을 알게 되었다.

어휘 quantity 수량   reconsider 재고하다

해설 세부 사항 관련 – 화자가 주문하려고 기다린 이유
화자가 중반부에 방금 알았는데 목재 유통업체가 참나무 바닥재 가격을 낮췄다고 한다(I just found out that the hardwood distributor has lowered the price of the oak flooring)고 했고, 화자가 알기로 청자가 원래 참나무를 선호했는데 너무 비싸다고 판단했다(I think you originally preferred oak but decided it was too expensive)면서 할인율은 15 퍼센트 정도 되는 듯하다(The reduction looks to be about fifteen percent)고 한 것으로 보아 변화된 상황에서 청자가 결정을 어떻게 할지 다시 생각하기를 바란다는 것을 알 수 있다. 따라서 정답은 (B)이다.

92-94 소개

W-Am **92Welcome to the Central Valley Environmental Center. 92,93We're so grateful to** all of you, our volunteers, for coming out today to help with this project to install bluebird nest boxes. The Eastern bluebird is a native species that plays an important role in our environment, but it's threatened by habitat loss and predation. **⁹⁴We have numerous donated nest boxes here that will help protect our local bluebird population. Remember that bluebirds prefer open woodlands and grasslands with scattered trees. Some suitable locations are already identified on the maps you've received.**

센트럴 밸리 환경 센터에 오신 것을 환영합니다. 파랑새 둥지 상자를 설치하는 이번 프로젝트를 돕기 위해 오늘 나와 주신 자원봉사자 여러분 모두에게 진심으로 감사합니다. 동부 파랑새는 토종으로 우리 환경에서 중요한 역할을 하고 있지만, 서식지 감소와 포식 때문에 위협을 받고 있습니다. 이곳에 기부받은 둥지 상자가 많습니다. 우리 지역의 파랑새 개체군을 보호하는 데 도움이 될 상자들이죠. 파랑새는 탁 트인 삼림지와 나무들이 여기저기 흩어져 있는 초원을 선호한다는 사실을 명심하세요. 받으신 지도에 적합한 위치들이 이미 식별되어 있습니다.

어휘 native species 토종　threaten 위협하다　habitat 서식지　predation 포식　numerous 많은　donate 기부하다 population 개체군　scattered 흩어진　suitable 적합한

92

Who most likely is the speaker?
(A) A teacher in a classroom
(B) A worker at an environmental center
(C) A salesperson in a sporting goods store
(D) A guide in a natural history museum

화자는 누구인 것 같은가?
(A) 수업 중인 교사
(B) 환경 센터 직원
(C) 스포츠 용품점 판매원
(D) 자연사 박물관 안내자

해설 전체 내용 관련 – 화자의 직업

화자가 초반부에 센트럴 밸리 환경 센터에 오신 것을 환영한다(Welcome to the Central Valley Environmental Center)며 파랑새 둥지 상자를 설치하는 이번 프로젝트를 돕기 위해 오늘 나와 주신 자원봉사자 여러분 모두에게 진심으로 감사하다(We're so grateful to all of you, our volunteers, for coming out today to help with this project to install bluebird nest boxes)고 한 것으로 보아 정답은 (B)이다.

93

What is the purpose of the project?
(A) To recruit volunteers
(B) To release bluebirds into the wild
(C) To provide shelter for bluebirds
(D) To educate people about bluebirds

프로젝트의 목적은 무엇인가?
(A) 자원봉사자를 모집하려고
(B) 파랑새를 야생 방사하려고
(C) 파랑새에게 은신처를 제공하려고
(D) 사람들에게 파랑새에 관해 교육하려고

어휘 shelter 은신처

해설 전체 내용 관련 – 프로젝트의 목적

화자가 초반부에 파랑새 둥지 상자를 설치하는 이번 프로젝트를 돕기 위해 오늘 나와 주신 자원봉사자 여러분 모두에게 진심으로 감사하다(We're so grateful to all of you, our volunteers, for coming out today to help with this project to install bluebird nest boxes)고 했으므로 정답은 (C)이다.

> **Paraphrasing** 담화의 install bluebird nest boxes
> → 정답의 provide shelter for bluebirds

94

What is marked on some maps?
(A) Locations where work can be done
(B) Flight patterns of bluebirds
(C) The location of nearby attractions
(D) Directions to the environmental center

지도에 표시된 것은 무엇인가?
(A) 작업을 수행할 수 있는 위치
(B) 파랑새의 비행 패턴
(C) 주변 명소 위치
(D) 환경 센터로 가는 길 안내

어휘 attraction (관광) 명소　directions 길 안내

해설 세부 사항 관련 – 지도에 표시된 것

화자가 후반부에 이곳에 우리 지역의 파랑새 개체군을 보호하는 데 도움이 될 둥지 상자들이 많다(We have numerous donated nest boxes here ~)면서, 파랑새는 탁 트인 삼림지와 나무들이 여기저기 흩어져 있는 초원을 선호한다는 사실을 명심하라(Remember that bluebirds prefer open woodlands and grasslands with scattered trees)고 한 뒤, 받은 지도에 적합한 위치들이 벌써 식별되어 있다(Some suitable locations are already identified on the maps you've received)고 했으므로, 파랑새 둥지를 설치하기에 좋은 위치가 표시되어 있다는 것을 알 수 있다. 따라서 정답은 (A)이다.

95-97 담화 + 목록

W-Br　Hi, everyone! **⁹⁵I want to update you on sales of our lines of dishware after the introduction of our holiday-themed patterns.** Our everyday dishware continues to perform as expected. Also, I am pleased to report that our New Year plates are a resounding success: total wholesale orders have outpaced those of our popular Dawn series of fine china. **⁹⁶We spent a lot on the design for New Year, so our CEO will be** happy to learn that the investment has paid off. **97Looks like we will need to rethink the Harvest Festival brand, though. Unless total sales reach those of our Café series by next year, we may even discontinue it.**

안녕하세요 여러분! 휴일을 주제로 한 무늬를 도입한 뒤, 당사 식기류 제품군의 판매 현황에 대해 새로운 소식을 알려 드리려고 합니다. 일상 식기류는 기대했던 대로 계속 팔리고 있습니다. 또한 새해 접시가 대성공을 거두고 있다는 점, 알려 드리게 되어 기쁩니다. 총도매 주문이 인기 있는 새벽 시리즈 고급 도자기 주문을 앞질렀습니다. 새해 디자인을 위해 돈을 많이 썼기 때문에, 투자가 성과를 거두었다는 사실을 CEO가 아시면 기뻐하실 겁니다. 그렇지만 추수제 브랜드는 재고해야 할 것 같습니다. 내년까지 총매출이 카페 시리즈 매출에 도달하지 않는다면, 심지어 단종해야 할지도 모릅니다.

어휘 introduction 도입 resounding 완전한 outpace 앞지르다 pay off 성과를 내다 discontinue 단종하다

Pattern	Wholesale Orders (Number of complete sets)
Everyday	7,000
Dawn	5,000
97Café	2,000
Holiday	6,200
New Year	6,000
Harvest Festival	200

무늬	도매 주문(온전한 세트 수)
일상	7,000
새벽	5,000
97카페	**2,000**
휴일	6,200
새해	6,000
추수제	200

95

What product does the speaker's company sell?
(A) Bath towels
(B) Dishware
(C) Tablecloths
(D) Drinking glasses

화자의 회사는 어떤 제품을 판매하는가?
(A) 목욕 수건
(B) 식기류
(C) 식탁보
(D) 유리잔

해설 세부 사항 관련 – 화자의 회사가 판매하는 제품
화자가 초반부에 휴일을 주제로 한 무늬를 도입한 뒤, 자신의 회사 식기류 제품군의 판매 현황에 대해 새로운 소식을 알리려고 한다(I want to

---

update you on sales of our lines of dishware ~ patterns)고 했으므로 정답은 (B)이다.

96

Why will the CEO be pleased?
(A) The company bought a new warehouse.
(B) Customer reviews have been positive.
(C) Shipping costs have gone down.
(D) An investment was successful.

CEO는 왜 기뻐할 것인가?
(A) 회사에서 새 창고를 샀다.
(B) 고객 후기가 긍정적이다.
(C) 운송비가 내렸다.
(D) 투자가 성공적이었다.

해설 세부 사항 관련 – CEO가 기뻐할 이유
화자가 중반부에 새해 디자인을 위해 돈을 많이 썼기 때문에, 투자가 성과를 거두었다는 사실을 CEO가 알면 기뻐할 것(We spent a lot on the design for New Year, so our CEO will be happy to learn that the investment has paid off)이라고 했으므로 정답은 (D)이다.

> **Paraphrasing** 담화의 the investment has paid off
> → 정답의 An investment was successful

97

Look at the graphic. What number of orders does the speaker say the Harvest Festival pattern must reach?
(A) 5,000
(B) 2,000
(C) 6,000
(D) 200

시각 정보에 의하면, 화자는 추수제 무늬 주문이 몇 개에 도달해야 한다고 말하는가?
(A) 5,000
(B) 2,000
(C) 6,000
(D) 200

해설 시각 정보 연계 – 추수제 무늬 주문이 도달해야 하는 개수
화자가 마지막에 그렇지만 추수제 브랜드는 재고해야 할 것 같다(Looks like we will need to rethink the Harvest Festival brand, though) 면서 내년까지 총매출이 카페 시리즈 매출에 도달하지 않는다면, 단종해야 할지도 모른다(Unless total sales reach those of our Café series by next year, we may even discontinue it)고 했고, 목록에 카페는 2,000이라고 나와 있으므로 정답은 (B)이다.

98-100 회의 발췌 + 도표

M-Au **98I'd like to welcome all of you to your first day of work at the Wildcats customer service office.** Baseball season starts in exactly one month.

⁹⁹**We expect ticket sales to be very good because the Wildcats had such a great season last year**. As you can see on the chart, we have four packages. ¹⁰⁰**Make sure you let our customers know about the new Sunday package**. It includes tickets for every Sunday home game throughout the season. Our Friday night package, holiday package, and discount package were available last year and should remain popular.

와일드캣츠 고객 서비스 사무실에 처음 출근하신 여러분 모두 환영합니다. 정확히 한 달 뒤면 야구 시즌이 시작됩니다. **지난해 시즌에 와일드캣츠가 대단히 잘했기 때문에 티켓 판매가 아주 잘 되리라 기대합니다.** 도표에서 보듯이, 4가지 패키지가 있습니다. **고객들에게 새로 나온 일요일 패키지에 대해 꼭 알려 주세요.** 거기에는 시즌 내내 모든 일요일 홈경기 티켓이 포함되어 있습니다. 금요일 밤 패키지, 휴일 패키지, 할인 패키지는 지난해에 이용할 수 있었는데 앞으로도 계속 인기가 많을 겁니다.

어휘 expect 기대하다　include 포함하다　remain 계속 ~이다

Package Name	Number of Games Included
Holiday package	6
¹⁰⁰Sunday package	16
Friday night package	19
Discount package	36

패키지 이름	포함된 경기 수
휴일 패키지	6
¹⁰⁰일요일 패키지	16
금요일 밤 패키지	19
할인 패키지	36

98

Who most likely is the speaker?
(A) A baseball player
(B) A travel agent
(C) A new job applicant
(D) A customer service trainer

화자는 누구인 것 같은가?
(A) 야구 선수
(B) 여행사 직원
(C) 새로운 취업 지원자
(D) 고객 서비스 교육 담당자

해설 전체 내용 관련 – 화자의 직업

화자가 도입부에 와일드캣츠 고객 서비스 사무실에 처음 출근하신 여러분 모두를 환영한다(I'd like to welcome all of you to your first day of work at the Wildcats customer service office)고 한 것으로 보아 정답은 (D)이다.

99

Why are ticket sales expected to be good?
(A) The prices have been reduced.
(B) The team's previous season was successful.
(C) There is a new advertising campaign.
(D) The team has many new players.

티켓 판매는 왜 잘 되리라 예상되는가?
(A) 가격이 인하되었다.
(B) 팀의 지난 시즌이 성공적이었다.
(C) 새로운 광고 캠페인이 있다.
(D) 팀에 새로운 선수가 많다.

어휘 previous 이전의

해설 세부 사항 관련 – 티켓 판매가 잘 되리라 예상되는 이유

화자가 중반부에 지난해 시즌에 와일드캣츠가 잘했기 때문에 티켓 판매가 아주 잘 되리라 기대한다(We expect ticket sales to be very good because the Wildcats had such a great season last year)고 했으므로 정답은 (B)이다.

> **Paraphrasing** 담화의 the Wildcats had such a great season last year → 정답의 The team's previous season was successful

100

Look at the graphic. How many games are included in the new ticket package that the speaker describes?
(A) 6
(B) 16
(C) 19
(D) 36

시각 정보에 의하면, 화자가 설명하는 새로운 티켓 패키지에 포함된 경기 수는 몇 개인가?
(A) 6
(B) 16
(C) 19
(D) 36

해설 시각 정보 연계 – 화자가 설명하는 새로운 티켓 패키지에 포함된 경기 수

화자가 후반부에 고객들에게 새로 나온 일요일 패키지에 대해 꼭 알려 주라(Make sure you let our customers know about the new Sunday package)면서 이에 대한 설명을 이어 갔고, 도표에서 일요일 패키지에 포함된 경기 수는 16이므로 정답은 (B)이다.

실전 TEST 3

1 (C)	2 (D)	3 (B)	4 (C)	5 (B)
6 (A)	7 (B)	8 (A)	9 (A)	10 (A)
11 (C)	12 (C)	13 (A)	14 (B)	15 (B)
16 (C)	17 (C)	18 (C)	19 (B)	20 (C)
21 (A)	22 (B)	23 (C)	24 (C)	25 (A)
26 (B)	27 (B)	28 (C)	29 (A)	30 (B)
31 (C)	32 (B)	33 (C)	34 (D)	35 (A)
36 (B)	37 (C)	38 (B)	39 (D)	40 (A)
41 (B)	42 (A)	43 (D)	44 (B)	45 (C)
46 (C)	47 (B)	48 (D)	49 (A)	50 (C)
51 (A)	52 (D)	53 (A)	54 (B)	55 (D)
56 (B)	57 (C)	58 (B)	59 (B)	60 (C)
61 (A)	62 (C)	63 (B)	64 (D)	65 (C)
66 (B)	67 (A)	68 (A)	69 (C)	70 (B)
71 (C)	72 (B)	73 (B)	74 (C)	75 (C)
76 (D)	77 (C)	78 (A)	79 (D)	80 (C)
81 (A)	82 (D)	83 (D)	84 (A)	85 (D)
86 (C)	87 (A)	88 (D)	89 (B)	90 (D)
91 (B)	92 (B)	93 (A)	94 (C)	95 (C)
96 (A)	97 (D)	98 (A)	99 (C)	100 (D)

PART 1

1 W-Br

(A) A man is standing in a road.
(B) A man is wearing a coat.
(C) A man with tools is bending over.
(D) A man is putting on a hat.

(A) 남자가 도로에 서 있다.
(B) 남자가 코트를 입고 있다.
(C) 공구를 든 남자가 몸을 숙이고 있다.
(D) 남자가 모자를 쓰고 있다.

어휘 bend over 몸을 앞으로 숙이다

해설 1인 등장 사진 – 사람의 동작/상태 묘사

(A) 동사 오답. 남자가 도로에 서 있는(is standing in a road) 모습이 아니므로 오답.
(B) 사진에 없는 명사를 이용한 오답. 사진에 코트(a coat)가 보이지 않으므로 오답.
(C) 정답. 공구를 든 남자(A man with tools)가 몸을 숙이고 있는(is bending over) 모습이므로 정답.

(D) 동사 오답. 남자가 모자를 쓰고 있는(is putting on a hat) 동작을 하는 것이 아니라 모자를 쓰고 있는(is wearing) 상태이므로 오답.

2 M-Cn

(A) There's long grass behind a fence.
(B) There's a door open beneath a light.
(C) There's a pot with flowers by the door.
(D) There's a window overlooking a garden.

(A) 울타리 뒤에 긴 풀이 있다.
(B) 전등 아래에 열린 문이 있다.
(C) 문 옆에 꽃 화분이 있다.
(D) 정원이 내려다보이는 창문이 있다.

어휘 overlook 내려다보다

해설 사물/풍경 사진 – 풍경 묘사

(A) 사진에 없는 명사를 이용한 오답. 사진에 울타리(a fence)의 모습이 보이지 않으므로 오답.
(B) 형용사 오답. 전등 아래에 문이 열려 있는(open beneath a light) 모습이 아니므로 오답.
(C) 사진에 없는 명사를 이용한 오답. 사진에 꽃 화분(a pot with flowers)의 모습이 보이지 않으므로 오답.
(D) 정답. 창문(a window)이 정원을 내려다보고 있는(overlooking a garden) 모습이므로 정답.

3 W-Br

(A) A man is looking in a mirror.
(B) A man is using an exercise machine.
(C) A stairway is being cleaned.
(D) A basket is hanging from the ceiling.

(A) 남자가 거울을 보고 있다.
(B) 남자가 운동 기구를 사용하고 있다.
(C) 계단이 청소되고 있다.
(D) 바구니가 천장에 매달려 있다.

어휘 ceiling 천장

해설 혼합 사진 – 사람/사물/풍경 혼합 묘사

(A) 사진에 없는 명사를 이용한 오답. 사진에 거울(a mirror)의 모습이 보이지 않으므로 오답.
(B) 정답. 남자가 운동 기구를 사용하고 있는(is using an exercise machine) 모습이므로 정답.

(C) 동사 오답. 계단(A stairway)이 청소되고 있는(is being cleaned) 모습이 아니므로 오답.

(D) 동사 오답. 바구니(A basket)가 천장에 매달려 있는(is hanging from the ceiling) 모습이 아니므로 오답.

4 W-Am

(A) A woman is cleaning the floor.
(B) Bottles are being placed on shelves.
(C) A woman is holding a bowl.
(D) A customer is reading a menu.

(A) 여자가 바닥을 청소하고 있다.
(B) 병들이 선반 위에 놓이고 있다.
(C) 여자가 그릇을 들고 있다.
(D) 손님이 메뉴를 읽고 있다.

해설 혼합 사진 – 사람/사물/풍경 혼합 묘사

(A) 동사 오답. 여자가 바닥을 청소하고 있는(is cleaning the floor) 모습이 아니므로 오답.

(B) 동사 오답. 병들(Bottles)이 선반 위에 놓이고 있는(are being placed on shelves) 모습이 아니므로 오답.

(C) 정답. 여자가 그릇을 들고 있는(is holding a bowl) 모습이므로 정답.

(D) 동사 오답. 손님(A customer)이 메뉴를 읽고 있는(is reading a menu) 모습이 아니므로 오답.

5 M-Au

(A) A tablecloth is folded on a chair.
(B) A dining area is prepared for a meal.
(C) Some chairs are being moved to a different room.
(D) Cups and plates are being filled.

(A) 식탁보가 의자 위에 접혀 있다.
(B) 식당이 식사를 위해 준비되어 있다.
(C) 의자들이 다른 방으로 옮겨지고 있다.
(D) 컵과 접시들이 채워지고 있다.

어휘 tablecloth 식탁보 prepare 준비하다

해설 사물/풍경 사진 – 사물 묘사

(A) 동사 오답. 식탁보(A tablecloth)가 의자 위에 접혀 있는(is folded on a chair) 모습이 아니므로 오답.

(B) 정답. 식당(A dining area)이 식사를 위해 준비되어 있는(is prepared for a meal) 모습이므로 정답.

(C) 동사 오답. 의자들(Some chairs)이 다른 방으로 옮겨지고 있는(are being moved to a different room) 모습이 아니므로 오답.

(D) 동사 오답. 컵과 접시들(Cups and plates)이 채워지고 있는(are being filled) 모습이 아니므로 오답.

6 M-Cn

(A) Some people have gathered in an outdoor seating area.
(B) Umbrellas are covering a buffet counter.
(C) Some chairs are stacked on the lawn.
(D) Some people are laughing at a performance.

(A) 사람들이 야외 좌석 구역에 모여 있다.
(B) 파라솔들이 뷔페 진열대를 가리고 있다.
(C) 의자들이 잔디밭에 쌓여 있다.
(D) 사람들이 공연을 보고 웃고 있다.

어휘 gather 모이다 stack 쌓다 lawn 잔디(밭) performance 공연

해설 혼합 사진 – 사람/사물/풍경 혼합 묘사

(A) 정답. 사람들이 야외 좌석 구역에 모여 있는(have gathered in an outdoor seating area) 모습이므로 정답.

(B) 사진에 없는 명사를 이용한 오답. 사진에 뷔페 진열대(a buffet counter)의 모습이 보이지 않으므로 오답.

(C) 동사 오답. 의자들(Some chairs)이 잔디밭에 쌓여 있는(are stacked on the lawn) 모습이 아니므로 오답.

(D) 사진에 없는 명사를 이용한 오답. 사진에 공연(a performance)을 하는 모습이 보이지 않으므로 오답.

PART 2

7

W-Br How was the security audit today?

M-Au (A) I can secure them.
(B) Very productive.
(C) If you like.

오늘 보안 감사는 어땠나요?
(A) 제가 그것들을 지킬 수 있습니다.
(B) 결실이 있었어요.
(C) 원하신다면요.

어휘 security 보안 audit 감사 secure 안전하게 지키다 productive 결실이 있는

해설 보안 감사가 어땠는지를 묻는 How 의문문

(A) 파생어 오답. 질문의 security와 파생 관계인 secure를 이용한 오답.

(B) 정답. 보안 검사가 어땠는지를 묻는 질문에 결실이 있었다는 결과를 알리고 있으므로 정답.

(C) 질문과 상관없는 오답. 제안이나 권유에 대한 응답이므로 오답.

8

M-Cn   What dinner specials do you have today?

W-Am   (A) We have baked salmon.
　　　　(B) For the first time.
　　　　(C) No, I haven't.

오늘 저녁 특선 요리는 뭔가요?

(A) 구운 연어가 있습니다.
(B) 처음이에요.
(C) 아니요, 전 안 했어요.

해설 특선 요리가 무엇인지를 묻는 What 의문문

(A) 정답. 오늘 저녁 특선 요리가 무엇인지를 묻는 질문에 구운 연어라고 구체적으로 응답하고 있으므로 정답.
(B) 질문과 상관없는 오답.
(C) Yes/No 불가 오답. What 의문문에는 Yes/No 응답이 불가능하므로 오답.

9

M-Au   When will the order be delivered?

W-Br   (A) Not until Wednesday afternoon.
　　　　(B) It's time to put them away.
　　　　(C) The light is on in the mail room.

주문품은 언제 배달되나요?

(A) 수요일 오후나 돼야 해요.
(B) 그것들을 치울 시간이에요.
(C) 우편물실에 불이 켜져 있어요.

어휘 put ~ away ~을 치우다[집어넣다]

해설 주문품이 배달되는 시점을 묻는 When 의문문

(A) 정답. 주문품이 배달되는 시점을 묻는 질문에 수요일 오후나 돼야 한다며 구체적인 시점으로 응답하고 있으므로 정답.
(B) 연상 단어 오답. 질문의 When에서 연상 가능한 time을 이용한 오답.
(C) 연상 단어 오답. 질문의 order와 delivered에서 연상 가능한 mail을 이용한 오답.

10

W-Am   What's the monthly membership fee for that service?

M-Au   (A) Twenty euros.
　　　　(B) Next month.
　　　　(C) Don't let me forget.

그 서비스에 대한 월 회비가 얼마인가요?

(A) 20유로입니다.
(B) 다음 달이에요.
(C) 제가 잊어버리지 않게 해 주세요.

어휘 membership fee 회비

해설 월 회비를 묻는 What 의문문

(A) 정답. 서비스의 월 회비를 묻는 질문에 20유로라며 구체적인 금액으로 알려 주고 있으므로 정답.
(B) 파생어 오답. 질문의 monthly와 파생어 관계인 month를 이용한 오답.

(C) 유사 발음 오답. 질문의 for that과 부분적으로 발음이 유사한 forget을 이용한 오답.

11

W-Br   Did you receive the e-mail I sent?

W-Am   (A) I need a receipt for that.
　　　　(B) Call a delivery service.
　　　　(C) I haven't looked at my computer today.

제가 보낸 이메일 받으셨나요?

(A) 영수증이 필요해요.
(B) 배달 서비스업체에 전화하세요.
(C) 오늘은 컴퓨터를 안 봤어요.

어휘 receive 받다   receipt 영수증, 수령

해설 이메일 수신을 확인하는 조동사(Did) 의문문

(A) 파생어 오답. 질문의 receive와 파생어 관계인 receipt를 이용한 오답.
(B) 연상 단어 오답. 질문의 receive에서 연상 가능한 delivery를 이용한 오답.
(C) 정답. 자신이 보낸 이메일을 받았는지를 묻는 질문에 오늘은 컴퓨터를 안 봤다며 확인해 봐야 함을 우회적으로 말하고 있으므로 정답.

12

M-Au   Why don't you have the meeting this afternoon?

M-Cn   (A) Just past the library and across the street.
　　　　(B) Otherwise, I think it's fine.
　　　　(C) Because we have a lot to do today.

오늘 오후에 왜 회의를 안 하시죠?

(A) 도서관을 지나 길 건너편이에요.
(B) 그 외에는 괜찮은 것 같아요.
(C) 왜냐하면 우리가 오늘 할 일이 많아서요.

어휘 past ~을 지나서   otherwise 그 외에는, 그렇지 않으면

해설 회의를 안 하는 이유를 묻는 Why 의문문

(A) 질문과 상관없는 오답. Where 의문문에 대한 응답이므로 오답.
(B) 질문과 상관없는 오답.
(C) 정답. 오늘 오후에 회의를 안 하는 이유를 묻는 질문에 오늘 할 일이 많기 때문이라고 이유를 제시하고 있으므로 정답.

13

W-Br   Where did you post the schedule?

M-Cn   (A) I hung a copy on the conference room door.
　　　　(B) In a few hours.
　　　　(C) Are you sure you submitted it?

일정을 어디에 게시했나요?

(A) 회의실 문에 복사본을 걸어 두었어요.
(B) 몇 시간 후에요.
(C) 제출하신 게 확실한가요?

어휘 post (안내문 등을) 게시[공고]하다   schedule 일정(표)   submit
제출하다

해설 일정을 게시한 장소를 묻는 Where 의문문

(A) 정답. 일정을 게시한 장소를 묻는 질문에 회의실 문에 복사본을 걸었
다며 구체적인 장소를 알려 주고 있으므로 정답.

(B) 연상 단어 오답. 질문의 schedule에서 연상 가능한 hours를 이용한
오답.

(C) 연상 단어 오답. 질문의 schedule에서 연상 가능한 submitted를 이
용한 오답.

14

M-Au   Who is leading the safety seminar?

W-Am   (A) That's what he said.
(B) Elizabeth will do it.
(C) Whenever management prefers.

안전 세미나는 누가 주도하나요?
(A) 그가 그렇게 말했어요.
(B) 엘리자베스가 할 거예요.
(C) 경영진이 원할 때 언제든지요.

어휘 management 경영(진)

해설 세미나를 주도할 사람을 묻는 Who 의문문

(A) 연상 단어 오답. 질문의 Who에서 연상 가능한 대명사 he를 이용한
오답.

(B) 정답. 안전 세미나를 주도할 사람을 묻는 질문에 사람 이름을 제시하
고 있으므로 정답.

(C) 연상 단어 오답. 질문의 leading에서 연상 가능한 management를
이용한 오답.

15

M-Cn   Could you please fill out your time sheet by
3 P.M. today?

W-Br   (A) How much time do you have?
(B) OK, I'll make a note to do that.
(C) I will place the order as soon as possible.

오늘 오후 3시까지 근무 기록표를 작성해 주시겠어요?
(A) 시간이 얼마나 있으세요?
(B) 네, 그렇게 하도록 기억해 둘게요.
(C) 최대한 빨리 주문할게요.

어휘 fill out 작성하다   time sheet 근무 기록표   make a note
기억[명심]하다, 메모하다

해설 부탁/요청의 의문문

(A) 단어 반복 오답. 질문의 time을 반복 이용한 오답.

(B) 정답. 오늘 오후 3시까지 근무 기록표를 작성해 달라는 요청에 네
(OK)라고 대답한 뒤, 그렇게 하도록 기억하겠다며 긍정 답변과 일관
된 내용을 덧붙이고 있으므로 정답.

(C) 유사 발음 오답. 질문의 please와 부분적으로 발음이 유사한 place
를 이용한 오답.

16

W-Am   When is the electrician supposed to get here?

M-Cn   (A) The package got here last night.
(B) I didn't drive to work today.
(C) She just let me know she's running late.

전기 기사가 언제 여기 오기로 했나요?
(A) 소포가 어젯밤에 여기 도착했어요.
(B) 전 오늘 차를 몰고 출근하지 않았어요.
(C) 그녀가 방금 늦는다고 나한테 알려 줬어요.

어휘 electrician 전기 기사   be supposed to ~하기로 되어 있다

해설 전기 기사의 방문 시점을 묻는 When 의문문

(A) 단어 반복 오답. 질문의 get here를 반복 이용한 오답.

(B) 연상 단어 오답. 질문의 get here에서 연상 가능한 drive를 이용한
오답.

(C) 정답. 전기 기사가 여기에 오는 시점을 묻는 질문에 방금 늦는다고 자
신에게 알려 줬다며 더 기다려야 한다는 것을 우회적으로 알려 주고
있으므로 정답.

17

W-Am   I'd like to schedule your performance review
meeting.

M-Au   (A) That is a high-performing team.
(B) The food here is very good.
(C) OK, let me look at my calendar.

업무 평가 면담 일정을 잡고 싶습니다.
(A) 성과가 좋은 팀이에요.
(B) 여기 음식은 정말 맛있어요.
(C) 알겠습니다, 제 일정표를 한번 볼게요.

어휘 performance review 업무 평가

해설 부탁/요청의 평서문

(A) 파생어 오답. 평서문의 performance와 파생어 관계인 performing
을 이용한 오답.

(B) 연상 단어 오답. 평서문의 review에서 연상 가능한 good을 이용한
오답.

(C) 정답. 업무 평가 면담 일정을 잡고 싶다는 요청에 대해 알겠다(OK)고
수락한 뒤, 일정표를 한번 보겠다며 긍정 답변과 일관된 내용을 덧붙
이고 있으므로 정답.

18

M-Cn   Haven't you been trained to use this machine?

W-Br   (A) I can get them to take a look.
(B) We need to finish before noon.
(C) I use it all the time.

이 기계 사용하는 법을 교육 받지 않으셨나요?
(A) 제가 가져와서 볼게요.
(B) 우리는 정오 전에 끝내야 해요.
(C) 전 늘 그걸 쓰고 있어요.

해설 기계 사용법 교육 여부를 확인하는 부정 의문문

(A) 연상 단어 오답. 질문의 machine에서 연상 가능한 take a look을 이용한 오답.
(B) 질문과 상관없는 오답. When 의문문에 대한 응답이므로 오답.
(C) 정답. 기계를 사용하는 법을 교육 받았는지 여부를 묻는 질문에 자신은 늘 그걸 쓰고 있다며 교육을 받을 필요가 없음을 우회적으로 나타내고 있으므로 정답.

19

W-Am Did you bring your computer home or leave it at work?

M-Au (A) Yes, last week.
(B) I left it at the office.
(C) In ten minutes.

컴퓨터를 집에 가져왔나요, 아니면 직장에 두고 왔나요?
(A) 네, 지난주에요.
(B) 사무실에 두고 왔어요.
(C) 10분 뒤에요.

해설 컴퓨터가 있는 장소를 묻는 선택 의문문

(A) Yes/No 불가 오답. 컴퓨터가 있는 장소를 묻는 선택 의문문에 Yes/No 응답은 불가능하므로 오답.
(B) 정답. 컴퓨터가 있는 장소를 묻는 선택 의문문에 사무실에 두고 왔다며 제시된 장소 중 하나를 선택해 응답하고 있으므로 정답.
(C) 질문과 상관없는 오답. When 의문문에 대한 응답이므로 오답.

20

M-Cn Why don't we create a video tour of the convention space?

W-Br (A) I lost it yesterday.
(B) That film has been very popular.
(C) I thought you already did that.

컨벤션 공간을 둘러보는 동영상을 만드는 건 어떨까요?
(A) 제가 어제 잃어버렸어요.
(B) 그 영화는 인기가 아주 많았어요.
(C) 당신이 이미 한 줄 알았어요.

해설 제안/권유의 의문문

(A) 질문과 상관없는 오답.
(B) 연상 단어 오답. 질문의 video에서 연상 가능한 film을 이용한 오답.
(C) 정답. 컨벤션 공간을 둘러보는 동영상 제작을 제안하는 질문에 이미 한 줄 알았다며 제안에 호응하는 의사를 우회적으로 표현하고 있으므로 정답.

21

M-Cn Isn't the food usually served at this time?

M-Au (A) There's been a schedule change.
(B) The reviews of that product have been negative.
(C) I'll go tomorrow instead.

보통 이 시간에 음식이 나오지 않나요?
(A) 일정에 변경이 있었어요.
(B) 그 제품에 대한 후기는 부정적이었어요.
(C) 제가 대신 내일 갈게요.

해설 음식이 나오는지 여부를 확인하는 부정 의문문

(A) 정답. 특정 시간에 음식이 나오는지 여부를 확인하는 질문에 일정에 변경이 있었다며 부정 답변을 생략하고 음식이 나오지 않는 이유를 제시하고 있으므로 정답.
(B) 연상 단어 오답. 질문의 food에서 연상 가능한 reviews를 이용한 오답.
(C) 연상 단어 오답. 질문의 this time에서 연상 가능한 tomorrow를 이용한 오답.

22

W-Br Do you take the bus or train to work?

M-Au (A) I love to travel.
(B) I prefer to drive.
(C) I only work on Tuesdays.

버스로 출근하세요, 아니면 기차로 출근하세요?
(A) 전 여행을 좋아해요.
(B) 전 운전하는 편을 더 좋아해요.
(C) 전 화요일에만 일해요.

해설 출근 방법을 묻는 선택 의문문

(A) 연상 단어 오답. 질문의 bus와 train에서 연상 가능한 travel을 이용한 오답.
(B) 정답. 출근 방법을 묻는 선택 의문문에서 운전하는 편을 더 좋아한다며 제시된 교통편 둘 다를 선택하지 않음을 우회적으로 표현하고 있으므로 정답.
(C) 단어 반복 오답. 질문의 work을 반복 이용한 오답.

23

W-Am Would you like me to make the reservation for you?

M-Cn (A) The hotel has a fitness club.
(B) No, I haven't heard of it.
(C) Sure, let me find the form.

제가 당신을 위해 예약해 드릴까요?
(A) 호텔에 피트니스 클럽이 있어요.
(B) 아니요, 전 못 들었어요.
(C) 네, 양식을 찾아볼게요.

어휘 reservation 예약

해설 제안/권유의 의문문

(A) 연상 단어 오답. 질문의 reservation에서 연상 가능한 hotel을 이용한 오답.
(B) 연상 단어 오답. 질문의 Would you like ~?에서 연상 가능한 대답인 No를 이용한 오답.
(C) 정답. 예약을 해 주겠다고 제안하는 질문에 네(Sure)라고 대답한 뒤, 양식을 찾아보겠다고 말하고 있으므로 정답.

24

W-Am Why are you cleaning the laboratory?

W-Br (A) Just stack the books against the wall.
(B) I will attend if I have to.
(C) Haven't you seen the inspection report?

왜 실험실을 청소하고 있나요?
(A) 그냥 책들을 벽에 기대어 쌓으세요.
(B) 꼭 참석해야 한다면 참석할게요.
(C) 점검 보고서 못 보셨어요?

어휘 laboratory 실험실 stack 쌓다 inspection 점검

해설 실험실을 청소하는 이유를 묻는 Why 의문문
(A) 연상 단어 오답. 질문의 cleaning에서 연상 가능한 stack the books를 이용한 오답.
(B) 질문과 상관없는 오답.
(C) 정답. 실험실을 청소하는 이유를 묻는 질문에 점검 보고서를 보았는지 되물으며 점검 보고서를 보면 알 수 있을 것임을 우회적으로 말하고 있으므로 정답.

25

M-Au What do you think of the highlighted paragraphs in this document?

W-Am (A) I think they need further revisions.
(B) There's some storage space upstairs.
(C) This room has very good lighting.

이 문서에서 강조 표시된 단락에 대해 어떻게 생각하세요?
(A) 수정이 더 필요한 것 같아요.
(B) 위층에 수납 공간이 좀 있어요.
(C) 이 방은 조명이 아주 밝네요.

어휘 highlight 강조 표시를 하다 paragraph 단락, 문단 revision 수정 storage 수납

해설 강조 표시된 단락에 대한 의견을 묻는 What 의문문
(A) 정답. 문서에서 강조 표시된 단락에 대한 의견을 묻는 질문에 수정이 더 필요한 것 같다며 부정적인 의견을 우회적으로 밝히고 있으므로 정답.
(B) 질문과 상관없는 오답.
(C) 유사 발음 오답. 질문의 highlighted와 부분적으로 발음이 유사한 lighting을 이용한 오답.

26

M-Cn Who's going to receive the final delivery?

W-Am (A) When everyone leaves the office.
(B) I can wait for it.
(C) Yes, but only on Fridays.

최종 배송은 누가 받나요?
(A) 모두 퇴근할 때요.
(B) 제가 기다릴 수 있어요.
(C) 네, 하지만 금요일에만요.

해설 배송을 받을 사람을 묻는 Who 의문문
(A) 연상 단어 오답. 질문의 Who에서 연상 가능한 everyone을 이용한 오답.
(B) 정답. 배송을 받을 사람을 묻는 질문에 자신이 기다릴 수 있다며 자신이 배송을 받겠다는 뜻을 우회적으로 알리고 있으므로 정답.
(C) Yes/No 불가 오답. Who 의문문에는 Yes/No 응답이 불가능하므로 오답.

27

W-Br I could book our flights now, right?

M-Au (A) It's a long flight.
(B) The trade show hasn't been confirmed.
(C) It's in the other room.

제가 지금 비행기를 예약하면 되겠죠?
(A) 비행 시간이 길어요.
(B) 무역 박람회는 아직 확정되지 않았어요.
(C) 그건 다른 방에 있어요.

해설 비행기를 예약할지 확인하는 부가 의문문
(A) 단어 반복 오답. 질문의 flights를 반복 이용한 오답.
(B) 정답. 지금 비행기를 예약하면 되는지 여부를 확인하는 질문에 무역 박람회는 아직 확정되지 않았다면서 아직 예약하지 말아야 함을 우회적으로 알리고 있으므로 정답.
(C) 질문과 상관없는 오답. Where 의문문에 대한 응답이므로 오답.

28

W-Am Why do we have to reschedule this event?

M-Cn (A) This weekend or maybe early next week.
(B) I will do it as soon as possible.
(C) My doctor's appointment couldn't be moved.

왜 이번 행사 일정을 다시 잡아야 하죠?
(A) 이번 주말이나 아마 다음 주 초예요.
(B) 제가 가능한 빨리 할게요.
(C) 제 진료 예약을 옮길 수 없었어요.

어휘 reschedule 일정을 다시 잡다[변경하다] appointment 예약

해설 행사 일정을 다시 잡아야 하는 이유를 묻는 Why 의문문
(A) 연상 단어 오답. 질문의 reschedule에서 연상 가능한 weekend와 next week를 이용한 오답.
(B) 연상 단어 오답. 질문의 do we have to에서 연상 가능한 I will do it을 이용한 오답.
(C) 정답. 이번 행사 일정을 다시 잡아야 하는 이유를 묻는 질문에 자신의 진료 예약을 옮길 수 없었다고 이유를 제시하고 있으므로 정답.

29

M-Au We should really consider expanding our storefront.

W-Br (A) Didn't you see the contract for the work?
(B) I don't know how far it is.
(C) We could borrow one for you.

매장 앞에 딸린 공간을 확장할지 정말 고려해 봐야겠어요.

(A) 공사 계약서 못 보셨어요?

(B) 얼마나 먼지 모르겠어요.

(C) 우리가 당신을 위해 하나 빌리면 돼요.

어휘 expand 확장하다   storefront 매장 앞에 딸린 공간   borrow 빌리다

해설 제안/권유의 평서문

(A) 정답. 매장 앞에 딸린 공간을 확장할지 고려해 봐야겠다고 제안하는 평서문에 공사 계약서를 못 보았냐고 되물으며 이미 공간을 확장하기로 했음을 우회적으로 알리고 있으므로 정답.

(B) 연상 단어 오답. 평서문의 expanding에서 연상 가능한 범위 표현 (how far)을 이용한 오답.

(C) 단어 반복 오답. 평서문의 We를 반복 이용한 오답.

30

M-Cn Do you know whose jacket that is in the conference room?

W-Am (A) Sure, if they're already planning to go.
(B) A few people have blue ones like that.
(C) Yes, Janelle usually orders them for us.

회의실에 있는 재킷이 누구 것인지 아세요?

(A) 물론이죠, 그들이 벌써 갈 계획이라면요.

(B) 몇 사람이 그런 파란 재킷을 가지고 있어요.

(C) 네, 보통 자넬이 우리를 위해 주문해요.

해설 재킷이 누구 것인지를 묻는 조동사(Do) 의문문

(A) 연상 단어 오답. 질문의 Do you know에서 연상 가능한 Sure를 이용한 오답.

(B) 정답. 회의실에 있는 재킷이 누구 것인지 묻는 질문에 몇 사람이 그런 파란 재킷을 가지고 있다며 누구 것인지 정확히는 모르겠음을 우회적으로 말하고 있으므로 정답.

(C) 연상 단어 오답. 질문의 whose에서 연상 가능한 사람 이름 Janelle을 이용한 오답.

31

W-Br When do you usually exercise?

M-Au (A) Fitness is important for everyone.
(B) An affordable machine.
(C) My doctor has suggested that I stop for a while.

보통 언제 운동하세요?

(A) 신체 단련은 모두에게 중요해요.

(B) 저렴한 기계예요.

(C) 의사가 저한테 잠시 운동을 쉬라고 권유했어요.

어휘 fitness 신체 단련, 건강   affordable 저렴한

해설 운동을 언제 하는지를 묻는 When 의문문

(A) 연상 단어 오답. 질문의 exercise에서 연상 가능한 fitness를 이용한 오답.

(B) 연상 단어 오답. 질문의 exercise에서 연상 가능한 machine을 이용한 오답.

(C) 정답. 운동을 언제 하는지 묻는 질문에 의사가 잠시 쉬라고 권했다며 현재 운동을 하지 않음을 우회적으로 말하고 있으므로 정답.

PART 3

32-34

W-Br Hello. I heard an announcement on the radio about the garden show you're organizing. They said it's running all week, and ³²**there will be several demonstrations about innovative gardening tools. Could I attend the demonstration scheduled for Wednesday?**

M-Au ³³**Sorry, but that session's just been canceled. The person leading it had another commitment.**

W-Br Oh, too bad. So are all of the demonstrations canceled?

M-Au No, the demonstration for Saturday is still on. That's at 1 P.M. ³⁴**I can register you for that session. Just get there about 15 minutes before it starts so you'll get a good seat.**

여   안녕하세요. 라디오에서 당신이 준비하고 있는 정원 박람회에 관한 공지를 들었어요. 일주일 내내 진행되고, **혁신적인 원예 도구에 관해 몇 차례 시연한다고 하던데요. 수요일로 예정된 시연회에 참석할 수 있을까요?**

남   **죄송하지만 그 시간은 방금 취소됐어요. 진행하는 사람에게 다른 일이 생겼거든요.**

여   아, 저런. 그럼 시연회 전부가 취소됐나요?

남   아니요, 토요일 시연회는 아직 진행하고 있어요. 오후 1시에요. **그 시간에 등록해 드릴 수 있어요. 시작하기 15분 전쯤에만 오시면 좋은 자리를 잡으실 수 있어요.**

어휘 organize 준비하다   run 진행되다, 운영되다   demonstration 시연(회)   innovative 혁신적인   session (특정 활동을 위한) 시간   cancel 취소하다   commitment 약속(한 일), 책무   register 등록하다

32

Why is the woman talking to the man?

(A) She wants to cancel a reservation.

(B) She wants to watch a demonstration.

(C) She wants to rent some equipment.

(D) She wants to hire a gardener.

여자는 왜 남자에게 이야기하고 있는가?

(A) 예약을 취소하고 싶어 한다.

(B) 시연회를 보고 싶어 한다.

(C) 장비를 빌리고 싶어 한다.

(D) 정원사를 고용하고 싶어 한다.

어휘 equipment 장비

해설 전체 내용 관련 – 대화의 목적

여자가 첫 대사에서 혁신적인 원예 도구에 관해 몇 차례 시연한다고 하더라(there will be several demonstrations about innovative gardening tools)면서 수요일로 예정된 시연회에 참석할 수 있을지(Could I attend the demonstration scheduled for Wednesday?)를 묻고 있으므로 정답은 (B)이다.

> **Paraphrasing** 대화의 attend the demonstration
> → 정답의 watch a demonstration

33

What problem does the man mention?
(A) A garden show has been canceled.
(B) A radio program was discontinued.
(C) A presenter is not available.
(D) Some equipment is late arriving.

남자는 어떤 문제를 언급하는가?
(A) 정원 박람회가 취소되었다.
(B) 라디오 프로그램이 중단되었다.
(C) 진행자 시간이 안 된다.
(D) 장비가 늦게 도착하고 있다.

어휘 discontinue 중단하다

해설 세부 사항 관련 – 남자가 언급하는 문제

남자가 첫 번째 대사에서 미안하지만 그 시간은 방금 취소됐다(Sorry, but that session's just been canceled)며 진행하는 사람에게 다른 일이 생겼다(The person leading it had another commitment)고 했으므로 정답은 (C)이다.

> **Paraphrasing** 대화의 The person leading it had another commitment
> → 정답의 A presenter is not available

34

What does the man advise the woman to do?
(A) Talk to the manager on Saturday
(B) Sign up for a class online
(C) Place an order for some tools
(D) Arrive early for an event

남자는 여자에게 무엇을 하라고 조언하는가?
(A) 토요일에 매니저와 대화하기
(B) 온라인으로 수강 신청하기
(C) 공구 주문하기
(D) 행사에 일찍 도착하기

해설 세부 사항 관련 – 남자가 여자에게 하는 조언

남자가 마지막 대사에서 그 시간에 등록해 줄 수 있다(I can register you for that session)고 했고, 시작하기 15분 전쯤에만 오면 좋은 자리를 잡을 수 있다(Just get there about 15 minutes before it starts so you'll get a good seat)고 알려 준 것으로 보아 행사에 미리 와 있으라는 조언을 하고 있다는 것을 알 수 있다. 따라서 정답은 (D)이다.

> **Paraphrasing** 대화의 get there about 15 minutes before it starts → 정답의 Arrive early for an event

35-37

> W-Am ³⁵I have all these estimates from different companies for repairing the brick work in the front of our office building, and they're all really similar. How can I decide?
>
> M-Au ³⁶We're just having the patio at the entrance repaired, right?
>
> W-Am Well, ³⁶we also need a new retaining wall around the garden and to have some additional pathways laid out across the lawn. It's actually quite a complex job.
>
> M-Au Oh. ³⁷Maybe talk to Mr. Lukich in sales. His background is in construction, so maybe he has familiarity with some of the firms and can help you pick one.
>
> W-Am That's a good idea.

> 여 사무실 건물 앞에 있는 벽돌 건조물 수리를 위해 여러 회사에서 이 많은 견적서를 받았어요. 그런데 정말 모두 거기서 거기예요. 어떻게 결정하죠?
>
> 남 입구에 있는 테라스만 수리하는 거죠?
>
> 여 어, 정원 주위에 새 옹벽도 해야 돼요. 그리고 잔디밭을 가로지르는 추가 보도도 깔아야 하고요. 사실 꽤 복잡한 작업이에요.
>
> 남 아. 영업부 루키치 씨와 얘기해 보세요. 건설 분야에 경력이 있죠. 그러니 일부 회사는 훤하게 꿰고 있을 거예요. 한 군데를 선택하는 데 도움이 될 겁니다.
>
> 여 좋은 생각이에요.

어휘 estimate 견적(서) similar 비슷한 patio 테라스 retaining wall 옹벽 pathway 보도 familiarity 잘 알고 있음, 친숙함

35

What does the woman need advice about?
(A) Which company to hire
(B) Which materials to use
(C) When to begin some repair work
(D) Where to lay down some paths

여자는 무엇에 대한 조언이 필요한가?
(A) 어떤 회사를 채용할지
(B) 어떤 재료를 사용할지
(C) 언제 수리 작업을 시작할지
(D) 어디에 길을 놓을지

해설 세부 사항 관련 – 여자에게 필요한 조언 사항

여자가 첫 대사에서 사무실 건물 앞에 있는 벽돌 건조물 수리를 위해 여러 회사에서 많은 견적서를 받았는데 모두 비슷하다(I have all these estimates from different companies ~ and they're all really similar)며 어떻게 결정할지(How can I decide?) 남자에게 의견을 묻는 것으로 보아 작업을 맡길 회사를 고르고 있다는 것을 알 수 있다. 따라서 정답은 (A)이다.

36

According to the woman, why is some repair work complicated?
(A) It will take place during the winter.
(B) It is part of a larger job.
(C) It has been postponed.
(D) It requires a special permit.

여자에 따르면, 수리 작업은 왜 복잡한가?
(A) 겨울철에 할 것이다.
(B) 더 큰 작업의 일부이다.
(C) 연기되었다.
(D) 특별 허가가 필요하다.

어휘 postpone 연기하다 permit 허가(증)

해설 세부 사항 관련 – 여자가 언급한 수리 작업이 복잡한 이유
남자가 첫 번째 대사에서 입구에 있는 테라스만 수리하는 건지(We're just having the patio at the entrance repaired, right?) 묻자 여자가 정원 주위에 새 옹벽도 필요하고 잔디밭을 가로지르는 보도도 추가로 깔아야 한다(we also need a new retaining wall ~ additional pathways laid out across the lawn)고 답하면서 사실 꽤 복잡한 작업(It's actually quite a complex job)이라고 덧붙인 것으로 보아 수리 작업 외에 다른 작업도 해야 함을 알 수 있다. 따라서 정답은 (B)이다.

37

Why does the man tell the woman to talk to Mr. Lukich?
(A) He can perform some construction work.
(B) His sales record is excellent.
(C) His background is relevant to the woman's needs.
(D) He was assigned to the woman's project.

남자는 여자에게 왜 루키치 씨와 이야기해 보라고 말하는가?
(A) 그는 건축 공사를 할 수 있다.
(B) 그의 판매 실적이 훌륭하다.
(C) 그의 경력이 여자에게 필요한 것과 관련이 있다.
(D) 그는 여자의 프로젝트에 배정되었다.

어휘 background 경력, 배경 relevant to ~와 관련이 있는
    be assigned to ~에 배정되다

해설 세부 사항 관련 – 루키치 씨와 이야기해야 하는 이유
남자가 마지막 대사에서 영업부 루키치 씨와 얘기해 보라(Maybe talk to Mr. Lukich in sales)면서 건설 분야에 경력이 있어 일부 회사는 훤하게 꿰고 있을 것이고 한 군데를 선택하는 데 도움이 될 것(His background is in construction, ~ and can help you pick one)이라고 했으므로 루키치 씨는 여자에게 필요한 경력과 정보를 가지고 있다는 것을 알 수 있다. 따라서 정답은 (C)이다.

38-40

W-Am Hi. I'm the general manager of the Sunrise Mall Shopping Center in town. **38I heard your band playing last month at the town fair and got your contact information. I really enjoyed your music.**

M-Cn Thank you! We're a local band and it's always a pleasure to hear from our audience.

W-Am The reason I'm calling is that **39I'm wondering if you'd be interested in playing music at the shopping center on a Saturday afternoon sometime.** The date can be flexible.

M-Cn Sure. We can play the first Saturday of March. But where exactly will we be performing?

W-Am **40There's a detailed map of the shopping center on our Web site. It'll show you where our event space is.**

여 안녕하세요. 저는 시내에 있는 선라이즈 몰 쇼핑센터 총지배인입니다. **지난달 도시 축제에서 선생님 밴드가 연주하는 것을 듣고 연락처를 얻었어요. 음악 정말 잘 들었어요.**

남 감사합니다! 저희는 지역 밴드라서 관객 여러분이 연락 주시면 언제나 반갑습니다.

여 제가 전화를 드리는 이유는 **토요일 오후 언젠가 쇼핑센터에서 음악을 연주해 주실 수 있을지 궁금해서요.** 날짜는 유동적이고요.

남 그럼요. 3월 첫째 주 토요일에 연주할 수 있어요. 그런데 정확히 어디서 공연하게 될까요?

여 **웹사이트에 쇼핑센터 지도가 자세히 나와 있어요. 행사장이 어디 있는지 보일 거예요.**

어휘 fair 축제, 박람회 contact information 연락처
    flexible 유동적인, 변경될 수 있는 detailed 자세한

38

Who is the man?
(A) A marketing agent
(B) A musician
(C) An event organizer
(D) A journalist

남자는 누구인가?
(A) 마케팅 대행사 직원
(B) 음악가
(C) 행사 주최자
(D) 기자

해설 전체 내용 관련 – 남자의 직업
여자가 첫 대사에서 지난달 도시 축제에서 남자의 밴드가 연주하는 것을

듣고 연락처를 얻었다(I heard your band playing last month at the town fair and got your contact information)고 했고, 음악 정말 잘 들었다(I really enjoyed your music)고 한 것으로 보아 정답은 (B)이다.

39

What does the woman want to do?
(A) Host an international fair
(B) Create a new parking area
(C) Organize a concert
(D) Give an interview

여자는 무엇을 하고 싶어 하는가?
(A) 국제 박람회 개최
(B) 새 주차 공간 조성
(C) 콘서트 기획
(D) 인터뷰

해설 세부 사항 관련 – 여자가 하고 싶어 하는 일

여자가 두 번째 대사에서 토요일 오후 언젠가 쇼핑센터에서 음악을 연주해 줄 수 있을지(I'm wondering if you'd be interested in playing music at the shopping center on a Saturday afternoon sometime) 묻고 있는 것으로 보아 정답은 (C)이다.

40

What does the woman suggest the man do?
(A) View a map
(B) Schedule a meeting
(C) Provide references
(D) Decorate a space

여자는 남자에게 무엇을 하라고 권하는가?
(A) 지도 보기
(B) 회의 일정 잡기
(C) 추천서 제공하기
(D) 공간 장식하기

어휘 view 보다 schedule 일정을 잡다 reference 추천서

해설 세부 사항 관련 – 여자의 권유 사항

여자가 마지막 대사에서 웹사이트에 쇼핑센터 지도가 자세히 나와 있다(There's a detailed map of the shopping center on our Web site)며 행사장이 어디 있는지 보일 것(It'll show you where our event space is)이라고 했으므로 정답은 (A)이다.

41-43

M-Au	Hi, Kirstin! ⁴¹**I'm glad to finally see you.** Looks like you've been busy!
W-Br	Yes, ⁴¹**this show is particularly popular.** ⁴¹,⁴²**Jose's paintings really draw a crowd.** ⁴²**He's selling a lot of them, too!**

M-Au Oh, they're great. ⁴²**I'm thinking of buying one myself.**

W-Br You should... sorry I've been so busy lately. I've been swamped at school, plus it's taken a lot to plan this show. Hey, ⁴³**would you want to get together with Janet and Miko for lunch next week?**

M-Au ⁴³**Sure, sounds great.**

남	안녕, 커스틴! **드디어 만나게 돼서 기뻐요.** 바쁘셨나 보네요!
여	네, **이번 전시회는 특히 인기가 많아요. 호세의 그림이 사람들을 많이 불러 모으고 있어요. 그림도 많이 팔리고 있어요!**
남	그림이 훌륭하죠. **저도 한 점 살까 해요.**
여	그러셔야죠… 미안해요. 최근에 너무 바빴어요. 학교 일이 산더미였고, 게다가 이 전시회를 기획하는 데도 시간이 많이 걸렸어요. **다음 주에 자넷, 미코랑 만나서 점심 같이 먹을래요?**
남	**그럼요, 좋아요.**

어휘	show 전시회, 전람회 particularly 특히 draw 끌어들이다 crowd 군중, 사람들 swamp (일이) 넘치다, 쇄도하다

41

Where most likely are the speakers?
(A) At a café
(B) At an art gallery
(C) At a school
(D) At an art supply store

화자들은 어디에 있는 것 같은가?
(A) 카페
(B) 미술관
(C) 학교
(D) 미술용품점

해설 전체 내용 관련 – 대화의 장소

남자가 첫 대사에서 여자에게 드디어 만나게 돼서 기쁘다(I'm glad to finally see you)고 했고, 여자가 이번 전시회는 특히 인기가 많다(this show is particularly popular)며 호세의 그림이 사람들을 많이 불러 모으고 있다(Jose's paintings really draw a crowd)고 한 것으로 보아 미술관에서 대화가 이루어지고 있음을 알 수 있으므로 정답은 (B)이다.

42

What does the man say he might do?
(A) Buy a painting
(B) Speak to Jose
(C) Invite friends to a show
(D) Go home

남자는 무엇을 할 수도 있다고 말하는가?

(A) 그림 구매하기
(B) 호세와 대화하기
(C) 전시회에 친구들 초대하기
(D) 집에 가기

해설 세부 사항 관련 – 남자가 할 수도 있다고 말하는 것

여자가 첫 대사에서 호세의 그림이 사람들을 많이 불러 모으고 있고 그림도 많이 팔리고 있다(Jose's paintings really draw a crowd. He's selling a lot of them, too!)고 하자 남자가 자신도 한 점 살까 한다(I'm thinking of buying one myself)고 했으므로 정답은 (A)이다.

> **Paraphrasing** 대화의 buying one → 정답의 Buy a painting

43

What plan do the speakers make?
(A) To visit some artists
(B) To organize a show
(C) To meet some sponsors
(D) To go out to lunch

화자들은 어떤 계획을 세우는가?
(A) 예술가들 방문하기
(B) 전시회 준비하기
(C) 후원자 만나기
(D) 점심 먹으러 가기

해설 세부 사항 관련 – 화자들의 계획

여자가 마지막 대사에서 다음 주에 자넷, 미코랑 만나서 점심을 같이 먹을지(would you want to get together with Janet and Miko for lunch next week?) 묻자, 남자가 좋다(Sure, sounds great)고 했으므로 정답은 (D)이다.

> **Paraphrasing** 대화의 get together with Janet and Miko for lunch → 정답의 go out to lunch

44-46

W-Am ⁴⁴**Thanks for stopping by, Lin. I'd like to discuss the candidates we interviewed yesterday for the legal assistant position.** ⁴⁵**I was very impressed with Mr. Smith's work history.**

M-Au ⁴⁵**Yeah, he has a lot of relevant experience in the legal field, but he didn't answer our questions very clearly.**

W-Am Still, I think he'd be a great help preparing the legal briefs for our clients.

M-Au ⁴⁶**I'd push for Ms. Wong. Not only was she clear and direct, but I called one of her references, and her former supervisor couldn't praise her enough.**

W-Am That's good to know.... ⁴⁶**Let me take another look at her work history.**

여 와 줘서 고마워요, 린. 어제 면접한 법률 보조직 지원자에 대해 의논을 좀 했으면 해요. 스미스 씨 근무 이력이 정말 인상 깊던데요.

남 네, 그는 법률 분야에서 관련 경험이 풍부하죠. 그런데 우리 질문에 명확하게 대답하지 않았어요.

여 그래도 의뢰인들을 위해 법률 브리핑을 준비하는 데 크게 도움이 될 것 같아요.

남 저는 웡 씨를 적극 추천합니다. 분명하고 솔직했을 뿐 아니라, 제가 추천인 한 사람에게 전화해 봤는데 이전 상사가 침이 마르도록 칭찬했어요.

여 그렇다면 잘됐네요…. 그녀의 근무 이력을 다시 한 번 살펴볼게요.

어휘 stop by 들르다 candidate 지원자 legal 법률의 relevant 관련된, 적절한 push for ~을 추진하다 reference 신원 보증인, (신원 보증인의) 추천서 former 이전의 supervisor 상사 praise 칭찬하다

44

Where do the speakers most likely work?
(A) At a hospital
(B) At a law firm
(C) At a university
(D) At a manufacturing company

화자들은 어디에서 일하는 것 같은가?
(A) 병원
(B) 법률 회사
(C) 대학
(D) 제조 회사

어휘 manufacturing 제조(업)

해설 전체 내용 관련 – 화자들의 근무지

여자가 첫 대사에서 남자에게 와 줘서 고맙다(Thanks for stopping by)며, 어제 면접한 법률 보조직 지원자에 대해 의논을 했으면 한다(I'd like to discuss the candidates we interviewed yesterday for the legal assistant position)고 한 것으로 보아 정답은 (B)이다.

45

Why does the man object to Mr. Smith?
(A) He does not have an extensive work history.
(B) He was late for the interview.
(C) He did not answer questions clearly.
(D) He did not dress appropriately.

남자는 왜 스미스 씨를 반대하는가?
(A) 근무 이력이 많지 않다.
(B) 면접에 늦었다.
(C) 질문에 명확하게 대답하지 않았다.
(D) 복장이 적절하지 않았다.

어휘 extensive 많은, 광범위한 appropriately 적절하게

해설 세부 사항 관련 – 남자가 스미스 씨를 반대하는 이유

여자가 첫 대사에서 스미스 씨 근무 이력이 정말 인상 깊다(I was very

impressed with Mr. Smith's work history)고 하자, 남자가 법률 분야에서 관련 경험이 풍부하지만 질문에 명확하게 대답하지 않았다(Yeah, he has a lot of relevant experience in the legal field, but he didn't answer our questions very clearly)고 했으므로 정답은 (C)이다.

46

What will the woman do next?
(A) Double-check Ms. Wong's references
(B) Answer Ms. Wong's question
(C) Review Ms. Wong's employment history
(D) Bring Ms. Wong in for another interview

여자는 다음에 무엇을 할 것인가?
(A) 웡 씨의 추천서 다시 확인하기
(B) 웡 씨의 질문에 대답하기
(C) 웡 씨의 채용 이력 검토하기
(D) 웡 씨를 다른 면접에 부르기

어휘 double-check 재확인하다

해설 세부 사항 관련 – 여자가 다음에 할 일
남자가 마지막 대사에서 자신은 웡 씨를 적극 추천한다(I'd push for Ms. Wong)면서 분명하고 솔직했을 뿐 아니라, 추천인 한 사람에게 전화해 봤는데 이전 상사가 침이 마르도록 칭찬했다(Not only was she clear and direct, but ~ couldn't praise her enough)고 하자 여자가 그녀의 근무 이력을 다시 한 번 살펴보겠다(Let me take another look at her work history)고 답하는 것으로 보아 여자가 웡 씨의 서류를 다시 살펴볼 것임을 알 수 있다. 따라서 정답은 (C)이다.

> **Paraphrasing** 대화의 take another look at her work history → 정답의 Review Ms. Wong's employment history

47-49

M-Au	Good morning! **⁴⁷This is the front desk. How may I help you?**
W-Am	Yes... Hi... **⁴⁷it's 7 A.M., and I am hearing drilling in the room above me.**
M-Au	That's right. **⁴⁸We are doing bathroom renovations on that floor. We posted notices about the project near the check-in desk and around the lobby.**
W-Am	I have a conference call at 8 A.M.
M-Au	**⁴⁹Let me see about finding an alternate accommodation for you in another wing.**
W-Am	That would be great. Due to a schedule change, I will be working from my room all day.

남	안녕하세요! **프런트입니다. 무엇을 도와드릴까요?**
여	네… 안녕하세요… **아침 7시인데 위층 방에서 드릴 소리가 들려요.**

남	맞습니다. **해당 층에서 욕실 개보수 작업을 하고 있어요. 체크인 데스크와 로비 주변에 공사를 알리는 공지를 붙였는데요.**
여	오전 8시에 전화 회의가 있어요.
남	**다른 동에 손님을 위한 대체 숙소를 알아보겠습니다.**
여	그래 주시면 좋죠. 일정이 변경돼서 하루 종일 제 방에서 일할 예정이거든요.

어휘	alternate 대체하는 accommodation 숙소 wing (건물의) 동[부속 건물] due to ~ 때문에

47

Where most likely is the conversation taking place?
(A) In an office building
(B) In a hotel
(C) In an apartment complex
(D) In a hospital

대화는 어디에서 이루어지고 있는 것 같은가?
(A) 사무실 건물
(B) 호텔
(C) 아파트 단지
(D) 병원

어휘 complex (건물) 단지

해설 전체 내용 관련 – 대화의 장소
남자가 첫 대사에서 프런트(This is the front desk)라며 무엇을 도와줄지(How may I help you?) 묻자 여자가 아침 7시인데 위층 방에서 드릴 소리가 들린다(it's 7 A.M., and I am hearing drilling in the room above me)고 한 것으로 보아 숙박 시설 직원과 투숙객의 대화임을 알 수 있다. 따라서 정답은 (B)이다.

48

What does the woman imply when she says, "I have a conference call at 8 A.M."?
(A) She will not be able to meet the man.
(B) She would like a faster Internet connection.
(C) She would like to check out early.
(D) She cannot work because of some noise.

여자가 "오전 8시에 전화 회의가 있어요"라고 말할 때 무엇을 의도하는가?
(A) 남자를 만날 수 없을 것이다.
(B) 더 빠른 인터넷 연결을 원한다.
(C) 일찍 퇴실하고 싶다.
(D) 소음 때문에 일을 할 수 없다.

해설 화자의 의도 파악 – 오전 8시에 전화 회의가 있다는 말의 의도
남자가 두 번째 대사에서 해당 층에서 욕실 개보수 작업을 하고 있다(We are doing bathroom renovations on that floor)며 체크인 데스크와 로비 주변에 공사를 알리는 공지를 붙였다(We posted notices about the project near the check-in desk and around the lobby)고 말하자 여자가 인용문을 언급한 것이므로, 공사 소음 때문에 일을 하기가 곤란하다는 의도로 한 말이라고 볼 수 있다. 따라서 정답은 (D)이다.

49

What does the man say he will do?

(A) Try to find the woman another room
(B) Give the woman a refund
(C) Bring the notice to the woman's room
(D) Ask that the drilling be stopped

남자는 무엇을 할 것이라고 말하는가?

(A) 여자에게 다른 방 찾아주기
(B) 여자에게 환불해 주기
(C) 여자의 방으로 공지 가져다주기
(D) 드릴 작업 중지 요청하기

어휘 give a refund 환불해 주다

해설 세부 사항 관련 – 남자가 할 것이라고 말하는 일
남자가 마지막 대사에서 다른 동에 여자를 위한 대체 숙소를 알아보겠다 (Let me see about finding an alternate accommodation for you in another wing)고 했으므로 정답은 (A)이다.

> **Paraphrasing** 대화의 an alternate accommodation
> → 정답의 another room

50-52 3인 대화

> W-Br **⁵⁰I like your idea, Mark, about producing a new line of touchless, voice-activated smart lamps. But if we were going to do that, ⁵⁰,⁵¹we'd need to hire a new consultant familiar with that technology, which would not be cheap.**
>
> W-Am **⁵¹Given that we went over on our production costs last year, it doesn't seem likely we'd have the budget.**
>
> M-Au **⁵²What if we reduced our spending on advertising temporarily and used the savings to hire the new consultant?** The decrease in advertising might cause a temporary drop in revenue, but I think we should make up for it when we launch the lamps.
>
> ---
>
> 여1 마크, 비접촉식 음성 작동 스마트 전등의 신제품군 제작에 대한 아이디어가 마음에 들어요. 하지만 그렇게 하려면 그 기술에 정통한 새 컨설턴트를 고용해야 하는데, 비용이 저렴하지는 않을 거예요.
>
> 여2 지난해에 생산 비용을 초과한 점을 고려하면, 예산이 있을 것 같지는 않아요.
>
> 남 광고 지출을 일시적으로 줄이고 절감분을 새 컨설턴트를 고용하는 데 쓰면 어떨까요? 광고가 줄면 수익도 잠시 떨어지겠지만, 전등을 출시할 때 만회할 수 있을 겁니다.
>
> ---
>
> 어휘 voice-activated 음성으로 작동되는 familiar with ~에 정통한 go over 초과하다 reduce 줄이다

> temporarily 일시적으로 decrease 감소 revenue 수익 make up for ~을 만회[벌충]하다

50

What are the speakers mainly discussing?

(A) Employee responsibilities
(B) An advertising campaign
(C) Developing a new product
(D) A type of phone

화자들은 주로 무엇에 대해 논의하고 있는가?

(A) 직원 책무
(B) 광고 캠페인
(C) 신제품 개발
(D) 전화기 종류

해설 전체 내용 관련 – 대화의 주제
첫 번째 여자가 첫 대사에서 남자의 비접촉식 음성 작동 스마트 전등의 신제품군 제작에 대한 아이디어가 마음에 든다(I like your idea, Mark, about producing a new line of touchless, voice-activated smart lamps)고 한 뒤, 하지만 그렇게 하려면 그 기술에 정통한 새 컨설턴트를 고용해야 하는데, 비용이 저렴하지는 않을 것(But if we were going to do that, we'd need to hire a new consultant familiar with that technology, which would not be cheap)이라며 문제점을 제기한 후, 신제품 개발에 대한 다른 화자들의 의견을 들으며 이야기를 이어 가고 있으므로 정답은 (C)이다.

> **Paraphrasing** 대화의 producing a new line
> → 정답의 Developing a new product

51

What do the women imply about hiring a new consultant?

(A) It would be expensive.
(B) It might not solve their problem.
(C) It will be challenging to find someone with the right skills.
(D) It has already happened.

여자들은 새 컨설턴트 고용에 대해 무엇을 암시하는가?

(A) 비용이 많이 들 것이다.
(B) 문제를 해결하지 못할 수도 있다.
(C) 적합한 역량을 가진 사람을 찾기가 어려울 것이다.
(D) 이미 고용했다.

어휘 challenging 어려운

해설 세부 사항 관련 – 새 컨설턴트 고용에 대해 여자들이 암시하는 것
첫 번째 여자가 첫 대사에서 그 기술에 정통한 새 컨설턴트를 고용해야 하는데, 비용이 저렴하지는 않을 것(we'd need to hire a new consultant familiar with that technology, which would not be cheap)이라고 지적하자 두 번째 여자가 지난해에 생산 비용을 초과한 점을 고려하면, 예산이 없을 것 같다(Given that we went over on our production costs last year, it doesn't seem likely we'd have the budget)고 맞장구를 치고 있으므로 정답은 (A)이다.

52

What does the man suggest they do?
(A) Stop production
(B) Hire temporary employees
(C) Review costs
(D) Spend less on advertising

남자는 무엇을 하자고 제안하는가?
(A) 생산 중지
(B) 임시직 직원 채용
(C) 비용 검토
(D) 광고 비용 절감

해설 세부 사항 관련 – 남자의 제안 사항

마지막 대사에서 남자가 광고 지출을 일시적으로 줄이고 절감분을 새 컨설턴트를 고용하는 데 쓰면 어떨지(What if we reduced our spending on advertising temporarily and used the savings to hire the new consultant?) 제안하고 있으므로 정답은 (D)이다.

53-55

M-Au	53Have you been having any problems with the therapeutic ultrasound machine? My patient just said he didn't feel his muscles were responding as usual.
W-Am	It has been acting funny. Perhaps we should call the technician?
M-Au	Maybe. I'm afraid it's getting pretty old, though. We may need to replace it.
W-Am	OK. 54I'll notify Barbara since she has to sign off on all purchases.
M-Au	By the way, 55can you see Mr. Cohen for me tomorrow? He just needs to do some exercises for his wrist. He's been responding well to the treatment.

남	치료용 초음파 기계에 무슨 문제라도 있었나요? 방금 환자가 그러는데 근육이 평소처럼 반응하지 않는 것 같다네요.
여	이상하게 작동하고 있긴 해요. 기사를 불러야 할까요?
남	아마도요. 그런데 꽤 낡아서 그런 것 같아요. 교체해야 할 수도 있어요.
여	네. 구매 건은 바바라가 모두 승인해야 하니까 제가 바바라에게 알릴게요.
남	그건 그렇고, 내일 저 대신 코헨 씨 좀 봐주시겠어요? 손목 운동만 하면 돼요. 치료에 대한 차도를 보이고 있고요.

53

Where most likely are the speakers?
(A) In a medical office
(B) At a repair shop
(C) At a department store
(D) In a warehouse

화자들은 어디에 있는 것 같은가?
(A) 진료소
(B) 수리점
(C) 백화점
(D) 창고

해설 전체 내용 관련 – 대화의 장소

남자가 첫 대사에서 치료용 초음파 기계에 무슨 문제라도 있었는지(Have you been having any problems with the therapeutic ultrasound machine?) 물으며 방금 환자가 말하는데 근육이 평소처럼 반응하지 않는 것 같다(My patient just said he didn't feel his muscles were responding as usual)고 했으므로 화자들은 의료 기관에서 대화를 나누고 있음을 알 수 있다. 따라서 정답은 (A)이다.

54

Who most likely is Barbara?
(A) A technician
(B) A manager
(C) A salesperson
(D) A fitness instructor

바바라는 누구인 것 같은가?
(A) 기술자
(B) 매니저
(C) 판매원
(D) 피트니스 강사

해설 세부 사항 관련 – 바바라의 직업

여자가 두 번째 대사에서 구매 건은 바바라가 모두 승인해야 하니까 자신이 바바라에게 알리겠다(I'll notify Barbara since she has to sign off on all purchases)고 한 것으로 보아 바바라는 관리직에 있는 직원임을 알 수 있다. 따라서 정답은 (B)이다.

55

What does the man ask the woman to do?
(A) Order some supplies
(B) Call Barbara
(C) Reserve an exercise room
(D) Help a patient tomorrow

남자는 여자에게 무엇을 해 달라고 요청하는가?

(A) 비품 주문하기
(B) 바바라에게 전화하기
(C) 운동실 예약하기
(D) 내일 환자 돕기

해설 세부 사항 관련 – 남자의 요청 사항

남자가 마지막 대사에서 여자에게 내일 자신 대신 코헨 씨를 봐줄 수 있는지(can you see Mr. Cohen for me tomorrow?) 물었고, 손목 운동만 하면 된다(He just needs to do some exercises for his wrist)고 자신의 환자인 코헨 씨에 대해 도움을 요청하고 있음을 알 수 있다. 따라서 정답은 (D)이다.

> Paraphrasing 대화의 see Mr. Cohen for me
> → 정답의 Help a patient

56-58

M-Au **[58]I'm preparing the budget report for our monthly meeting, but [56]can I ask you about the bill for landscaping? It seems very high.**

W-Br Keep in mind that they maintain the parking area and outdoor lighting.

M-Au Well, **[57,58]the real issue is that we share the expenses with the medical clinic next door. With patients coming to the clinic, they use far more parking spaces than we do. And the way we divide the cost should reflect that.**

W-Br I think you're right. **[58]I'll e-mail the clinic about it.**

남 제가 월례 회의를 위해 예산 보고서를 준비하고 있는데요, 조경 비용 청구서에 관해 좀 여쭤봐도 될까요? 너무 비싼 것 같아요.

여 유념하세요. 그들이 주차장과 실외 조명 유지 관리를 맡고 있어요.

남 어, 진짜 문제는 우리가 이웃하고 있는 병원과 비용을 분담한다는 사실이에요. 환자들이 병원에 오면서 우리보다 주차 공간을 훨씬 더 많이 쓰고 있어요. 그러니 비용을 나누는 방식에 이 사실을 반영해야 해요.

여 일리가 있네요. **병원에 이메일을 보낼게요.**

어휘 budget 예산 landscaping 조경 maintain 유지 관리하다 expense 비용 patient 환자 reflect 반영하다

56

What does the woman imply when she says, "they maintain the parking area and outdoor lighting"?

(A) Items were mistakenly added to a bill.
(B) Some costs might be reasonable.
(C) New rates went into effect.
(D) A billing period is longer than one month.

여자가 "그들이 주차장과 실외 조명 유지 관리를 맡고 있어요"라고 말할 때 무엇을 의미하는가?

(A) 실수로 청구서에 항목들이 추가되었다.
(B) 비용이 합리적일 수 있다.
(C) 새로운 요금이 시행되었다.
(D) 청구 기간이 한 달보다 길다.

어휘 go into effect 시행되다, 발효되다

해설 화자의 의도 파악 – 그들이 주차장과 실외 조명 유지 관리를 맡고 있다는 말의 의도

인용문은 남자가 조경 비용 청구서에 관해 좀 물어봐도 될지(can I ask you about the bill for landscaping?)라면서 너무 비싼 것 같다(It seems very high)는 의견에 대한 대답이므로 청구 비용이 포함하는 서비스에 비하면 사실상 비싸지 않을 수도 있다는 뜻을 전하려는 의도로 볼 수 있다. 따라서 정답은 (B)이다.

57

What does the man think a medical clinic should do?

(A) Hire more employees
(B) Use fewer parking spaces
(C) Pay a larger share of a bill
(D) Move to a new building

남자는 병원이 무엇을 해야 한다고 생각하는가?

(A) 추가 직원 채용하기
(B) 주차 공간 더 적게 사용하기
(C) 청구서의 더 많은 부담금 지불하기
(D) 새 건물로 이전하기

어휘 share 부담(금), 할당량

해설 세부 사항 관련 – 남자가 병원이 해야 한다고 생각하는 것

남자가 두 번째 대사에서 진짜 문제는 자신들이 이웃하고 있는 병원과 비용을 분담한다는 사실(the real issue is that we share the expenses with the medical clinic next door)이라고 했고, 환자들이 병원에 오면서 자신들보다 주차 공간을 훨씬 더 많이 쓰고 있다(With patients coming to the clinic, they use far more parking spaces than we do)며 비용을 나누는 방식에 이 사실을 반영해야 한다(And the way we divide the cost should reflect that)고 했으므로 병원이 비용을 더 분담해야 한다고 생각하고 있음을 알 수 있다. 따라서 정답은 (C)이다.

> Paraphrasing 대화의 the way we divide the cost should reflect that
> → 정답의 Pay a larger share of a bill

58

What will the woman most likely do at the monthly meeting?

(A) Choose a new landscaping company
(B) Discuss a payment arrangement
(C) Suggest enlarging the parking lot
(D) Review a plan for new outdoor lighting

여자는 월례 회의에서 무엇을 할 것 같은가?
(A) 새 조경 회사 선택
(B) 지급 방식 논의
(C) 주차장 확장 제안
(D) 새로운 실외 조명 계획 검토

어휘 arrangement (처리) 방식　enlarge 확장하다

해설 세부 사항 관련 – 여자가 월례 회의에서 할 일
남자가 첫 대사에서 월례 회의를 위해 예산 보고서를 준비하고 있다(I'm preparing the budget report for our monthly meeting)고 했고, 두 번째 대사에서 자신들이 이웃하고 있는 병원과 비용을 분담(we share the expenses with the medical clinic next door)하는데 환자들이 병원에 오면서 자신들보다 주차 공간을 훨씬 더 많이 쓰고 있다(With patients coming to the clinic, they use far more parking spaces than we do)면서 비용을 나누는 방식에 이 사실을 반영해야 한다(And the way we divide the cost should reflect that)고 문제 제기를 하자 여자가 그것에 대해 병원에 이메일을 보내겠다(I'll e-mail the clinic about it)고 했다. 따라서 여자는 월례 회의에 참가해 비용을 나누는 방식에 대해 논의를 할 것임을 알 수 있으므로 정답은 (B)이다.

59-61 3인 대화

W-Am Thank you both for that lovely dinner. **⁵⁹What a nice way to celebrate that our two companies will be working together in the future.**

M-Cn We've often held business dinners here. Say, **⁶⁰I wanted to mention how much I liked the speech you gave at our meeting today.** Very inspiring!

W-Am Ah, thank you... So, I'm in town until tomorrow afternoon. **⁶¹Ms. Rice, should I come by your office in the morning to sign the last few papers?**

W-Br **⁶¹Yes,** I'll be in at eight thirty... well, actually, make that nine. Does that give you enough time before your flight?

W-Am Yes, that should be plenty of time.

여1 두 분 다 고마워요. 저녁 맛있게 잘 먹었어요. **앞으로 우리 두 회사가 함께 일하게 된 것을 이렇게 축하하다니 얼마나 멋진지 몰라요.**

남 저희는 종종 이곳에서 사업상 식사를 하곤 해요. 어, **오늘 회의에서 하신 연설이 얼마나 좋았는지 말하고 싶었어요.** 너무 고무적이었어요!

여1 아, 고마워요… 전 내일 오후까지 시내에 있을 거예요. **라이스 씨, 제가 오전에 사무실에 들러서 마지막 서류 몇 장에 서명해도 될까요?**

여2 네, 제가 8시 30분에는 회사에 나와 있을 거예요… 음, 실은, 9시로 해요. 그렇게 하면 비행기 타기 전까지 시간이 충분한가요?

여1 네, 시간은 충분할 거예요.

59

Why are the speakers celebrating?
(A) A new restaurant is opening.
(B) Their companies will be working together.
(C) They have received an important loan.
(D) They have received an award.

화자들은 왜 축하하고 있는가?
(A) 새 레스토랑이 문을 연다.
(B) 회사들이 협업할 것이다.
(C) 중요한 대출을 받았다.
(D) 상을 받았다.

해설 세부 사항 관련 – 화자들이 축하하는 이유
첫 번째 여자가 첫 대사에서 앞으로 자신들의 두 회사가 함께 일하게 된 것을 이렇게 축하하게 되어 멋지다(What a nice way to celebrate that our two companies will be working together in the future)고 했으므로 정답은 (B)이다.

60

What does the man say he liked about a meeting today?
(A) Some unexpected news
(B) Some photos from a presentation
(C) A speech that was given
(D) A change to the agenda

남자는 오늘 회의에 관해 무엇이 좋았다고 말하는가?
(A) 뜻밖의 소식
(B) 프레젠테이션 사진
(C) 연설
(D) 의제 변경

어휘 unexpected 뜻밖의, 의외의

해설 세부 사항 관련 – 남자가 오늘 회의에 관해 좋았다고 말하는 것
남자가 첫 대사에서 오늘 회의에서 한 연설이 얼마나 좋았는지 말하고 싶었다(I wanted to mention how much I liked the speech you gave at our meeting today)고 했으므로 정답은 (C)이다.

> **Paraphrasing** 대화의 the speech you gave
> → 정답의 A speech that was given

61

What will the women do tomorrow morning?
(A) Finalize some paperwork
(B) Meet at the airport
(C) Make sure the office is locked up
(D) Compare some reports

여자들은 내일 아침에 무엇을 할 것인가?

(A) 서류 작업 마무리하기
(B) 공항에서 만나기
(C) 사무실이 잠겼는지 확인하기
(D) 보고서 비교하기

해설 세부 사항 관련 – 여자들이 내일 아침에 할 일

첫 번째 여자가 두 번째 대사에서 두 번째 여자인 라이스 씨(Ms. Rice)에게 자신이 오전에 사무실에 들러서 마지막 서류 몇 장에 서명해도 될지(should I come by your office in the morning to sign the last few papers?)를 묻자 두 번째 여자가 네(Yes)라고 대답한 것으로 보아 정답은 (A)이다.

> **Paraphrasing** 대화의 sign the last few papers
> → 정답의 Finalize some paperwork

62-64 대화 + 일정표

M-Au **⁶²Are we all set for the event? The food is prepared, and the beverages are ready. They're loading the truck now.** I confirmed the music and other entertainment. And I think we'll arrive early.

W-Am That's good because **⁶³I was actually worried that one hour wouldn't have been enough to get everything ready.**

M-Au I agree. How does the rest of the schedule look?

W-Am The timing looks good. **⁶⁴I wonder if we could actually finish up early at the end of the night. Why don't you tell Pierre to bring the truck back at eleven thirty?**

M-Au OK. He should be finished with his hotel delivery by then.

남 **행사 준비는 다 됐나요? 음식은 준비됐고, 음료도 준비됐군요. 지금 사람들이 트럭에 싣고 있어요.** 음악과 기타 여흥은 제가 확인했어요. 그리고 우리가 일찍 도착할 것 같네요.

여 잘됐네요. **전부 준비하려면 한 시간으로는 부족할까 봐 사실 걱정했거든요.**

남 동감이에요. 나머지 일정은 어때 보여요?

여 시간 배분이 잘된 것 같아요. **우리가 실제로 자정 전에 빨리 끝낼 수 있을지 궁금하네요. 피에르에게 11시 30분에 트럭을 가져오라고 하는 게 어때요?**

남 그럴게요. 그때쯤이면 피에르가 호텔 배달을 마칠 거예요.

어휘 be set for ~할 준비가 되다　load 짐을 싣다　confirm 확인하다

Time	Task
5:00	Arrive
⁶³5:00–6:00	Set up
7:00–10:00	Reception
10:00–10:30	Entertainment
10:30–midnight	Clean up

시간	업무
5:00	도착
⁶³5:00-6:00	준비
7:00-10:00	연회
10:00-10:30	여흥
10:30-자정	청소

62

What industry do the speakers most likely work in?
(A) Shipping
(B) Music recording
(C) Catering
(D) Tourism

화자들은 어떤 업종에서 일하는 것 같은가?
(A) 배송
(B) 음악 녹음
(C) 출장 연회
(D) 관광

해설 전체 내용 관련 – 화자들의 근무 업계

남자가 첫 대사에서 여자에게 행사 준비는 다 됐는지(Are we all set for the event?) 묻고 음식은 준비됐고, 음료도 준비됐다(The food is prepared, and the beverages are ready)면서 지금 사람들이 트럭에 싣고 있다(They're loading the truck now)고 한 것으로 보아 정답은 (C)이다.

63

Look at the graphic. What task in the schedule does the woman express concern about?
(A) Arrive
(B) Set up
(C) Entertainment
(D) Clean up

시각 정보에 의하면, 여자는 일정에서 어떤 업무를 걱정하는가?
(A) 도착
(B) 준비
(C) 여흥
(D) 청소

해설 시각 정보 연계 – 여자가 걱정하는 업무

여자가 첫 번째 대사에서 전부 준비하려면 한 시간으로는 부족할까 봐 걱정했다(I was actually worried that one hour wouldn't have been enough to get everything ready)고 했고, 일정표에서 한 시간이 소요되는 작업은 준비(Set up)이므로 정답은 (B)이다.

64

What does the woman ask the man to do?
(A) Check on a hotel delivery
(B) Help to prepare some food
(C) Help to load some supplies
(D) Arrange for the truck to arrive early

여자는 남자에게 무엇을 하라고 요청하는가?
(A) 호텔 배달 확인하기
(B) 음식 준비 돕기
(C) 비품 적재 돕기
(D) 트럭이 일찍 도착하도록 준비하기

해설 세부 사항 관련 – 여자가 남자에게 요청하는 것
여자가 마지막 대사에서 자신들이 자정 전에 빨리 끝낼 수 있을지 궁금하다(I wonder if we could actually finish ~ night)며 피에르에게 11시 30분에 트럭을 가져오라고 하는 게 어떨지(Why don't you tell Pierre to bring the truck back at eleven thirty?) 남자에게 묻고 있으므로 정답은 (D)이다.

> **Paraphrasing** 대화의 tell Pierre to bring the truck back at eleven thirty → 정답의 Arrange for the truck to arrive early

65-67 대화 + 지도

> W-Am ⁶⁵,⁶⁷**Are you all set for the environmental fair our company is putting on at the park this weekend?** I just finished finding supplies for my game about recycling.
>
> M-Cn Yes, I've finished writing the questions for the environmental trivia game I'm leading. Hey, I wanted to check with you: ⁶⁶**What else can I do to be helpful that day?** Would you like me to hang signs or something? Help decorate?
>
> W-Am ⁶⁶**One thing we could use is someone to stand at the park entrance and direct people to the pavilion where the fair will take place.**
>
> M-Cn Wait, ⁶⁷**aren't there several entrances to the park?**
>
> W-Am Yes, but ⁶⁷**only the entrance on Court Street is open on weekends.**

> 여 이번 주말에 우리 회사가 공원에서 여는 환경 박람회 준비는 다 됐나요? 전 방금 재활용 게임용 비품 찾는 일을 마쳤어요.
> 남 네, 전 제가 진행할 환경 상식 퀴즈 질문 작성을 마쳤어요. 저, 확인하고 싶은 게 있었어요. 그날 제가 도움이 될 만한 일이 또 뭐가 있을까요? 표지판 같은 걸 걸까요? 장식하는 일을 도울까요?
> 여 도움이 될 만한 게 하나 있는데 누가 공원 입구에 서서 박람회가 열리는 파빌리온으로 사람들을 안내하는 거예요.
> 남 잠깐만요, 공원 입구가 여러 군데 있지 않나요?

여 네, 하지만 주말에는 코트 가에 있는 입구만 열어요.

> 어휘 environmental 환경의 fair 박람회 put on (전람회 등을) 개최하다 supplies 비품 recycling 재활용 trivia 퀴즈, 잡학 direct 길을 안내하다 pavilion (공원의) 파빌리온, 정자 take place 열리다

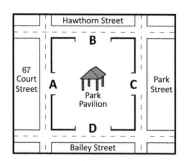

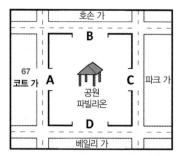

65

What event will the speakers attend at the park this weekend?
(A) A picnic
(B) An athletic event
(C) An environmental fair
(D) A volunteer trash cleanup

화자들은 이번 주말 공원에서 열리는 어떤 행사에 참석할 것인가?
(A) 소풍
(B) 체육 행사
(C) 환경 박람회
(D) 쓰레기 줍기 자원봉사

어휘 athletic 체육의 trash 쓰레기

해설 전체 내용 관련 – 화자들이 이번 주말에 참석할 행사
여자가 첫 대사에서 남자에게 이번 주말에 자신들의 회사가 공원에서 여는 환경 박람회 준비는 다 됐는지(Are you all set for the environmental fair our company is putting on at the park this weekend?)를 묻고 있으므로 정답은 (C)이다.

66

What does the woman ask the man to do the day of the event?
(A) Hand out prizes
(B) Direct people where to go
(C) Decorate the park pavilion
(D) Hang up signs

여자는 남자에게 행사 당일 무엇을 해 달라고 요청하는가?
(A) 상품 나눠 주기
(B) 사람들에게 가는 길 안내하기
(C) 공원 파빌리온 장식하기
(D) 표지판 걸기

해설 세부 사항 관련 – 여자가 남자에게 행사 당일 요청하는 일

남자가 첫 번째 대사에서 그날 자신이 도움이 될 만한 일이 또 뭐가 있을지(What else can I do to be helpful that day?) 묻자 여자가 누가 공원 입구에 서서 박람회가 열리는 파빌리온으로 사람들을 안내하면 좋겠다(One thing we could use is someone to stand at the park entrance and direct people to the pavilion where the fair will take place)고 했으므로 정답은 (B)이다.

> **Paraphrasing** 대화의 direct people to the pavilion
> → 정답의 Direct people where to go

67

Look at the graphic. Which entrance will participants use for the event?
(A) Entrance A
(B) Entrance B
(C) Entrance C
(D) Entrance D

시각 정보에 의하면, 참가자들은 행사에 어느 입구를 이용할 것인가?
(A) 입구 A
(B) 입구 B
(C) 입구 C
(D) 입구 D

해설 시각 정보 연계 – 참가자들이 행사에 이용할 입구

여자가 첫 대사에서 환경 박람회는 이번 주말(this weekend)에 열린다고 했고, 남자가 마지막 대사에서 공원 입구가 여러 군데 있지 않은지(aren't there several entrances to the park?) 묻자, 여자가 주말에는 코트 가에 있는 입구만 연다(only the entrance on Court Street is open on weekends)고 했으므로 환경 박람회는 코트 가의 입구만 이용할 수 있다는 것을 알 수 있다. 따라서 지도에서 코트 가를 찾으면 정답은 (A)이다.

68-70 대화 + 프로젝트 계획표

W-Br   I came by in person to see how the construction of my town house is proceeding. ⁶⁸**I was a bit worried after that text you sent me yesterday.**

M-Cn   Yes, ⁶⁸,⁶⁹**we finished stage three of the project last week, but as I said in my text, there'll be a delay for stage four.**

W-Br   I understand there's a problem with the supply of drywall sheets?

M-Cn   There's a delay right now. But we should get them next week.

W-Br   ⁷⁰**Is there anything we can do while we wait?**

M-Cn   ⁷⁰**I suggest you start working with your interior designer to decide on the finishing touches.** As soon as the drywall arrives, we'll be ready to finish the interior.

여   티운하우스 공사가 어떻게 진행되고 있는지 직접 보려고 들렀어요. **어제 보내신 문자를 받고 조금 걱정이 돼서요.**

남   네, **지난주에 3단계 공사를 마쳤는데, 제가 문자로 말씀드렸듯이 4단계는 지연됩니다.**

여   석고 보드 판 공급에 문제가 있다고 알고 있는데요?

남   지금은 지체되고 있어요. 하지만 다음 주에는 받을 겁니다.

여   **기다리는 동안 우리가 할 수 있는 일이 있을까요?**

남   **인테리어 디자이너와 마무리 작업 결정하는 일을 시작하세요.** 석고 보드가 도착하는 대로 내부 작업이 마무리될 수 있게 준비가 될 겁니다.

어휘   in person 직접   proceed 진행되다   supply 공급 drywall 석고 보드   finishing touch 마무리 작업

Stage 1	Framing
Stage 2	Plumbing
⁶⁹Stage 3	Insulation
Stage 4	Drywall Installation
Stage 5	Finish Interior

1단계	골조
2단계	배관
⁶⁹3단계	단열
4단계	석고 보드 벽 설치
5단계	내부 마감

68

What did the man do yesterday?
(A) Communicated with the woman about the schedule
(B) Contacted an electrician
(C) Changed an aspect of the house's design
(D) Ordered some supplies

남자는 어제 무엇을 했는가?
(A) 일정에 관해 여자와 연락
(B) 전기 기사에게 연락
(C) 주택 디자인 일부 변경
(D) 비품 주문

해설 세부 사항 관련 – 남자가 어제 한 일

여자가 첫 대사에서 남자에게 어제 보낸 문자를 받고 조금 걱정이 됐다(I was a bit worried after that text you sent me yesterday)고 하자 남자가 지난주에 3단계 공사를 마쳤는데, 자신이 문자로 말했듯이 4단계는 지연된다(we finished stage three of the project last week, but as I said in my text, there'll be a delay for stage four)고 한 것으로 보아, 남자가 어제 일정에 관한 문자를 여자에게 보냈음을 알 수 있다. 따라서 정답은 (A)이다.

69

Look at the graphic. What stage has recently been completed?
(A) Framing
(B) Plumbing
(C) Insulation
(D) Drywall installation

시각 정보에 의하면, 어떤 단계가 최근에 완료되었는가?
(A) 골조
(B) 배관
(C) 단열
(D) 석고 보드 설치

해설 시각 정보 연계 – 최근에 완료된 단계
남자가 첫 번째 대사에서 지난주에 3단계 공사를 마쳤는데, 자신이 문자로 말했듯이 4단계는 지연될 것이다(we finished stage three ~ a delay for stage four)고 했으므로, 최근에 완료된 단계는 3단계이고 계획표에서 3단계는 단열(Insulation)로 나와 있으므로 정답은 (C)이다.

70

What does the man suggest the woman do?
(A) Cancel an order
(B) Make some design decisions
(C) Pay a bill in advance
(D) Change suppliers

남자는 여자에게 무엇을 하라고 제안하는가?
(A) 주문 취소
(B) 디자인 결정
(C) 대금 선불 지불
(D) 공급업체 변경

어휘 in advance 미리, 선금[선지급]으로

해설 세부 사항 관련 – 남자가 여자에게 제안하는 일
여자가 마지막 대사에서 기다리는 동안 자신들이 할 수 있는 일이 있을지(Is there anything we can do while we wait?) 묻자 남자가 인테리어 디자이너와 마무리 작업 결정하는 일을 시작하라(I suggest you start working with your interior designer to decide on the finishing touches)고 권하고 있으므로 정답은 (B)이다.

> Paraphrasing 대화의 decide on the finishing touches
> → 정답의 Make some design decisions

PART 4

71-73 광고

> M-Au And now ⁷¹**let me thank our sponsor, Perfect Tea. Take a deep breath and give yourself a break with Perfect Tea! Their distinctive blend of relaxing teas was born on a farm in northeastern India,** where ⁷²**the ideal mix of rain and sun gives**

> **Perfect Tea its strong and aromatic flavor. Believe me, you won't find this taste anywhere else!** Plus, ⁷³**you can now sign up for a membership to have your favorite teas delivered to you automatically each month.**

> 자, 저희 후원 업체인 퍼펙트 티에게 감사드립니다. 심호흡하시고 퍼펙트 티로 휴식을 취하세요! 특유의 혼합 방식으로 긴장을 풀어 주는 차들은 인도 북동부에 있는 농장에서 탄생했습니다. 이 지역은 비와 태양이 완벽하게 어우러져 퍼펙트 티에 진하고 향긋한 풍미를 부여합니다. 절 믿으세요. 이 맛은 어디에서도 찾을 수 없을 겁니다! 더욱이 이제 회원 가입하면 매달 좋아하는 차들이 자동으로 배달됩니다.

> 어휘 take a deep breath 심호흡을 하다 distinctive 특유의, 독특한 blend 혼합, 조합 ideal 이상적인 aromatic 향긋한 flavor 풍미, 맛 taste 맛 sign up for ~에 (회원) 가입하다

71

What is being advertised?
(A) An online supermarket
(B) A travel guide
(C) A beverage product
(D) A hotel chain

무엇이 광고되고 있는가?
(A) 온라인 슈퍼마켓
(B) 여행 안내서
(C) 음료 제품
(D) 호텔 체인

해설 전체 내용 관련 – 광고되고 있는 것
화자가 도입부에 자신들의 후원 업체인 퍼펙트 티에게 감사드린다면서(let me thank our sponsor, Perfect Tea) 퍼펙트 티를 소개한 후, 심호흡을 하고 퍼펙트 티로 휴식을 취하라(Take a deep breath and give yourself a break with Perfect Tea!)고 하고, 특유의 혼합 방식으로 긴장을 풀어 주는 차들은 인도 북동부에 있는 농장에서 탄생했다(Their distinctive blend of relaxing teas was born on a farm in northeastern India)며 차 제품을 홍보하는 것으로 보아 정답은 (C)이다.

> Paraphrasing 담화의 Their distinctive blend of relaxing teas → 정답의 A beverage product

72

What does the speaker emphasize?
(A) The eco-friendly policy of a business
(B) The superior flavor of a product
(C) The extensive selection on a Web site
(D) The positive reviews of a brand

화자는 무엇을 강조하는가?
(A) 기업의 친환경 정책
(B) 제품의 뛰어난 풍미
(C) 웹사이트에 구비된 폭넓은 제품
(D) 브랜드에 대한 긍정적인 평가

어휘 eco-friendly 친환경인 superior 뛰어난 extensive 폭넓은

해설 세부 사항 관련 – 화자가 강조하는 것

화자가 중반부에 그 지역은 비와 태양이 완벽하게 어우러져 퍼펙트 티에 진하고 향긋한 풍미를 부여한다(the ideal mix of rain and sun gives Perfect Tea its strong and aromatic flavor)고 했고, 이 맛은 어디에서도 찾을 수 없다는 자신의 말을 믿으라(Believe me, you won't find this taste anywhere else!)고 퍼펙트 티 제품의 풍미를 강조하고 있으므로 정답은 (B)이다.

> **Paraphrasing** 담화의 its strong and aromatic flavor
> → 정답의 The superior flavor

73

What is a benefit of membership?
(A) It provides a discount.
(B) It makes ordering more efficient.
(C) It includes access to an online chat room.
(D) It comes with a gift.

회원 가입의 혜택은 무엇인가?
(A) 할인을 제공한다.
(B) 주문이 더 효율적이다.
(C) 온라인 채팅방에 들어갈 수 있다.
(D) 선물이 딸려 있다.

어휘 efficient 효율적인 access 접근, 이용 가능함 come with ~이 딸려 있다

해설 세부 사항 관련 – 회원 가입의 혜택

화자가 마지막에 이제 회원 가입하면 매달 좋아하는 차들이 자동으로 배달된다(you can now sign up for a membership to have your favorite teas delivered to you automatically each month)고 했으므로 주문하는 것이 더 쉽고, 효율적일 것이라는 점을 알 수 있다. 따라서 정답은 (B)이다.

74-76 방송

M-Cn Welcome to *The Money Hour* on WWBC, Alberta. Today, ^{74,75}**I'll discuss the topic of preparing for retirement with my guest Sarah Levinson. She's the author of the book *All You Need to Know About Retirement Investments*.** ⁷⁵**We will delve into the broad range of investment options and discuss how to choose a financial advisor.** But first, ⁷⁶**let me send a shout-out to our sponsors over at Pinnacle's, and their brand-new vitamin C supplement.** Pinnacle's vitamin C formula supports a healthy immune system. So make sure to check it out. And now, Sarah, where should we begin?

앨버타주, WWBC 〈머니 아워〉에 오신 것을 환영합니다. 오늘은 **게스트 사라 레빈슨과 함께 은퇴 준비를 주제로 이야기하겠습니다.** 레빈슨 씨는 〈은퇴 투자에 대해 알아야 할 모든 것〉을 쓴 저자입니다. 우리는

광범위한 투자 옵션들을 자세히 탐색하고 금융 자문을 선택하는 방법에 대해 논의하려고 합니다. 하지만 먼저 피너클에 있는 우리 후원자들과 그들의 새로 나온 비타민 C 보충제에 감사의 말씀을 드리겠습니다. 피너클의 비타민 C 제조법은 건강한 면역 체계를 뒷받침합니다. 그러니 꼭 확인해 보세요. 자, 사라, 어디서부터 시작할까요?

어휘 delve into ~을 자세히 탐색하다 shout-out 감사의 표시[함성] brand-new 새로운, 완전 새 것인 supplement 보충(제), 보조 식품 formula 제조법 immune 면역의

74

Who is Sarah Levinson?
(A) A university professor
(B) A coach
(C) A computer scientist
(D) A book author

사라 레빈슨은 누구인가?
(A) 대학교수
(B) 코치
(C) 컴퓨터 과학자
(D) 저자

해설 세부 사항 관련 – 사라 레빈슨의 직업

화자가 초반부에 게스트 사라 레빈슨과 함께 은퇴 준비를 주제로 이야기하겠다(I'll discuss the topic of preparing for retirement with my guest Sarah Levinson)며 레빈슨 씨는 〈은퇴 투자에 대해 알아야 할 모든 것〉을 쓴 저자(She's the author of the book *All You Need to Know About Retirement Investments*)라고 소개했으므로 정답은 (D)이다.

75

What is the main topic of the broadcast?
(A) Digital trends in publishing
(B) Qualities of a good bank
(C) How to save for retirement
(D) Best jobs in finance

방송의 주제는 무엇인가?
(A) 출판의 디지털 동향
(B) 좋은 은행의 특징
(C) 은퇴에 대비한 저축 방법
(D) 금융 분야 최고의 직업

해설 전체 내용 관련 – 방송의 주제

화자가 초반부에 게스트 사라 레빈슨과 함께 은퇴 준비를 주제로 이야기하겠다(I'll discuss the topic of preparing for retirement with my guest Sarah Levinson)고 했고, 광범위한 투자 옵션들을 자세히 탐색하고 금융 자문을 선택하는 방법에 대해 논의하려고 한다(We will delve into the broad range of investment options and discuss how to choose a financial advisor)고 한 것으로 보아 은퇴 준비를 위한 재정 관리가 주제임을 알 수 있다. 따라서 정답은 (C)이다.

76

What kind of company sponsors the broadcast?
(A) A local store
(B) A publishing company
(C) A technology firm
(D) A health supplement manufacturer

어떤 업종의 회사가 방송을 후원하는가?
(A) 지역 매장
(B) 출판사
(C) 기술 회사
(D) 건강 보조 식품 제조업체

해설 세부 사항 관련 – 방송을 후원하는 업체

화자가 후반부에 피너클에 있는 후원자들과 그들의 새로 나온 비타민 C 보충제에 감사의 말씀을 전한다(let me send a shout-out to our sponsors over at Pinnacle's, and their brand-new vitamin C supplement)고 한 것으로 보아 정답은 (D)이다.

77-79 회의 발췌

M-Au Good morning. Welcome to Western Seed and Gardening Supplies. **77You've all been hired to help out for the next six weeks. During our annual spring sale, we never have enough permanent workers to handle everything. 78Your supervisor, Margaret Malin, will explain how to take customers' orders. 79First, I want to make sure that we have the information we need to set up your direct deposit. We prefer to send your paychecks directly to your bank accounts.** There's a white folder on the table in front of you. So, let's get started there.

안녕하세요. 웨스턴 시드 앤드 가드닝 서플라이즈에 오신 것을 환영합니다. 여러분은 앞으로 6주 동안 돕기 위해 채용되었습니다. 연례 봄맞이 할인 기간에는 모든 일을 처리할 정규직 직원이 늘 부족하거든요. 상사인 마가렛 말린이 고객 주문을 받는 방법을 설명할 거예요. 우선 계좌 입금을 설정하는 데 필요한 정보부터 확인하고 싶습니다. 당사는 급여를 은행 계좌로 직접 보내는 방식을 선호합니다. 앞에 있는 탁자 위에 흰색 폴더가 있죠. 그럼 거기부터 시작합시다.

어휘 annual 연례의 permanent 정규직인 handle 처리하다 direct deposit (급여의) 계좌 입금 paycheck 급여

77

Why did the company hire temporary workers?
(A) It has opened a new office.
(B) It is selling a wider variety of products.
(C) It is very busy this time of year.
(D) It is installing a new computer system.

회사는 왜 임시직 직원을 채용했는가?
(A) 새 사무실을 열었다.
(B) 더 다양한 제품을 판매하고 있다.
(C) 연중 이맘때는 무척 바쁘다.
(D) 새로운 컴퓨터 시스템을 설치하고 있다.

해설 세부 사항 관련 – 회사가 임시직 직원을 채용한 이유

화자가 초반부에 여러분은 앞으로 6주 동안 돕기 위해 채용되었다(You've all been hired to help out for the next six weeks)면서 연례 봄맞이 할인 기간에는 모든 일을 처리할 정규직 직원이 늘 부족하다(During our annual spring sale, we never have enough permanent workers to handle everything)고 한 것으로 보아 할인 기간에는 일손이 모자를 만큼 바쁘다는 것을 알 수 있다. 따라서 정답은 (C)이다.

78

What will Margaret Malin discuss?
(A) How to take customers' orders
(B) How to open a bank account
(C) How to close the store each night
(D) How to handle customer complaints

마가렛 말린은 무엇에 대해 논의할 것인가?
(A) 고객의 주문을 받는 방법
(B) 은행 계좌를 개설하는 방법
(C) 매일 밤 가게를 닫는 방법
(D) 고객 불만을 처리하는 방법

해설 세부 사항 관련 – 마가렛 말린이 논의할 것

화자가 중반부에 상사인 마가렛 말린이 고객의 주문을 받는 방법을 설명할 것(Your supervisor, Margaret Malin, will explain how to take customers' orders)이라고 했으므로 정답은 (A)이다.

79

Why does the speaker say, "There's a white folder on the table in front of you"?
(A) To review a gardening supplies price list
(B) To share some company history
(C) To introduce some job duties
(D) To ask for some banking information

화자는 왜 "앞에 있는 탁자 위에 흰색 폴더가 있죠"라고 말하는가?
(A) 원예용품 가격표를 검토하려고
(B) 회사 연혁을 공유하려고
(C) 직무에 대해 소개하려고
(D) 은행 정보를 요청하려고

해설 화자의 의도 파악 – 앞에 있는 탁자 위에 흰색 폴더가 있다는 말의 의도

인용문 앞에서 우선 계좌 입금을 설정하는 데 필요한 정보부터 확인하고 싶다(First, I want ~ information we need to set up your direct deposit)고 했고 당사는 급여를 은행 계좌로 직접 보내는 방식을 선호한다(We prefer to send your paychecks directly to your bank accounts)고 했으므로, 인용문은 은행 정보를 적어 달라는 의도로 볼 수 있다. 따라서 정답은 (D)이다.

80-82 방송

W-Am Before we get back to our program, ⁸⁰**the organization called On the Farm is proud to announce a new training program for people who work with livestock.** ⁸¹**The Livestock Operations Program provides trainees with the most up-to-date techniques in raising cattle.** You'll learn about the latest methods of proper fencing, feeding, and medical care. The training is delivered at your workplace and is tailored to suit your needs. The course takes one year and leads to a Certificate in Livestock Operations. ⁸²**Call On the Farm at 555-0128 for more information or to register!**

프로그램으로 돌아가기 전에, **온 더 팜이라는 단체에서 가축을 다루는 사람들을 위한 새로운 훈련 프로그램을 자랑스럽게 발표합니다. 가축 운영 프로그램은 훈련생들에게 소 사육에 관한 최신 기술을 제공합니다.** 적절한 울타리 치기, 먹이 주기, 의료 관리 등 최신 기법에 대해 배우게 됩니다. 교육은 여러분의 일터에서 제공되며 수강생의 요구에 맞춰 조정됩니다. 이 과정은 1년이 걸리며 가축 운영 자격증을 취득할 수 있습니다. **자세한 정보나 등록을 원하시면 555-0128로 온 더 팜에 전화하세요!**

어휘 livestock 가축 up-to-date 최신의 cattle 소 fence 울타리를 치다 feed 먹이다 tailor (목적, 요구에) 맞춰 조정하다 suit one's need ~의 필요[요구]에 맞다 certificate 자격증

80

What is the speaker discussing?
(A) A supermarket sale
(B) An agricultural show
(C) An educational program
(D) An outdoor festival

화자는 무엇을 논의하고 있는가?
(A) 슈퍼마켓 할인
(B) 농업 박람회
(C) 교육 프로그램
(D) 야외 축제

해설 전체 내용 관련 – 화자가 논의하는 사항
화자가 초반부에 온 더 팜이라는 단체에서 가축을 다루는 사람들을 위한 새로운 훈련 프로그램을 자랑스럽게 발표한다(the organization called On the Farm is proud to announce a new training program for people who work with livestock)고 한 후, 이 프로그램에 대한 설명을 이어 가고 있으므로 정답은 (C)이다.

> **Paraphrasing** 담화의 a new training program
> → 정답의 An educational program

81

Who is the announcement intended for?
(A) Cattle farmers
(B) Foresters
(C) College students
(D) Restaurant cooks

누구를 대상으로 한 발표인가?
(A) 목축업자
(B) 수목 관리원
(C) 대학생
(D) 식당 요리사

해설 세부 사항 관련 – 청자의 직업
화자가 중반부에 가축 운영 프로그램은 훈련생들에게 소 사육에 관한 최신 기술을 제공한다(The Livestock Operations Program provides trainees with the most up-to-date techniques in raising cattle)고 했으므로 정답은 (A)이다.

82

How can a person get more information?
(A) By going to a farm
(B) By sending an e-mail
(C) By going to a Web site
(D) By calling a phone number

더 자세한 정보를 어떻게 얻을 수 있는가?
(A) 농장에 가서
(B) 이메일을 보내서
(C) 웹사이트에 가서
(D) 전화번호로 전화해서

해설 세부 사항 관련 – 더 자세한 정보를 얻는 방법
화자가 마지막에 자세한 정보나 등록을 원하면 555-0128로 온 더 팜에 전화하라(Call On the Farm at 555-0128 for more information or to register!)고 알려 주고 있으므로 정답은 (D)이다.

83-85 전화 메시지

W-Br Hello, Mr. Juma. ⁸³**This is the Municipal Water Department.** We have been investigating flooding on Bozeman Street that was reported over the phone Sunday night. ⁸⁴**Our technicians ruled out a water main break. They determined that a pipe had burst on the grounds of your bakery.** They turned off the water supply to your business. ⁸⁵**Please be aware that it is your responsibility to repair the pipe.** Your insurance may cover the cost. ⁸⁵**We will turn the water back on once the pipe is fixed.**

안녕하세요, 주마 씨. **시 수도국입니다.** 저희는 일요일 밤에 전화로 신고된 보즈먼 가 누수를 조사해 왔습니다. **기술자들은 상수도 본관이 파열됐을 가능성은 배제했습니다. 그들은 주마 씨의 제과점 바닥에서 배**

관이 터졌다는 것을 알아냈습니다. 그들이 주마 씨의 사업장으로 가는 수도 공급을 차단했습니다. **배관 수리는 업주 책임이라는 점 유념해 주시기 바랍니다.** 보험으로 비용을 충당할 수 있으실 겁니다. **배관이 수리되면 물을 다시 공급하겠습니다.**

어휘 municipal 시의 investigate 조사하다 flooding 누수, 범람 rule out 가능성을 배제하다 water main 수도[급수] 본관 break 파열, 고장 determine 알아내다, 밝히다 burst 터지다 responsibility 책임 insurance 보험

83

Who is the speaker?
(A) A plumber
(B) A shop owner
(C) A reporter
(D) A city employee

화자는 누구인가?
(A) 배관공
(B) 가게 주인
(C) 기자
(D) 시 공무원

어휘 plumber 배관공 city employee 시 공무원, 시 직원

해설 전체 내용 관련 – 화자의 직업
화자가 메시지 도입부에서 인사를 한 후 자신을 시 수도국(This is the Municipal Water Department)이라고 밝힌 것으로 보아 정답은 (D)이다.

> **Paraphrasing** 담화의 the Municipal Water Department
> → 정답의 A city employee

84

What problem does the speaker identify?
(A) A broken water pipe
(B) A heavy rainstorm
(C) A change to an insurance policy
(D) A misleading phone call

화자는 어떤 문제를 확인하는가?
(A) 파열된 수도관
(B) 심한 폭풍우
(C) 보험 약관 변경
(D) 오해의 소지가 있는 전화

어휘 misleading 오해의 소지가 있는

해설 세부 사항 관련 – 화자가 확인하는 문제
화자가 중반부에 수도국 기술자들은 상수도 본관이 파열됐을 가능성은 배제했다(Our technicians ruled out a water main break)며 그들은 제과점 바닥에서 배관이 터졌다는 것을 알아냈다(They determined that a pipe had burst on the grounds of your bakery)고 했으므로 정답은 (A)이다.

> **Paraphrasing** 담화의 a pipe had burst
> → 정답의 A broken water pipe

85

What will the listener most likely do after listening to the message?
(A) Cancel his insurance policy
(B) Move his bakery
(C) Open his store for business
(D) Arrange for a repair

청자는 메시지를 들은 뒤 무엇을 할 것 같은가?
(A) 보험 해지
(B) 제과점 이전
(C) 매장 개업
(D) 수리 준비

해설 세부 사항 관련 – 청자가 메시지를 들은 뒤 할 일
화자가 후반부에 배관 수리는 업주 책임이라는 점 유념해 달라(Please be aware that it is your responsibility to repair the pipe)고 하였고, 배관이 수리되면 물을 다시 공급하겠다(We will turn the water back on once the pipe is fixed)고 한 것으로 보아 정답은 (D)이다.

86-88 소개

M-Cn I hope that everyone enjoyed the delightful meal. **86It's almost time for us to present this year's awards to our athletes here at the National Tennis Conference.** However, before we do so, **87I am honored to welcome a very special speaker up to the stage—Brigitte Rollin.** This moment is such a thrill for me. **87Ms. Rollin is a superb competitor.** She has won multiple tournaments and is also renowned for her charity work and sponsorships. Before she comes to the podium, **88I'd like to remind you that photographs of tonight's event are prohibited.** But everyone in attendance will receive a signed photograph of our guest at the end of the event.

모두 기분 좋은 식사를 즐기셨기 바랍니다. **전국 테니스 연맹에서 여기 있는 우리 선수들에게 올해의 상을 수여할 시간이 다가왔네요.** 하지만 그 전에, **매우 특별한 강연자인 브리짓 롤린 씨를 무대로 모시게 되어 영광입니다.** 지금 이 순간 너무 설렙니다. **롤린 씨는 탁월한 선수입니다.** 여러 대회에서 우승했으며 자선 활동과 후원으로도 유명합니다. 롤린 씨가 연단에 오르기 전에, **오늘 밤 행사는 촬영이 금지되어 있다는 점 상기시켜 드리고 싶습니다.** 하지만 행사가 끝날 때 참석하신 모든 분들은 게스트의 서명이 있는 사진을 받게 될 겁니다.

어휘 athlete 선수 conference 연맹 be honored to ~하게 되어 영광으로 여기다 competitor 선수, 경쟁자 tournament 대회, 시합 renowned for ~로 유명한 charity 자선 podium 연단 prohibit 금지하다 in attendance 참석한

86

What type of event is taking place?

(A) A writers' workshop
(B) A debate competition
(C) A sports awards ceremony
(D) A book signing

어떤 종류의 행사가 열리고 있는가?

(A) 저자 워크숍
(B) 토론 대회
(C) 스포츠 시상식
(D) 도서 사인회

해설 전체 내용 관련 – 행사의 종류

화자가 초반부에 전국 테니스 연맹에서 여기 있는 우리 선수들에게 올해의 상을 수여할 시간이 다가왔다(It's almost time for us to present this year's awards to our athletes here at the National Tennis Conference)고 했으므로 정답은 (C)이다.

> **Paraphrasing** 담화의 present this year's awards to our athletes
> → 정답의 A sports awards ceremony

87

What does the speaker mean when he says, "This moment is such a thrill for me"?

(A) He admires a guest speaker.
(B) He likes speaking to audiences.
(C) He is enjoying a meal.
(D) He is pleased to win an award.

화자가 "지금 이 순간 너무 설렙니다"라고 말할 때 무엇을 의미하는가?

(A) 초청 연사를 존경한다.
(B) 청중에게 연설하는 것을 좋아한다.
(C) 식사를 즐기고 있다.
(D) 상을 받아서 기쁘다.

어휘 admire 존경하다

해설 화자의 의도 파악 – 지금 이 순간 너무 설렌다는 말의 의도

인용문 앞에서 매우 특별한 강연자인 브리짓 롤린 씨를 무대로 모시게 되어 영광(I am honored to welcome a very special speaker up to the stage—Brigitte Rollin)이라고 했고, 인용문에 이어 롤린 씨는 탁월한 선수(Ms. Rollin is a superb competitor)라고 한 것으로 보아 팬으로서 강연자를 좋아한다는 표현을 하려는 의도로 볼 수 있다. 따라서 정답은 (A)이다.

88

What are the listeners reminded to do?

(A) Hold their applause until the end
(B) Finish their meals
(C) Turn off their phones
(D) Avoid taking pictures

청자들은 무엇을 하라고 주의를 받는가?

(A) 끝날 때까지 박수갈채 자제하기
(B) 식사 끝내기
(C) 전화기 끄기
(D) 사진 찍지 않기

어휘 hold 지제하다 applause 박수갈채

해설 세부 사항 관련 – 청자들이 주의를 받은 일

화자가 후반부에 오늘 밤 행사는 촬영이 금지되어 있다는 점 상기시키고 싶다(I'd like to remind you that photographs of tonight's event are prohibited)고 했으므로 정답은 (D)이다.

> **Paraphrasing** 담화의 photographs of tonight's event are prohibited → 정답의 Avoid taking pictures

89-91 방송

W-Am Welcome to the WLED Radio traffic report. **89There's heavy traffic in Bellevue's city center this afternoon as organizers prepare for tomorrow's annual marathon.** Runners and their families are arriving in town, and excitement is in the air. **90Remember, you can log in to our Web site to follow the race, where we will post updates regularly. 91For those of you planning on coming to the city center to watch the marathon tomorrow, I suggest you use the Bellevue bicycle rental system.** You can take public transportation to the city center and then get one of the city bicycles located at Central Train Station to move around.

WLED 라디오 교통 안내 방송에 오신 것을 환영합니다. **주최 측이 내일 열리는 연례 마라톤을 준비하면서 오늘 오후 벨뷰 도심은 교통 체증이 심합니다.** 주자들과 가족들이 시에 도착하고 있고, 흥분된 분위기가 감돌고 있습니다. **경주 진행 상황을 지켜보시려면 정기적으로 새로운 소식을 알려 드리는 저희 웹사이트에 로그인하세요. 내일 마라톤을 보기 위해 도심에 올 계획인 분들은 벨뷰 자전거 대여 시스템을 이용하시기를 권해 드립니다.** 도심까지는 대중교통을 타고 오시고 그 다음부터는 중앙 기차역에 위치한 시 자전거 한 대를 타고 이동하시면 됩니다.

어휘 organizer 주최자 annual 연례의, 매년의 in the air 분위기가 감도는 post 게시하다, 공표하다 public transportation 대중교통

89

What is causing heavy traffic in the city center?

(A) Road construction
(B) Preparation for an event
(C) Bad weather conditions
(D) A disabled vehicle

무엇이 도심 교통 체증을 일으키고 있는가?

(A) 도로 공사
(B) 행사 준비
(C) 악천후
(D) 고장 차량

어휘 disabled 고장 난

해설 세부 사항 관련 – 도심 교통 체증을 일으키고 있는 원인
화자가 초반부에 주최 측이 내일 열리는 연례 마라톤을 준비하면서 오늘 오후 벨뷰 도심은 교통 체증이 심하다(There's heavy traffic in Bellevue's city center this afternoon as organizers prepare for tomorrow's annual marathon)고 한 것으로 보아 정답은 (B)이다.

> Paraphrasing 담화의 prepare for tomorrow's annual marathon → 정답의 Preparation for an event

90

Why should the listeners visit the radio station's Web site?

(A) To enter a contest
(B) To request some music
(C) To ask some questions about city planning
(D) To learn about the progress of a sporting event

청자들은 왜 라디오 방송국 웹사이트를 방문해야 하는가?

(A) 경연에 참가하려고
(B) 음악을 신청하려고
(C) 도시 계획에 대해 질문하려고
(D) 스포츠 행사의 진행 상황을 알아보려고

해설 세부 사항 관련 – 청자들이 라디오 방송국 웹사이트를 방문해야 하는 이유
화자가 중반부에 경주 진행 상황을 지켜보려면, 정기적으로 새로운 소식을 알려 주는 자사 웹사이트에 로그인하라(Remember, you can log in to our Web site to follow the race, where we will post updates regularly)고 했으므로 정답은 (D)이다.

> Paraphrasing 담화의 updates → 정답의 the progress of a sporting event

91

What does the speaker recommend the listeners do?

(A) Work from home
(B) Avoid driving into the city center
(C) Wait for another traffic report
(D) Take a different exit

화자는 청자들에게 무엇을 하라고 추천하는가?

(A) 재택근무하기
(B) 도심 운전 피하기
(C) 다른 교통 안내 방송 기다리기
(D) 다른 출구로 나가기

해설 세부 사항 관련 – 화자가 청자들에게 추천하는 일
화자가 후반부에 내일 마라톤을 보기 위해 도심에 올 계획인 사람들은 벨

뷰 자전거 대여 시스템을 이용하길 권한다(For those of you planning on coming to the city center to watch the marathon tomorrow, I suggest you use the Bellevue bicycle rental system)고 한 것으로 보아 정답은 (B)이다.

92-94 전화 메시지

M-Cn Hi. This message is for Josephine Sanders. **92This is Chang-Soo from Lindmar Dental.** I took your dental X-rays this morning. **93After you left the office, I found a necklace in the X-ray room.** I'm pretty sure that it's yours. **93I remember asking you to take it off before I took your X-rays. I must have forgotten to return it to you.** I apologize for the inconvenience. But, our office is open until seven tonight. **94If I'm not here, just ask the receptionist.**

안녕하세요. 조세핀 샌더스에게 보내는 메시지입니다. **저는 린드마 치과에서 근무하는 창수라고 합니다.** 제가 오늘 아침에 치과 엑스레이를 찍었습니다. **고객님이 나가고 나서, 엑스레이실에서 목걸이를 발견했습니다.** 고객님 목걸이가 틀림없다고 생각합니다. **엑스레이를 찍기 전에 제가 목걸이를 벗어 달라고 부탁했던 게 기억나거든요. 제가 깜박하고 고객님께 돌려주지 않았나 봅니다.** 불편을 드려 죄송합니다. 하지만 진료실은 오늘 저녁 7시까지 열려 있습니다. 제가 여기 없으면 접수원에게 문의하세요.

어휘 necklace 목걸이 return 돌려주다 inconvenience 불편 receptionist 접수원

92

Where does the speaker work?

(A) At a jewelry store
(B) At a dental office
(C) At a medical supply store
(D) At a hotel chain

화자는 어디에서 일하는가?

(A) 보석 매장
(B) 치과
(C) 의료용품점
(D) 호텔 체인

해설 전체 내용 관련 – 화자의 근무지
화자가 초반부에 린드마 치과에서 근무하는 창수(This is Chang-Soo from Lindmar Dental)라고 자신을 소개하고 있으므로 정답은 (B)이다.

93

What did the speaker forget to do?

(A) Give back a necklace
(B) Write down a phone number
(C) Send some X-ray results
(D) Call a receptionist

화자는 무엇을 잊어버렸는가?

(A) 목걸이 돌려주기
(B) 전화번호 적기
(C) 엑스레이 결과 보내기
(D) 접수원에게 전화하기

해설 세부 사항 관련 – 화자가 잊어버린 일

화자가 중반부에 청자가 나가고 나서, 엑스레이실에서 목걸이를 발견했다 (After you left the office, I found a necklace in the X-ray room)고 했고, 엑스레이를 찍기 전에 자신이 목걸이를 벗어 달라고 부탁했던 게 기억난다(I remember asking you to take it off before I took your X-rays)면서 자신이 깜박하고 청자에게 돌려주지 않은 것 같다(I must have forgotten to return it to you)고 했으므로 정답은 (A)이다.

> Paraphrasing 담화의 return it
> → 정답의 Give back a necklace

94

Why does the speaker say, "our office is open until seven tonight"?
(A) To remind the listener about a delivery
(B) To recommend that a contract be signed quickly
(C) To ask the listener to return to an office
(D) To indicate that a sale is ending

화자는 왜 "진료실은 오늘 저녁 7시까지 열려 있습니다"라고 말하는가?
(A) 청자에게 배달에 대해 다시 알리려고
(B) 계약을 빨리 체결하라고 권하려고
(C) 청자가 진료실에 다시 가도록 요청하려고
(D) 판매가 끝난다고 알리려고

어휘 return 다시 가다, 되돌아가다

해설 화자의 의도 파악 – 진료실은 오늘 저녁 7시까지 열려 있다는 말의 의도

화자가 인용문 바로 뒤 문장에서 자신이 여기 없으면 접수원에게 문의하라 (If I'm not here, just ask the receptionist)고 한 것으로 보아 청자에게 진료실에 들러 달라는 부탁을 하려는 것임을 알 수 있다. 따라서 정답은 (C)이다.

95-97 회의 발췌 + 도표

M-Au **⁹⁵Our workers haul soil, garden mulch, and plants every day to make our customers' yards look beautiful.** They need strong handcarts to move these heavy items. The Classic Handcarts we have now are poor quality. They fall apart, and our workers constantly repair them. ⁹⁶**We need the strongest handcarts available.** ⁹⁶,⁹⁷**I recommend we purchase the 150-dollar model because it will not break easily.** It's so durable that we'll save money in the end. If you agree, I'll order twenty of them.

우리 직원들은 고객의 마당을 아름답게 만들기 위해 매일 흙, 정원용 부엽토, 식물을 나릅니다. 이런 무거운 물건들을 옮기려면 튼튼한 손수

레가 필요합니다. 지금 우리가 보유하고 있는 클래식 핸드카트는 품질이 형편없습니다. 잘 망가져서 직원들이 계속 고칩니다. **여기 나와 있는 것 중 가장 튼튼한 손수레가 필요합니다. 쉽게 망가지지 않을 것이기 때문에 150달러짜리 모델 구매를 추천합니다.** 내구성이 무척 좋아서 결국에는 돈이 절약될 겁니다. 동의하시면 제가 20개 주문하겠습니다.

어휘 haul 나르다 mulch 부엽토 poor 형편없는 fall apart 망가지다 constantly 계속 durable 내구성이 좋은 in the end 결국에는

ROCKNOSE HANDCARTS	
Models	**Cost**
Classic Handcart	$ 50
Superior Handcart	$ 80
Deluxe Handcart	$110
⁹⁷Super Duty Handcart	$150

로크노즈 핸드카트	
모델	**가격**
클래식 핸드카트	50달러
슈페리어 핸드카트	80달러
디럭스 핸드카트	110달러
⁹⁷슈퍼 듀티 핸드카트	150달러

95

Where does the speaker most likely work?
(A) At a hardware store
(B) At a tool manufacturer
(C) At a landscaping service
(D) At a construction company

화자는 어디에서 일하는 것 같은가?
(A) 철물점
(B) 공구 제조업체
(C) 조경 서비스업체
(D) 건설 회사

해설 전체 내용 관련 – 화자의 근무지

화자가 도입부에 자신들의 직원들은 고객의 마당을 아름답게 만들기 위해 매일 흙, 정원용 부엽토, 식물을 나른다(Our workers haul soil, garden mulch, and plants every day to make our customers' yards look beautiful)고 했으므로 정답은 (C)이다.

96

What is the speaker's highest priority?
(A) Buying a long-lasting product
(B) Spending as little money as possible
(C) Having the order delivered quickly
(D) Getting the largest product available

화자가 최우선으로 여기는 것은 무엇인가?

(A) 오래가는 제품 구매하기
(B) 가능한 한 돈 적게 쓰기
(C) 주문품 신속 배달 받기
(D) 입수할 수 있는 가장 큰 제품 구하기

해설 세부 사항 관련 – 화자가 최우선으로 여기는 것

화자가 중반부에 여기 나와 있는 것 중 가장 튼튼한 손수레가 필요하다 (We need the strongest handcarts available)면서 쉽게 망가지지 않을 것이기 때문에 150달러짜리 모델 구매를 추천한다(I recommend we purchase the 150-dollar model because it will not break easily)고 주장하는 것으로 보아 정답은 (A)이다.

> Paraphrasing 담화의 the strongest handcarts
> → 정답의 a long-lasting product

97

Look at the graphic. Which handcart does the speaker want to buy?

(A) Classic Handcart
(B) Superior Handcart
(C) Deluxe Handcart
(D) Super Duty Handcart

시각 정보에 의하면, 화자는 어떤 손수레를 구매하고 싶어 하는가?

(A) 클래식 핸드카트
(B) 슈페리어 핸드카트
(C) 디럭스 핸드카트
(D) 슈퍼 듀티 핸드카트

해설 시각 정보 연계 – 화자가 구매하고 싶은 손수레

화자가 후반부에 쉽게 망가지지 않을 것이기 때문에 150달러짜리 모델 구매를 추천한다(I recommend we purchase the 150-dollar model because it will not break easily)고 했고, 도표에서 150달러짜리는 슈퍼 듀티 핸드카트이므로 정답은 (D)이다.

98-100 강연 + 도표

> W-Br [98]**Thank you all for being here. I'd like to go over our next training module.** By now you should all be familiar with how to create a lead, contact your potential customers, and close on a deal. [98]**As a sales representative you're used to focusing on your own leads and clients,** and that's terrific. However, [99]**there is strength in teamwork, and that's what we'll work on now.** Let's get started. [100]**I'd like you to create three groups, and we're going to take on the roles of different characters in typical scenarios involving clients.**

> 모두 와 주셔서 감사합니다. 다음 교육 과정을 검토하고자 합니다. 이제 여러분 모두 잠재 고객을 형성하고 연락하여 거래를 성사시키는 방법을 잘 알고 있을 것입니다. **영업 담당자로서 여러분은 자신의 잠재 고**

객과 고객에게 집중하는 데 익숙합니다. 정말 대단합니다. 하지만 **팀워크에는 강점이 있는데 지금 우리가 할 일이 바로 그 일입니다.** 시작해 볼까요. **세 그룹을 만들고 고객을 포함한 전형적인 시나리오에서 다양한 인물의 역할을 맡아서 해 보겠습니다.**

> 어휘 lead (상품, 서비스에 관심 있는) 잠재 고객 potential 잠재적인, 가능성 있는 terrific 대단한, 훌륭한 strength 강점 typical 전형적인 involve 포함하다

TRAINING MODULES	DURATION
Plan and Organize Your Work	25 min.
From Opportunities to Deals	30 min.
[99]Work as a Team	20 min.
Visualize Success	10 min.

교육 과정	시간
업무 계획과 구상	25분
기회부터 거래까지	30분
[99]**팀으로 일하기**	**20분**
성공을 머릿속에 그리기	10분

98

Who is the training intended for?

(A) Sales personnel
(B) Executive officers
(C) Human Resource employees
(D) Product developers

누구를 대상으로 한 교육인가?

(A) 영업 사원
(B) 임원
(C) 인사과 직원
(D) 제품 개발자

해설 전체 내용 관련 – 청자의 직업

화자가 초반부에 모두 와 주어 감사하다(Thank you all for being here)며 다음 교육 과정을 검토하고자 한다(I'd like to go over our next training module)고 했고, 영업 담당자로서 여러분은 자신의 잠재 고객과 고객에게 집중하는 데 익숙하다(As a sales representative you're used to focusing on your own leads and clients)고 했으므로 영업 사원 대상 교육임을 알 수 있다. 따라서 정답은 (A)이다.

> Paraphrasing 담화의 a sales representative
> → 정답의 Sales personnel

99

Look at the graphic. How long will the training be?
(A) 25 minutes
(B) 30 minutes
(C) 20 minutes
(D) 10 minutes

시각 정보에 의하면, 교육은 얼마나 걸릴 것인가?

(A) 25분
(B) 30분
(C) 20분
(D) 10분

해설 시각 정보 연계 – 교육에 걸리는 시간

화자가 중반부에 팀워크에는 강점이 있는데 지금 우리가 할 일이 바로 그 일(there is strength in teamwork, and that's what we'll work on now)이라고 했고, 도표에 팀워크에 관한 과정은 팀으로 일하기(Work as a Team)로 교육 시간은 20분이므로 정답은 (C)이다.

100

What does the speaker tell the listeners to do?
(A) Turn off their phones
(B) Get some refreshments
(C) Ask questions often
(D) Role-play a situation

화자는 청자들에게 무엇을 하라고 말하는가?

(A) 전화기 끄기
(B) 다과 먹기
(C) 자주 질문하기
(D) 상황에 맞춰 역할극하기

해설 세부 사항 관련 – 화자가 청자들에게 하라고 하는 일

화자가 마지막에 세 그룹을 만들고 고객을 포함한 전형적인 시나리오에서 다양한 인물의 역할을 맡아서 해 보겠다(I'd like you to create three groups, and we're going to take on the roles of different characters in typical scenarios involving clients)고 했으므로 정답은 (D)이다.

> **Paraphrasing** 담화의 take on the roles of different characters in typical scenarios
> → 정답의 Role-play a situation

1 (C)	**2** (B)	**3** (D)	**4** (C)	**5** (C)
6 (A)	**7** (B)	**8** (C)	**9** (A)	**10** (B)
11 (A)	**12** (B)	**13** (A)	**14** (C)	**15** (A)
16 (B)	**17** (C)	**18** (C)	**19** (C)	**20** (A)
21 (C)	**22** (B)	**23** (C)	**24** (A)	**25** (B)
26 (B)	**27** (A)	**28** (A)	**29** (B)	**30** (A)
31 (A)	**32** (B)	**33** (B)	**34** (A)	**35** (C)
36 (B)	**37** (A)	**38** (A)	**39** (B)	**40** (D)
41 (D)	**42** (A)	**43** (B)	**44** (B)	**45** (A)
46 (C)	**47** (B)	**48** (D)	**49** (A)	**50** (B)
51 (C)	**52** (D)	**53** (B)	**54** (A)	**55** (C)
56 (D)	**57** (A)	**58** (B)	**59** (A)	**60** (D)
61 (D)	**62** (B)	**63** (C)	**64** (A)	**65** (B)
66 (C)	**67** (A)	**68** (A)	**69** (C)	**70** (D)
71 (C)	**72** (B)	**73** (D)	**74** (B)	**75** (A)
76 (D)	**77** (D)	**78** (C)	**79** (A)	**80** (D)
81 (B)	**82** (C)	**83** (C)	**84** (B)	**85** (D)
86 (A)	**87** (D)	**88** (A)	**89** (D)	**90** (A)
91 (C)	**92** (C)	**93** (D)	**94** (A)	**95** (B)
96 (D)	**97** (C)	**98** (D)	**99** (C)	**100** (A)

PART 1

1 M-Au

(A) A man is looking out a window.
(B) A man is fixing a ceiling tile.
(C) A man is reaching for a coat.
(D) A man is installing a wooden floor.

(A) 남자가 창밖을 내다보고 있다.
(B) 남자가 천장 타일을 고치고 있다.
(C) 남자가 코트를 잡으려고 손을 뻗고 있다.
(D) 남자가 나무 바닥을 설치하고 있다.

어휘 fix 고치다   reach for ~을 잡으려고 손을 뻗다

해설 1인 등장 사진 – 사람의 동작/상태 묘사
(A) 동사 오답. 남자가 창밖을 내다보고 있는(is looking out a window) 모습이 아니므로 오답.
(B) 동사 오답. 남자가 천장 타일을 고치고 있는(is fixing a ceiling tile) 모습이 아니므로 오답.
(C) 정답. 남자가 코트를 잡으려고 손을 뻗고 있는(is reaching for a coat) 모습이므로 정답.

(D) 동사 오답. 남자가 나무 바닥을 설치하고 있는(is installing a wooden floor) 모습이 아니므로 오답.

2 W-Br

(A) A wall is covered with vines.
(B) A tree is near a sign.
(C) There are puddles on the road.
(D) A tree has fallen onto the pavement.

(A) 담이 덩굴로 덮여 있다.
(B) 나무 한 그루가 표지판 가까이에 있다.
(C) 도로에 물웅덩이들이 있다.
(D) 나무 한 그루가 인도 위로 넘어져 있다.

어휘 vine 덩굴, 포도나무   puddle 물웅덩이   fall 넘어지다
    pavement 인도

해설 사물/풍경 사진 – 풍경 묘사
(A) 동사 오답. 담(A wall)이 덩굴로 덮여 있는(is covered with vines) 모습이 아니므로 오답.
(B) 정답. 나무(A tree)가 표지판 가까이에 있는(is near a sign) 모습이므로 정답.
(C) 사진에 없는 명사를 이용한 오답. 사진에 물웅덩이(puddles)의 모습이 보이지 않으므로 오답.
(D) 동사 오답. 나무(A tree)가 인도 위로 넘어져 있는(has fallen onto the pavement) 모습이 아니므로 오답.

3 W-Am

(A) A construction worker is repairing a fence.
(B) A set of cones is blocking an entrance.
(C) Some lines are being painted on a roadway.
(D) A man is working outdoors.

(A) 건설 인부가 울타리를 수리하고 있다.
(B) 원뿔형 교통 표지들이 입구를 막고 있다.
(C) 차선이 도로 위에 도색되고 있다.
(D) 남자가 실외에서 일하고 있다.

어휘 construction 건설   repair 수리하다   cone 원뿔형 교통 표지
    block 막다   entrance 입구

해설 혼합 사진 – 사람/사물/풍경 혼합 묘사

(A) 동사 오답. 건설 인부(A construction worker)가 울타리를 수리하고 있는(is repairing a fence) 모습이 아니므로 오답.

(B) 동사 오답. 원뿔형 교통 표지들(A set of cones)이 입구를 막고 있는 (is blocking an entrance) 모습이 아니므로 오답.

(C) 동사 오답. 차선(Some lines)이 도로 위에 도색되고 있는(are being painted on a roadway) 모습이 아니므로 오답.

(D) 정답. 남자(A man)가 실외에서 일하고 있는(is working outdoors) 모습이므로 정답.

---

4 M-Cn

(A) A cupboard is filled with kitchen utensils.
(B) A woman is looking at an electrical outlet.
(C) Some papers have been placed on a counter.
(D) Some shelves are being adjusted.

(A) 찬장에 주방용품이 가득 채워져 있다.
(B) 여자가 전기 콘센트를 보고 있다.
(C) 서류들이 카운터 위에 놓여 있다.
(D) 선반들이 조정되고 있다.

어휘 utensil (주방)용품 electrical outlet 전기 콘센트 adjust 조정하다

해설 혼합 사진 – 사람/사물/풍경 혼합 묘사

(A) 사진에 없는 명사를 이용한 오답. 사진에 주방용품(kitchen utensils)이 보이지 않으므로 오답.

(B) 동사 오답. 여자(A woman)가 전기 콘센트를 보고 있는(is looking at an electrical outlet) 모습이 아니라 찬장 안을 들여다보고 있는 (is looking into a cupboard) 모습이므로 오답.

(C) 정답. 서류들(Some papers)이 카운터 위에 놓여 있는(have been placed on a counter) 모습이므로 정답.

(D) 동사 오답. 선반들(Some shelves)이 조정되고 있는(are being adjusted) 모습이 아니므로 오답.

---

5 W-Br

(A) Magazines are on a rack on the wall.
(B) A bookcase is next to a sofa.
(C) A plant has been placed next to a chair.
(D) A ceiling lamp hangs over a carpet.

(A) 잡지들이 벽에 걸려 있는 선반 위에 있다.
(B) 책장이 소파 옆에 있다.
(C) 식물이 의자 옆에 놓여 있다.
(D) 천장 전등이 카펫 위에 걸려 있다.

어휘 rack 선반, 걸이 hang over ~ 위에 걸려 있다

해설 사물/풍경 사진 – 사물 묘사

(A) 사진에 없는 명사를 이용한 오답. 사진에 벽에 걸려 있는 선반(a rack on the wall)의 모습이 보이지 않으므로 오답.

(B) 사진에 없는 명사를 이용한 오답. 사진에 책장(A bookcase)의 모습이 보이지 않으므로 오답.

(C) 정답. 식물(A plant)이 의자 옆에 놓여 있는(has been placed next to a chair) 모습이므로 정답.

(D) 동사 오답. 천장 전등(A ceiling lamp)이 카펫 위에 걸려 있는 (hangs over a carpet) 모습이 아니므로 오답.

---

6 M-Cn

(A) A man is crouching down next to a wall.
(B) A man is taking measurements of a room.
(C) A man is attaching a door to a frame.
(D) A man is standing on a ladder.

(A) 남자가 벽 옆에 쭈그리고 앉아 있다.
(B) 남자가 방의 치수를 재고 있다.
(C) 남자가 틀에 문을 달고 있다.
(D) 남자가 사다리 위에 서 있다.

어휘 crouch 쭈그리고 앉다 take a measurement 치수를 재다 frame 틀, 골조 ladder 사다리

해설 2인 이상 등장 사진 – 사람의 동작/상태 묘사

(A) 정답. 남자가 벽 옆에 쭈그리고 앉아 있는(is crouching down next to a wall) 모습이므로 정답.

(B) 동사 오답. 남자가 방의 치수를 재고 있는(is taking measurements of a room) 모습이 아니므로 오답.

(C) 동사 오답. 남자가 틀에 문을 달고 있는(is attaching a door to a frame) 모습이 아니므로 오답.

(D) 동사 오답. 남자가 사다리 위에 서 있는(is standing on a ladder) 모습이 아니므로 오답.

PART 2

7

W-Br   Which flowers should we get for Ms. Jones?

M-Au   (A) I'm sure she'll be happy to switch with you.
　　　 (B) She would like the yellow ones.
　　　 (C) She's the only one who received the report.

존스 씨를 위해 어떤 꽃을 사야 할까요?

(A) 그녀는 틀림없이 기꺼이 당신과 바꿔 줄 거예요.

(B) 그녀는 노란색 꽃을 좋아할 거예요.

(C) 그녀가 보고서를 받은 유일한 사람이에요.

어휘 switch (근무 시간을) 바꾸다   receive 받다

해설 구입해야 할 꽃을 묻는 Which 의문문

(A) 연상 단어 오답. 질문의 flowers와 for Ms. Jones에서 연상 가능한 she'll be happy를 이용한 오답.

(B) 정답. 존스 씨를 위해 어떤 꽃을 사야 할지를 묻는 질문에 그녀는 노란색을 좋아할 것이라며 사야 할 꽃의 색상을 제안하고 있으므로 정답.

(C) 연상 단어 오답. 질문의 Ms. Jones에서 연상 가능한 대명사 She를 이용한 오답.

8

M-Cn   Did you put paper in the copy machine?

W-Am   (A) I remember that manager very well.

(B) I use notebooks for taking notes.

(C) No, someone already did that.

복사기에 종이를 넣었나요?

(A) 그 매니저를 또렷이 기억해요.

(B) 메모할 때 공책을 사용해요.

(C) 아니요, 누가 벌써 했던데요.

어휘 take a note 메모하다, 필기하다

해설 상대방이 복사기에 종이를 넣었는지 확인하는 조동사(Did) 의문문

(A) 질문과 상관없는 오답.

(B) 연상 단어 오답. 질문의 paper에서 연상 가능한 notebooks를 이용한 오답.

(C) 정답. 상대방이 복사기에 종이를 넣었는지를 묻는 질문에 아니요(No)라고 대답한 뒤, 누군가 벌써 했다며 부정 답변과 일관된 내용을 덧붙이고 있으므로 정답.

9

W-Br   Can you help me test the new voice mail system?

M-Cn   (A) No, I have a meeting that's about to start.

(B) I wasn't aware that he sent an e-mail.

(C) Yes, I pay my phone bill online.

새 음성 메일 시스템 테스트하는 것 좀 도와주실 수 있나요?

(A) 아니요, 전 곧 시작되는 회의가 있어요.

(B) 저는 그가 이메일을 보냈는지 몰랐어요.

(C) 네, 저는 온라인으로 전화 요금을 내요.

어휘 be about to 막 ~하려는 참이다   aware 알고 있는   bill 고지서

해설 부탁/요청의 의문문

(A) 정답. 새 음성 메일 시스템 테스트를 도와줄 수 있는지 요청하는 질문에 아니요(No)라고 거절하며 구체적인 이유를 제시하고 있으므로 정답.

(B) 유사 발음 오답. 질문의 mail과 부분적으로 발음이 유사한 e-mail을 이용한 오답.

(C) 연상 단어 오답. 질문의 Can you ~?에서 연상 가능한 대답인 Yes를 이용한 오답.

10

M-Cn   Why is the marketing team in the conference room?

W-Br   (A) The office near the lobby.

(B) Because they are attending a training seminar.

(C) Those reports are highly regarded.

마케팅팀이 왜 회의실에 있죠?

(A) 로비 근처 사무실이에요.

(B) 연수 세미나에 참석하고 있기 때문이에요.

(C) 그 보고서들은 평가가 아주 좋아요.

어휘 highly regarded 높이 평가되는

해설 마케팅팀이 회의실에 있는 이유를 묻는 Why 의문문

(A) 연상 단어 오답. 질문의 marketing team과 conference room에서 연상 가능한 office를 이용한 오답.

(B) 정답. 마케팅팀이 회의실에 있는 이유를 묻는 질문에 연수 세미나에 참석하고 있기 때문이라며 이유를 제시하고 있으므로 정답.

(C) 연상 단어 오답. 질문의 marketing team과 conference room에서 연상 가능한 reports를 이용한 오답.

11

M-Cn   Who is the new committee member going to be?

W-Am   (A) A lawyer from New York.

(B) At the shop next door.

(C) Most of his clients.

누가 새 위원이 되나요?

(A) 뉴욕에서 온 변호사요.

(B) 옆 가게에서요.

(C) 그의 고객 대부분이요.

어휘 committee 위원회

해설 새 위원이 될 사람을 묻는 Who 의문문

(A) 정답. 새 위원이 될 사람을 묻는 질문에 뉴욕에서 온 변호사라고 알려 주고 있으므로 정답.

(B) 질문과 상관없는 오답. Where 의문문에 대한 응답이므로 오답.

(C) 연상 단어 오답. 질문의 Who에서 연상 가능한 his clients가 있지만 his를 나타내는 구체적인 대상이 없으므로 오답.

12

M-Au   Why didn't we order more of the same chairs?

W-Br   (A) You heard all of them?

(B) Because they're very expensive.

(C) I don't think I'll make it.

같은 의자를 왜 더 주문하지 않았죠?

(A) 전부 들었어요?

(B) 아주 비싸서요.

(C) 저는 못 갈 것 같아요.

어휘 make it 가다, 참가하다

해설 같은 의자를 더 주문하지 않은 이유를 묻는 Why 의문문

(A) 질문과 상관없는 오답.

(B) 정답. 같은 의자를 더 주문하지 않은 이유를 묻는 질문에 비싸기 때문이라고 이유를 제시하고 있으므로 정답.

(C) 연상 단어 오답. 질문의 didn't에서 연상 가능한 don't를 이용한 오답.

13

M-Cn How many projects have been approved?

W-Br (A) One for each department.
(B) I'm going to cook my specialty tonight.
(C) Just a projector, please.

얼마나 많은 프로젝트가 승인되었나요?

(A) 부서별로 1개씩이요.
(B) 오늘 밤에 저는 특별 요리를 만들려고 해요.
(C) 그냥 프로젝터만 주세요.

어휘 approve 승인하다   specialty (식당의) 특별 요리, 전문 음식

해설 승인된 프로젝트의 개수를 묻는 How many 의문문

(A) 정답. 승인된 프로젝트의 개수를 묻는 질문에 부서별로 1개씩이라고 응답하고 있으므로 정답.

(B) 질문과 상관없는 오답.

(C) 파생어 오답. 질문의 projects와 파생어 관계인 projector를 이용한 오답.

14

M-Au Were you running late this morning?

W-Am (A) Yes, two please.
(B) She enjoys exercising in the park.
(C) No, I've been here for an hour.

오늘 아침에 늦으셨어요?

(A) 네, 두 개 주세요.
(B) 그녀는 공원에서 운동하는 걸 즐겨요.
(C) 아니요, 여기 온 지 한 시간 됐어요.

어휘 run late 늦어지다, 지각하다

해설 아침에 늦었는지 묻는 Be동사 의문문

(A) 연상 단어 오답. 질문의 Were you ~?에서 연상 가능한 대답인 Yes를 이용한 오답.

(B) 연상 단어 오답. 질문의 running에서 연상 가능한 exercising을 이용한 오답.

(C) 정답. 아침에 늦었는지 묻는 질문에 아니요(No)라고 대답한 뒤, 온 지 한 시간 됐다며 부정 답변과 일관된 내용을 덧붙이고 있으므로 정답.

15

M-Cn We should leave early for the restaurant.

W-Br (A) Yes, it can be difficult to find parking.
(B) A detailed process.
(C) I started the design early in the day.

식당으로 일찍 출발해야겠어요.

(A) 네, 주차할 곳을 찾기가 어려울지도 몰라요.
(B) 자세한 과정이요.
(C) 저는 그날 일찌감치 디자인을 시작했어요.

어휘 detailed 자세한

해설 제안/권유의 평서문

(A) 정답. 식당으로 일찍 출발해야겠다고 권유하는 평서문에 네(Yes)라고 대답한 뒤, 주차할 곳을 찾기가 어려울지도 모른다고 이유를 덧붙이며 호응하고 있으므로 정답.

(B) 평서문과 상관없는 오답.

(C) 단어 반복 오답. 평서문의 early를 반복 이용한 오답.

16

M-Au Why did the price of these shoes increase?

W-Br (A) Not after what happened last week.
(B) There is a new manufacturing process.
(C) Everyone who heard the announcement.

이 신발 가격이 왜 올랐나요?

(A) 지난주에 있었던 일 이후로는 아니에요.
(B) 새로운 제조 공정이 있어요.
(C) 발표를 들은 사람 모두요.

어휘 increase (가격이) 오르다   manufacturing 제조   process 공정, 과정

해설 신발 가격이 상승한 이유를 묻는 Why 의문문

(A) 질문과 상관없는 오답.

(B) 정답. 신발 가격이 상승한 이유를 묻는 질문에 Because를 생략하고 새로운 제조 공정이 있다며 이유를 제시하고 있으므로 정답.

(C) 질문과 상관없는 오답. Who 의문문에 대한 응답이므로 오답.

17

W-Br Have you written down the instructions for how to operate the machine?

M-Cn (A) A recent development.
(B) Thank you for doing that.
(C) Yes, I placed them beside it.

기계 작동법에 관한 사용 설명서를 작성하셨나요?

(A) 최근 개발품이에요.
(B) 그렇게 해 주셔서 고마워요.
(C) 네, 기계 옆에 뒀어요.

어휘 instructions 사용 설명서   recent 최근의   development 개발(품)   beside 옆에

해설 사용 설명서를 작성했는지 묻는 조동사(Have) 의문문

(A) 연상 단어 오답. 질문의 machine에서 연상 가능한 development를 이용한 오답.

(B) 단어 반복 오답. 질문의 for를 반복 이용한 오답.

(C) 정답. 기계 작동법에 관한 사용 설명서를 작성했는지 묻는 질문에 네(Yes)라고 답한 뒤, 기계 옆에 뒀다며 긍정 답변과 일관된 내용을 덧붙이고 있으므로 정답.

18

M-Au　How did you choose your dentist?

W-Am　(A) I have a new doctor.
　　　(B) I once wanted to be a teacher.
　　　(C) A friend recommended one to me.

치과 의사는 어떻게 선택하셨나요?
(A) 의사를 바꿨어요.
(B) 전 한때 교사가 되고 싶었어요.
(C) 친구가 한 분을 저에게 추천해 줬어요.

어휘 recommend 추천하다

해설 치과 의사를 선택한 경로를 묻는 How 의문문
(A) 연상 단어 오답. 질문의 dentist에서 연상 가능한 직업 단어 doctor를 이용한 오답.
(B) 연상 단어 오답. 질문의 dentist에서 연상 가능한 직업 단어 teacher를 이용한 오답.
(C) 정답. 치과 의사를 선택한 경로를 묻는 질문에 친구가 자신에게 추천해 주었다고 알려 주고 있으므로 정답.

19

M-Cn　We should send out the invitations for her retirement party.

W-Br　(A) Actually, I don't remember.
　　　(B) I didn't see who wrote it.
　　　(C) I already did that.

그녀의 퇴임 파티 초대장을 보내야 해요.
(A) 실은 기억이 안 나요.
(B) 누가 썼는지 전 못 봤어요.
(C) 제가 벌써 했어요.

어휘 invitation 초대(장)　retirement 퇴임, 은퇴

해설 제안/권유의 평서문
(A) 평서문과 상관없는 오답.
(B) 연상 단어 오답. 평서문의 invitations에서 연상 가능한 wrote를 이용한 오답.
(C) 정답. 퇴임 파티 초대장을 보내야 한다고 제안하는 평서문에 자신이 벌써 했다며 초대장을 보낼 필요가 없음을 우회적으로 알리고 있으므로 정답.

20

W-Am　Have you begun planning a vacation?

M-Cn　(A) I've already used all of my time off.
　　　(B) It's a nice place to visit.
　　　(C) It seems unlikely they did.

휴가 계획은 짜기 시작하셨나요?
(A) 전 연차를 벌써 다 써 버렸어요.
(B) 방문하기에 멋진 장소예요.
(C) 그들이 했을 것 같지 않아요.

어휘 time off 연[월]차, 휴가　unlikely ~할[일] 것 같지 않은

해설 휴가 계획을 짜기 시작했는지 묻는 조동사(Have) 의문문
(A) 정답. 휴가 계획을 짜기 시작했는지 묻는 질문에 자신은 연차를 벌써 다 써 버렸다며 휴가 계획을 짤 필요가 없음을 우회적으로 응답하고 있으므로 정답.
(B) 연상 단어 오답. 질문의 vacation에서 연상 가능한 place와 visit을 이용한 오답.
(C) 질문과 상관없는 오답.

21

M-Cn　Where should I look for a used car?

M-Au　(A) A low price.
　　　(B) Sorry, I'm not very hungry.
　　　(C) I have a friend who is selling one.

중고차를 어디에서 찾아봐야 할까요?
(A) 저렴한 가격이요.
(B) 미안해요, 전 배가 별로 안 고프네요.
(C) 차를 팔고 있는 친구가 있어요.

해설 중고차를 찾아볼 장소를 묻는 Where 의문문
(A) 연상 단어 오답. 질문의 used car에서 연상 가능한 low price를 이용한 오답.
(B) 질문과 상관없는 오답.
(C) 정답. 구입을 위해 중고차를 찾아볼 마땅한 장소를 묻는 질문에 중고차를 팔고 있는 친구가 있다며 그 친구가 파는 차를 보러 갈 것을 우회적으로 추천하고 있으므로 정답.

22

W-Br　Didn't Insook move into that office four months ago?

M-Au　(A) I don't think Insook has copies of those.
　　　(B) I think that's what I heard.
　　　(C) A four o'clock departure.

인숙 씨가 넉 달 전에 그 사무실로 이사하지 않았나요?
(A) 인숙 씨한테는 사본이 없을 거예요.
(B) 저도 그렇게 들은 것 같아요.
(C) 4시 출발이에요.

어휘 departure 출발

해설 인숙 씨가 그 사무실로 이사했는지를 확인하는 부정 의문문
(A) 단어 반복 오답. 질문의 Insook을 반복 이용한 오답.
(B) 정답. 인숙 씨가 넉 달 전에 그 사무실로 이사했는지를 묻는 질문에 자신도 그렇게 들은 것 같다며 우회적으로 확인해 주고 있으므로 정답.
(C) 단어 반복 오답. 질문의 four를 반복 이용한 오답.

23

M-Au　Would you like me to type up the proposal for you?

W-Am　(A) Which kind did you buy?
　　　(B) Yes, they saw it.
　　　(C) That would be very helpful.

제가 제안서를 타이핑해 드릴까요?

(A) 어떤 종류로 사셨어요?
(B) 네, 그들이 봤어요.
(C) 그렇게 해 주시면 크게 도움이 될 거예요.

어휘 proposal 제안(서)

해설 제안/권유의 의문문
(A) 단어 반복 오답. 질문의 you를 반복 이용한 오답.
(B) 연상 단어 오답. 질문의 Would you like ~?에서 연상 가능한 대답 Yes를 이용한 오답.
(C) 정답. 제안서를 타이핑해 줄지를 제안하는 질문에 그러면 크게 도움이 될 것이라고 호응하고 있으므로 정답.

24

W-Am　We should print more business cards.

M-Cn　(A) I'm not sure how useful they would be.
　　　(B) A candlemaker.
　　　(C) Let me know if she arrives.

명함을 더 인쇄해야겠어요.

(A) 그것들이 얼마나 유용할지 모르겠어요.
(B) 양초 제조업자예요.
(C) 그녀가 도착하면 알려 주세요.

해설 제안/권유의 평서문
(A) 정답. 명함을 더 인쇄해야 한다고 제안하는 평서문에 그것들이 얼마나 유용할지 모르겠다며 더 인쇄할 필요가 없다는 반대의 의사를 우회적으로 표현하고 있으므로 정답.
(B) 연상 단어 오답. 평서문의 business cards에서 연상 가능한 candlemaker를 이용한 오답.
(C) 평서문과 상관없는 오답.

25

W-Am　Can I have a copy of the sales report?

W-Br　(A) Only the original location.
　　　(B) The printer is broken.
　　　(C) She helps the senior manager.

매출 보고서 사본 한 부를 받을 수 있을까요?

(A) 원래 지점만이요.
(B) 프린터가 고장 났어요.
(C) 그녀는 선임 관리자를 도와요.

해설 부탁/요청의 의문문
(A) 연상 단어 오답. 질문의 copy에서 연상 가능한 original을 이용한 오답.
(B) 정답. 매출 보고서 사본을 받을 수 있을지 요청하는 질문에 프린터가 고장 났다며 보고서를 줄 수 없음을 우회적으로 표현하고 있으므로 정답.
(C) 연상 단어 오답. 질문의 sales와 report에서 연상 가능한 manager를 이용한 오답.

26

M-Cn　When do you need to renew your passport?

W-Br　(A) Not since I was at university.
　　　(B) It won't expire for a while yet.
　　　(C) I completed more than I expected.

당신은 언제 여권을 갱신해야 하나요?

(A) 제가 대학에 다녔을 때 이후로는 없어요.
(B) 당분간은 아직 만료되지 않아요.
(C) 제가 예상했던 것보다 더 많이 끝냈어요.

어휘 renew 갱신하다　expire 만료되다

해설 여권의 갱신 기한을 묻는 When 의문문
(A) 연상 단어 오답. 질문의 When에서 연상 가능한 Not since를 이용한 오답.
(B) 정답. 여권의 갱신 기한을 묻는 질문에 당분간은 만료되지 않는다고 응답하고 있으므로 정답.
(C) 질문과 상관없는 오답.

27

W-Br　Do you have this shirt in a larger size?

M-Cn　(A) I don't work here.
　　　(B) I brought some more hangers.
　　　(C) A very suitable color.

이 셔츠 더 큰 사이즈 있나요?

(A) 저 여기서 일하는 사람 아니에요.
(B) 제가 옷걸이를 좀 더 가져왔어요.
(C) 아주 어울리는 색이네요.

어휘 suitable 어울리는, 적당한

해설 더 큰 사이즈가 있는지 여부를 확인하는 조동사(Do) 의문문
(A) 정답. 더 큰 사이즈의 셔츠가 있는지 여부를 묻는 질문에 자신은 이곳에서 일하는 사람이 아니라며 더 큰 사이즈의 셔츠가 있는지를 확인해 줄 수 없음을 우회적으로 알리고 있으므로 정답.
(B) 연상 단어 오답. 질문의 shirt에서 연상 가능한 hangers를 이용한 오답.
(C) 연상 단어 오답. 질문의 shirt에서 연상 가능한 color를 이용한 오답.

28

W-Am　Aren't you planning to buy some supplies today?

M-Au　(A) I have a very busy schedule this afternoon.
　　　(B) The closet down the hall.
　　　(C) A member of the committee.

오늘 비품을 구매할 계획 아닌가요?

(A) 오늘 오후 일정이 아주 바빠요.
(B) 복도 끝에 있는 벽장이요.
(C) 위원회 위원이에요.

어휘 supplies 비품　committee 위원회

해설 비품을 구매할 계획인지를 확인하는 부정 의문문
(A) 정답. 오늘 비품을 구매할 계획인지를 묻는 질문에 자신은 오늘 오후 일정이 아주 바쁘다며 비품을 구매하지 않을 것임을 우회적으로 응답하고 있으므로 정답.
(B) 질문과 상관없는 오답. Where 의문문에 대한 응답이므로 오답.

(C) 연상 단어 오답. 질문의 planning에서 연상 가능한 committee를 이용한 오답.

29

W-Br Mary's promotion was well deserved, don't you think?

M-Au (A) Yes, they've known each other for about ten years.
(B) Yes, Mary has put in a lot of overtime lately.
(C) Mary will go on vacation next month.

메리의 승진은 자격이 충분했어요, 그렇죠?
(A) 네, 그들은 10년 가까이 서로 알고 지냈어요.
(B) 네, 메리는 최근에 초과 근무를 많이 했죠.
(C) 메리는 다음 달에 휴가를 가요.

어휘 promotion 승진   well deserved 자격이 충분한

해설 동료의 승진 자격이 충분했다는 의견에 동의 여부를 확인하는 부정 의문문
(A) 연상 단어 오답. 질문의 don't you think?에서 연상 가능한 대답 Yes를 이용한 오답.
(B) 정답. 메리의 승진은 자격이 충분했다는 의견에 대한 동의 여부를 확인하는 질문에 네(Yes)라고 대답하고, 최근에 초과 근무를 많이 했다며 동의하는 이유를 제시하고 있으므로 정답.
(C) 단어 반복 오답. 질문의 Mary를 반복 이용한 오답.

30

W-Am Should we go ahead with the project or postpone it?

M-Au (A) Let's check the budget first.
(B) That's a really good idea.
(C) She'll be at that meeting.

프로젝트를 진행해야 할까요, 아니면 연기해야 할까요?
(A) 먼저 예산부터 확인합시다.
(B) 정말 좋은 생각이에요.
(C) 그녀는 그 회의에 참석할 거예요.

어휘 go ahead 계속 진행하다   postpone 연기하다   budget 예산

해설 프로젝트의 향후 계획을 묻는 선택 의문문
(A) 정답. 프로젝트의 향후 계획을 묻는 선택 의문문에서 먼저 예산부터 확인하자며 두 가지 선택 사항 중 어느 것도 선택할 수 없음을 우회적으로 응답하고 있으므로 정답.
(B) 연상 단어 오답. 질문의 Should we ~?에서 연상 가능한 That's a good idea를 이용한 오답.
(C) 유사 발음 오답. 질문의 Should와 발음이 유사한 She'll을 이용한 오답.

31

W-Am Is Mr. Hernandez joining us for dinner?

M-Cn (A) Haven't you seen the guest list?
(B) Can he turn it in tomorrow instead?
(C) I'll put it upstairs for now.

에르난데스 씨도 우리와 저녁 식사 같이 하나요?
(A) 손님 명단 못 보셨어요?
(B) 그가 대신 내일 제출해도 될까요?
(C) 일단 제가 위층에 갖다 놓을게요.

어휘 turn in ~을 제출하다

해설 저녁 식사 참석 유무를 묻는 Be동사 의문문
(A) 정답. 에르난데스 씨가 저녁 식사에 참석하는지를 묻는 질문에 손님 명단을 못 보았는지 되물으며 손님 명단을 확인하면 알 수 있다는 것을 우회적으로 말하고 있으므로 정답.
(B) 연상 단어 오답. 질문의 Mr. Hernandez에서 연상 가능한 he를 이용한 오답.
(C) 단어 반복 오답. 질문의 for를 반복 이용한 오답.

PART 3

32-34

W-Br [32]Hi, Mr. Davies. This is Becca Griffith. [32]Thanks again for retiling our bathrooms. I noticed a mark or a scratch, though, on a tile near the bottom of the shower.

M-Au It's probably just a mark that one of my tools left. Sorry about that. [33]I have an industrial-strength cleaning agent that a construction friend of mine told me about. [33,34]Can I come on Thursday morning or Friday afternoon? No extra charge of course.

W-Br Great! [34]I am home in the mornings.

여 **안녕하세요, 데이비스 씨. 베카 그리피스예요. 욕실 타일을 재시공해 줘서 다시 한 번 감사드려요.** 그런데 샤워기 바닥 근처에 있는 타일에 자국인지 흠집이 있더군요.

남 제 공구들 중 하나가 남긴 자국일 겁니다. 죄송해요. **건설업계에 있는 친구가 알려 준 아주 강력한 세정제가 있어요. 목요일 오전이나 금요일 오후에 가도 될까요?** 물론 추가 요금은 없습니다.

여 잘됐네요! **오전에는 제가 집에 있어요.**

어휘 retile 타일을 다시 깔다   mark 자국   scratch 흠집, 긁힌 자국   industrial-strength 아주 강력한, 고성능인   cleaning agent 세정제, 세제

32

Who most likely is the man?
(A) A delivery person
(B) A contractor
(C) A salesperson
(D) A house cleaner

남자는 누구일 것 같은가?

(A) 배달원
(B) 시공업자
(C) 판매원
(D) 집 청소부

어휘 contractor 시공업자, 도급업자

해설 전체 내용 관련 – 남자의 직업

여자가 첫 대사에서 남자에게 인사(Hi, Mr. Davies)를 하면서 욕실 타일을 재시공해 줘서 다시 한 번 감사하다(Thanks again for retiling our bathrooms)고 한 것으로 보아 남자는 시공업자임을 알 수 있다. 따라서 정답은 (B)이다.

33

What will the man most likely bring when he returns?
(A) An updated invoice
(B) A product recommended to him
(C) A new tool
(D) A replacement tile

남자는 재방문 시 무엇을 가져올 것 같은가?

(A) 수정된 청구서
(B) 자신이 추천받은 제품
(C) 새로운 공구
(D) 대체 타일

어휘 replacement 대체(품)

해설 세부 사항 관련 – 남자가 재방문 시 가져올 것

남자가 건설업계에 있는 친구가 알려 준 아주 강력한 세정제가 있다(I have an industrial-strength cleaning agent that a construction friend of mine told me about)며 목요일 오전이나 금요일 오후에 가도 될지(Can I come on Thursday morning or Friday afternoon?) 묻고 있으므로 친구가 추천해 준 세정제를 가지고 방문할 것임을 알 수 있다. 따라서 정답은 (B)이다.

> **Paraphrasing** 대화의 told me about
> → 정답의 recommended to him

34

When will the man most likely return to the woman's house?
(A) On Thursday morning
(B) On Thursday afternoon
(C) On Friday morning
(D) On Friday afternoon

남자는 언제 여자의 집을 재방문할 것 같은가?

(A) 목요일 오전
(B) 목요일 오후
(C) 금요일 오전
(D) 금요일 오후

해설 세부 사항 관련 – 남자가 여자의 집을 재방문하는 시점

남자가 목요일 오전이나 금요일 오후에 가도 될지(Can I come on Thursday morning or Friday afternoon?) 묻자 여자가 오전에는 자

신이 집에 있다(I am home in the mornings)고 한 것으로 보아 정답은 (A)이다.

35-37

M-Au	**35How is the new recycling initiative going? Are people using the new recycling bins we've placed along the forest paths for their bottles?**
W-Am	**35It's going OK. 36I still find recyclable materials mixed in with regular waste, which concerns me.**
M-Au	**37I watched a great documentary about the benefits of recycling** last night. **Maybe we could play it in the visitor center.** If people see even a little of it before they begin hiking, maybe we'll see different results.
남	새로운 재활용 계획은 어떻게 돼 가고 있나요? 병을 버리라고 우리가 숲길을 따라 놓아둔 새 재활용 쓰레기통을 사람들이 쓰고 있나요?
여	잘 되어 가고 있어요. 아직도 재활용품들이 일반 쓰레기와 섞여 있는 게 보여서 걱정이에요.
남	어젯밤에 재활용의 이점을 다룬 정말 괜찮은 다큐멘터리를 봤어요. 관광 안내소에서 틀어도 될 듯해요. 사람들이 하이킹을 시작하기 전에 조금이라도 본다면, 어쩌면 결과가 달라질지도 몰라요.
어휘	initiative 계획 bin 쓰레기통 recyclable material 재활용품 concern 걱정스럽게[우려하게] 만들다 benefit 이점

35

What are the speakers mainly discussing?
(A) The condition of forest paths
(B) Hiking options
(C) A recycling program
(D) Vending machines

화자들은 주로 무엇에 대해 논의하고 있는가?

(A) 숲길의 상태
(B) 하이킹 선택 사항
(C) 재활용 프로그램
(D) 자동판매기

해설 전체 내용 관련 – 대화의 주제

남자가 첫 대사에서 새로운 재활용 계획은 어떻게 돼 가고 있는지(How is the new recycling initiative going?) 묻고 이어서 병을 버리라고 자신들이 숲길을 따라 놓아둔 새 재활용 쓰레기통을 사람들이 쓰고 있는지(Are people using the new recycling bins ~ for their bottles?) 묻자 여자가 잘 되어 가고 있다(It's going OK)면서 재활용 계획에 대한 대화를 이어 가고 있으므로 정답은 (C)이다.

36

What is the woman concerned about?

(A) The condition of the visitor center

(B) Materials being disposed of properly

(C) The need for new plastic bins

(D) Her work schedule

여자는 무엇을 우려하는가?

(A) 관광 안내소의 상태

(B) 제대로 처리되고 있어야 하는 물품

(C) 새로운 플라스틱 쓰레기통의 필요성

(D) 자신의 근무 일정

어휘 dispose of ~을 처리하다[버리다] properly 제대로, 적절히

해설 세부 사항 관련 – 여자의 우려 사항

여자가 아직도 재활용품들이 일반 쓰레기와 섞여 있는 게 보여서 걱정 (I still find recyclable materials mixed in with regular waste, which concerns me)이라고 했으므로 정답은 (B)이다.

37

What does the man suggest?

(A) Showing a video

(B) Purchasing a television

(C) Recording some instructions

(D) Hiring additional workers

남자는 무엇을 제안하는가?

(A) 동영상 보여 주기

(B) 텔레비전 구매하기

(C) 설명 녹화하기

(D) 추가 인력 채용하기

해설 세부 사항 관련 – 남자의 제안 사항

남자가 마지막 대사에서 재활용의 이점을 다룬 정말 괜찮은 다큐멘터리를 봤다(I watched a great documentary about the benefits of recycling)며 관광 안내소에서 틀어도 될 듯하다(Maybe we could play it in the visitor center)고 한 것으로 보아 정답은 (A)이다.

> **Paraphrasing** 대화의 play it → 정답의 Showing a video

38-40

> M-Cn Audrey, I saw you at the training session this morning. What did you think?
>
> W-Am ³⁸,³⁹**For me and some of the other managers, it really didn't apply to the work we do.** ³⁹**The session stressed working face-to-face with employees in your section.** ³⁸,³⁹**Well, I manage a group of salespeople spread across the country.** Some salespeople I only see once a year.
>
> M-Cn You know, ³⁹**Takeshi told me the same thing.** All the teams that he oversees need to work independently. ⁴⁰**I'm going to talk**

---

to our training coordinators and see if we can arrange some training sessions about management strategies for remote workers.

> 남 오드리, 오늘 아침 교육 시간에 봤어요. 어땠어요?
>
> 여 저와 다른 매니저 몇 명에게는 우리가 하는 일에 썩 잘 적용되진 않았어요. 교육 시간에는 부서 직원과 직접 대면해서 하는 작업을 강조했어요. 음, 저는 전국에 흩어져 있는 영업 사원 집단을 관리하고 있어요. 일부 영업 사원들은 일 년에 한 번밖에 안 봐요.
>
> 남 타케시도 같은 말을 했어요. 타케시가 감독하는 팀들은 전부 독립적으로 일해야 하거든요. **교육 담당자와 얘기해서 원격 근무자를 위한 관리 전략을 다루는 교육 시간을 마련할 수 있는지 알아봐야겠어요.**

어휘 apply to ~에 적용되다 stress 강조하다 face-to-face 대면으로 oversee 감독하다 independently 독립적으로 coordinator (기획, 진행) 책임자 arrange 마련하다 strategy 전략 remote 원격의

38

Who most likely is the woman?

(A) A manager

(B) A consultant

(C) A salesperson

(D) A trainer

여자는 누구일 것 같은가?

(A) 매니저

(B) 컨설턴트

(C) 영업 사원

(D) 교육 담당자

해설 전체 내용 관련 – 여자의 직업

여자가 첫 대사에서 교육 시간(training session)에 대한 평가로 자신과 다른 매니저 몇 명에게는 자신들이 하는 일에 썩 잘 적용되진 않았다(For me and some of the other managers, it really didn't apply to the work we do)고 언급한 후, 대사 후반에 자신은 전국에 흩어져 있는 영업 사원 집단을 관리하고 있다(Well, I manage a group of salespeople spread across the country)고 했으므로 여자는 매니저임을 알 수 있다. 따라서 정답은 (A)이다.

39

What did Takeshi tell the man?

(A) The training session will increase sales.

(B) The training session was not useful.

(C) Some people prefer independent work.

(D) More salespeople will be hired.

타케시는 남자에게 무슨 말을 했는가?

(A) 교육 시간이 매출을 늘릴 것이다.

(B) 교육 시간이 유용하지 않았다.

(C) 일부는 단독 작업을 선호한다.

(D) 영업 사원이 더 고용될 것이다.

해설 세부 사항 관련 – 타케시가 남자에게 한 말

여자가 자신과 다른 매니저 몇 명에게는 자신들이 하는 일에 썩 잘 적용되진 않았다(For me and some of the other managers, it really didn't apply to the work we do)고 했고, 교육 시간에는 부서 직원과 직접 대면해서 하는 작업을 강조(The session stressed working face-to-face with employees in your section)했는데 자신은 전국에 흩어져 있는 영업 사원 집단을 관리하고 있다(Well, I manage a group of salespeople spread across the country)고 하자 남자가 타케시도 같은 말을 했다(Takeshi told me the same thing)고 한 것으로 보아 여자와 타케시에게는 교육 내용이 도움이 되지 않았음을 알 수 있다. 따라서 정답은 (B)이다.

> **Paraphrasing** 대화의 it really didn't apply to the work we do → 정답의 The training session was not useful

40

What will the man most likely do next?

(A) Meet with the salespeople face-to-face
(B) Ask Takeshi to talk to his teams
(C) Cancel this week's sales meeting
(D) Discuss future training sessions

남자는 다음에 무엇을 할 것 같은가?

(A) 영업 사원과 대면 면담하기
(B) 타케시에게 팀들과 대화하도록 요청하기
(C) 이번 주 영업 회의 취소하기
(D) 향후 교육 시간에 관해 논의하기

해설 세부 사항 관련 – 남자가 다음에 할 일

남자가 마지막 대사에서 교육 담당자와 얘기해서 원격 근무자를 위한 관리 전략을 다루는 교육 시간을 마련할 수 있는지 알아보려고 한다(I'm going to talk to our training coordinators and see if we can arrange some training sessions about management strategies for remote workers)고 했으므로 정답은 (D)이다.

41-43

M-Cn	Wow, that meeting was fast. Not sure I got all the details of our assignments. **41, 42I think I am supposed to provide an update on sales of our company's latest nonfiction releases, right?**
W-Br	**41, 42Actually, I got the nonfiction assignment.** Anna wants you to prepare a report on sales of our latest hardcover fiction, in bookstores and at regional trade shows.
M-Cn	Oh, that's right. My handwriting is a mess. I should take notes on my laptop—which reminds me, **43do you think you could help me create the spreadsheet Anna wants?**
W-Br	**43I don't think I have the time;** I am

behind on a few tasks, plus I have my new assignment. Support staff should be able to help you!

남	와, 회의가 빨랐어요. 업무 세부 사항을 제가 전부 이해했는지 모르겠어요. **제가 우리 회사에서 최근에 발간한 논픽션의 판매에 대한 최신 정보를 제공해야 하는 것 같은데, 맞죠?**
여	**실은 제가 그 논픽션 업무를 맡았어요.** 안나는 당신에게 최근에 나온 하드커버 소설의 매출이 서점과 지역 무역 박람회에서 어떤지 보고서를 준비하라고 했어요.
남	아, 맞아요. 제 글씨가 아주 엉망이네요. 노트북으로 메모해야 하는데. 생각난 김에 **안나가 원하는 스프레드시트 만드는 일 좀 도와주실 수 있겠어요?**
여	**시간이 안 될 것 같아요.** 몇 가지 일이 밀려 있는데다 새로운 업무도 있거든요. 지원팀 직원이 도와줄 수 있을 거예요!

어휘	assignment (할당 받은) 업무, 과제 be supposed to ~해야 한다, ~하기로 되어 있다 release 발간, 출시(작) regional 지역의 handwriting 글씨, 필체 mess 엉망인 상태 behind 뒤처진 support 지원팀

41

Where do the speakers most likely work?

(A) At an accounting firm
(B) At a warehouse
(C) At a university bookstore
(D) At a book-publishing company

화자들은 어디에서 일하는 것 같은가?

(A) 회계 법인
(B) 창고
(C) 대학교 서점
(D) 출판사

해설 전체 내용 관련 – 화자들의 근무지

남자가 첫 대사에서 자신이 회사에서 최근에 발간한 논픽션의 판매에 대한 최신 정보를 제공해야 하는지(I think I am supposed to provide an update on sales of our company's latest nonfiction releases, right?)를 묻자 여자가 실은 자신이 그 논픽션 업무를 맡았다(Actually, I got the nonfiction assignment)고 했으므로 이들이 출판업계에서 일하고 있음을 알 수 있다. 따라서 정답은 (D)이다.

42

What is the woman's assignment?

(A) To prepare a sales report
(B) To train recently hired employees
(C) To take notes during staff meetings
(D) To proofread reports

여자의 업무 과제는 무엇인가?

(A) 매출 보고서 준비하기
(B) 최근에 채용된 직원 교육하기
(C) 직원 회의 중에 메모하기
(D) 보고서 교정하기

어휘 proofread 교정하다

해설 세부 사항 관련 – 여자의 업무

남자가 첫 대사에서 자신이 회사에서 최근에 발간한 논픽션의 판매에 대한 최신 정보를 제공해야 하는지(I think I am supposed to provide an update on sales of our company's latest nonfiction releases, right?)를 묻자 여자가 실은 자신이 그 논픽션 업무를 맡았다(Actually, I got the nonfiction assignment)고 했으므로 여자의 업무가 논픽션의 판매에 대한 정보를 제공하는 것임을 알 수 있다. 따라서 정답은 (A)이다.

> **Paraphrasing** 대화의 provide an update on sales
> → 정답의 prepare a sales report

43

Why will the woman be unable to help the man?
(A) She lacks the technical training.
(B) She is too busy.
(C) She is unsure of what Anna really wants.
(D) She sent her laptop to be serviced.

여자는 왜 남자를 도울 수 없는가?
(A) 기술 훈련이 부족하다.
(B) 너무 바쁘다.
(C) 안나가 정말 원하는 것이 무엇인지 잘 모른다.
(D) 노트북을 수리 맡겼다.

어휘 lack 부족하다   unsure of ~을 확신하지 못하는

해설 세부 사항 관련 – 여자가 남자를 도울 수 없는 이유

남자가 두 번째 대사에서 여자에게 안나가 원하는 스프레드시트 만드는 일 좀 도와 달라고(do you think you could help me create the spreadsheet Anna wants?) 요청하자 여자가 시간이 안 될 것 같다(I don't think I have the time)고 답하고 이유를 설명하고 있으므로 정답은 (B)이다.

> **Paraphrasing** 대화의 I don't think I have the time
> → 정답의 She is too busy

44-46

M-Au	**44, 45We got the architectural plans back for the new learning center. It's going to be in the southern part of our nature preserve.**
W-Br	**44, 45Isn't that the owl territory?**
M-Au	**45I hadn't thought of that.**
W-Br	I think we can build it somewhere else. **46I'll set up a meeting with the preserve board. Can you book us a meeting room in the community center?**
M-Au	**46Why don't we do it in our offices here instead?** That way we can walk out to any proposed sites.

남	새 학습 센터를 위한 건축 계획을 다시 받았습니다. 센터는 자연 보존 구역 남쪽에 위치할 예정입니다.
여	**거기는 올빼미 영역 아닌가요?**
남	**그건 미처 생각하지 못했어요.**
여	다른 곳에 지을 수 있을 거예요. **보존 위원회와 회의를 잡을게요. 주민 센터 회의실을 예약해 주시겠어요?**
남	**대신 여기 사무실에서 하는 게 어때요?** 그렇게 하면 제안된 부지가 어디든 걸어서 갈 수 있어요.

어휘 architectural 건축의 preserve 보존[보호] (구역)
territory 영역, 영토 set up (계획 등을) 세우다, 준비하다
board 위원회 proposed 제안된

44

Who most likely are the speakers?
(A) School teachers
(B) Employees of a nature area
(C) Members of a bird-watching club
(D) Construction workers

화자들은 누구일 것 같은가?
(A) 학교 교사
(B) 자연 구역 직원
(C) 조류 관찰 동호회 회원
(D) 건설 인부

해설 전체 내용 관련 – 화자들의 직업

남자가 첫 대사에서 새 학습 센터를 위한 건축 계획을 다시 받았다(We got the architectural plans back for the new learning center)며 센터는 자연 보존 구역 남쪽에 위치할 예정(It's going to be in the southern part of our nature preserve)이라고 하자 여자가 거기는 올빼미 영역이 아닌지(Isn't that the owl territory?) 묻는 것으로 보아 정답은 (B)이다.

45

What problem are the speakers discussing?
(A) The proposed location of a building
(B) The schedule of a community event
(C) Some recently completed construction
(D) Damage caused by animals

화자들은 어떤 문제를 논의하고 있는가?
(A) 제안된 건축 장소
(B) 지역 사회 행사 일정
(C) 최근에 완공된 건축물
(D) 동물에 의한 피해

어휘 recently 최근에 completed 완성된, 완료된 damage 피해,
손상 cause 야기하다

해설 전체 내용 관련 – 화자들이 논의하고 있는 문제

남자가 첫 대사에서 새 학습 센터를 위한 건축 계획을 다시 받았다(We got the architectural plans back for the new learning center)며 센터는 자연 보존 구역 남쪽에 위치할 예정(It's going to be in the southern part of our nature preserve)이라고 하자 여자가 거기는 올

빼미 영역이 아닌지(Isn't that the owl territory?) 물었고 남자가 그건 미처 생각하지 못했다(I hadn't thought of that)면서 건축을 위한 장소에 대해 대화를 이어 가고 있으므로 정답은 (A)이다.

46

What does the man suggest the speakers do?
(A) Contact some builders
(B) Conduct a tour of a nature preserve
(C) Hold a meeting at their workplace
(D) Post an announcement at the community center

남자는 화자들이 무엇을 할 것을 제안하는가?
(A) 건축업자에게 연락하기
(B) 자연 보존 구역 견학하기
(C) 근무지에서 회의 개최하기
(D) 주민 센터에 공지 게시하기

어휘 tour 견학 workplace 근무지 post 게시[공고]하다

해설 세부 사항 관련 – 남자의 제안 사항
여자가 두 번째 대사에서 보존 위원회와 회의를 잡겠다(I'll set up a meeting with the preserve board)며 주민 센터 회의실을 예약해 주겠는지(Can you book us a meeting room in the community center?) 묻자 남자가 대신 여기 사무실에서 하는 게 어떤지(Why don't we do it in our offices here instead?) 제안하고 있으므로 정답은 (C)이다.

> **Paraphrasing** 대화의 do it in our offices here
> → 정답의 Hold a meeting at their workplace

47-49

M-Cn ⁴⁷I wanted to leave a little time at the end of this meeting to discuss our decision to advertise for and hire a new, full-time data entry assistant. I'm not sure this is the best way to go. The work in that department isn't steady. Sometimes they're overworked, and other times it's very slow.

W-Am ⁴⁸Maybe we should contact an employment agency that specializes in temporary workers. We used one two years ago to get factory help during the summer.

M-Cn Oh yes. I remember that. ⁴⁹Janet Olsen is head of personnel. Why don't we walk to her office later and see what she thinks?

남 새 상근직 데이터 입력 보조 직원을 구하는 광고를 내고 채용하기로 한 결정에 대해 회의 마지막에 잠시 논의할 시간을 가졌으면 했어요. 이게 최선인지 잘 모르겠거든요. 그 부서는 업무가 들쭉날쭉해요. 때로는 과중한 업무에 시달리기도 하고, 때로는 아주 한가해요.

여 **임시직 전문 직업 소개소에 연락해 봐야 할 것 같아요.** 2년 전 여름 동안 공장이 도움을 얻어야 해서 한 곳을 이용했어요.

남 맞아요. 저도 기억나요. **자넷 올슨이 인사부장이잖아요. 나중에 올슨 씨 사무실로 가서 어떻게 생각하는지 알아보는 게 어때요?**

어휘 discuss 논의하다 decision 결정 assistant 보조 직원, 조교 steady 꾸준한 overworked 과중한 업무에 시달리는 employment agency 직업 소개소 temporary 임시의 personnel 인사부

47

What does the man say about hiring a new employee?
(A) The hiring process is already finished.
(B) Hiring may not be necessary.
(C) There are no qualified applicants.
(D) There is no money in the budget.

남자는 새 직원 채용에 관해 무엇이라고 말하는가?
(A) 채용 절차는 이미 끝났다.
(B) 채용할 필요가 없을 수도 있다.
(C) 자격을 갖춘 지원자가 없다.
(D) 예산에 돈이 없다.

어휘 qualified 자격을 갖춘 applicant 지원자

해설 세부 사항 관련 – 새 직원 채용에 대해 남자가 언급한 말
남자가 첫 대사에서 새 상근직 데이터 입력 보조 직원을 구하는 광고를 내고 채용하기로 한 결정에 대해 회의 마지막에 잠시 논의할 시간을 가졌으면 했다(I wanted ~ to discuss our decision to advertise for and hire a new, full-time data entry assistant)고 하고, 이것이 최선인지 잘 모르겠다(I'm not sure this is the best way to go)며 그 부서는 업무가 들쭉날쭉하다(The work in that department isn't steady)고 한 것으로 보아 상근직 채용을 재고해야 한다는 말임을 알 수 있다. 따라서 정답은 (B)이다.

48

What does the woman suggest?
(A) Contracting some advertising work
(B) Discussing the problem at the next meeting
(C) Training new factory team workers
(D) Hiring a temporary employee

여자는 무엇을 제안하는가?
(A) 광고 작업 계약하기
(B) 다음 회의에서 문제 논의하기
(C) 새로운 공장 팀원 교육하기
(D) 임시직 채용하기

해설 세부 사항 관련 – 여자의 제안 사항
여자가 임시직 전문 직업 소개소에 연락해 봐야 할 것 같다(Maybe we should contact an employment agency that specializes in temporary workers)고 제안하고 있으므로 정답은 (D)이다.

> **Paraphrasing** 대화의 temporary workers
> → 정답의 a temporary employee

49

Why will the speakers talk to Janet Olsen?
(A) To get her opinion about an issue
(B) To ask how a problem was solved previously
(C) To learn whether they can use her office
(D) To ask about a recently hired team member

화자들은 왜 자넷 올슨과 대화할 것인가?
(A) 어떤 문제에 대한 그녀의 의견을 듣기 위해
(B) 이전에 문제가 어떻게 해결되었는지 묻기 위해
(C) 그들이 그녀의 사무실을 사용할 수 있는지 알아보기 위해
(D) 최근에 고용된 팀원에 대해 문의하기 위해

해설 세부 사항 관련 – 화자들이 자넷 올슨과 대화하려는 이유
남자가 마지막 대사에서 자넷 올슨이 인사부장(Janet Olsen is head of personnel)이라며 나중에 올슨 씨 사무실로 가서 어떻게 생각하는지 알아보는 게 어떨지(Why don't we walk to her office later and see what she thinks?) 제안하고 있으므로 정답은 (A)이다.

> Paraphrasing 대화의 see what she thinks
> → 정답의 get her opinion about an issue

50-52

W-Br	Hello. ⁵⁰**I purchased tickets online for the sculpture exhibit this Saturday, but the parade is going to make it hard to get to the museum.** What's your refund policy?
M-Cn	The museum will remain open during the parade. ⁵¹**We only offer full refunds in the event of a closure.**
W-Br	⁵¹**Could I exchange the tickets?**
M-Cn	⁵¹**You can do that on the Web site.** But actually, ⁵²**if you plan to visit again in the near future, a membership would save you money over the course of the year.**
W-Br	Oh, I have too many financial commitments at the moment.

여	안녕하세요. **이번 주 토요일 조각전 입장권을 온라인으로 구매했어요. 그런데 퍼레이드 때문에 미술관에 가기 힘들 것 같아요.** 환불 정책이 어떻게 되나요?
남	미술관은 퍼레이드 동안 계속 문을 열 예정입니다. **폐관 시에만 전액 환불해 드려요.**
여	**표를 교환할 수 있을까요?**
남	**웹사이트에서 할 수 있습니다.** 하지만 **머지않아 다시 방문할 계획이시면, 회원권으로 일 년간 돈을 절약할 수 있어요.**
여	아, 지금은 돈 나가는 곳이 너무 많아요.

어휘	sculpture 조각 exhibit 전시(회) refund 환불 policy 정책 in the event of ~의 경우에 closure 폐관, 폐점 over the course of ~ 동안 financial 재정의 commitment (돈의) 사용, 책무[의무]

50

What may prevent the woman from seeing the exhibit?
(A) The exhibit will close early.
(B) A parade will be held.
(C) The buses are not running.
(D) She has a work commitment.

무엇이 여자가 전시회를 보지 못하게 가로막을 수 있는가?
(A) 전시회가 일찍 끝날 것이다.
(B) 퍼레이드가 열릴 것이다.
(C) 버스가 운행되지 않는다.
(D) 그녀는 해야 할 일이 있다.

해설 세부 사항 관련 – 여자가 전시회를 보지 못하게 가로막을 것
여자가 첫 대사에서 이번 주 토요일 조각전 입장권을 온라인으로 구매했는데 퍼레이드 때문에 미술관에 가기 힘들 것 같다(I purchased tickets online for the sculpture exhibit this Saturday, but the parade is going to make it hard to get to the museum)고 했으므로 정답은 (B)이다.

51

What does the man tell the woman she can do?
(A) Get a full refund
(B) Donate the cost of her tickets
(C) Exchange her tickets for another date
(D) Give her tickets to family members

남자는 여자가 무엇을 할 수 있다고 말하는가?
(A) 전액 환불받기
(B) 입장권 비용 기부하기
(C) 입장권을 다른 날짜로 교환하기
(D) 입장권을 가족에게 양도하기

해설 세부 사항 관련 – 여자가 할 수 있다고 남자가 언급하는 것
남자가 첫 대사에서 폐관 시에만 전액 환불해 준다(We only offer full refunds in the event of a closure)고 환불 정책을 설명하자 여자가 표를 교환할 수는 있는지(Could I exchange the tickets?)를 물었고 남자가 웹사이트에서 할 수 있다(You can do that on the Web site)고 답했으므로 정답은 (C)이다.

52

What does the woman imply when she says, "Oh, I have too many financial commitments at the moment"?
(A) She will call the man back later.
(B) She will not visit the gift shop.
(C) She will not attend a special event.
(D) She will not purchase a membership.

여자가 "아, 지금은 돈 나가는 곳이 너무 많아요"라고 말할 때 무엇을 의도하는가?
(A) 나중에 남자에게 다시 전화할 것이다.
(B) 선물 가게를 방문하지 않을 것이다.
(C) 특별 행사에 참석하지 않을 것이다.
(D) 회원권을 구매하지 않을 것이다.

해설 화자의 의도 파악 – 아, 지금은 돈 나가는 곳이 너무 많다는 말의
의도

앞에서 남자가 머지않아 다시 방문할 계획이라면, 회원권으로 일 년간 돈
을 절약할 수 있다(if you plan to visit again in the near future, a
membership would save you money over the course of the
year)는 말에 대한 답으로 인용문을 언급했으므로 회원권을 구입할 만한
여유가 없음을 알려 주려는 의도로 볼 수 있다. 따라서 정답은 (D)이다.

53-55 3인 대화

> M-Cn Hi, Shufen. **⁵⁴Is that the new brochure
> we're getting printed?**
>
> W-Am **⁵³Petra just picked it up from the print
> shop.**
>
> W-Br Yes, **⁵³I stopped there on my way to the
> office.** This copy is just for us to review
> and approve. I have to give the printers our
> OK by five o'clock.
>
> M-Cn **⁵⁴I love the way the colors just pop out.**
> The last time we printed this kind of
> information, it looked so boring.
>
> W-Am But wait, **⁵⁵isn't that our old logo on the
> brochure?**
>
> W-Br **⁵⁵I know I gave them the new logo. I'm
> going to call them up now and make sure
> they fix this.**

> 남 안녕하세요, 슈펜. 그게 우리가 인쇄 맡겨 놓은 새
> 소책자인가요?
>
> 여1 페트라가 방금 인쇄소에서 가져왔어요.
>
> 여2 네, 사무실로 오는 길에 거기 들렀어요. 이 인쇄본은 우리가
> 검토하고 승인하기 위한 용도예요. 5시까지는 인쇄소에
> 승인해 줘야 해요.
>
> 남 색깔이 튀어서 마음에 들어요. 지난번에 이런 종류의
> 정보지를 인쇄했을 때는 너무 따분해 보였거든요.
>
> 여1 잠깐만요, 소책자에 있는 게 이전 로고 아닌가요?
>
> 여2 저는 분명히 새 로고를 줬는데요. 지금 전화해서 이것을
> 고쳐 달라고 확실히 해 놓을게요.

> 어휘 pick up ~을 가져가다[찾아가다] print shop 인쇄소
> approve 승인하다 give one's[the] OK 승인하다,
> 오케이하다 pop out 튀다, 튀어나오다 boring 따분한

53

What did Petra do on her way to the office?
(A) She dropped a brochure off at a local store.
(B) She stopped at a printing shop.
(C) She shopped at an office store for some supplies.
(D) She contacted a repair technician.

페트라는 사무실로 가는 길에 무엇을 했는가?
(A) 지역 매장에 소책자를 가져다줬다.
(B) 인쇄소에 들렀다.
(C) 사무용품점에서 비품을 구매했다.
(D) 수리 기사에게 연락했다.

어휘 drop off ~을 가져다주다 stop at ~에 들르다 supplies 비품,
물품

해설 세부 사항 관련 – 페트라가 사무실로 가는 길에 한 일

첫 번째 여자가 첫 번째 대사에서 페트라가 방금 인쇄소에서 가져왔다
(Petra just picked it up from the print shop)고 하자, 두 번째 여자
인 페트라가 뒤이어 사무실로 오는 길에 거기 들렀다(I stopped there
on my way to the office)고 했으므로 정답은 (B)이다.

> Paraphrasing 대화의 stopped there
> → 정답의 stopped at a printing shop

54

What does the man say about the brochure the
speakers are discussing?
(A) He likes the bright colors.
(B) He already approved it.
(C) It contains too much information.
(D) It was redesigned several times.

화자들이 논의하고 있는 소책자에 관해 남자는 무엇이라고 말하는가?
(A) 밝은 색깔이 마음에 든다.
(B) 이미 승인했다.
(C) 정보가 너무 많다.
(D) 디자인을 여러 번 다시 했다.

해설 세부 사항 관련 – 소책자에 관해 남자가 언급하는 말

남자가 첫 번째 대사에서 그게 자신들이 인쇄 맡겨 놓은 새 소책자인지(Is
that the new brochure we're getting printed?) 물은 후 남자가 색깔
이 튀어서 마음에 든다(I love the way the colors just pop out)고 했
으므로 정답은 (A)이다.

> Paraphrasing 대화의 the colors just pop out
> → 정답의 the bright colors

55

Why will Petra make a phone call?
(A) To order copies
(B) To change a deadline
(C) To get a mistake corrected
(D) To try to get a price reduced

페트라는 왜 전화를 할 것인가?
(A) 인쇄본을 주문하려고
(B) 마감일을 변경하려고
(C) 오류를 바로잡으려고
(D) 가격을 낮추어 보려고

해설 세부 사항 관련 – 페트라가 전화를 하려는 이유

첫 번째 여자가 두 번째 대사에서 소책자에 있는 게 이전 로고가 아닌지

(isn't that our old logo on the brochure?) 묻자 두 번째 여자인 페트라가 자신은 분명히 새 로고를 줬다(I know I gave them the new logo)며 지금 전화해서 이것을 고쳐 달라고 확실히 해 놓겠다(I'm going to call them up now and make sure they fix this)고 한 것으로 보아 페트라는 로고 문제 해결을 위해 전화할 것임을 알 수 있다. 따라서 정답은 (C)이다.

Paraphrasing 대화의 fix this
→ 정답의 get a mistake corrected

56-58

M-Cn	**56Did you have time to order furniture for the new meeting room?**
W-Br	**56I have the office furniture price list, but I** haven't had a chance to look at it. **56,57With the convention next month, I've been so busy working on travel arrangements.**
M-Cn	**57Oh, that's right. That's a lot of work.**
W-Br	When I was hired as office manager, I was told that was one of my responsibilities.
M-Cn	**58Maybe you should talk to the area director to see if that can be taken off your plate.**
W-Br	There's no need. The fact is, I like working on travel plans.

남	새 회의실에 놓을 가구를 주문할 시간이 있었나요?
여	사무용 가구 가격표는 있는데 들여다볼 기회가 없었어요. 다음 달 컨벤션 때문에 출장 준비하느라 너무 바빴어요.
남	맞아요. 일이 많죠.
여	제가 사무장으로 채용되었을 때, 그게 제가 맡은 업무 중 하나라고 들었어요.
남	지부장과 상의해서 그 일을 덜 수 있는지 알아보세요.
여	그럴 필요 없어요. 사실 전 출장 계획 짜는 일이 좋아요.

어휘	arrangement 준비 be told that ~라고 듣다 responsibility 맡은 일, 책무 take off one's plate 일[부담]을 덜다

56

What does the woman imply when she says, "I haven't had a chance to look at it"?
(A) She is not interested in the price list.
(B) She likes the old furniture in the meeting room.
(C) The furniture prices are very high.
(D) The office furniture has not been ordered.

여자가 "들여다볼 기회가 없었어요"라고 말할 때 무엇을 의미하는가?
(A) 그녀는 가격표에 관심이 없다.
(B) 그녀는 회의실에 있는 낡은 가구를 좋아한다.
(C) 가구 가격이 매우 비싸다.
(D) 사무용 가구는 주문되지 않았다.

해설 화자의 의도 파악 – 들여다볼 기회가 없었다는 말의 의도
앞에서 남자가 새 회의실에 놓을 가구를 주문할 시간이 있었는지(Did you have time to order furniture for the new meeting room?) 묻자 사무용 가구 가격표는 있는데(I have the office furniture price list, but) 라면서 인용문을 덧붙이고, 그 뒤에 바로 다음 달 컨벤션 때문에 출장 준비하느라 너무 바빴다(With the convention next month, I've been so busy working on travel arrangements)고 했으므로 주문할 시간이 없었다는 의도로 볼 수 있다. 따라서 정답은 (D)이다.

57

What is most likely true about the travel arrangements that the woman is working on?
(A) They are taking more time than expected.
(B) They will be finished tomorrow.
(C) There are only two people working on them.
(D) The man is responsible for managing them.

여자가 하고 있는 출장 준비에 관해 무엇이 사실일 것 같은가?
(A) 예상보다 시간이 더 걸리고 있다.
(B) 내일 끝날 것이다.
(C) 그 일을 하는 사람이 두 사람뿐이다.
(D) 남자는 출장 준비 관리를 담당한다.

어휘 responsible for ~을 담당하는, ~에 책임이 있는

해설 세부 사항 관련 – 여자가 하고 있는 출장 준비에 대해 사실인 것
여자가 첫 번째 대사에서 다음 달 컨벤션 때문에 출장 준비하느라 너무 바빴다(With the convention next month, I've been so busy working on travel arrangements)고 했고 뒤이어 남자가 맞다(Oh, that's right)고 호응하며 일이 많다(That's a lot of work)고 한 것으로 보아 출장 준비로 많은 시간을 쓰고 있다는 것을 알 수 있다. 따라서 정답은 (A)이다.

58

What does the man suggest that the woman do?
(A) Train a coworker to order furniture
(B) Ask whether a responsibility can be removed
(C) Find somebody to help with travel planning
(D) Apply for a management position

남자는 여자에게 무엇을 하라고 제안하는가?
(A) 가구 주문을 위해 동료 교육하기
(B) 한 가지 책무를 배재할 수 있는지 문의하기
(C) 출장 계획을 도와줄 사람 찾기
(D) 관리직에 지원하기

어휘 planning 계획 (세우기) management position 관리직

해설 세부 사항 관련 – 남자의 제안 사항
남자가 마지막 대사에서 여자에게 지부장과 상의해서 그 일을 덜 수 있는지 알아보라(Maybe you should talk to the area director to see if that can be taken off your plate)고 제안하고 있으므로 정답은 (B)이다.

Paraphrasing 대화의 if that can be taken off your plate
→ 정답의 whether a responsibility can be removed

59-61 3인 대화

M-Au **60Can you please tell my supervisor what we discussed about the pop-up box my company would like to add to a Web page we're designing?**

W-Br Sure. **59Though we're mainly a consulting service, 60we do have Web developers who can be hired for hourly work.** Our developers all have the most current certifications.

M-Cn OK, well, none of our Web developers have experience with pop-up boxes, but if some of yours do, we'd be interested. Though, did Felix already explain that **61we'd like the pop-up box to be available when the site goes live next Monday?** I'm not sure how long drawing up the contract for this arrangement will take.

남1 우리가 디자인하고 있는 웹페이지에 회사가 추가하려는 팝업 상자에 대해 논의한 내용을 관리자에게 설명해 주시겠어요?

여 네. 저희는 컨설팅 서비스에 주력하고 있지만, 시간제 작업에 채용할 수 있는 웹 개발자들이 있어요. 저희 개발자들은 모두 최신 자격증을 보유하고 있습니다.

남2 그렇군요. 우리 웹 개발자들 중에는 팝업 상자 관련 경험이 있는 사람은 없지만, 그쪽에 그런 사람이 있다면 우리도 관심이 있어요. 그런데 펠릭스가 벌써 설명했나요? 다음 주 월요일에 사이트가 가동될 때 팝업 상자를 쓸 수 있으면 합니다. 이 협의를 위한 계약서 작성이 얼마나 걸릴지 모르겠네요.

어휘 pop-up box 팝업 상자 add 추가하다 developer 개발자 hourly 시간제의, 시간당 certification 자격증 available 사용할 수 있는 go live (컴퓨터 시스템이) 가동되다 draw up 작성하다 arrangement 협의

59

Who most likely is the woman?
(A) A consulting company employee
(B) A Web developer
(C) A supervisor
(D) A certified trainer

여자는 누구일 것 같은가?
(A) 컨설팅 회사 직원
(B) 웹 개발자
(C) 관리자
(D) 자격증이 있는 교육 담당자

어휘 certified 자격증이 있는, 공인 받은

해설 전체 내용 관련 – 여자의 직업
여자가 자신들은 컨설팅 서비스에 주력하고 있지만(Though we're mainly a consulting service)이라고 말한 것으로 보아 정답은 (A)이다.

60

What does the woman tell Felix' supervisor?
(A) She can provide some paperwork.
(B) She is paid hourly.
(C) She is not familiar with a feature.
(D) She has employees who can complete a task.

여자는 펠릭스의 관리자에게 무엇을 알려 주는가?
(A) 그녀는 서류 작업을 제공할 수 있다.
(B) 그녀는 시급을 받는다.
(C) 그녀는 어떤 기능 하나에 익숙하지 않다.
(D) 그녀에게 일을 완료할 수 있는 직원들이 있다.

어휘 familiar with ~에 익숙한 feature 기능

해설 세부 사항 관련 – 여자가 펠릭스의 관리자에게 언급하는 말
첫 번째 남자가 자신들이 디자인하고 있는 웹페이지에 회사가 추가하려는 팝업 상자에 대해 논의한 내용을 관리자에게 설명해 달라(Can you please tell my supervisor what we discussed about the pop-up box my company would like to add to a Web page we're designing?)고 요청하자 여자가 자신들에게 시간제 작업에 채용할 수 있는 웹 개발자들이 있다(we do have Web developers who can be hired for hourly work)고 한 것으로 보아 여자의 회사에는 팝업 상자와 관련하여 일을 할 수 있는 웹 개발자가 있음을 알 수 있다. 따라서 정답은 (D)이다.

> Paraphrasing 대화의 Web developers → 정답의 employees who can complete a task

61

When will a Web site be launched?
(A) Once a feature is added
(B) Later that day
(C) After two companies merge
(D) In the coming week

웹사이트는 언제 출시되는가?
(A) 기능이 추가되면
(B) 그날 늦게
(C) 두 회사가 합병한 후에
(D) 다음 주에

어휘 merge 합병하다 coming 다음의, 다가오는

해설 세부 사항 관련 – 웹사이트가 출시되는 시점
두 번째 남자가 다음 주 월요일에 사이트가 가동될 때 팝업 상자를 쓸 수 있으면 한다(we'd like the pop-up box to be available when the site goes live next Monday)고 했으므로 정답은 (D)이다.

> Paraphrasing 대화의 next Monday → 정답의 In the coming week

M-Au	Stevenson's Supplies and Distributing, Andy speaking.
W-Am	Hello, this is Carolina, from Monarch Pottery. ⁶²**There's an issue with the delivery we received from you this morning.** ^{62,63}**The invoice shows that we ordered two buckets of clear glaze, but there was none in our shipment.**
M-Au	Oh, ⁶³**I noticed that there were two buckets left behind on the loading dock after the delivery truck left!** I'll have the glaze delivered to you within an hour.
W-Am	I'd appreciate it. ⁶⁴**I need that glaze for a demonstration I'm doing in my adult wheel-throwing class this evening.**

남	스티븐슨 공급과 유통의 앤디입니다.
여	안녕하세요, 저는 모나크 도자기의 캐롤라이나예요. **저희가 오늘 아침에 받은 배송품에 문제가 있어요. 송장에는 투명 유약을 두 통 주문했다고 나오는데, 한 통도 배송되지 않았어요.**
남	아, **배송 트럭이 떠난 뒤에 하역장에 통 두 개가 남겨져 있는 걸 알았어요!** 한 시간 안에 유약을 배달해 드리겠습니다.
여	그렇게 해 주시면 감사하겠습니다. **오늘 저녁 성인 물레 성형 수업에서 시연을 하는 데 유약이 필요하거든요.**

어휘 pottery 도자기 invoice 송장 bucket 통, 양동이 glaze 유약 left behind (잊어버려서) 뒤에 남겨진, 두고 간 loading dock 하역장 demonstration 시연 wheel-throwing 물레 성형

Monarch Pottery Weekly Schedule	
Monday	Hand Building (adults)
⁶⁴Tuesday	Wheel Throwing (adults)
Wednesday	Hand Building (children)
Thursday	Wheel Throwing (children)
Friday	No classes

모나크 도자기 주간 일정	
월요일	손으로 빚기 (성인)
⁶⁴화요일	물레 성형 (성인)
수요일	손으로 빚기 (아동)
목요일	물레 성형 (아동)
금요일	수업 없음

62

What problem does the woman mention?
(A) Her order arrived late.
(B) Her order is missing an item.
(C) She did not order enough of an item.
(D) She did not receive an invoice.

여자는 어떤 문제를 언급하는가?
(A) 주문한 물건이 늦게 도착했다.
(B) 주문한 물건이 하나 빠져 있다.
(C) 물건을 충분히 주문하지 않았다.
(D) 송장을 받지 못했다.

해설 세부 사항 관련 – 여자가 언급하는 문제

여자가 첫 번째 대사에서 자신들이 아침에 받은 배송품에 문제가 있다(There's an issue with the delivery we received from you this morning)며 송장에는 투명 유약을 두 통 주문했다고 나오는데, 한 통도 배송되지 않았다(The invoice shows that we ordered two buckets of clear glaze, but there was none in our shipment)고 했으므로 정답은 (B)이다.

> Paraphrasing 대화의 there was none in our shipment → 정답의 Her order is missing an item

63

What does the man say about some buckets of glaze?
(A) They contain the wrong color glaze.
(B) They are on the delivery truck now.
(C) They were left behind.
(D) They are heavier than they look.

남자는 유약 통에 관해 무엇이라고 말하는가?
(A) 엉뚱한 색깔의 유약이 들어 있다.
(B) 지금 배달 트럭에 있다.
(C) 두고 갔다.
(D) 보기보다 더 무겁다.

어휘 contain 들어 있다

해설 세부 사항 관련 – 유약 통에 관해 남자가 언급한 말

여자가 첫 번째 대사에서 송장에는 투명 유약을 두 통 주문했다고 나오는데, 한 통도 배송되지 않았다(The invoice shows that we ordered two buckets of clear glaze, but there was none in our shipment)고 했고, 남자가 뒤이어 배송 트럭이 떠난 뒤에 하역장에 통 두 개가 남겨져 있는 걸 알았다(I noticed that there were two buckets left behind on the loading dock after the delivery truck left!)고 설명하고 있으므로 정답은 (C)이다.

> Paraphrasing 대화의 there were two buckets left behind → 정답의 They were left behind

64

Look at the graphic. On which day is the conversation taking place?
(A) Tuesday
(B) Wednesday
(C) Thursday
(D) Friday

시각 정보에 의하면, 어떤 요일에 대화가 이루어지고 있는가?

(A) 화요일
(B) 수요일
(C) 목요일
(D) 금요일

해설 시각 정보 연계 – 대화가 이루어지고 있는 요일

여자가 마지막 대사에서 오늘 저녁 성인 물레 성형 수업에서 시연을 하는데 유약이 필요하다(I need that glaze for a demonstration I'm doing in my adult wheel-throwing class this evening)고 했고, 일정표를 보면 물레 성형 성인 수업은 화요일로 나와 있으므로 정답은 (A)이다.

65-67 대화 + 목록

M-Au	**65,66I found a place that I think we can use for the conference our company is hosting this summer. 66It's a hotel ballroom, but it can be set up for business events.**
W-Br	OK. **65What's their catering like?**
M-Au	Well, **66they don't provide meals, but the hotel will provide snacks and beverages throughout the day.**
W-Br	And how many participants are we expecting?
M-Au	**67Last year's conference was hosted by a different company, and there were about 100 registrants. I'd expect about the same this year.**

남	이번 여름 우리 회사에서 주최하는 회의에 쓸 만한 곳을 찾았어요. 호텔 무도회장이지만, 업무 행사용으로 준비될 수 있어요.
여	네. 그곳 음식은 어떤가요?
남	식사는 제공하지 않지만 호텔에서 하루 종일 간식과 음료를 제공할 거예요.
여	그럼 참가자는 몇 명이나 될까요?
남	지난해 회의는 다른 회사에서 주최했는데, 100명 정도 등록 인원이 있었어요. 제 예상으로는 올해도 거의 같을 것이라고 봐요.

어휘	host 주최하다 ballroom 무도회장 be set up for ~을 위해 준비[마련]되다 catering 음식 공급 participant 참가자 registrant 등록자

Monaco Hotel

Host your business event with us!

⚓ Package	Number of guests ⚓
67Bronze	125
Silver	150
Gold	175
Platinum	200

모나코 호텔

업무 행사는 저희와 함께하세요!

⚓ 패키지	손님 수 ⚓
67브론즈	125
실버	150
골드	175
플래티넘	200

65

What are the speakers mainly discussing?
(A) A conference hosted by another company
(B) A location for an upcoming conference
(C) The purpose of an annual conference
(D) A conference speaker they both admire

화자들은 주로 무엇에 관해 논의하고 있는가?
(A) 다른 회사에서 주최하는 회의
(B) 곧 있을 회의의 장소
(C) 연례 회의의 목적
(D) 두 사람 모두 존경하는 강연자

해설 전체 내용 관련 – 대화의 주제

남자가 첫 대사에서 이번 여름 자신들의 회사에서 주최하는 회의에 쓸 만한 곳을 찾았다(I found a place that I think we can use for the conference our company is hosting this summer)며 장소에 대해 설명하자 여자가 그곳 음식은 어떤지(What's their catering like?) 물으며 회의 장소에 대한 대화를 이어 가고 있으므로 정답은 (B)이다.

Paraphrasing	대화의 a place → 정답의 A location 대화의 the conference our company is hosting this summer → 정답의 an upcoming conference

66

What does the man imply about conference participants?
(A) They will choose food options from a menu.
(B) They will eat breakfast together.
(C) They will not be provided with meals.
(D) They must buy snacks from a nearby store.

남자는 회의 참가자들에 대해 무엇을 암시하는가?
(A) 메뉴에서 음식을 선택할 것이다.
(B) 함께 아침을 먹을 것이다.
(C) 식사를 제공받지 않을 것이다.
(D) 근처 가게에서 간식을 사야 한다.

해설 세부 사항 관련 – 회의 참가자들에 대해 남자가 암시하는 것

남자가 첫 번째 대사에서 이번 여름 자신들의 회사에서 주최하는 회의에 쓸 만한 곳을 찾았다(I found a place that I think we can use for the conference our company is hosting this summer)면서 호텔 무도회장이지만, 업무 행사용으로 준비될 수 있다(It's a hotel ballroom, but it can be set up for business events)고 했고, 두 번째 대사에서 식사는 제공하지 않지만 호텔에서 하루 종일 간식과 음료를 제공할 것

(they don't provide meals, but the hotel will provide snacks and beverages throughout the day)이라고 했으므로 회의 참가자들에게 식사가 제공되지 않는다는 것을 알 수 있다. 따라서 정답은 (C)이다.

67

Look at the graphic. Which package will the speakers most likely purchase?
(A) Bronze
(B) Silver
(C) Gold
(D) Platinum

시각 정보에 의하면, 화자들은 어떤 패키지를 구매할 것 같은가?
(A) 브론즈
(B) 실버
(C) 골드
(D) 플래티넘

해설 시각 정보 연계 – 화자들이 구매할 패키지

남자가 대화의 마지막에 지난해 회의는 다른 회사에서 주최했는데, 100명 정도 등록 인원이 있었다(Last year's conference was hosted by a different company, and there were about 100 registrants)며 자신의 예상으로는 올해도 거의 같을 것으로 본다(I'd expect about the same this year)고 했다. 목록을 보면 브론즈의 손님 수가 125명으로 남자가 언급한 100명 정도의 참가자 수와 가장 근접하므로 정답은 (A)이다.

68-70 대화 + 지도

> **W-Am** Good morning. **68We've just parked our truck and we have a lot of equipment and furniture to move in. If you let us know the rooms where we can put the boxes, you won't have to move things again.**
>
> **M-Cn** The furniture will go in the reception area. Right near the front door.
>
> **W-Am** **69We also have five very heavy boxes.**
>
> **M-Cn** **69Those are the rowing machines. They go in the exercise area near the pool.**
>
> **W-Am** This looks like it's going to be a very nice gym. **70I see you already have the weight-lifting equipment set up.**
>
> **M-Cn** **70It was delivered yesterday.** We decided to put it right here near the entrance.

여	안녕하세요. **저희가 방금 트럭을 주차했는데 안으로 옮길 장비와 가구가 많네요. 상자를 놓을 수 있는 방을 알려 주시면 물건을 다시 옮기시지 않아도 될 거예요.**
남	가구는 안내실에 놓일 거예요. 현관 바로 근처예요.
여	**아주 무거운 상자도 다섯 개 있어요.**
남	**그건 로잉 머신입니다. 수영장 근처 운동 구역에 놓으세요.**
여	아주 멋진 헬스장이 될 것 같네요. **웨이트 리프팅 기구는 벌써 설치하셨군요.**

| 남 | **그건 어제 배송됐어요.** 바로 여기 입구 근처에 두기로 했답니다. |

| 어휘 | equipment 장비 reception area 안내실, 로비 front door 현관 rowing machine 로잉 머신(노 젓기 운동 기구) weight-lifting 웨이트 리프팅, 역도 |

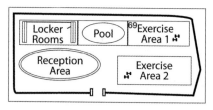

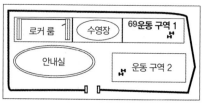

68

Where most likely does the woman work?
(A) At a delivery company
(B) At a fitness center
(C) At a truck repair facility
(D) At an exercise equipment manufacturer

여자는 어디에서 일할 것 같은가?
(A) 택배 회사
(B) 헬스장
(C) 트럭 수리 시설
(D) 운동 장비 제조업체

어휘 manufacturer 제조업체

해설 전체 내용 관련 – 여자의 근무지

여자가 첫 대사에서 자신들이 방금 트럭을 주차했는데 안으로 옮길 장비와 가구가 많다(We've just parked our truck and we have a lot of equipment and furniture to move in)며 상자를 놓을 수 있는 방을 알려 주면 물건을 다시 옮기지 않아도 된다(If you let us know the rooms where we can put the boxes, you won't have to move things again)고 한 것으로 보아 정답은 (A)이다.

69

Look at the graphic. Where will the five heavy boxes be put?
(A) In the reception area
(B) In the locker rooms
(C) In exercise area 1
(D) In exercise area 2

시각 정보에 의하면, 무거운 상자 다섯 개는 어디에 놓이겠는가?
(A) 안내실
(B) 로커 룸
(C) 운동 구역 1
(D) 운동 구역 2

해설 시각 정보 연계 – 무거운 상자 다섯 개가 놓일 장소

여자가 두 번째 대사에서 아주 무거운 상자도 다섯 개 있다(We also have five very heavy boxes)고 하자 남자가 그건 로잉 머신(Those are the rowing machines)이라며 수영장 근처 운동 구역에 놓아 달라(They go in the exercise area near the pool)고 했고, 지도에 수영장 근처 운동 구역은 운동 구역 1이므로 정답은 (C)이다.

70

What equipment was delivered yesterday?
(A) Rowing machines
(B) Furniture
(C) Pool supplies
(D) Weight-lifting equipment

어떤 장비가 어제 배송되었는가?
(A) 로잉 머신
(B) 가구
(C) 수영장 용품
(D) 웨이트 리프팅 기구

해설 세부 사항 관련 – 어제 배송된 장비

여자가 세 번째 대사에서 웨이트 리프팅 기구는 벌써 설치되어 있다(I see ~ the weight-lifting equipment set up)고 하자 남자가 뒤이어 그건 어제 배송됐다(It was delivered yesterday)고 했으므로 정답은 (D)이다.

PART 4

71-73 소개

M-Au Good morning, everyone! **71I'm Joshua, a volunteer guide here in beautiful Rosedale Sculpture Park.** My background is in art history, so I'll do my best to answer all your questions. But first, let me give you an overview of this amazing property. It was purchased in the nineteenth century by a local family who had spent many years abroad. **72During their years overseas they collected many statues and other types of sculptures... some ancient, some modern, which you'll see around the gardens today. 73And now take out your cameras as you follow me along our first trail.**

모두 안녕하세요! 저는 여기 아름다운 로즈데일 조각 공원에서 자원봉사 가이드로 일하는 조슈아입니다. 제가 미술사를 전공했으니 어떤 질문이든 최선을 다해 답해 드리겠습니다. 하지만 먼저, 이 놀라운 부지에 대해 간략히 알려 드리겠습니다. 이곳은 19세기에 해외에서 여러 해를 보낸 현지 가족에 의해 매입되었습니다. 그들은 해외에 있는 동안 많은 조각상과 다른 유형의 조각품들을 수집했죠. 몇 점은 아주 오래됐고, 몇 점은 현대적인데 오늘 정원 여기저기에서 보실 겁니다. 자, 이제 첫 번째 코스로 저를 따라오면서 카메라를 준비하세요.

어휘 sculpture 조각   background (개인의) 학력, 경력, 소양   do one's best 최선을 다하다   give an overview of ~을 간략히 설명하다   property 부지, 건물   purchase 매입하다   statue 조각상   ancient 아주 오래된, 고대의   trail 코스

71

Who is the speaker?
(A) A book author
(B) A park ranger
(C) A tour guide
(D) A painter

화자는 누구인가?
(A) 책 저자
(B) 공원 경비원
(C) 투어 가이드
(D) 화가

해설 전체 내용 관련 – 화자의 직업

화자가 초반부에 자신을 아름다운 로즈데일 조각 공원에서 자원봉사 가이드로 일하는 조슈아(I'm Joshua, a volunteer guide here in beautiful Rosedale Sculpture Park)라고 소개하고 있으므로 정답은 (C)이다.

72

What will the listeners mostly see during their visit?
(A) Rare plants
(B) Works of art
(C) Antique furnishing
(D) A nineteenth-century library

청자들은 방문 중에 주로 무엇을 볼 것인가?
(A) 희귀 식물
(B) 예술 작품
(C) 골동품 가구
(D) 19세기 도서관

어휘 rare 희귀한   work 작품   antique 골동품(의)

해설 세부 사항 관련 – 방문 중에 청자들이 볼 것

화자가 중반부에 그들은 해외에 있는 동안 많은 조각상과 다른 유형의 조각품들을 수집했는데 몇 점은 아주 오래됐고, 몇 점은 현대적으로 오늘 정원 여기저기에서 볼 것(During their years overseas they collected many statues and other types of sculptures... some ancient, some modern, which you'll see around the gardens today)이라고 했으므로 정답은 (B)이다.

Paraphrasing   담화의 statues and other types of sculptures → 정답의 Works of art

73

What does the speaker invite the listeners to do?
(A) Use a map
(B) Make a purchase
(C) Stay with the group
(D) Take pictures

화자는 청자들에게 무엇을 하라고 권하는가?
(A) 지도 사용하기
(B) 구입하기
(C) 단체에서 이탈하지 않기
(D) 사진 찍기

해설 세부 사항 관련 – 화자가 청자들에게 권하는 일

화자가 마지막에 이제 첫 번째 코스로 자신을 따라오면서 카메라를 준비하라(And now take out your cameras as you follow me along our first trail)고 한 것으로 보아 청자들에게 사진 찍기를 권하고 있음을 알 수 있다. 따라서 정답은 (D)이다.

74-76 방송

M-Cn Welcome to *Amir's Car Talk*! **74Let's discuss electric pickup trucks. I recommend that truck enthusiasts out there invest in one.** Most accelerate as quickly as sports cars, and electric pickups are super quiet. Plus, many have a towing capacity of over five tons! Sure, **75electric pickups are not cheap, but the environment will benefit.** Consider this, too: **76electric pickup trucks can even be used to power homes during an interruption in the supply of electricity.** That's pretty amazing, right?

〈아미르의 카 토크〉에 오신 걸 환영합니다! **전기 픽업트럭에 대해 이야기해 봅시다. 트럭 애호가들에게 한 대 투자하실 것을 권합니다.** 전기 픽업 대부분은 스포츠카만큼 가속이 빠르고 아주 조용합니다. 게다가 많은 경우 5톤 이상의 견인력을 지니고 있습니다! 물론 **전기 픽업이 저렴하지는 않지만, 환경에는 이로울 겁니다.** 이 점도 고려해 보세요. **전기 픽업트럭은 심지어 전기 공급이 중단되는 동안 가정에 전력을 공급하는 용도로도 활용될 수 있습니다.** 정말 놀랍죠?

어휘 electric 전기의 pickup truck 픽업트럭, 소형 오픈 트럭 enthusiast 애호가, 팬 invest in ~에 투자하다 accelerate 가속하다 towing capacity 견인력 power 전력[동력]을 공급하다 interruption 중단 supply 공급 electricity 전기

74

What does the speaker recommend doing?
(A) Creating more charging stations
(B) Buying an electric pickup truck
(C) Getting new tires
(D) Shopping for a sports car

화자는 무엇을 하라고 권하는가?
(A) 충전소 더 만들기
(B) 전기 픽업트럭 구매하기
(C) 새 타이어 구하기
(D) 스포츠카 쇼핑하기

해설 세부 사항 관련 – 화자의 추천 사항

화자가 초반부에 전기 픽업트럭에 대해 이야기해 보자(Let's discuss electric pickup trucks)고 운을 뗀 후, 트럭 애호가들에게 한 대 투자할 것을 권한다(I recommend that truck enthusiasts out there invest in one)고 한 것으로 보아 정답은 (B)이다.

> **Paraphrasing** 담화의 invest in one
> → 정답의 Buying an electric pickup truck

75

What disadvantage of electric pickup trucks does the speaker mention?
(A) Their high cost
(B) Their engine noise
(C) Their slow speed
(D) Their small size

화자는 전기 픽업트럭의 어떤 단점을 언급하는가?
(A) 비싼 가격
(B) 엔진 소음
(C) 느린 속도
(D) 작은 크기

해설 세부 사항 관련 – 전기 픽업트럭의 단점으로 화자가 언급하는 것

화자가 중반부에 전기 픽업이 저렴하지는 않지만, 환경에는 이로울 것(electric pickups are not cheap, but the environment will benefit)이라고 언급했으므로 정답은 (A)이다.

> **Paraphrasing** 담화의 not cheap → 정답의 high cost

76

What alternative use for electric pickup trucks does the speaker mention?
(A) Sheltering animals
(B) Generating radio signals
(C) Supporting building structures
(D) Powering homes

화자는 전기 픽업트럭의 어떤 대체 용도를 언급하는가?
(A) 동물 은신처 제공
(B) 무선 통신 신호 생성
(C) 건축 구조물 지지
(D) 가정에 전원 공급

어휘 alternative 대체의, 대안적인 shelter 은신처를 제공하다 generate 생성하다 radio 무선 (통신) signal 신호 structure 구조물

해설 세부 사항 관련 – 전기 픽업트럭의 대체 용도로 화자가 언급하는 것

화자가 후반부에 전기 픽업트럭은 심지어 전기 공급이 중단되는 동안 가정에 전력을 공급하는 용도로도 활용될 수 있다(electric pickup trucks can even be used to power homes during an interruption in the supply of electricity)고 했으므로 정답은 (D)이다.

77-79 회의 발췌

W-Am **77Welcome to the monthly staff meeting. As you might guess from the number of customers we get, Big Box Supermarket performed well this past year. 78To show us their appreciation for our hard work, the owners are inviting us to dinner at Wharton Restaurant.** Congratulations, everyone! Now, let's get back to business. We are increasing the amount of fruits and vegetables we receive. As a result, 79**I need two employees to arrive one hour early on Saturdays and Sundays.** There's a sign-up sheet in the staff room.

월례 직원 회의에 잘 오셨습니다. 우리가 확보한 고객 수에서 추측할 수 있듯이, 빅 박스 슈퍼마켓은 지난해 실적이 양호했습니다. 노고에 감사를 표하기 위해 점주들이 와튼 레스토랑 저녁 식사에 우리를 초대할 거예요. 축하합니다, 여러분! 자, 다시 일 이야기로 돌아갑시다. 우리가 납품받는 과일과 야채 양이 늘어나고 있어요. 그 결과 **토요일과 일요일에는 1시간 일찍 오는 직원 두 명이 필요합니다. 직원실에 신청서가 있습니다.**

어휘 monthly 월례의, 매월의   perform 실적을 내다
appreciation 감사   sign-up sheet 신청서

77

Who most likely is the speaker?
(A) A store cashier
(B) A produce supplier
(C) A restaurant owner
(D) A supermarket manager

화자는 누구일 것 같은가?
(A) 가게 계산원
(B) 농산물 공급업자
(C) 식당 주인
(D) 슈퍼마켓 관리자

해설 전체 내용 관련 – 화자의 직업
화자가 초반부에 월례 직원 회의에 잘 왔다(Welcome to the monthly staff meeting)며 자신들이 확보한 고객 수에서 추측할 수 있듯이, 빅 박스 슈퍼마켓은 지난해 실적이 양호했다(As you might guess from the number of customers we get, Big Box Supermarket performed well this past year)고 한 것으로 보아 정답은 (D)이다.

78

What are the owners doing?
(A) Increasing staff pay
(B) Introducing new products
(C) Hosting a dinner
(D) Hiring more employees

점주들은 무엇을 할 것인가?
(A) 직원 급여 인상
(B) 신제품 도입
(C) 저녁 식사 대접
(D) 직원 충원

해설 세부 사항 관련 – 점주들이 하려고 하는 일
화자가 중반부에 노고에 감사를 표하기 위해 점주들이 와튼 레스토랑 저녁 식사에 우리를 초대할 것이다(To show us their appreciation for our hard work, the owners are inviting us to dinner at Wharton Restaurant)고 했으므로 정답은 (C)이다.

> **Paraphrasing**   담화의 inviting us to dinner
> → 정답의 Hosting a dinner

79

What does the speaker imply when she says, "There's a sign-up sheet in the staff room"?
(A) The new work hours are voluntary.
(B) People who sign up get a reward.
(C) All employees must sign up for a shift.
(D) The meeting will continue in the staff room.

화자가 "직원실에 신청서가 있습니다"라고 말할 때 무엇을 의도하는가?
(A) 새 근무 시간은 자발적이다.
(B) 신청한 사람은 보상을 받는다.
(C) 모든 직원은 교대 근무를 신청해야 한다.
(D) 회의가 직원실에서 계속될 것이다.

어휘 voluntary 자발적으로   reward 보상

해설 화자의 의도 파악 – 직원실에 신청서가 있다는 말의 의도
인용문 앞에서 토요일과 일요일에는 1시간 일찍 오는 직원 두 명이 필요하다(I need two employees to arrive one hour early on Saturdays and Sundays)며 앞당겨진 출근 시간을 언급하면서 신청서가 비치되어 있는 곳을 가리키는 것으로 보아, 앞당겨진 시간에 출근하는 것은 신청에 의한 자발적인 것임을 알리려고 한 말임을 알 수 있다. 따라서 정답은 (A)이다.

80-82 광고

W-Br **80Homeowners, is your heating system over ten years old? Are you paying too much for your heating bills?** Honest Heating has the solution! Whether you need just a tune-up or an entirely new system, Honest Heating can help. 81**We're the only heating company in the area that uses infrared cameras. They let us see holes, cracks, and rust that regular color cameras miss.** Call today for a low-cost checkup. 82**Mention that you heard about us on KNXY News Radio, and you'll receive a five percent discount.** Don't delay; call Honest Heating today!

주택 소유주 여러분, 난방 시스템이 10년 넘었나요? 난방비를 너무 많이 내고 있나요? 어니스트 히팅에 해결책이 있습니다! 정비만 필요하든 완전히 새로운 시스템이 필요하든 어니스트 히팅이 도와드릴 수 있습니다. 당사는 이 지역에서 적외선 카메라를 사용하는 유일한 난방 업체입니다. 적외선 카메라로 일반 컬러 카메라가 놓치는 구멍, 균열, 녹을 확인할 수 있습니다. 저렴한 비용의 점검을 받으시려면 오늘 전화 주세요. KNXY 뉴스 라디오에서 들었다고 말씀하시면 5퍼센트 할인을 받으실 수 있습니다. 지체하지 말고 오늘 어니스트 히팅에 전화하세요!

어휘 heating 난방 bill 고지서 solution 해결책 tune-up 정비 entirely 완전히 infrared 적외선의 crack 균열 rust 녹 checkup 점검 delay 지체하다, 미루다

80
What is being advertised?
(A) A solar heating system for homes
(B) A contest for a new heating system
(C) A home cleaning service
(D) A service for home heating systems

무엇이 광고되고 있는가?
(A) 가정용 태양열 난방 시스템
(B) 새로운 난방 시스템 대회
(C) 가정 청소 서비스
(D) 가정 난방 시스템 서비스

해설 전체 내용 관련 – 광고되고 있는 것
화자가 도입부에서 청자들을 주택 소유주(Homeowners)라고 부르며 난방 시스템이 10년 넘었는지(is your heating system over ten years old?) 그리고 난방비를 너무 많이 내고 있는지(Are you paying too much for your heating bills?)를 묻고, 어니스트 히팅에 해결책이 있다(Honest Heating has the solution!)고 한 것으로 보아 주택용 난방 시스템을 광고하고 있다는 것을 알 수 있다. 따라서 정답은 (D)이다.

81
What does the advertisement emphasize about the company?
(A) Its 24-hour service
(B) Its special cameras
(C) Its low prices
(D) Its customer service

광고는 회사에 대해 어떤 점을 강조하는가?
(A) 24시간 서비스
(B) 특수 카메라
(C) 저렴한 가격
(D) 고객 서비스

해설 세부 사항 관련 – 광고가 회사에 대해 강조하는 점
화자가 중반부에 자신의 회사는 이 지역에서 적외선 카메라를 사용하는 유일한 난방업체(We're the only heating company in the area that uses infrared cameras)라며 적외선 카메라로 일반 컬러 카메라가 놓치는 구멍, 균열, 녹을 확인할 수 있다(They let us see holes, cracks, and rust that regular color cameras miss)고 했으므로 정답은 (B)

이다. 뒤에서 저렴한 점검(a low-cost checkup)을 언급했지만, 광고에서 강조한 것은 적외선 카메라를 통한 서비스 품질이지 가격이라고 볼 수 없으므로 (C)는 답이 되지 않는다.

Paraphrasing 담화의 infrared cameras
→ 정답의 special cameras

82
How can the listeners get a discount?
(A) By presenting a coupon
(B) By scheduling an appointment online
(C) By mentioning a radio advertisement
(D) By joining a mailing list

청자들은 어떻게 할인받을 수 있는가?
(A) 쿠폰을 제시해서
(B) 온라인으로 예약을 잡아서
(C) 라디오 광고를 언급해서
(D) 우편물 수신자 명단에 올려서

어휘 present 제시하다

해설 세부 사항 관련 – 청자들이 할인을 받을 수 있는 방법
화자가 후반부에 KNXY 뉴스 라디오에서 들었다고 하면 5퍼센트 할인을 받을 수 있다(Mention that you heard about us on KNXY News Radio, and you'll receive a five percent discount)고 알려 주고 있으므로 정답은 (C)이다.

Paraphrasing 담화의 Mention that you heard about us on KNXY News Radio → 정답의 mentioning a radio advertisement

83-85 회의 발췌

M-Cn 83**I am pleased to report on progress at our newest cement plant.** Local mines began delivering raw materials, and by the end of the month, 84**the plant delivered its first cement shipment to Regent construction company. The plant is not earning a profit yet.** But we hope to be a strong partner with Regent during this construction boom. Also, all 60 employees recently completed safety training. In addition, 85**five new employees received advanced safety training and certification.** They will work with our safety program supervisors to ensure that appropriate procedures are followed.

당사 최신 시멘트 공장의 진행 상황을 보고하게 되어 기쁩니다. 지역 광산에서 원자재를 배송하기 시작했고, 월말에는 공장에서 리젠트 건설사로 첫 시멘트 수송품을 배송했습니다. 아직은 공장이 수익을 내지 못하고 있습니다. 하지만 이번 건설 경기 호황 동안 리젠트의 탄탄한 협력업체가 됐으면 합니다. 또한 직원 60명 전원이 최근 안전 교육을 마쳤습

니다. 아울러 **신입 사원 5명이 상급 안전 교육을 이수하고 자격증을 받았습니다.** 그들은 적절한 절차가 지켜지는지 확실히 하기 위해 안전 프로그램 감독관들과 협력할 것입니다.

> **어휘** progress 진행 상황, 경과   mine 광산   raw material 원자재   earn 벌다   profit 수익   boom 호황, 붐   certification 자격증   appropriate 적절한   procedure 절차   follow (규칙, 절차 등을) 지키다, 따르다

83

What is the purpose of the meeting?
(A) To welcome new managers
(B) To fix a problem with a training program
(C) To provide an update
(D) To announce a change in strategy

회의의 목적은 무엇인가?
(A) 새로운 관리자를 환영하려고
(B) 교육 프로그램의 문제점을 해결하려고
(C) 최근 소식을 제공하려고
(D) 전략의 변경 사항을 알리려고

해설 전체 내용 관련 – 회의의 목적
화자가 도입부에서 자신들의 최신 시멘트 공장의 진행 상황을 보고하게 되어 기쁘다(I am pleased to report on progress at our newest cement plant)고 했으므로 정답은 (C)이다.

> **Paraphrasing** 담화의 report on progress
> → 정답의 provide an update

84

What does the speaker imply when he says, "But we hope to be a strong partner with Regent during this construction boom"?
(A) Regent is a new construction company.
(B) The plant may earn profits soon.
(C) The plant needs to create new products.
(D) The company needs to build more plants.

남자는 "하지만 이번 건설 경기 호황 동안 리젠트의 탄탄한 협력업체가 됐으면 합니다"라고 말할 때 무엇을 의도하는가?
(A) 리젠트는 신생 건설 회사이다.
(B) 공장은 곧 수익을 낼 수도 있다.
(C) 공장은 새로운 제품을 만들어야 한다.
(D) 회사는 공장을 더 많이 지어야 한다.

해설 화자의 의도 파악 – 하지만 이번 건설 경기 호황 동안 리젠트의 탄탄한 협력업체가 됐으면 한다는 말의 의도
화자가 중반부에 공장에서 리젠트 건설사에 첫 시멘트 수송품을 배송했다(the plant delivered its first cement shipment to Regent construction company)며 아직은 공장이 수익을 내지 못하고 있다(The plant is not earning a profit yet)고 한 뒤 인용문을 언급했으므로, 리젠트와의 꾸준한 거래를 통해 공장이 수익을 낼 수 있을 것이라는 의도로 볼 수 있다. 따라서 정답은 (B)이다.

85

What did new employees do?
(A) They inspected local mines.
(B) They delivered raw materials.
(C) They constructed a building.
(D) They acquired certification.

신입 사원들은 무엇을 했는가?
(A) 지역 광산들을 시찰했다.
(B) 원자재를 배송했다.
(C) 건물을 지었다.
(D) 자격증을 취득했다.

어휘 acquire 취득하다

해설 세부 사항 관련 – 신입 사원들이 한 일
화자가 후반부에 신입 사원 5명이 상급 안전 교육을 이수하고 자격증을 받았다(five new employees received advanced safety training and certification)고 했으므로 정답은 (D)이다.

> **Paraphrasing** 담화의 received → 정답의 acquired

86-88 광고

> W-Br **86This weekend, Coleman's Downtown Theater will present a marathon of science fiction films.** Some of the films being shown are over 100 years old. **87Fans may even learn something about the history of science fiction films, since the films will be shown in chronological order.** The marathon will run on Saturday and Sunday from ten A.M. to ten P.M. **88On Sunday afternoon, makeup artist Sara Wills, who has created some of film's scariest space monsters, will be in the lobby giving a demonstration.**

> 이번 주말, 콜먼즈 다운타운 극장에서 공상 과학 영화들의 연속 상영을 선보입니다. 상영되는 영화들의 일부는 100년이 넘었습니다. 영화들이 연대순으로 상영되므로 팬들은 공상 과학 영화의 역사까지 배울 수 있습니다. 이번 연속 상영은 토요일과 일요일 오전 10시부터 오후 10시까지 계속됩니다. 일요일 오후에는 영화에서 가장 무시무시한 우주 괴물을 만들어 낸 메이크업 아티스트 사라 윌스가 로비에서 시연합니다.

> **어휘** marathon 연속 상영[방영]   science fiction film 공상 과학 영화   chronological order 연대순   scary 무서운   demonstration 시연

86

What will happen at Coleman's Downtown Theater this weekend?
(A) Movies of a special type will be shown.
(B) An actor will sign autographs.
(C) Collectors will gather for a trade show.
(D) An outdoor seating area will be opened.

이번 주말에 콜먼즈 다운타운 극장에서 무슨 일이 일어날 것인가?
(A) 특정 종류의 영화가 상영된다.
(B) 배우가 사인회를 연다.
(C) 수집가들이 무역 박람회에 모인다.
(D) 야외 좌석 공간이 개방된다.

어휘 autograph 사인 collector 수집가

해설 전체 내용 관련 – 콜먼즈 다운타운 극장에서 이번 주말에 일어날 일

화자가 도입부에서 이번 주말, 콜먼즈 다운타운 극장에서 공상 과학 영화들의 연속 상영을 선보이다(This weekend, Coleman's Downtown Theater will present a marathon of science fiction films)고 했으므로 정답은 (A)이다.

> **Paraphrasing** 담화의 present a marathon of science fiction films → 정답의 Movies of a special type will be shown

87

What might people learn this weekend?
(A) How to prepare to run a marathon
(B) How the city has grown in 100 years
(C) The history of space exploration
(D) The history of an art form

이번 주말에 사람들은 무엇을 배울 수 있는가?
(A) 마라톤 경주를 준비하는 방법
(B) 100년 동안 도시가 어떻게 성장해 왔는가
(C) 우주 탐험의 역사
(D) 한 예술 형태의 역사

어휘 exploration 탐험

해설 세부 사항 관련 – 이번 주말에 사람들이 배울 수 있는 것

화자가 중반부에 영화들이 연대순으로 상영되므로 팬들은 공상 과학 영화의 역사까지 배울 수 있다(Fans may even learn something about the history of science fiction films, since the films will be shown in chronological order)고 했고, 공상 과학 영화는 예술의 한 형태이므로 정답은 (D)이다.

> **Paraphrasing** 담화의 science fiction films → 정답의 an art form

88

Who will be in the lobby on Sunday?
(A) A professional who works in the movies
(B) A writer who has released a new book
(C) A historian from a nearby university
(D) An astronaut who has been to space

일요일 로비에 누가 있을 것인가?
(A) 영화업계에서 일하는 전문가
(B) 신간을 낸 저자
(C) 인근 대학의 역사학자
(D) 우주에 가 본 우주 비행사

어휘 astronaut 우주 비행사

해설 세부 사항 관련 – 일요일 로비에서 볼 수 있는 사람

화자가 마지막에 일요일 오후에는 영화에서 가장 무시무시한 우주 괴물을 만들어 낸 메이크업 아티스트 사라 윌스가 로비에서 시연한다(On Sunday afternoon, makeup artist Sara Wills, who has created some of film's scariest space monsters, will be in the lobby giving a demonstration)고 했으므로 정답은 (A)이다.

> **Paraphrasing** 담화의 makeup artist Sara Wills, who has created some of film's scariest space monsters → 정답의 A professional who works in the movies

89-91 회의 발췌

W-Am **89Helping investors keep a long-term perspective is part of our role as financial consultants. 90Before today's meeting ends, I want to remind everyone about tonight's security update to our computer systems.** As you know, **91the security of our clients' personal and financial data is our highest priority. I hope you already viewed the online training video so you're ready to use the new security features tomorrow. If not, be sure to do so this afternoon.** We are the most trusted company in the industry, and we want to stay that way.

투자자들이 장기적인 관점을 견지하도록 돕는 일이 재무 컨설턴트로서 우리가 하는 역할의 일부입니다. 오늘 회의가 끝나기 전에 여러분 모두에게 오늘 밤 컴퓨터 시스템 보안 업데이트 관련해서 다시 한 번 주의를 환기하고자 합니다. 알다시피 고객의 개인 및 재무 데이터 보안은 우리가 최우선으로 하는 사항입니다. 내일 새로운 보안 기능을 사용할 수 있도록 온라인 교육 동영상을 이미 보셨기를 바랍니다. 아니라면 오늘 오후에 꼭 보도록 하세요. 우리는 업계에서 가장 신뢰도가 높은 회사이고, 앞으로도 계속 그러길 바랍니다.

어휘 investor 투자자 long-term 장기적인 perspective 관점 remind 상기시키다 security 보안 priority 우선 사항 view 보다, 시청하다 feature 기능

89

What work do the listeners do?
(A) Train security guards
(B) Make advertisements
(C) Create security software
(D) Provide financial advice

청자들은 어떤 일을 하는가?
(A) 경비원 교육
(B) 광고 제작
(C) 보안 소프트웨어 제작
(D) 재무 조언 제공

해설 전체 내용 관련 – 청자들의 업무

화자가 도입부에서 투자자들이 장기적인 관점을 견지하도록 돕는 일이 재무 컨설턴트로서 자신들이 하는 역할의 일부(Helping investors keep a long-term perspective is part of our role as financial consultants)라고 했으므로 정답은 (D)이다.

90

What will happen tonight?
(A) Security systems will be updated.
(B) More security guards will be on duty.
(C) Financial data will be revised.
(D) New computers will be purchased.

오늘 밤에 무슨 일이 일어날 것인가?
(A) 보안 시스템이 업데이트된다.
(B) 더 많은 경비원들이 근무한다.
(C) 재무 데이터가 수정된다.
(D) 새 컴퓨터를 구입한다.

어휘 on duty 근무 중인   revise 수정하다

해설 세부 사항 관련 – 오늘 밤에 있을 일

화자가 중반부에 오늘 회의가 끝나기 전에 모두에게 오늘 밤 컴퓨터 시스템 보안 업데이트 관련해서 다시 한 번 주의를 환기하고자 한다(Before today's meeting ends, I want to remind everyone about tonight's security update to our computer systems)고 했으므로 정답은 (A)이다.

> **Paraphrasing** 담화의 security update to our computer systems → 정답의 Security systems will be updated

91

Why does the speaker say, "We are the most trusted company in the industry, and we want to stay that way"?
(A) To congratulate a colleague
(B) To show appreciation to clients
(C) To motivate the listeners to act
(D) To introduce the next speaker

화자는 왜 "우리는 업계에서 가장 신뢰도가 높은 회사이고, 앞으로도 계속 그러길 바랍니다"라고 말하는가?
(A) 동료를 축하하려고
(B) 고객에게 감사를 표하려고
(C) 청자들이 행동하도록 동기 부여를 하려고
(D) 다음 연사를 소개하려고

어휘 motivate 동기를 부여하다, 자극하다

해설 화자의 의도 파악 – 우리는 업계에서 가장 신뢰도가 높은 회사이고, 앞으로도 계속 그러길 바란다는 말의 의도

인용문 앞에서 고객의 개인 및 재무 데이터 보안은 자신들이 최우선으로 하는 사항(the security of our clients' personal and financial data is our highest priority)이며, 내일 새로운 보안 기능을 사용할 수 있도록 온라인 교육 동영상을 이미 보았기를 바란다(I hope you already

viewed the online training video so you're ready to use the new security features tomorrow)면서 아니라면 오늘 오후에 꼭 보도록 하라(If not, be sure to do so this afternoon)고 했으므로 인용문은 청자들이 교육 동영상을 보고 새로운 보안 기능에 대비하도록 동기를 부여하려는 의도로 볼 수 있다. 따라서 정답은 (C)이다.

92-94 방송

> M-Au Greetings, listeners! Welcome to another episode of *Eating Central*. **⁹²I recently tried two Italian restaurants that opened in the area: Arno's Bistro and Maria's Kitchen.** Arno's Bistro features an elegant dining space with a nice view of South River. **⁹³Maria's Kitchen offers only an unappetizing view of a parking area,** but something was to my taste there: the chicken. It was moist and savory, with a fresh tomato sauce, and isn't to be missed. Sadly, the chicken at Arno's Bistro was dry, with sauce similar to what can be bought at the grocery store. **⁹⁴Looking for some tasty Italian? Maria's Kitchen isn't pretty, but the food is superb!**

안녕하세요, 청취자 여러분! 〈이팅 센트럴〉의 또 다른 에피소드에 오신 것을 환영합니다. 제가 최근에 이 지역에 문을 연 이탈리아 식당 두 곳에 가 봤습니다. 아르노즈 비스트로와 마리아즈 키친인데요. 아르노즈 비스트로는 사우스 리버가 보이는 멋진 전망과 함께 품격 있는 식사 공간이 특징입니다. 마리아즈 키친은 주차 구역만 보이는 보잘것없는 전망을 제공하지만, 제 입맛에 맞는 무언가가 있었으니 바로 닭 요리입니다. 신선한 토마토 소스를 끼얹은 닭 요리는 촉촉하고 풍미가 있었습니다. 그러므로 놓쳐서는 안 되는 것입니다. 아쉽게도 아르노즈 비스트로의 닭 요리는 퍽퍽했고 소스는 식료품점에서 살 수 있는 것과 비슷했습니다. 맛있는 이탈리아 음식을 찾으시나요? 마리아즈 키친은 예쁘지는 않지만, 음식은 최고입니다!

> 어휘 episode 1회 방송분 recently 최근에 feature 특징으로 하다 elegant 품격 있는, 고상한 unappetizing 매력 없는, 입맛 떨어지게 하는 taste 입맛, 취향 moist 촉촉한 savory 풍미가 있는 tasty 맛있는 superb 최고의, 훌륭한

92

What is the purpose of the broadcast?
(A) To promote healthy eating habits
(B) To describe new recipes
(C) To review local restaurants
(D) To promote Italian culture

방송의 목적은 무엇인가?
(A) 건강한 식습관 장려
(B) 새로운 조리법 설명
(C) 지역 식당 평가
(D) 이탈리아 문화 홍보

어휘 promote 장려하다, 홍보하다 describe 설명하다 recipe 조리법

해설 전체 내용 관련 – 방송의 목적

화자가 초반부에 자신이 최근에 이 지역에 문을 연 이탈리아 식당인 아르노즈 비스트로와 마리아즈 키친 두 곳에 가 봤다(I recently tried two Italian restaurants that opened in the area: Arno's Bistro and Maria's Kitchen)며 각 식당에 대한 설명을 이어 가고 있으므로 정답은 (C)이다.

93

What does the speaker criticize about Maria's Kitchen?
(A) The cost
(B) The service
(C) The parking
(D) The view

화자는 마리아즈 키친에 대해 무엇을 비판하는가?
(A) 가격
(B) 서비스
(C) 주차
(D) 전망

해설 세부 사항 관련 – 화자가 마리아즈 키친에 대해 비판하는 것

화자가 중반부에 마리아즈 키친은 주차 구역만 보이는 보잘것없는 전망을 제공한다(Maria's Kitchen offers only an unappetizing view of a parking area)고 했으므로 정답은 (D)이다.

94

What does the speaker recommend that the listeners do?
(A) Try the Italian food at Maria's Kitchen
(B) Cook Italian food at home
(C) Order the chicken at Arno's Bistro
(D) Travel outside the area for the best Italian food

화자는 청자들에게 무엇을 하라고 권하는가?
(A) 마리아즈 키친에서 이탈리아 음식 먹어 보기
(B) 집에서 이탈리아 음식 요리하기
(C) 아르노즈 비스트로에서 닭 요리 주문하기
(D) 최고의 이탈리아 음식을 찾아 타지로 여행 가기

해설 세부 사항 관련 – 화자가 청자들에게 권하는 일

화자가 후반부에 청자들에게 맛있는 이탈리아 음식을 찾고 있는지 (Looking for some tasty Italian?) 물은 뒤, 마리아즈 키친은 예쁘지는 않지만 음식은 최고(Maria's Kitchen isn't pretty, but the food is superb!)라고 추천하고 있으므로 정답은 (A)이다.

95-97 녹음 메시지 + 초대장

W-Br Hello, Evelyn. It's Sophia, ⁹⁵**calling about my wedding arrangements**. My wedding is five days away, and ⁹⁶**the forecast has changed dramatically. It was originally supposed to be sunny, but a huge storm is going to arrive on my wedding day.** ^{95,97}**Could you work with the Newfield Hotel to move our five o'clock reception indoors? Please reserve the Gold Room, if it's still available.** It has a wonderful dance floor and plenty of room for the band. Let me know which room you reserve so that I can let guests know about the change in plans.

안녕하세요, 에블린. 소피아인데요, **결혼 준비 때문에 전화했어요.** 제 결혼식이 닷새 앞인데, **일기 예보가 딴판으로 바뀌었네요. 원래는 날씨가 맑겠다고 했는데, 결혼식 날 엄청난 폭풍우가 닥친다고 해요. 뉴필드 호텔과 얘기해서 5시 피로연을 실내로 옮겨 주실래요? 아직 비어 있다면 골드 룸으로 예약해 주세요.** 멋진 무도장이 있고 밴드가 들어갈 공간이 넉넉하거든요. 하객들에게 계획에서 변동된 사항을 알릴 수 있도록 어떤 방을 예약했는지 알려 주세요.

어휘 arrangement 준비 forecast 일기 예보 be supposed to ~하기로 되어 있다 reception 피로연 reserve 예약하다 available 비어 있는, 이용할 수 있는 room 공간

⟡ **Save Our Date** ⟡
◯◯
Sophia and Randy

June 2
Newfield Hotel
⁹⁷5:00 P.M. reception in the Rose Garden
Music by Moderne Heart

⟡ **이 날은 비워 두세요** ⟡
◯◯
소피아와 랜디

6월 2일
뉴필드 호텔
⁹⁷**오후 5시 피로연 로즈 가든**
음악 연주 머데언 하트

95

Who most likely is the listener?
(A) A band leader
(B) A wedding planner
(C) A restaurant worker
(D) A professional printer

청자는 누구일 것 같은가?

(A) 밴드 리더

(B) 웨딩 플래너

(C) 식당 종업원

(D) 전문 인쇄업자

해설 진제 내용 관련 – 청자의 직업

화자가 초반부에 자신의 결혼 준비 때문에 전화했다(calling about my wedding arrangements)고 언급한 뒤, 중반부에 뉴필드 호텔과 얘기해서 5시 피로연을 실내로 옮기고, 아직 비어 있다면 골드 룸을 예약해 달라(Could you work with the Newfield Hotel to move our five o'clock reception indoors? Please reserve the Gold Room, if it's still available)고 변경 요청을 하는 것으로 보아 청자는 결혼 준비를 총괄하는 웨딩 플래너임을 알 수 있다. 따라서 정답은 (B)이다.

96

What problem does the speaker mention?

(A) A delayed flight

(B) An unavailable musician

(C) Additional guests

(D) A change in weather

화자는 어떤 문제를 언급하는가?

(A) 지연된 비행기

(B) 부를 수 없는 음악가

(C) 추가 하객

(D) 날씨 변화

어휘 unavailable 이용할 수 없는, 시간이 안 되는

해설 세부 사항 관련 – 화자가 언급하는 문제

화자가 중반부에 일기 예보가 딴판으로 바뀌었다(the forecast has changed dramatically)고 한 뒤 원래는 날씨가 맑겠다고 했는데, 결혼식 날 엄청난 폭풍우가 닥친다고 한다(It was originally supposed to be sunny, but a huge storm is going to arrive on my wedding day)는 문제를 언급하고 있으므로 정답은 (D)이다.

97

Look at the graphic. What information will most likely be changed?

(A) Newfield Hotel

(B) 5:00 P.M.

(C) Rose Garden

(D) Moderne Heart

시각 정보에 의하면, 어떤 정보가 변경될 것 같은가?

(A) 뉴필드 호텔

(B) 오후 5시

(C) 로즈 가든

(D) 머데언 하트

해설 시각 정보 연계 – 변경될 정보

화자가 중반부에 뉴필드 호텔과 얘기해서 5시 피로연을 실내로 옮겨 줄지(Could you work with the Newfield Hotel to move our five o'clock reception indoors?)를 물으며, 아직 비어 있다면 골드 룸으로

예약해 달라(Please reserve the Gold Room, if it's still available)고 요청했는데, 초대장에 오후 5시 피로연은 로즈 가든이라고 나와 있으므로 정답은 (C)이다.

98-100 회의 발췌 + 차트

M-Au Welcome, everyone. **98I've invited Ms. Sayan Mitra from Solve Now Consulting. She specializes in solving process optimization issues. 99Our automobile production process is too slow. According to Solve Now's analysis, the delay is in the painting process.** We're wasting too much time cleaning the spraying tool when changing to a different paint color between cars. They recommend using a more powerful cleaning solution on the spraying tool. **100Ms. Mitra has some slides that take us through the study and recommendations.** So, please welcome Ms. Mitra.

모두 잘 오셨습니다. 제가 솔브 나우 컨설팅의 사얀 미트라 씨를 초청했습니다. 미트라 씨는 공정 최적화 문제를 해결하는 전문가입니다. 당사의 자동차 생산 공정은 무척 느립니다. 솔브 나우 분석에 따르면, 도장 과정에서 지연이 일어납니다. 차량들 간의 페인트 색상 변경 시 분무 장비를 청소하는 데 시간을 지나치게 낭비하고 있어요. 그들은 분무 장비에 더 강력한 세척 용액을 사용하라고 권합니다. 미트라 씨는 우리가 연구와 권장 사항을 이해하는 데 도움이 되는 슬라이드를 가지고 오셨습니다. 자, 미트라 씨를 반갑게 맞아 주세요.

어휘 specialize in ~을 전문으로 하다 process 공정, 과정 optimization 최적화 production 생산 analysis 분석 solution 용액 take ~ through ~가 …을 익히도록 돕다 recommendation 권장 사항

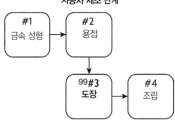

Car Production Stages

#1 Metal pressing → #2 Welding
↓
99#3 Painting → #4 Assembly

자동차 제조 단계

#1 금속 성형 → #2 용접
↓
99#3 도장 → #4 조립

98

Who is Sayan Mitra?
(A) A customer service representative
(B) An accountant
(C) A car dealer
(D) A consultant

사얀 미트라는 누구인가?
(A) 고객 서비스 담당자
(B) 회계사
(C) 자동차 판매업자
(D) 컨설턴트

해설 세부 사항 관련 – 사얀 미트라의 직업
화자가 초반부에 자신이 솔브 나우 컨설팅의 사얀 미트라 씨를 초청했다(I've invited Ms. Sayan Mitra from Solve Now Consulting)면서 미트라 씨는 공정 최적화 문제를 해결하는 전문가(She specializes in solving process optimization issues)라고 소개하는 것으로 보아 정답은 (D)이다.

99

Look at the graphic. Which stage of car production is the speaker discussing?
(A) Stage 1
(B) Stage 2
(C) Stage 3
(D) Stage 4

시각 정보에 의하면, 화자는 자동차 생산의 어느 단계에 대해 논의하고 있는가?
(A) 1단계
(B) 2단계
(C) 3단계
(D) 4단계

해설 시각 정보 연계 – 화자가 논의하고 있는 자동차 생산의 단계
화자가 중반부에 자신들 회사의 자동차 생산 공정은 무척 느리다(Our automobile production process is too slow)고 말한 뒤, 솔브 나우 분석에 따르면, 도장 과정에서 지연이 일어난다(According to Solve Now's analysis, the delay is in the painting process)고 하면서 관련된 이야기를 이어 가고 있으므로 화자가 논의하고 있는 단계는 도장 과정임을 알 수 있다. 차트에 따르면 도장 과정은 3단계이므로 정답은 (C)이다.

100

What will the listeners most likely do next?
(A) View a presentation
(B) Ask some questions
(C) Review some specifications
(D) Return to their desks

청자들은 다음에 무엇을 할 것 같은가?
(A) 프레젠테이션 보기
(B) 질문하기
(C) 사양 검토하기
(D) 업무에 복귀하기

어휘 specification 사양

해설 세부 사항 관련 – 청자들이 다음에 할 일
화자가 후반부에 미트라 씨는 연구와 권장 사항을 이해하는 데 도움이 되는 슬라이드를 가지고 왔다(Ms. Mitra has some slides that take us through the study and recommendations)면서 미트라 씨를 반갑게 맞아 달라(So, please welcome Ms. Mitra)고 한 것으로 보아 미트라 씨가 슬라이드를 보여 주며 설명을 할 것임을 알 수 있다. 따라서 정답은 (A)이다.

1 (A)	2 (C)	3 (A)	4 (D)	5 (B)
6 (B)	7 (B)	8 (C)	9 (A)	10 (C)
11 (A)	12 (C)	13 (A)	14 (B)	15 (B)
16 (C)	17 (C)	18 (B)	19 (C)	20 (B)
21 (B)	22 (A)	23 (C)	24 (B)	25 (B)
26 (A)	27 (B)	28 (C)	29 (A)	30 (C)
31 (C)	32 (A)	33 (D)	34 (B)	35 (A)
36 (B)	37 (B)	38 (B)	39 (C)	40 (A)
41 (B)	42 (A)	43 (D)	44 (B)	45 (A)
46 (C)	47 (B)	48 (D)	49 (C)	50 (A)
51 (B)	52 (C)	53 (B)	54 (B)	55 (D)
56 (D)	57 (B)	58 (B)	59 (C)	60 (D)
61 (D)	62 (A)	63 (C)	64 (B)	65 (C)
66 (B)	67 (D)	68 (A)	69 (C)	70 (D)
71 (C)	72 (A)	73 (D)	74 (C)	75 (D)
76 (B)	77 (B)	78 (B)	79 (C)	80 (D)
81 (C)	82 (D)	83 (D)	84 (B)	85 (A)
86 (D)	87 (B)	88 (B)	89 (A)	90 (C)
91 (D)	92 (C)	93 (C)	94 (A)	95 (A)
96 (C)	97 (C)	98 (A)	99 (C)	100 (B)

PART 1

1 W-Br

(A) He's working on a puzzle.
(B) He's lying on a sofa.
(C) He's reaching for a book.
(D) He's putting on a sweater.

(A) 남자가 퍼즐을 맞추고 있다.
(B) 남자가 소파에 누워 있다.
(C) 남자가 책을 잡으려고 손을 뻗고 있다.
(D) 남자가 스웨터를 입고 있다.

어휘 lie 누워 있다 reach for ~을 잡으려고 손을 뻗다

해설 1인 등장 사진 – 사람의 동작/상태 묘사
(A) 정답. 남자가 퍼즐을 맞추고 있는(is working on a puzzle) 모습이므로 정답.
(B) 동사 오답. 남자가 소파에 누워 있는(is lying on a sofa) 모습이 아니므로 오답.
(C) 동사 오답. 남자가 책을 잡으려고 손을 뻗고 있는(is reaching for a book) 모습이 아니므로 오답.

(D) 동사 오답. 남자가 스웨터를 입고 있는(is putting on a sweater) 동작을 하고 있는 것이 아니므로 오답.

2 M-Au

(A) She's organizing some books.
(B) She's buying a toothbrush.
(C) She's holding some products.
(D) She's talking to a store employee.

(A) 여자가 책들을 정리하고 있다.
(B) 여자가 칫솔을 사고 있다.
(C) 여자가 상품들을 들고 있다.
(D) 여자가 매장 직원과 이야기하고 있다.

어휘 organize 정리하다

해설 1인 등장 사진 – 사람의 동작/상태 묘사
(A) 동사 오답. 여자가 책들을 정리하고 있는(is organizing some books) 모습이 아니므로 오답.
(B) 동사 오답. 여자가 칫솔을 사고 있는(is buying a toothbrush) 모습이 아니므로 오답.
(C) 정답. 여자가 상품들을 들고 있는(is holding some products) 모습이므로 정답.
(D) 동사 오답. 여자가 매장 직원과 이야기하고 있는(is talking to a store employee) 모습이 아니므로 오답.

3 M-Cn

(A) He's wearing safety glasses.
(B) He's cleaning some equipment.
(C) He's picking up a hammer.
(D) He's laying stones on a driveway.

(A) 남자가 보안경을 쓰고 있다.
(B) 남자가 장비를 청소하고 있다.
(C) 남자가 망치를 집어 들고 있다.
(D) 남자가 진입로에 돌을 깔고 있다.

어휘 safety glasses 보안경 equipment 장비 lay 놓다
driveway 진입로

해설 1인 등장 사진 – 사람의 동작/상태 묘사
(A) 정답. 남자가 보안경을 쓰고 있는(is wearing safety glasses) 모습이므로 정답.

(B) 동사 오답. 남자가 장비를 청소하고 있는(is cleaning some equipment) 모습이 아니므로 오답.

(C) 동사 오답. 남자가 망치를 집어 들고 있는(is picking up a hammer) 모습이 아니므로 오답.

(D) 동사 오답. 남자가 진입로에 돌을 깔고 있는(is laying stones on a driveway) 모습이 아니므로 오답.

4 W-Br

(A) Some flowerpots have been placed along a walkway.
(B) The gate of a fence was left open.
(C) Some stairway railings are being installed.
(D) The building entrance has columns.

(A) 화분들이 통로를 따라 놓여 있다.
(B) 울타리 문이 열려 있었다.
(C) 계단 난간이 설치되고 있다.
(D) 건물 입구에 기둥들이 있다.

어휘 flowerpot 화분 walkway 통로, 보도 stairway 계단 railing 난간 install 설치하다 entrance 입구 column 기둥

해설 사물/풍경 사진 – 사물 묘사

(A) 사진에 없는 명사를 이용한 오답. 사진에 통로를 따라 놓여 있는(have been placed along a walkway) 화분들(Some flowerpots)의 모습이 보이지 않으므로 오답.

(B) 사진에 없는 명사를 이용한 오답. 사진에 울타리(a fence)의 모습이 보이지 않으므로 오답.

(C) 동사 오답. 계단 난간(Some stairway railings)이 설치되고 있는 (are being installed) 모습이 아니므로 오답.

(D) 정답. 건물 입구(The building entrance)에 기둥들이 있는(has columns) 모습이므로 정답.

5 M-Au

(A) Two people are standing around a buffet counter.
(B) Two people are having a meal together.
(C) A server is bringing dishes to a customer.
(D) A server is pouring water into glasses.

(A) 두 사람이 뷔페 진열대 주위에 서 있다.
(B) 두 사람이 함께 식사를 하고 있다.
(C) 종업원이 손님에게 음식을 가져다주고 있다.
(D) 종업원이 유리잔에 물을 따르고 있다.

어휘 have a meal 식사하다 pour 따르다, 붓다

해설 2인 이상 등장 사진 – 사람의 동작/상태 묘사

(A) 동사 오답. 두 사람이 뷔페 진열대 주위에 서 있는(are standing around a buffet counter) 모습이 아니므로 오답.

(B) 정답. 두 사람이 함께 식사를 하고 있는(are having a meal together) 모습이므로 정답.

(C) 사진에 없는 명사를 이용한 오답. 사진에 손님에게 음식을 가져다주고 있는(is bringing dishes to a customer) 종업원(A server)의 모습이 보이지 않으므로 오답.

(D) 사진에 없는 명사를 이용한 오답. 사진에 유리잔에 물을 따르고 있는 (is pouring water into glasses) 종업원(A server)의 모습이 보이지 않으므로 오답.

6 W-Am

(A) Electrical cables have been stacked on the floor.
(B) Stools have been placed around the room.
(C) Cabinets are being emptied.
(D) The floor of the workshop is being swept.

(A) 전기 케이블이 바닥에 쌓여 있다.
(B) 등받이 없는 의자들이 방 여기저기에 놓여 있다.
(C) 캐비닛을 비우고 있다.
(D) 작업장 바닥을 쓸고 있다.

어휘 electrical 전기의 stack 쌓다 empty 비우다 workshop 작업장 sweep 쓸다, 청소하다

해설 사물/풍경 사진 – 사물 묘사

(A) 동사 오답. 전기 케이블(Electrical cables)이 바닥에 쌓여 있는 (have been stacked on the floor) 모습이 아니므로 오답.

(B) 정답. 등받이 없는 의자들(Stools)이 방 여기저기에 놓여 있는(have been placed around the room) 모습이므로 정답.

(C) 동사 오답. 캐비닛(Cabinets)이 비워지고 있는(are being emptied) 모습이 아니므로 오답.

(D) 동사 오답. 작업장 바닥(The floor of the workshop)이 쓸리고 있는 (is being swept) 모습이 아니므로 오답.

PART 2

7

M-Cn Where can I buy tickets for the orchestra's fund-raiser?

W-Br (A) Over the next week.
　　　(B) On the fifth floor.
　　　(C) I suppose; if you want to.

오케스트라 모금 행사 입장권은 어디에서 살 수 있나요?

(A) 다음 한 주 동안이요.

(B) 5층에서요.

(C) 그렇겠죠, 원하시면요.

어휘 fund-raiser 모금 행사

해설 입장권의 구입 장소를 묻는 Where 의문문

(A) 질문과 상관없는 오답. When 또는 How long 의문문에 어울리는 응답이므로 오답.

(B) 정답. 모금 행사 입장권 구입 장소를 묻는 질문에 5층이라는 구체적인 장소를 제시하고 있으므로 정답.

(C) 질문과 상관없는 오답.

8

W-Br How long does your commute take?

W-Am (A) The gym opens early.

(B) I've been working here since March.

(C) About an hour lately.

통근 시간이 얼마나 걸리나요?

(A) 체육관은 일찍 문을 열어요.

(B) 저는 3월부터 여기서 일하고 있어요.

(C) 요즘에는 한 시간 정도요.

어휘 commute 통근 lately 요즘, 최근에

해설 통근에 걸리는 시간을 묻는 How long 의문문

(A) 질문과 상관없는 오답.

(B) 연상 단어 오답. 질문의 How long에서 연상 가능한 since March를 이용한 오답.

(C) 정답. 통근에 걸리는 시간을 묻는 질문에 한 시간 정도라고 구체적으로 알려 주고 있으므로 정답.

9

W-Am What's good to order at this café?

W-Br (A) I recommend the coffee and baked goods.

(B) Your food is on the way.

(C) It was sent this morning.

이 카페에서 뭘 주문하면 좋을까요?

(A) 커피와 제과류를 추천해 드립니다.

(B) 음식이 곧 나옵니다.

(C) 오늘 아침에 발송되었습니다.

어휘 order 주문하다 on the way 도중에

해설 무엇을 주문하면 좋을지 묻는 What 의문문

(A) 정답. 카페에서 무엇을 주문하면 좋을지 묻는 질문에 커피와 제과류를 추천한다며 구체적으로 응답하고 있으므로 정답.

(B) 연상 단어 오답. 질문의 order와 café에서 연상 가능한 food를 이용한 오답.

(C) 연상 단어 오답. 질문의 order에서 연상 가능한 was sent를 이용한 오답.

10

W-Am When's the new office furniture going to be delivered?

M-Cn (A) At the end of the report.

(B) I already finished the revision.

(C) It'll be here next week.

새 사무용 가구는 언제 배송되나요?

(A) 보고서 끝부분에요.

(B) 저는 이미 수정을 마쳤어요.

(C) 다음 주에 도착해요.

어휘 deliver 배달하다 revision 수정

해설 가구의 배송 시점을 묻는 When 의문문

(A) 연상 단어 오답. 질문의 office에서 연상 가능한 report를 이용한 오답.

(B) 질문과 상관없는 오답.

(C) 정답. 새 사무용 가구가 언제 배송되는지 묻는 질문에 다음 주에 도착한다며 배송 시점을 언급하고 있으므로 정답.

11

W-Br Who's holding the training session on Thursday?

M-Cn (A) Marcela's leading it.

(B) I exercise regularly.

(C) He was late today.

목요일 교육 과정은 누가 진행하나요?

(A) 마르셀라가 진행할 거예요.

(B) 저는 규칙적으로 운동해요.

(C) 그는 오늘 지각했어요.

어휘 training session 교육 (과정) regularly 규칙적으로

해설 교육 과정 진행자를 묻는 Who 의문문

(A) 정답. 목요일 교육 과정을 진행할 사람을 묻는 질문에 Marcela라는 사람 이름을 제시하고 있으므로 정답.

(B) 연상 단어 오답. 질문의 training에서 연상 가능한 exercise를 이용한 오답.

(C) 연상 단어 오답. Who 의문문에 대한 답으로 연상 가능한 대명사 He를 이용한 오답.

12

W-Am When should we hire extra help for the holidays?

M-Au (A) A helpful assistant.

(B) A fun party.

(C) As soon as possible.

연휴를 대비해 추가 인력은 언제 고용해야 할까요?

(A) 도움이 되는 보조원이요.

(B) 즐거운 파티예요.

(C) 가능한 한 빨리요.

어휘 extra help 추가 인력 helpful 도움이 되는 assistant 보조원

TEST 5

(A) 파생어 오답. 질문의 help와 파생어 관계인 helpful을 이용한 오답.
(B) 연상 단어 오답. 질문의 holidays에서 연상 가능한 party를 이용한 오답.
(C) 정답. 연휴를 대비해서 추가 인력을 언제 고용할지 묻는 질문에 '가능한 한 빨리요.'라고 응답하고 있으므로 정답.

13

M-Cn Why did you pick the color green for the product packaging?

W-Br (A) Because it matches our uniforms.
　　　(B) I will pick it up tomorrow.
　　　(C) Not until we know the menu options.

제품 포장으로 왜 초록색을 선택하셨나요?
(A) 저희 유니폼과 잘 어울리거든요.
(B) 제가 내일 가지러 갈게요.
(C) 메뉴 선택 사항부터 알아야 해요.

어휘 packaging 포장(재)　match 어울리다

해설 초록색 포장을 선택한 이유를 묻는 Why 의문문
(A) 정답. 초록색 포장을 선택한 이유를 묻는 질문에 자신들의 유니폼과 잘 어울리기 때문이라며 이유를 제시하고 있으므로 정답.
(B) 단어 반복 오답. 질문의 pick을 반복 이용한 오답.
(C) 질문과 상관없는 오답.

14

W-Am When's the budget report due?

W-Br (A) Sounds too expensive.
　　　(B) By end of day on Friday.
　　　(C) I can pay you back tomorrow.

예산 보고서 마감일이 언제인가요?
(A) 너무 비싼 것 같네요.
(B) 금요일 퇴근 전까지요.
(C) 내일 갚을 수 있어요.

어휘 budget 예산　pay ~ back ~에게 (빌린 돈을) 갚다, 상환하다

해설 예산 보고서의 마감일을 묻는 When 의문문
(A) 연상 단어 오답. 질문의 budget에서 연상 가능한 expensive를 이용한 오답.
(B) 정답. 예산 보고서의 마감일을 묻는 질문에 금요일 퇴근 전까지라며 구체적 시점으로 응답하고 있으므로 정답.
(C) 연상 단어 오답. 질문의 due에서 연상 가능한 tomorrow를 이용한 오답.

15

M-Cn Which shopping bag should I bring?

W-Am (A) Just outside the store.
　　　(B) The large one.
　　　(C) No, it isn't.

어떤 쇼핑백을 가지고 가야 하나요?
(A) 가게 바로 밖에요.
(B) 큰 거요.
(C) 아니요, 그렇지 않아요.

해설 가져가야 할 쇼핑백을 묻는 Which 의문문
(A) 연상 단어 오답. 질문의 shopping에서 연상 가능한 store를 이용한 오답.
(B) 정답. 어떤 쇼핑백을 가져가야 할지 묻는 질문에 큰 거라며 특정하여 알려 주고 있으므로 정답.
(C) Yes/No 불가 오답. Which 의문문에는 Yes/No 응답이 불가능하므로 오답.

16

M-Cn Don't forget to add another table to the conference room.

M-Au (A) Probably the yoga class.
　　　(B) No, they didn't.
　　　(C) OK, I'll do that now.

잊지 말고 회의실에 탁자를 하나 더 놓으세요.
(A) 아마 요가 수업일 거예요.
(B) 아니요, 그들은 하지 않았어요.
(C) 네, 지금 할게요.

어휘 conference room 회의실　probably 아마

해설 부탁/요청의 평서문
(A) 연상 단어 오답. 평서문의 room에서 연상 가능한 class를 이용한 오답.
(B) 연상 단어 오답. 평서문의 Don't에서 연상 가능한 didn't를 이용한 오답.
(C) 정답. 회의실에 탁자 하나를 더 추가해 달라는 요청에 대해 OK라고 승낙한 뒤, 지금 하겠다고 덧붙이고 있으므로 정답.

17

M-Au Who from our office is going to the conference?

W-Br (A) I am enjoying our new assignment.
　　　(B) At the hotel downtown.
　　　(C) Leslie and her support staff.

우리 사무실에서 누가 회의에 참석하나요?
(A) 저는 우리의 새 업무를 즐겁게 하고 있어요.
(B) 시내에 있는 호텔에서요.
(C) 레슬리와 보조 직원이요.

어휘 assignment 임무, 과제

해설 회의 참석자를 묻는 Who 의문문
(A) 연상 단어 오답. 질문의 office에서 연상 가능한 assignment를 이용한 오답.
(B) 연상 단어 오답. 질문의 conference에서 연상 가능한 hotel을 이용한 오답.
(C) 정답. 회의 참석자를 묻는 질문에 레슬리와 보조 직원이라며 사람 이름과 동행인을 제시하고 있으므로 정답.

18

W-Am Where are the signs for the sale?

M-Au (A) We are advertising a fifteen percent discount.
(B) On the porch.
(C) I didn't know we had sold those items.

판매 표지판은 어디에 있죠?
(A) 우리는 15퍼센트 할인을 광고하고 있어요.
(B) 현관에요.
(C) 저는 우리가 그 물건들을 팔았는지 몰랐어요.

어휘 porch 현관

해설 판매 표지판의 위치를 묻는 Where 의문문
(A) 연상 단어 오답. 질문의 sale에서 연상 가능한 advertising과 discount를 이용한 오답.
(B) 정답. 판매 표지판의 위치를 묻는 질문에 현관이라고 위치를 알려 주고 있으므로 정답.
(C) 연상 단어 오답. 질문의 sale에서 연상 가능한 sold를 이용한 오답.

19

W-Br Do you think we should place an advertisement in the newspaper?

M-Au (A) That's not what happened.
(B) No, I already have a subscription.
(C) Our budget is quite limited this month.

신문에 광고를 내야 한다고 생각하세요?
(A) 그렇지 않았어요.
(B) 아니요, 전 이미 구독하고 있어요.
(C) 이번 달 우리 예산이 매우 제한돼 있어요.

어휘 subscription 구독

해설 신문 광고의 필요성 여부를 묻는 조동사(Do) 의문문
(A) 질문과 상관없는 오답.
(B) 연상 단어 오답. 질문의 newspaper에서 연상 가능한 subscription을 이용한 오답.
(C) 정답. 신문에 광고를 내야 하는지 여부를 묻는 질문에 이번 달 예산이 제한적이라며 광고를 할 수 없음을 우회적으로 알리고 있으므로 정답.

20

W-Br I don't remember where I put my copy of the contract.

M-Cn (A) My calendar is up-to-date.
(B) I can look around for it.
(C) I don't think that's the best idea.

계약서 사본을 어디에 두었는지 기억이 안 나요.
(A) 제 일정표는 최신이에요.
(B) 제가 찾아볼게요.
(C) 그게 최선의 생각은 아닌 것 같아요.

어휘 contract 계약서 up-to-date 최신의

해설 정보 전달의 평서문
(A) 연상 단어 오답. 평서문의 contract에서 연상 가능한 up-to-date를 이용한 오답.
(B) 정답. 계약서 사본을 어디에 두었는지 기억나지 않는다는 평서문에 자신이 찾아보겠다며 해결 방안을 제시하고 있으므로 정답.
(C) 단어 반복 오답. 평서문의 don't를 반복 이용한 오답.

21

M-Cn What should we order for dinner?

M-Au (A) Yes, I ate some of that yesterday.
(B) I'd like something we haven't tried before.
(C) That makes sense to me.

저녁으로 뭘 주문할까요?
(A) 네, 전 어제 그걸 좀 먹었어요.
(B) 우리가 전에 먹어 보지 않은 게 좋겠어요.
(C) 일리가 있네요.

해설 저녁 메뉴를 묻는 What 의문문
(A) Yes/No 불가 오답. What 의문문에는 Yes/No 응답이 불가능하므로 오답.
(B) 정답. 저녁으로 무엇을 주문할지 묻는 질문에 전에 먹어 보지 않은 게 좋겠다는 의견을 제시하고 있으므로 정답.
(C) 질문과 상관없는 오답.

22

M-Au I thought the new safety training was supposed to start tomorrow.

W-Am (A) Yes, you're right.
(B) An old computer.
(C) The ones on the counter.

저는 새 안전 교육이 내일 시작되는 줄 알았어요.
(A) 네, 맞아요.
(B) 오래된 컴퓨터예요.
(C) 카운터에 있는 것들이요.

어휘 safety training 안전 교육 be supposed to ~하기로 되어 있다

해설 정보 전달의 평서문
(A) 정답. 새 안전 교육이 내일 시작되는 줄 알았다는 평서문에 네(Yes)라고 대답한 뒤, 맞다면서 정보를 확인해 주고 있으므로 정답.
(B) 연상 단어 오답. 평서문의 new에서 연상 가능한 old를 이용한 오답.
(C) 평서문과 상관없는 오답.

23

M-Au Should we buy desktop computers or laptops for the office?

W-Br (A) The Web site is working now.
(B) You can buy them at any store.
(C) Most of our staff travel a lot.

사무용으로 데스크톱 컴퓨터를 사야 할까요, 아니면 노트북을 사야 할까요?

(A) 웹사이트는 지금 작동하고 있어요.

(B) 그것들은 어느 가게에서나 살 수 있어요.

(C) 우리 직원 대다수는 출장을 많이 가요.

해설 구입할 컴퓨터의 종류를 묻는 선택 의문문

(A) 연상 단어 오답. 질문의 computers와 laptops에서 연상 가능한 Web site를 이용한 오답.

(B) 단어 반복 오답. 질문의 buy를 반복 이용한 오답.

(C) 정답. 구입할 컴퓨터의 종류를 묻는 선택 의문문에 직원 대다수가 출장을 많이 간다며 휴대가 용이한 노트북 구입의 의사를 우회적으로 표현하고 있으므로 정답.

24

M-Au Will you be attending the reception tomorrow?

W-Am (A) Just another day or so.

(B) Can you remind me what the topic is?

(C) I heard that they ran out of them.

내일 리셉션에 참석하실 건가요?

(A) 하루 정도 더요.

(B) 주제가 무엇인지 다시 한번 알려 주시겠어요?

(C) 그들이 그것들을 다 써 버렸다고 들었어요.

어휘 reception 환영[축하] 연회 run out of ~을 다 써 버리다

해설 리셉션 참석 여부를 확인하는 조동사(Will) 의문문

(A) 연상 단어 오답. 질문의 tomorrow에서 연상 가능한 day를 이용한 오답.

(B) 정답. 내일 리셉션에 참석할지를 묻는 질문에 리셉션의 주제가 무엇인지 상기시켜 줄 수 있는지 되물으며 우회적으로 응답하고 있으므로 정답.

(C) 질문과 상관없는 오답.

25

M-Au Did you buy your ticket to the baseball game?

W-Br (A) Sure, after the game is over.

(B) I thought admission was free.

(C) A sports tournament.

야구 경기 입장권을 사셨나요?

(A) 네, 경기가 끝난 후에요.

(B) 입장이 무료인 줄 알았는데요.

(C) 스포츠 토너먼트예요.

어휘 admission 입장

해설 경기 입장권 구입 여부를 확인하는 조동사(Did) 의문문

(A) 단어 반복 오답. 질문의 game을 반복 이용한 오답.

(B) 정답. 야구 경기 입장권을 구입했는지를 묻는 질문에 입장이 무료인 줄 알았다며 입장권을 구입하지 않았음을 우회적으로 응답하고 있으므로 정답.

(C) 연상 단어 오답. 질문의 baseball game에서 연상 가능한 sports tournament를 이용한 오답.

26

M-Cn How can I get more information about the employee party?

M-Au (A) A phone number is included in the invitation.

(B) The chef is from Italy.

(C) Where is the employment office?

직원 파티에 대한 더 많은 정보는 어떻게 얻을 수 있나요?

(A) 초대장에 전화번호가 포함되어 있어요.

(B) 요리사는 이탈리아 출신이에요.

(C) 직업소개소는 어디에 있나요?

어휘 employment office 직업소개소

해설 파티에 대한 정보 입수 방법을 묻는 How 의문문

(A) 정답. 직원 파티에 대한 정보를 얻는 방법을 묻는 질문에 초대장에 전화번호가 포함되어 있다며 전화를 걸어 정보를 얻을 수 있음을 우회적으로 알리고 있으므로 정답.

(B) 연상 단어 오답. 질문의 party에서 연상 가능한 chef를 이용한 오답.

(C) 파생어 오답. 질문의 employee와 파생어 관계인 employment를 이용한 오답.

27

W-Br Could you show me how to transfer funds?

M-Cn (A) No, it's the other one.

(B) Let me just finish this first.

(C) Sure, that seems like a reasonable price.

이체하는 방법 좀 가르쳐 주시겠어요?

(A) 아니요, 그건 다른 거예요.

(B) 이것만 먼저 끝내고요.

(C) 물론이죠, 적당한 가격 같네요.

어휘 transfer 옮기다, 이체하다 reasonable (가격이) 적정한

해설 부탁/요청의 의문문

(A) 연상 단어 오답. 질문의 Could you ~?에서 연상 가능한 대답인 No를 이용한 오답.

(B) 정답. 이체하는 방법을 가르쳐 달라는 요청에 하던 일부터 먼저 끝내겠다면서 기다리면 가르쳐 줄 수 있음을 우회적으로 표현하고 있으므로 정답.

(C) 유사 발음 오답. 질문의 show와 부분적으로 발음이 유사한 Sure를 이용한 오답.

28

W-Br Will our gym memberships renew automatically?

M-Au (A) They just saw that.

(B) About our manager.

(C) That's what I was told.

헬스클럽 회원권은 자동 갱신되나요?

(A) 그들이 방금 봤어요.

(B) 매니저에 대해서요.

(C) 그렇다고 들었어요.

어휘 renew 갱신되다   automatically 자동으로

해설 회원권의 자동 갱신 여부를 확인하는 조동사(Will) 의문문
(A) 질문과 상관없는 오답.
(B) 연상 단어 오답. 질문의 gym에서 연상 가능한 manager를 이용한 오답.
(C) 정답. 헬스클럽 회원권의 자동 갱신 여부를 묻는 질문에 그렇다고 들었다며 자동으로 갱신됨을 우회적으로 확인해 주고 있으므로 정답.

29

M-Au   Isn't Shinji scheduled to work at the cash register?

W-Am   (A) Yes, he just arrived.
        (B) The price hasn't changed.
        (C) How much does it cost?

신지가 계산대에서 일할 예정 아닌가요?
(A) 네, 그는 방금 도착했어요.
(B) 가격은 바뀌지 않았어요.
(C) 비용이 얼마나 드나요?

해설 계산대에서의 근무 예정 여부를 확인하는 부정 의문문
(A) 정답. 신지가 계산대에서 일할 예정인지 여부를 묻는 질문에 네(Yes)라고 대답한 뒤, 그가 방금 도착했다며 긍정 답변과 일관된 내용을 덧붙였으므로 정답.
(B) 연상 단어 오답. 질문의 cash에서 연상 가능한 price를 이용한 오답.
(C) 연상 단어 오답. 질문의 cash에서 연상 가능한 cost를 이용한 오답.

30

W-Am   Do you have all the ingredients for the recipe?

M-Cn   (A) We will plant a garden soon.
        (B) Yes, my oven is working again.
        (C) I need to buy some onions.

조리법에 필요한 재료가 전부 있나요?
(A) 우리는 곧 정원을 가꿀 거예요.
(B) 네, 제 오븐이 다시 작동하고 있어요.
(C) 양파를 좀 사야 해요.

어휘 ingredient 재료   plant a garden 정원을 가꾸다

해설 필요한 재료가 전부 있는지를 묻는 조동사(Do) 의문문
(A) 질문과 상관없는 오답.
(B) 연상 단어 오답. 질문의 ingredients와 recipe에서 연상 가능한 oven을 이용한 오답.
(C) 정답. 조리법에 필요한 재료가 전부 있는지를 묻는 질문에 양파를 좀 사야 한다며 양파가 필요함을 우회적으로 알리고 있으므로 정답.

31

W-Am   You're in charge of the supplier discount program, right?

M-Au   (A) The coupons are on the kitchen counter.
        (B) We have all the supplies we need.
        (C) Horatio is the one you want to talk to.

납품업체 할인 프로그램 담당이시죠, 그렇죠?
(A) 쿠폰은 주방 카운터에 있어요.
(B) 우리한테 필요한 비품이 전부 있어요.
(C) 호레이쇼와 얘기하시면 돼요.

어휘 in charge of ~을 담당하는   supplier 납품[공급]업체

해설 할인 프로그램의 담당자인지를 확인하는 부가 의문문
(A) 연상 단어 오답. 질문의 discount에서 연상 가능한 coupons를 이용한 오답.
(B) 파생어 오답. 질문의 supplier와 파생어 관계인 supplies를 이용한 오답.
(C) 정답. 할인 프로그램의 담당자인지 여부를 확인하는 질문에 얘기할 사람은 호레이쇼라며 호레이쇼가 담당자임을 우회적으로 알려 주고 있으므로 정답.

PART 3

32-34

W-Br   Hi, Martin. It's Lillian. **[32]Are you still planning to read from your book of poetry at the arts festival next weekend?** You're one of this publishing company's most accomplished writers.

M-Cn   **[32,33]I just need directions to the festival site. It's in a park, right?**

W-Br   Yes. Just know that once you get there, our table will be the one closest to the entrance. **[34]I can text you the address when we finish this call**.

여   안녕하세요, 마틴. 릴리안이에요. **다음 주말 예술제에서 시집을 낭독하실 계획은 그대로인 거죠?** 선생님은 이 출판사에서 가장 뛰어난 작가로 손꼽히는 분이시잖아요.

남   **축제 장소로 가는 길만 알려 주시면 됩니다. 공원에 있는 거 맞죠?**

여   네. 일단 도착하시면 입구에서 가장 가까운 자리가 저희 테이블이라는 점만 알아 두세요. **통화가 끝나면 제가 주소를 문자로 보내 드릴게요.**

어휘   poetry 시   publishing 출판   accomplished 뛰어난   directions 길 안내

32

What are the speakers discussing?
(A) Plans for an upcoming event
(B) The quality of the man's poems
(C) The publishing company they work for
(D) A problem with the woman's phone

화자들은 무엇을 논의하고 있는가?
(A) 다가오는 행사 계획
(B) 남자가 쓴 시의 질
(C) 그들이 일하는 출판사
(D) 여자의 전화기 문제

해설 전체 내용 관련 – 대화의 주제
여자가 첫 대사에서 다음 주말 예술제에서 시집을 낭독할 계획이 그대로인지(Are you still planning to read from your book of poetry at the arts festival next weekend?)를 물었고, 이에 남자가 축제 장소로 가는 길만 알려 주면 된다(I just need directions to the festival site)며 계획대로 참여할 것임을 우회적으로 표현하고 있으므로 정답은 (A)이다.

> **Paraphrasing** 대화의 the arts festival next weekend
> → 정답의 an upcoming event

33

What does the man need?
(A) Permission from his company
(B) Contact information
(C) An extra table
(D) The location of a park

남자는 무엇이 필요한가?
(A) 회사의 허가
(B) 연락처 정보
(C) 여분의 탁자
(D) 공원의 위치

어휘 permission 허가

해설 세부 사항 관련 – 남자가 필요한 것
남자가 축제 장소로 가는 길만 알려 주면 된다(I just need directions to the festival site)며 공원에 있는 것이 맞는지(It's in a park, right?)를 묻는 것으로 보아 축제 장소인 공원의 위치를 확인할 필요가 있음을 알 수 있다. 따라서 정답은 (D)이다.

34

What will the woman do next?
(A) Call the man's manager
(B) Send a text message
(C) Talk with an editor
(D) Check a schedule

여자는 다음에 무엇을 할 것인가?
(A) 남자의 매니저에게 전화하기
(B) 문자 메시지 보내기
(C) 편집자와 이야기하기
(D) 일정 확인하기

해설 세부 사항 관련 – 여자가 다음에 할 일
여자가 마지막 대사에서 통화가 끝나면 주소를 문자로 보내 주겠다(I can text you the address when we finish this call)고 했으므로 정답은 (B)이다.

> **Paraphrasing** 대화의 text → 정답의 Send a text message

35-37

W-Br	Mr. Guzman? I'm calling from Powell Advertising. As I'm sure you know, ³⁵**your contract with us expires next month. I was hoping we could take some time to discuss renewal terms.**
M-Au	Quite honestly, ³⁶**we're not seeing the increase in sales we were hoping for.** Advertising in buses and trains just isn't working for us.
W-Br	Hmm. ³⁷**I know you've been hesitant to get into Web advertising. But maybe now the time is right.**
M-Au	OK. ³⁷**Let's set up a time to talk about this.** I'm going to ask a few of my colleagues here to join us.

여	구즈만 씨? 파월 광고에서 전화 드립니다. 아시겠지만, **다음 달이면 저희와 맺은 계약이 만료됩니다. 시간을 좀 내서 갱신 조건에 대해 논의하고 싶었어요.**
남	솔직히 말해서, **우리가 기대한 매출 증가를 보고 있지는 않아요.** 버스와 열차 광고는 우리에게 효과가 없네요.
여	흠. **웹 광고를 시작하는 데 주저하시는 점 알아요. 하지만 지금이 적기일지 모릅니다.**
남	알겠습니다. **시간을 정해서 이 문제를 논의해 보죠.** 여기 동료 몇 명에게 함께하자고 부탁하겠습니다.

어휘	expire 만료되다 renewal 갱신 terms (계약) 조건 increase 증가 hesitant 주저하는

35

Why does the woman call the man?
(A) To discuss renewing a contract
(B) To discuss a transportation issue
(C) To announce a change in price
(D) To announce a personnel change

여자는 남자에게 왜 전화하는가?
(A) 계약 갱신을 논의하기 위해
(B) 운송 문제를 논의하기 위해
(C) 가격 변동을 알리기 위해
(D) 인사 변동을 알리기 위해

해설 전체 내용 관련 – 여자가 남자에게 전화하는 목적
여자가 첫 대사에서 다음 달이면 계약이 만료된다(your contract with us expires next month)면서 시간을 내서 갱신 조건에 대해 논의하고 싶다(I was hoping we could take some time to discuss renewal terms)고 했으므로 정답은 (A)이다.

> **Paraphrasing** 대화의 discuss renewal terms
> → 정답의 discuss renewing a contract

36

What does the man say about the current advertising?
(A) It is a good low-cost option.
(B) It has not led to a significant increase in sales.
(C) His colleagues have decided to cancel it.
(D) His colleagues do not have time to discuss it.

남자는 현재 광고에 관해 무엇이라고 말하는가?
(A) 훌륭한 저비용 옵션이다.
(B) 상당한 매출 증가로 이어지지 않았다.
(C) 동료들이 광고를 취소하기로 결정했다.
(D) 동료들이 광고에 대해 논의할 시간이 없다.

해설 세부 사항 관련 – 남자가 현재 광고에 대해 언급하는 것
남자가 첫 번째 대사에서 기대한 매출 증가를 보지 못하고 있다(we're not seeing the increase in sales we were hoping for)고 했으므로 정답은 (B)이다.

> Paraphrasing 대화의 not seeing the increase in sales
> → 정답의 not led to a significant increase in sales

37

What will the speakers discuss in their next meeting?
(A) Hiring a celebrity
(B) Advertising on the Internet
(C) Expanding an advertising budget
(D) Changing advertising companies

화자들은 다음 회의에서 무엇을 논의할 것인가?
(A) 유명인사 고용
(B) 인터넷 광고
(C) 광고 예산 확대
(D) 광고 회사 변경

어휘 celebrity 유명인사 expand 확대하다

해설 세부 사항 관련 – 화자들이 다음 회의에서 논의할 것
여자가 두 번째 대사에서 웹 광고 진입에 주저하는 점 알고 있지만(I know you've been hesitant to get into Web advertising) 지금이 적기일지 모른다(But maybe now the time is right)고 했고, 남자가 뒤이어 시간을 정해 이 문제를 논의하자(Let's set up a time to talk about this)고 대답한 것으로 보아 화자들이 이후에 웹 광고에 대해 논의할 것임을 알 수 있다. 따라서 정답은 (B)이다.

> Paraphrasing 대화의 Web advertising
> → 정답의 Advertising on the Internet

38-40 3인 대화

W-Am ³⁸,³⁹**Did Mr. Okamura really order all these carrots for the café? I signed for the delivery, but now I'm worried that there was a mistake.**

W-Br ³⁹**I don't know, Miho.** ³⁸**I saw the list of specials we're offering this weekend**

and didn't see anything that has a lot of carrots in it.

M-Cn It's OK. ⁴⁰**Mr. Okamura told me that we need them for a special private dinner tonight. I'll start preparing them now.**

W-Am OK. ⁴⁰**Once I finish the baking, I should be able to do some.**

M-Cn Thanks, Miho.

여1 오카무라 씨가 정말 카페를 위해 이 당근을 전부 주문했나요? 배송 수령 서명을 했는데, 착오가 있었을까 봐 걱정이 돼요.
여2 모르겠어요, 미호. 이번 주말에 제공하는 특별요리 목록을 봤는데 당근이 많이 들어가는 건 못 봤어요.
남 괜찮아요. 오카무라 씨가 오늘 밤 비공개 특별 만찬에 필요하다고 했어요. 제가 지금 준비하려고 해요.
여1 그렇군요. 일단 베이킹이 끝나면, 저도 좀 할 수 있을 거예요.
남 고마워요, 미호.

어휘 sign for ~을 수령했다고 서명하다 private 비공개의

38

Where does the conversation most likely take place?
(A) At a farmers market
(B) In a restaurant kitchen
(C) In a grocery store
(D) At a shipping company

대화는 어디에서 이루어지는 것 같은가?
(A) 농산물 시장
(B) 식당 주방
(C) 식료품점
(D) 운송회사

해설 전체 내용 관련 – 대화의 장소
첫 번째 여자가 첫 대사에서 오카무라 씨가 정말 카페를 위해 이 당근을 전부 주문했는지(Did Mr. Okamura really order all these carrots for the café?) 물었고 두 번째 여자가 이번 주말에 제공하는 특별요리 목록을 봤는데 당근이 많이 들어가는 건 못 봤다(I saw the list of specials we're offering this weekend and didn't see anything that has a lot of carrots in it)고 한 것으로 보아 식당 직원들이 배송된 식재료에 대해 이야기하는 대화임을 알 수 있다. 따라서 정답은 (B)이다.

39

Why is Miho concerned about the delivery?
(A) It seems too small.
(B) It arrived late.
(C) It contains a large quantity of one item.
(D) One type of item is missing from it.

미호는 왜 배송과 관련하여 걱정하는가?
(A) 너무 작아 보인다.
(B) 늦게 도착했다.
(C) 한 가지 품목의 수량이 많다.
(D) 한 가지 유형의 품목이 누락되었다.

해설 세부 사항 관련 – 미호가 배송과 관련하여 걱정하는 이유

첫 번째 여자가 첫 대사에서 오카무라 씨가 정말 카페를 위해 이 당근을 전부 주문했는지(Did Mr. Okamura really order all these carrots for the café?) 물으며 배송 수령 서명을 했는데 착오가 있었을까 봐 걱정된다 (I signed for the delivery, but now I'm worried that there was a mistake)고 하자 두 번째 여자가 첫 번째 여자의 이름을 부르며 모르겠다 (I don't know, Miho)고 한 것으로 보아 미호가 당근이 많이 배송되어 걱정하는 상황임을 알 수 있다. 따라서 정답은 (C)이다.

40

What does Miho offer to do?
(A) Help the man with his task
(B) Contact Mr. Okamura
(C) Sign for a delivery
(D) Find a replacement worker

미호는 무엇을 해 주겠다고 제안하는가?
(A) 남자의 일 돕기
(B) 오카무라 씨에게 연락하기
(C) 배송 수령 서명하기
(D) 대체 작업자 찾기

어휘 replacement 대체

해설 세부 사항 관련 – 미호의 제안 사항

남자가 첫 대사에서 오카무라 씨가 오늘 밤 비공개 특별 만찬에 필요하다고 했다(Mr. Okamura ~ we need them for a special private dinner tonight)면서 자신이 지금 준비하려고 한다(I'll start preparing them now)고 하자, 뒤이어 첫 번째 여자인 미호가 베이킹이 끝나면 자신도 좀 할 수 있을 것(Once I finish the baking, I should be able to do some)이라며 도와줄 것을 제안하고 있으므로 정답은 (A)이다.

> **Paraphrasing** 대화의 do some
> → 정답의 Help the man with his task

41-43

> W-Am Hi. ⁴¹**I'm calling from Dr. Jankovic's office to confirm your appointment tomorrow morning.**
>
> M-Au ⁴¹**Sure. I'll be there at eleven o'clock.**
>
> W-Am ⁴²**Since you're a new patient, please complete all the online forms before you arrive.** I sent you an e-mail last week with the link to our medical portal.
>
> M-Au Oh, I must have missed it. Sorry about that. I'll do it right away.
>
> W-Am No problem. ⁴³**And one reminder: our regular parking area is unavailable because it's being renovated.** You can park in front of the insurance company next door to us. We have an agreement with them.

여 안녕하세요. **야코비치 박사님 진료실에서 내일 오전 예약 확인차 전화 드립니다.**

남 네. **11시에 갈게요.**

여 **신규 환자이시기 때문에 도착하기 전에 온라인 양식들을 모두 작성해 주세요.** 지난주에 저희 의료 포털 링크가 포함된 이메일을 보내 드렸습니다.

남 아, 제가 놓쳤나 봐요. 미안합니다. 지금 바로 할게요.

여 괜찮습니다. 그리고 한 가지 알려 드리자면, **저희 정기 주차장이 보수 중이어서 이용하실 수 없습니다.** 옆 건물 보험회사 앞에 주차하시면 됩니다. 그 회사와 합의되었습니다.

어휘 confirm 확인하다 appointment (병원 등의) 예약 patient 환자 complete 작성하다 reminder 상기시키는 것 unavailable 이용할 수 없는 renovate 보수하다 agreement 합의

41

What will the man do tomorrow morning?
(A) Meet with a client
(B) Visit a doctor's office
(C) Relocate to a different office
(D) Attend a presentation

남자는 내일 오전에 무엇을 할 것인가?
(A) 고객 만나기
(B) 진료실 방문하기
(C) 다른 사무실로 이전하기
(D) 프레젠테이션에 참석하기

어휘 relocate 이전하다

해설 세부 사항 관련 – 남자가 내일 오전에 할 일

여자가 첫 대사에서 야코비치 박사님 진료실에서 내일 오전 예약 확인차 전화했다(I'm calling from Dr. Jankovic's office to confirm your appointment tomorrow morning)고 하자 남자가 네(Sure)라고 하며 11시에 가겠다(I'll be there at eleven o'clock)고 했으므로 정답은 (B)이다.

> **Paraphrasing** 대화의 be there
> → 정답의 Visit a doctor's office

42

What does the woman tell the man to do?
(A) Fill in some forms
(B) Update a contact number
(C) Make a payment
(D) Choose a menu item

여자는 남자에게 무엇을 하라고 말하는가?
(A) 양식 작성
(B) 연락처 번호 업데이트
(C) 비용 납부
(D) 메뉴 항목 선택

어휘 fill in ~을 작성하다

해설 세부 사항 관련 – 여자가 남자에게 하라고 언급하는 일

여자가 두 번째 대사에서 남자에게 신규 환자이므로 도착하기 전에 온라인 양식들을 모두 작성해 달라(Since you're a new patient, please complete all the online forms before you arrive)고 요청하고 있으므로 정답은 (A)이다.

> **Paraphrasing** 대화의 complete all the online forms
> → 정답의 Fill in some forms

43

What reminder does the woman give the man?
(A) A colleague is out of town.
(B) A price has changed.
(C) Some software must be updated.
(D) A parking area is closed.

여자는 남자에게 무엇을 상기시켜 주는가?
(A) 동료가 출타 중이다.
(B) 가격이 변경되었다.
(C) 소프트웨어가 업데이트되어야 한다.
(D) 주차장이 폐쇄되었다.

해설 세부 사항 관련 – 여자가 남자에게 상기시키는 것

여자가 마지막 대사에서 그리고 한 가지 알려 주면, 정기 주차장이 보수 중이어서 이용할 수 없다(And one reminder: our regular parking area is unavailable because it's being renovated)고 했으므로 정답은 (D)이다.

> **Paraphrasing** 대화의 our regular parking area is
> unavailable → 정답의 A parking area is
> closed

44-46

W-Br	Hi. **44I'm flying to Munich.** The name's Goldenberg. I have one suitcase.
M-Cn	**44I see your reservation, Ms. Goldenberg. I'll print your boarding pass.**
W-Br	Actually, **45I was wondering if you could change my seat. I'd rather have an aisle one.** It's easier if I have to move around.
M-Cn	Unfortunately, this flight is full. In fact, it's overbooked. So, **46if you're interested, I can offer you an aisle seat on tomorrow's flight and upgrade you to business class.**
W-Br	**46Tomorrow? I'm the guest speaker at a conference.**
M-Cn	OK. We'll ask some other passengers. Here's your boarding pass. Have a good trip!

여	안녕하세요. **뮌헨으로 가려고요.** 이름은 골든버그예요. 여행가방은 하나고요.
남	**예약하셨군요, 골든버그 씨. 탑승권을 출력해 드릴게요.**
여	실은 **자리를 바꿔 주실 수 있는지 궁금했어요. 통로 자리가 좋겠어요.** 돌아다녀야 한다면 그쪽이 더 수월하죠.
남	안타깝게도 이 비행기는 만석이에요. 사실 초과 예약됐어요. 그래서 **원하신다면 내일 비행기의 통로 자리를 제공하고 비즈니스석으로 업그레이드해 드릴 수 있습니다.**
여	**내일이요?** 제가 학회 초청 연사거든요.
남	네. 다른 승객들에게 물어보겠습니다. 탑승권 여기 있습니다. 즐거운 여행 되세요!

어휘	reservation 예약 boarding pass 탑승권 aisle 통로 overbooked 초과 예약된

44

Where is the conversation most likely taking place?
(A) At a bus terminal
(B) At an airport
(C) In a hotel lobby
(D) In a conference hall

대화는 어디에서 이루어지고 있는 것 같은가?
(A) 버스터미널
(B) 공항
(C) 호텔 로비
(D) 회의장

해설 전체 내용 관련 – 대화의 장소

여자가 첫 대사에서 뮌헨까지 비행기로 가려고 한다(I'm flying to Munich)고 했고, 남자가 뒤이어 여자의 예약을 확인해(I see your reservation, Ms. Goldenberg) 주면서 탑승권을 출력해 주겠다(I'll print your boarding pass)고 한 것으로 보아 정답은 (B)이다.

45

What does the woman ask for?
(A) A different seat
(B) A name badge
(C) A room upgrade
(D) A special menu

여자는 무엇을 요청하는가?
(A) 다른 자리
(B) 이름 배지
(C) 객실 업그레이드
(D) 특별 메뉴

해설 세부 사항 관련 – 여자의 요청 사항

여자가 두 번째 대사에서 자리를 바꿔 줄 수 있는지 궁금했다(I was wondering if you could change my seat)며 통로 자리가 좋겠다(I'd rather have an aisle one)고 했으므로 정답은 (A)이다.

> **Paraphrasing** 대화의 an aisle one → 정답의 A different seat

46

Why does the woman say, "I'm the guest speaker at a conference"?

(A) To confirm her conference attendance
(B) To introduce herself
(C) To refuse an offer
(D) To clarify a misunderstanding

여자는 왜 "제가 학회 초청 연사거든요"라고 말하는가?

(A) 회의 참석을 확정하기 위해
(B) 자신을 소개하기 위해
(C) 제안을 거절하기 위해
(D) 오해를 해명하기 위해

어휘 clarify 해명하다 misunderstanding 오해, 착오

해설 화자의 의도 파악 – 학회 초청 연사라는 말의 의도
앞에서 남자가 원하신다면 내일 비행기의 통로 자리를 제공하고 비즈니스석으로 업그레이드해 줄 수 있다(if you're interested, I can offer you an aisle seat on tomorrow's flight and upgrade you to business class)고 제안하자 내일인지(Tomorrow?) 되물으며 자신이 학회 초청 연사라고 말한 것으로 보아 초청 연사이기 때문에 내일 출발할 수 없다는 의도로 볼 수 있다. 따라서 정답은 (C)이다.

47-49

M-Au	Hi, I'm calling from Gwan Construction. **⁴⁷We were originally scheduled to transport the tower crane to your building this weekend for upcoming construction.** As you know, we will use it to lift large steel beams onto the roof for renovations on the top floor. **⁴⁷But I'm afraid we're going to have to bring it and set it up this Wednesday instead.**
W-Am	Well, **⁴⁸the weekend would have been better, since most of the offices are usually empty. But if you have to, I'll send a notice that employees should use the side-street entrance.**
M-Au	OK. **⁴⁹I'll go ahead and contact the city to request a change to the start date of our construction permit.**
남	안녕하세요, 관 건설에서 전화드립니다. **곧 있을 공사를 위해 원래 이번 주말에 타워크레인을 건물로 운송할 예정이었습니다.** 아시다시피, 꼭대기 층 보수를 위해 대형 철재를 지붕 위로 들어올리는 데 크레인을 사용하려고 합니다. 그런데 아무래도 이번 주 수요일에 대신 가져와서 설치해야 할 것 같아요.
여	음, 주말이 더 나았을 것 같아요. 보통 사무실 대부분이 비어 있거든요. 하지만 꼭 그렇게 하셔야 한다면, 직원들에게 골목 쪽 입구를 이용하라고 공지하겠습니다.
남	네. 제가 진행해서 시에 연락하여 건축 허가 시작일을 변경해 달라고 요청하겠습니다.

어휘	be scheduled to ~하기로 예정되어 있다 transport 운송하다 tower crane 타워크레인 upcoming 곧 있을, 다가오는 side-street 골목의, 옆길의 go ahead 진행하다 permit 허가(증)

47

What issue does the man discuss with the woman?

(A) His employees need access to the roof.
(B) Part of his plan needs to be rescheduled.
(C) A shipment of steel was incomplete.
(D) A renovation project is over budget.

남자는 여자와 어떤 문제를 논의하는가?

(A) 그의 직원들이 지붕에 접근해야 한다.
(B) 그의 계획 일부는 일정이 조정되어야 한다.
(C) 강철 선적이 완료되지 않았다.
(D) 보수 프로젝트가 예산을 초과한다.

해설 전체 내용 관련 – 남자가 여자와 논의하는 것
남자가 첫 대사에서 원래 이번 주말에 타워크레인을 건물로 운송할 예정이었다(We were originally scheduled to transport the tower crane to your building this weekend ~)고 한 후, 그런데 이번 주 수요일에 가져와서 설치해야 할 것 같다(But I'm afraid we're going to have to bring it and set it up this Wednesday instead)며 여자에게 일정 변경에 대해 이야기하고 있으므로 정답은 (B)이다.

48

Who most likely is the woman?

(A) An architect
(B) A financial analyst
(C) A construction worker
(D) A building manager

여자는 누구일 것 같은가?

(A) 건축가
(B) 재무 분석가
(C) 건설 인부
(D) 건물 관리인

해설 전체 내용 관련 – 여자의 직업
여자가 보통 사무실 대부분이 비어 있기 때문에 주말이 더 나았을 것 같다(the weekend would have been better, since most of the offices are usually empty)고 말한 뒤, 하지만 꼭 그렇게 해야 한다면 직원들에게 골목 쪽 입구를 이용하라고 공지하겠다(But if you have to, I'll send a notice that employees should use the side-street entrance)고 한 것으로 보아 여자는 사무실들이 있는 건물의 관리소에서 일하고 있음을 알 수 있다. 따라서 정답은 (D)이다.

49

What will the man do next?

(A) Close the building temporarily
(B) Get approval from his supervisor
(C) Reach out to city officials
(D) Arrange a new payment schedule

남자는 다음에 무엇을 할 것인가?
(A) 건물 임시 폐쇄하기
(B) 상사의 승인받기
(C) 시 공무원에게 연락하기
(D) 새로운 지급 일정 정하기

어휘 temporarily 임시로　approval 승인　reach out to ~에게
연락을 취하다

해설 세부 사항 관련 – 남자가 다음에 할 일
남자가 마지막 대사에서 시에 연락하여 건축 허가 시작일을 변경해 달라고
요청하겠다(I'll go ahead and contact the city to request a change
to the start date of our construction permit)고 했으므로 정답은
(C)이다.

> **Paraphrasing** 대화의 contact the city
> → 정답의 Reach out to city officials

50-52 3인 대화

M-Au	As you all know, ⁵⁰**our bookstore has a new inventory system for keeping track of what books we have in the store. We were going to start using it just after the holidays when the store is closed to customers, but we need to start using it now.**
W-Br	⁵⁰**Mr. Jones,** ⁵¹**you mean we'll be entering inventory into the system and helping customers at the same time? That's a lot.**
M-Au	⁵¹**I understand your concern,** but Marc has been attending training and will be able to lead the transition so that salespeople can concentrate on customer service. ⁵²**Marc, anything you want to say?**
M-Cn	The system isn't difficult to use. ⁵²**And most importantly, I think it will make filling online orders much quicker.**

남1	다들 알다시피, 저희 서점에는 매장에 어떤 책이 있는지 추적할 수 있는 새로운 재고 관리 시스템이 있습니다. 원래는 서점이 문을 닫는 연휴 이후에 사용하려고 했는데, 지금부터 쓰기 시작해야 할 것 같아요.
여	존스 씨, 그러니까 우리가 시스템에 재고를 입력하면서 동시에 고객을 돕는다는 건가요? 일이 많은데요.
남1	걱정은 이해하지만, 마크가 교육에 참석했으니 영업 사원이 고객 서비스에 집중할 수 있도록 전환 과정을 주도할 수 있을 겁니다. 마크, 하고 싶은 말이 있나요?
남2	이 시스템은 사용하기 어렵지 않습니다. 그리고 가장 중요한 것은 온라인 주문을 훨씬 더 빠르게 처리할 수 있을 겁니다.

어휘	inventory 재고 (관리)　keep track of ~을 추적하다 enter 입력하다　at the same time 동시에　concern 걱정　transition 전환　concentrate on ~에 집중하다 fill an order 주문을 처리하다

50

What does Mr. Jones announce?
(A) A change of plans
(B) A book-signing event
(C) New store hours
(D) A price change

존스 씨는 무엇을 알리는가?
(A) 계획 변경
(B) 도서 사인회
(C) 새로운 매장 영업시간
(D) 가격 변동

해설 세부 사항 관련 – 존스 씨가 알리는 것
첫 번째 남자가 첫 대사에서 서점에는 매장에 어떤 책이 있는지 추적할
수 있는 새로운 재고 관리 시스템이 있다(our bookstore has a new
inventory system for keeping track of what books we have in
the store)면서 원래는 서점이 문을 닫는 연휴 이후에 사용하려고 했는
데, 지금부터 쓰기 시작해야 할 것 같다(We were going to start using
it just after the holidays when the store is closed to customers,
but we need to start using it now)고 했고, 여자가 뒤이어 존스 씨
(Mr. Jones)라고 칭하며 대화를 이어가는 것으로 보아 존스 씨가 계획의
변경 사항을 알리고 있음을 알 수 있다. 따라서 정답은 (A)이다.

51

What is the woman concerned about?
(A) The accuracy of some software
(B) An increased workload
(C) Customer complaints
(D) Running out of supplies

여자는 무엇을 걱정하는가?
(A) 소프트웨어의 정확성
(B) 늘어난 업무량
(C) 고객 불만
(D) 비품 소진

어휘 accuracy 정확성　workload 업무량

해설 세부 사항 관련 – 여자의 우려 사항
여자가 시스템에 재고를 입력하면서 동시에 고객을 돕는다는 것인지(you
mean we'll be entering inventory into the system and helping
customers at the same time?) 되물으며 일이 많다(That's a lot)고
하자 첫 번째 남자가 걱정은 이해한다(I understand your concern)고
했으므로 정답은 (B)이다.

> **Paraphrasing** 대화의 That's a lot
> → 정답의 An increased workload

52

What does Marc emphasize?
(A) Reduced operating expenses
(B) Greater inventory availability
(C) The efficiency of a new system
(D) The need for extra training

TEST 5 **129**

마크는 무엇을 강조하는가?
(A) 절감된 운영비
(B) 재고 가용성 향상
(C) 새로운 시스템의 효율성
(D) 추가 교육의 필요성

어휘 availability 가용성 efficiency 효율성

해설 세부 사항 관련 – 마크가 강조하는 것

첫 번째 남자가 두 번째 대사에서 마크에게 하고 싶은 말이 있는지(Marc, anything you want to say?) 묻자 두 번째 남자인 마크가 가장 중요한 것은 온라인 주문을 훨씬 더 빠르게 처리할 수 있을 것(And most importantly, I think it will make filling online orders much quicker)이라며 새로운 시스템의 장점으로 빠른 일 처리, 즉 효율성을 강조하고 있으므로 정답은 (C)이다.

53-55

W-Br	Hi, I'm Tina Mackin, from the television program *Sunrise Scotland*. ⁵³**I just received an e-mail with information on the musical that's opening next month, *The Fields of Dumbarton*.**
M-Cn	Yes, the director asked me to send that— some photos and information. ⁵⁴**So you got the e-mail with all the attachments?**
W-Br	⁵⁴**I did, but I was expecting a short video from one of the rehearsals.** We'd like to show a clip on our morning television program.
M-Cn	I wasn't aware of that. ⁵⁵**I'll talk to the musical's director, Michael Byrne.**
W-Br	OK. ⁵⁵**And when you speak to him, please advise him to arrive early for his appearance on our show this Friday.** There's road construction around the studio, so it may take longer to get here than he expects.

여 안녕하세요, 저는 텔레비전 프로그램 〈선라이즈 스코틀랜드〉의 티나 맥킨입니다. **다음 달에 초연하는 뮤지컬 〈덤바턴의 들판〉에 관한 정보가 담긴 이메일을 방금 받았어요.**

남 네, 감독님이 제게 사진과 정보를 보내라고 요청하셨어요. **그래서 첨부 파일 전부와 이메일을 받으셨나요?**

여 **받았는데, 저는 리허설 중 하나를 보여 주는 짧은 동영상을 기대했어요.** 저희 아침 텔레비전 프로그램에서 클립 영상을 보여 주고 싶거든요.

남 그건 미처 생각 못 했네요. **뮤지컬 감독님인 마이클 번과 얘기해 볼게요.**

여 좋아요. 그리고 감독님과 얘기하실 때 이번 금요일 저희 프로그램에 출연할 때 일찍 도착하실 수 있도록 알려 주세요. 스튜디오 주변에서 도로 공사를 해서 이곳에 도착하는 데 예상보다 오래 걸릴 수 있어요.

어휘 director 감독 attachment 첨부(물) rehearsal 리허설 advise 알리다, 조언하다 appearance 출연 construction 공사

53

What will begin next month?
(A) A television show
(B) A musical
(C) A photo exhibition
(D) A rehearsal for a music video

다음 달에 무엇이 시작될 것인가?
(A) 텔레비전 프로그램
(B) 뮤지컬
(C) 사진전
(D) 뮤직비디오 리허설

해설 세부 사항 관련 – 다음 달에 시작되는 것

여자가 첫 대사에서 다음 달에 초연하는 뮤지컬 〈덤바턴의 들판〉에 관한 정보가 담긴 이메일을 방금 받았다(I just received an e-mail with information on the musical that's opening next month, *The Fields of Dumbarton*)고 했으므로 정답은 (B)이다.

54

What does the woman say about the e-mail?
(A) She is not happy with the attached photos.
(B) She expected it to contain a video.
(C) She thought it would arrive earlier.
(D) She has not had time to read it.

여자는 이메일에 관해 무엇이라고 말하는가?
(A) 첨부된 사진에 만족하지 않는다.
(B) 동영상이 들어 있을 것이라고 기대했다.
(C) 더 일찍 도착할 것이라고 생각했다.
(D) 이메일을 읽을 시간이 없었다.

어휘 contain 들어 있다

해설 세부 사항 관련 – 여자가 이메일에 관해 언급하는 것

남자가 첫 대사에서 첨부 파일 전부와 이메일을 받았는지(So you got the e-mail with all the attachments?) 묻자 여자가 받았지만 리허설을 보여 주는 짧은 동영상을 기대했다(I did, but I was expecting a short video from one of the rehearsals)고 대답했으므로 정답은 (B)이다.

> **Paraphrasing** 대화의 was expecting a short video
> → 정답의 expected it to contain a video

55

What does the woman suggest that Michael Byrne do on Friday?
(A) Talk with her on the phone about a video
(B) Share some ideas for a new musical
(C) Help her with a problem at the studio
(D) Allow extra time to get to his appointment

여자는 마이클 번에게 금요일에 무엇을 하라고 권하는가?

(A) 그녀와 전화로 동영상에 대해 이야기하기

(B) 새 뮤지컬에 대한 아이디어 공유하기

(C) 스튜디오에서 그녀의 문제를 도와주기

(D) 약속 장소까지 도착하는 시간을 넉넉하게 잡기

해설 세부 사항 관련 – 여자가 마이클 번에게 금요일에 하라고 권하는 것

남자가 두 번째 대사에서 뮤지컬 감독인 마이클 번과 얘기해 보겠다(I'll talk to the musical's director, Michael Byrne)고 했고, 여자가 뒤이어 감독님과 얘기할 때 이번 금요일 프로그램에 출연할 때 일찍 도착하도록 알려 주라(And when you speak to him, please advise him to arrive early for his appearance on our show this Friday)고 했으므로 정답은 (D)이다.

Paraphrasing	대화의 arrive early for his appearance on our show → 정답의 Allow extra time to get to his appointment

56-58

W-Am	**⁵⁷Have you had a chance to look at the survey results?**
M-Au	**⁵⁷I wasn't surprised. ⁵⁶,⁵⁷We've known for a while that our customers really don't like the music in our video games.**
W-Am	**⁵⁶The trend is to have popular music with vocals rather than the electronic sounds we've always used.**
M-Au	I'm sure using popular music in our games will increase sales. **⁵⁶,⁵⁸I think we should start to make this change now, don't you?**
W-Am	Well, **⁵⁸what's popular today may not be popular tomorrow, and we want our games to keep selling for a long time. So, let's not rush this decision.**
M-Au	I see, OK. Let's discuss this further with our division leaders.

여	설문 조사 결과를 볼 기회가 있었나요?
남	놀랍지 않았어요. 고객들이 비디오 게임에 나오는 음악을 탐탁지 않아 한다는 걸 얼마 전부터 알고 있었으니까요.
여	우리가 늘 사용해 오던 전자음보다는 보컬이 들어가는 대중음악을 넣는 추세예요.
남	우리 게임에 대중음악을 사용하면 매출이 증가할 거라고 확신합니다. 지금 당장 바꿔야 할 것 같은데, 어때요?
여	음, 오늘 유행이라 해도 내일은 아닐 수 있어요. 그리고 우리 게임이 오랫동안 팔리는 게 좋잖아요. 그러니까 결정을 서두르지 말죠.
남	알겠어요. 이 문제는 부서장들과 좀 더 논의해 봅시다.

어휘	electronic 전자의 increase 증가시키다 rush 서두르다 decision 결정 division leader 부서장

56

What are the speakers mainly discussing?

(A) A musician who has become successful

(B) A company decision to stop offering a service

(C) A licensing agreement with a popular singer

(D) A possible change to a product

화자들은 주로 무엇에 대해 논의하고 있는가?

(A) 성공한 음악가

(B) 서비스 제공을 중단하기로 한 회사 결정

(C) 인기 가수와의 라이선스 계약

(D) 제품의 변경 가능성

해설 전체 내용 관련 – 대화의 주제

남자가 첫 대사에서 고객들이 비디오 게임에 나오는 음악을 탐탁지 않아 한다는 걸 얼마 전부터 알고 있었다(We've known for a while that our customers really don't like the music in our video games)고 했고, 여자가 뒤이어 늘 사용해 오던 전자음보다는 보컬이 들어가는 대중음악을 넣는 추세(The trend is to have popular music with vocals rather than the electronic sounds we've always used)라고 하자 남자가 지금 당장 바꿔야 할 것 같은데, 어떤지(I think we should start to make this change now, don't you?) 묻고 있으므로 게임 음악을 변경하는 문제에 대해 논의하고 있음을 알 수 있다. 따라서 정답은 (D)이다.

57

What problem was identified in a customer survey about video games?

(A) Some video games are too difficult.

(B) Customers do not like the music.

(C) Some games only work with expensive equipment.

(D) Some games are completely defective.

비디오 게임에 대한 고객 설문 조사에서 어떤 문제가 확인되었는가?

(A) 일부 비디오 게임이 너무 어렵다.

(B) 고객들이 음악을 좋아하지 않는다.

(C) 일부 게임이 비싼 장비로만 작동한다.

(D) 일부 게임이 결함투성이다.

어휘 completely 완전히 defective 결함이 있는

해설 세부 사항 관련 – 고객 설문 조사에서 확인된 문제

여자가 첫 대사에서 설문 조사 결과를 볼 기회가 있었는지(Have you had a chance to look at the survey results?) 묻자 남자가 놀랍지 않았다(I wasn't surprised)면서 고객들이 비디오 게임에 나오는 음악을 탐탁지 않아 한다는 걸 얼마 전부터 알고 있었다(We've known for a while that our customers really don't like the music in our video games)고 했으므로 정답은 (B)이다.

58

Why does the woman say, "So, let's not rush this decision"?

(A) To request more funding from the division leaders

(B) To reject the man's suggestion

(C) To obtain a replacement product

(D) To recommend a different musician

여자는 왜 "그러니까 결정을 서두르지 말죠"라고 말하는가?
(A) 부서장들에게 자금을 더 요청하려고
(B) 남자의 제안을 거절하려고
(C) 대체 제품을 입수하려고
(D) 다른 음악가를 추천하려고

어휘 reject 거절하다   obtain 입수하다

해설 화자의 의도 파악 – 그러니까 결정을 서두르지 말자는 말의 의도
앞에서 남자가 지금 당장 바꿔야 할 것 같은데, 어떤지(I think we should start to make this change now, don't you?) 여자에게 의견을 묻자 여자가 오늘 유행이라 해도 내일은 아닐 수 있고 게임이 오랫동안 팔리는 게 좋다(what's popular today may not be popular tomorrow, and we want our games to keep selling for a long time)고 말한 뒤 인용문을 언급하고 있으므로, 바꿔야 한다는 남자의 의견에 동의하지 않는다는 의도로 볼 수 있다. 따라서 정답은 (B)이다.

59-61

M-Cn	Good morning, Dr. An! In case you have forgotten, ⁵⁹**today I am going to start transferring patients' paper records to electronic files.**
W-Am	Oh, right! Thanks! Who will be handling phone calls and greeting patients while you're in the back office?
M-Cn	I arranged for a temporary office assistant to come in and help out.
W-Am	OK. ⁶⁰,⁶¹**But the system we use for scheduling appointments can be tricky to operate.**
M-Cn	Well, ⁶¹**the office assistant is coming from an agency that specializes in the medical profession, so I think we should be fine.**

남	안녕하세요, 안 박사님! 혹시 잊으셨을까 봐 말씀드리는데, **오늘부터 제가 환자의 문서 기록을 전자 파일로 옮기려고 합니다.**
여	참, 그렇죠! 고마워요! 당신이 사무실에서 업무를 보는 동안 누가 전화를 받고 환자를 응대하나요?
남	임시 사무 보조원이 와서 돕도록 처리해 두었어요.
여	그렇군요. **그런데 예약 일정을 관리하는 데 사용하는 시스템이 조작하기 까다로울 수도 있을 텐데요.**
남	음, 사무 보조원이 의료업을 전문으로 하는 업체에서 오기 때문에 괜찮을 것 같아요.

어휘	in case ~할 경우에 대비해서 transfer 옮기다, 이전하다 greet 맞이하다 back office (고객에게 노출되지 않는) 사무실 arrange (일을) 처리[주선]하다 temporary 임시의 tricky 까다로운 agency 대행업체 specialize in ~을 전문으로 하다 medical profession 의료업

59

What does the man say he will do today?
(A) Greet patients
(B) Train a new employee
(C) Transfer medical records
(D) Make appointments

남자는 오늘 무엇을 할 것이라고 말하는가?
(A) 환자 응대하기
(B) 신입 사원 교육하기
(C) 진료 기록 옮기기
(D) 예약 잡기

해설 세부 사항 관련 – 남자가 오늘 할 것이라고 말하는 일
남자가 첫 대사에서 오늘부터 환자의 문서 기록을 전자 파일로 옮기려고 한다(today I am going to start transferring patients' paper records to electronic files)고 했으므로 정답은 (C)이다.

Paraphrasing	대화의 transferring patients' paper records to electronic files → 정답의 Transfer medical records

60

What is the woman concerned about?
(A) The cost of hiring a new office assistant
(B) Maintaining the security of electronic files
(C) The privacy of patients in the office
(D) Using a scheduling system

여자는 무엇을 걱정하는가?
(A) 새 사무 보조원을 고용하는 비용
(B) 전자 파일의 보안 유지
(C) 진료실 환자들의 사생활
(D) 일정 관리 시스템의 사용

해설 세부 사항 관련 – 여자의 우려 사항
여자가 두 번째 대사에서 그러나 예약 일정을 관리하는 데 사용하는 시스템이 조작하기 까다로울 수도 있을 것(But the system we use for scheduling appointments can be tricky to operate)이라며 우려를 표현하고 있으므로 정답은 (D)이다.

Paraphrasing	대화의 the system we use for scheduling appointments → 정답의 a scheduling system

61

Why does the man feel confident in the temporary office assistant?
(A) He will be able to help the assistant if the office gets busy.
(B) He has worked with the assistant on other projects.
(C) The doctor recommended that he hire the assistant.
(D) The assistant comes from an agency that specializes in medical work.

남자는 왜 임시 사무 보조원에 확신을 가지는가?
(A) 사무실이 바빠지면 남자가 보조원을 도울 수 있을 것이다.
(B) 남자는 다른 프로젝트에서 보조원과 일한 적이 있다.
(C) 의사가 그에게 보조원을 고용하라고 권했다.
(D) 보조원은 의료 업무를 전문으로 하는 업체에서 온다.

해설 세부 사항 관련 – 남자가 임시 사무 보조원에 확신을 가지는 이유

여자가 두 번째 대사에서 예약 일정을 관리하는 데 사용하는 시스템이 조작하기 까다로울 수도 있을 것(But the system we use for scheduling appointments can be tricky to operate)이라며 우려를 표하자 남자가 뒤이어 사무 보조원이 의료업을 전문으로 하는 업체에서 오기 때문에 괜찮을 것 같다(the office assistant is coming from an agency that specializes in the medical profession, so I think we should be fine)며 여자를 안심시키고 있으므로 정답은 (D)이다.

> **Paraphrasing** 대화의 the medical profession
> → 정답의 medical work

62-64 대화 + 송장

W-Am	Hi, Ian. This is Michelle from Michelle's Flower Shop. ⁶²**We just received our wholesale order, but the tulips are missing.**
M-Cn	Oh sorry, ⁶³**I forgot to let you know that my supplier can't get them to me until tomorrow.**
W-Am	I've had a number of customers requesting tulips recently. So could you please ship them as soon as you can?
M-Cn	Absolutely. I'll send the truck back to you tomorrow with the tulips.
W-Am	And actually, ⁶⁴**I've ordered 100 flowers, but could you double that, please?** I'm sure I'll need at least 200.
M-Cn	⁶⁴**Sure. And I'll send you a revised invoice as well.**

여	안녕하세요, 이안. 미셸 꽃집의 미셸이에요. **방금 도매 주문품을 받았는데, 튤립이 빠졌네요.**
남	아, 죄송합니다. **납품업체가 내일이나 돼야 제게 튤립을 가져다줄 수 있는데, 잊어버리고 얘기를 못 했네요.**
여	최근에 튤립을 요청하는 손님들이 많았어요. 그러니 가능한 한 빨리 배송해 주시겠어요?
남	물론이죠. 내일 튤립을 실은 트럭을 다시 보내겠습니다.
여	그리고 실은 **100송이를 주문했는데, 두 배로 주시겠어요?** 틀림없이 적어도 200송이는 필요할 거예요.
남	**그럼요. 수정된 송장도 같이 보내겠습니다.**

어휘 wholesale 도매의 supplier 공급업자[체] ship 배송하다 at least 적어도 revised 수정된

Invoice	
From: Prebble Flower Distributors To: Michelle's Flower Shop	
Roses (125)	$155
⁶⁴Tulips (100)	$130
Calla lilies (75)	$180
Carnations (50)	$85

송장	
발신: 프레블 꽃 유통 수신: 미셸 꽃집	
장미 (125)	155달러
⁶⁴**튤립(100)**	**130달러**
칼라 (75)	180달러
카네이션 (50)	85달러

62

Why is the woman calling?
(A) To report that an order is incomplete
(B) To report that some flowers are damaged
(C) To ask for a discount
(D) To check on a client

여자는 왜 전화하고 있는가?
(A) 주문이 전부 오지 않았다고 알리려고
(B) 일부 꽃이 손상되었다고 알리려고
(C) 할인을 요청하려고
(D) 고객 상태를 확인하려고

어휘 incomplete 불완전한 check on (문제가 없는지) 확인하다, 살펴보다

해설 전체 내용 관련 – 여자가 전화하는 이유

여자가 첫 대사에서 방금 도매 주문품을 받았는데, 튤립이 빠졌다(We just received our wholesale order, but the tulips are missing)고 한 것으로 보아 받지 못한 주문품 때문에 전화한 것임을 알 수 있다. 따라서 정답은 (A)이다.

> **Paraphrasing** 대화의 the tulips are missing
> → 정답의 an order is incomplete

63

What did the man forget to do?
(A) To provide a discount
(B) To meet with some clients
(C) To report a delay
(D) To correct an invoice

남자는 무엇을 하는 것을 잊어버렸는가?
(A) 할인 제공하기
(B) 고객 만나기
(C) (배송) 지연 보고하기
(D) 송장 정정하기

해설 세부 사항 관련 – 남자가 잊어버린 일

남자가 첫 번째 대사에서 납품업체가 내일이나 돼야 튤립을 가져다줄 수 있는데, 잊어버리고 얘기를 못 했다(I forgot to let you know that my supplier can't get them to me until tomorrow)고 했으므로 정답은 (C)이다.

> **Paraphrasing** 대화의 my supplier can't get them to me until tomorrow → 정답의 a delay

64

Look at the graphic. Which price will change on the invoice?
(A) $155
(B) $130
(C) $180
(D) $85

시각 정보에 의하면, 송장에서 어떤 가격이 변경될 것인가?
(A) 155달러
(B) 130달러
(C) 180달러
(D) 85달러

해설 시각 정보 연계 – 송장에서 변경될 가격

여자가 세 번째 대사에서 100송이를 주문했는데, 두 배로 줄 수 있는지 (I've ordered 100 flowers, but could you double that, please?) 묻자 남자가 승낙(Sure)하면서 수정된 송장도 같이 보내겠다(And I'll send you a revised invoice as well)고 했으므로, 100송이를 주문하는 가격이 변경될 것임을 알 수 있다. 송장에 100송이의 튤립 가격이 130달러로 나와 있으므로 정답은 (B)이다.

65-67 대화 + 제어 패널

W-Am ⁶⁵I hear that we've received complaints about the display panel on the Handimax coffee maker we just introduced. Have you looked into it?

M-Au ⁶⁵,⁶⁷It's the warning light that lets people know that more water needs to be added. On the Handimax, it's right next to the Keep Warm light and some customers become confused when using the machine.

W-Am ⁶⁶The warning light was much bigger on previous models, which made it easier to see. Should we enlarge it? Would that solve the problem?

M-Au ⁶⁷I think we should move the warning light to the right of the words Add Water. That could avoid the issue.

여 얼마 전에 출시한 핸디맥스 커피 메이커의 디스플레이 패널에 관한 불만이 접수됐다고 들었어요. 조사해 봤어요?

남 물을 더 추가해야 한다는 것을 알려 주는 경고등이에요. 핸디맥스에는 '보온' 라이트 바로 옆에 있어서 일부 고객이 기계를 사용할 때 혼란스러워해요.

여 이전 모델은 경고등이 훨씬 커서 보기가 더 쉬웠죠. 크기를 키워야 할까요? 그러면 문제가 해결될까요?

남 경고등을 '물 추가' 글자 오른쪽으로 옮겨야 할 것 같아요. 그러면 문제를 피할 수 있어요.

어휘 complaint 불만, 항의 introduce 출시하다 look into ~을 조사하다 confused 혼란스러운 previous 이전의 enlarge 확대하다 avoid 피하다

Handimax Coffee Maker
On Light 1
Keep Warm Light 2   67   Light 4 Add Water
Off Light 3

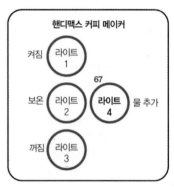

핸디맥스 커피 메이커
켜짐 라이트 1
보온 라이트 2   67   라이트 4 물 추가
꺼짐 라이트 3

65

What is the problem with the coffee maker?
(A) It often needs to be refilled with water.
(B) It turns off unexpectedly.
(C) Its display panel causes confusion.
(D) The lights are not bright enough.

커피 메이커의 문제점은 무엇인가?
(A) 물을 자주 다시 채워야 한다.
(B) 갑자기 꺼진다.
(C) 디스플레이 패널이 혼동된다.
(D) 라이트가 충분히 밝지 않다.

어휘 unexpectedly 갑자기, 뜻밖에

해설 전체 내용 관련 – 커피 메이커의 문제점

여자가 첫 대사에서 얼마 전에 출시한 핸디맥스 커피 메이커의 디스플레이 패널에 관한 불만이 접수됐다고 들었다(I hear that we've received complaints about the display panel ~ we just introduced)고 하자 남자가 물을 더 추가해야 한다는 것을 알려 주는 경고등(It's the warning light that lets people know that more water needs to be added)이라면서 핸디맥스에는 '보온' 라이트 바로 옆에 있어서 일부 고객이 기계를 사용할 때 혼란스러워한다(On the Handimax, it's right next to the Keep Warm light and some customers become confused when using the machine)고 했으므로 정답은 (C)이다.

66

What was different about previous models?
(A) They had more lights.
(B) They had larger lights.
(C) They had multicolor lights.
(D) They had flashing lights.

이전 모델이 다른 점은 무엇이었는가?
(A) 라이트가 더 많았다.
(B) 라이트가 더 컸다.
(C) 라이트 색상이 다양했다.
(D) 깜박이는 라이트가 있었다.

어휘 multicolor 색깔이 다채로운 flashing 깜박이는, 번쩍이는

해설 세부 사항 관련 – 이전 모델의 다른 점
여자가 두 번째 대사에서 이전 모델은 경고등이 훨씬 커서 보기가 더 쉬웠다(The warning light was much bigger on previous models, which made it easier to see)고 했으므로 정답은 (B)이다.

67

Look at the graphic. Which light does the man suggest moving?
(A) Light 1
(B) Light 2
(C) Light 3
(D) Light 4

시각 정보에 의하면, 남자는 어떤 라이트를 옮기자고 제안하는가?
(A) 라이트 1
(B) 라이트 2
(C) 라이트 3
(D) 라이트 4

해설 시각 정보 연계 – 남자가 옮기자고 제안하는 라이트
남자가 첫 대사에서 물을 더 추가해야 한다는 것을 알려 주는 경고등(It's the warning light that lets people know that more water needs to be added)이라면서 핸디맥스에는 '보온' 라이트 바로 옆에 있어서 일부 고객이 기계를 사용할 때 혼란스러워한다(On the Handimax, it's right next to the Keep Warm light and some customers become confused when using the machine)고 했고, 마지막 대사에서 경고등을 '물 추가' 글자 오른쪽으로 옮겨야 할 것 같다(I think we should move the warning light to the right of the words Add Water)고 했다. 제어 패널을 보면 보온 라이트 2 옆에 있는 라이트 4가 경고등이라는 것을 알 수 있으므로 정답은 (D)이다.

68-70 대화 + 일정

M-Cn Thanks for stopping by, Petra. Last week, I got the schedule for the rollout of Langenfeld's new oatmeal raisin cookies.

W-Br Oh, yes. It's about time. **68Customers have been complaining about how dry the current ones are.**

M-Cn Well, I just got an e-mail update from headquarters. **69,70They want to extend the window of time the product will be discounted. We had originally planned to offer the discount only two days—March fifth and sixth, but now they'd like to extend that window by two more days.**

W-Br **70OK, that should help win back some customers. We should also post about the change on our social media accounts.**

남 들러 줘서 고마워요, 페트라. 지난주에 랑겐펠드의 새 오트밀 건포도 쿠키의 출시 일정표를 받았어요.

여 아, 네. 때가 됐죠. 현재 제품들이 너무 퍼석하다고 고객들이 불평해 왔잖아요.

남 방금 본사에서 이메일로 최신 정보를 받았어요. 본사에서는 제품이 할인되는 기간을 연장하고 싶어 해요. 원래 우리는 3월 5일과 6일 이틀만 할인을 제공하려 했는데, 지금 본사는 할인 기간을 이틀 더 늘리려고 하네요.

여 좋아요, 그러면 고객들을 되찾는 데 도움이 될 거예요. 우리 소셜 미디어 계정들에도 변경 사항을 올려야겠어요.

어휘 stop by 잠시 들르다 rollout (신제품) 출시 raisin 건포도 extend 연장하다 window (of time) 기간, 시간(대) win back 되찾다 post (웹사이트에) 게시하다

Langenfeld Bakery, Inc. Multiphase Schedule Product: oatmeal raisin cookies		
Phase 1	Final internal taste test (corporate–level only)	March 1
Phase 2	Shipping to local stores	March 2–4
Phase 3	Free sample distribution and 10% discount	March 5–6
Phase 4	Resumption of full–price sales	March 7

랑겐펠드 제과 주식회사 다단계 일정 제품: 오트밀 건포도 쿠키		
1단계	최종 내부 맛 테스트 (회사 차원에서만)	3월 1일
2단계	지역 매장에 발송	3월 2–4일
3단계	**무료 샘플 배포 및 10퍼센트 할인**	**3월 5–6일**
4단계	정가 판매 재개	3월 7일

68

What does the woman say about the bakery's customers?

(A) They are dissatisfied with the quality of a product.
(B) They think the bakery's products are overpriced.
(C) They are now aware of the bakery's social media accounts.
(D) They sometimes arrive before the bakery opens.

여자는 제과점 고객들에 대해 무엇이라고 말하는가?

(A) 제품 품질에 불만이 있다.
(B) 제과점 제품들이 너무 비싸다고 생각한다.
(C) 이제 제과점의 소셜 미디어 계정을 알고 있다.
(D) 때때로 제과점이 문을 열기 전에 도착한다.

어휘 dissatisfied with ~에 불만인 overpriced 너무 비싼

해설 세부 사항 관련 – 여자가 제과점 고객들에 관해 언급하는 것
여자가 첫 대사에서 현재 제품들이 너무 퍼석하다고 고객들이 불평해 왔다 (Customers have been complaining about how dry the current ones are)고 했으므로 정답은 (A)이다.

> **Paraphrasing** 대화의 have been complaining about how dry the current ones are → 정답의 are dissatisfied with the quality of a product

69

Look at the graphic. Which phase is being extended?

(A) Phase 1
(B) Phase 2
(C) Phase 3
(D) Phase 4

시각 정보에 의하면, 어떤 단계가 연장될 것인가?

(A) 1단계
(B) 2단계
(C) 3단계
(D) 4단계

해설 시각 정보 연계 – 연장될 단계
남자가 두 번째 대사에서 본사에서 제품이 할인되는 기간을 연장하고 싶어 한다(They want to extend the window of time the product will be discounted)며 원래는 3월 5일과 6일 이틀만 할인을 제공하려고 했는데, 본사는 할인 기간을 이틀 더 늘리려고 한다(We had originally planned to offer the discount only two days—March fifth and sixth, but now they'd like to extend that window by two more days)고 했고, 일정에 따르면 3월 5일과 6일 할인은 3단계이므로 정답은 (C)이다.

70

What does the woman say the bakery should do?

(A) Ship a product early
(B) Sell a wider range of products
(C) Hold a contest
(D) Advertise a discount

여자는 제과점이 무엇을 해야 한다고 말하는가?

(A) 제품 조기 발송
(B) 더 다양한 제품 판매
(C) 대회 개최
(D) 할인 광고

해설 세부 사항 관련 – 여자가 제과점이 해야 한다고 언급하는 것
남자가 두 번째 대사에서 본사에서 제품이 할인되는 기간을 연장하고 싶어한다(They want to extend the window of time the product will be discounted)고 하자 여자가 그러면 고객들을 되찾는 데 도움이 될 것 (OK, that should help win back some customers)이라면서 소셜 미디어 계정에 변경 사항을 올려야겠다(We should also post about the change on our social media accounts)고 한 것으로 보아 할인 기간의 연장을 알리려 한다는 것을 알 수 있다. 따라서 정답은 (D)이다.

> **Paraphrasing** 대화의 post about the change on our social media accounts
> → 정답의 Advertise a discount

PART 4

71-73 전화 메시지

M-Cn Hi, Chara. This is Joe. **⁷¹I found a very nice space for your restaurant.** It has everything you're looking for, including an outdoor terrace. **⁷²It's a bit over your budget, but don't worry. The owners like the idea that you're such a successful chef. So they are willing to sit down and come to a compromise on the rent. ⁷³This place is not downtown, but it's located in the neighborhood of Peckham, which, as you know, is a busy, vibrant area.** I think you'll like it.

안녕하세요, 캐라. 조예요. 당신 식당을 위한 아주 멋진 공간을 찾았어요. 야외 테라스를 포함해 찾으시는 게 전부 갖춰져 있어요. 예산을 조금 초과하기는 하지만, 걱정하지 마세요. 주인들은 당신이 크게 성공한 요리사여서 좋대요. 그래서 기꺼이 협상에 응해서 임대료를 절충할 의향을 가지고 있어요. 이곳이 시내는 아니지만 페컴 근처에 있어요. 알다시피 번화하고 활기찬 지역이죠. 마음에 드실 거예요.

어휘 budget 예산 be willing to 기꺼이 ~하다 come to a compromise 절충[타협]에 이르다 vibrant 활기찬

71

Who is the speaker?

(A) An investment banker
(B) An attorney
(C) A real estate agent
(D) An architect

화자는 누구인가?
(A) 투자 은행가
(B) 변호사
(C) 부동산 중개인
(D) 건축가

해설 전체 내용 관련 – 화자의 직업

화자가 초반부에 청자의 식당을 위한 아주 멋진 공간을 찾았다(I found a very nice space for your restaurant)고 하면서 그 장소에 대한 설명을 이어 가고 있는 것으로 보아 화자는 부동산 중개인임을 알 수 있다. 따라서 정답은 (C)이다.

72

What does the speaker reassure the listener about?
(A) A price is negotiable.
(B) Some supplies have arrived.
(C) A job applicant is qualified.
(D) Clients are satisfied.

화자는 청자에게 무엇에 대해 안심시키는가?
(A) 가격은 협상의 여지가 있다.
(B) 물품이 도착했다.
(C) 구직자는 자격을 갖추고 있다.
(D) 고객들이 만족해한다.

어휘 negotiable 협상의 여지가 있는 qualified 자격을 갖춘

해설 세부 사항 관련 – 화자가 청자에게 안심시키는 것

화자가 중반부에 예산을 조금 초과하지만 걱정하지 말라(It's a bit over your budget, but don't worry)고 했고, 주인들이 청자가 크게 성공한 요리사라서 좋아한다(The owners like the idea that you're such a successful chef)면서 기꺼이 협상에 응해서 임대료를 절충할 의향이 있다(So they are willing to sit down and come to a compromise on the rent)고 했으므로 정답은 (A)이다.

> **Paraphrasing** 담화의 come to a compromise on the rent → 정답의 A price is negotiable

73

What is an advantage of Peckham?
(A) It has beautiful scenery.
(B) It has several parks.
(C) It is a safe neighborhood.
(D) It is popular.

페컴의 장점은 무엇인가?
(A) 경치가 아름답다.
(B) 공원이 여러 개 있다.
(C) 안전한 동네이다.
(D) 많은 사람이 찾는다.

해설 세부 사항 관련 – 페컴의 장점

화자가 후반부에 이곳이 시내는 아니지만 페컴 근처에 있어서 번화하고 활기찬 지역(This place is not downtown, but it's located in the neighborhood of Peckham, which, as you know, is a busy, vibrant area)이라고 했으므로 정답은 (D)이다.

> **Paraphrasing** 담화의 is a busy, vibrant area
> → 정답의 is popular

74-76 담화

> **W-Br** Good morning, **[74]new Catrin's Fitness staff!** Having you working on a rotating basis at the front desk in the mornings will be really helpful! Plan to arrive at five A.M. to turn on the lights and the exercise machines. Oh, be sure to turn on the steam rooms in the men's and women's locker rooms. **[75]The steam rooms can malfunction as they warm up, and members have been complaining,** so I always double-check that the steam is working OK just before we open. **[76]Please unlock the entrance at about five twenty-five and be ready to scan IDs as the guests come in.**

> 안녕하세요, 캐트린스 피트니스 신입 사원 여러분! 여러분이 아침에 프런트에서 교대 근무하면 정말 도움이 될 것입니다! 새벽 5시에 도착해서 전등과 운동기구를 켜도록 계획을 잡으세요. 아, 남녀 로커룸에 있는 한증실을 꼭 켜 주세요. 한증실이 예열 도중 오작동할 수 있어서 회원들이 불만을 토로하고 있어요. 그래서 영업 개시 직전에 저는 증기가 제대로 작동하는지 항상 재차 확인합니다. 5시 25분쯤에 문을 열고 고객이 들어오면 신분증을 스캔할 수 있도록 준비해 주세요.

> **어휘** on a rotating basis 교대로 steam room 한증실
> malfunction 제대로 작동하지 않다

74

Where does the talk most likely take place?
(A) At a physical therapy office
(B) At a primary school
(C) At a gym
(D) At a hospital

담화는 어디에서 이루어지는 것 같은가?
(A) 물리치료실
(B) 초등학교
(C) 헬스장
(D) 병원

어휘 physical therapy 물리치료

해설 전체 내용 관련 – 담화의 장소

화자가 초반부에 캐트린스 피트니스 신입 사원 여러분(new Catrin's Fitness staff!)이라며 청자들을 호명했고, 아침에 여러분이 프런트에서 교대로 일하면 정말 도움이 될 것(Having you working on a rotating basis at the front desk in the mornings will be really helpful!)이라며 새벽 5시에 도착해서 전등과 운동기구를 켜도록 계획을 잡으라(Plan to arrive at five A.M. to turn on the lights and the exercise machines)고 했으므로, 담화가 이루어지고 있는 장소는 헬스장임을 알 수 있다. 따라서 정답은 (C)이다.

75

What does the speaker imply when she says, "I always double-check that the steam is working OK"?
(A) She deserves a promotion.
(B) She does not enjoy doing extra work.
(C) Some complaints are unreasonable.
(D) A task is important.

화자가 "저는 증기가 제대로 작동하는지 항상 재차 확인합니다"라고 말할 때 무엇을 의도하는가?
(A) 그녀는 승진할 자격이 있다.
(B) 그녀는 잔업을 좋아하지 않는다.
(C) 일부 불평은 부당하다.
(D) 업무가 중요하다.

해설 화자의 의도 파악 – 증기가 제대로 작동하는지 항상 재차 확인한다는 말의 의도

앞에서 한증실이 예열 도중 오작동할 수 있어 회원들이 불만을 토로하고 있다(The steam rooms can malfunction as they warm up, and members have been complaining)고 한 뒤, 결과의 so와 함께 인용문을 언급했으므로 확인 작업이 필수적임을 알리려는 의도로 볼 수 있다. 따라서 정답은 (D)이다.

76

What will the listeners do after opening the facility?
(A) Rent lockers to guests
(B) Check membership identification cards
(C) Fold towels
(D) Answer phones

청자들은 시설을 개방한 후 무엇을 할 것인가?
(A) 고객들에게 사물함 대여하기
(B) 회원 카드 확인하기
(C) 수건 개기
(D) 전화 받기

해설 세부 사항 관련 – 청자들이 시설을 개방한 후 할 일

화자가 마지막에 5시 25분쯤에 문을 열고 고객이 들어오면 신분증을 스캔할 수 있도록 준비하라(Please unlock the entrance at about five twenty-five and be ready to scan IDs as the guests come in)고 할 일을 알려 주고 있으므로 정답은 (B)이다.

> **Paraphrasing** 담화의 IDs → 정답의 membership identification cards

77-79 방송

> M-Au Welcome back. ⁷⁷I'm Hongwei Shen, back with you live for today's airing of *Science Today*. From biology to physics, *Science Today* is your source of accurate science news. ^{77,78}We've been talking about the meteor shower that will be visible in the night sky on Saturday and Sunday. It's going to be a big event, and I hope you have the chance to see it. ⁷⁹I'm going to open the line to

> callers now. If you have a question about astronomy and this weekend's event—and I'm going to restrict questions to those topics only—the number is 555-0156.

> 어서 오세요. **오늘의 〈사이언스 투데이〉 생방송으로 여러분에게 돌아온 홍웨이 센입니다.** 생물학에서 물리학에 이르기까지 〈사이언스 투데이〉는 정확한 과학 뉴스를 전달해 드립니다. **토요일과 일요일에 밤하늘에서 볼 수 있는 유성우에 대해 이야기하고 있었는데요.** 큰 이벤트가 될 테니 기회를 잡아 꼭 보시면 좋겠습니다. **지금부터 전화를 연결해 보겠습니다.** 천문학과 이번 주말 이벤트에 대해 질문 있으시면, 질문은 이 주제로만 제한할게요, 번호는 555-0156입니다.

> 어휘 airing 방송 accurate 정확한 meteor shower 유성우 astronomy 천문학 restrict 제한하다

77

What is the topic of today's broadcast?
(A) Weather
(B) Astronomy
(C) Gardening
(D) Sports

오늘 방송의 주제는 무엇인가?
(A) 날씨
(B) 천문학
(C) 정원 가꾸기
(D) 스포츠

해설 전체 내용 관련 – 오늘 방송의 주제

화자가 초반부에 오늘의 〈사이언스 투데이〉 생방송으로 여러분에게 돌아온 홍웨이 센(I'm Hongwei Shen, back with you live for today's airing of *Science Today*)이라고 자신을 소개한 뒤, 토요일과 일요일에 밤하늘에서 볼 수 있는 유성우에 대해 이야기하고 있었다(We've been talking about the meteor shower that will be visible in the night sky on Saturday and Sunday)고 했으므로 정답은 (B)이다.

78

What can the listeners do this weekend?
(A) Learn to improve their vision
(B) Watch a meteor shower
(C) Go to a musical event
(D) Listen to a special program

청자들은 이번 주말에 무엇을 할 수 있는가?
(A) 시력 올리는 법 배우기
(B) 유성우 보기
(C) 음악 행사 보러 가기
(D) 특별 프로그램 듣기

해설 세부 사항 관련 – 청자들이 이번 주말에 할 수 있는 일

화자가 중반부에 토요일과 일요일에 밤하늘에서 볼 수 있는 유성우에 대해 이야기하고 있었다(We've been talking about the meteor shower that will be visible in the night sky on Saturday and Sunday)고 했으므로 정답은 (B)이다.

79

What does the speaker say some listeners can do?
(A) Win a prize
(B) Request advice
(C) Ask questions
(D) Call again later

화자는 청자들이 무엇을 할 수 있다고 말하는가?
(A) 수상하기
(B) 조언 요청하기
(C) **질문하기**
(D) 나중에 다시 전화하기

해설 세부 사항 관련 – 청자들이 할 수 있다고 화자가 언급하는 것
화자가 후반부에 지금부터 전화를 연결해 보겠다(I'm going to open the line to callers now)며 천문학과 이번 주말 이벤트에 대해 질문이 있으면, 질문은 이 주제로만 제한하고 번호는 555-0156(If you have a question about astronomy and this weekend's event—and I'm going to restrict questions to those topics only—the number is 555-0156)이라고 했으므로 정답은 (C)이다.

80-82 연설

W-Am Good afternoon, everyone, and ⁸⁰**welcome to the Panecks Corporation's ten-year anniversary luncheon.** We have had so many achievements: ⁸¹**just this past year we sold our five millionth unit. That makes five million cars on the road today equipped with Panecks radios.** As you might know, our president, Mr. Strohmeyer, has been in Japan all this month negotiating with Navasota Motors. ⁸²**He couldn't be here today, but he sent a video greeting to thank you for all your hard work.** We have three monitors here in the front of the room. Let's get started.

여러분, 안녕하세요. **패넥스 사 10주년 기념 오찬에 오신 것을 환영합니다.** 우리는 수많은 성과를 거두어 왔습니다. **바로 지난해에 우리는 500만 번째 제품을 판매했습니다. 이것으로 오늘날 패넥스 라디오를 장착한 자동차 500만 대가 도로 위를 달리고 있습니다.** 아시겠지만 스트로마이어 회장님은 이번 달 내내 일본에서 나바소타 자동차와 협상을 진행하고 계십니다. **회장님은 오늘 여기 오시지 못했지만, 여러분의 모든 노고에 감사하기 위해 동영상으로 인사말을 보내셨습니다.** 여기 연회실 앞에 모니터 세 대가 있습니다. 시작하겠습니다.

어휘 anniversary 기념일 luncheon 오찬 achievement 성과 millionth 100만 번째의 equipped with ~을 장착한 negotiate 협상하다

80

What is the purpose of the luncheon?
(A) To announce a merger
(B) To introduce a new company president
(C) To launch a new product
(D) To celebrate a company's anniversary

오찬의 목적은 무엇인가?
(A) 합병 발표
(B) 신임 회장 소개
(C) 신제품 출시
(D) **회사 창립기념일 축하**

해설 전체 내용 관련 – 오찬의 목적
화자가 초반부에 패넥스 사 10주년 기념 오찬에 오신 것을 환영한다(welcome to the Panecks Corporation's ten-year anniversary luncheon)고 말한 뒤 회사의 성과와 회장의 인사말 동영상에 대해 말하고 있으므로 정답은 (D)이다.

81

What does the speaker say about the Panecks Corporation?
(A) It opened an office in Japan.
(B) It designed a new type of car.
(C) It sold a large number of car radios.
(D) It made a video of the company's history.

화자는 패넥스 사에 관해 무엇이라고 말하는가?
(A) 일본에 사무실을 열었다.
(B) 새로운 유형의 차를 디자인했다.
(C) **차량용 라디오를 많이 팔았다.**
(D) 회사의 연혁을 동영상으로 만들었다.

해설 세부 사항 관련 – 화자가 패넥스 사에 대해 언급하는 것
화자가 중반부에 바로 지난해에 500만 번째 제품을 판매했다(just this past year we sold our five millionth unit)며 이것으로 오늘날 패넥스 라디오를 장착한 자동차 500만 대가 도로 위를 달리고 있다(That makes five million cars on the road today equipped with Panecks radios)고 했으므로 정답은 (C)이다.

82

Why does the speaker say, "We have three monitors here in the front of the room"?
(A) To introduce new staff
(B) To remind the listeners to be careful
(C) To emphasize technology improvements
(D) To direct the listeners to watch a video

화자는 왜 "여기 연회실 앞에 모니터 세 대가 있습니다"라고 말하는가?
(A) 새 직원을 소개하려고
(B) 청자들에게 주의할 것을 상기시키려고
(C) 기술 개선을 강조하려고
(D) **청자들이 동영상을 시청하도록 안내하려고**

해설 화자의 의도 파악 – 연회실 앞에 모니터 세 대가 있다는 말의 의도
앞에서 회장님은 오늘 여기 오지 못했지만, 여러분의 모든 노고에 감사하기 위해 동영상으로 인사말을 보냈다(He couldn't be here today, but he sent a video greeting to thank you for all your hard work)고 한 뒤 인용문을 언급했으므로, 모니터를 통해 동영상을 볼 수 있음을 알리려는 의도로 볼 수 있다. 따라서 정답은 (D)이다.

83-85 회의 발췌

M-Cn Thanks for attending this all-staff meeting today. **83First on the agenda is our new restaurant reservation app, Faster Now. 84We have competition from other technology companies, but our app is the only one that specializes in business luncheons.** You'll see that the app will allow the user not only to reserve a table but also to make menu choices in advance. That way, when people get to the restaurant, they won't have to wait long for their meal. **85Here's Johanna, our lead IT researcher, who'll describe the app specifications and show us how it works.**

오늘 전 직원 회의에 참석해 주셔서 감사합니다. **첫 번째 안건은 당사의 새로운 식당 예약 앱인 패스터 나우입니다. 다른 기술 회사와 경쟁하고 있지만, 비즈니스 오찬 전문 앱은 당사 앱이 유일합니다.** 보면 아시겠지만 앱으로 사용자는 테이블을 예약할 수 있을 뿐만 아니라 메뉴도 미리 선택할 수 있습니다. 그렇게 하면 사람들은 식당에 도착해서 식사를 오래 기다릴 필요가 없습니다. **여기 조해나 수석 IT 연구원이 앱 사양을 설명하고 작동 방식을 보여 드리겠습니다.**

어휘 agenda 안건   reservation 예약   in advance 미리   describe 설명하다   specification 사양

83

What is Faster Now?
(A) Job-recruiting software
(B) An online Web site builder
(C) A self-paced training program
(D) A reservation app for restaurants

패스터 나우는 무엇인가?
(A) 채용 소프트웨어
(B) 온라인 웹사이트 구축기
(C) 각자 진도에 맞춘 교육 프로그램
(D) 식당 예약 앱

해설 세부 사항 관련 – 패스터 나우의 정체
화자가 초반부에 첫 번째 안건은 당사의 새로운 식당 예약 앱인 패스터 나우(First on the agenda is our new restaurant reservation app, Faster Now)라고 했으므로 정답은 (D)이다.

> **Paraphrasing** 담화의 our new restaurant reservation app
> → 정답의 A reservation app for restaurants

84

What type of business do the listeners work for?
(A) A catering service
(B) A technology company
(C) A law firm
(D) A supermarket

청자들은 어떤 업종에 일하는가?
(A) 출장 연회 서비스
(B) 기술 회사
(C) 법률 사무소
(D) 슈퍼마켓

해설 전체 내용 관련 – 청자들의 근무지
화자가 중반부에 다른 기술 회사와 경쟁하고 있지만, 비즈니스 오찬 전문 앱은 당사 앱이 유일하다(We have competition from other technology companies, but our app is the only one that specializes in business luncheons)고 한 것으로 보아 정답은 (B)이다.

85

What will happen next in the meeting?
(A) A product demonstration
(B) A brainstorming session
(C) A job interview
(D) A client introduction

회의에서 다음에 무슨 일이 일어날 것인가?
(A) 제품 시연
(B) 브레인스토밍 시간
(C) 취업 면접
(D) 고객 소개

해설 세부 사항 관련 – 회의에서 다음에 일어날 일
마지막에 여기 조해나 수석 IT 연구원이 앱 사양을 설명하고 작동 방식을 보여 주겠다(Here's Johanna, our lead IT researcher, who'll describe the app specifications and show us how it works)고 했으므로 회의에서 시연이 있을 것임을 알 수 있다. 따라서 정답은 (A)이다.

> **Paraphrasing** 담화의 show us how it works
> → 정답의 A product demonstration

86-88 회의 발췌

W-Am **86I called this meeting because next week this team is scheduled to begin installing windows in the new building on Bellevue Avenue.** Originally, you were going to install the M-FIT on all floors. **87Our supplier just raised the price on those frames, so we had to change them. 88The new type, the M-25, has the same dimensions, but it's installed differently.** I'll send a link to the supplier's Web site where you're going to sign up to watch a video demonstration on how to install this model. I know this is a last-minute request. Still, this way we'll stay on budget.

86

What project is the speaker discussing?
(A) The grand opening of a shopping center
(B) The maintenance of a city park
(C) The repair of a highway
(D) The construction of a building

화자는 어떤 프로젝트에 대해 논의하고 있는가?
(A) 쇼핑센터 개장
(B) 도시공원 정비
(C) 고속도로 보수
(D) 건물 건축

해설 전체 내용 관련 – 화자가 논의하는 프로젝트
화자가 도입부에서 다음 주에 이 팀이 벨뷰 가에 있는 새 건물에 창문 설치를 시작할 예정이어서 이 회의를 소집했다(I called this meeting because next week this team is scheduled to begin installing windows in the new building on Bellevue Avenue)고 한 후, 건물에 창문을 설치하는 사항에 대한 이야기를 이어 가고 있으므로 정답은 (D)이다.

87

What problem does the speaker mention?
(A) Some heavy machinery is broken.
(B) A price has changed.
(C) There is a labor shortage.
(D) Some supplies are late.

화자는 어떤 문제점을 언급하는가?
(A) 중장비가 고장 났다.
(B) 가격이 변경되었다.
(C) 인력이 부족하다.
(D) 일부 공급 물품이 늦었다.

어휘 labor shortage 인력 부족

해설 세부 사항 관련 – 화자가 말하는 문제
화자가 중반부에 납품업체가 방금 틀 가격을 인상해서 어쩔 수 없이 변경했다(Our supplier just raised the price on those frames, so we had to change them)고 했으므로 정답은 (B)이다.

> **Paraphrasing** 담화의 raised the price
> → 정답의 A price has changed

88

Why does the speaker say, "I know this is a last-minute request"?
(A) To refuse an upgrade deal
(B) To apologize for an inconvenience
(C) To cancel a merchandise order
(D) To express her surprise

화자는 왜 "막바지에 촉박한 요청이라는 점 알고 있습니다"라고 말하는가?
(A) 승급 협의를 거절하려고
(B) 불편에 대해 사과하려고
(C) 상품 주문을 취소하려고
(D) 놀라움을 표현하려고

어휘 refuse 거절하다 inconvenience 불편 merchandise 상품

해설 화자의 의도 파악 – 막바지에 촉박한 요청이라는 점 알고 있다는 말의 의도
앞에서 새로운 타입인 M-25는 치수는 같지만 설치 방식이 다르다(The new type, the M-25, has the same dimensions, but it's installed differently)면서 납품업체의 웹사이트 링크를 보내는데 가입하면 이 모델의 설치 방법에 관한 동영상 시연을 볼 수 있다(I'll send a link to the supplier's Web site ~ how to install this model)고 한 것으로 보아 인용문은 설치 방식을 급하게 익히도록 요청하는 것에 대한 유감을 표현하는 의도로 볼 수 있다. 따라서 정답은 (B)이다.

89-91 녹음 메시지

M-Au Thank you for calling Forest Apartments. Press one to speak to our on-site manager. **89All residents should be aware that next week we will start updating the laundry facilities in each of our buildings.** **90While the work is going on, tenants will not be able to access the laundry facilities in their building. The Maple building will be first.** Tenants of the Maple building may use the laundry room in any other building while their facilities are being renovated. **91Please note that new doors and locks will also be installed, so all tenants will need a new key. Please stop at the main office to pick that up.**

포레스트 아파트에 전화 주셔서 감사합니다. 1번을 누르면 현장 관리소장과 통화하실 수 있습니다. **모든 주민은 다음 주에 각 동마다 세탁 시설 개보수가 시작된다는 것을 알아 두시기 바랍니다. 공사가 진행되는 동안 입주민은 거주하는 동에 있는 세탁 시설을 이용하실 수 없습니다. 메이플 동이 첫 번째입니다.** 메이플 동 입주민은 시설이 개보수되는 동안에 다른 동에 있는 세탁실을 이용하시면 됩니다. **문과 잠금 장치도 새로 설치되므로 입주민 모두 새 열쇠가 필요하다는 점에 유념해 주십시오. 관리사무소에 들러 열쇠를 가져가세요.**

어휘 on-site 현장의 resident 주민 laundry 세탁 tenant 입주민, 세입자 access 이용하다 renovate 개보수하다

89

According to the speaker, what will happen next week?

(A) Some laundry rooms will be updated.
(B) The main office of the apartment complex will be closed.
(C) Some new tenants will move into a vacant apartment.
(D) A parking area will become unavailable.

화자에 따르면, 다음 주에 무슨 일이 일어날 것인가?

(A) 일부 세탁실이 개보수될 것이다.
(B) 아파트 단지 관리사무소가 문을 닫을 것이다.
(C) 일부 신규 입주민들이 비어 있는 아파트로 이사할 것이다.
(D) 주차 공간을 사용할 수 없게 될 것이다.

어휘 vacant 비어 있는 unavailable 사용할 수 없는

해설 세부 사항 관련 – 다음 주에 일어날 일

화자가 초반부에 모든 주민은 다음 주에 각 동마다 세탁 시설 개보수가 시작된다는 것을 알아 두라(All residents should be aware that next week we will start updating the laundry facilities in each of our buildings)고 했으므로 정답은 (A)이다.

Paraphrasing 담화의 updating the laundry facilities
→ 정답의 laundry rooms will be updated

90

What does the speaker say about the Maple building?

(A) It has more tenants than the other buildings.
(B) It is the only building with a laundry room.
(C) It is first in the project schedule.
(D) It is where the main office is located.

화자는 메이플 동에 관해 무엇이라고 말하는가?

(A) 다른 동들보다 입주민이 더 많다.
(B) 세탁실이 있는 유일한 동이다.
(C) 프로젝트 일정 중 첫 번째이다.
(D) 관리사무소가 있는 곳이다.

해설 세부 사항 관련 – 화자가 메이플 동에 관해 언급하는 것

화자가 중반부에 공사하는 동안 입주민은 거주 동에 있는 세탁 시설을 이용할 수 없다(While the work is going on, tenants will not be able to access the laundry facilities in their building)며 메이플 동이 첫 번째(The Maple building will be first)라고 했으므로 정답은 (C)이다.

91

Why should tenants stop at the main office?

(A) To pay a laundry fee
(B) To pick up a questionnaire
(C) To sign a permission form
(D) To receive a new key

입주민들은 왜 관리사무소에 들러야 하는가?

(A) 세탁비를 지불하려고
(B) 설문지를 가져가려고
(C) 허가 양식에 서명하려고
(D) 새 열쇠를 받으려고

해설 세부 사항 관련 – 입주민들이 관리사무소에 들러야 하는 이유

화자가 후반부에 문과 잠금 장치도 새로 설치되므로 입주민 모두 새 열쇠가 필요하다(new doors and locks will also be installed, so all tenants will need a new key)며 관리사무소에 들러 가져가라(Please stop at the main office to pick that up)고 했으므로 정답은 (D)이다.

Paraphrasing 담화의 pick that up
→ 정답의 receive a new key

92-94 전화 메시지

W-Am This message is for Mr. Yun. I'm calling from the rental office. 92I received the signed contract, and as we confirmed earlier, your rental of the retail space here in the shopping center will begin on the first of October. There are a few more things. You need to schedule a city inspection before the electricity can be turned on. 93And the owner has agreed to your request to add a storage room, and construction will begin within the week. 94I think everything can be done by the first of October, and you can open your doors and welcome new customers.

윤 선생님께 드리는 메시지입니다. 임대 사무실에서 전화드려요. 서명된 계약서는 잘 받았습니다. 그런데 앞서 확인했듯이 이곳 쇼핑센터에 있는 소매 공간 임대는 10월 1일부터 시작됩니다. 몇 가지 사항이 더 있습니다. 전기를 켤 수 있으려면 그 전에 시 점검 일정부터 잡으셔야 합니다. 그리고 창고를 추가해 달라는 요청에 소유주가 동의해, 이번 주 안에 공사가 시작될 예정입니다. 10월 1일까지는 모두 마칠 수 있을 듯하니 문을 열고 새로운 고객을 맞이하실 수 있을 겁니다.

어휘 retail 소매의 inspection 점검 storage room 창고

92

Who most likely is the listener?

(A) A city inspector
(B) An electrician
(C) A business owner
(D) A lawyer

청자는 누구일 것 같은가?

(A) 시 조사관
(B) 전기 기사
(C) 사업주
(D) 변호사

해설 전체 내용 관련 – 청자의 직업

화자가 초반부에 청자에게 서명된 계약서는 잘 받았고 앞서 확인했듯이 이곳 쇼핑센터에 있는 소매 공간 임대는 10월 1일부터 시작된다(I received the signed contract, and as we confirmed earlier, your rental of the retail space here in the shopping center will begin on the first of October)고 한 것으로 보아 청자는 쇼핑센터에서 소매업을 운영할 것임을 알 수 있다. 따라서 정답은 (C)이다.

93

What does the speaker say about a storage room?
(A) It will be used for electrical equipment.
(B) It is available for rent.
(C) It has not been built yet.
(D) It was recently repaired.

화자는 창고에 관해 무엇이라고 말하는가?
(A) 전기 장비에 사용될 것이다.
(B) 임대할 수 있다.
(C) 아직 건축되지 않았다.
(D) 최근에 수리되었다.

해설 세부 사항 관련 – 화자가 창고에 관해 언급하는 것
화자가 중반부에 창고를 추가해 달라는 요청에 소유주가 동의했고, 이번 주 안에 공사가 시작될 예정(And the owner has agreed to your request to add a storage room, and construction will begin within the week)이라고 했으므로 정답은 (C)이다.

94

What does the speaker believe will happen on the first of October?
(A) The store will open.
(B) The contract will be signed.
(C) The inspection will take place.
(D) Construction work will start.

화자는 10월 1일에 무슨 일이 일어날 것이라고 믿는가?
(A) 가게가 문을 열 것이다.
(B) 계약이 체결될 것이다.
(C) 점검이 이루어질 것이다.
(D) 공사가 시작될 것이다.

해설 세부 사항 관련 – 화자가 10월 1일에 일어날 것이라고 믿는 일
화자가 마지막에 10월 1일까지는 모두 마칠 수 있을 듯하니 문을 열고 새로운 고객을 맞이할 수 있을 것(I think everything can be done by the first of October, and you can open your doors and welcome new customers)이라고 했으므로 정답은 (A)이다.

Paraphrasing	담화의 you can open your doors and welcome new customers → 정답의 The store will open

95-97 공지 + 쿠폰

M-Cn Greetings, Carsin's cashiers! **95Let's take a look at the coupon we just mailed out to rewards members this week.** **96Our local rival, Gilroy's,** has been offering a similar discount to its customers, and business there has been booming. So it's time we try something similar—but, of course, even better! Our discount offer is ten percent, while theirs is only five percent. Please spend some time looking over the four rules of use at the bottom.

97We may need to revisit the one about using multiple discounts. Our customers do love manufacturer coupons! We will monitor customer complaints.

안녕하세요, 카신즈 계산원 여러분! **이번 주에 리워드 회원들에게 발송한 쿠폰을 한번 살펴봅시다.** 지역 경쟁업체인 길로이즈도 고객들에게 비슷한 할인을 제공해 왔고, 장사가 잘되고 있죠. 그러니 이제 우리도 비슷한 것을 시도해 볼 때가 됐어요. 물론, 더 나은 것으로요! 우리가 제공하는 할인은 10퍼센트이지만 그쪽은 5퍼센트밖에 안 됩니다. 잠시 시간을 내서 맨 밑에 있는 네 가지 사용 규칙을 살펴봐 주세요. **여러 할인을 중복 사용하는 데 대한 규칙은 다시 논의해야 할 수도 있습니다.** 고객들은 제조사 쿠폰을 정말 좋아하죠! 고객 불만 사항도 지켜보겠습니다.

어휘 mail out 발송하다 boom 번창하다 revisit 다시 논의하다
multiple 다수[복수]의 manufacturer 제조사

Carsin's Food Shop
10% Off Your Total Order
Rewards Coupon
Rules of Use 1. Coupon must be presented at time of purchase. 2. Stamps, milk, and gift cards excluded. 973. May not be used with other discounts. 4. Only one coupon per customer.

카신즈 푸드 숍
총 주문에서 10% 할인
보상 쿠폰
사용 규칙 1. 구매 시 쿠폰을 제시해야 합니다. 2. 스탬프, 우유, 상품권은 제외됩니다. **973. 다른 할인과 함께 사용할 수 없습니다.** 4. 고객 1인당 쿠폰 1매로 제한됩니다.

95

What is the purpose of the announcement?
(A) To describe a new customer discount
(B) To introduce new employees to the team
(C) To announce the end of a rewards program
(D) To review customer-complaint policies

공지의 목적은 무엇인가?
(A) 새로운 고객 할인에 대해 설명하려고
(B) 신입 사원을 팀에 소개하려고
(C) 보상 프로그램의 종료를 알리려고
(D) 고객 불만 관련 정책을 검토하려고

어휘 rewards 보상 policy 정책

화자가 초반부에 이번 주에 리워드 회원들에게 발송한 쿠폰을 한번 살펴보자(Let's take a look at the coupon we just mailed out to rewards members this week)고 한 후, 할인에 대한 설명을 이어 가고 있으므로 정답은 (A)이다.

96

What does the speaker say about Gilroy's?
(A) It does not offer discounts.
(B) It operates outside the local area.
(C) It is a competitor.
(D) It has strict rules for employees.

화자는 길로이즈에 관해 무엇이라고 말하는가?
(A) 할인을 제공하지 않는다.
(B) 지역 밖에서 운영된다.
(C) 경쟁업체이다.
(D) 직원 관련 규정이 엄격하다.

해설 세부 사항 관련 – 화자가 길로이즈에 관해 언급하는 것

화자가 초반부에 자신들의 지역 경쟁업체인 길로이즈(Our local rival, Gilroy's)라고 언급했으므로 정답은 (C)이다.

Paraphrasing 담화의 Our local rival → 정답의 a competitor

97

Look at the graphic. Which rule might be changed?
(A) Rule 1
(B) Rule 2
(C) Rule 3
(D) Rule 4

시각 정보에 의하면, 어떤 규칙이 변경될 수 있는가?
(A) 규칙 1
(B) 규칙 2
(C) 규칙 3
(D) 규칙 4

해설 시각 정보 연계 – 변경될 수 있는 규칙

화자가 후반부에 여러 할인을 중복 사용하는 데 대한 규칙은 다시 논의해야 할 수도 있다(We may need to revisit the one about using multiple discounts)고 했고, 쿠폰에 중복 사용과 관련된 사항은 규칙 3에 나와 있으므로 정답은 (C)이다.

98-100 회의 발췌 + 목록

M-Au Good morning. **98I hope you are settling in to your new offices here at Golden Glove Insurance Company. Let's plan something fun to get to know each other.** On the wall, there's a list of team-building activities. **99After this meeting, put a check mark next to the activity you want to do together next Friday afternoon. 100It would be**

energizing and fun to use our volleyball court, but I shouldn't influence you! Please make your own choice, and we'll do the one with the most votes.

안녕하세요. 이곳 골든 글러브 보험사 새 사무실에 잘 자리잡고 있기를 바랍니다. 서로 친해질 수 있는 재미있는 행사를 계획해 봅시다. 벽면에 단합 활동 목록이 있습니다. 이 회의가 끝나면 다음 주 금요일 오후에 같이 했으면 하는 활동 옆에 체크하세요. 배구장을 이용하면 활력도 넘치고 재미있겠지만, 제가 여러분에게 영향을 주면 안 되겠죠! 각자 선택하면 가장 많은 표를 얻은 활동을 하도록 하겠습니다.

어휘 settle in to ~에 자리잡다   vote 표

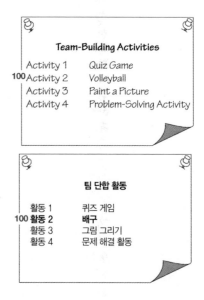

Team-Building Activities

Activity 1   Quiz Game
100Activity 2   Volleyball
Activity 3   Paint a Picture
Activity 4   Problem-Solving Activity

팀 단합 활동

활동 1   퀴즈 게임
100 **활동 2   배구**
활동 3   그림 그리기
활동 4   문제 해결 활동

98

Who most likely is the speaker?
(A) An office manager
(B) A sports coach
(C) An accountant
(D) A computer technician

화자는 누구일 것 같은가?
(A) 사무장
(B) 스포츠 코치
(C) 회계사
(D) 컴퓨터 기술자

해설 전체 내용 관련 – 화자의 직업

화자가 초반부에 이곳 골든 글러브 보험사 새 사무실에 잘 자리잡고 있기를 바란다(I hope you are settling in to your new offices here at Golden Glove Insurance Company)고 말한 뒤, 서로 친해질 수 있는 재미있는 행사를 계획해 보자(Let's plan something fun to get to know each other)며 단합 활동 설문 조사를 안내하는 것으로 보아 사무실의 직원을 이끌고 관리하는 일을 한다는 것을 알 수 있다. 따라서 정답은 (A)이다.

99

When will the group have a team-building activity?
(A) This afternoon
(B) Tomorrow morning
(C) Next Friday
(D) Next Saturday

단체는 언제 팀 단합 활동을 할 것인가?
(A) 오늘 오후
(B) 내일 오전
(C) 다음 주 금요일
(D) 다음 주 토요일

해설 세부 사항 관련 – 팀 단합 활동을 할 시점
화자가 중반부에 이 회의가 끝나면 다음 주 금요일 오후에 같이 했으면 하는 활동 옆에 체크하라(After this meeting, put a check mark next to the activity you want to do together next Friday afternoon)고 했으므로 정답은 (C)이다.

100

Look at the graphic. Which activity does the speaker most likely prefer?
(A) Activity 1
(B) Activity 2
(C) Activity 3
(D) Activity 4

시각 정보에 의하면, 화자는 어떤 활동을 가장 선호할 것 같은가?
(A) 활동 1
(B) 활동 2
(C) 활동 3
(D) 활동 4

해설 시각 정보 연계 – 화자가 가장 선호하는 활동
화자가 후반부에 배구장을 이용하면 활력도 넘치고 재미있겠지만, 자신이 청자들에게 영향을 주면 안 된다(It would be energizing and fun to use our volleyball court, but I shouldn't influence you!)고 했으므로 화자가 선호하는 활동은 배구임을 알 수 있다. 목록에서 배구는 활동 2 이므로 정답은 (B)이다.

1 (A)	2 (C)	3 (A)	4 (D)	5 (B)
6 (A)	7 (B)	8 (B)	9 (B)	10 (C)
11 (C)	12 (A)	13 (B)	14 (C)	15 (B)
16 (A)	17 (A)	18 (B)	19 (C)	20 (A)
21 (C)	22 (C)	23 (A)	24 (A)	25 (B)
26 (A)	27 (B)	28 (B)	29 (A)	30 (B)
31 (C)	32 (A)	33 (B)	34 (C)	35 (A)
36 (B)	37 (D)	38 (A)	39 (D)	40 (C)
41 (C)	42 (D)	43 (B)	44 (A)	45 (D)
46 (B)	47 (C)	48 (A)	49 (A)	50 (A)
51 (B)	52 (C)	53 (D)	54 (C)	55 (A)
56 (B)	57 (A)	58 (C)	59 (D)	60 (C)
61 (B)	62 (B)	63 (D)	64 (C)	65 (C)
66 (B)	67 (A)	68 (C)	69 (D)	70 (B)
71 (D)	72 (B)	73 (C)	74 (A)	75 (C)
76 (D)	77 (C)	78 (B)	79 (D)	80 (C)
81 (D)	82 (D)	83 (D)	84 (B)	85 (A)
86 (B)	87 (A)	88 (D)	89 (C)	90 (A)
91 (C)	92 (D)	93 (B)	94 (C)	95 (A)
96 (D)	97 (D)	98 (B)	99 (A)	100 (B)

PART 1

1 W-Br

(A) A man is carrying a backpack.
(B) A man is tying his shoelace.
(C) A woman is purchasing a snack.
(D) A woman is picking up a ticket from the ground.

(A) 남자가 배낭을 메고 있다.
(B) 남자가 신발 끈을 묶고 있다.
(C) 여자가 스낵을 사고 있다.
(D) 여자가 바닥에서 표를 줍고 있다.

어휘 tie 묶다, 매다   shoelace 신발 끈   purchase 사다

해설 2인 이상 등장 사진 – 사람의 동작/상태 묘사
(A) 정답. 남자가 배낭을 메고 있는(is carrying a backpack) 모습이므로 정답.
(B) 동사 오답. 남자가 신발 끈을 묶고 있는(is tying his shoelace) 모습이 아니므로 오답.
(C) 동사 오답. 여자가 스낵을 사고 있는(is purchasing a snack) 모습이 아니므로 오답.
(D) 동사 오답. 여자가 바닥에서 표를 줍고 있는(is picking up a ticket from the ground) 모습이 아니므로 오답.

2 W-Am

(A) She's wiping off a counter.
(B) She's putting dishes in a sink.
(C) She's using a microwave oven.
(D) She's rinsing a cloth under a faucet.

(A) 여자가 조리대를 닦고 있다.
(B) 여자가 싱크대에 접시를 넣고 있다.
(C) 여자가 전자레인지를 사용하고 있다.
(D) 여자가 수도꼭지 아래에서 천을 헹구고 있다.

어휘 wipe off ~을 닦다   rinse (물에) 헹구다   faucet 수도꼭지

해설 1인 등장 사진 – 사람의 동작/상태 묘사
(A) 동사 오답. 여자가 조리대를 닦고 있는(is wiping off a counter) 모습이 아니므로 오답.
(B) 동사 오답. 여자가 싱크대에 접시를 넣고 있는(is putting dishes in a sink) 모습이 아니므로 오답.
(C) 정답. 여자가 전자레인지를 사용하고 있는(is using a microwave oven) 모습이므로 정답.
(D) 동사 오답. 여자가 수도꼭지 밑에서 천을 헹구고 있는(is rinsing a cloth under a faucet) 모습이 아니므로 오답.

3 W-Br

(A) A man is walking behind some parked cars.
(B) A woman is cleaning snow off a walkway.
(C) A man is maintaining a fence.
(D) A woman is taking off a snow jacket.

(A) 남자가 주차된 차들 뒤에서 걸어가고 있다.
(B) 여자가 보도에 쌓인 눈을 치우고 있다.
(C) 남자가 울타리를 수리하고 있다.
(D) 여자가 스노 재킷을 벗고 있다.

어휘 maintain 수리하다, 정비하다

해설 2인 이상 등장 사진 – 사람의 동작/상태 묘사
(A) 정답. 남자가 주차된 차들 뒤에서 걸어가고 있는(is walking behind some parked cars) 모습이므로 정답.
(B) 위치 오답. 여자가 보도(a walkway)에 쌓인 눈을 치우고 있는(is cleaning snow off) 모습이 아니라 차에 쌓인 눈을 치우고 있는 모습이므로 오답.
(C) 동사 오답. 남자가 울타리를 수리하고 있는(is maintaining a fence) 모습이 아니므로 오답.
(D) 동사 오답. 여자가 스노 재킷을 벗고 있는(is taking off a snow jacket) 모습이 아니므로 오답.

4 M-Au

(A) He's placing a pan in an oven.
(B) He's hanging up an apron.
(C) Some pots are stacked on the floor.
(D) Some jars are arranged on shelves.

(A) 남자가 팬을 오븐에 넣고 있다.
(B) 남자가 앞치마를 걸고 있다.
(C) 냄비들이 바닥에 쌓여 있다.
(D) 병들이 선반에 배열되어 있다.

어휘 stack 쌓다 jar 병, 단지 arrange 배열하다

해설 혼합 사진 – 사람/사물/풍경 혼합 묘사

(A) 동사 오답. 남자가 팬을 오븐에 넣고 있는(is placing a pan in an oven) 모습이 아니므로 오답.
(B) 동사 오답. 남자가 앞치마를 걸고 있는(is hanging up an apron) 모습이 아니므로 오답.
(C) 위치 오답. 냄비들(Some pots)이 바닥에 쌓여 있는(are stacked on the floor) 모습이 아니므로 오답.
(D) 정답. 병들(Some jars)이 선반에 배열되어 있는(are arranged on shelves) 모습이므로 정답.

5 M-Cn

(A) A building is under construction.
(B) A metal bench is unoccupied.
(C) A bicycle is propped against a tree.
(D) A tree has fallen down.

(A) 건물이 공사 중이다.
(B) 금속 벤치가 비어 있다.
(C) 자전거가 나무에 기대어져 있다.
(D) 나무가 쓰러져 있다.

어휘 under construction 공사[건설] 중인 unoccupied 비어 있는 prop ~ against ... ~을 …에 기대 놓다

해설 사물/풍경 사진 – 풍경 묘사

(A) 동사 오답. 건물(A building)이 공사 중인(is under construction) 모습이 아니므로 오답.
(B) 정답. 금속 벤치(A metal bench)가 비어 있는(is unoccupied) 모습이므로 정답.

(C) 사진에 없는 명사를 이용한 오답. 사진에 자전거(A bicycle)의 모습이 보이지 않으므로 오답.
(D) 동사 오답. 나무(A tree)가 쓰러진(has fallen down) 모습이 아니므로 오답.

6 M-Au

(A) A customer is standing near a shopping cart.
(B) Some bags have been left on the floor.
(C) A shopping cart has been left in a parking area.
(D) A customer is leaning into a freezer.

(A) 고객이 쇼핑 카트 옆에 서 있다.
(B) 봉지들이 바닥에 놓여 있다.
(C) 쇼핑 카트가 주차장에 놓여 있다.
(D) 고객이 냉동고 안으로 몸을 기울이고 있다.

어휘 freezer 냉동고

해설 혼합 사진 – 사람/사물/풍경 혼합 묘사

(A) 정답. 고객(A customer)이 쇼핑 카트 옆에 서 있는(is standing near a shopping cart) 모습이므로 정답.
(B) 위치 오답. 봉지들(Some bags)이 바닥에 놓여 있는(have been left on the floor) 모습이 아니므로 오답.
(C) 위치 오답. 쇼핑 카트(A shopping cart)가 주차장에 놓여 있는(has been left in a parking area) 모습이 아니므로 오답.
(D) 사진에 없는 명사를 이용한 오답. 사진에 냉동고(a freezer)의 모습이 보이지 않으므로 오답.

PART 2

7

W-Am Have you made an appointment with your dentist yet?

M-Cn (A) I'll put it upstairs for now.
(B) Yes, last week.
(C) A new supply order.

치과 진료 예약을 했나요?
(A) 일단 위층에 놓겠습니다.
(B) 네, 지난주에요.
(C) 신규 공급 주문입니다.

어휘 make an appointment 예약하다 for now 일단, 우선은

해설 진료 예약을 했는지 여부를 묻는 조동사(Have) 의문문

(A) 질문과 상관없는 오답.
(B) 정답. 치과 진료 예약을 했는지 여부를 확인하는 질문에 지난주에 했다고 밝히고 있으므로 정답.
(C) 질문과 상관없는 오답.

8

M-Cn Do you want to buy the blue sofa or the yellow one?

W-Br (A) A three-bedroom apartment.
(B) I like the yellow one.
(C) I've already been there.

파란색 소파를 사고 싶습니까, 아니면 노란색 소파를 사고 싶습니까?
(A) 침실이 세 개인 아파트요.
(B) 저는 노란색이 좋아요.
(C) 저는 이미 거기에 가 봤어요.

해설 구입하기를 원하는 소파 색상을 묻는 선택 의문문
(A) 연상 단어 오답. 질문의 sofa에서 연상 가능한 three-bedroom apartment를 이용한 오답.
(B) 정답. 파란색과 노란색 중 구입하기를 원하는 소파 색상을 묻는 질문에 노란색을 좋아한다며 하나를 선택해 응답하고 있으므로 정답.
(C) 질문과 상관없는 오답.

9

W-Am When is your restaurant going to open for business?

M-Au (A) These are new clothes.
(B) By the end of the month.
(C) Yes, it's a large rest area.

식당은 언제 영업을 시작하나요?
(A) 이것들은 새 옷입니다.
(B) 이달 말에요.
(C) 네, 넓은 휴게소예요.

어휘 rest area 휴게소

해설 식당을 개업하는 시점을 묻는 When 의문문
(A) 질문과 상관없는 오답.
(B) 정답. 식당을 개업하는 시점을 묻는 질문에 이달 말이라고 시점을 밝히고 있으므로 정답.
(C) Yes/No 불가 오답. When 의문문에는 Yes/No 응답이 불가능하므로 오답.

10

W-Am Why won't my computer turn on?

M-Cn (A) No, it's a small font.
(B) Turn right at the corner.
(C) Because the battery is old.

컴퓨터가 왜 켜지지 않죠?
(A) 아니요, 작은 글씨체예요.
(B) 모퉁이에서 오른쪽으로 도세요.
(C) 배터리가 오래됐기 때문이에요.

어휘 turn on 켜지다

해설 컴퓨터가 켜지지 않는 이유를 묻는 Why 의문문
(A) Yes/No 불가 오답. Why 의문문에는 Yes/No 응답이 불가능하므로 오답.

(B) 단어 반복 오답. 질문의 turn을 반복 이용한 오답.
(C) 정답. 컴퓨터가 켜지지 않는 이유를 묻는 질문에 배터리가 오래됐기 때문이라고 이유를 제시하고 있으므로 정답.

11

M-Au Do you like the renovations we did to the office?

M-Cn (A) The construction company down the street.
(B) He's in the cafeteria.
(C) Yes, it's very spacious now.

우리가 사무실을 개조한 것이 마음에 드나요?
(A) 길 아래쪽에 있는 건설 회사예요.
(B) 그는 구내식당에 있어요.
(C) 네, 이제 아주 넓네요.

어휘 renovation 개조, 수리 spacious 넓은

해설 사무실 개조가 마음에 드는지 묻는 조동사(Do) 의문문
(A) 연상 단어 오답. 질문의 renovations에서 연상 가능한 construction company를 이용한 오답.
(B) 질문과 상관없는 오답.
(C) 정답. 사무실 개조가 마음에 드는지 묻는 질문에 그렇다(Yes)고 대답한 뒤 넓다고 의견을 덧붙이고 있으므로 정답.

12

M-Au Which conference room is the accountant using?

W-Am (A) The one on the first floor.
(B) It went well, thanks.
(C) That was a lot of money.

회계사는 어느 회의실을 사용하고 있습니까?
(A) 1층에 있는 거요.
(B) 잘됐어요, 감사합니다.
(C) 큰돈이었죠.

어휘 accountant 회계사

해설 회계사가 사용하는 회의실을 묻는 Which 의문문
(A) 정답. 회계사가 어떤 회의실을 사용하고 있는지 묻는 질문에 1층에 있는 회의실이라고 알려 주고 있으므로 정답.
(B) 연상 단어 오답. 질문의 conference에서 연상 가능한 went well을 이용한 오답.
(C) 연상 단어 오답. 질문의 accountant에서 연상 가능한 a lot of money를 이용한 오답.

13

M-Cn The Internet isn't working.

W-Am (A) There's the cleaning crew's checklist.
(B) We should call the IT department.
(C) Several copies, please.

인터넷이 안 돼요.

(A) 청소 작업반의 점검표가 있어요.

(B) IT 부서에 전화해야겠어요.

(C) 몇 부 복사해 주세요.

해설 정보 전달의 평서문

(A) 연상 단어 오답. 평서문의 isn't working에서 연상 가능한 checklist 를 이용한 오답.

(B) 정답. 인터넷이 안 된다는 평서문에 IT 부서에 전화해야 한다며 대처 방안을 제시하고 있으므로 정답.

(C) 평서문과 상관없는 오답.

14

M-Cn Would you like to present first, or should I?

W-Br (A) About twenty dollars each.

(B) No, it's the second train.

(C) I'm ready to start.

먼저 발표하시겠어요, 아니면 제가 할까요?

(A) 각 20달러 정도입니다.

(B) 아니요, 두 번째 열차예요.

(C) 전 시작할 준비됐어요.

어휘 present 발표하다

해설 발표 순서를 묻는 선택 의문문

(A) 질문과 상관없는 오답. How much 의문문에 대한 응답이므로 오답.

(B) 연상 단어 오답. 질문의 first에서 연상 가능한 second를 이용한 오답.

(C) 정답. 발표 순서를 묻는 질문에 준비가 됐다며 먼저 하겠다는 의사를 나타내고 있으므로 정답.

15

M-Au The concert tickets are on sale now, aren't they?

W-Am (A) The new director of marketing.

(B) Yes, and they're selling fast.

(C) One of my favorite bands.

콘서트 티켓 지금 판매 중이죠?

(A) 신임 마케팅 이사예요.

(B) 네, 그리고 빠르게 팔려 나가고 있어요.

(C) 제가 좋아하는 밴드 중 하나예요.

해설 티켓 판매 여부를 확인하는 부가 의문문

(A) 연상 단어 오답. 질문의 on sale에서 연상 가능한 marketing을 이용한 오답.

(B) 정답. 콘서트 티켓 판매 여부를 확인하는 질문에 그렇다(Yes)고 대답한 뒤 표가 빠르게 팔려 나가고 있다며 관련 내용을 덧붙이고 있으므로 정답.

(C) 연상 단어 오답. 질문의 concert에서 연상 가능한 bands를 이용한 오답.

16

M-Au Do you have any feedback about Yumiko's performance?

W-Br (A) Yes, her work is excellent.

(B) Near the back of the room.

(C) It's nice to meet you.

유미코의 공연에 대한 의견이 있으신가요?

(A) 네, 그녀의 공연은 훌륭해요.

(B) 방 뒤쪽 근처예요.

(C) 만나서 반가워요.

어휘 performance 공연

해설 공연에 대한 의견이 있는지 묻는 조동사(Do) 의문문

(A) 정답. 공연에 대한 의견이 있는지 여부를 묻는 질문에 그렇다(Yes)고 대답한 뒤 훌륭하다며 구체적으로 의견을 밝히고 있으므로 정답.

(B) 유사 발음 오답. 질문의 feedback과 부분적으로 발음이 비슷한 back 을 이용한 오답.

(C) 연상 단어 오답. 질문의 feedback, performance에서 연상 가능한 nice를 이용한 오답.

17

W-Am Why don't we reassign Silvia to the evening shift in the stockroom?

M-Cn (A) Sure—I expect she'll be OK with that.

(B) I sent my assignment to the instructor.

(C) The new office furniture is comfortable.

실비아에게 창고 저녁 근무를 다시 맡기는 게 어때요?

(A) 좋아요. 그녀는 그 결정을 괜찮다고 할 거예요.

(B) 저는 강사에게 과제를 보냈어요.

(C) 새 사무용 가구는 편안해요.

어휘 reassign 다시 맡기다 shift 교대 근무 stockroom 창고 assignment 과제 comfortable 편안한

해설 제안/권유의 의문문

(A) 정답. 실비아에게 창고 저녁 근무를 다시 맡기자는 제안에 좋다(Sure) 고 대답한 뒤 그녀는 그 결정을 괜찮다고 할 것이라고 관련 내용을 덧붙이고 있으므로 정답.

(B) 유사 발음 오답. 질문의 reassign과 부분적으로 발음이 비슷한 assignment를 이용한 오답.

(C) 연상 단어 오답. 질문의 stockroom에서 연상 가능한 furniture를 이용한 오답.

18

M-Au How can we find extra seasonal help?

W-Am (A) Spring is my favorite season.

(B) Let's post some job listings on our Web site.

(C) Because he left early today.

시즌에 도와줄 추가 일손을 어떻게 구하죠?

(A) 봄은 제가 가장 좋아하는 계절이에요.

(B) 우리 웹사이트에 구인 목록을 올리도록 하죠.

(C) 그가 오늘 일찍 떠났기 때문이에요.

TEST
6

어휘 seasonal 시즌[계절]의   job listing 구인 목록

해설 추가 일손을 구하는 방법을 묻는 How 의문문

(A) 연상 단어/파생어 오답. 질문의 seasonal에서 연상 가능한 Spring, 질문의 seasonal과 파생어 관계인 season을 이용한 오답.

(B) 정답. 추가 일손을 구하는 방법을 묻는 질문에 웹사이트에 구인 목록을 올리는 방안을 제시하고 있으므로 정답.

(C) 질문과 상관없는 오답.

19

W-Am Do you know if there's a bus from here to New York City?

M-Cn (A) That's a great idea.
(B) No, he studied in London.
(C) Yes, there's one every day around nine o'clock.

여기서 뉴욕시로 가는 버스가 있는지 혹시 아세요?

(A) 좋은 생각이에요.
(B) 아니요, 그는 런던에서 공부했어요.
(C) 네, 매일 9시쯤에 한 대 있어요.

해설 버스 운행 여부를 묻는 조동사(Do) 의문문

(A) 질문과 상관없는 오답.

(B) 연상 단어 오답. 질문의 New York City에서 연상 가능한 London을 이용한 오답.

(C) 정답. 버스가 있는지 묻는 질문에 그렇다(Yes)고 대답한 뒤 버스가 오는 시간을 덧붙이고 있으므로 정답.

20

M-Cn Who's driving you to the airport?

W-Br (A) The hotel has a free shuttle.
(B) She just received her pilot's license.
(C) About twenty minutes late.

누가 공항까지 태워다 주나요?

(A) 호텔에 무료 셔틀이 있어요.
(B) 그녀는 얼마 전에 조종사 면허증을 받았어요.
(C) 20분 정도 늦어요.

해설 누가 공항까지 태워다 주는지 묻는 Who 의문문

(A) 정답. 누가 공항까지 태워다 주는지 묻는 질문에 호텔에 무료 셔틀이 있다며 태워다 줄 사람이 필요 없음을 우회적으로 밝히고 있으므로 정답.

(B) 연상 단어 오답. 질문의 airport에서 연상 가능한 pilot을 이용한 오답.

(C) 질문과 상관없는 오답.

21

W-Am How often should I replace the water filter?

M-Cn (A) A new coffeemaker.
(B) Can I have more ice, please?
(C) There's a manual in the cabinet.

정수기 필터를 얼마나 자주 교체해야 하나요?

(A) 새 커피 메이커예요.
(B) 얼음 좀 더 주시겠어요?
(C) 캐비닛 안에 설명서가 있어요.

어휘 replace 교체하다   manual 설명서

해설 정수기 필터 교체 빈도를 묻는 How often 의문문

(A) 연상 단어 오답. 질문의 filter에서 연상 가능한 coffeemaker를 이용한 오답.

(B) 연상 단어 오답. 질문의 water에서 연상 가능한 ice를 이용한 오답.

(C) 정답. 정수기 필터 교체 빈도를 묻는 질문에 캐비닛 안에 설명서가 있다고 우회적으로 응답하고 있으므로 정답.

22

W-Br Aren't you still on the event-planning committee?

M-Au (A) There's an orange sign at the entrance.
(B) Check the bookshelf by the window.
(C) Members are replaced every year.

아직 행사 기획 위원회에 계시지 않나요?

(A) 입구에 주황색 표지판이 있어요.
(B) 창가에 있는 책장을 확인하세요.
(C) 위원은 해마다 교체돼요.

어휘 planning 기획   committee 위원회   entrance 입구

해설 행사 기획 위원회에 있는지 여부를 확인하는 부정 의문문

(A) 연상 단어 오답. 질문의 event에서 연상 가능한 sign at the entrance를 이용한 오답.

(B) 질문과 상관없는 오답.

(C) 정답. 아직 행사 기획 위원회에 있는지 여부를 묻는 질문에 위원이 해마다 교체된다며 지금은 위원이 아님을 우회적으로 나타내고 있으므로 정답.

23

M-Au Would you like to join us for tea now in the cafeteria?

W-Am (A) I have a client meeting in ten minutes.
(B) Actually, I joined a different gym.
(C) Some tables and chairs.

지금 구내식당에서 차 마실 건데 같이 갈래요?

(A) 10분 후에 고객 면담이 있어요.
(B) 사실 저는 다른 헬스클럽에 등록했어요.
(C) 몇 개의 탁자와 의자요.

어휘 join 함께하다; 가입하다

해설 제안/권유의 의문문

(A) 정답. 차를 마시러 같이 가자는 권유에 고객 면담이 있다면서 거절의 의사를 우회적으로 표현하고 있으므로 정답.

(B) 단어 반복 오답. 질문의 join을 반복 이용한 오답.

(C) 연상 단어 오답. 질문의 cafeteria에서 연상 가능한 tables and chairs를 이용한 오답.

24

M-Cn How do you think the new robotics technician is doing?

W-Br (A) I've been working off-site for a few weeks.
(B) The tools are on my desk.
(C) Because the team won first place.

새로 온 로봇 기술자는 어떻게 지내고 있는 것 같아요?
(A) 저는 몇 주째 외부에서 일하고 있어요.
(B) 도구는 제 책상 위에 있어요.
(C) 왜냐하면 그 팀이 1등을 했기 때문이에요.

어휘 technician 기술자 off-site 외부에서

해설 새로 온 로봇 기술자가 어떻게 지내고 있는지 묻는 How 의문문

(A) 정답. 새로 온 로봇 기술자가 어떻게 지내고 있는지 묻는 질문에 몇 주째 외부에서 일하고 있다며 의견을 제시할 수 없음을 우회적으로 나타내고 있으므로 정답.
(B) 연상 단어 오답. 질문의 technician에서 연상 가능한 tools를 이용한 오답.
(C) 질문과 상관없는 오답. Why 의문문에 대한 응답이므로 오답.

25

W-Am I hope the building inspector will arrive soon.

M-Cn (A) No, not as much as we expected.
(B) Traffic is heavy on Highway 90.
(C) A multilevel apartment complex.

건축물 검사원이 빨리 도착하면 좋겠어요.
(A) 아니요, 우리가 기대한 것만큼은 아닙니다.
(B) 90번 간선 도로가 많이 막혀요.
(C) 다층식 아파트 단지예요.

어휘 building inspector 건축물 검사원 multilevel 다층(식)의

해설 의사 전달의 평서문

(A) 연상 단어 오답. 평서문의 hope에서 연상 가능한 expected를 이용한 오답.
(B) 정답. 건축물 검사원이 빨리 도착하면 좋겠다는 평서문에 간선 도로가 많이 막힌다며 도착이 늦어진다는 것을 우회적으로 알려 주고 있으므로 정답.
(C) 연상 단어 오답. 평서문의 building에서 연상 가능한 apartment complex를 이용한 오답.

26

W-Am We should order a cake for the company picnic.

M-Au (A) Some of the staff don't eat sweets.
(B) The bank is on Twelfth Street.
(C) About five kilometers.

우리는 회사 야유회를 위해 케이크를 주문해야 해요.
(A) 일부 직원들은 단것을 먹지 않아요.
(B) 은행은 12번가에 있습니다.
(C) 5킬로미터 정도예요.

어휘 sweet 단것, 디저트

해설 제안/권유의 평서문

(A) 정답. 회사 야유회를 위해 케이크를 주문해야 한다는 평서문에 단것을 먹지 않는 직원도 있다며 주문 시 고려해야 할 사항을 제시하고 있으므로 정답.
(B) 평서문과 상관없는 오답. Where 의문문에 대한 응답이므로 오답.
(C) 평서문과 상관없는 오답. How far 의문문에 대한 응답이므로 오답.

27

W-Am Does the rental vehicle have automatic or manual transmission?

M-Cn (A) It's on the shelf in the office.
(B) Bradley will be driving the vehicle.
(C) The lights turn on automatically.

렌트 차량이 자동 변속기인가요, 아니면 수동 변속기인가요?
(A) 그것은 사무실 선반에 있어요.
(B) 브래들리가 차량을 운전할 겁니다.
(C) 라이트가 자동으로 들어와요.

어휘 automatic 자동의 manual 수동의 transmission 변속기

해설 렌트 차량의 변속기 종류를 묻는 선택 의문문

(A) 질문과 상관없는 오답. Where 의문문에 대한 응답이므로 오답.
(B) 정답. 렌트 차량의 변속기 종류를 묻는 질문에 브래들리가 차량을 운전한다며 자신은 모르는 사항임을 우회적으로 나타내고 있으므로 정답.
(C) 파생어 오답. 질문의 automatic과 파생어 관계인 automatically를 이용한 오답.

28

W-Br I'd like to have some jackets altered.

M-Au (A) I prefer 100 percent cotton.
(B) When would you like to pick them up?
(C) Yes, it's a much shorter trip.

재킷을 수선하고 싶어요.
(A) 저는 면 100퍼센트를 선호해요.
(B) 언제 찾으러 오시겠어요?
(C) 네, 훨씬 더 짧은 여행입니다.

어휘 alter (옷을) 고치다, 수선하다

해설 부탁/요청의 평서문

(A) 연상 단어 오답. 평서문의 jacket에서 연상 가능한 100 percent cotton을 이용한 오답.
(B) 정답. 재킷을 수선하고 싶다는 평서문에 재킷을 찾으러 올 날짜를 되물으며 요청에 응하겠다는 의사를 우회적으로 표현하고 있으므로 정답.
(C) 유사 발음 오답. 평서문의 altered와 부분적으로 발음이 유사한 shorter를 이용한 오답.

29

M-Cn Where should we unload the kitchen tiles?

W-Br (A) The client isn't at home right now.
(B) Not long ago.

(C) Sorry I spilled the water.

부엌 타일을 어디에 내릴까요?

(A) 고객이 지금 집에 없어요.
(B) 얼마 전이에요.
(C) 죄송해요. 물을 쏟았어요.

어휘 unload (짐을) 내리다 spill 쏟다

해설 부엌 타일을 내릴 장소를 묻는 Where 의문문

(A) 정답. 부엌 타일을 내릴 장소를 묻는 질문에 고객이 집에 없다며 짐을 내릴 수 없음을 우회적으로 밝히고 있으므로 정답.
(B) 질문과 상관없는 오답.
(C) 연상 단어 오답. 질문의 kitchen에서 연상 가능한 water를 이용한 오답.

30

M-Au Are you using the older version of the software or the one that was just released?

W-Am (A) I'm using brass hardware in the kitchen.
(B) Were we supposed to update the program?
(C) Yes, he has a used computer.

이전 버전 소프트웨어를 사용하고 있나요, 아니면 방금 출시된 소프트웨어를 사용하고 있나요?

(A) 저는 부엌에 황동 철제를 사용하고 있어요.
(B) 프로그램을 업데이트해야 했나요?
(C) 네, 그는 중고 컴퓨터를 가지고 있어요.

어휘 release 출시하다 brass 황동[놋쇠]으로 만든 hardware 철물; 하드웨어 be supposed to ~해야 한다 used 중고의

해설 사용하고 있는 소프트웨어 버전을 묻는 선택 의문문

(A) 연상 단어/유사 발음 오답. 질문의 software에서 연상 가능하며 부분적으로 발음이 유사한 hardware를 이용한 오답.
(B) 정답. 사용하고 있는 소프트웨어 버전을 묻는 질문에 프로그램을 업데이트해야 했는지 되물으며 이전 버전을 사용하고 있음을 간접적으로 나타내고 있으므로 정답.
(C) 연상 단어 오답. 질문의 older와 software에서 연상 가능한 used computer를 이용한 오답.

31

M-Cn Could you help me access my e-mail account before you leave?

W-Br (A) On the top shelf.
(B) Did you check the storage closet?
(C) Several technicians are working late tonight.

가시기 전에 제 이메일 계정에 접속할 수 있게 도와주시겠어요?

(A) 맨 위 선반이에요.
(B) 수납장을 확인하셨어요?
(C) 기술자 몇 명이 오늘 밤 늦게까지 일해요.

어휘 access 접속하다 account 계정 storage 저장, 보관 closet 벽장

해설 부탁/요청의 의문문

(A) 질문과 상관없는 오답. Where 의문문에 대한 응답이므로 오답.

(B) 연상 단어 오답. 질문의 e-mail에서 연상 가능한 check, storage를 이용한 오답.
(C) 정답. 도움을 요청하는 질문에 기술자 몇 명이 늦게까지 일한다며 도움을 받을 수 있는 대안을 제시하고 있으므로 정답.

PART 3

32-34

M-Cn Hello. ³²**I've come to close my bank account.** ³³**I received an e-mail informing me that the bank is going to start charging a monthly maintenance fee**, and I'd rather keep my money in an account with no fee.

W-Br Yes, ³³**that's our new policy.** Are you aware, though, that we'll waive the fee if you maintain a minimum balance of 500 dollars?

M-Cn OK. That shouldn't be a problem. ³⁴**Where can I find a printed copy of the policy?**

W-Br ³⁴**I can print one out for you right now.**

남 안녕하세요. 통장을 해지하려고 왔습니다. 은행에서 매달 유지 수수료를 부과하기 시작한다는 이메일을 받았는데, 수수료가 없는 계좌에 돈을 넣어 두고 싶어요.

여 네, 새로운 정책이에요. 하지만 최소 잔고 500달러를 유지하면 수수료를 면제해 주는데 알고 계시나요?

남 그렇군요. 그러면 문제없겠네요. **인쇄된 정책 사본은 어디에 있나요?**

여 **지금 바로 출력해 드릴게요.**

어휘 bank account 은행 계좌 charge 청구하다 maintenance 유지 fee 수수료 waive 면제하다 balance 잔고

32

What does the man want to do at the bank?
(A) Close an account
(B) Make a deposit
(C) Apply for a loan
(D) Interview for a job

남자는 은행에서 무엇을 하고 싶어 하는가?

(A) 계좌 해지
(B) 입금
(C) 대출 신청
(D) 입사 면접

어휘 make a deposit 입금하다 loan 대출

해설 세부 사항 관련 – 남자가 은행에서 하고 싶어 하는 일
남자가 첫 대사에서 통장을 해지하려고 왔다(I've come to close my bank account)고 했으므로 정답은 (A)이다.

33

What new policy are the speakers discussing?
(A) Extending business hours
(B) Charging a maintenance fee
(C) Increasing online security
(D) Offering membership benefits

화자들은 어떤 새로운 정책에 관해 논의하고 있는가?
(A) 영업시간 연장
(B) 유지 수료료 청구
(C) 온라인 보안 강화
(D) 회원 혜택 제공

어휘 extend 연장하다 security 보안 benefit 혜택

해설 전체 내용 관련 – 대화의 주제
남자가 첫 대사에서 은행에서 매달 유지 수료료를 부과하기 시작한다는 이메일을 받았다(I received an e-mail ~ charging a monthly maintenance fee)고 했고 여자가 그것이 새로운 정책(that's our new policy)이라고 했으므로 화자들은 유지 수료료 부과 정책을 논의하고 있음을 알 수 있다. 따라서 정답은 (B)이다.

34

What will the woman do next?
(A) Go to lunch
(B) Speak to her manager
(C) Provide a document
(D) Schedule an appointment

여자는 다음에 무엇을 할 것인가?
(A) 점심 먹으러 가기
(B) 매니저와 대화하기
(C) 문서 제공하기
(D) 예약 잡기

어휘 appointment 예약, 약속

해설 세부 사항 관련 – 여자가 다음에 할 일
남자가 인쇄된 정책 사본이 있는 곳을 묻자(Where can I find a printed copy of the policy?) 여자가 바로 출력해 주겠다고(I can print one out for you right now)고 했으므로 여자는 출력물을 제공할 것임을 알 수 있다. 따라서 정답은 (C)이다.

> **Paraphrasing** 대화의 a printed copy of the policy
> → 정답의 a document

35-37

M-Au	Hi, Bianca. It's Matthew. ³⁵,³⁶**I'm here at Mariano's East for Lauren's surprise retirement dinner**, but nobody else is here.
W-Br	Hi, Matthew. ³⁶**We're here at Mariano's West, on Tenth Avenue**. We've been wondering where you are.
M-Au	Oh, no. ³⁶**I went to the wrong place**, but I'll

be there soon. ³⁷**I just realized I left the gift I bought for her at the office, so I can stop and pick it up on the way.**

남	안녕하세요, 비앙카. 매튜예요. **로렌의 깜짝 은퇴 만찬을 위해 마리아노즈 이스트에 왔는데**, 다른 사람은 아무도 여기 없네요.
여	안녕하세요, 매튜. **우리는 10번가에 있는 마리아노즈 웨스트에 있어요**. 어디 계신지 의아했어요.
남	아, 이런. **제가 엉뚱한 곳에 왔네요**. 곧 갈게요. **그녀를 위해 산 선물을 사무실에 두고 온 걸 이제야 알았으니, 가는 길에 들러 가져가면 돼요.**

어휘 retirement 은퇴 realize 알다, 깨닫다

35

What event is taking place?
(A) A retirement dinner
(B) A client meeting
(C) An industry conference
(D) An award ceremony

어떤 행사가 열리고 있는가?
(A) 은퇴 만찬
(B) 고객 면담
(C) 업계 회의
(D) 시상식

해설 세부 사항 관련 – 행사의 종류
남자가 첫 대사에서 로렌의 깜짝 은퇴 만찬을 위해 마리아노즈 이스트에 왔다(I'm here at Mariano's East for Lauren's surprise retirement dinner)고 했으므로 정답은 (A)이다.

36

What problem does the man have?
(A) His car broke down.
(B) He is at the wrong location.
(C) He forgot some tickets.
(D) He has a schedule conflict.

남자는 어떤 문제를 가지고 있는가?
(A) 차가 고장 났다.
(B) 엉뚱한 장소에 있다.
(C) 표를 깜박했다.
(D) 일정이 겹친다.

어휘 schedule conflict 일정 겹침

해설 세부 사항 관련 – 남자의 문제
남자가 첫 대사에서 마리아노즈 이스트에 왔다(I'm here at Mariano's East)고 했고 여자가 우리는 10번가에 있는 마리아노즈 웨스트에 있다(We're here at Mariano's West, on Tenth Avenue)고 하자 남자가 자신이 엉뚱한 곳에 왔다(I went to the wrong place)고 대답했으므로 정답은 (B)이다.

37

Why will the man go to his office?
(A) To sign for a delivery
(B) To meet a colleague
(C) To print out a document
(D) To pick up a gift

남자는 왜 사무실에 갈 것인가?
(A) 배송 확인 서명을 하기 위해
(B) 동료를 만나기 위해
(C) 문서를 인쇄하기 위해
(D) 선물을 가지러 가기 위해

해설 세부 사항 관련 – 남자가 사무실에 가는 이유
남자가 마지막 대사에서 로렌을 위해 산 선물을 사무실에 두고 온 것이 생각났다(I just realized I left the gift I bought for her at the office)면서 가는 길에 들러 가져가겠다(I can stop and pick it up on the way)고 했으므로 정답은 (D)이다.

38-40

W-Am	Fritz, ³⁸**Kelfern Limited just called. They received the fabric for their new line of sofas.** ³⁹**They ordered brown but received the green sofa fabric instead.**
M-Cn	Hmm. Let me check our records. ³⁹**Looks like the product code was entered wrong when the order was processed.** It's our fault.
W-Am	OK. I'll call them right away to apologize and tell them to return the order. We'll get a new shipment out as soon as possible, and ⁴⁰**I'll offer them a twenty percent discount for the inconvenience.**

여	프리츠, 방금 켈펀 유한회사에서 전화가 왔어요. 소파 신제품군에 쓸 원단을 받았대요. 갈색을 주문했는데 대신 녹색 소파 원단을 받았다네요.
남	흠. 기록을 확인해 볼게요. **주문이 처리될 때 제품 코드가 잘못 입력된 것 같네요.** 우리 잘못이에요.
여	그렇군요. 제가 바로 전화해서 사과하고 주문품을 반품하라고 말할게요. 가능한 한 빨리 새로운 배송을 보내고, **불편을 끼친 것에 대해 20퍼센트 할인을 제공할게요.**

어휘	fabric 원단 instead 대신 enter 입력하다 process 처리하다 fault 잘못, 책임 apologize 사과하다 inconvenience 불편

38

What type of business is Kelfern Limited?
(A) A furniture company
(B) An automobile manufacturer
(C) A restaurant supply store
(D) An architectural design firm

켈펀 유한회사는 어떤 종류의 업체인가?
(A) 가구 회사
(B) 자동차 제조업체
(C) 식당용품점
(D) 건축 설계 사무소

어휘 manufacturer 제조업체 architectural 건축의

해설 전체 내용 관련 – 회사의 업종
여자가 첫 대사에서 켈펀 유한회사에서 전화가 왔다(Kelfern Limited just called)면서 소파 신제품군에 쓸 원단을 받았다(They received the fabric for their new line of sofas)고 했으므로 켈펀 유한회사는 가구 회사임을 알 수 있다. 따라서 정답은 (A)이다.

39

According to the man, what was the cause of a problem?
(A) A delivery was late.
(B) A part was missing.
(C) A product was damaged.
(D) A code was entered incorrectly.

남자에 따르면, 문제의 원인은 무엇인가?
(A) 배송이 늦었다.
(B) 부품이 누락되었다.
(C) 제품이 손상되었다.
(D) 코드가 잘못 입력되었다.

어휘 incorrectly 틀리게, 잘못

해설 세부 사항 관련 – 남자가 말하는 문제의 원인
여자가 도입부에서 켈펀 유한회사가 갈색 원단을 주문했는데 대신 녹색 원단을 받았다(They ordered brown but received the green sofa fabric instead)고 하자 남자가 주문이 처리될 때 제품 코드가 잘못 입력된 것 같다(Looks like the product code was entered wrong when the order was processed)고 했으므로 정답은 (D)이다.

40

What will the woman offer Kelfern Limited?
(A) Free installation
(B) Next-day delivery
(C) A discount
(D) A full refund

여자는 켈펀 유한회사에 무엇을 제공할 것인가?
(A) 무료 설치
(B) 익일 배송
(C) 할인
(D) 전액 환불

어휘 installation 설치

해설 세부 사항 관련 – 여자가 제공할 것

여자가 마지막 대사에서 불편을 끼친 것에 대해 20퍼센트 할인을 제공하겠다(I'll offer them a twenty percent discount ~)고 했으므로 정답은 (C)이다.

41-43

M-Cn	Pauline, [41]**have you thought about where we should park our food truck for business next weekend?**
W-Br	[41]**I was thinking Schiller Park would be a good location.** [41,42]**A neighborhood festival is being held there on Saturday.** [41]**I'm sure a lot of people going to the festival will want to buy our fried noodles and dumplings.**
M-Cn	That's a good idea—but [43]**I'm worried about having the proper permit to sell food there.** Does the one we already have cover that?
W-Br	It does. I already checked on that.
남	폴린, 다음 주말에 영업을 위해 푸드 트럭을 어디에 주차해야 할지 생각해 봤어요?
여	제 생각에는 쉴러 공원이 좋을 것 같아요. 토요일에 그곳에서 동네 축제가 열릴 거예요. 축제에 오는 많은 사람들이 분명 우리 볶음면과 만두를 사고 싶어 할 거예요.
남	좋은 생각이에요. 하지만 **거기에서 음식을 팔 수 있는 적절한 허가증을 받는 것이 걱정이네요.** 우리가 이미 가지고 있는 허가증으로 될까요?
여	돼요. 제가 이미 확인했어요.
어휘	dumpling 만두 proper 적절한 permit 허가(증)

41

What industry do the speakers work in?
(A) Transportation
(B) Tourism
(C) Food service
(D) Journalism

화자들은 어떤 업계에서 일하는가?
(A) 교통
(B) 관광
(C) 음식 서비스
(D) 언론

해설 전체 내용 관련 – 화자들의 근무 업계

남자가 첫 대사에서 다음 주말에 푸드 트럭을 어디에 주차해야 할지 생각해 봤는지(have you thought about ~ our food truck for business next weekend?) 물었고 여자가 쉴러 공원이 좋을 것 같다(I was thinking Schiller Park would be a good location)면서 토요일에 쉴러 공원에서 동네 축제가 열린다(A neighborhood festival ~ on Saturday)고 대답했다. 그러면서 축제에 오는 많은 사람들이 분명 우리 볶음면과 만두를 사고 싶어 할 것(I'm sure a lot of people ~ to buy our fried noodles and dumplings)이라고 대답했으므로 정답은 (C)이다.

> **Paraphrasing** 대화의 fried noodles and dumplings
> → 정답의 Food

42

According to the woman, what event will be held on Saturday?
(A) A farmers market
(B) A theater performance
(C) A sports competition
(D) A community festival

여자에 따르면, 토요일에 어떤 행사가 열릴 것인가?
(A) 농산물 직판장
(B) 연극 공연
(C) 스포츠 대회
(D) 지역 사회 축제

해설 세부 사항 관련 – 여자가 말하는 토요일에 열릴 행사

여자가 첫 번째 대사에서 토요일에 그곳에서 동네 축제가 열린다(A neighborhood festival is being held there on Saturday)고 했으므로 정답은 (D)이다.

> **Paraphrasing** 대화의 A neighborhood festival
> → 정답의 A community festival

43

What is the man concerned about?
(A) Getting enough tickets
(B) Having the appropriate permit
(C) Publicizing an event
(D) Preparing for rain

남자는 무엇을 걱정하는가?
(A) 충분한 표 구하기
(B) 적절한 허가증 보유하기
(C) 행사 홍보하기
(D) 비에 대비하기

어휘 appropriate 적절한 publicize 홍보하다

해설 세부 사항 관련 – 남자의 우려 사항

남자가 두 번째 대사에서 그곳에서 음식을 팔 수 있는 적절한 허가증을 받는 것이 걱정(I'm worried about having the proper permit to sell food there)이라고 했으므로 정답은 (B)이다.

44-46

M-Au	Hi. **⁴⁴I'm interested in having an antique looked at to determine its value, and I heard your shop provides free appraisals. Are you available for one now?**
W-Br	**⁴⁴Yes.** What do you have?
M-Au	It's this picture frame. **⁴⁵I want to put it up for sale at an auction next month,** and I need some help deciding on the starting bid.
W-Br	I see. This frame is nicely crafted and should sell for quite a lot. There's some damage on it here that decreases the value, but that can easily be fixed. **⁴⁶I'll give you a list of local people who do this kind of restoration.**

남	안녕하세요. **골동품을 보여 드리고 가치를 판단 받고 싶은데, 이 가게에서 무료로 감정을 해 준다고 들었어요. 지금 가능하신가요?**
여	**네.** 어떤 물건인가요?
남	이 액자예요. **다음 달 경매에 내놓아 팔고 싶은데,** 시작 입찰가를 결정하는 데 도움이 필요해요.
여	알겠습니다. 이 액자는 정교하게 만들어져서 꽤 비싼 값에 팔릴 거예요. 여기 손상된 부분이 있어서 가치가 떨어지지만 쉽게 수리할 수 있어요. **지역에서 이런 종류의 복원 작업을 하는 분들의 명단을 드릴게요.**

어휘	antique 골동품 determine 판단하다 appraisal 감정, 평가 available 시간이 있는 auction 경매 bid (경매) 입찰가 craft 정교하게 만들다 decrease 떨어뜨리다 restoration 복원

44

Who most likely is the woman?
(A) An antiques appraiser
(B) An interior decorator
(C) A graphic artist
(D) A repair technician

여자는 누구인 것 같은가?
(A) 골동품 감정사
(B) 실내 장식가
(C) 그래픽 아티스트
(D) 수리 기사

어휘 appraiser 감정사

해설 전체 내용 관련 – 여자의 직업
남자가 첫 대사에서 골동품 가치를 판단 받고 싶은데, 이 가게에서 무료로 감정을 해 준다고 들었다(I'm interested in having an antique looked at to determine its value, and I heard your shop provides free appraisals)며 가능한지(Are you available for one now?) 물었고 여자가 그렇다(Yes)고 대답했으므로 정답은 (A)이다.

45

What does the man say he plans to do with an item?
(A) Give it to a family member
(B) Donate it to a museum
(C) Display it in his home
(D) Sell it at an auction

남자는 물건으로 무엇을 할 계획이라고 말하는가?
(A) 가족에게 주기
(B) 박물관에 기부하기
(C) 집에 전시하기
(D) 경매에서 판매하기

어휘 donate 기부하다

해설 세부 사항 관련 – 남자가 할 것이라고 말하는 일
남자가 두 번째 대사에서 다음 달 경매에 내놓아 팔고 싶다(I want to put it up for sale at an auction next month)고 했으므로 정답은 (D)이다.

46

What will the woman give the man?
(A) A brochure
(B) A list of contacts
(C) A bill
(D) An event schedule

여자는 남자에게 무엇을 줄 것인가?
(A) 소책자
(B) 연락처 목록
(C) 계산서
(D) 행사 일정

해설 세부 사항 관련 – 여자가 남자에게 줄 것
여자가 마지막 대사에서 지역에서 이런 종류의 복원 작업을 하는 분들의 명단을 주겠다(I'll give you a list of local people who do this kind of restoration)고 했으므로 정답은 (B)이다.

M-Au	Nalini, ⁴⁷**another patient missed an appointment today. A lot of our patients have been forgetting about their scheduled slots lately,** even though we call the week before to remind them.
W-Br	⁴⁷**Yes, I've noticed that this is becoming a problem.** But we have so many patients that we don't have enough time to make more-frequent calls.
M-Au	⁴⁸**We should seriously consider automated appointment reminders. There are lots of software programs that do it.**
W-Br	That's a great idea. But let's make sure we invest in a good one. I know many offices already use them. ⁴⁹**I'll ask for some recommendations now.**

남	날리니, **오늘 다른 환자가 또 예약한 시간을 놓쳤어요.** 일주일 전에 전화를 걸어 다시 알려 주는데도 **최근 들어 많은 환자들이 예정된 시간을 깜박하네요.**
여	네, 이게 문제가 되고 있다는 것을 저도 알고 있어요. 하지만 환자가 너무 많아서 더 자주 전화하기에는 시간이 부족해요.
남	**자동 예약 알림을 진지하게 고려해야 해요. 그런 기능을 하는 소프트웨어 프로그램들이 많이 있어요.**
여	좋은 생각이에요. 하지만 괜찮은 프로그램에 투자하도록 합시다. 이미 많은 사무실에서 사용하고 있다고 알고 있어요. **지금 추천해 달라고 요청할게요.**

어휘	appointment 예약 slot 시간, 자리 lately 최근 remind 다시 알리다 frequent 잦은 invest 투자하다 recommendation 추천

47

What problem are the speakers discussing?
(A) An office space is too small.
(B) Some medical forms are incomplete.
(C) Some patients are missing appointments.
(D) The wrong supplies were delivered.

화자들은 어떤 문제를 논의하고 있는가?
(A) 사무실 공간이 너무 협소하다.
(B) 일부 의료 양식이 다 작성되지 않았다.
(C) 일부 환자들이 예약 시간을 놓치고 있다.
(D) 엉뚱한 비품이 배송되었다.

어휘 incomplete 불완전한 supplies 비품

해설 전체 내용 관련 – 대화의 주제
남자가 첫 대사에서 오늘 다른 환자가 또 예약한 시간을 놓쳤다(another patient missed an appointment today)며 최근 들어 많은 환자들이 예정된 시간을 깜박한다(A lot of our patients have been forgetting about their scheduled slots lately)고 하자 여자가 이게 문제가 되고 있다는 것을 알고 있다(Yes, I've noticed ~ a problem)고 했으므로 정답은 (C)이다.

48

What does the man suggest doing?
(A) Purchasing some software
(B) Hiring an additional staff member
(C) Contacting an equipment vendor
(D) Locating a confirmation number

남자는 무엇을 하자고 제안하는가?
(A) 소프트웨어 구매하기
(B) 직원 추가로 채용하기
(C) 장비 공급업체에 연락하기
(D) 확인 번호 찾기

어휘 purchase 구매하다 additional 추가의 equipment 장비 vendor 공급업체, 판매상 locate 찾다

해설 세부 사항 관련 – 남자의 제안 사항
남자가 두 번째 대사에서 자동 예약 알림을 진지하게 고려해야 한다(We should seriously consider automated appointment reminders)며 그런 기능을 하는 소프트웨어 프로그램들이 많다(There are lots of software programs that do it)고 했으므로 정답은 (A)이다.

49

What does the woman say she will do next?
(A) Get recommendations
(B) Confirm a budget
(C) Call in a prescription order
(D) Update patient contact details

여자는 다음에 무엇을 할 것이라고 말하는가?
(A) 추천 받기
(B) 예산 확정하기
(C) 전화로 처방전 요청하기
(D) 환자 연락처 세부 정보 업데이트하기

어휘 budget 예산 prescription 처방전

해설 세부 사항 관련 – 여자가 다음에 할 것이라고 말하는 일
여자가 마지막 대사에서 지금 추천해 달라고 요청하겠다(I'll ask for some recommendations now)고 했으므로 정답은 (A)이다.

> Paraphrasing 대화의 ask for some recommendations
> → 정답의 Get recommendations

50-52 3인 대화

W-Br	Welcome! How can I help you?
M-Cn	Hi. ⁵⁰**We own a small commercial fishing company in the area.**
M-Au	A friend of ours referred us to you. You see, ⁵¹**one of our boat's anchor engines isn't retracting the chain completely.**
M-Cn	⁵¹**And we have to finish pulling it in manually.**

W-Br	Hmm. We might need to send your boat to a dry dock to make that kind of repair.
M-Cn	OK. But this is our peak season. We really need to have the engine fixed as quickly as possible.
W-Br	⁵²**The marina posts its dry-dock availability on its Web site. Let's see how soon they can fit you in.**

여	어서 오세요! 무엇을 도와드릴까요?
남1	안녕하세요. **저희는 이 지역에서 조그만 상업용 수산업 회사를 소유하고 있습니다.**
남2	친구가 여기를 추천해 줬어요. 보시다시피, **배에 있는 닻 엔진 중 하나가 체인을 끝까지 되감지 못해요.**
남1	**그래서 체인을 수동으로 당겨 마무리해야 합니다.**
여	흠. 그런 종류를 수리하려면 배를 건선거에 보내야 할지도 모릅니다.
남1	좋습니다. 하지만 지금은 성수기예요. 우리는 엔진을 가능한 빨리 수리해야 합니다.
여	**계류장에서 건선거 이용 가능 시간을 웹사이트에 게시해요. 얼마나 빨리 날을 잡을 수 있는지 봅시다.**

어휘	commercial 상업의 refer ~ to ... (도움을 위해) ~을 …로 보내다 anchor 닻 retract 뒤로 끌어당기다 manually 수동으로 dry dock 건선거(배를 수리하는 곳) marina 계류장, 항구 availability 이용 가능함 fit ~ in ~을 만나기 위해 시간을 내다

50

What industry do the men work in?

(A) Fishing
(B) Tourism
(C) Trucking
(D) Manufacturing

남자들은 어떤 업계에서 일하는가?

(A) 수산업
(B) 관광업
(C) 트럭 운송업
(D) 제조업

해설 전체 내용 관련 – 남자들의 근무 업계

첫 번째 남자가 첫 대사에서 우리는 이 지역에서 조그만 상업용 수산업 회사를 소유하고 있다(We own a small commercial fishing company in the area)고 했으므로 정답은 (A)이다.

51

What problem are the speakers discussing?

(A) The weather is unpredictable.
(B) A machine is broken.
(C) An employee is absent.
(D) Operating costs have risen.

화자들은 어떤 문제를 논의하고 있는가?

(A) 날씨가 예측할 수 없다.
(B) 기계가 고장 났다.
(C) 직원이 결근했다.
(D) 운영비가 증가했다.

어휘 unpredictable 예측할 수 없는 absent 결근한 operating cost 운영비

해설 전체 내용 관련 – 대화의 주제

두 번째 남자가 배에 있는 닻 엔진 중 하나가 체인을 끝까지 되감지 못한다(one of our boat's anchor engines isn't retracting the chain completely)고 했고 첫 번째 남자가 그래서 체인을 수동으로 당겨 마무리해야 한다(And we have to finish pulling it in manually)면서 기계 결함과 관련하여 대화를 이어 가고 있으므로 정답은 (B)이다.

Paraphrasing	대화의 one of our boat's anchor engines → 정답의 A machine 대화의 isn't retracting the chain completely → 정답의 is broken

52

What will the woman most likely do next?

(A) Lead a group outing
(B) Open a weather application
(C) Check a schedule
(D) Negotiate a discount

여자는 다음에 무엇을 할 것 같은가?

(A) 단체 소풍 인도하기
(B) 날씨 앱 열기
(C) 일정 확인하기
(D) 할인 협상하기

어휘 outing 소풍 negotiate 협상하다

해설 세부 사항 관련 – 여자가 다음에 할 일

여자가 마지막 대사에서 계류장에서 건선거 이용 가능한 시간을 웹사이트에 게시한다(The marina posts its dry-dock availability on its Web site)면서 얼마나 빨리 날을 잡을 수 있는지 확인하자(Let's see how soon they can fit you in)고 했으므로 정답은 (C)이다.

Paraphrasing	대화의 see how soon they can fit you in → 정답의 Check a schedule

53-55

W-Am	Good morning, Lewis. ⁵³**Are you excited to go to the annual conference?**
M-Au	⁵³**Yes! I'm looking forward to learning about any new software that we could use to develop our smart kitchen appliances.** ⁵⁴**I just wish I could get there earlier so I'd have time to explore the city.**
W-Am	Well, there are no presentations in the evenings.

M-Au	That's a good point. I should see how late museums are open.
W-Am	⁵⁵**Don't forget to keep all your receipts—** I use an app to help me manage mine. It makes getting reimbursed a lot easier.

여	안녕하세요, 루이스. **연례 회의에 참석하게 되어서 설레죠?**
남	네! **저는 스마트 주방 기기 개발에 활용할 수 있는 새로운 소프트웨어에 대해 배우기를 기대하고 있어요.** 다만 좀 더 일찍 도착해서 도시를 둘러볼 시간이 있었으면 좋겠어요.
여	음, 저녁에는 설명회가 없어요.
남	좋네요. 박물관이 얼마나 늦게까지 문을 여는지 봐야겠어요.
여	**잊지 말고 꼭 영수증을 모두 보관하세요.** 저는 앱을 사용해 영수증을 관리해요. 그러면 환급받기가 한결 수월해요.

어휘 annual 연례의 kitchen appliance 주방 기기 explore 둘러보다 receipt 영수증 reimburse 환급하다

53

Why is the man going to a conference?
(A) To promote his products
(B) To earn a certification
(C) To facilitate a workshop
(D) To learn about new technology

남자는 왜 회의에 가는가?
(A) 자신의 제품을 홍보하기 위해
(B) 자격증을 취득하기 위해
(C) 워크숍 진행을 돕기 위해
(D) 새로운 기술을 배우기 위해

어휘 certification 자격증 facilitate 진행을 돕다, 수월하게 하다

해설 세부 사항 관련 – 남자가 회의에 가는 이유
여자가 첫 대사에서 연례 회의에 참석하게 되어서 설레는지(Are you excited to go to the annual conference?) 묻자 남자가 그렇다(Yes!)고 대답한 뒤 스마트 주방 기기 개발에 활용할 수 있는 새로운 소프트웨어에 대해 배우기를 기대하고 있다(I'm looking forward to learning about any new software that we could use to develop our smart kitchen appliances)고 했으므로 정답은 (D)이다.

> **Paraphrasing** 대화의 new software
> → 정답의 new technology

54

Why does the woman say, "there are no presentations in the evenings"?
(A) To decline an invitation
(B) To express surprise
(C) To make a suggestion
(D) To complain about an event

여자는 왜 "저녁에는 설명회가 없어요"라고 말하는가?
(A) 초대를 거절하기 위해
(B) 놀라움을 표현하기 위해
(C) 제안하기 위해
(D) 행사에 대해 불평하기 위해

어휘 decline 거절하다

해설 화자의 의도 파악 – 저녁에 설명회가 없다는 말의 의도
앞에서 남자가 좀 더 일찍 도착해서 도시를 둘러봤으면 좋겠다(I just wish I could get there earlier so I'd have time to explore the city)고 희망 사항을 말한 뒤 인용문을 언급했으므로 저녁에 시간이 있으니 도시를 둘러보라고 제안하기 위해 한 말임을 알 수 있다. 따라서 정답은 (C)이다.

55

What does the woman remind the man to do?
(A) Keep some receipts
(B) Confirm a reservation
(C) Make a phone call
(D) Check a map

여자는 남자에게 무엇을 상기시키는가?
(A) 영수증 보관하기
(B) 예약 확인하기
(C) 전화 걸기
(D) 지도 확인하기

해설 세부 사항 관련 – 여자가 남자에게 상기시키는 것
여자가 마지막 대사에서 잊지 말고 꼭 영수증을 모두 보관하라(Don't forget to keep all your receipts)고 했으므로 정답은 (A)이다.

56-58 3인 대화

W-Br	Thanks for having this meeting with us, Maksim. As you know, ⁵⁶**we want to increase the monitoring of wildlife movement in our park.**
M-Cn	You mentioned that you have some cameras already installed, correct?
W-Am	^{56, 57}**We have some motion-detection cameras to capture movement in some areas. But we'd like to track wildlife at a greater distance.** Motion-detector cameras don't really work for that.
M-Cn	⁵⁷**You'd need to buy continuous-recording cameras for that.** You'll probably get some great videos.
W-Br	And actually, ⁵⁸**we could post those online. That would be great publicity for the park.**
W-Am	⁵⁸**Yes, that would be another advantage of installing the cameras.**

<table>
<tr><td>여1</td><td>이번 회의에 함께해 줘서 고마워요, 막심. 아시다시피, 우리는 공원 내 야생 동물의 이동에 대한 추적 감시를 더 강화하고 싶어요.</td></tr>
<tr><td>남</td><td>카메라가 이미 설치되어 있다고 하셨죠, 맞나요?</td></tr>
<tr><td>여2</td><td>일부 구역에 움직임을 포착하는 동작 감지 카메라가 있어요. 하지만 더 먼 거리까지 야생 동물을 추적하고 싶어요. 동작 감지 카메라는 그렇게는 작동하지 않거든요.</td></tr>
<tr><td>남</td><td>그러려면 연속 녹화 카메라를 구입해야 합니다. 아마도 멋진 동영상을 얻을 겁니다.</td></tr>
<tr><td>여1</td><td>그리고 사실, 동영상들을 온라인에 올릴 수도 있죠. 그러면 공원 홍보에도 좋을 거예요.</td></tr>
<tr><td>여2</td><td>네, 그것도 카메라를 설치하는 또 다른 장점이네요</td></tr>
</table>

어휘	monitoring 감시 wildlife 야생 동물 detection 감지 capture 포착하다 track 추적하다 distance 거리 continuous 연속적인 publicity 홍보

56

Where do the women work?
(A) At a research laboratory
(B) At a wildlife park
(C) At a newspaper
(D) At an event venue

여자들은 어디에서 일하는가?
(A) 연구실
(B) 야생 동물 공원
(C) 신문사
(D) 행사장

해설 전체 내용 관련 – 여자들의 근무지

첫 번째 여자가 첫 대사에서 공원 내 야생 동물의 이동에 대한 추적 감시를 좀 더 강화하고 싶다(we want to increase the monitoring of wildlife movement in our park)고 했고 두 번째 여자가 일부 구역에 움직임을 포착하는 동작 감지 카메라가 있지만 더 먼 거리까지 야생 동물을 추적하고 싶다(We have some motion-detection cameras ～ track wildlife at a greater distance)고 했으므로 두 사람은 야생 동물 공원에서 일하고 있음을 알 수 있다. 따라서 정답은 (B)이다.

57

What will the women most likely purchase from the man?
(A) Outdoor cameras
(B) Construction supplies
(C) Printing materials
(D) Safety equipment

여자들은 남자에게서 무엇을 구매할 것 같은가?
(A) 실외 카메라
(B) 건설 자재
(C) 인쇄 재료
(D) 안전 장비

해설 세부 사항 관련 – 여자들이 남자에게 구매할 것

두 번째 여자가 일부 구역에 움직임을 포착하는 동작 감지 카메라가 있

지만(We have some motion-detection cameras ～ in some areas) 더 먼 거리까지 야생 동물을 추적하고 싶다(But we'd like to track wildlife at a greater distance)고 하자 남자가 그러려면 연속 녹화 카메라를 사야 한다(You'd need to buy continuous-recording cameras for that)고 제안했으므로 정답은 (A)이다.

58

What advantage do the women mention?
(A) Training opportunities
(B) Cost savings
(C) Increased publicity
(D) Efficient staff scheduling

여자들은 어떤 장점을 언급하는가?
(A) 교육 기회
(B) 비용 절감
(C) 홍보 강화
(D) 효율적인 직원 일정 관리

어휘 opportunity 기회 efficient 효율적인

해설 세부 사항 관련 – 여자들이 언급하는 장점

첫 번째 여자가 두 번째 대사에서 동영상을 온라인에 올릴 수 있다(we could post those online)고 하면서 그러면 공원 홍보에도 좋을 것(That would be great publicity for the park)이라고 하자 두 번째 여자가 카메라를 설치하는 또 다른 장점(Yes, that would be another advantage of installing the cameras)이라며 호응했으므로 정답은 (C)이다.

59-61

M-Au	[59]**I spoke to Representative Kimura from the city council today.** [59,60]**He's joining us in the studio on Tuesday so we can interview him about the city council's budget plans.**
W-Am	Great! [59]**Our listeners always appreciate those interviews.** [60]**I already have a list of questions to ask him.** By the way, do you have time to listen to the recordings of last week's shows and compare them to the transcripts—make any changes that need to be made? I'd like to post them to the Web site tomorrow.
M-Au	[61]**Doesn't the voice-recognition software generate the transcripts?**
W-Am	Yes, but the program isn't completely accurate.

남	오늘 시 의회 키무라 의원과 이야기했습니다. 의원이 화요일에 스튜디오에 합류한다고 해요. 그러니 시 의회 예산 계획에 대해 의원과 인터뷰할 수 있어요.
여	잘됐네요! 청취자들은 늘 그런 인터뷰를 높이 평가하죠. 저한테 의원에게 물어볼 질문 목록이 이미 있어요. 그나저나 지난주 방송 녹화 파일을 들으면서 대본과 대조하고 수정해야

할 부분이 있으면 수정해야 하는데 시간이 있나요? 내일 웹사이트에 녹화 파일을 올리고 싶어서요.

남 **음성 인식 소프트웨어가 대본을 생성하지 않나요?**

여 맞아요, **하지만 그 프로그램이 완전히 정확하지는 않아요.**

어휘 representative 의원 budget plan 예산 계획 appreciate 높이 평가하다 compare 대조하다 transcript 대본 recognition 인식 generate 생성하다 accurate 정확한

59

Where do the speakers most likely work?
(A) At an electronics store
(B) At a bank
(C) At a medical clinic
(D) At a radio station

화자들은 어디에서 일하는 것 같은가?
(A) 전자 제품 매장
(B) 은행
(C) 병원
(D) 라디오 방송국

해설 전체 내용 관련 – 화자들의 근무지
남자가 도입부에서 오늘 시 의회 키무라 의원과 이야기했다(I spoke ~ the city council today)고 했고 의원이 화요일에 스튜디오에 합류하니 시 의회 예산 계획에 대해 의원과 인터뷰할 수 있다(He's joining us in the studio on Tuesday so we can interview him ~ budget plans)고 하자 여자가 청취자들은 그런 인터뷰를 높이 평가한다(Our listeners always appreciate those interviews)고 말하는 것으로 보아 화자들은 라디오 방송국에서 근무하고 있음을 알 수 있다. 따라서 정답은 (D)이다.

60

What will the woman do on Tuesday?
(A) Take inventory
(B) Speak at a convention
(C) Conduct an interview
(D) Respond to e-mails

여자는 화요일에 무엇을 할 것인가?
(A) 재고 조사하기
(B) 회의에서 연설하기
(C) 인터뷰하기
(D) 이메일에 답장하기

어휘 inventory 재고 (조사) convention 회의

해설 세부 사항 관련 – 여자가 화요일에 할 일
남자가 도입부에서 의원이 화요일에 스튜디오에 합류하니 시 의회 예산 계획에 대해 의원과 인터뷰할 수 있다(He's joining us in the studio on Tuesday so we can interview him ~ budget plans)고 했고 여자가 자신한테 의원에게 물어볼 질문 목록이 이미 있다(I already have a list of questions to ask him)고 했으므로 여자는 화요일에 의원을 인터뷰할 예정임을 알 수 있다. 따라서 정답은 (C)이다.

61

What does the woman mean when she says, "but the program isn't completely accurate"?
(A) Some software needs to be upgraded.
(B) Some transcripts should be checked.
(C) There was a mistake in the budget.
(D) A schedule will need to be confirmed.

여자가 "하지만 그 프로그램이 완전히 정확하지는 않아요"라고 말할 때 무엇을 의미하는가?
(A) 소프트웨어를 업그레이드해야 한다.
(B) 대본을 확인해야 한다.
(C) 예산에 착오가 있었다.
(D) 일정을 확인해야 한다.

어휘 confirm 확인하다

해설 화자의 의도 파악 – 프로그램이 완전히 정확하지 않다는 말의 의도
앞에서 남자가 음성 인식 소프트웨어가 대본을 생성하지 않느냐(Doesn't the voice-recognition software generate the transcripts?)고 물은 뒤 인용문을 언급하고 있으므로, 프로그램이 생성하더라도 한 번 더 대본을 확인해야 한다는 의도임을 알 수 있다. 따라서 정답은 (B)이다.

62-64 대화 + 상품 목록

W-Am Hi, Marcos. **⁶²Are you available to review this media release? I'd like another opinion.**

M-Cn Sure, I'll take a look. Is this the announcement about the outdoor lights?

W-Am Yes, **⁶³the company wants us to write a release about its most successful landscaping light products of the year— solar-powered outdoor lights.**

M-Cn That's interesting. They've outsold all the other kinds, including wired landscaping lights. **⁶⁴I think consumers like how easy the lights are to install.** They don't require any special tools or knowledge to set up.

여 안녕하세요, 마르코스. **이 언론 보도 자료를 검토할 시간 있을까요? 다른 의견을 듣고 싶어서요.**

남 물론이죠, 한번 볼게요. 실외 조명에 대한 보도인가요?

여 네, **회사에서 올해 가장 성공한 조경 조명 제품에 관해 보도 자료를 작성하길 원하네요. 태양열 실외 조명이요.**

남 흥미롭군요. 그 제품이 유선 조경 조명까지 포함해서 다른 어떤 종류보다 많이 팔렸죠. **제 생각에 소비자들은 설치하기가 쉬워서 그 조명을 좋아해요.** 그 제품은 설치하는 데 특별한 도구나 지식이 필요 없거든요.

어휘 release 보도 자료 opinion 의견 landscaping 조경 outsell ~보다 많이 팔리다 set up 설치하다

Model	Power Source
10G	Gas-powered
15EW	Electric (wired)
20AB	Battery (traditional)
[63]50SP	Solar (rechargeable)

모델	동력
10G	휘발유 동력
15EW	전기 (유선)
20AB	배터리 (기존 방식)
[63]50SP	태양열 (충전 가능)

62

What is the woman preparing?
(A) An owner's manual
(B) A media release
(C) A financial report
(D) A questionnaire

여자는 무엇을 준비하고 있는가?
(A) 사용 설명서
(B) 언론 보도 자료
(C) 재무 보고서
(D) 설문지

해설 세부 사항 관련 – 여자가 준비하고 있는 것
여자가 첫 대사에서 이 언론 보도 자료를 검토할 시간 있는지(Are you available to review this media release?) 물으면서 다른 의견을 듣고 싶다(I'd like another opinion)고 했으므로 정답은 (B)이다.

63

Look at the graphic. According to the woman, which is the most successful model?
(A) 10G
(B) 15EW
(C) 20AB
(D) 50SP

시각 정보에 의하면, 여자가 가장 성공한 모델이라고 말하는 것은 무엇인가?
(A) 10G
(B) 15EW
(C) 20AB
(D) 50SP

해설 시각 정보 연계 – 여자가 말하는 가장 성공한 모델
여자가 두 번째 대사에서 회사에서 올해 가장 성공한 조경 조명 제품인 태양열 실외 조명에 관해 보도 자료를 작성하길 원한다(the company wants us to write a release about its most successful landscaping light products of the year—solar-powered outdoor lights)고 했고, 상품 목록에 따르면 태양열 조명의 모델명은 50SP이므로 정답은 (D)이다.

64

What does the man think consumers like about a product?
(A) It has an extended warranty.
(B) It is widely available.
(C) It is easy to install.
(D) It is reasonably priced.

남자는 소비자들이 제품에서 무엇을 좋아한다고 생각하는가?
(A) 보증 기간이 연장되었다.
(B) 쉽게 구할 수 있다.
(C) 설치가 용이하다.
(D) 가격이 합리적이다.

어휘 extended 연장된 warranty 보증 (기간) reasonably 합리적으로

해설 세부 사항 관련 – 남자가 말하는 소비자들이 제품에서 좋아하는 점
남자가 마지막 대사에서 소비자들이 설치하기가 쉬워서 그 조명을 좋아한다고 생각한다(I think consumers like how easy the lights are to install)고 했으므로 정답은 (C)이다.

65-67 대화 + 물품 유형

M-Cn Thank you for meeting with me at your studio. **65I've just been commissioned to decorate a hotel lobby**, and I think a pair of your large floor vases will look great there—especially on each side of the front desk.

W-Br Sure, Mr. Kwon. We have a few designs available right now. The most popular one is this tall vase with a wide opening in the middle.

M-Cn Hmm, that looks great, but **66I think I'll go with the one with the handles on both sides.** It'll match the classic style of the lobby nicely.

W-Br Wonderful! Great choice. **67Let me check with an associate about when we can deliver the vases to you.**

남 작업실에서 저를 만나 주셔서 감사합니다. **얼마 전에 호텔 로비 장식하는 일을 의뢰받았는데요.** 바닥에 놓는 커다란 꽃병 한 쌍이 거기에 아주 잘 어울릴 것 같아요. 특히 프런트 양쪽에 놓으면 근사할 겁니다.

여 그럼요, 권 선생님. 저희한테 당장 구할 수 있는 디자인이 몇 가지 있어요. 가장 인기 있는 꽃병은 가운데에 넓은 구멍이 있고 키가 큰 이 꽃병이에요.

남 흠, 괜찮아 보이기는 하는데, **양쪽에 손잡이가 있는 걸로 할게요.** 클래식한 스타일의 로비와 잘 어울릴 것 같거든요.

여 멋진데요! 잘 고르셨어요. **언제 꽃병을 배달할 수 있는지 동료에게 확인해 볼게요.**

어휘 commission 의뢰하다 vase 꽃병 associate 동료

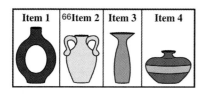

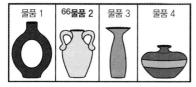

65

What has the man been hired to decorate?
(A) A museum entrance
(B) A client's office
(C) A hotel lobby
(D) A rooftop garden

남자는 무엇을 장식하기 위해 고용되었는가?
(A) 박물관 입구
(B) 고객 사무실
(C) 호텔 로비
(D) 옥상 정원

해설 세부 사항 관련 – 남자가 장식할 것
남자가 첫 대사에서 얼마 전에 호텔 로비 장식하는 일을 의뢰받았다(I've just been commissioned to decorate a hotel lobby)고 했으므로 정답은 (C)이다.

66

Look at the graphic. Which item does the man choose?
(A) Item 1
(B) Item 2
(C) Item 3
(D) Item 4

시각 정보에 의하면, 남자는 어떤 물품을 선택하는가?
(A) 물품 1
(B) 물품 2
(C) 물품 3
(D) 물품 4

해설 시각 정보 연계 – 남자가 선택하는 물품
남자가 두 번째 대사에서 양쪽에 손잡이가 있는 것으로 하겠다(I think I'll go with the one with the handles on both sides)고 했고, 물품 유형에 따르면 양쪽에 손잡이가 있는 꽃병은 2번이므로 정답은 (B)이다.

67

What will the woman talk to a colleague about?
(A) A delivery date
(B) An employee discount
(C) A payment method
(D) A product substitution

여자는 동료에게 무엇에 관해 이야기할 것인가?
(A) 배송 날짜
(B) 직원 할인
(C) 결제 방법
(D) 제품 대체

어휘 substitution 대체

해설 세부 사항 관련 – 여자가 동료에게 이야기할 것
여자가 마지막 대사에서 언제 꽃병을 배달할 수 있는지 동료에게 확인해 보겠다(Let me check with an associate about when we can deliver the vases to you)고 했으므로 정답은 (A)이다.

> **Paraphrasing** 대화의 when we can deliver
> → 정답의 A delivery date

68-70 대화 + 일정표

M-Au	I heard you offer tours of the city. **68I'm a travel agent, and I like to try out different tour companies before recommending them to my clients.** How long do your tours last?
W-Am	They generally take between one and two hours. **69The Riverside tour is our most popular.** It's one and a half hours long.
M-Au	I think I'd prefer to take a shorter one right now.
W-Am	OK. And **70would you like to rent a headset? That way, you can listen to the recorded information on your bus tour.**
M-Au	**70That's a good option.**

남	도시 투어를 제공한다고 들었어요. **저는 여행사 직원인데, 고객들에게 추천하기 전에 다양한 여행사를 한번 체험해 보고 싶어요.** 투어에 얼마나 걸리죠?
여	보통 1시간에서 2시간 정도 걸려요. **리버사이드 투어가 우리 회사에서 가장 인기가 많아요.** 한 시간 반 걸리고요.
남	이번에는 좀 더 짧은 투어가 좋을 것 같아요.
여	알겠습니다. 그리고 헤드셋을 대여하시겠어요? 그렇게 하면 버스 투어 시 녹음된 정보를 들을 수 있어요.
남	**좋은 옵션이네요.**

어휘 travel agent 여행사 직원 try out (판단하기 위해) 시험 삼아 해 보다 recommend 추천하다 prefer 선호하다

Somerville Tours 🚌

	Time	Length
Downtown West	9 A.M.	1 hour
Downtown East	10 A.M.	1 hour
69Riverside	11 A.M.	1 ½ hours
Combination tour	12 P.M.	2 hours

서머빌 투어		
	시간	소요 시간
다운타운 웨스트	오전 9시	1시간
다운타운 이스트	오전 10시	1시간
69 리버사이드	**오전 11시**	1시간 30분
복합 투어	오후 12시	2시간

68

Why is the man interested in taking a tour?
(A) To do research for a book
(B) To choose an area to live in
(C) To evaluate a company's service
(D) To take photographs for a Web site

남자는 왜 관광에 관심이 있는가?
(A) 책을 위한 조사를 하기 위해
(B) 거주할 지역을 고르기 위해
(C) 회사의 서비스를 평가하기 위해
(D) 웹사이트에 올릴 사진을 찍기 위해

어휘 research 조사하다   evaluate 평가하다

해설 세부 사항 관련 – 남자가 관광에 관심 있는 이유
남자가 첫 대사에서 자신을 여행사 직원(I'm a travel agent)이라고 밝힌 뒤 고객들에게 추천하기 전에 다양한 여행사를 체험해 보고 싶다(I like to try out different tour companies before recommending them to my clients)고 했다. 따라서 회사의 서비스를 평가하기 위해 관광에 나섰음을 알 수 있으므로 정답은 (C)이다.

69

Look at the graphic. What time does the most popular tour begin?
(A) At 9 A.M.
(B) At 10 A.M.
(C) At 11 A.M.
(D) At 12 P.M.

시각 정보에 의하면, 가장 인기 있는 투어는 몇 시에 시작하는가?
(A) 오전 9시
(B) 오전 10시
(C) 오전 11시
(D) 오후 12시

해설 시각 정보 연계 – 가장 인기 있는 투어가 시작하는 시간
여자가 첫 대사에서 리버사이드 투어가 회사에서 가장 인기가 많다(The Riverside tour is our most popular)고 했고, 일정표에 따르면 리버사이드 투어가 시작하는 시간은 오전 11시이므로 정답은 (C)이다.

70

What will the man most likely do?
(A) Book tickets in advance
(B) Rent an audio device
(C) Visit the library
(D) Wait for cooler weather

남자는 무엇을 할 것 같은가?
(A) 티켓 사전 예약하기
(B) 오디오 장치 대여하기
(C) 도서관 방문하기
(D) 날씨가 더 선선해질 때까지 기다리기

해설 세부 사항 관련 – 남자가 할 일
대화 후반부에서 여자가 헤드셋을 대여하겠는지(would you like to rent a headset?) 물으면서 그렇게 하면 버스 투어 시 녹음된 정보를 들을 수 있다(That way, you can listen to the recorded information on your bus tour)고 제안하자 남자가 좋은 옵션(That's a good option)이라며 긍정적으로 대답했으므로 정답은 (B)이다.

> **Paraphrasing** 대화의 a headset → 정답의 an audio device

PART 4

71-73 광고

M-Cn **71 Are you tired of relying on noisy, bulky fans to cool you down on hot days? Then look no further than the Deluxe Cool.** Its revolutionary design cools you off without the usual noise! Unlike typical rotating fans, the Deluxe Cool fan uses vibrations to move a single blade to push air. **72 And we're proud to say that it's now the quietest fan on the market!** Now's the time to buy, as **73 we are offering a special discount when you type in the code "DELUXE" at online checkout.**

더운 날 시끄럽고 부피가 큰 선풍기에 의존해 더위를 식히는 게 지겨우신가요? 그러면 디럭스 쿨만 보시면 됩니다. 혁신적인 디자인으로 늘 듣던 소음 없이 시원하게 해 줍니다! 일반적인 회전 선풍기와 달리 디럭스 쿨 선풍기는 진동을 사용해 날개 하나를 움직여 공기를 밀어냅니다. 그리고 우리는 디럭스 쿨 선풍기가 현재 시장에서 가장 조용한 선풍기라고 자신 있게 말할 수 있습니다! 지금이 구매할 때입니다. 온라인 결제 창에 "DELUX" 코드를 입력하면 특별 할인 혜택을 드리니까요.

어휘 rely on ~에 의존하다   bulky 부피가 큰   revolutionary 혁신적인   rotate 회전하다   vibration 진동   blade 날

71

What product is being advertised?
(A) A refrigerator
(B) An automobile
(C) A blender
(D) A fan

어떤 제품이 광고되고 있는가?
(A) 냉장고
(B) 자동차
(C) 믹서기
(D) 선풍기

해설 전체 내용 관련 – 광고되고 있는 것

화자가 초반부에 시끄럽고 부피가 큰 선풍기로 더위를 식히는 것이 지겨우면(Are you tired of relying on noisy, bulky fans to cool you down on hot days?) 디럭스 쿨만 보라(Then look no further than the Deluxe Cool)고 한 뒤 혁신적인 디자인으로 소음 없이 시원하게 한다(Its revolutionary design cools you off without the usual noise!)며 소음 없는 선풍기를 광고하고 있으므로 정답은 (D)이다.

72

Why is the company proud of the product?
(A) It is available worldwide.
(B) It is quiet.
(C) It is affordable.
(D) It won an award.

회사는 왜 제품에 자부심을 느끼는가?
(A) 전 세계 어디에서나 구할 수 있다.
(B) 조용하다.
(C) 가격이 저렴하다.
(D) 상을 받았다.

어휘 affordable 저렴한

해설 세부 사항 관련 – 회사가 제품에 자부심을 느끼는 이유

화자가 중반부에서 디럭스 쿨 선풍기가 현재 시장에서 가장 조용한 선풍기라고 자신 있게 말할 수 있다(And we're proud to say that it's now the quietest fan on the market!)고 말하고 있으므로 정답은 (B)이다.

73

How can the listeners receive a discount?
(A) By creating an online profile
(B) By purchasing multiple products
(C) By using a special code
(D) By writing a product review

청자들은 어떻게 할인을 받을 수 있는가?
(A) 온라인 프로필을 만들어서
(B) 여러 제품을 구매해서
(C) 특수 코드를 사용해서
(D) 제품 후기를 작성해서

해설 세부 사항 관련 – 청자들이 할인받을 수 있는 방법

화자가 후반부에서 온라인 결제 창에 "DELUX" 코드를 입력하면 특별 할인 혜택을 준다(we are offering a special discount when you type in the code "DELUXE" at online checkout)고 했으므로 정답은 (C)이다.

> **Paraphrasing** 담화의 type in the code "DELUXE"
> → 정답의 using a special code

74-76 회의 발췌

M-Au **⁷⁴This is an update for all dining room staff. Next month we're going to stop handing out**

---

printed menus to customers. Instead, we will place a sign with a QR code on each table. Customers can scan the code with their smartphones to open a digital menu. **⁷⁵The owners feel that scanned menus are more environmentally friendly and will use less paper. ⁷⁶Now, we know that not all customers will be familiar with this process. Please be sure to help any customers who need assistance.**

식당 직원 전원에게 최근에 바뀐 정보를 알려 드립니다. 다음 달부터는 고객들에게 인쇄된 메뉴판을 나누어 주지 않습니다. 대신 테이블마다 QR코드가 있는 표지판을 설치할 예정입니다. 고객들은 스마트폰으로 코드를 스캔해 디지털 메뉴판을 열 수 있습니다. **식당 주인들은 스캔 방식 메뉴판이 더 환경친화적이고 종이를 덜 사용하리라 생각합니다.** 잘 아시겠지만 모든 고객이 이 절차에 익숙하지는 않을 겁니다. 도움이 필요한 고객은 반드시 돕도록 하세요.

어휘 hand out ~을 나누어 주다 environmentally friendly 환경친화적인 familiar with ~에 익숙한 assistance 도움

74

Where does the talk most likely take place?
(A) At a restaurant
(B) At a print shop
(C) At a computer store
(D) At a manufacturing plant

담화는 어디에서 이루어지는 것 같은가?
(A) 식당
(B) 인쇄소
(C) 컴퓨터 매장
(D) 제조 공장

해설 전체 내용 관련 – 담화의 장소

화자가 초반부에서 식당 직원 전원에게 최근 바뀐 정보를 알린다(This is an update for all dining room staff)고 한 뒤 다음 달부터는 고객들에게 인쇄된 메뉴판을 배포하지 않는다(Next month we're going to stop handing out printed menus to customers)고 했으므로 정답은 (A)이다.

> **Paraphrasing** 담화의 dining room → 정답의 restaurant

75

According to the speaker, why is a change being made?
(A) To save storage space
(B) To address customer feedback
(C) To be environmentally responsible
(D) To improve employee satisfaction

화자에 따르면, 변화는 왜 이루어지고 있는가?
(A) 저장 공간을 절약하기 위해
(B) 고객의 의견에 대처하기 위해
(C) 환경에 책임감을 갖기 위해
(D) 직원 만족도를 개선하기 위해

어휘 address 처리하다 responsible 책임지는 satisfaction
　　　만족(도)

해설 세부 사항 관련 – 변화를 도모하는 이유
화자가 중반부에서 식당 주인들은 스캔 방식 메뉴판이 더 환경친화적이
고 종이를 덜 사용한다고 생각한다(The owners feel that scanned
menus are more environmentally friendly and will use less
paper)고 했으므로 정답은 (C)이다.

> Paraphrasing 담화의 environmentally friendly
> → 정답의 environmentally responsible

76

What does the speaker ask the listeners to do?
(A) Review a safety manual
(B) Record time accurately
(C) Wear appropriate clothing
(D) Assist customers with a process

화자는 청자들에게 무엇을 하라고 요청하는가?
(A) 안전 매뉴얼 검토하기
(B) 시간 정확하게 기록하기
(C) 적절한 복장 착용하기
(D) 고객이 절차를 잘 따라가도록 돕기

해설 세부 사항 관련 – 화자의 요청 사항
화자가 후반부에 모든 고객이 이 절차에 익숙하지는 않다(we know that
not all customers will be familiar with this process)고 밝힌 뒤
도움이 필요한 고객은 반드시 도우라(Please be sure to help any
customers who need assistance)고 당부하고 있으므로 정답은 (D)이
다.

> Paraphrasing 담화의 help any customers
> → 정답의 Assist customers

77-79 회의 발췌

> M-Cn ⁷⁷I'd like to start this meeting by sharing
> the results of the promotional campaign we ran
> last quarter for our new line of bottled juices
> and teas. As you know, ⁷⁸Claudia was the one
> who suggested advertising our products on
> popular social media channels. And you all put
> that plan into action. As a result of this campaign,
> awareness of our brand among younger
> consumers is up by 30 percent. ⁷⁹Because of this
> success, we're going to be able to reward each of

> you with a bonus that's a percentage of your base
> salary. You'll see it in your June third paycheck.

지난 분기에 우리가 실시한 병 주스와 차 신제품 라인을 알리는 홍보 캠
페인의 결과를 공유하는 것으로 이번 회의를 시작하려고 합니다. 아시
다시피, 클라우디아가 인기 있는 소셜 미디어 채널에 우리 제품을 광고
하자고 제안했죠. 그리고 여러분 모두 그 계획을 실행에 옮겼습니다.
이 캠페인 결과, 젊은 소비자들 사이에서 우리 브랜드 인지도가 30퍼센
트 상승했습니다. 이렇게 성공한 덕분에 여러분 모두에게 기본급 비율
에 해당하는 보너스를 지급할 수 있게 됐어요. 6월 3일 급여에서 확인
하실 수 있습니다.

어휘 promotional 홍보의 put ~ into action ~을 실행에
옮기다 awareness 인지도 reward 보상하다 base salary
기본급 paycheck 급여

77

What does the speaker's company sell?
(A) Children's clothing
(B) Office furniture
(C) Bottled drinks
(D) Sports equipment

화자의 회사는 무엇을 판매하는가?
(A) 아동복
(B) 사무용 가구
(C) 병 음료
(D) 스포츠 용품

해설 세부 사항 관련 – 화자의 회사가 판매하는 것
화자가 초반부에 지난 분기에 실시한 병에 든 주스와 차 신제품 라인을 알
리는 홍보 캠페인의 결과를 공유하는 것으로 회의를 시작하겠다(I'd like
to start this meeting by sharing the results of the promotional
campaign we ran last quarter for our new line of bottled juices
and teas)고 했으므로 병 음료를 판매하는 회사임을 알 수 있다. 따라서
정답은 (C)이다.

> Paraphrasing 담화의 bottled juices and teas
> → 정답의 Bottled drinks

78

What did Claudia suggest doing?
(A) Holding a contest for customers
(B) Placing advertisements on social media
(C) Hiring a celebrity spokesperson
(D) Sponsoring a music festival

클라우디아는 무엇을 하자고 제안했는가?
(A) 고객 대상 공모전 개최하기
(B) 소셜 미디어에 광고하기
(C) 유명 인사를 대변인으로 채용하기
(D) 음악 축제 후원하기

어휘 celebrity 유명 인사 spokesperson 대변인 sponsor 후원하다

해설 세부 사항 관련 – 클라우디아의 제안 사항

화자가 중반부에 클라우디아가 인기 있는 소셜 미디어 채널에 우리 제품을 광고하자고 제안했다(Claudia was the one who suggested advertising our products on popular social media channels)고 밝혔으므로 정답은 (B)이다.

> **Paraphrasing** 담화의 advertising our products on popular social media channels → 정답의 Placing advertisements on social media

79

What will the listeners receive on June 3?
(A) A salary bonus
(B) A day off
(C) A new ID card
(D) A product sample

청자들은 6월 3일에 무엇을 받을 것인가?
(A) 급여 보너스
(B) 휴가
(C) 새 신분증
(D) 제품 샘플

해설 세부 사항 관련 – 청자들이 6월 3일에 받을 것

화자가 후반부에서 캠페인 성공 덕분에 모두에게 기본급 비율에 해당하는 보너스를 지급하겠다(Because of this success, we're going to be able to reward each of you with a bonus that's a percentage of your base salary)고 발표하면서 6월 3일 급여에서 확인할 수 있다(You'll see it in your June third paycheck)고 했으므로 정답은 (A)이다.

80-82 설명

> M-Au We'd like to welcome you to our archive of ancient manuscripts. **80Given the delicate condition of the items in our archive, we have a specific protocol that you must follow to protect the material as you conduct your research. 81Please store all personal belongings in the large filing cabinet against that wall.** After you do, I will be distributing gloves that must be worn at all times. Finally, at noon we'll be breaking for lunch. **82See you all in the cafeteria. It's on the first floor of this building.**

> 고문서 보관소에 오신 여러분을 환영합니다. **저희 보관소에 있는 물품들의 취약한 상태를 고려하여, 연구를 수행할 때 자료를 보호하기 위해 지켜야 하는 특별 요강이 있습니다. 개인 소지품은 전부 저기 벽에 있는 큰 서류함에 보관해 주세요.** 그렇게 하신 다음, 제가 장갑을 나눠 드릴 텐데요, 항상 착용해야 합니다. 마지막으로 정오에 점심시간이 있습니다. **다들 구내식당에서 만나요. 구내식당은 이 건물 1층에 있습니다.**

어휘 archive 보관소 ancient 고대의 manuscript 문서 given ~을 고려하여 delicate 취약한, 손상되기 쉬운 protocol 요강, 규정 protect 보호하다 store 보관하다 distribute 나누어 주다

80

Why do the listeners have to follow a protocol?
(A) To secure the building
(B) To ensure accurate data
(C) To protect delicate items
(D) To obtain certification

청자들은 왜 요강을 지켜야 하는가?
(A) 건물 보안을 위해
(B) 데이터의 정확성을 보장하기 위해
(C) 취약한 물품을 보호하기 위해
(D) 자격증을 취득하기 위해

어휘 accurate 정확한 obtain 취득하다 certification 자격증

해설 세부 사항 관련 – 청자들이 요강을 지켜야 하는 이유

화자가 초반부에 보관소에 있는 물품들의 취약한 상태를 고려해 연구 수행 시 자료를 보호하기 위해 지켜야 하는 특별 요강이 있다(Given the delicate condition of the items in our archive, we have a specific protocol that you must follow to protect the material as you conduct your research)고 했으므로 정답은 (C)이다.

81

Where should the listeners place their belongings?
(A) On a shelf
(B) In lockers
(C) On study tables
(D) In a filing cabinet

청자들은 어디에 소지품을 두어야 하는가?
(A) 선반 위
(B) 사물함 안
(C) 책상 위
(D) 서류함 안

해설 세부 사항 관련 – 청자들이 소지품을 두어야 하는 장소

화자가 중반부에 개인 소지품은 전부 저기 벽에 있는 큰 서류함에 보관하라(Please store all personal belongings in the large filing cabinet against that wall)고 했으므로 정답은 (D)이다.

82

What information does the speaker provide about the cafeteria?
(A) Its menu
(B) Its seating capacity
(C) Its hours of operation
(D) Its location

TEST 6

화자는 구내식당에 관해 어떤 정보를 제공하는가?

(A) 메뉴
(B) 좌석 수
(C) 운영 시간
(D) 위치

어휘 capacity 정원, 수용력

해설 세부 사항 관련 – 구내식당에 관해 제공하는 정보

화자가 후반부에서 구내식당에서 만나자(See you all in the cafeteria)고 한 뒤 구내식당은 이 건물 1층에 있다(It's on the first floor of this building)고 위치를 알려 주고 있으므로 정답은 (D)이다.

> **Paraphrasing** 담화의 on the first floor of this building
> → 정답의 location

83-85 전화 메시지

> **W-Br** Hi. ⁸³**This is Raya calling from Toprak Editing Services. I wanted to let you know that the copy editor has completed reviewing the draft of your manuscript, and it's now with the proofreader.** ⁸⁴**When the final copy of the manuscript is ready, you will receive an automatic e-mail notification from the cloud management system.** By the way, ⁸⁵**you requested that the manuscript be ready within seven days.** We guarantee a turnaround time of ten days.
>
> 안녕하세요. 저는 탑프락 에디팅 서비스의 라야입니다. 원고 편집자가 귀하의 원고 초안에 대한 검토를 마쳤으며, 이제는 교정 담당자에게 넘어갔다는 사실을 알려 드리고 싶습니다. 원고 최종본이 준비되면 클라우드 관리 시스템에서 자동 이메일 알림을 받게 됩니다. 그런데 7일 이내에 원고를 준비해 달라고 요청하셨죠. 열흘 안에는 반드시 작업을 마치겠습니다.
>
> **어휘** draft 초안 manuscript 원고 proofreader 교정 담당자 notification 알림 turnaround time 작업 완료 시간

83

What type of business does the speaker work for?

(A) An accounting firm
(B) A law firm
(C) A graphic design service
(D) An editing service

화자는 어떤 유형의 업체에서 일하는가?

(A) 회계 사무소
(B) 법률 사무소
(C) 그래픽 디자인 서비스
(D) 편집 서비스

해설 전체 내용 관련 – 화자의 근무 업체

화자가 초반부에서 탑프락 에디팅 서비스의 라야(This is Raya calling from Toprak Editing Services)라고 자신을 소개한 뒤 원고 편집자

가 원고 초안 검토를 마쳤고 원고가 교정 담당자에게 넘어갔다(the copy editor has completed reviewing the draft of your manuscript, and it's now with the proofreader)고 편집 진행 상황을 설명하고 있으므로 정답은 (D)이다.

84

According to the speaker, what will the listener receive by e-mail?

(A) An updated price list
(B) A system notification
(C) A calendar invitation
(D) A revised agenda

화자에 따르면, 청자는 이메일로 무엇을 받을 것인가?

(A) 최신 가격 목록
(B) 시스템 알림
(C) 일정 초대 메시지
(D) 수정된 안건

어휘 calendar invitation (일정 관리 앱에서 제공하는) 일정 초대 메시지 revise 수정하다

해설 세부 사항 관련 – 청자가 이메일로 받을 것

화자가 중반부에서 원고 최종본이 준비되면 클라우드 관리 시스템에서 자동 이메일 알림을 받게 된다(When the final copy of the manuscript is ready, you will receive an automatic e-mail notification from the cloud management system)고 했으므로 정답은 (B)이다.

> **Paraphrasing** 담화의 an automatic e-mail notification ~
> system → 정답의 A system notification

85

What does the speaker imply when she says, "We guarantee a turnaround time of ten days"?

(A) A request may not be met.
(B) A refund will be issued soon.
(C) Additional staff is needed.
(D) High rates are justified.

화자가 "열흘 안에는 반드시 작업을 마치겠습니다"라고 말할 때 무엇을 의미하는가?

(A) 요청에 맞추지 못할 수도 있다.
(B) 곧 환불될 것이다.
(C) 직원이 추가로 필요하다.
(D) 비싼 요금이 타당하다.

어휘 rate 요금 justified 타당한

해설 화자의 의도 파악 – 열흘 안에는 반드시 작업을 마치겠다는 말의 의도

앞에서 7일 이내에 원고를 준비해 달라는 요청을 받았다(you requested that the manuscript be ready within seven days)고 한 뒤 인용문을 언급하고 있으므로, 고객의 요청 대로 7일 안에 작업을 마치지 못할 수도 있다는 의도임을 알 수 있다. 따라서 정답은 (A)이다.

W-Am **86Welcome to the Forestry Today podcast, a show about managing the health of trees and the productivity of woodlands.** Today's guest is Jessica Williams, who works as a consulting forester for landowners. I was chatting with Jessica before the show about her work, and **87she said that one benefit of her job is she gets to interact with many different landowners in her area and learn about their woodlands.** I know many of my listeners are interested in careers in forestry, so **88I'll begin by asking Jessica about the education she needed to get started in her career.**

포레스트리 투데이 팟캐스트에 오신 것을 환영합니다. 포레스트리 투데이는 나무의 건강과 삼림지의 생산성 관리에 관해 이야기하는 방송입니다. 오늘 손님은 제시카 윌리엄스인데요, 지주들을 위한 수목 관리 상담가로 일하고 있습니다. 방송 전에 제시카와 그녀의 일에 대해 이야기를 나누었는데요, **제시카는 직업의 장점 하나로 지역에 있는 여러 지주들과 교류하고 그들의 삼림에 대해 배울 수 있다는 점을 꼽았습니다.** 많은 청취자가 삼림 분야 직업에 관심을 갖고 있다는 것을 압니다. **제시카에게 경력을 시작하면서 필요했던 교육에 대해 질문하면서 방송을 시작하겠습니다.**

어휘 productivity 생산성 woodland 삼림지, 숲 consult 상담하다 forester 수목 관리원 landowner 지주 benefit 이점 interact with ~와 교류하다

86

What is the podcast about?
(A) Real estate
(B) Forestry
(C) Sports management
(D) Solar energy

팟캐스트는 무엇에 관한 것인가?
(A) 부동산
(B) 삼림
(C) 스포츠 매니지먼트
(D) 태양 에너지

해설 전체 내용 관련 – 팟캐스트의 주제
화자가 초반부에서 포레스트리 투데이 팟캐스트에 오신 것을 환영한다(Welcome to the Forestry Today podcast)면서 나무의 건강과 삼림지의 생산성 관리에 관해 이야기하는 방송(a show about managing the health of trees and the productivity of woodlands)이라고 했으므로 정답은 (B)이다.

87

What job benefit does Jessica Williams mention?
(A) Meeting new people
(B) Having flexible hours
(C) Being outdoors
(D) Working remotely

제시카 윌리엄스는 직업의 장점으로 무엇을 언급하는가?
(A) 새로운 사람들과의 만남
(B) 유연한 근무 시간
(C) 야외에 있는 것
(D) 원격 근무

어휘 flexible 유연한 remotely 원격으로

해설 세부 사항 관련 – 제시카 윌리엄스가 언급하는 직업의 장점
화자가 중반부에서 제시카는 직업의 장점 하나로 지역에 있는 여러 지주들과 교류하고 그들의 삼림에 대해 배울 수 있다는 점을 꼽았다(she said that one benefit of her job is she gets to interact with many different landowners in her area and learn about their woodlands)고 했으므로 정답은 (A)이다.

> Paraphrasing 담화의 interact with many different landowners → 정답의 Meeting new people

88

What will the speaker ask Jessica Williams about?
(A) Her teaching experience
(B) Her publications
(C) Her travels
(D) Her education

화자는 제시카 윌리엄스에게 무엇에 관해 물어볼 것인가?
(A) 가르친 경험
(B) 출판물
(C) 여행
(D) 교육

해설 세부 사항 관련 – 화자가 제시카 윌리엄스에게 물어볼 것
화자가 후반부에서 제시카에게 경력을 시작하면서 필요했던 교육에 대해 질문하면서 방송을 시작하겠다(I'll begin by asking Jessica about the education she needed to get started in her career)고 했다. 따라서 정답은 (D)이다.

89-91 안내 방송

M-Au Good afternoon, and welcome aboard the Winding Creek Express. **89In just a few moments our scenic train ride will begin.** We'll be traveling 60 kilometers from the pine forests of Winding Creek to the coastal town of Wendell Shores. This route has been carrying cargo and passengers since 1885, and **90I'll tell you about its fascinating history along the way. 91We were planning to stop**

for a hike to the Wendell Shores lighthouse, but the path is too wet from last night's rain.

안녕하세요, 와인딩 크릭 익스프레스에 탑승하신 것을 환영합니다. **잠시 후에 경치를 감상하는 기차 여행이 시작됩니다.** 와인딩 크릭 소나무 숲에서 웬델 쇼어스 해안 마을까지 60킬로미터를 여행하겠습니다. 이 노선은 1885년부터 화물과 승객을 실어 나르고 있죠. **가면서 흥미진진한 역사에 대해 말씀드리겠습니다.** 잠시 멈춰서 웬델 쇼어스 등대로 도보 여행을 할 계획이었지만, 어젯밤 비로 길이 너무 젖었네요.

어휘 scenic 경치가 좋은 pine 소나무 coastal 해안의 cargo 화물 passenger 승객 hike 도보 여행 lighthouse 등대 path 길

89

Where is the announcement taking place?
(A) On a boat
(B) On a bus
(C) On a train
(D) On an airplane

안내 방송은 어디에서 나오고 있는가?
(A) 배
(B) 버스
(C) 기차
(D) 비행기

해설 전체 내용 관련 – 안내 방송의 장소
화자가 초반부에서 잠시 후에 경치를 감상하는 기차 여행이 시작된다(In just a few moments our scenic train ride will begin)고 했으므로 정답은 (C)이다.

90

What information does the speaker say he will provide?
(A) Historical facts
(B) Sightseeing suggestions
(C) Details about special events
(D) Safety instructions

화자는 어떤 정보를 제공할 것이라고 말하는가?
(A) 역사적 사실
(B) 관광 추천
(C) 특별 행사에 관한 세부 정보
(D) 안전 지침

어휘 sightseeing 관광 instructions 지침, 지시

해설 세부 사항 관련 – 화자가 제공할 정보
화자가 후반부에 가면서 흥미진진한 역사에 대해 이야기하겠다(I'll tell you about its fascinating history along the way)고 했으므로 정답은 (A)이다.

Paraphrasing 담화의 fascinating history
→ 정답의 Historical facts

91

Why does the speaker say, "the path is too wet from last night's rain"?
(A) To request directions
(B) To make a recommendation
(C) To announce a change of plans
(D) To decline an invitation

화자는 왜 "어젯밤 비로 길이 너무 젖었네요"라고 말하는가?
(A) 길을 묻기 위해
(B) 추천하기 위해
(C) 계획 변경을 알리기 위해
(D) 초대를 거절하기 위해

어휘 decline 거절하다

해설 화자의 의도 파악 – 어젯밤 비로 길이 너무 젖었다는 말의 의도
앞에서 잠시 멈춰서 웬델 쇼어스 등대로 도보 여행을 할 계획이었다 (We were planning to stop for a hike to the Wendell Shores lighthouse)고 한 뒤 인용문을 언급하고 있으므로, 길이 젖어 도보 여행이 취소되었다는 것을 알리려는 의도임을 알 수 있다. 따라서 정답은 (C)이다.

92-94 연설

W-Am Thanks for coming to this press conference. **92We often have container ships lined up at the port waiting to be unloaded for several days. So today the Port Authority is announcing a modernization plan to utilize more automation, including automated cranes and driverless vehicles, to speed up the unloading process. 93Whenever automation is introduced, employees become worried about being replaced by machines.** But we'll always need workers here. And we're setting aside funds to offer career retraining programs for our dockworkers. **94I've made a timeline for this modernization program. I'll distribute copies of it now.**

기자 회견에 와 주셔서 감사합니다. 컨테이너선들이 며칠째 하역을 기다리며 항구에 늘어서 있는 모습을 종종 봅니다. 따라서 오늘 항만 관리 위원회는 하역 과정의 속도를 높이기 위해 자동 크레인과 무인 차량을 포함한 자동화를 더 많이 활용하는 현대화 계획을 발표합니다. 자동화가 도입될 때마다 직원들은 기계로 대체되지 않을까 걱정합니다. 하지만 우리에게는 언제나 직원이 필요할 것입니다. 그리고 우리는 모두 작업자들을 위한 직업 재교육 프로그램을 제공하기 위해 기금을 따로 적립하고 있습니다. 제가 이번 현대화 프로그램의 일정표를 만들었습니다. 지금 사본을 배포하겠습니다.

어휘 press conference 기자 회견 unload (짐을) 내리다 modernization 현대화 utilize 활용하다 automation 자동화 introduce 도입하다 replace 대체하다 set aside 따로 떼어 두다 fund 기금 distribute 배포하다

92

What industry does the speaker most likely work in?
(A) Aviation
(B) Construction
(C) Automotive
(D) Shipping

화자는 어떤 업계에서 일하는 것 같은가?
(A) 항공
(B) 건설
(C) 자동차
(D) 운송

해설 전체 내용 관련 – 화자의 근무 업계
화자가 초반부에 컨테이너선들이 며칠째 하역을 기다리며 항구에 늘어서 있는 모습을 종종 본다(We often have container ships ~ for several days)면서 문제점을 밝힌 뒤 오늘 항만 관리 위원회는 하역 과정의 속도를 높이기 위해 자동 크레인과 무인 차량을 포함한 자동화를 더 많이 활용하는 현대화 계획을 발표한다(So today the Port Authority is announcing ~ to speed up the unloading process)고 했다. 따라서 화자는 운송업체에서 근무하고 있음을 알 수 있으므로 정답은 (D)이다.

93

Why does the speaker say, "But we'll always need workers here"?
(A) To complain about a staff shortage
(B) To address a concern
(C) To suggest a schedule change
(D) To disagree with a proposal

화자는 왜 "하지만 우리에게는 언제나 직원이 필요할 것입니다"라고 말하는가?
(A) 직원 부족에 관해 불평하기 위해
(B) 우려를 해소하기 위해
(C) 일정 변경을 제안하기 위해
(D) 제안에 이의를 제기하기 위해

어휘 address 해소하다, 처리하다   disagree with ~에 이의를 제기하다

해설 화자의 의도 파악 – 언제나 직원이 필요하다는 말의 의도
앞에서 자동화가 도입될 때마다 직원들이 기계로 대체되지 않을까 걱정한다(Whenever automation is introduced, employees become worried about being replaced by machines)고 한 뒤 인용문을 언급하고 있으므로, 자동화에 대한 우려를 불식하려는 의도임을 알 수 있다. 따라서 정답은 (B)이다.

94

What will the speaker do next?
(A) Distribute a document
(B) Begin a slideshow
(C) Demonstrate a product
(D) Hand out awards

화자는 다음에 무엇을 할 것인가?
(A) 문서 배포하기
(B) 슬라이드 쇼 시작하기
(C) 제품 시연하기
(D) 상 나눠 주기

해설 세부 사항 관련 – 화자가 다음에 할 일
화자가 후반부에서 이번 현대화 프로그램의 일정표를 만들었다(I've made a timeline for this modernization program)고 하면서 지금 사본을 배포하겠다(I'll distribute copies of it now)고 했으므로 정답은 (A)이다.

95-97 담화 + 평면도

W-Br All right. Now that **95we've concluded the guided portion of our tour, you all have the remaining hour to explore the museum at your leisure.** In the Klein Gallery, you'll find an assortment of classical sculptures. **96There's also a short film in the auditorium about local artist Matteo Rossi. I highly recommend it.** And if anyone wants to grab a bite to eat, the café has an assortment of sandwiches, coffees, and pastries. **97We'll meet back at the entrance outside of the gift shop in one hour.** From there, we'll go on to the next stop on our city tour.

좋습니다. 이제 **가이드가 안내하는 투어 부분은 마쳤으니, 여러분 모두 남은 시간은 한가롭게 박물관을 둘러보시면 됩니다.** 클라인 갤러리에는 다양한 고전주의 조각품이 모여 있습니다. **강당에서 지역 예술가 마테오 로시에 관한 단편 영화도 상영되고 있습니다. 강력 추천합니다.** 그리고 간단히 요기하고 싶은 분은 카페에 샌드위치, 커피, 페이스트리가 다양하게 준비되어 있습니다. **한 시간 후에 선물 가게 밖 입구에서 다시 만나겠습니다.** 거기서 시티 투어 다음 목적지로 가겠습니다.

어휘 conclude 마치다   remaining 남은   explore 둘러보다
at one's leisure 한가하게, 느긋하게   an assortment of 다양한
sculpture 조각품   auditorium 강당   grab a bite to eat
간단히 요기하다

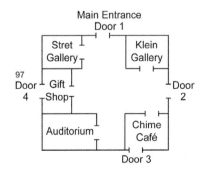

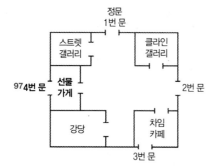

정문
1번 문

스트렛 갤러리 | 클라인 갤러리

97 4번 문 · 선물 가게 · 2번 문

강당 | 차임 카페

3번 문

95

Who most likely is the speaker?
(A) A tour guide
(B) An artist
(C) A security guard
(D) An exhibit curator

화자는 누구인 것 같은가?
(A) 투어 가이드
(B) 예술가
(C) 경비원
(D) 전시 큐레이터

해설 전체 내용 관련 – 화자의 직업

화자가 초반부에서 가이드가 안내하는 투어는 마쳤으니, 남은 시간은 한가롭게 박물관을 둘러보라(we've concluded the guided portion of our tour, you all have the remaining hour to explore the museum at your leisure)고 권하고 있으므로 정답은 (A)이다.

96

What does the speaker recommend?
(A) Eating outside on a terrace
(B) Becoming museum members
(C) Purchasing souvenirs
(D) Viewing a film

화자는 무엇을 추천하는가?
(A) 테라스에서 실외 식사하기
(B) 박물관 회원 되기
(C) 기념품 구매하기
(D) 영화 보기

해설 세부 사항 관련 – 화자의 추천 사항

화자가 중반부에서 강당에서 지역 예술가 마테오 로시에 관한 단편 영화도 상영되고 있다(There's also a short film in the auditorium about local artist Matteo Rossi)면서 강력 추천한다(I highly recommend it)고 했다. 따라서 정답은 (D)이다.

97

Look at the graphic. Where will the listeners meet in one hour?
(A) At Door 1
(B) At Door 2
(C) At Door 3
(D) At Door 4

시각 정보에 의하면, 청자들은 한 시간 후에 어디에서 만날 것인가?
(A) 1번 문
(B) 2번 문
(C) 3번 문
(D) 4번 문

해설 시각 정보 연계 – 청자들이 한 시간 후에 만날 장소

화자가 후반부에서 한 시간 후에 선물 가게 밖 입구에서 다시 만나자(We'll meet back at the entrance outside of the gift shop in one hour)고 했고, 평면도에 따르면 선물 가게 밖 입구는 4번 문이므로 정답은 (D)이다.

98-100 전화 메시지 + 일정표

W-Am Hello, Mr. Brown. You were referred to Brighter Smiles by your regular dentist. **98I see you've already checked in for your 11:00 A.M. appointment tomorrow. 99I'm calling to explain what will happen when you come in for your procedure.** We'll start by doing some x-rays of your mouth, and then we'll use the digital scan to create your crown. We'll put in a temporary crown, and you'll come in for your follow-up appointment in three weeks. By the way, **100our parking area is being repaved this week. So I suggest you use the free street parking on Morrison Avenue.**

안녕하세요, 브라운 씨. 담당 치과 의사가 브라운 씨에게 브라이트 스마일즈를 추천했습니다. 내일 오전 11시 예약으로 이미 등록하셨네요. 내일 시술을 위해 오시면 어떻게 진행되는지 설명하려고 전화했습니다. 먼저 구강 엑스레이를 찍은 후 디지털 스캔을 사용해 치관을 만듭니다. 임시 치관을 씌워 드리니 3주 후에 후속 진료를 받으러 오세요. 참, 이번 주에 저희 주차장이 재포장 공사 중입니다. 그러니 모리슨 가에 있는 무료 주차장을 이용하시는 것을 제안드립니다.

어휘 refer ~ to ... (도움을 위해) ~을 …로 보내다 check in 등록하다 procedure 시술 (절차) crown 치관 temporary 임시의 follow-up 후속의 repave (도로를) 재포장하다

Daily Schedule	
Appointment Time	**Doctor**
9:30 A.M.	Dr. Sugiyama
⁹⁸11:00 A.M.	Dr. Stewart
12:00 P.M.	Dr. Kim
12:30 P.M.	Dr. Alabi

일일 일정	
예약 시간	**의사**
오전 9시 30분	스기야마 박사
⁹⁸오전 11시	**스튜어트 박사**
오후 12시	김 박사
오후 12시 30분	알라비 박사

98

Look at the graphic. Which dentist will the listener see?

(A) Dr. Sugiyama
(B) Dr. Stewart
(C) Dr. Kim
(D) Dr. Alabi

시각 정보에 의하면, 청자는 어떤 치과 의사에게 진료받을 것인가?

(A) 스기야마 박사
(B) 스튜어트 박사
(C) 김 박사
(D) 알라비 박사

해설 시각 정보 연계 – 청자가 진료받을 치과 의사

화자가 초반부에서 내일 오전 11시 예약으로 이미 등록했다(I see you've already checked in for your 11:00 A.M. appointment tomorrow)면서 청자의 예약 상태를 확인하고 있고, 일정표에 따르면 오전 11시에 진료하는 의사는 스튜어트 박사이므로 정답은 (B)이다.

99

Why is the speaker calling?

(A) To explain a procedure
(B) To reschedule an appointment
(C) To ask about a payment
(D) To confirm insurance information

화자는 왜 전화를 하고 있는가?

(A) 시술 절차를 설명하기 위해
(B) 예약을 다시 잡기 위해
(C) 결제에 대해 묻기 위해
(D) 보험 정보를 확인하기 위해

어휘 insurance 보험

해설 전체 내용 관련 – 화자가 전화하는 목적

화자가 초반부에서 내일 시술을 위해 오면 어떻게 진행되는지 설명하려고 전화했다(I'm calling to explain what will happen when you come in for your procedure)고 했으므로 정답은 (A)이다.

100

What does the speaker recommend that the listener do?

(A) Review the dentist's instructions
(B) Park on the street
(C) Fill out some paperwork
(D) Use a different credit card

화자는 청자에게 무엇을 하라고 권하는가?

(A) 치과 의사의 지침 검토하기
(B) 거리에 주차하기
(C) 서류 작성하기
(D) 다른 신용 카드 사용하기

해설 세부 사항 관련 – 화자의 권장 사항

화자가 후반부에서 이번 주에 주차장이 재포장 공사 중(our parking area is being repaved this week)이라고 하면서 모리슨 가에 있는 무료 주차장을 이용할 것을 제안한다(I suggest you use the free street parking on Morrison Avenue)고 했으므로 정답은 (B)이다.

Paraphrasing	담화의 use the free street parking on Morrison Avenue → 정답의 Park on the street

1 (D)	**2** (A)	**3** (C)	**4** (B)	**5** (B)
6 (D)	**7** (A)	**8** (A)	**9** (A)	**10** (C)
11 (B)	**12** (B)	**13** (C)	**14** (C)	**15** (C)
16 (B)	**17** (A)	**18** (A)	**19** (A)	**20** (C)
21 (A)	**22** (C)	**23** (C)	**24** (B)	**25** (C)
26 (A)	**27** (A)	**28** (C)	**29** (C)	**30** (B)
31 (B)	**32** (B)	**33** (D)	**34** (A)	**35** (B)
36 (C)	**37** (B)	**38** (A)	**39** (C)	**40** (D)
41 (D)	**42** (C)	**43** (A)	**44** (B)	**45** (B)
46 (C)	**47** (D)	**48** (B)	**49** (C)	**50** (C)
51 (B)	**52** (C)	**53** (C)	**54** (B)	**55** (A)
56 (B)	**57** (D)	**58** (A)	**59** (D)	**60** (C)
61 (B)	**62** (B)	**63** (C)	**64** (D)	**65** (B)
66 (B)	**67** (C)	**68** (C)	**69** (A)	**70** (D)
71 (C)	**72** (A)	**73** (D)	**74** (B)	**75** (D)
76 (A)	**77** (C)	**78** (C)	**79** (D)	**80** (D)
81 (C)	**82** (A)	**83** (B)	**84** (D)	**85** (D)
86 (D)	**87** (B)	**88** (A)	**89** (D)	**90** (D)
91 (C)	**92** (D)	**93** (B)	**94** (A)	**95** (B)
96 (B)	**97** (A)	**98** (D)	**99** (B)	**100** (D)

PART 1

1 W-Am

(A) The woman is tying her shoe.
(B) The woman is putting on some sunglasses.
(C) The woman is polishing her vehicle.
(D) The woman is unloading some bags.

(A) 여자가 신발 끈을 묶고 있다.
(B) 여자가 선글라스를 끼고 있다.
(C) 여자가 차를 닦고 있다.
(D) 여자가 가방을 내리고 있다.

어휘 tie 묶다   polish 닦다   vehicle 차량   unload (짐을) 내리다

해설 1인 등장 사진 – 사람의 동작/상태 묘사

(A) 동사 오답. 여자가 신발 끈을 묶고 있는(is tying her shoe) 모습이 아니므로 오답.
(B) 동사 오답. 여자가 선글라스를 끼고 있는(is putting on some sunglasses) 모습이 아니므로 오답. 참고로, putting on은 무언가를 착용하는 동작을 가리키는 말로 이미 착용 중인 상태를 나타내는 wearing과 혼동하지 않도록 주의한다.

(C) 동사 오답. 여자가 차를 닦고 있는(is polishing her vehicle) 모습이 아니므로 오답.
(D) 정답. 여자가 가방을 내리고 있는(is unloading some bags) 모습이므로 정답.

2 M-Cn

(A) Some artwork is mounted on a wall.
(B) A dresser drawer has been left open.
(C) Some chairs are stacked in a corner.
(D) Magazines are scattered on the floor.

(A) 미술품들이 벽에 걸려 있다.
(B) 옷장 서랍이 열려 있다.
(C) 의자들이 구석에 쌓여 있다.
(D) 잡지들이 바닥에 흩어져 있다.

어휘 artwork 미술품   mount 고정시키다   dresser 찬장, 옷장   drawer 서랍   stack 쌓다   scatter 뿌리다

해설 사물/풍경 사진 – 사물 묘사

(A) 정답. 미술품들(Some artwork)이 벽에 걸려 있는(is mounted on a wall) 모습이므로 정답.
(B) 사진에 없는 명사를 이용한 오답. 사진에 옷장(A dresser)의 모습이 보이지 않으므로 오답.
(C) 동사 오답. 의자들(Some chairs)이 구석에 쌓여 있는(are stacked in a corner) 모습이 아니므로 오답.
(D) 위치 오답. 잡지들(Magazines)이 바닥에 흩어져 있는(are scattered on the floor) 모습이 아니므로 오답.

3 M-Au

(A) She's getting on a bus.
(B) She's grasping a door handle.
(C) She's pulling some wheeled luggage.
(D) She's walking through an outdoor park entrance.

(A) 여자가 버스에 올라타고 있다.
(B) 여자가 문손잡이를 잡고 있다.
(C) 여자가 바퀴가 달린 짐을 끌고 있다.
(D) 여자가 야외 공원 입구를 통과하고 있다.

어휘 grasp 쥐다, 잡다   luggage 짐(수하물)   entrance 입구, 문

해설 1인 등장 사진 – 사람의 동작/상태 묘사

(A) 사진에 없는 명사를 이용한 오답. 사진에 버스(a bus)의 모습이 보이지 않으므로 오답.
(B) 사진에 없는 명사를 이용한 오답. 사진에 문손잡이(a door handle)의 모습이 보이지 않으므로 오답.
(C) 정답. 여자가 바퀴가 달린 짐을 끌고 있는(is pulling some wheeled luggage) 모습이므로 정답.
(D) 사진에 없는 명사를 이용한 오답. 사진에 야외 공원(an outdoor park)의 모습이 보이지 않으므로 오답.

해설 혼합 사진 – 사람/사물/풍경 혼합 묘사

(A) 동사 오답. 사람들이 땅에서 물건을 줍고 있는(are picking items up off the ground) 모습이 아니므로 오답.
(B) 정답. 파라솔들(Some umbrellas)이 펴져 있는(have been opened) 모습이므로 정답.
(C) 사진에 없는 명사를 이용한 오답. 사진에 호텔 로비(a hotel lobby)의 모습이 보이지 않으므로 오답.
(D) 동사 오답. 사람들이 전등을 걸고 있는(hanging up lights) 모습이 아니므로 오답.

4 M-Cn

(A) One of the men is seated underneath a window.
(B) One of the men is reading in front of a shelf.
(C) Some women are writing on a whiteboard.
(D) One of the women is using a laptop computer.

(A) 남자들 중 한 명이 창문 아래에 앉아 있다.
(B) 남자들 중 한 명이 선반 앞에서 책을 읽고 있다.
(C) 여자들이 화이트보드에 글을 쓰고 있다.
(D) 여자들 중 한 명이 노트북 컴퓨터를 사용하고 있다.

어휘 seat 앉히다   underneath ~아래에   shelf 선반, 책꽂이

해설 2인 이상 등장 사진 – 사람의 동작/상태 묘사

(A) 동사 오답. 남자들 중 한 명(One of the men)이 창문 아래에 앉아 있는(is seated underneath a window) 모습이 아니므로 오답.
(B) 정답. 남자들 중 한 명(One of the men)이 선반 앞에서 책을 읽고 있는(is reading in front of a shelf) 모습이므로 정답.
(C) 사진에 없는 명사를 이용한 오답. 사진에 화이트보드(a whiteboard)의 모습이 보이지 않으므로 오답.
(D) 동사 오답. 여자들 중 한 명(One of the women)이 노트북 컴퓨터를 사용하고 있는(is using a laptop computer) 모습이 아니므로 오답.

5 W-Br

(A) Some people are picking items up off the ground.
(B) Some umbrellas have been opened.
(C) There's some furniture in a hotel lobby.
(D) There are some people hanging up lights.

(A) 사람들이 땅에서 물건을 줍고 있다.
(B) 파라솔들이 펴져 있다.
(C) 호텔 로비에 가구가 있다.
(D) 전등을 걸고 있는 사람들이 있다.

어휘 pick up ~을 집다   umbrella 파라솔   hang up ~을 걸다

6 W-Am

(A) Some safety cones are being removed from a work site.
(B) Some helmets have been placed on the ground.
(C) Some workers are directing traffic.
(D) A road is being dug up by some workers.

(A) 안전 고깔들이 작업장에서 제거되고 있다.
(B) 헬멧들이 바닥에 놓여 있다.
(C) 작업자들이 교통정리를 하고 있다.
(D) 작업자들이 도로를 파고 있다.

어휘 safety cone 안전 고깔   remove 치우다   place 놓다, 두다   direct 지휘하다   dig 파다

해설 혼합 사진 – 사람/사물/풍경 혼합 묘사

(A) 동사 오답. 안전 고깔들(Some safety cones)이 작업장에서 제거되고 있는(are being removed from a work site) 모습이 아니므로 오답.
(B) 동사 오답. 헬멧들(Some helmets)이 바닥에 놓여 있는(have been placed on the ground) 모습이 아니므로 오답.
(C) 동사 오답. 작업자들(Some workers)이 교통정리를 하고 있는(are directing traffic) 모습이 아니므로 오답.
(D) 정답. 작업자들(some workers)이 도로(A road)를 파고 있는(is being dug up) 모습이므로 정답.

PART 2

7

W-Am When will the office be open after the renovations?

M-Au (A) Tuesday morning.
       (B) Some inventory control.
       (C) I'll wear a business suit.

사무실은 수리 후에 언제 문을 열 예정인가요?
(A) 화요일 아침이요.
(B) 재고 관리요.
(C) 비즈니스 정장을 입을 것입니다.

어휘 renovation 보수, 수리　inventory control 재고 관리　suit 정장

해설 사무실이 문을 여는 시점을 묻는 When 의문문
(A) 정답. 수리 후에 사무실이 문을 여는 시점을 묻는 질문에 화요일 아침이라고 구체적인 시점으로 응답하고 있으므로 정답.
(B) 연상 단어 오답. 질문의 office에서 연상 가능한 inventory를 이용한 오답.
(C) 연상 단어 오답. 질문의 office에서 연상 가능한 business와 suit를 이용한 오답.

8

W-Am　Why didn't we order more watches for the store?

W-Br　(A) Because we haven't sold many lately.
　　　(B) I can watch that for you.
　　　(C) In alphabetical order, please.

왜 매장에 놓을 시계를 더 주문하지 않았나요?
(A) 최근에 많이 팔리지 않았기 때문에요.
(B) 제가 지켜봐 줄 수 있어요.
(C) 알파벳 순서로 부탁해요.

어휘 lately 최근에　alphabetical 알파벳순의

해설 매장에 놓을 시계를 더 주문하지 않은 이유를 묻는 Why 의문문
(A) 정답. 매장에 놓을 시계를 더 주문하지 않은 이유를 묻는 질문에 최근에 많이 팔리지 않았기 때문이라고 이유를 제시하고 있으므로 정답.
(B) 단어 반복 오답. 질문의 watches를 반복 이용한 오답.
(C) 단어 반복 오답. 질문의 order를 반복 이용한 오답.

9

W-Br　Which workshop do you want to attend?

M-Au　(A) I'd prefer the one on leadership skills.
　　　(B) His office is upstairs.
　　　(C) Sure, that works for me.

어떤 워크숍에 참석하고 싶나요?
(A) 리더십 기술에 관한 것을 선호해요.
(B) 그의 사무실은 위층에 있어요.
(C) 물론이죠, 저에게 잘 맞아요.

어휘 attend 참석하다

해설 참석하고 싶은 워크숍을 묻는 Which 의문문
(A) 정답. 참석하고 싶은 워크숍을 묻는 질문에 리더십 기술에 관한 것을 선호한다고 알려 주고 있으므로 정답.
(B) 연상 단어 오답. 질문의 workshop에서 연상 가능한 office를 이용한 오답.
(C) 유사 발음 오답. 질문의 workshop과 부분적으로 발음이 유사한 works를 이용한 오답.

10

M-Au　Who else needs to approve the logo design?

W-Am　(A) Every page is numbered.
　　　(B) Yes, let me get you a pen instead.
　　　(C) I'm waiting for a call from our marketing department.

그 외에 누가 또 로고 디자인을 승인해야 하나요?
(A) 모든 페이지에 번호가 매겨져 있어요.
(B) 네, 대신 볼펜을 드릴게요.
(C) 마케팅 부서에서 올 전화를 기다리고 있어요.

어휘 approve 승인하다　number 번호를 매기다

해설 로고 디자인을 승인하는 사람을 묻는 Who 의문문
(A) 질문과 상관없는 오답.
(B) Yes/No 불가 오답. Who 의문문에는 Yes/No 응답이 불가능하므로 오답.
(C) 정답. 로고 디자인을 승인하는 사람을 묻는 질문에 마케팅 부서에서 올 전화를 기다리고 있다며 마케팅 부서에 소속된 사람이 승인 담당자라는 것을 간접적으로 알려 주고 있으므로 정답.

11

W-Br　Can you please turn up the lights so I can take a photograph?

M-Cn　(A) This isn't very heavy.
　　　(B) Sure, no problem.
　　　(C) The music is quite loud.

사진을 찍을 수 있도록 조명의 밝기를 좀 올려 주시겠어요?
(A) 별로 무겁지 않아요.
(B) 그럼요, 문제없어요.
(C) 음악이 꽤 시끄러워요.

어휘 turn up (소리, 온도 등) 높이다, 올리다

해설 부탁/요청의 의문문
(A) 연상 단어 오답. 질문의 lights를 light(가벼운)로 착각했을 때 연상 가능한 heavy를 이용한 오답.
(B) 정답. 사진을 찍을 수 있도록 조명의 밝기를 올려 달라는 요청에 그럼요(Sure)라고 수락한 뒤, 문제없다며 긍정 답변과 일관된 내용을 덧붙이고 있으므로 정답.
(C) 연상 단어 오답. 질문의 turn up에서 연상 가능한 music과 loud를 이용한 오답.

12

M-Au　Where can I get my passport renewed?

W-Am　(A) Two hours long.
　　　(B) There's a list of locations online.
　　　(C) Yes, I travel frequently.

어디에서 여권을 갱신할 수 있나요?
(A) 2시간이 걸려요.
(B) 온라인에 위치들이 나온 목록이 있어요.
(C) 네, 자주 여행해요.

어휘 renew 갱신하다 frequently 자주, 흔히

해설 여권을 갱신할 수 있는 장소를 묻는 Where 의문문

(A) 질문과 상관없는 오답. How long 의문문에 대한 응답이므로 오답.
(B) 정답. 여권을 갱신할 수 있는 장소를 묻는 질문에 온라인에 위치들이 나온 목록이 있다고 원하는 정보를 찾을 수 있는 장소를 알려 주며 우회적으로 응답하고 있으므로 정답.
(C) Yes/No 불가 오답. Where 의문문에는 Yes/No 응답이 불가능하므로 오답.

13

M-Cn How are we going to increase our sales?

W-Am (A) He works in the accounting office.
(B) Yes, I am going there.
(C) By advertising on social media.

매출은 어떻게 늘릴 계획인가요?
(A) 그는 회계 사무소에서 일해요.
(B) 네, 거기에 갈 거예요.
(C) 소셜 미디어에 광고를 해서요.

어휘 accounting 회계

해설 매출을 늘릴 방법을 묻는 How 의문문

(A) 연상 단어 오답. 질문의 sales에서 연상 가능한 accounting을 이용한 오답.
(B) Yes/No 불가 오답. How 의문문에는 Yes/No 응답이 불가능하므로 오답.
(C) 정답. 매출을 늘릴 방법을 묻는 질문에 소셜 미디어에 광고를 한다는 구체적인 방법을 제시하고 있으므로 정답.

14

M-Au Why did you replace the coffee machine in the break room?

W-Am (A) She installed new software.
(B) A company credit card.
(C) There was a sale.

왜 휴게실에 있는 커피 머신을 교체했나요?
(A) 그녀가 새 소프트웨어를 설치했어요.
(B) 회사 신용 카드요.
(C) 할인 행사가 있었어요.

어휘 replace 교체하다 break room 휴게실 install 설치하다

해설 커피 머신을 교체한 이유를 묻는 Why 의문문

(A) 연상 단어 오답. 질문의 machine에서 연상 가능한 installed를 이용한 오답.
(B) 연상 단어 오답. 질문의 break room에서 연상 가능한 company를 이용한 오답.
(C) 정답. 휴게실에 있는 커피 머신을 교체한 이유를 묻는 질문에 할인 행사가 있었다고 이유를 제시하고 있으므로 정답.

15

M-Cn Where is Mr. Kim meeting with the new interns?

W-Am (A) I've conducted several workshops.
(B) We met when we were in college.
(C) Didn't you get the memo?

김 씨는 어디에서 신입 인턴들을 만날 예정인가요?
(A) 워크숍을 여러 번 진행했어요.
(B) 우리는 대학 때 만났어요.
(C) 메모를 못 받았나요?

어휘 conduct 실시하다

해설 신입 인턴들을 만나는 장소를 묻는 Where 의문문

(A) 연상 단어 오답. 질문의 meeting을 '회의'로 해석했을 때 연상 가능한 workshops를 이용한 오답.
(B) 파생어 오답. 질문의 meeting과 파생어 관계인 met을 이용한 오답.
(C) 정답. 김 씨가 신입 인턴들을 만날 장소를 묻는 질문에 메모를 못 받았는지 물으며 장소를 알 수 있는 방법을 우회적으로 제시하므로 정답.

16

M-Cn When will the client sign the contract?

M-Au (A) No, my desk is made from solid wood.
(B) We're scheduled to do that this afternoon.
(C) Fourteen new employees is a record!

고객은 언제 계약서에 서명할까요?
(A) 아니요, 제 책상은 원목으로 만들어졌습니다.
(B) 오늘 오후에 할 예정입니다.
(C) 14명의 신입 사원은 기록입니다!

어휘 contract 계약(서) solid wood 원목

해설 계약서에 서명할 시점을 묻는 When 의문문

(A) Yes/No 불가 오답. How 의문문에는 Yes/No 응답이 불가능하므로 오답.
(B) 정답. 고객이 계약서에 서명할 시점을 묻는 질문에 오늘 오후라고 구체적인 시점을 알려 주고 있으므로 정답.
(C) 질문과 상관없는 오답.

17

W-Am Can I order some dessert?

M-Cn (A) The kitchen closed an hour ago.
(B) To start the meal.
(C) She usually walks there.

디저트를 주문해도 될까요?
(A) 한 시간 전에 주방이 마감했어요.
(B) 식사를 시작하기 위해서입니다.
(C) 그녀는 보통 그곳에서 산책해요.

해설 부탁/요청의 의문문

(A) 정답. 디저트를 주문해도 될지 묻는 요청에 주방이 마감했다며 요청을 거절해야 하는 상황을 우회적으로 표현하고 있으므로 정답.
(B) 연상 단어 오답. 질문의 order와 dessert에서 연상 가능한 meal을 이용한 오답.
(C) 질문과 상관없는 오답.

TEST 7

18

M-Au Isn't Mr. Romero managing the storeroom inventory?

M-Cn (A) No, he's working with a different team.
(B) The warehouse on Mill Street.
(C) OK, I'll be there soon.

로메로 씨가 창고 재고를 관리하고 있지 않나요?
(A) 아니요, 그는 다른 팀에서 일하고 있어요.
(B) 밀 가에 있는 창고입니다.
(C) 좋아요, 곧 갈게요.

어휘 storeroom 창고, 저장실 inventory 재고 warehouse 창고

해설 로메로 씨의 재고 관리 업무 여부를 확인하는 부정 의문문
(A) 정답. 로메로 씨가 창고 재고를 관리하는지를 묻는 질문에 아니요(No)라고 대답한 뒤, 다른 팀에서 일한다며 부정 답변과 일관된 내용을 덧붙이고 있으므로 정답.
(B) 연상 단어 오답. 질문의 storeroom과 inventory에서 연상 가능한 warehouse를 이용한 오답.
(C) 질문과 상관없는 오답.

19

W-Am Will the new software be installed tonight or tomorrow?

M-Cn (A) Your computer is already fully updated.
(B) The password is confidential.
(C) About twenty minutes.

새 소프트웨어 설치는 오늘 밤인가요, 아니면 내일인가요?
(A) 컴퓨터는 벌써 완전히 업데이트가 되었어요.
(B) 암호는 기밀입니다.
(C) 약 20분입니다.

어휘 fully 완전히, 충분히 confidential 기밀의, 비밀의

해설 소프트웨어 설치 시기를 묻는 선택 의문문
(A) 정답. 오늘 밤과 내일 중 새 소프트웨어 설치 시기가 언제인지를 묻는 질문에 컴퓨터는 벌써 업데이트가 되었다며 둘 다 아니라는 것을 우회적으로 응답하고 있으므로 정답.
(B) 연상 단어 오답. 질문의 software에서 연상 가능한 password를 이용한 오답.
(C) 연상 단어 오답. 질문의 installed에서 연상 가능한 걸리는 시간 표현 twenty minutes를 이용한 오답.

20

W-Br When do you need me to return the projector?

M-Au (A) At the company headquarters.
(B) Turn right at the light.
(C) By the end of the week.

언제 프로젝터를 반납해야 합니까?
(A) 회사 본사에 있어요.
(B) 신호등에서 우회전하세요.
(C) 이번 주말까지입니다.

어휘 headquarters 본사

해설 프로젝터의 반납 시점을 묻는 When 의문문
(A) 연상 단어 오답. 질문의 projector에서 연상 가능한 company와 headquarters를 이용한 오답.
(B) 파생어 오답. 질문의 return과 파생어 관계인 turn을 이용한 오답.
(C) 정답. 프로젝터의 반납 시점을 묻는 질문에 이번 주말까지라며 구체적인 시점을 제시하고 있으므로 정답.

21

W-Am I don't think we'll need the large conference room.

W-Br (A) Only ten people registered.
(B) We'll take the large shirts, please.
(C) I'm going to Milan this year.

큰 회의실이 필요하지 않을 것 같아요.
(A) 겨우 10명만 등록했어요.
(B) 큰 셔츠를 주세요.
(C) 올해 밀라노에 갈 예정입니다.

어휘 conference room 회의실 register 등록하다

해설 의사 전달의 평서문
(A) 정답. 큰 회의실이 필요하지 않을 것이라는 평서문에 겨우 10명만 등록했다며 호응하는 의도를 우회적으로 표현하고 있으므로 정답.
(B) 단어 반복 오답. 평서문의 large를 반복 이용한 오답.
(C) 연상 단어 오답. 평서문의 conference에서 연상 가능한 개최 장소(Milan)를 이용한 오답.

22

W-Br There's going to be a coffee break, isn't there?

M-Au (A) No, the plastic cups won't break.
(B) I'll just look in the directory. Thanks.
(C) It is a six-hour conference.

휴식 시간이 있겠죠?
(A) 아니요, 플라스틱 컵은 깨지지 않아요.
(B) 그냥 명부를 볼게요. 감사해요.
(C) 6시간 길이의 회의입니다.

어휘 coffee break 휴식 시간 directory 명부, 인명록

해설 휴식 시간 존재 여부를 확인하는 부가 의문문
(A) 단어 반복 오답. 질문의 break를 반복 이용한 오답.
(B) 질문과 상관없는 오답.
(C) 정답. 휴식 시간 존재 여부를 확인하는 질문에 6시간 길이의 회의라며 휴식 시간이 당연히 있을 장시간 회의임을 우회적으로 표현하고 있으므로 정답.

23

W-Br Has next quarter's budget been approved?

W-Am (A) I saw that film last week.
(B) Three kilometers away.
(C) It's still being reviewed.

다음 분기의 예산이 승인되었습니까?

(A) 지난주에 그 영화를 보았어요.
(B) 3킬로미터 떨어져 있어요.
(C) 아직 검토 중입니다.

어휘 budget 예산 approve 승인하다 review 검토하다

해설 다음 분기의 예산이 승인되었는지 여부를 묻는 조동사(Has) 의문문

(A) 연상 단어 오답. 질문의 next에서 연상 가능한 last를 이용한 오답.
(B) 연상 단어 오답. 질문의 quarter를 '4분의 1'로 해석했을 때 연상 가능한 Three를 이용한 오답.
(C) 정답. 다음 분기의 예산이 승인되었는지 여부를 묻는 질문에 아직 검토 중이라고 알려 주고 있으므로 정답.

24

W-Am Do you like the new carpet in the lobby?

M-Au (A) The car is parked outside.
  (B) No, not at all.
  (C) Yes, I have several hobbies.

로비의 새 카펫이 마음에 드나요?

(A) 차는 밖에 주차되어 있어요.
(B) 아니요, 전혀 그렇지 않아요.
(C) 네, 취미가 몇 가지 있어요.

해설 새 카펫이 마음에 드는지 여부를 묻는 조동사(Do) 의문문

(A) 유사 발음 오답. 질문의 carpet과 부분적으로 발음이 유사한 car를 이용한 오답.
(B) 정답. 로비의 새 카펫이 마음에 드는지를 묻는 질문에 아니요(No)라고 대답한 뒤, 전혀 그렇지 않다며 부정 답변과 일관된 내용을 덧붙이고 있으므로 정답.
(C) 유사 발음 오답. 질문의 lobby와 부분적으로 발음이 유사한 hobbies를 이용한 오답.

25

W-Br We should go and get some lunch now.

M-Au (A) It's a new approach.
  (B) I bought these shoes on sale.
  (C) I have a dentist's appointment at noon.

지금 가서 점심을 먹어야 합니다.

(A) 새로운 접근 방식입니다.
(B) 이 신발을 할인 행사에서 샀어요.
(C) 정오에 치과 예약이 있어요.

어휘 approach 접근 (방식) appointment 예약

해설 제안/권유의 평서문

(A) 연상 단어 오답. 평서문의 go에서 연상 가능한 approach를 이용한 오답.
(B) 연상 단어 오답. 평서문의 get을 '마련하다'로 해석했을 때 연상 가능한 bought와 shoes를 이용한 오답.
(C) 정답. 지금 가서 점심을 먹자고 제안하는 평서문에 정오에 치과 예약이 있다며 우회적으로 제안을 거절하고 있으므로 정답.

26

W-Am Would you be interested in a magazine subscription?

W-Br (A) Definitely—how much is it?
  (B) A full-page ad.
  (C) No, it's my own recipe.

잡지 구독에 관심이 있으십니까?

(A) 확실히 그렇습니다—얼마입니까?
(B) 전면 광고입니다.
(C) 아니요, 제 자신의 조리법입니다.

어휘 subscription 구독 full-page ad 전면 광고 recipe 조리법

해설 잡지 구독에 관심이 있는지 여부를 묻는 조동사(Would) 의문문

(A) 정답. 잡지 구독에 관심이 있는지 묻는 질문에 확실히 그렇다(Definitely)고 대답한 뒤, 얼마인지 추가 정보를 물으며 긍정 답변과 일관된 내용을 덧붙이고 있으므로 정답.
(B) 연상 단어 오답. 질문의 magazine에서 연상 가능한 full-page와 ad를 이용한 오답.
(C) 질문과 상관없는 오답.

27

M-Cn I don't think Mr. Beck will like the new production plan.

M-Au (A) You don't think so?
  (B) To visit the plant tomorrow.
  (C) About an hour on Tuesday.

벡 씨가 새로운 생산 계획을 마음에 들어 할 것이라고 생각하지 않아요.

(A) 그렇게 생각하지 않는다고요?
(B) 내일 공장을 방문하기 위해서입니다.
(C) 화요일에 한 시간 정도요.

어휘 production 생산 plant 공장

해설 의사 전달의 평서문

(A) 정답. 벡 씨가 새로운 생산 계획을 마음에 들어 할 것이라고 생각하지 않는다는 평서문에 그렇게 생각하지 않는지 되물어보고 있으므로 정답.
(B) 유사 발음 오답. 평서문의 plan과 부분적으로 발음이 유사한 plant를 이용한 오답.
(C) 평서문과 상관없는 오답. How long 의문문에 대한 응답이므로 오답.

28

M-Cn Shouldn't we discuss the advertising campaign now?

W-Am (A) On the radio.
  (B) A roundtable discussion.
  (C) No, we have other priorities.

이제 광고 캠페인에 대해 논의해야 하지 않을까요?

(A) 라디오에서요.
(B) 원탁 토론입니다.
(C) 아니요, 다른 우선 사항이 있어요.

어휘 advertising 광고 priority 우선 사항

해설 제안/권유의 의문문
(A) 연상 단어 오답. 질문의 advertising에서 연상 가능한 radio를 이용한 오답.
(B) 파생어 오답. 질문의 discuss와 파생어 관계인 discussion을 이용한 오답.
(C) 정답. 광고 캠페인에 대해 논의하자고 제안하는 질문에 아니요(No)라고 대답한 뒤, 다른 우선 사항이 있다며 부정 답변에 대한 이유를 제시하고 있으므로 정답.

29

W-Br Where should I put this box of report binders?

M-Au (A) The delivery truck is late.
(B) Our team report contains a lot of interesting data.
(C) The cabinet in my office is full.

보고서 바인더가 들어 있는 이 상자는 어디에 두어야 하나요?
(A) 배달 트럭이 늦었어요.
(B) 우리 팀의 보고서에는 흥미로운 데이터가 많이 있어요.
(C) 제 사무실의 캐비닛은 다 찼어요.

해설 상자를 둘 장소를 묻는 Where 의문문
(A) 연상 단어 오답. 질문의 box에서 연상 가능한 delivery를 이용한 오답.
(B) 단어 반복 오답. 질문의 report를 반복 이용한 오답.
(C) 정답. 보고서 바인더가 든 상자를 둘 장소를 묻는 질문에 자신의 사무실 캐비닛은 다 찼다며 상자를 둘 수 없다는 것을 우회적으로 알려 주고 있으므로 정답.

30

W-Br Have you seen our orientation video for new employees?

M-Cn (A) Seven new employees.
(B) Yes, I watched it this morning.
(C) We still haven't met.

신입 사원을 위한 오리엔테이션 비디오 영상을 보셨나요?
(A) 신입 사원 7명이요.
(B) 네, 오늘 아침에 보았어요.
(C) 우리는 아직 만나 보지 못했어요.

해설 오리엔테이션 비디오 영상을 보았는지 여부를 묻는 조동사(Have) 의문문
(A) 단어 반복 오답. 질문의 new employees를 반복 이용한 오답.
(B) 정답. 신입 사원을 위한 오리엔테이션 비디오 영상을 보았는지 여부를 묻는 질문에 네(Yes)라고 대답한 뒤, 오늘 아침에 보았다며 긍정 답변과 어울리는 내용을 덧붙이고 있으므로 정답.
(C) 유사 발음 오답. 질문의 Have와 부분적으로 발음이 유사한 haven't를 이용한 오답.

31

M-Cn When are you planning to take a vacation?

W-Br (A) She planned the event herself.
(B) I'm working on three projects.
(C) Could you take our picture, please?

언제 휴가를 가실 계획인가요?
(A) 그녀는 행사를 직접 계획했어요.
(B) 세 개의 프로젝트를 진행하고 있어요.
(C) 사진 좀 찍어 주시겠어요?

어휘 take a vacation 휴가를 내다

해설 휴가를 갈 시점을 묻는 When 의문문
(A) 파생어 오답. 질문의 planning과 파생어 관계인 planned를 이용한 오답.
(B) 정답. 휴가를 갈 시점을 묻는 질문에 세 개의 프로젝트를 진행하고 있다며 당장은 바빠서 휴가 계획을 세울 수 없음을 우회적으로 알려 주고 있으므로 정답.
(C) 단어 반복 오답. 질문의 take를 반복 이용한 오답.

PART 3

32-34

M-Au Fernanda, **32I know we were hoping to have the walls in the office repainted next month. But do you think it'll be too much of a disruption for the employees?**

W-Br **32I think it'll be fine. 33I asked the team when they'd like to work from home the next few months.** Most people prefer Mondays and Fridays, so we could have the painters come on those days.

M-Au Sounds good. **34I'll reach out to some companies to see who's available to do the work.**

남 페르난다, 다음 달에 사무실 벽을 다시 칠하기를 바라고 있다는 걸 알아요. 하지만 직원들에게 크게 방해가 될 것 같나요?

여 괜찮을 것 같아요. 팀원들에게 앞으로 몇 달 동안 언제 재택근무를 하고 싶은지 물었어요. 대부분이 월요일과 금요일을 선호하니, 도장공들이 그날에 오도록 하면 됩니다.

남 좋아요. **업체 몇 군데에 연락해서 누가 작업을 할 수 있는지 알아볼게요.**

어휘 disruption 지장, 방해 reach out 연락을 취하다

32

What are the speakers discussing?
(A) Moving to a new office
(B) Painting some walls
(C) Purchasing some furniture
(D) Raising employee salaries

화자들은 무엇을 논의하고 있는가?
(A) 새 사무실로 이사하기
(B) 벽에 페인트칠하기
(C) 가구 구입하기
(D) 직원 급여 인상하기

어휘 raise (월급 등을) 인상하다, 올리다

해설 전체 내용 관련 – 대화의 주제

남자가 첫 대사에서 다음 달에 사무실 벽을 다시 칠할 것(I know we were hoping to have the walls in the office repainted next month)이라며 직원들에게 방해가 될지(But do you think it'll be too much of a disruption for the employees?)를 묻자, 여자가 괜찮다(I think it'll be fine)고 대답하면서 페인트칠과 관련하여 대화를 이어 가고 있으므로 정답은 (B)이다.

> **Paraphrasing** 대화의 have the walls in the office repainted → 정답의 Painting some walls

33

What did the woman ask a team about?
(A) Group assignments
(B) Vacation schedules
(C) Software preferences
(D) Work-from-home dates

여자는 팀에게 무엇에 대해 물었는가?
(A) 그룹 과제
(B) 휴가 일정
(C) 소프트웨어 선호도
(D) 재택근무 날짜

어휘 assignment 과제, 임무   preference 선호(도)

해설 세부 사항 관련 – 여자가 팀에게 물어본 것

여자가 첫 대사에서 팀원들에게 언제 재택근무를 하고 싶은지 물었다(I asked the team when they'd like to work from home the next few months)고 말하고 있으므로 정답은 (D)이다.

> **Paraphrasing** 대화의 when they'd like to work from home → 정답의 Work-from-home dates

34

What does the man offer to do?
(A) Contact some businesses
(B) Get a manager's approval
(C) Calculate some costs
(D) Send a notification e-mail

남자는 무엇을 하겠다고 제안하는가?
(A) 업체에 연락하기
(B) 관리자의 승인받기
(C) 비용 계산하기
(D) 알림 이메일 보내기

어휘 approval 승인   calculate 계산하다   notification 알림, 통보

해설 세부 사항 관련 – 남자의 제안 사항

남자가 마지막 대사에서 업체 몇 군데에 연락해서 가능한 작업자를 알아보겠다(I'll reach out to some companies to see who's available to do the work)고 말하고 있으므로 정답은 (A)이다.

> **Paraphrasing** 대화의 reach out to some companies → 정답의 Contact some businesses

35-37

W-Br	Hi, Gregor. ³⁵The customers at table 23 wanted to let you know they really enjoyed their meal. They had the vegetable stew.
M-Au	³⁵Thanks for letting me know. ³⁶Unfortunately, Rajeev just informed me that he has to leave early. We won't have enough cooks to cover the evening rush.
W-Br	Oh. ³⁷I'll let the customers know that some of their food might take longer than usual to come out.
M-Au	That's a good idea.

여	안녕하세요, 그레고르. 23번 테이블 손님들이 식사를 정말 맛있게 했다고 전해 주길 원하네요. 야채 스튜를 드신 손님들이요.
남	전해 주셔서 감사해요. 안타깝게도 라지브가 일찍 퇴근해야 한다고 방금 알려 주었어요. 바쁜 저녁 시간을 감당하기에는 요리사가 부족할 거예요.
여	오. 손님들에게 식사 준비가 평소보다 더 오래 걸릴 수 있다고 알릴게요.
남	좋은 생각입니다.

어휘	inform 알리다 cover (일을) 감당하다

35

Where do the speakers most likely work?
(A) At an appliance store
(B) At a restaurant
(C) At a food-manufacturing plant
(D) At a cooking school

화자들은 어디에서 일하는 것 같은가?
(A) 가전제품 매장
(B) 식당
(C) 식품 제조 공장
(D) 요리 학교

해설 전체 내용 관련 – 화자들의 근무지

여자가 첫 대사에서 남자에게 손님들이 식사를 맛있게 했다(The customers ~ they really enjoyed their meal)며 야채 스튜를 먹은 손님(They had the vegetable stew)이라고 알렸고, 남자가 전해 주어 고맙다(Thanks for letting me know)고 대답한 것으로 보아 화자들은 식당 직원이라는 것을 알 수 있다. 따라서 정답은 (B)이다.

36

What problem does the man mention?
(A) Some uniforms have not been delivered.
(B) Some paperwork was misfiled.
(C) A business will be understaffed.
(D) A permit has not been approved.

남자는 어떤 문제를 언급하는가?
(A) 유니폼이 배송되지 않았다.
(B) 서류가 잘못 정리되었다.
(C) 사업장에 인력이 부족할 것이다.
(D) 허가가 승인되지 않았다.

어휘 paperwork 서류 misfile (서류 등을) 잘못 철하다, 정리하다
understaffed 인원이 부족한 permit 허가(증)

해설 세부 사항 관련 – 남자가 언급하는 문제

남자가 첫 대사에서 안타깝게도 라지브가 일찍 퇴근해야 한다(Unfortunately, Rajeev just informed ~ leave early)며 바쁜 저녁 시간을 감당하기에는 요리사가 부족할 것(We won't have enough cooks ~ rush)이라고 말하는 것으로 보아 요리사 한 명이 일찍 퇴근을 해서 저녁 시간에 일손이 부족할 것을 언급하고 있으므로 정답은 (C)이다.

> Paraphrasing 대화의 won't have enough cooks to cover
> the evening rush
> → 정답의 will be understaffed

37

What does the woman say she will do?
(A) Schedule an upcoming training session
(B) Inform customers of a potential delay
(C) Work an extra shift
(D) Contact a vendor

여자는 무엇을 할 것이라고 말하는가?
(A) 곧 있을 교육 일정 잡기
(B) 손님들에게 잠재적인 지연에 대해 알리기
(C) 추가 근무하기
(D) 공급업체에 연락하기

어휘 upcoming 다가오는, 곧 있을 potential 잠재적인 shift (교대)
근무 vendor 판매 회사, 노점상

해설 세부 사항 관련 – 여자가 할 것이라고 말하는 일

여자가 두 번째 대사에서 손님들에게 식사 준비가 평소보다 더 오래 걸릴 수 있다고 알리겠다(I'll let the customers know that some of their food might take longer than usual to come out)고 말하고 있으므로 정답은 (B)이다.

> Paraphrasing 대화의 might take longer than usual to
> come out → 정답의 a potential delay

38-40

M-Au **38Thank you, Amany, for agreeing to come in and test out our new video game. Given your expertise in the field, we're excited for you to play it and let us know what you think.**

W-Am It's my pleasure. I love playing games that are in development and sharing ideas for improvements. **39I heard that this game was designed to be used as a training tool for delivery drivers, right?**

M-Au **39Correct. It's designed to teach drivers to choose the most efficient routes. Oh, and by the way, 40it's nearly lunchtime— would you like me to take you over to the cafeteria before you get started? All the food is complimentary.**

남 아마니, 이렇게 오셔서 우리의 최신 비디오 게임을 테스트하는 데 동의해 주셔서 감사합니다. 이 분야에 대해 가지고 계신 전문 지식을 생각하면, 직접 이 게임을 해 보시고 어떤 의견을 주실지 무척 기대가 됩니다.

여 천만에요. 저도 개발 중인 게임을 해 보고 개선을 위한 아이디어를 공유하는 것을 정말 좋아해요. 이 게임이 배달 운전기사의 훈련 도구로 사용하기 위해 설계가 되었다고 들었는데, 맞나요?

남 맞습니다. 운전기사가 가장 효율적인 경로를 선택할 수 있게 가르치도록 설계되었어요. 아, 그런데 거의 점심시간이네요. 시작하기 전에 구내식당으로 안내해 드릴까요? 모든 음식은 무료입니다.

어휘 given ~을 고려해 볼 때 expertise 전문 지식
improvement 개선, 향상 efficient 효율적인
complimentary 무료의

38

What was the woman hired to do for a video game?
(A) Provide feedback
(B) Create some animations
(C) Compose a musical score
(D) Write a script

여자는 비디오 게임을 위해 무엇을 하도록 고용되었는가?
(A) 피드백 제공하기
(B) 애니메이션 만들기
(C) 음악 작곡하기
(D) 대본 쓰기

어휘 compose 작곡하다 score 악보, (음악) 작품 script 대본, 원고

해설 세부 사항 관련 – 여자가 비디오 게임을 위해 고용된 목적

남자가 첫 대사에서 여자에게 최신 비디오 게임을 테스트하는 데 동의해 주어 고맙다(Thank you, Amany, for agreeing to come in and test out our new video game)며 직접 이 게임을 해 보고 어떤 의견을 줄 지 무척 기대가 된다(Given your expertise ~ let us know what you think)고 말하고 있으므로 정답은 (A)이다.

> **Paraphrasing** 대화의 let us know what you think
> → 정답의 Provide feedback

39

According to the man, who has a video game been designed for?

(A) Medical personnel
(B) Human resource specialists
(C) Delivery drivers
(D) Assembly-line workers

남자에 따르면, 비디오 게임은 누구를 위해 설계되었는가?

(A) 의료진
(B) 인사 전문가
(C) 배달 운전기사
(D) 조립 라인 작업자

어휘 personnel 직원 human resource 인사, 인적 자원
specialist 전문가 assembly 조립

해설 세부 사항 관련 – 남자가 말하는 비디오 게임 설계의 대상

여자가 첫 대사에서 게임이 배달 운전기사의 훈련 도구로 사용하기 위해 설계가 되었는지(I heard that this game was designed to be used as a training tool for delivery drivers, right?) 묻자 남자가 맞다(Correct)면서 운전기사가 가장 효율적인 경로를 선택할 수 있게 가르치도록 설계되었다(It's designed to teach drivers to choose the most efficient routes)고 말하고 있으므로 정답은 (C)이다.

40

What does the man invite the woman to do?

(A) Store her items in a locker
(B) Tour a building
(C) Choose a place to work
(D) Get some food

남자는 여자에게 무엇을 하라고 권하는가?

(A) 사물함에 물건 보관하기
(B) 건물 견학하기
(C) 작업할 장소 선택하기
(D) 식사하기

해설 세부 사항 관련 – 남자가 여자에게 권하는 것

남자가 마지막 대사에서 점심시간이라며 구내식당으로 안내해 줄지(it's nearly lunchtime—would you like me to take you over to the cafeteria before you get started?) 물으면서 음식이 무료(All the food is complimentary)라고 말하는 것으로 보아 여자에게 점심 식사를 권하고 있음을 알 수 있다. 따라서 정답은 (D)이다.

41-43

W-Br **41I really appreciate you coming to my office to help fix my printer, Malik.** I tried going through the troubleshooting steps on my own, but it still jams up on me every time I try to print double-sided copies.

M-Cn **41No problem. I can help you. 42Can you try printing a test document for me so I can see what's happening?**

W-Br Sure. I'll print the first two pages of the budget report I'm working on.

M-Cn Hmm. **43It looks like you're using paper that's a nonstandard size.** That may be why it's not going through smoothly, but I'll take a closer look to see what else could be wrong.

여 프린터 수리를 돕기 위해 제 사무실로 이렇게 와 줘서 정말 고마워요, 말릭. 혼자서 문제 해결 단계를 시도해 보았지만 양면 인쇄를 하려고 할 때마다 여전히 종이가 걸리네요.

남 문제없어요. 제가 도와드릴게요. 상황이 어떤지 파악할 수 있도록 테스트 문서를 인쇄해 주시겠어요?

여 물론이죠. 작업 중인 예산 보고서의 처음 두 페이지를 인쇄해 볼게요.

남 흠. 일반 사이즈가 아닌 용지를 사용하고 있는 것 같네요. 그래서 원활하게 작동하지 않는 것일 수도 있지만, 그 외에 어떤 부분이 잘못된 것인지 좀 더 자세히 봐야겠어요.

어휘 appreciate 고마워하다 troubleshooting 문제 해결
on one's own 혼자 힘으로 jam (기계 등이 막혀서)
움직이지 않다 double-sided 양면의 nonstandard
비표준의, 보통 크기[유형]가 아닌

41

Why did the man come to the woman's office?

(A) To discuss a report
(B) To deliver some tools
(C) To review job applications
(D) To make a repair

남자는 왜 여자의 사무실에 왔는가?

(A) 보고서에 대해 논의하기 위해
(B) 도구를 전달하기 위해
(C) 입사 지원서를 검토하기 위해
(D) 수리를 하기 위해

해설 세부 사항 관련 – 남자가 여자의 사무실에 온 이유

여자가 첫 대사에서 남자에게 프린터 수리를 위해 사무실로 와 줘서 고맙다(I really appreciate you coming to my office to help fix my printer, Malik)고 하자 남자가 문제없다(No problem)며 자신이 도와주겠다(I can help you)고 말하고 있으므로 정답은 (D)이다.

> **Paraphrasing** 대화의 fix → 정답의 make a repair

42

What does the man ask the woman to do?
(A) Provide a signature
(B) Confirm a budget
(C) Print a document
(D) Clear a work space

남자는 여자에게 무엇을 해 달라고 요청하는가?
(A) 서명
(B) 예산 확정
(C) 문서 인쇄
(D) 작업 공간 정리

어휘 signature 서명 confirm 확정하다, 확인하다

해설 세부 사항 관련 – 남자의 요청 사항

남자가 첫 대사에서 여자에게 상황을 파악할 수 있도록 테스트 문서를 인쇄해 달라고(Can you try printing a test document for me so I can see what's happening?) 요청했으므로 정답은 (C)이다.

> **Paraphrasing** 대화의 try printing a test document
> → 정답의 Print a document

43

What does the man notice?
(A) An item is not a standard size.
(B) Some information is missing.
(C) A cord is unplugged.
(D) A manual is not accurate.

남자는 무엇을 알아채는가?
(A) 제품이 표준 사이즈가 아니다.
(B) 정보가 누락되었다.
(C) 코드가 뽑혀 있다.
(D) 설명서가 정확하지 않다.

어휘 unplug (전기) 플러그를 뽑다 accurate 정확한

해설 세부 사항 관련 – 남자가 알아채는 것

남자가 마지막 대사에서 일반 사이즈가 아닌 용지를 사용하고 있는 것 같다(It looks like you're using paper that's a nonstandard size)고 말하고 있으므로 정답은 (A)이다.

> **Paraphrasing** 대화의 paper that's a nonstandard size
> → 정답의 An item is not a standard size

44-46

M-Cn	Elson Electric Service. How can I help you?
W-Br	Hi. My name's Kriti Bora. **44I'm calling because I received an electricity bill from your company in the mail. But I don't understand why, since my bills are paid automatically through my bank account.**

M-Cn	Let me check your customer account, Ms. Bora. Hmm... It looks like the payment didn't go through. Have you changed anything recently?
W-Br	Well, **45I changed banks about a month ago**, but I thought that I'd informed you about it.
M-Cn	I don't see any recent updates here. So, I'm sorry, but **46I'll need you to update your bank account information on our Web site. I'll send you the link to the form.**

남	엘슨 전기 서비스입니다. 어떻게 도와드릴까요?
여	안녕하세요. 제 이름은 크리티 보라입니다. **우편으로 전기 요금 고지서를 받아서 전화를 했어요.** 그런데 요금은 은행 계좌에서 자동 이체가 되기 때문에 영문을 모르겠네요.
남	보라 씨, 고객 계정을 확인해 보겠습니다. 음… 결제가 안 된 것 같군요. 최근에 변경 사항이 있었습니까?
여	음, **한 달 전쯤에 은행을 바꿨는데**, 그것에 대해 알린 것으로 알고 있어요.
남	여기에는 최근 변경 사항이 보이지 않습니다. 그러니, 죄송하지만, **저희 웹사이트에서 고객님의 은행 계좌 정보를 업데이트해 주셔야 합니다. 양식 링크를 보내 드리겠습니다.**

어휘	bill 고지서, 청구서; 청구 금액 account 계좌, 계정 payment 결제, 납입 go through 통과[성사]되다

44

Why is the woman calling?
(A) To report a power outage
(B) To inquire about a bill
(C) To get advice about energy savings
(D) To transfer a service to a new location

여자는 왜 전화를 하고 있는가?
(A) 정전을 신고하기 위해
(B) 고지서에 대해 문의하기 위해
(C) 에너지 절약에 대한 조언을 얻기 위해
(D) 서비스 시설을 새로운 장소로 이전하기 위해

어휘 power outage 정전 inquire 문의하다 transfer 옮기다, 이전하다

해설 전체 내용 관련 – 여자가 전화하는 목적

여자가 첫 대사에서 우편으로 전기 요금 고지서를 받아서 전화를 했다(I'm calling because I received an electricity bill from your company in the mail)고 했고 요금은 자동 이체가 되는 데 영문을 모르겠다(But I don't understand why, since my bills are paid automatically through my bank account)고 말하고 있으므로 전기 요금 고지서에 대해 의문을 가지고 있음을 알 수 있다. 따라서 정답은 (B)이다.

45

What did the woman do a month ago?
(A) She had solar panels installed.
(B) She changed banks.
(C) She took a vacation.
(D) She opened a business.

여자는 한 달 전에 무엇을 했는가?
(A) 태양 전지판을 설치했다.
(B) **은행을 바꾸었다.**
(C) 휴가를 갔다.
(D) 사업을 시작했다.

해설 세부 사항 관련 – 여자가 한 달 전에 한 일
여자가 두 번째 대사에서 한 달 전쯤에 은행을 바꿨다(I changed banks about a month ago)고 말하고 있으므로 정답은 (B)이다.

46

What does the man say the woman needs to do?
(A) Schedule an inspection
(B) Talk to a building manager
(C) Complete an online form
(D) Pay an extra fee

남자는 여자가 무엇을 해야 한다고 말하는가?
(A) 검사 일정 잡기
(B) 건물 관리자에게 말하기
(C) **온라인 양식 작성하기**
(D) 추가 요금 지불하기

어휘 inspection 검사

해설 세부 사항 관련 – 여자가 해야 한다고 남자가 말하는 것
남자가 마지막 대사에서 여자에게 웹사이트에서 은행 계좌 정보를 업데이트해야 한다(I'll need you to update your bank account information on our Web site)며 양식 링크를 보내겠다(I'll send you the link to the form)고 했으므로 정답은 (C)이다.

> **Paraphrasing** 대화의 update your bank account information on our Web site
> → 정답의 Complete an online form

47-49 3인 대화

M-Au ⁴⁷**Hi, Dr. Patel.** Thanks for contacting us for a second meeting.

W-Br Good to see you both again. As you know, ⁴⁷**my dental practice has been growing,** ⁴⁸**so I've decided to purchase the latest carbon dioxide dental laser your company makes.**

M-Au Excellent news!

W-Br But I do have a question. While I'm convinced of the benefits of this machine for my dental patients, this is a huge financial commitment. ⁴⁹**Do you offer any payment plans?**

M-Au ⁴⁹**Yes, and Mr. Kim here can help you with that.**

M-Cn ⁴⁹**Sure.** Just give me a minute to bring up the relevant information on my tablet. I'll go over each option with you in detail.

남1 **안녕하세요, 파텔 박사님.** 두 번째 회의를 위해 연락 주셔서 감사합니다.

여 두 분 모두 다시 만나서 반갑습니다. 아시다시피, **제 치과가 잘되고 있어서 귀사에서 만든 최신 이산화탄소 치과용 레이저를 구입하기로 결정했어요.**

남1 아주 좋은 소식입니다!

여 하지만 궁금한 점이 하나 있어요. 이 기계가 우리 치과 환자들에게 이로움을 줄 것은 확신하지만, 금전적으로 큰 부담이 됩니다. **할부를 제공하나요?**

남1 **그럼요, 그리고 김 씨가 이것에 대해 도와줄 것입니다.**

남2 **물론이죠.** 잠시만 기다려 주시면 태블릿에서 관련 정보를 불러오겠습니다. 각 옵션에 대해 같이 상세하게 살펴볼게요.

어휘 practice (의사, 변호사 등의) 사무실 latest 최신의 carbon dioxide 이산화탄소 convince 확신시키다 financial 재정적인 commitment 책임 payment plan 할부, 분할 납부 relevant 관련 있는, 적절한 go over 살펴보다

47

Who most likely is the woman?
(A) A research scientist
(B) An advertising executive
(C) A software engineer
(D) A dentist

여자는 누구인 것 같은가?
(A) 연구 과학자
(B) 광고 책임자
(C) 소프트웨어 기술자
(D) **치과 의사**

해설 전체 내용 관련 – 여자의 직업
첫 번째 남자가 첫 대사에서 안녕하세요, 파텔 박사님(Hi, Dr. Patel)이라고 인사를 했고 여자가 자신의 치과가 잘되고 있다(my dental practice has been growing)고 말하는 것으로 보아 정답은 (D)이다.

48

What does the woman say she has decided to do?
(A) Accept a job offer
(B) Purchase some equipment
(C) Move to a new office
(D) Take a training course

여자는 무엇을 하기로 결정했다고 말하는가?
(A) 일자리 제안 수락하기
(B) 장비 구입하기
(C) 새 사무실로 이사하기
(D) 교육 과정 수강하기

어휘 accept 받아들이다   job offer 일자리 제의   equipment 장비

해설 세부 사항 관련 – 여자가 하기로 결정했다고 말하는 것
여자가 첫 대사에서 이산화탄소 치과용 레이저를 구입하기로 결정했다(so I've decided to purchase the latest carbon dioxide dental laser your company makes)고 말하고 있으므로 정답은 (B)이다.

> **Paraphrasing** 대화의 the latest carbon dioxide dental laser → 정답의 some equipment

49

What do the men say are available?
(A) Some preliminary sketches
(B) Some consultation services
(C) Payment plans
(D) User manuals

남자들은 무엇이 가능하다고 말하는가?
(A) 사전 개요
(B) 상담 서비스
(C) 할부
(D) 사용자 매뉴얼

어휘 preliminary 예비의   sketch 개요   consultation 상담, 협의

해설 세부 사항 관련 – 남자들이 가능하다고 말하는 것
여자가 두 번째 대사에서 할부를 제공하는지(Do you offer any payment plans?) 물었고 첫 번째 남자가 그렇다며 김 씨가 도와줄 것(Yes, and Mr. Kim here can help you with that)이라고 하자 뒤이어 두 번째 남자가 물론이다(Sure)라고 답하고 있으므로 정답은 (C)이다.

50-52

M-Au	⁵⁰**I've had a chance to look at your commercial dishwasher. Unfortunately, the drain pump needs to be replaced, and I don't have the part on hand.**
W-Am	But we're about to open for dinner, and all our tables are booked this evening. ⁵¹**There's nothing you can do now?**
M-Au	I'm afraid not. ⁵¹**I'll request that the replacement part be sent by express shipping**, but it could still take a couple of hours to complete the repair.
W-Am	All right—but please let me know as soon as you get the part. We're really going to be busy this evening, and ⁵²**I'm concerned we won't have enough tableware to last the whole evening.**

남	여기 상업용 식기세척기를 좀 살펴보았어요. 안타깝게도 배수펌프를 교체해야 하는데 지금 당장은 부품이 없네요.
여	하지만 저녁 식사를 위해 곧 문을 열 예정이고 오늘 저녁에는 모든 테이블이 예약되어 있어요. **지금 해 주실 수 있는 일이 없을까요?**
남	유감이지만 할 수 있는 게 없어요. **교체 부품을 특급 배송으로 보내 달라고 요청하겠지만** 수리를 마칠 때까지 여전히 두어 시간이 걸릴 수 있어요.
여	알겠어요. 하지만 부품을 받는 대로 알려 주세요. 오늘 저녁에 정말 바쁠 것이고 **저녁 내내 사용할 식기가 부족할까 걱정되네요.**

어휘 commercial 상업용의   dishwasher 식기세척기   drain 배수관   replace 교체하다   on hand 수중에   be about to 막 ～하려고 하다   tableware 식탁용 식기류

50

Who most likely is the man?
(A) A sales representative
(B) A restaurant chef
(C) A repair technician
(D) A health inspector

남자는 누구인 것 같은가?
(A) 영업 사원
(B) 레스토랑 셰프
(C) 수리 기술자
(D) 위생 감독관

해설 전체 내용 관련 – 남자의 직업
남자가 첫 대사에서 식기세척기를 살펴보았다(I've had a chance to look at your commercial dishwasher)며 배수펌프를 교체해야 하는데 지금 당장은 부품이 없다(Unfortunately, the drain pump needs to be replaced, and I don't have the part on hand)고 말하고 있으므로 남자는 기계를 수리하는 사람임을 알 수 있다. 따라서 정답은 (C)이다.

51

What does the man offer to do?
(A) Reduce a price
(B) Expedite an order
(C) Post an online notice
(D) Photograph some items

남자는 무엇을 하겠다고 제안하는가?
(A) 가격 인하하기
(B) 주문을 신속히 처리하기
(C) 온라인 공지 올리기
(D) 상품 사진 촬영하기

해설 세부 사항 관련 – 남자의 제안 사항
여자가 첫 대사에서 지금 해 줄 수 있는 일이 있는지(There's nothing you can do now?) 묻자 남자가 교체 부품을 특급 배송으로 요청하겠다(I'll request that the replacement part be sent by express shipping)고 제안하고 있으므로 정답은 (B)이다.

52

Why does the woman say she is concerned?
(A) Profits have decreased.
(B) A competitor has recently opened.
(C) Some supplies may run out.
(D) Her business Web site is down.

여자는 왜 걱정된다고 말하는가?
(A) 이익이 감소했다.
(B) 경쟁업체가 최근에 문을 열었다.
(C) 일부 물품이 소진될 수 있다.
(D) 회사 웹사이트가 다운되었다.

어휘 decrease 감소하다 competitor 경쟁업체 supplies 물품

해설 세부 사항 관련 – 여자가 걱정하는 이유
여자가 마지막 대사에서 저녁 내내 사용할 식기가 부족할까 걱정(I'm concerned we won't have enough tableware to last the whole evening)이라고 말하고 있으므로 정답은 (C)이다.

Paraphrasing	대화의 won't have enough tableware → 정답의 Some supplies may run out

53-55 3인 대화

M-Cn	Good morning, Ms. Phillips. We're glad to be working with you. 53**Is this the space that you want us to redesign?**
W-Br	Yes, this is it—the waiting room. 53**We want patients to relax while they wait here.** We'd like the space to have soothing colors and comfortable furniture.
M-Au	You know, 54**one thing that's been very popular in health-care facilities is aquariums.**
M-Cn	54**Children especially enjoy watching fish swim around in the tank.**
W-Br	That'd be great—if I can afford it.
M-Au	55**We'll need to know the size of the space before we can tell you how much it'll cost. Let's start by measuring the room.**

남1	안녕하세요, 필립스 씨. 함께 작업을 하게 되어 기쁩니다. **이곳이 다시 디자인하기를 원하는 공간입니까?**
여	네, 여기가 바로 대기실입니다. **환자들이 이곳에서 기다리는 동안 편히 쉴 수 있기를 바랍니다.** 차분한 색상과 편안한 가구가 있는 공간이 되었으면 합니다.

남2	아시다시피, **의료 시설에서 매우 인기 있는 것 중 하나는 수족관입니다.**
남1	**특히 아이들이 수조에서 헤엄치는 물고기를 구경하는 것을 좋아합니다.**
여	그러면 좋겠네요. 제가 금전적으로 여유가 된다면요.
남2	**비용이 얼마인지 알려 드리기 전에 이곳의 크기를 알아야 합니다. 먼저 방을 측정하는 것으로 시작하겠습니다.**

어휘	patient 환자 soothing 진정시키는 facility 시설 afford (금전적으로) 여유가 있다 measure 측정하다

53

Where does the woman most likely work?
(A) At an elementary school
(B) At a pet store
(C) At a medical clinic
(D) At a department store

여자는 어디에서 근무하는 것 같은가?
(A) 초등학교
(B) 애완동물 가게
(C) 병원
(D) 백화점

해설 전체 내용 관련 – 여자의 근무지
첫 번째 남자가 이곳이 다시 디자인하기를 원하는 공간인지(Is this the space that you want us to redesign?) 묻자 여자가 환자들이 이곳에서 기다리는 동안 편히 쉴 수 있기를 바란다(We want patients to relax while they wait here)고 말하는 것으로 보아 여자는 병원에서 근무하고 있음을 알 수 있다. 따라서 정답은 (C)이다.

54

What do the men suggest doing?
(A) Upgrading a sound system
(B) Installing a fish tank
(C) Changing a color scheme
(D) Replacing some flooring

남자들은 무엇을 하라고 제안하는가?
(A) 음향 시스템 업그레이드하기
(B) 수조 설치하기
(C) 배색 변경하기
(D) 바닥 교체하기

어휘 color scheme 배색, 색채 배합 flooring 바닥재

해설 세부 사항 관련 – 남자들의 제안 사항
두 번째 남자가 첫 대사에서 의료 시설에서 수족관이 인기가 많다(one thing that's been very popular in health-care facilities is aquariums)고 하자 첫 번째 남자가 특히 아이들이 수조에서 헤엄치는 물고기를 구경하는 것을 좋아한다(Children especially enjoy watching fish swim around in the tank)며 맞장구를 치는 것으로 보아, 남자들은 수족관 설치를 제안하고 있음을 알 수 있다. 따라서 정답은 (B)이다.

Paraphrasing	대화의 aquariums → 정답의 a fish tank

55

How will some measurements be used?

(A) To draft a cost estimate
(B) To purchase some bookshelves
(C) To decide what materials to use
(D) To apply for a building permit

측정값은 어떻게 사용될 것인가?

(A) 비용 견적을 작성하기 위해
(B) 책장을 구입하기 위해
(C) 사용할 재료를 결정하기 위해
(D) 건축 허가를 신청하기 위해

어휘 draft 초안을 작성하다   estimate 견적서   material 재료
permit 허가(증)

해설 세부 사항 관련 – 측정값의 사용 목적
두 번째 남자가 마지막 대사에서 비용을 알려 주기 전에 크기를 알아야 한다(We'll need to know the size of the space before we can tell you how much it'll cost)며 방을 측정하는 것으로 시작하겠다(Let's start by measuring the room)고 말하고 있으므로 정답은 (A)이다.

> **Paraphrasing** 대화의 how much it'll cost
> → 정답의 a cost estimate

56-58

W-Br	⁵⁶**Welcome to our career-fair booth.** Can I answer any questions for you?
M-Cn	Yes, thank you. What sort of jobs do you have available?
W-Br	We have several open positions for graphic designers and related jobs.
M-Cn	Great. I'd like to learn more.
W-Br	⁵⁷**Do you have a background in graphic design?**
M-Cn	Um, I'm very interested in learning.
W-Br	I see. Well, we do have a few entry-level positions for people like yourself. And we cover tuition costs for people who need job-related schooling. ⁵⁸**Here's a brochure with some information about our company.**

여	**채용 박람회에서 저희 회사 부스에 오신 것을 환영합니다.** 질문에 답변해 드릴까요?
남	네, 감사합니다. 어떤 종류의 직무가 있습니까?
여	그래픽 디자이너와 관련 업무에 대한 공석이 몇 개 있습니다.
남	좋네요. 더 알고 싶습니다.
여	**그래픽 디자인 경력이 있으신가요?**
남	음, 배우고 싶은 마음은 매우 있습니다.

여	알겠습니다. 그래요, 당신과 같은 사람들을 위한 초급 직책이 몇 개 있습니다. 그리고 업무 관련 교육이 필요한 사람들을 위해 수업료도 지원합니다. **저희 회사에 대한 정보가 포함된 안내 책자가 여기 있습니다.**
어휘	background 경력 entry-level 초보적인, 견습적인 cover (비용 등을) 부담하다 tuition 수업(료)

56

Where most likely are the speakers?

(A) At a car show
(B) At a job fair
(C) At a training workshop
(D) At a product launch

화자들은 어디에 있는 것 같은가?

(A) 자동차 쇼
(B) 채용 박람회
(C) 교육 워크숍
(D) 제품 출시 행사

해설 전체 내용 관련 – 대화의 장소
여자가 첫 대사에서 채용 박람회에서 자신의 회사 부스에 온 것을 환영한다(Welcome to our career-fair booth)고 말하고 있으므로 정답은 (B)이다.

57

What does the man imply when he says, "I'm very interested in learning"?

(A) He met a deadline earlier than expected.
(B) He requires more product information.
(C) He has many hobbies.
(D) He lacks experience.

남자가 "배우고 싶은 마음은 매우 있습니다"라고 말할 때 무엇을 의미하는가?

(A) 예상보다 일찍 마감일을 맞추었다.
(B) 제품 정보를 더 요구한다.
(C) 취미가 많다.
(D) 경력이 부족하다.

어휘 require 필요[요구]하다   lack 부족하다

해설 화자의 의도 파악 – 배우는 것에 관심이 많다는 말의 의도
앞에서 여자가 그래픽 디자인 경력이 있는지(Do you have a background in graphic design?) 묻자 인용문을 언급한 것이므로, 경력이 없어서 배울 의향이 있다는 의도로 한 말임을 알 수 있다. 따라서 정답은 (D)이다.

58

What does the woman give the man?

(A) A brochure
(B) A business card
(C) A company T-shirt
(D) An event schedule

여자는 남자에게 무엇을 주는가?

(A) 안내 책자
(B) 명함
(C) 회사 티셔츠
(D) 행사 일정표

해설 세부 사항 관련 – 여자가 남자에게 주는 것

여자가 마지막 대사에서 자신의 회사에 대한 정보가 포함된 안내 책자가 여기 있다(Here's a brochure with some information about our company)고 말하는 것으로 보아 정답은 (A)이다.

59-61

W-Am	Tarrington Events. Silvia speaking.
M-Cn	Hello. This is Marcel Breton. ⁵⁹**I'd like to inquire about hosting a company gathering at your lakeside resort.**
W-Am	Great. Can you tell me how many people would be attending, Mr. Breton?
M-Cn	We'd have about 50 employees there. ⁶⁰**I specifically selected your venue because I saw that you've received excellent reviews.**
W-Am	I'm glad to hear that! ⁶¹**And what dates were you thinking of?**
M-Cn	⁶¹**Maybe the first week of April?**
W-Am	Ah, ⁶¹**that could be a problem.** We book at least six months in advance.

여	태링턴 이벤트의 실비아입니다.
남	안녕하세요. 저는 마르셀 브레톤입니다. **귀사의 호숫가 휴양지에서 회사 모임을 주최하는 것에 대해 문의하고 싶습니다.**
여	좋아요. 몇 명이 참석할지 말씀해 주시겠습니까, 브레톤 씨?
남	약 50명의 직원이 참석할 것입니다. **훌륭한 평가를 받은 것을 보고 일부러 이곳을 선택했습니다.**
여	그렇다니 기쁘네요! **그러면 날짜를 언제로 생각하고 계셨나요?**
남	**아마 4월 첫째 주가 될 것 같은데요?**
여	아, **그게 문제가 될 것 같습니다. 저희는 최소 6개월 전에 예약을 받습니다.**

어휘	gathering 모임 lakeside 호숫가 specifically 특별히, 특히 venue 장소 in advance 미리, 사전에

59

What is the man organizing?
(A) A client meeting
(B) A trade show
(C) An awards banquet
(D) A company outing

남자는 무엇을 준비하고 있는가?
(A) 고객 미팅
(B) 무역 박람회
(C) 시상식 만찬
(D) 회사 야유회

어휘 banquet 연회, 만찬 company outing 회사 야유회

해설 세부 사항 관련 – 남자가 준비하는 것

남자가 첫 대사에서 호숫가 휴양지에서 회사 모임을 주최하는 것에 대해 문의한다(I'd like to inquire about hosting a company gathering at your lakeside resort)고 말하는 것으로 보아 남자가 회사에서 하는 행사를 준비하고 있다는 것을 알 수 있다. 따라서 정답은 (D)이다.

> **Paraphrasing** 대화의 company gathering
> → 정답의 company outing

60

What factor influenced the man's selection?
(A) Affordability
(B) Proximity
(C) Positive reviews
(D) Catering options

어떤 요인이 남자의 선택에 영향을 주었는가?
(A) 가격 적절성
(B) 근접성
(C) 긍정적인 평가
(D) 음식 공급업체 옵션

어휘 affordability 감당할 수 있는 비용

해설 세부 사항 관련 – 남자의 선택에 영향을 준 요인

남자가 두 번째 대사에서 훌륭한 평가를 받은 것을 보고 이곳을 선택했다(I specifically selected your venue because I saw that you've received excellent reviews)고 말하고 있으므로 정답은 (C)이다.

> **Paraphrasing** 대화의 excellent reviews
> → 정답의 Positive reviews

61

What does the woman imply when she says, "We book at least six months in advance"?
(A) A colleague is mistaken about a date.
(B) A request might not be accommodated.
(C) A decision needs to be made soon.
(D) A cancellation will not be possible.

여자가 "저희는 최소 6개월 전에 예약을 받습니다"라고 말할 때 무엇을 의미하는가?
(A) 동료가 날짜에 대해 착각하고 있다.
(B) 요청이 수용되지 않을 수도 있다.
(C) 결정을 빨리 내려야 한다.
(D) 취소가 불가능할 것이다.

어휘 colleague 동료 accommodate 수용하다 cancellation 취소

해설 화자의 의도 파악 – 최소 6개월 전에 예약을 받는다는 말의 의도 앞에서 여자가 날짜를 언제로 생각하고 있는지(And what dates were you thinking of?) 물었고 남자가 4월 첫째 주가 될 것 같다(Maybe the first week of April?)고 하자 여자가 그게 문제가 될 것 같다(that could be a problem)면서 인용문을 언급한 것이므로, 남자가 원하는 날짜에 예약이 안 될 수도 있다는 것을 알리려고 한 말임을 알 수 있다. 따라서 정답은 (B)이다.

62-64 대화 + 가격표

Professional Cleaning!

Cost by size of business

100 square meters	$70
200 square meters	$140
[63]300 square meters	$200
400 square meters	$300

W-Br	A friend of mine recommended your business and said you're the best. But [62]**I'm not sure if you clean on the weekends.**
M-Au	I have staff available seven days a week. Tell me a little about what you need.
W-Br	Well, [63]**my store is about 300 square meters**. That includes the storage room.
M-Au	OK. So you'd like the fixtures dusted and the floors cleaned?
W-Br	That's right. And there are three fitting rooms with mirrors that need cleaning and some large display windows at the front of the store.
M-Au	[64]**We'll clean the mirrors, but we don't do exterior work. You'll have to get a specialist for the outside of your windows. I'd recommend Star Services.**

프로페셔널 클리닝!

사업장 크기별 비용

100평방미터	70달러
200평방미터	140달러
[63]300평방미터	200달러
400평방미터	300달러

여	친구가 귀사를 추천했고 최고라고 말했어요. 그런데 **주말에도 청소를 하시는지 잘 모르겠네요.**
남	일주일 내내 근무하는 직원이 있습니다. 필요한 사항에 대해 말씀해 주세요.
여	음, 제 가게는 약 300평방미터이고요. 여기에는 창고가 포함됩니다.
남	좋아요. 설비의 먼지를 털고 바닥을 청소하고 싶으신가요?
여	맞아요. 그리고 청소가 필요한 거울이 있는 탈의실 3개와 매장 전면에 대형 진열창이 몇 개 있어요.
남	**거울 청소는 하겠지만 외부 작업은 하지 않아요. 창의 바깥 면은 다른 전문가를 구해야 할 거예요. 스타 서비스를 추천합니다.**

어휘	storage 저장, 보관소 fixture (천장, 벽 등의) 고정물, 설비 dust 먼지를 털다 fitting room 탈의실 exterior 외부의 specialist 전문가

62

What was the woman uncertain about?
(A) Transportation costs
(B) Weekend availability
(C) A company's reputation
(D) Membership fees

여자는 무엇에 대해 확신이 없었는가?
(A) 운송비
(B) 주말에 이용 가능
(C) 회사의 평판
(D) 회비

어휘 reputation 명성, 평판

해설 세부 사항 관련 – 여자가 불확실해 한 것
여자가 첫 대사에서 주말에도 청소를 하는지 잘 모르겠다(I'm not sure if you clean on the weekends)고 말하고 있으므로 정답은 (B)이다.

> **Paraphrasing** 대화의 clean on the weekends
> → 정답의 Weekend availability

63

Look at the graphic. How much will the woman be charged?
(A) $70
(B) $140
(C) $200
(D) $300

시각 정보에 의하면, 여자는 얼마를 지불할 것인가?
(A) 70달러
(B) 140달러
(C) 200달러
(D) 300달러

여자가 두 번째 대사에서 가게는 약 300평방미터(my store is about 300 square meters)라고 말하고 있고, 가격표에 따르면 300평방미터는 200달러이므로 정답은 (C)이다.

64

What does the man recommend Star Services to do?
(A) Manage payroll
(B) Install mirrors
(C) Shampoo the carpets
(D) Clean the windows

남자는 스타 서비스에게 무엇을 하라고 권하는가?
(A) 급여 관리
(B) 거울 설치
(C) 카펫 청소
(D) 창문 청소

어휘 payroll 급여, 급여 지급 명부   shampoo (카펫 등을) 특수 세제로 세척하다

해설 세부 사항 관련 – 남자가 스타 서비스에게 하라고 권하는 것
남자가 마지막 대사에서 거울 청소는 하지만 외부 작업은 하지 않는다(We'll clean the mirrors, but we don't do exterior work)고 했고 창의 바깥 면은 다른 전문가를 구해야 할 것이다(You'll have to get a specialist for the outside of your windows)라며 스타 서비스를 추천한다(I'd recommend Star Services)고 말하고 있으므로 남자는 스타 서비스에게 창의 바깥 면을 청소하도록 권할 것임을 알 수 있다. 따라서 정답은 (D)이다.

65-67 대화 + 상품 진열

M-Au	Hi. **[65]I'd like to have a frame made for a vintage family photograph.** I was wondering if you could help me select something that would be appropriate for an old photo.
W-Br	Sure—**[66]let's see the photo. Wow, it's not very often that we see this type of round shape.**
M-Au	**[66]Yes, it's quite unique.** I'd like to give it to my mother for her birthday next Friday.
W-Br	**[67]Since it's a birthday present, I can wrap it for you free of charge.**

남	안녕하세요. **오래된 가족사진을 위한 액자를 가지고 싶어요.** 오래된 사진에 적합한 것을 선택하도록 도와줄 수 있는지 궁금하네요.
여	물론이죠. **사진을 좀 볼게요. 와우, 이런 유형의 둥근 모양을 보는 것은 그리 흔한 일이 아니지요.**
남	네, **꽤 독특하죠.** 다음 주 금요일 어머니의 생신에 드리고 싶어요.
여	**생신 선물이니까 무료로 포장해 드릴 수 있어요.**

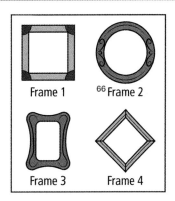

Frame 1   [66]Frame 2
Frame 3   Frame 4

1번 액자   [66]2번 액자
3번 액자   4번 액자

65

What is the man having framed?
(A) An invitation
(B) A photograph
(C) A diploma
(D) A painting

남자는 무엇을 액자에 넣을 계획인가?
(A) 초대장
(B) 사진
(C) 졸업장
(D) 그림

해설 세부 사항 관련 – 남자가 액자에 넣을 것
남자가 첫 대사에서 오래된 가족사진을 위한 액자를 가지고 싶다(I'd like to have a frame made for a vintage family photograph)고 말하고 있으므로 정답은 (B)이다.

66

Look at the graphic. Which frame will the man most likely select?
(A) Frame 1
(B) Frame 2
(C) Frame 3
(D) Frame 4

TEST 7

시각 정보에 의하면, 남자는 어떤 액자를 선택할 것 같은가?
(A) 1번 액자
(B) 2번 액자
(C) 3번 액자
(D) 4번 액자

해설 시각 정보 연계 – 남자가 선택할 액자

여자가 첫 대사에서 사진을 보자(let's see the photo)고 요청한 후 이런 둥근 모양을 보는 것은 흔한 일이 아니다(Wow, it's not very often that we see this type of round shape)라고 놀라자 남자가 꽤 독특하다(Yes, it's quite unique)고 응답하는 것으로 보아 남자는 사진의 모양과 동일한 둥근 액자를 선택할 것임을 알 수 있다. 상품 진열에 따르면 둥근 액자는 2번 액자이므로 정답은 (B)이다.

67

What is included in the price?
(A) Delivery
(B) Labor
(C) Gift wrapping
(D) UV glass

가격에는 무엇이 포함되는가?
(A) 배송비
(B) 인건비
(C) 선물 포장비
(D) UV 유리 비용

해설 세부 사항 관련 – 가격에 포함되는 것

여자가 마지막 대사에서 생신 선물이니까 무료로 포장해 줄 수 있다(Since it's a birthday present, I can wrap it for you free of charge)고 한 것으로 보아 정답은 (C)이다.

68-70 대화 + 차트

W-Br　Jinyu, [68]**I'm sorry I missed your update on the sales of our air-conditioner models. I was busy leading the new-employee training.**

M-Cn　Oh, yeah. That's OK—I heard the training went really well. But [69]**the main takeaway from my update was that our newest air-conditioner model was this month's top seller.**

W-Br　[69,70]**A lot of customers have mentioned they prefer that model because it's affordable**, so I'm not surprised it was our best-selling product.

여　진유, 에어컨 판매에 대한 업데이트를 놓쳐서 미안해요. 신입 사원 교육을 진행하느라 바빴어요.

남　아, 그래요. 괜찮아요. 교육이 아주 잘 진행되었다고 들었어요. 그런데 **제 업데이트에서 가장 중요한 점은 우리의 최신형 에어컨 모델이 이번 달에 가장 잘 팔린 제품이라는 것입니다.**

여　**저렴한 가격 때문에 많은 고객들이 그 모델을 선호한다고 했어요.** 그래서 그 제품이 가장 잘 팔렸다는 사실이 놀랍지 않네요.

어휘　takeaway 요점　affordable 저렴한

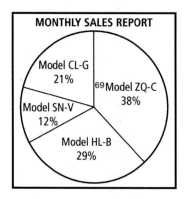

MONTHLY SALES REPORT
- Model CL-G 21%
- [69]Model ZQ-C 38%
- Model SN-V 12%
- Model HL-B 29%

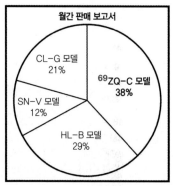

월간 판매 보고서
- CL-G 모델 21%
- [69]ZQ-C 모델 38%
- SN-V 모델 12%
- HL-B 모델 29%

68

Why did the woman miss an update?
(A) She was on vacation.
(B) She was meeting with clients.
(C) She was training new employees.
(D) She was at a medical appointment.

여자는 왜 업데이트를 놓쳤는가?
(A) 휴가 중이었다.
(B) 고객들을 만나고 있었다.
(C) 신입 사원을 교육하고 있었다.
(D) 진료 예약으로 병원에 있었다.

어휘　appointment 예약

해설 세부 사항 관련 – 여자가 업데이트를 놓친 이유

여자가 첫 대사에서 에어컨 판매에 대한 업데이트를 놓쳐서 미안하다(I'm sorry I missed your update on the sales of our air-conditioner models)면서 신입 사원 교육을 진행하느라 바빴다(I was busy leading the new-employee training)고 말하고 있으므로 정답은 (C)이다.

Paraphrasing　대화의 leading the new-employee training
→ 정답의 training new employees

69

Look at the graphic. Which model are the speakers discussing?
(A) Model ZQ-C
(B) Model HL-B
(C) Model SN-V
(D) Model CL-G

시각 정보에 의하면, 화자들은 어떤 모델에 대해 논의하고 있는가?

(A) ZQ-C 모델
(B) HL-B 모델
(C) SN-V 모델
(D) CL-G 모델

해설 시각 정보 연계 – 화자들이 논의하는 모델

남자가 첫 대사에서 업데이트에서 가장 중요한 점은 우리의 최신형 에어컨 모델이 이번 달에 가장 잘 팔렸다는 것(the main takeaway from my update was that our newest air-conditioner model was this month's top seller)이라고 하자 여자가 저렴한 가격 때문에 많은 고객들이 그 모델을 선호한다(A lot of customers have mentioned they prefer that model because it's affordable)고 말하고 있으므로 화자들이 가장 잘 팔린 모델에 대해 논의하고 있음을 알 수 있다. 차트에 따르면 가장 잘 팔린 모델은 ZQ-C 모델이므로 정답은 (A)이다.

70

According to the woman, what do customers like about an air-conditioner model?
(A) It is quiet.
(B) It is easy to install.
(C) It is energy efficient.
(D) It is inexpensive.

여자에 따르면, 고객들은 에어컨의 어떤 점에 대해 좋아하는가?

(A) 조용하다.
(B) 설치가 쉽다.
(C) 에너지 효율이 높다.
(D) 저렴하다.

어휘 efficient 효율적인

해설 세부 사항 관련 – 여자가 말하는 고객들이 에어컨에 대해 좋아하는 점

여자가 마지막 대사에서 저렴한 가격 때문에 많은 고객들이 그 모델을 선호한다(A lot of customers have mentioned they prefer that model because it's affordable)고 말하고 있으므로 정답은 (D)이다.

> **Paraphrasing** 대화의 **affordable** → 정답의 **inexpensive**

PART 4

71-73 회의 발췌

> **M-Au** I called this special meeting because I have some great news to share with everyone. As you know, [71]**we've been wanting to do some renovation work for the city government.** [72]**The bidding process was competitive, but I was just told our firm has been awarded a large contract for work on city offices and courtrooms. This is a big deal for us!** Our first move will be adding staff and workers in anticipation of these projects. [73]**I will be posting job listings on the company Web site later this week.**

> 모두와 공유할 좋은 소식이 있어서 특별히 이 회의를 소집했습니다. 아시다시피, 우리는 시 정부를 위한 개보수 공사를 하고 싶어 했습니다. **입찰 과정이 치열했지만 우리 회사가 시청과 법원 개보수 공사의 대규모 계약을 따냈다는 소식을 방금 들었습니다. 이것은 우리에게 대단한 성과입니다!** 먼저 할 일은 이러한 프로젝트에 대비하여 직원과 인부를 추가하는 것입니다. **이번 주 후반에 회사 웹사이트에 채용 공고를 게시하겠습니다.**

> **어휘** renovation 보수 bidding 입찰, 경매 competitive 경쟁이 치열한 courtroom 법정 in anticipation of ~을 대비하여

71

What type of company does the speaker work for?
(A) A technology consulting firm
(B) A landscaping company
(C) A construction company
(D) A law firm

화자는 어떤 업종에서 일하는가?

(A) 기술 컨설팅 회사
(B) 조경 회사
(C) 건설 회사
(D) 법무 법인

해설 전체 내용 관련 – 화자의 근무 업종

화자가 초반부에 우리는 시 정부를 위한 개보수 공사를 하고 싶어했다(we've been wanting to do some renovation work for the city government)라고 말하고 있으므로 화자는 공사를 하는 업종에서 일하고 있음을 알 수 있다. 따라서 정답은 (C)이다.

72

What good news does the speaker share about the company?
(A) It won a city contract.
(B) It will expand its headquarters.
(C) It has won an industry award.
(D) Its profits have increased.

화자는 회사에 대해 어떤 좋은 소식을 공유하는가?
(A) 시 계약을 따냈다.
(B) 본사를 확장할 것이다.
(C) 업계 상을 받았다.
(D) 이익이 증가했다.

어휘 expand 확장하다

해설 세부 사항 관련 – 화자가 회사에 대해 공유하는 좋은 소식
화자가 중반부에 입찰 과정이 치열했지만 우리 회사가 시청과 법원 개보수 공사 계약을 따냈다(The bidding process was competitive, but I was just told our firm has been awarded a large contract for work on city offices and courtrooms)면서 이것은 우리에게 대단한 성과(This is a big deal for us!)라고 말하는 것으로 보아 정답은 (A)이다.

> **Paraphrasing** 담화의 has been awarded → 정답의 won
> 담화의 contract for work on city offices and courtrooms → 정답의 city contract

73

What does the speaker say he will do later this week?
(A) Purchase new equipment
(B) Update some software
(C) Contact an advertising agency
(D) Post some job openings

화자는 이번 주 후반에 무엇을 할 것이라고 말하는가?
(A) 새 장비 구입하기
(B) 소프트웨어 업데이트하기
(C) 광고 대행사에 연락하기
(D) 구인 광고 게시하기

어휘 advertising agency 광고 대행사   job openings 구인, 채용 공고

해설 세부 사항 관련 – 화자가 이번 주 후반에 할 것이라고 말하는 일
화자가 마지막에 이번 주 후반에 회사 웹사이트에 채용 공고를 게시하겠다(I will be posting job listings on the company Web site later this week)고 말하고 있으므로 정답은 (D)이다.

> **Paraphrasing** 담화의 posting job listings
> → 정답의 Post some job openings

74-76 담화

> W-Br ⁷⁴**I hope you're all enjoying this year's Gamesfest event! Thanks for stopping by our booth for this product demo.** I'm really excited to share the updated version of our video game, *Lively Pilot*. ⁷⁵**Previous versions were available only on computers, but we redesigned** *Lively Pilot* **so that it's compatible with your smartphone.** Now you can play it anywhere you go! In fact, ⁷⁶**following this presentation, you can download the new version to your phones for a limited-**

> **time free trial. I'll give you an access code to get started.**

> 여러분 모두 올해 게임즈페스트 행사에서 즐거운 시간을 보내고 계시길 바랍니다! 제품 시연을 위해 저희 부스를 방문해 주셔서 감사합니다. 저희 비디오 게임인 〈라이블리 파일럿〉의 업데이트 버전을 함께 경험하게 되어 정말 기쁩니다. 이전 버전은 컴퓨터에서만 사용할 수 있었지만 〈라이블리 파일럿〉은 스마트폰과 호환되도록 다시 설계되었습니다. 이제 어디에서나 게임을 할 수 있습니다! 실제로 이 프레젠테이션 후에, 새 버전을 휴대폰에 다운로드하여 제한된 시간 동안 무료 체험판을 사용할 수 있습니다. 시작할 수 있도록 액세스 코드를 알려 드리겠습니다.

> 어휘 product demo 제품 시연   previous 이전의   compatible 호환이 되는   following ~ 후에   trial 체험판

74

Where does the talk most likely take place?
(A) At a press conference
(B) At a trade show
(C) At an award ceremony
(D) At a sports competition

담화는 어디에서 이루어지는 것 같은가?
(A) 기자 회견
(B) 무역 박람회
(C) 시상식
(D) 스포츠 경기

해설 전체 내용 관련 – 담화의 장소
화자가 도입부에 올해 게임즈페스트 행사에서 즐거운 시간을 보내고 있길 바란다(I hope you're all enjoying this year's Gamesfest event!)며 제품 시연을 위해 저희 부스를 방문해 주어 고맙다(Thanks for stopping by our booth for this product demo)고 말하는 것으로 보아, 화자는 박람회에서 말을 하고 있다는 것을 알 수 있다. 따라서 정답은 (B)이다.

75

What aspect of a product does the speaker mention?
(A) Its improved graphics
(B) Its fast download speeds
(C) Its high-quality audio
(D) Its smartphone compatibility

화자는 제품의 어떤 측면을 언급하는가?
(A) 향상된 그래픽
(B) 빠른 다운로드 속도
(C) 고품질 오디오
(D) 스마트폰 호환성

어휘 improve 향상하다   compatibility 호환성

해설 세부 사항 관련 – 화자가 제품에 대해 언급하는 것
화자가 중반부에 이전 버전은 컴퓨터에서만 사용했지만 〈라이블리 파일럿〉은 스마트폰과 호환된다(Previous versions ~ but we redesigned *Lively Pilot* so that it's compatible with your smartphone)고 말하고 있으므로 정답은 (D)이다.

어휘 forklift 지게차 operator (기계 등의) 운전자, 조작자 clerk 점원, 직원 warehouse 창고 measure 조치 mandatory 의무적인 attire 복장, 의복 nonslip 미끄러짐을 방지하는 promptly 신속히, 즉시 hectic 정신없이 바쁜

76

What does the speaker say the listeners can do after the talk?
(A) Start a free trial
(B) Speak to a representative
(C) Enjoy some refreshments
(D) Enter a contest

화자는 청자들이 담화 후에 무엇을 할 수 있다고 말하는가?
(A) 무료 체험판 시작하기
(B) 담당자와 통화하기
(C) 다과 즐기기
(D) 대회 참가하기

어휘 representative 직원 refreshment 다과

해설 세부 사항 관련 – 청자들이 담화 후에 할 수 있다고 화자가 말하는 것
화자가 후반부에 이 프레젠테이션 이후에, 새 버전을 휴대폰에 다운로드하여 제한된 시간 동안 무료 체험판을 사용할 수 있다(following this presentation, you can download the new version to your phones for a limited-time free trial)면서 시작할 수 있도록 액세스 코드를 알려 주겠다(I'll give you an access code to get started)고 말하고 있으므로 정답은 (A)이다.

77

Where is the meeting most likely taking place?
(A) At a farm
(B) At a cafeteria
(C) At a warehouse
(D) At a grocery store

회의는 어디에서 열리고 있는 것 같은가?
(A) 농장
(B) 구내식당
(C) 창고
(D) 식료품점

해설 전체 내용 관련 – 회의의 장소
화자가 도입부에 참석해 주어서 고맙다(Thank you for attending)고 했고 지게차 기사들과 배송 직원들이 바쁘므로 회의는 짧게 끝내겠다(I know that all the forklift operators and shipping clerks are quite busy, so I'll keep this meeting short)면서 창고 직원들은 작업하는 동안 반드시 안전 조치를 실천해야 한다(We need to ensure that warehouse employees practice safe measures while working)고 말하는 것으로 보아, 화자는 창고에서 열리는 회의에서 말하고 있다는 것을 알 수 있다. 따라서 정답은 (C)이다.

77-79 회의 발췌

M-Cn **⁷⁷Thank you for attending. I know that all the forklift operators and shipping clerks are quite busy, so I'll keep this meeting short. We need to ensure that warehouse employees practice safe measures while working. ⁷⁸Management would like me to remind you to always wear the mandatory attire while at work, including gloves and nonslip shoes. One other thing: ⁷⁹this week it has come to my attention that some of you are taking breaks that are longer than scheduled. Please be sure to return promptly from your 30-minute breaks, as it gets hectic around here.**

참석해 주셔서 감사합니다. 지게차 기사들과 배송 직원들이 모두 바쁘다는 것을 알고 있어서, 회의는 짧게 끝내겠습니다. 창고 직원들은 작업하는 동안 반드시 안전 조치를 실천해야 합니다. 장갑과 미끄럼 방지 신발을 포함하여 작업 중에 항상 필수 복장을 착용하도록 상기시켜 달라는 경영진의 요청이 있었습니다. 다른 한 가지가 또 있습니다. 이번 주에 여러분 중 일부가 정해진 시간보다 더 길게 휴식을 취하고 있다는 것을 알게 되었습니다. 정신없이 바빠지므로 30분간 휴식을 취한 후에는 반드시 신속히 복귀하시기 바랍니다.

78

What does the speaker say is required?
(A) Requesting vacation time in advance
(B) Updating employee contact information
(C) Wearing the appropriate clothing
(D) Completing some employee training

화자는 무엇이 필요하다고 말하는가?
(A) 사전에 휴가 신청하기
(B) 직원 연락처 정보 업데이트하기
(C) 적절한 의복 착용하기
(D) 직원 교육 완료하기

어휘 in advance 사전에, 미리 appropriate 적절한

해설 세부 사항 관련 – 화자가 필요하다고 말하는 것
화자가 중반부에 장갑과 미끄럼 방지 신발을 포함하여 작업 중에 항상 필수 복장을 착용하도록 상기시켜 달라는 경영진의 요청이 있었다(Management would like me to remind you to always wear the mandatory attire while at work, including gloves and nonslip shoes)고 말하는 것으로 보아 정답은 (C)이다.

79

What did the speaker find out about this week?
(A) Business has been slower than usual.
(B) Inventory has been running low.
(C) Employees have been missing meetings.
(D) Workers have been taking extended breaks.

화자는 이번 주에 무엇에 대해 알게 되었는가?
(A) 사업이 평소보다 더디다.
(B) 재고가 부족하다.
(C) 직원들이 회의에 빠지고 있다.
(D) 직원들이 휴식을 더 길게 취하고 있다.

어휘 inventory 재고   extended 연장된

해설 세부 사항 관련 – 화자가 이번 주에 알게 된 것

화자가 후반부에 이번 주에 여러분 중 일부가 정해진 시간보다 더 길게 휴식을 취한다는 것을 알게 되었다(this week it has come to my attention that some of you are taking breaks that are longer than scheduled)고 말하고 있으므로 정답은 (D)이다.

> Paraphrasing 담화의 breaks that are longer than
> scheduled → 정답의 extended breaks

80-82 방송

> W-Am And now for the local business news.
> **80Electronics manufacturer Chelan Systems has announced it will be opening a new manufacturing facility here in the region.** It will employ an estimated five thousand people. **81Company executives chose the area due to its proximity to the local technical school.** Chelan Systems will be partnering with the school to create internships and jobs for students and graduates. **82An information session where attendees can learn about available positions is scheduled to take place at the Front Street Hotel at the end of the month.**
>
> 그리고 이제 지역 비즈니스 뉴스입니다. **전자 제품 제조업체인 첼랜 시스템즈가 이 지역에 새로운 제조 시설을 열 것이라고 발표했습니다.** 약 5,000명을 고용할 예정입니다. **회사 임원들은 지역 기술 학교와 가깝다는 이유로 이곳을 선택했습니다.** 첼랜 시스템즈는 학교와 협력하여 재학생과 졸업생을 위한 인턴십과 일자리를 창출할 것입니다. **참석자들이 모집 중인 직책에 대해 알 수 있는 설명회가 이달 말 프런트 스트리트 호텔에서 열릴 예정입니다.**
>
> 어휘 manufacturer 제조업체 manufacturing facility 제조 시설, 공장 region 지방, 지역 estimated 약, 어림잡아 executive 임원 proximity 근접성 partner with ~와 협력[제휴]하다 graduate 졸업생 attendee 참석자

80

What type of business is coming to an area?
(A) A research facility
(B) A delivery service
(C) A computer repair company
(D) An electronics manufacturer

어떤 유형의 업체가 지역에 들어올 예정인가?
(A) 연구 시설
(B) 배송 서비스 업체
(C) 컴퓨터 수리 업체
(D) 전자 제품 제조업체

해설 세부 사항 관련 – 지역에 들어올 예정인 업체

화자가 초반부에 전자 제품 제조업체인 첼랜 시스템즈가 이 지역에 새로운 제조 시설을 열 것이라고 알리고 있다(Electronics manufacturer ~ has announced it will be opening a new manufacturing facility here in the region)고 알리고 있으므로 정답은 (D)이다.

81

Why was a specific location chosen?
(A) It is near public transportation.
(B) It is affordable.
(C) It is near an educational institution.
(D) It will attract a lot of customers.

특정 위치는 왜 선택되었는가?
(A) 대중교통이 가깝다.
(B) 저렴하다.
(C) 교육 기관이 가깝다.
(D) 많은 고객을 끌어들일 것이다.

어휘 affordable 저렴한   institution 기관   attract 끌어들이다

해설 세부 사항 관련 – 특정 위치가 선택된 이유

화자가 중반부에 회사 임원들은 지역 기술 학교와 가깝다는 이유로 이곳을 선택했다(Company executives chose the area due to its proximity to the local technical school)고 말하고 있으므로 정답은 (C)이다.

> Paraphrasing 담화의 proximity to the local technical
> school → 정답의 near an educational
> institution

82

How can the listeners find out more information?
(A) By attending an event
(B) By visiting a Web site
(C) By contacting a city official
(D) By subscribing to a newsletter

청자들은 어떻게 자세한 정보를 알 수 있는가?
(A) 행사에 참석해서
(B) 웹사이트에 방문해서
(C) 시 공무원에게 연락해서
(D) 소식지를 구독해서

어휘 subscribe 구독하다 newsletter 소식지

해설 세부 사항 관련 – 청자들이 자세한 정보를 알 수 있는 방법
화자가 마지막에 참석자들이 모집 중인 직책에 대해 알 수 있는 설명회가 이달 말 프런트 스트리트 호텔에서 열릴 예정(An information session where attendees can learn about available positions is scheduled to take place at the Front Street Hotel at the end of the month)이라고 하는 것으로 보아, 설명회에 참석하면 직책에 대한 정보를 얻을 수 있다는 것을 알 수 있다. 따라서 정답은 (A)이다.

> **Paraphrasing** 담화의 information session → 정답의 event

83-85 방송

> M-Au **83The cross-harbor tunnel building project is scheduled for completion today, and the tunnel will be open for travel this weekend.** The tunnel will link Springfield Island to the mainland. This will reduce reliance on the Springfield ferry, which has been the only means of transportation for island residents. **84This tunnel will also make it possible for more people to attend the yearly island musical festival. Good news for local tourism:** **85the fee for using the tunnel is fifteen dollars. Now that may seem like a steep price— but remember**, that's less than taking the ferry.
>
> 항구를 가로지르는 터널 건설 프로젝트가 오늘 완료될 것이며 터널은 이번 주말에 개통될 예정입니다. 터널은 스프링필드 섬과 육지를 연결할 것입니다. 이것은 섬 주민들의 유일한 교통수단이었던 스프링필드 페리에 대한 의존도를 덜어 줄 것입니다. 또한 이 터널 덕분에 매년 열리는 섬 음악 축제에 더 많은 사람들이 참석할 수 있을 것입니다. 지역 관광에 희소식입니다. 터널 사용료는 15달러입니다. 지금은 비싼 요금처럼 보일 수 있지만 기억하세요, 페리를 타는 것보다 저렴합니다.
>
> 어휘 harbor 항구 completion 완료 mainland 대륙 reliance 의존, 의지 ferry 페리, 여객선 means 수단 steep 터무니없이 비싼

83
What is the broadcast mainly about?
(A) The announcement of a sporting competition
(B) The completion of a construction project
(C) The closing of a local business
(D) The election of a city official

방송은 주로 무엇에 관한 것인가?
(A) 스포츠 경기의 발표
(B) 건설 프로젝트의 완료
(C) 지역 사업체의 폐업
(D) 시 공무원의 선출

어휘 competition 경기, 시합 closing 폐업 election 선출

해설 전체 내용 관련 – 방송의 주제
화자가 도입부에 항구를 가로지르는 터널 건설 프로젝트가 오늘 완료될 것이며 터널은 이번 주말에 개통될 예정(The cross-harbor tunnel building project is scheduled for completion today, and the tunnel will be open for travel this weekend)이라고 말하며 터널 건설과 관련된 이야기를 이어 가고 있으므로 정답은 (B)이다.

> **Paraphrasing** 담화의 cross-harbor tunnel building project → 정답의 construction project

84
According to the speaker, which industry will benefit from an event?
(A) Technology
(B) Manufacturing
(C) Fishing
(D) Tourism

화자에 따르면, 어떤 업종이 행사로부터 혜택을 받을 것인가?
(A) 기술업
(B) 제조업
(C) 어업
(D) 관광업

해설 세부 사항 관련 – 행사로부터 혜택을 받을 업종
화자가 중반부에 터널 덕분에 매년 열리는 섬 음악 축제에 더 많은 사람들이 참석할 것(This tunnel will also make it possible for more people to attend the yearly island musical festival)이라며 지역 관광에 희소식(Good news for local tourism)이라고 하는 것으로 보아 정답은 (D)이다.

85
Why does the speaker say, "that's less than taking the ferry"?
(A) To show surprise
(B) To stress a disadvantage
(C) To acknowledge a mistake
(D) To offer a counterargument

화자는 왜 "페리를 타는 것보다 저렴합니다"라고 말하는가?
(A) 놀람을 나타내기 위해
(B) 단점을 강조하기 위해
(C) 실수를 인정하기 위해
(D) 반론을 제시하기 위해

어휘 stress 강조하다 disadvantage 단점 acknowledge 인정하다 counterargument 반대론, 반론

해설 화자의 의도 파악 – 페리를 타는 것보다 저렴하다는 말의 의도
앞에서 터널 사용료는 15달러(the fee for using the tunnel is fifteen dollars)라며 지금은 비싼 요금처럼 보일 수 있지만 기억하라(Now that may seem like a steep price—but remember)고 말한 뒤 인용문을 언급한 것으로 보아, 요금이 비싸다고 생각하는 사람들에게 그렇지 않다는 것을 상기시키려는 의도로 한 말임을 알 수 있다. 따라서 정답은 (D)이다.

W-Br **86,87Starting next year, plastic shopping bags will no longer be used in grocery stores like ours, as a new regulation takes effect nationwide. 87We need to come up with a plan to phase them out.** Now, perhaps there's a business opportunity for us in this. There'll always be people who don't bring their own bags. We could put a modest price tag on reusable canvas tote bags of our own and display them near the checkout counter. If so, we could have our logo on them, which would get us free publicity as a side benefit. **88Who would like to reach out to our marketing department and ask them to come up with design ideas?**

내년부터 전국적으로 새로운 규정이 시행됨에 따라 우리와 같은 식료품 매장에서는 비닐 쇼핑백을 더 이상 사용하지 않을 것입니다. 단계적으로 중단하는 계획을 세워야 합니다. 자, 아마도 여기에 우리를 위한 사업 기회가 있을 것입니다. 가방을 가져오지 않는 사람들이 꼭 있을 것입니다. 재사용 가능한 캔버스 토트백에 저렴한 가격표를 붙여 계산대 근처에 진열하면 됩니다. 만약 그렇다면, 우리의 로고를 달 수 있고, 부수적인 이익으로 무료 홍보도 할 수 있을 것입니다. **누가 마케팅 부서에 연락해서 디자인 아이디어를 요청하겠습니까?**

어휘 regulation 규정, 규제 take effect 시행되다 nationwide 전국적으로 come up with ~을 생각해 내다 phase out 단계적으로 중단하다 modest 비싸지 않은 reusable 다시 사용할 수 있는 checkout counter 계산대 publicity 홍보 reach out 연락하다

86

What kind of business does the speaker work for?
(A) A publicity agency
(B) A plastic bag manufacturer
(C) An accounting firm
(D) A grocery store

화자는 어떤 업종에서 일하는가?
(A) 광고 대행사
(B) 비닐봉지 제조업체
(C) 회계 법인
(D) 식료품점

해설 전체 내용 관련 – 화자의 근무 업종
화자가 도입부에 내년부터 새로운 규정이 시행됨에 따라 우리와 같은 식료품 매장에서 비닐 쇼핑백을 사용하지 않을 것(Starting next year, plastic shopping bags will no longer be used in grocery stores like ours, as a new regulation takes effect nationwide)이라고 말하는 것으로 보아 식료품 매장에서 일을 하고 있음을 알 수 있다. 따라서 정답은 (D)이다.

87

What does the speaker mainly discuss?
(A) Upgrading the bookkeeping system
(B) Preparing for a new regulation
(C) Revising a company logo
(D) Increasing online advertising

화자는 주로 무엇에 대해 논의하는가?
(A) 부기 시스템 업그레이드하기
(B) 새로운 규정에 대해 준비하기
(C) 회사 로고 수정하기
(D) 온라인 광고 늘리기

어휘 bookkeeping 부기(수입과 지출을 장부에 정리하는 방법) revise 수정하다

해설 전체 내용 관련 – 담화의 주제
화자가 도입부에 내년부터 새로운 규정이 시행됨에 따라 우리와 같은 식료품 매장에서 비닐 쇼핑백을 사용하지 않을 것(Starting next year, ~ as a new regulation takes effect nationwide)이라고 말했고 단계적으로 중단하는 계획을 세워야 한다(We need to come up with a plan to phase them out)면서 구체적인 계획과 관련된 이야기를 이어 가고 있으므로 정답은 (B)이다.

88

What does the speaker expect one of the listeners to do?
(A) Contact another department
(B) Draft a timeline
(C) Find a new supplier
(D) Design a showroom layout

화자는 청자 중 한 명이 무엇을 해 주기를 기대하는가?
(A) 다른 부서에 연락하기
(B) 일정 초안 작성하기
(C) 새로운 공급업체 찾기
(D) 전시실 배치 디자인하기

어휘 timeline 일정표, 시간표 supplier 공급자 layout 배치

해설 세부 사항 관련 – 화자가 청자 중 한 명이 해 주기를 기대하는 것
화자가 마지막에 누가 마케팅 부서에 연락해서 디자인 아이디어를 요청하겠는지(Who would like to reach out to our marketing department and ask them to come up with design ideas?) 묻고 있으므로 정답은 (A)이다.

Paraphrasing 담화의 reach out to our marketing department → 정답의 Contact another department

89-91 전화 메시지

W-Am Hi, Luis. This is Claudia from Barton Services. **89As requested, I've created a spreadsheet to help you track the monthly expenses at your catering**

company and make sure you're staying within your budget. ⁹⁰I just need you to do one thing— if you can scan all of the receipts of your company's expenditures moving forward, I'll be able to include links to those receipts right in the spreadsheet. Oh, and before I forget, ⁹¹**you mentioned recently that you don't know much about cash flow forecasting and wanted to know the best way to learn more.** Well, we're offering a workshop on that topic next month. All the information is on our Web site.

안녕하세요, 루이스. 저는 바톤 서비스의 클라우디아입니다. 요청에 따라 귀하의 케이터링 회사에서 지출하는 월별 비용을 추적하고 예산 범위 내에서 지출하도록 도와줄 스프레드시트를 만들었습니다. 한 가지만 해 주시면 됩니다. 앞으로 회사 지출 영수증을 모두 스캔해 주시면 제가 해당 영수증에 대한 링크를 스프레드시트에 바로 포함시킬 수 있습니다. 아, 잊기 전에 최근에 현금 흐름의 예측에 대해 잘 모르셔서 더 많은 정보를 얻을 수 있는 최선의 방법을 알고 싶다고 하셨습니다. 음, 우리는 다음 달에 그 주제에 관한 워크숍을 제공할 예정입니다. 모든 정보는 우리 웹사이트에 있습니다.

어휘 track 추적하다 expense 비용 expenditure 지출, 비용 moving forward 앞으로 forecast 예측하다

89

Who most likely is the speaker?
(A) A journalist
(B) An accountant
(C) A restaurant owner
(D) A customer service representative

화자는 누구인 것 같은가?
(A) 기자
(B) 회계사
(C) 식당 주인
(D) 고객 서비스 담당자

해설 전체 내용 관련 – 화자의 직업
화자가 초반부에 요청에 따라 귀하의 케이터링 회사에서 지출하는 월별 비용을 추적하고 예산 범위 내에서 지출하도록 도와줄 스프레드시트를 만들었다(As requested, I've created a spreadsheet to help you track the monthly expenses ~ you're staying within your budget)고 말하는 것으로 보아 정답은 (B)이다.

90

What does the speaker say she needs the listener to do?
(A) Contact some clients
(B) Check an inventory list
(C) Create a marketing campaign
(D) Scan some information

화자는 청자가 무엇을 해야 한다고 말하는가?
(A) 고객에게 연락하기
(B) 재고 목록 확인하기
(C) 마케팅 캠페인 만들기
(D) 정보 스캔하기

어휘 inventory 재고

해설 세부 사항 관련 – 청자가 해야 한다고 화자가 말하는 것
화자가 중반부에 한 가지만 해 주면 된다(I just need you to do one thing)면서 앞으로 회사 지출 영수증을 스캔해 주면 해당 영수증에 대한 링크를 스프레드시트에 바로 포함시킬 수 있다(if you can scan ~ in the spreadsheet)고 말하고 있으므로 정답은 (D)이다.

Paraphrasing	담화의 all of the receipts → 정답의 some information

91

Why does the speaker say, "we're offering a workshop on that topic next month"?
(A) To reject an invitation
(B) To explain a delay
(C) To make a recommendation
(D) To ask for help

화자는 왜 "우리는 다음 달에 그 주제에 관한 워크숍을 제공할 예정입니다"라고 말하는가?
(A) 초대를 거절하려고
(B) 지연을 설명하려고
(C) 추천을 하려고
(D) 도움을 요청하려고

어휘 reject 거절하다

해설 화자의 의도 파악 – 우리는 다음 달에 그 주제에 관한 워크숍을 제공할 예정이라는 말의 의도
앞에서 최근에 현금 흐름의 예측에 대해 잘 알지 못하며 더 많은 정보를 얻을 수 있는 최선의 방법을 알고 싶어 한다(you mentioned recently that you don't know much about cash flow forecasting and wanted to know the best way to learn more)고 상기시키며 인용문을 언급한 것으로 보아, 청자가 원하는 정보를 얻을 수 있는 방법을 알려주려고 한 말임을 알 수 있다. 따라서 정답은 (C)이다.

92-94 회의 발췌

M-Cn ⁹²**We're in the process of ordering supplies we'll need for the next fiscal year.** ⁹²,⁹³**Some of our members have complained about poor ventilation by the treadmills, so we'll be getting additional fans.** ⁹²**We should also replace our old exercise mats and balance balls.** ⁹⁴**We need to place that order soon.** Tunji, I think you have a free hour tomorrow morning. Once that order is placed, all of our new supplies will be on their way!

다음 회계 연도에 필요한 물품 주문을 준비하는 중입니다. 러닝머신 주변에 환기가 잘 안된다고 회원들 몇 분이 불만을 토로해 환풍기를 추가로 확보할 예정입니다. 오래된 운동 매트와 밸런스 볼도 교체해야 합니다. 빨리 주문해야 합니다. 툰지, 내일 아침에 여유가 있는 것 같던데요. 주문이 완료되면 새 물품들의 배송이 바로 시작될 것입니다!

어휘 fiscal year 회계 연도 ventilation 환기 (장치) treadmill 트레드밀, 러닝머신 fan 환풍기 on one's way 오는[가는] 중인

92

What is the speaker discussing?
(A) Updating a database
(B) Hiring more staff
(C) Revising safety guidelines
(D) Purchasing supplies

화자는 무엇에 대해 논의하고 있는가?
(A) 데이터베이스 업데이트
(B) 직원 충원
(C) 안전 지침 개정
(D) 물품 구입

어휘 revise 변경하다

해설 전체 내용 관련 – 담화의 주제
화자가 도입부에 다음 회계 연도에 필요한 물품 주문을 준비하는 중(We're in the process of ordering supplies we'll need for the next fiscal year)이라면서 러닝머신 주변에 환기가 잘 안된다고 회원들이 불만을 토로해 환풍기를 추가로 확보할 예정(Some of our members ~ additional fans)이고 오래된 운동 매트와 밸런스 볼도 교체해야 한다(We should also replace ~ balance balls)고 말하고 있으므로 정답은 (D)이다.

93

Where does the speaker most likely work?
(A) At a warehouse
(B) At a fitness center
(C) At a home-improvement store
(D) At a cleaning service

화자는 어디에서 일하는 것 같은가?
(A) 창고
(B) 피트니스 센터
(C) 철물점
(D) 청소 서비스업체

해설 전체 내용 관련 – 화자의 근무지
화자가 초반부에 러닝머신 주변에 환기가 잘 안된다고 회원들이 불만을 토로해 환풍기를 추가로 확보할 예정(Some of our members ~ additional fans)이라며 오래된 운동 매트와 밸런스 볼도 교체해야 한다(We should also replace our old exercise mats and balance balls)고 말하는 것으로 보아 정답은 (B)이다.

94

What does the speaker mean when he says, "Tunji, I think you have a free hour tomorrow morning"?
(A) Tunji should complete the task.
(B) Tunji can attend the client meeting.
(C) Tunji's schedule needs to be corrected.
(D) Tunji can leave work early.

화자가 "툰지, 내일 아침에 여유가 있는 것 같던데요"라고 말할 때 무엇을 의미하는가?
(A) 툰지가 업무를 완료해야 한다.
(B) 툰지가 고객 회의에 참석할 수 있다.
(C) 툰지의 일정을 수정해야 한다.
(D) 툰지가 일찍 퇴근할 수 있다.

해설 화자의 의도 파악 – 내일 아침에 여유가 있는 것 같다는 말의 의도
앞에서 화자가 빨리 주문해야 한다(We need to place that order soon)고 말한 뒤 인용문을 언급하고 있으므로, 툰지에게 주문 업무를 시키려는 의도임을 알 수 있다. 따라서 정답은 (A)이다.

95-97 전화 메시지 + 주문 양식

W-Am Hello. 95I'm calling from Baxter's Car Repair. We rented some toy-vending machines from your company, and I'm pleased to say, they've been a big success! Some have completely sold out! 96Today I'm calling to order a box of toy cars. We'd like to get the mixed colors this time, instead of all red cars. I'm sure I'll be calling again soon to order key chains—we have plenty now, but they're also very popular. Finally, do you supply other types of vending machines? 97We're thinking of installing a cold-drink machine next to the toy machines.

안녕하세요. 백스터의 자동차 정비소에서 전화드렸습니다. 귀사에서 장난감 자판기를 대여했는데 큰 성공을 거두고 있다는 기쁜 소식을 전합니다! 어떤 제품은 완전히 매진되었습니다! 오늘은 장난감 자동차 한 상자를 주문하기 위해 전화했습니다. 이번에는 빨간색 자동차 대신 혼합 색상을 사고 싶습니다. 열쇠고리의 주문을 위해 곧 다시 전화를 할 것입니다. 지금은 많이 있지만 열쇠고리도 매우 인기가 높습니다. 마지막으로, 다른 종류의 자판기도 공급하십니까? 장난감 자판기 옆에 냉음료 자판기를 설치할까 생각하고 있습니다.

어휘 vending machine 자판기 supply 공급하다

Item Name	Color	Price per Box
Toy cars	Red	$15
Toy cars	Mixed colors	96$17
Plastic jewelry	Mixed colors	$18
Key chains	Blue	$14

품목명	색상	상자당 가격
장난감 자동차	빨간색	15달러
장난감 자동차	**혼합 색상**	**96 17달러**
플라스틱 장신구	혼합 색상	18달러
열쇠고리	파란색	14달러

95

Where does the speaker work?

(A) At a community center
(B) At a car repair shop
(C) At a supermarket
(D) At a department store

화자는 어디에서 근무하는가?

(A) 커뮤니티 센터
(B) 자동차 정비소
(C) 슈퍼마켓
(D) 백화점

해설 전체 내용 관련 – 화자의 근무지

화자가 초반부에 백스터의 자동차 정비소에서 전화했다(I'm calling from Baxter's Car Repair)고 밝히고 있으므로 정답은 (B)이다.

96

Look at the graphic. How much will the speaker pay for today's order?

(A) $15
(B) $17
(C) $18
(D) $14

시각 정보에 의하면, 화자는 오늘 주문에 대해 얼마를 지불할 것인가?

(A) 15달러
(B) 17달러
(C) 18달러
(D) 14달러

해설 시각 정보 연계 – 화자가 주문에 대해 지불할 금액

화자가 중반부에 장난감 자동차 한 상자를 주문하겠다(Today I'm calling to order a box of toy cars)며 빨간색 자동차 대신 혼합 색상을 사고 싶다(We'd like to get the mixed colors this time, instead of all red cars)고 말하고 있고, 주문 양식에 따르면 혼합 색상의 장난감 자동차는 17달러이므로 정답은 (B)이다.

97

What does the speaker want to install?

(A) A beverage vending machine
(B) An air-conditioning unit
(C) Some security cameras
(D) Some carpeting

화자는 무엇을 설치하길 원하는가?

(A) 음료 자판기
(B) 에어컨
(C) 보안 카메라
(D) 카펫

해설 세부 사항 관련 – 화자가 설치하고 싶어 하는 것

화자가 마지막에 장난감 자판기 옆에 냉음료 자판기를 설치할까 생각하고 있다(We're thinking of installing a cold-drink machine next to the toy machines)고 말하고 있으므로 정답은 (A)이다.

> **Paraphrasing** 담화의 cold-drink machine
> → 정답의 beverage vending machine

98-100 회의 발췌 + 이메일의 받은 메일함

M-Au First, I'd like to remind everyone about our company's new health initiative. **98I sent out an e-mail this morning with detailed information about the fitness program and instructions for setting your fitness goals.** If you haven't seen the e-mail yet, please check your inbox after this meeting. **99This year, employees will be rewarded for meeting their goals. Employees who achieve three or more of their personal goals will get two extra days off work this year, with pay.** Now, **100let's go over a few examples of goals that you can set for yourself in your employee portal.**

먼저, 우리 회사의 새로운 건강 계획 프로젝트에 대해 모두에게 다시 한 번 알리고자 합니다. **오늘 아침에 피트니스 프로그램에 대한 자세한 정보와 피트니스 목표 설정 지침이 포함된 이메일을 보냈습니다.** 아직 이메일을 보지 못했다면 회의가 끝난 후 받은 메일함을 확인하십시오. 올해에는 목표를 달성한 직원들은 포상을 받게 될 것입니다. 개인 목표 중 3개 이상을 달성한 직원들은 올해 추가적으로 이틀의 유급 휴가를 받게 됩니다. 이제 **직원 포털에서 스스로 설정할 수 있는 목표의 몇 가지 예를 살펴보겠습니다.**

어휘 initiative 계획 instruction 설명, 지시 inbox 받은 메일함 reward 보상하다 go over ~을 살펴보다

Inbox

✉	**Takanori Kimura** Discuss new account	11:45
✉	**Ozan Demir** Retirement lunch	11:21
✉	**Robert Wilson** Sales tips	10:09
✉	**98Ivan Stepanov** Create your fitness plan	9:52

받은 메일함

	타카노리 키무라 새 계정 논의하기	11:45
	오잔 데미르 퇴직 기념 오찬	11:21
	로버트 윌슨 영업 팀	10:09
	98 이반 스테파노프 피트니스 계획 만들기	9:52

Paraphrasing 담화의 days off work this year, with pay
→ 정답의 paid time off

98

Look at the graphic. Who is the speaker?
(A) Takanori Kimura
(B) Ozan Demir
(C) Robert Wilson
(D) Ivan Stepanov

시각 정보에 의하면, 화자는 누구인가?
(A) 타카노리 키무라
(B) 오잔 데미르
(C) 로버트 윌슨
(D) **이반 스테파노프**

해설 시각 정보 연계 – 화자의 이름

화자가 초반부에 오늘 아침에 피트니스 프로그램에 대한 자세한 정보와 피트니스 목표 설정 지침이 포함된 이메일을 보냈다(I sent out an e-mail this morning with detailed information about the fitness program and instructions for setting your fitness goals)고 말하고 있고, 받은 메일함에 따르면 피트니스 관련 메일은 이반 스테파노프가 보낸 것이므로 정답은 (D)이다.

99

How is the company trying to increase participation in a program?
(A) By offering free snacks
(B) By providing paid time off
(C) By awarding a salary increase
(D) By giving away a free trip

회사는 프로그램 참여도를 높이기 위해 어떻게 노력하고 있는가?
(A) 무료 간식을 제공해서
(B) **유급 휴가를 제공해서**
(C) 급여 인상을 지급해서
(D) 무료 여행을 제공해서

어휘 paid time off 유급 휴가 award 수여하다

해설 세부 사항 관련 – 회사가 참여도를 높이기 위해 하는 노력

화자가 중반부에 목표를 달성한 직원들은 포상을 받게 될 것(This year, employees will be rewarded for meeting their goals)이라면서 목표 중 3개 이상을 달성한 직원은 추가적으로 이틀의 유급 휴가를 받게 된다(Employees who achieve three or more of their personal goals will get two extra days off work this year, with pay)고 알리고 있으므로 정답은 (B)이다.

100

What will the speaker do next?
(A) Introduce some committee members
(B) Review some sales figures
(C) Pass out tickets to an upcoming event
(D) Give examples of employee goals

화자는 다음에 무엇을 할 것인가?
(A) 위원 소개하기
(B) 판매 수치 검토하기
(C) 예정된 행사 티켓 나눠 주기
(D) **직원 목표의 예시 제공하기**

어휘 committee 위원회 sales figure 판매 수치 pass out 나눠 주다

해설 세부 사항 관련 – 화자가 다음에 할 일

화자가 마지막에 직원 포털에서 스스로 설정할 수 있는 목표의 몇 가지 예를 살펴보겠다(let's go over a few examples of goals that you can set for yourself in your employee portal)고 말하고 있으므로 정답은 (D)이다.

Paraphrasing 담화의 go over a few examples of goals that you can set
→ 정답의 Give examples of employee goals

실전 TEST 8

1 (A)	**2** (D)	**3** (D)	**4** (C)	**5** (B)
6 (B)	**7** (C)	**8** (C)	**9** (B)	**10** (A)
11 (B)	**12** (C)	**13** (C)	**14** (A)	**15** (A)
16 (A)	**17** (C)	**18** (B)	**19** (B)	**20** (B)
21 (A)	**22** (A)	**23** (C)	**24** (C)	**25** (B)
26 (A)	**27** (C)	**28** (B)	**29** (C)	**30** (B)
31 (C)	**32** (D)	**33** (B)	**34** (C)	**35** (D)
36 (A)	**37** (B)	**38** (D)	**39** (B)	**40** (C)
41 (B)	**42** (C)	**43** (A)	**44** (A)	**45** (D)
46 (C)	**47** (B)	**48** (D)	**49** (C)	**50** (B)
51 (A)	**52** (C)	**53** (B)	**54** (D)	**55** (C)
56 (D)	**57** (C)	**58** (C)	**59** (B)	**60** (A)
61 (D)	**62** (C)	**63** (A)	**64** (B)	**65** (B)
66 (D)	**67** (A)	**68** (C)	**69** (A)	**70** (D)
71 (B)	**72** (A)	**73** (B)	**74** (D)	**75** (A)
76 (C)	**77** (A)	**78** (D)	**79** (B)	**80** (A)
81 (D)	**82** (D)	**83** (B)	**84** (C)	**85** (B)
86 (A)	**87** (A)	**88** (B)	**89** (D)	**90** (C)
91 (A)	**92** (D)	**93** (C)	**94** (C)	**95** (C)
96 (B)	**97** (B)	**98** (D)	**99** (C)	**100** (A)

PART 1

1 W-Br

(A) She's writing on a document.
(B) She's looking at some framed artwork.
(C) She's opening a folder.
(D) She's organizing a desk drawer.

(A) 여자가 문서에 글을 쓰고 있다.
(B) 여자가 액자에 넣은 작품을 보고 있다.
(C) 여자가 서류철을 열고 있다.
(D) 여자가 책상 서랍을 정리하고 있다.

어휘 framed 액자에 넣은 organize 정리하다 drawer 서랍

해설 1인 등장 사진 – 사람의 동작/상태 묘사
(A) 정답. 여자가 문서에 글을 쓰고 있는(is writing on a document) 모습이므로 정답.
(B) 동사 오답. 여자가 액자에 넣은 작품을 보고 있는(is looking at some framed artwork) 모습이 아니므로 오답.
(C) 동사 오답. 여자가 서류철을 열고 있는(is opening a folder) 모습이 아니므로 오답.
(D) 동사 오답. 여자가 책상 서랍을 정리하고 있는(is organizing a desk drawer) 모습이 아니므로 오답.

2 M-Cn

(A) He's driving a van.
(B) He's cutting some shrubs.
(C) He's moving some garden stones.
(D) He's operating a machine.

(A) 남자가 승합차를 운전하고 있다.
(B) 남자가 관목을 자르고 있다.
(C) 남자가 정원석을 옮기고 있다.
(D) 남자가 기계를 작동하고 있다.

어휘 van 승합차, 밴 shrub 관목, 키 작은 나무 operate 작동[조작]하다

해설 1인 등장 사진 – 사람의 동작/상태 묘사
(A) 사진에 없는 명사를 이용한 오답. 사진에 승합차(a van)의 모습이 보이지 않으므로 오답.
(B) 동사 오답. 남자가 관목을 자르고 있는(is cutting some shrubs) 모습이 아니므로 오답.
(C) 동사 오답. 남자가 정원석을 옮기고 있는(is moving some garden stones) 모습이 아니므로 오답.
(D) 정답. 남자가 기계를 작동하고 있는(is operating a machine) 모습이므로 정답.

3 W-Am

(A) They're swimming in the water.
(B) They're catching fish from a lake.
(C) They're waiting at a boat dock.
(D) They're paddling a canoe.

(A) 사람들이 물에서 수영하고 있다.
(B) 사람들이 호수에서 낚시를 하고 있다.
(C) 사람들이 보트 선착장에서 기다리고 있다.
(D) 사람들이 카누의 노를 젓고 있다.

어휘 dock 선착장, 부두 paddle 노를 젓다

해설 2인 이상 등장 사진 – 사람의 동작/상태 묘사
(A) 동사 오답. 사람들이 물에서 수영하고 있는(are swimming in the water) 모습이 아니므로 오답.
(B) 동사 오답. 사람들이 호수에서 낚시를 하고 있는(are catching fish from a lake) 모습이 아니므로 오답.
(C) 사진에 없는 명사를 이용한 오답. 사진에 보트 선착장(a boat dock)의 모습이 보이지 않으므로 오답.
(D) 정답. 사람들이 카누의 노를 젓고 있는(are paddling a canoe) 모습이므로 정답.

4 M-Cn

(A) A walkway is being swept clean.
(B) Some people are walking through an intersection.
(C) One of the people is leaning against a wall.
(D) One of the people is fixing a bicycle tire.

(A) 보도가 깨끗하게 청소되고 있다.
(B) 사람들이 교차로를 걷고 있다.
(C) 사람들 중 한 명이 벽에 기대어 있다.
(D) 사람들 중 한 명이 자전거 타이어를 고치고 있다.

어휘 walkway 보도, 통로 sweep (빗자루로) 쓸다, 청소하다
      intersection 교차로 lean 기대다

해설 혼합 사진 – 사람/사물/풍경 혼합 묘사
(A) 동사 오답. 보도(A walkway)가 청소되고 있는(is being swept clean) 모습이 아니므로 오답.
(B) 사진에 없는 명사를 이용한 오답. 사진에 교차로(an intersection)의 모습이 보이지 않으므로 오답.
(C) 정답. 사람들 중 한 명이 벽에 기대어 있는(is leaning against a wall) 모습이므로 정답.
(D) 동사 오답. 자전거 타이어를 고치고 있는(is fixing a bicycle tire) 사람의 모습이 보이지 않으므로 오답.

5 M-Au

(A) A customer is loading items into a shopping bag.
(B) Some products have been set out under tents.
(C) A bowl has been filled with water.
(D) Some baskets are hanging from a post.

(A) 고객이 쇼핑백에 물건을 넣고 있다.
(B) 물건들이 텐트 아래에 진열되어 있다.
(C) 그릇 하나가 물로 채워져 있다.
(D) 바구니들이 기둥에 매달려 있다.

어휘 load 넣다, 싣다 set out 진열하다 bowl 그릇 post 기둥

해설 혼합 사진 – 사람/사물/풍경 혼합 묘사
(A) 동사 오답. 고객(A customer)이 쇼핑백에 물건을 넣고 있는(is loading items into a shopping bag) 모습이 아니므로 오답.
(B) 정답. 물건들(Some products)이 텐트 아래에 진열되어 있는(have been set out under tents) 모습이므로 정답.
(C) 사진에 없는 명사를 이용한 오답. 사진에 물로 채워져 있는(has been filled with water) 그릇(A bowl)의 모습이 보이지 않으므로 오답.

(D) 동사 오답. 바구니들(Some baskets)이 기둥에 매달려 있는(are hanging from a post) 모습이 아니므로 오답.

6 W-Br

(A) There's a campfire underneath some shade trees.
(B) Some trees are providing shade for a picnic area.
(C) A flower bed has been planted near a park bench.
(D) Fallen branches are stacked next to a brick pathway.

(A) 나무 그늘 아래에 모닥불이 있다.
(B) 나무들이 피크닉장에 그늘을 드리우고 있다.
(C) 화단이 공원 벤치 근처에 조성되어 있다.
(D) 떨어진 나뭇가지들이 벽돌 길 옆에 쌓여 있다.

어휘 campfire 모닥불 underneath ~의 밑에 shade 그늘 picnic area 피크닉장 flower bed 화단 stack 쌓다 brick 벽돌 pathway 길, 통로

해설 사물/풍경 사진 – 풍경 묘사
(A) 사진에 없는 명사를 이용한 오답. 사진에 모닥불(a campfire)의 모습이 보이지 않으므로 오답.
(B) 정답. 나무들(Some trees)이 피크닉장에 그늘을 드리우고 있는(are providing shade for a picnic area) 모습이므로 정답.
(C) 사진에 없는 명사를 이용한 오답. 사진에 화단(A flower bed)의 모습이 보이지 않으므로 오답.
(D) 사진에 없는 명사를 이용한 오답. 사진에 떨어진 나뭇가지들(fallen branches)의 모습이 보이지 않으므로 오답.

PART 2

7

M-Cn When does your bus leave?

M-Au (A) The station is on Liberty Avenue.
      (B) A seat in the back.
      (C) At eight o'clock.

당신이 탑승할 버스는 언제 출발하나요?
(A) 역은 리버티 가에 있어요.
(B) 뒷좌석이요.
(C) 8시에요.

해설 버스가 출발하는 시점을 묻는 When 의문문
(A) 연상 단어 오답. 질문의 bus에서 연상 가능한 station을 이용한 오답.
(B) 연상 단어 오답. 질문의 bus에서 연상 가능한 seat를 이용한 오답.
(C) 정답. 탑승할 버스가 출발하는 시점을 묻는 질문에 8시라고 알려 주고 있으므로 정답.

8

M-Cn Who made the cake for the party?

W-Br (A) Just a cup of apple juice.
(B) I already ate.
(C) The baker on Second Street.

누가 파티를 위해 케이크를 만들었나요?
(A) 사과 주스 한 잔만요.
(B) 이미 먹었어요.
(C) 2번가에 있는 제과점입니다.

어휘 baker 제과점, 제빵사

해설 케이크를 만든 사람을 묻는 Who 의문문
(A) 연상 단어 오답. 질문의 cake와 party에서 연상 가능한 apple과 juice를 이용한 오답.
(B) 연상 단어 오답. 질문의 cake에서 연상 가능한 ate를 이용한 오답.
(C) 정답. 케이크를 만든 사람이 누구인지 묻는 질문에 2번가에 있는 제과점이라고 알려 주고 있으므로 정답.

9

W-Am Why are you taking French classes?

M-Cn (A) Do you have a reservation?
(B) Because I'm transferring to the Paris office.
(C) Two days a week.

왜 프랑스어 수업을 듣고 있어요?
(A) 예약을 하셨나요?
(B) 파리 사무실로 전근 갈 예정이라서요.
(C) 일주일에 이틀이요.

어휘 transfer 전근 가다, 옮기다

해설 프랑스어 수업을 수강하는 이유를 묻는 Why 의문문
(A) 단어 반복 오답. 질문의 you를 반복 이용한 오답.
(B) 정답. 프랑스어 수업을 왜 듣고 있는지 묻는 질문에 파리 사무실로 전근을 갈 예정이기 때문이라며 이유를 알려 주고 있으므로 정답.
(C) 연상 단어 오답. 질문의 classes에서 연상 가능한 수강 빈도 표현인 Two days a week를 이용한 오답.

10

W-Br What material is this shirt made of?

M-Cn **(A) It's a light cotton fabric.**
(B) No, I don't need any more supplies.
(C) In small, medium, and large sizes.

이 셔츠는 어떤 재질로 만들었나요?
(A) 가벼운 면직물이요.
(B) 아니요, 더 이상 물품이 필요하지 않아요.
(C) 소형, 중형, 대형 사이즈로 있어요.

어휘 material 재료 fabric 직물, 천 supplies 물품, 공급품

해설 셔츠의 재질을 묻는 What 의문문
(A) 정답. 셔츠의 재질이 무엇인지 묻는 질문에 가벼운 면직물이라고 응답하고 있으므로 정답.
(B) Yes/No 불가 오답. What 의문문에는 Yes/No 응답이 불가능하므로 오답.

11

W-Am How much will the jazz concert cost?

W-Br (A) Leaving from platform six.
(B) The ticket's 50 dollars.
(C) A seat on the aisle, please.

재즈 콘서트는 얼마일까요?
(A) 6번 플랫폼에서 출발하는 것이요.
(B) 표는 50달러입니다.
(C) 통로에 있는 좌석으로 부탁해요.

어휘 aisle 통로

해설 콘서트 비용을 묻는 How much 의문문
(A) 연상 단어 오답. 질문의 How much에서 연상 가능한 six를 이용한 오답.
(B) 정답. 재즈 콘서트가 얼마일지 묻는 질문에 표는 50달러라고 가격을 알려 주고 있으므로 정답.
(C) 연상 단어 오답. 질문의 concert에서 연상 가능한 seat를 이용한 오답.

12

W-Br Where's the robotics conference going to be held?

M-Au (A) I'll print your first chapter.
(B) At the end of June.
(C) It's in Boston.

로봇 공학 학회는 어디에서 열릴 예정인가요?
(A) 첫 번째 챕터를 인쇄할게요.
(B) 6월 말에요.
(C) 보스턴에서요.

어휘 robotics 로봇 공학 conference 회의, 학회 be held 열리다

해설 학회의 개최 장소를 묻는 Where 의문문
(A) 연상 단어 오답. 질문의 conference에서 연상 가능한 chapter를 이용한 오답.
(B) 질문과 상관없는 오답. When 의문문에 대한 응답이므로 오답.
(C) 정답. 로봇 공학 학회의 개최 장소를 묻는 질문에 보스턴이라는 구체적인 장소를 알려 주고 있으므로 정답.

13

W-Am Would you like me to turn on the air conditioner?

M-Cn (A) I bought shampoo and conditioner.
(B) He did an excellent job!
(C) No—let's open the windows.

TEST 8

에어컨 켜 드릴까요?

(A) 삼푸와 컨디셔너를 샀어요.

(B) 그가 일을 아주 잘했어요!

(C) 아니요–창문을 엽시다.

해설 제안/권유의 의문문

(A) 단어 반복 오답. 질문의 conditioner를 반복 이용한 오답.

(B) 질문과 상관없는 오답.

(C) 정답. 에어컨을 켜 줄지 제안하는 질문에 아니요(No)라고 거절한 뒤, 창문을 열자고 대안을 제시하며 부정 답변과 일관된 내용을 덧붙였으므로 정답.

14

W-Br　When do you need a copy of the contract?

M-Au　(A) As soon as possible.

(B) A savings account at the bank.

(C) Sure—here's my contact information.

계약서 사본은 언제 필요하세요?

(A) 가능한 한 빨리요.

(B) 은행의 예금 계좌요.

(C) 물론이죠. 여기 제 연락처가 있어요.

어휘 contract 계약서　savings account 보통 예금 (계좌)

해설 계약서 사본이 필요한 시점을 묻는 When 의문문

(A) 정답. 계약서 사본이 필요한 시점을 묻는 질문에 가능한 한 빨리라고 응답하고 있으므로 정답.

(B) 질문과 상관없는 오답.

(C) Yes/No 불가 응답. When 의문문에는 Yes/No 응답이 불가능한데, Sure도 일종의 Yes 응답이라고 볼 수 있으므로 오답.

15

M-Cn　I definitely think we should reschedule the picnic.

W-Am　(A) Is it supposed to rain?

(B) A company celebration.

(C) Some salad with a light dressing.

피크닉 일정을 꼭 다시 잡아야 할 것 같아요.

(A) 비가 오기로 되어 있나요?

(B) 회사 축하 행사입니다.

(C) 가벼운 드레싱을 곁들인 샐러드입니다.

어휘 be supposed to ~하기로 되어 있다　celebration 축하 행사

해설 제안/요청의 평서문

(A) 정답. 피크닉 일정을 다시 잡을 것을 제안하는 평서문에 비가 오기로 되어 있는지 물으며 일정을 다시 잡자는 제안에 대한 이유를 확인하고 있으므로 정답.

(B) 연상 단어 오답. 평서문의 reschedule에서 연상 가능한 celebration을 이용한 오답.

(C) 연상 단어 오답. 평서문의 picnic에서 연상 가능한 salad를 이용한 오답.

16

W-Am　How often is this filing cabinet organized?

W-Br　(A) About once every quarter.

(B) Yes, this is the right size.

(C) A fifteen-minute meeting.

파일 캐비닛을 얼마나 자주 정리하나요?

(A) 1분기마다 한 번 정도요.

(B) 네, 이게 맞는 사이즈예요.

(C) 15분 걸리는 회의입니다.

어휘 organize 정리하다, 준비하다　quarter 분기, 4분의 1

해설 캐비닛의 정리 빈도를 묻는 How often 의문문

(A) 정답. 파일 캐비닛을 얼마나 자주 정리하는지 묻는 질문에 1분기마다 한 번이라고 구체적인 빈도를 제시하고 있으므로 정답.

(B) Yes/No 불가 오답. How often 의문문에는 Yes/No 응답이 불가능하므로 오답.

(C) 연상 단어 오답. 질문의 organized를 '준비하다'로 해석했을 때 연상 가능한 meeting을 이용한 오답.

17

M-Au　Is Ms. Lee planning to run for mayor in the election?

W-Am　(A) I go there often, actually.

(B) An electronic reading device.

(C) Yes, she made the official announcement.

이 씨는 시장 선거에 출마할 계획인가요?

(A) 사실 거기 자주 갑니다.

(B) 전자 독서 장비입니다.

(C) 네, 공식적으로 발표를 했습니다.

어휘 run for ~에 입후보하다　mayor 시장　election 선거　electronic 전자의　device 장비, 기구　official 공식적인

해설 이 씨가 시장 선거에 출마할지 여부를 묻는 Be동사 의문문

(A) 연상 단어 오답. 질문의 run에서 연상 가능한 go를 이용한 오답.

(B) 유사 발음 오답. 질문의 election과 부분적으로 발음이 유사한 electronic을 이용한 오답.

(C) 정답. 이 씨가 시장 선거에 출마할 계획인지 묻는 질문에 네(Yes)라고 대답한 뒤, 공식적으로 발표를 했다며 긍정 답변과 일관된 내용을 덧붙이고 있으므로 정답.

18

W-Br　Are you looking for a one-bedroom or a two-bedroom apartment?

M-Au　(A) No, I've had enough coffee today.

(B) A two-bedroom apartment with a balcony.

(C) At the home-improvement store.

침실이 하나인 아파트를 찾고 있나요, 아니면 두 개인 아파트를 찾고 있나요?

(A) 아니요, 오늘 커피는 충분히 마셨어요.

(B) 발코니가 딸린 침실이 두 개인 아파트요.

(C) 집수리용품점에서요.

어휘 look for ~을 찾다　home-improvement store 집수리용품점, 철물점

해설 찾고 있는 아파트의 종류를 묻는 선택 의문문
(A) 연상 단어 오답. Are you ~? 의문문에서 연상 가능한 대답(No)을 이용한 오답.
(B) 정답. 침실 한 개와 두 개인 아파트 중 찾고 있는 아파트를 묻는 질문에 발코니가 딸린 침실이 두 개인 아파트를 찾고 있다며 둘 중 하나를 선택해 응답하고 있으므로 정답.
(C) 연상 단어 오답. 질문의 apartment에서 연상 가능한 home-improvement를 이용한 오답.

19

M-Cn　You should include an image on each page of the book.

M-Au　(A) The bookstore is closed.
　　　(B) Yes, that's a good idea.
　　　(C) A job as a graphic designer.

　　　책의 각 페이지에 이미지를 포함시켜야 해요.
　　　(A) 서점이 문을 닫았어요.
　　　(B) 네, 좋은 생각이에요.
　　　(C) 그래픽 디자이너로서 해야 할 일입니다.

어휘 job 해야 할 일, 책무

해설 제안/권유의 평서문
(A) 유사 발음 오답. 평서문의 book과 부분적으로 발음이 유사한 bookstore를 이용한 오답.
(B) 정답. 책의 각 페이지에 이미지를 포함시킬 것을 제안하는 평서문에 네(Yes)라고 대답한 뒤, 좋은 생각이라며 제안을 받아들이는 긍정 답변과 일관된 내용을 덧붙였으므로 정답.
(C) 연상 단어 오답. 평서문의 image에서 연상 가능한 graphic designer를 이용한 오답.

20

M-Cn　How do I make changes to this section of the Web site?

W-Br　(A) Only five more times.
　　　(B) Let me show you.
　　　(C) Can I preorder my meal?

　　　웹사이트의 이 부분은 어떻게 변경하나요?
　　　(A) 다섯 번만 더요.
　　　(B) 제가 알려 드릴게요.
　　　(C) 식사를 미리 주문할 수 있나요?

어휘 make a change to ~을 변경하다　preorder 선주문하다

해설 변경 방법을 묻는 How 의문문
(A) 질문과 상관없는 오답.
(B) 정답. 웹사이트의 특정 부분을 변경하는 방법을 묻는 질문에 직접 알려 주겠다며 응답하고 있으므로 정답.
(C) 질문과 상관없는 오답.

21

M-Au　Will you be working a half day or a full day?

W-Am　(A) My project deadline is tomorrow.
　　　(B) Here's an empty glass.
　　　(C) About 73 euros.

　　　반나절 근무를 하실 건가요, 아니면 하루 종일 근무하실 건가요?
　　　(A) 프로젝트 마감일이 내일입니다.
　　　(B) 여기 빈 잔이 있어요.
　　　(C) 약 73유로입니다.

해설 근무 시간의 양을 묻는 선택 의문문
(A) 정답. 반나절과 종일 근무 중 계획하고 있는 근무 시간을 묻는 질문에 프로젝트 마감일이 내일이라며 할 일이 많다는 것을 간접적으로 나타내어 하루 종일은 일해야 함을 우회적으로 응답하고 있으므로 정답.
(B) 연상 단어 오답. 질문의 half와 full에서 연상 가능한 empty를 이용한 오답.
(C) 질문과 상관없는 오답. How much 의문문에 대한 응답이므로 오답.

22

W-Br　There's an opening in my department for an accountant.

M-Au　(A) I have some experience with that.
　　　(B) They agreed to participate.
　　　(C) No, the store is closed.

　　　제 부서에 회계사를 위한 자리가 하나 났어요.
　　　(A) 제가 그쪽으로 경력이 있어요.
　　　(B) 그들은 참석하기로 동의했어요.
　　　(C) 아니요, 가게는 문을 닫았어요.

어휘 opening (취직) 자리, 공석　accountant 회계사　participate 참여하다

해설 정보 전달의 평서문
(A) 정답. 자신의 부서에 회계사를 위한 자리가 났다는 평서문에 그쪽으로 경력이 있다며 공석에 대한 관심을 표현하고 있으므로 정답.
(B) 연상 단어 오답. 평서문의 opening을 '개장, 개업식'으로 해석했을 때 연상 가능한 participate를 이용한 오답.
(C) 연상 단어 오답. 평서문의 opening에서 연상 가능한 closed를 이용한 오답.

23

M-Au　Isn't the shuttle between terminals fully automated?

W-Am　(A) The windows in this room don't open.
　　　(B) No, just a one-way ticket please.
　　　(C) I've actually never been to that airport.

　　　터미널 간의 셔틀은 완전히 자동화되지 않았나요?
　　　(A) 이 방 창문이 열리지 않아요.
　　　(B) 아니요, 그냥 편도 티켓으로 주세요.
　　　(C) 제가 실은 그 공항에 가 본 적이 없어요.

어휘 fully 완전히　automate 자동화하다

해설 셔틀의 완전 자동화 여부를 확인하는 부정 의문문

(A) 질문과 상관없는 오답.

(B) 연상 단어 오답. 질문의 terminals에서 연상 가능한 one-way와 ticket을 이용한 오답.

(C) 정답. 터미널 간의 셔틀이 완전히 자동화가 되었는지를 확인하는 질문에 그 공항에 가 본 적이 없다며 자동화 여부를 모른다고 우회적으로 응답하고 있으므로 정답.

24

M-Cn What's the product code for that item?

M-Au (A) I saw the advertisement on television.
(B) Batteries are included in the box.
(C) All the information is on the invoice.

해당 항목의 제품 코드는 무엇인가요?

(A) 텔레비전에서 그 광고를 보았어요.

(B) 배터리는 상자에 담겨 있어요.

(C) 모든 정보는 송장에 나와 있어요.

어휘 advertisement 광고 invoice 송장

해설 항목의 제품 코드를 묻는 What 의문문

(A) 연상 단어 오답. 질문의 product에서 연상 가능한 advertisement를 이용한 오답.

(B) 연상 단어 오답. 질문의 product에서 연상 가능한 batteries와 box를 이용한 오답.

(C) 정답. 해당 항목의 제품 코드가 무엇인지 묻는 질문에 모든 정보는 송장에 나와 있다고 응답하고 있으므로 정답.

25

W-Am Why don't we rent a bigger booth at this year's conference?

M-Cn (A) The conference call went really well.
(B) Our budget is very tight.
(C) I think the vent on the dryer is clogged.

올해 콘퍼런스에서는 더 큰 부스를 빌리는 게 어떨까요?

(A) 전화 회의가 아주 잘 진행되었어요.

(B) 예산이 아주 빠듯합니다.

(C) 건조기의 통풍구가 막힌 것 같아요.

어휘 conference call 전화 회의 budget 예산 vent 환기구, 통풍구 clog 막다

해설 제안/권유의 의문문

(A) 단어 반복 오답. 질문의 conference를 반복 이용한 오답.

(B) 정답. 콘퍼런스에서 더 큰 부스를 빌릴 것을 제안하는 질문에 예산이 아주 빠듯하다며 제안에 대한 부정적인 의사를 우회적으로 표현하고 있으므로 정답.

(C) 유사 발음 오답. 질문의 rent와 부분적으로 발음이 유사한 vent를 이용한 오답.

26

M-Cn Carmen's computer needs to be repaired, doesn't it?

W-Br (A) She bought a new one.
(B) I'll bring a pair of gloves on the hike.
(C) A degree in computer science.

카르멘의 컴퓨터는 수리를 해야겠죠?

(A) 그녀는 새것으로 하나 구입했어요.

(B) 하이킹할 때 장갑 한 켤레를 가져올게요.

(C) 컴퓨터 공학 학위예요.

어휘 on ~(할) 때[시] hike 하이킹, 등산 degree 학위 computer science 컴퓨터 공학

해설 카르멘의 컴퓨터 수리의 필요성 여부를 확인하는 부가 의문문

(A) 정답. 카르멘의 컴퓨터를 수리해야 하는지 여부를 확인하는 질문에 그녀는 새것으로 하나 구입했다며 컴퓨터를 수리할 필요가 없음을 우회적으로 알려 주고 있으므로 정답.

(B) 유사 발음 오답. 질문의 repaired와 부분적으로 발음이 유사한 pair를 이용한 오답.

(C) 단어 반복 오답. 질문의 computer를 반복 이용한 오답.

27

W-Br Who are the candidates for new branch manager?

M-Au (A) Yes, I do like my new office.
(B) No, I'm not available at that time.
(C) We're still accepting applications.

신임 지점장 후보는 누구인가요?

(A) 네, 새 사무실이 정말 마음에 듭니다.

(B) 아니요, 그때는 시간이 안 됩니다.

(C) 아직 지원서를 받고 있어요.

어휘 candidate 후보자 branch manager 지점장 application 지원(서)

해설 신임 지점장 후보를 묻는 Who 의문문

(A) Yes/No 불가 오답. Who 의문문에는 Yes/No 응답이 불가능하므로 오답.

(B) Yes/No 불가 오답. Who 의문문에는 Yes/No 응답이 불가능하므로 오답.

(C) 정답. 신임 지점장 후보가 누구인지 묻는 질문에 아직 지원서를 받고 있는 중이라며 현재는 누구인지 알 수 없다고 우회적으로 응답하고 있으므로 정답.

28

M-Au Did the focus group like the advertisement we designed?

W-Am (A) Some well-known magazines.
(B) We'll need to make some changes.
(C) Turn left at the stop sign.

표적 집단이 우리가 디자인한 광고를 맘에 들어 했나요?
(A) 유명한 잡지들입니다.
(B) 변경이 좀 필요할 거예요.
(C) 정지 표지판에서 좌회전하세요.

어휘 focus group 표적 집단 well-known 잘 알려진

해설 표적 집단이 광고를 좋아했는지를 묻는 조동사(Did) 의문문

(A) 연상 단어 오답. 질문의 advertisement에서 연상 가능한 magazines를 이용한 오답.
(B) 정답. 표적 집단이 자신들이 디자인한 광고를 맘에 들어 했는지를 묻는 질문에 변경이 필요할 것이라며 광고를 썩 맘에 들어하지 않았음을 간접적으로 표현하고 있으므로 정답.
(C) 유사 발음 오답. 질문의 designed와 부분적으로 발음이 유사한 sign을 이용한 오답.

29

W-Am Please let me know when you arrive in Osaka.

M-Cn (A) The clients are great to work with.
(B) How many did you buy?
(C) I always carry my smartphone with me.

오사카에 도착하면 연락 주세요.
(A) 그 고객들은 함께 일하기에 좋습니다.
(B) 몇 개를 샀어요?
(C) 항상 스마트폰을 가지고 다녀요.

해설 부탁/요청의 평서문

(A) 평서문과 상관없는 오답.
(B) 단어 반복 오답. 평서문의 you를 반복 이용한 오답.
(C) 정답. 오사카에 도착하면 연락 달라는 요청에 항상 스마트폰을 가지고 다닌다며 요청대로 연락하겠다고 간접적으로 표현하고 있으므로 정답.

30

M-Cn Where exactly is the employee cafeteria located?

W-Br (A) There's a new research report available.
(B) I'm headed over to lunch right now.
(C) Here's your ID badge.

직원 식당은 정확히 어디에 있나요?
(A) 이용 가능한 새 연구 보고서가 있어요.
(B) 지금 점심 먹으러 가려고요.
(C) 여기 신분증 배지입니다.

어휘 exactly 정확히 head 가다, 향하다

해설 직원 식당의 위치를 묻는 Where 의문문

(A) 연상 단어 오답. 질문의 employee에서 연상 가능한 research와 report를 이용한 오답.
(B) 정답. 직원 식당이 정확히 어디에 있는지 묻는 질문에 지금 점심 먹으러 가려고 한다며 식당 위치를 직접 가르쳐 줄 수 있음을 우회적으로 나타내고 있으므로 정답.
(C) 연상 단어 오답. 질문의 employee에서 연상 가능한 ID badge를 이용한 오답.

31

W-Am You're meeting with the clients on Thursday, aren't you?

M-Cn (A) Our software is updated every Wednesday.
(B) It's an all-vegetarian menu, without any meat.
(C) That contract is already signed.

목요일에 고객들과 만날 예정인 거죠?
(A) 저희 소프트웨어는 수요일마다 업데이트됩니다.
(B) 고기가 전혀 들어가지 않은 완전 채식 메뉴입니다.
(C) 그 계약은 이미 체결되었어요.

어휘 vegetarian 채식의

해설 목요일에 고객들과 만날지 여부를 확인하는 부가 의문문

(A) 연상 단어 오답. 질문의 Thursday에서 연상 가능한 Wednesday를 이용한 오답.
(B) 유사 발음 오답. 질문의 meeting과 부분적으로 발음이 유사한 meat를 이용한 오답.
(C) 정답. 목요일에 고객들과 만날지 여부를 확인하는 질문에 그 계약은 이미 체결되었다며 목요일에 고객들과 만날 필요가 없음을 우회적으로 표현하고 있으므로 정답.

PART 3

32-34

M-Cn Hi, Ling. **32I'm calling about the apartments you showed me last week.**

W-Am Hello, Jinyu. **32Did you like any of them?**

M-Cn Yes, **33I liked the one that was outside of town. It was so big—I would love to have that extra space. My current place is too small.**

W-Am Oh, unfortunately, that apartment's already been rented. But there's another one available in the same neighborhood, and it's nice and big. **34Would you like me to book a showing?**

M-Cn **34Yes, please!** I'm available every morning this week.

남 안녕하세요, 링. **지난주에 보여 주신 아파트에 관련해서 전화를 드렸어요.**

여 안녕하세요, 진유. **마음에 드는 것이 있었나요?**

남 네, **시 외곽에 있는 것이 괜찮았어요. 아주 컸거든요. 그 정도 여유 공간이 있으면 좋겠어요. 지금 사는 곳은 너무 작아서요.**

여	아, 안타깝게도 그 아파트는 이미 나갔어요. 하지만 같은 동네에 또 하나 나온 것이 있는데, 크고 좋아요. **둘러보는 것을 예약해 드릴까요?**
남	**네, 그렇게 해 주세요!** 이번 주는 오전에 다 시간이 돼요.

어휘	current 지금의 rent 임대하다 available 구할 수 있는 neighborhood 동네, 인근 showing (부동산 매물) 둘러보기

32

Who most likely is the woman?
(A) An architect
(B) A building manager
(C) An interior decorator
(D) A real estate agent

여자는 누구인 것 같은가?
(A) 건축가
(B) 건물 관리인
(C) 실내 장식가
(D) 부동산 중개인

해설 전체 내용 관련 – 여자의 직업

남자가 첫 대사에서 지난주에 보여 준 아파트에 관련해 전화했다(I'm calling about the apartments you showed me last week)고 하자 여자가 마음에 드는 것이 있었는지(Did you like any of them?) 묻는 것으로 보아 여자는 부동산 중개인임을 알 수 있다. 따라서 정답은 (D)이다.

33

Which feature is most important to the man?
(A) Location
(B) Size
(C) Appearance
(D) Room layout

어떤 특징이 남자에게 가장 중요한가?
(A) 위치
(B) 크기
(C) 외관
(D) 방 배치

해설 세부 사항 관련 – 남자에게 가장 중요한 특징

남자가 두 번째 대사에서 시 외곽에 있는 것이 좋았다(I liked the one that was outside of town)고 한 후, 아주 컸고 그 정도 여유 공간이 있으면 좋겠다(It was so big—I would love to have that extra space)면서 지금 사는 곳은 너무 작다(My current place is too small)고 말하는 것으로 보아 정답은 (B)이다.

34

What will the woman most likely do next?
(A) Process a payment
(B) Measure a room
(C) Schedule an appointment
(D) Order some furniture

여자는 다음에 무엇을 할 것 같은가?
(A) 결제 처리하기
(B) 방 측정하기
(C) 예약 잡기
(D) 가구 주문하기

어휘 payment 결제, 지불 appointment 약속, 예약

해설 세부 사항 관련 – 여자가 다음에 할 일

여자가 두 번째 대사에서 둘러보는 것을 예약해 줄지(Would you like me to book a showing?) 묻자 남자가 그렇게 해달라(Yes, please!)고 했으므로 정답은 (C)이다.

Paraphrasing	대화의 book a showing → 정답의 Schedule an appointment

35-37

M-Au	[35],[36]**We're getting a shipment of medical equipment today.** [35]**The new autorefractor machines for eye exams are coming in.**
W-Br	Great. [35]**They're going to make our patients' exams much more accurate.**
M-Au	[36]**I can unpack them when they get here.**
W-Br	That's OK. Just put them in the storage closet overnight. A company representative is coming in tomorrow, and we'll need them then.
M-Au	What time is the representative coming?
W-Br	[37]**He's coming at six P.M.** after the clinic closes. He'll be showing us how to use the new equipment.

남	오늘 의료 장비 배송을 받을 예정이에요. 시력 검사를 위한 새 자동 굴절 검사기가 올 겁니다.
여	잘됐네요. 환자를 훨씬 더 정확하게 검사할 수 있겠어요.
남	장비가 도착하면 제가 포장을 풀어놓을게요.
여	괜찮아요. 밤에는 수납장에 그냥 넣어 두세요. 회사 직원 한 분이 내일 올 예정인데 그때 필요해요.
남	그 직원은 몇 시에 오나요?
여	병원이 문을 닫은 후인 오후 6시에 올 거예요. 새 장비를 사용하는 방법을 알려 줄 것입니다.

어휘	shipment 배송(물) equipment 장비, 용품 autorefractor 자동 굴절 검사기 eye exam 시력 검사 accurate 정확한 unpack 포장을 풀다, 꺼내다 storage 수납, 보관 representative (담당) 직원, 대표 clinic 병원

35

Where is the conversation most likely taking place?
(A) At a fitness center
(B) At a warehouse
(C) At a hotel
(D) At an eye clinic

대화는 어디에서 이루어지고 있는 것 같은가?
(A) 피트니스 센터
(B) 창고
(C) 호텔
(D) 안과

해설 전체 내용 관련 – 대화의 장소
남자가 첫 대사에서 오늘 의료 장비 배송을 받을 예정(We're getting a shipment of medical equipment today)이라며 시력 검사를 위한 새 자동 굴절 검사기가 올 것(The new autorefractor machines for eye exams are coming in)이라고 말하자 여자가 환자를 더 정확하게 검사할 수 있겠다(They're going to make our patients' exams much more accurate)고 응답하고 있으므로 대화의 장소가 안과임을 알 수 있다. 따라서 정답은 (D)이다.

36

What does the man offer to do?
(A) Unpack a shipment
(B) Cancel some appointments
(C) Take inventory
(D) Process a payment

남자는 무엇을 하겠다고 제안하는가?
(A) 배송물의 포장 풀기
(B) 예약 취소하기
(C) 재고 조사하기
(D) 결제 처리하기

어휘 inventory 재고

해설 세부 사항 관련 – 남자의 제안 사항
남자가 첫 번째 대사에서 의료 장비 배송을 받을 예정(We're getting a shipment of medical equipment today)이라고 했고 두 번째 대사에서 장비가 도착하면 자신이 포장을 풀어놓겠다(I can unpack them when they get here)고 제안하고 있으므로 정답은 (A)이다.

> **Paraphrasing** 대화의 them → 정답의 a shipment

37

What will take place at 6 P.M. tomorrow?
(A) A safety inspection
(B) A training session
(C) A package delivery
(D) A job interview

내일 오후 6시에 무슨 일이 일어날 것인가?
(A) 안전 점검
(B) 교육 세션
(C) 소포 배송
(D) 취업 면접

해설 세부 사항 관련 – 내일 오후 6시에 일어날 일
여자가 마지막 대사에서 병원이 문을 닫은 후인 오후 6시에 직원이 올 예정(He's coming at six P.M. after the clinic closes)이라며 새 장비를 사용하는 방법을 알려 줄 것(He'll be showing us how to use the new equipment)이라고 말하고 있으므로 정답은 (B)이다.

> **Paraphrasing** 대화의 showing us how to use the new equipment → 정답의 A training session

38-40

M-Au Hi, Liliana. I've only worked here at the factory for six months, but [38]**I'm wondering if it's possible to change positions.** You've been here quite a while. [38]**What do you think?**

W-Am Good! I definitely encourage you to work your way up. [39]**I'll celebrate fifteen years of employment here next month.**

M-Au Congratulations! Right now I'm working as a package handler, but I'd like to be an assembly technician. What do I need to do?

W-Am Well, [40]**the first step would be to talk to your supervisor.** He'll be able to give you more details.

M-Au [40]**Thanks. Actually, I think he's in his office now.**

남 안녕하세요, 릴리아나. 여기 공장에서 일을 한 지 이제 6개월밖에 되지 않았지만 **직무 변경이 가능한지 궁금해요.** 여기서 근무한 지 꽤 오래되셨는데요. **어떻게 생각하세요?**

여 좋은데요! 꼭 진급하시기를 응원합니다. **전 다음 달에 이 회사 근무 15주년을 기념할 예정이에요.**

남 축하드립니다! 지금은 포장물 처리하는 일을 하고 있지만 조립 기술자가 되고 싶어요. 어떻게 해야 할까요?

여 음, **첫 번째 단계는 상사와 이야기를 나누는 것이에요.** 그분이 더 자세한 정보를 줄 수 있을 것입니다.

남 **감사합니다. 사실 지금 사무실에 계시는 것 같아요.**

어휘 encourage 격려하다 work one's way up 진급[승진]하다 package 소포, 포장물 handler 취급하는 사람 assembly 조립 technician 기술자, 기사 supervisor 상사, 관리자

38

What does the man ask the woman about?
(A) Safety regulations
(B) Security procedures
(C) Working weekend shifts
(D) Changing jobs

남자는 여자에게 무엇에 대해 물어보는가?
(A) 안전 규정
(B) 보안 절차
(C) 주말 교대 근무
(D) 업무 변경

해설 세부 사항 관련 – 남자가 여자에게 물어보는 것
남자가 첫 대사에서 여자에게 직무 변경이 가능한지 궁금하다(I'm wondering if it's possible to change positions)고 했고 어떻게 생각하는지(What do you think?) 물어보고 있으므로 정답은 (D)이다.

> **Paraphrasing** 대화의 positions → 정답의 jobs

39

What does the woman say she will do next month?
(A) Take a vacation
(B) Celebrate a work anniversary
(C) Retire from a job
(D) Transfer to another facility

여자는 다음 달에 무엇을 할 것이라고 말하는가?
(A) 휴가 가기
(B) 근무 기념일 축하하기
(C) 직장에서 퇴직하기
(D) 다른 시설로 전근 가기

어휘 anniversary 기념일 facility 시설

해설 세부 사항 관련 – 여자가 다음 달에 할 것이라고 말하는 일
여자가 첫 대사에서 다음 달에 이 회사 근무 15주년을 기념할 예정(I'll celebrate fifteen years of employment here next month)이라고 말하고 있으므로 정답은 (B)이다.

> **Paraphrasing** 대화의 fifteen years of employment here
> → 정답의 a work anniversary

40

What will the man most likely do next?
(A) Check a work schedule
(B) Review an operator's manual
(C) Speak with a supervisor
(D) Register for a course

남자는 다음에 무엇을 할 것 같은가?
(A) 근무 일정 확인하기
(B) 사용자 설명서 검토하기
(C) 상사와 이야기하기
(D) 과정에 등록하기

어휘 operator (기계, 장비를) 조작하는 사람 register 등록하다

해설 세부 사항 관련 – 남자가 다음에 할 일
여자가 두 번째 대사에서 첫 번째 단계는 상사와 이야기를 하는 것(the first step would be to talk to your supervisor)이라고 권하자 남자가 고맙다(Thanks)며 사실 지금 사무실에 있는 것 같다(Actually, I think he's in his office now)고 말하는 것으로 보아 남자가 그의 상사를 찾아가 그와 이야기를 할 것임을 알 수 있다. 따라서 정답은 (C)이다.

> **Paraphrasing** 대화의 talk to → 정답의 Speak with

41-43

> M-Cn Hi. My name is Hector Murray, and I'm a customer at your bank. **41I'm calling about getting a small-business loan.** My business is expanding, and I need an additional vehicle.
>
> W-Br Sure, we can help you with that. **42We'll need some financial information—your updated business plan, bank statements, and income and payroll tax statements.**
>
> M-Cn OK. Should I make an appointment to go over the information with you in person?
>
> W-Br No, there's no need to come in. **43You can just fill out our online application form.** I'll send you the link.

> 남 안녕하세요. 제 이름은 헥터 머레이이고 귀사 은행을 이용하고 있습니다. **소기업 대출을 받는 것에 관련해 전화드렸어요.** 제 사업이 커지고 있어서 차량이 추가적으로 필요합니다.
>
> 여 네, 도와드릴 수 있습니다. **최신 사업 계획서, 은행 입출금 내역서, 소득세 및 급여세 명세서와 같은 재정 정보가 필요합니다.**
>
> 남 좋아요. 직접 뵙고 정보를 함께 검토하기 위해 예약을 해야 할까요?
>
> 여 아니요, 오실 필요는 없습니다. **온라인 신청서를 작성하시면 됩니다.** 링크를 보내 드리겠습니다.

> 어휘 loan 대출 expand 확장하다 vehicle 차량 financial 재정의 bank statement 은행 입출금 내역서 income tax 소득세 payroll tax 급여세 make an appointment 예약하다 go over 검토하다 in person 직접 fill out 작성하다 application form 신청서

41

Why is the man calling?
(A) To dispute a charge
(B) To inquire about a loan
(C) To register a business
(D) To place an advertisement

남자는 왜 전화를 하고 있는가?
(A) 요금에 이의를 제기하기 위해
(B) 대출에 대해 문의하기 위해
(C) 사업자 등록을 하기 위해
(D) 광고를 게재하기 위해

어휘 dispute 이의를 제기하다, 반박하다 charge 요금 inquire 문의하다

해설 전체 내용 관련 – 남자가 전화하는 목적

남자가 첫 대사에서 소기업 대출을 받는 것에 관련해 전화했다(I'm calling about getting a small-business loan)고 말하고 있으므로 정답은 (B)이다.

Paraphrasing	대화의 calling about getting a small-business loan → 정답의 inquire about a loan

42

What does the woman say the man must provide?
(A) An inspection certificate
(B) A form of identification
(C) Financial records
(D) Product descriptions

여자는 남자가 무엇을 제공해야 한다고 말하는가?
(A) 검사 증명서
(B) 신분증
(C) 재정 기록 문서
(D) 제품 설명서

어휘 certificate 증명서

해설 세부 사항 관련 – 남자가 제공해야 한다고 여자가 말하는 것

여자가 첫 대사에서 남자에게 최신 사업 계획서, 입출금 내역서, 소득세 및 급여세 명세서와 같은 재정 정보가 필요하다(We'll need some financial information—your updated business plan, bank statements, and income and payroll tax statements)고 말하고 있으므로 정답은 (C)이다.

Paraphrasing	대화의 information → 정답의 records

43

What does the woman tell the man he can do online?
(A) Fill out an application
(B) Create an account
(C) View pricing options
(D) Print a mailing label

여자는 남자에게 온라인에서 무엇을 할 수 있다고 말하는가?
(A) 신청서 작성하기
(B) 계정 만들기
(C) 가격 옵션 보기
(D) 우편 라벨 인쇄하기

어휘 account 계정

해설 세부 사항 관련 – 남자가 온라인에서 할 수 있다고 여자가 말하는 것

여자가 마지막 대사에서 남자에게 온라인 신청서를 작성하면 된다(You can just fill out our online application form)고 말하고 있으므로 정답은 (A)이다.

44-46

W-Br Hi, Mr. Schneider. Thanks for agreeing to show me around your new facility. **44It will really help me with the article I'm writing. I think my magazine's readers will enjoy learning about indoor hydroponic farming.**

M-Au It's my pleasure. **45When we grow plants in water rather than soil, we actually end up needing much less water to grow the same amount of food. That surprises most people.**

W-Br Interesting. I'll be sure to include that information. By the way, **46is it all right if I take some pictures of your setup?** I brought a camera.

M-Au Of course. Let's get started.

여 안녕하세요, 슈나이더 씨. 새 시설 안내에 동의해 주셔서 감사합니다. **지금 쓰고 있는 기사에 큰 도움이 될 거예요. 저희 잡지 독자들이 실내 수경 재배에 대해 배우는 것을 좋아할 것 같아요.**

남 별말씀을요. **우리가 흙이 아닌 물에서 식물을 키울 때 사실 같은 양의 식량을 재배하기 위해 훨씬 적은 양의 물을 필요로 하게 됩니다. 그 점이 많은 사람들을 놀라게 하지요.**

여 흥미롭군요. 그 내용을 꼭 포함시켜야겠어요. 그건 그렇고, **여기 구조 사진 좀 찍어도 괜찮을까요?** 카메라를 가져왔어요.

남 물론이죠. 시작합시다.

어휘 article 기사 indoor 실내의 hydroponic 수경법의 farming 농사 soil 흙 end up (결국) ~하게 되다 include 포함하다 setup 구조, 설치

44

Which industry does the woman most likely work in?
(A) Journalism
(B) Marketing
(C) Entertainment
(D) Technology

여자는 어떤 업계에서 일하는 것 같은가?
(A) 언론
(B) 마케팅
(C) 연예
(D) 기술

해설 전체 내용 관련 – 여자의 근무 업계

여자가 첫 대사에서 지금 쓰고 있는 기사에 도움이 될 것(It will really help me with the article I'm writing)이라며 잡지의 독자들이 실내 수경 재배에 대해 배우는 것을 좋아할 것 같다(I think my magazine's readers will enjoy learning about indoor hydroponic farming)고 말하고 있으므로 정답은 (A)이다.

45

What does the man say is beneficial about a farming technique?
(A) It is easy to learn.
(B) It improves air quality.
(C) It reduces food waste.
(D) It requires less water.

남자는 농사 기술에 대해 무엇이 유익하다고 말하는가?
(A) 배우기 쉽다.
(B) 공기의 질을 향상시킨다.
(C) 음식물 쓰레기를 줄인다.
(D) 물이 덜 필요하다.

어휘 beneficial 유익한, 이로운 improve 향상시키다 quality 질
require 필요하다

해설 세부 사항 관련 – 남자가 농사 기술의 유익한 점이라고 말하는 것
남자가 첫 대사에서 흙이 아닌 물에서 식물을 키울 때 같은 양의 식량을 재배하기 위해 훨씬 적은 양의 물이 필요하다(When we grow plants in water rather than soil, we actually end up needing much less water to grow the same amount of food)며 그것에 사람들이 놀란다(That surprises most people)고 말하는 것으로 보아 정답은 (D)이다.

> Paraphrasing 대화의 needing much less water
> → 정답의 requires less water

46

What does the woman ask permission to do?
(A) Review some financial documents
(B) Taste some food samples
(C) Take some photographs
(D) Return on another day

여자는 무엇을 하도록 허락을 구하는가?
(A) 재정 문서 검토하기
(B) 음식 시식하기
(C) 사진 찍기
(D) 다른 날에 다시 오기

어휘 permission 허락, 허가 financial 재정의 taste 맛보다

해설 세부 사항 관련 – 여자가 허락을 구하는 일
여자가 두 번째 대사에서 여기 구조를 사진 찍어도 괜찮을지(is it all right if I take some pictures of your setup?) 허락을 구하고 있으므로 정답은 (C)이다.

> Paraphrasing 대화의 pictures → 정답의 photographs

47-49

M-Au Ms. Becker, ⁴⁷**I've walked around your property, and I think your home's a good candidate for solar panels. I can probably install them next month.**

W-Br Great! ⁴⁷**But aren't there too many trees around my house?**

M-Au Well, there's a spot in your back garden that gets enough sunlight to put some solar panels—⁴⁸**if you cut just a few of the branches off that maple tree.**

W-Br ⁴⁸**That tree's actually on my neighbors' property, so I'd better make sure it's OK. I'll ask them later.** By the way, ⁴⁹**my garage is pretty small, so I'm concerned about the size of the ten-kilowatt battery that goes with the panels. Can you look in there to make sure it'll fit?**

남 베커 씨, 집 주변을 걸어서 둘러보았는데, 집이 태양 전지판을 설치하기에 좋은 조건이라고 생각합니다. 다음 달에 설치할 수 있을 것 같습니다.

여 잘됐네요! 그런데 우리 집 주변에 나무가 너무 많지 않나요?

남 음, 태양 전지판을 설치하기에 햇빛을 충분히 받을 만한 장소가 뒤 정원에 있습니다, 단풍나무에서 가지 몇 개만 자르면요.

여 저 나무는 사실 이웃의 소유지에 있는 것이라 자르는 게 괜찮은지 확인하는 게 좋겠어요. 나중에 물어볼게요. 그나저나 제 차고가 꽤 작아서 패널에 딸려 오는 10킬로와트짜리 배터리의 크기가 걱정되네요. 맞을지 확인하기 위해 그곳을 좀 봐 주시겠어요?

어휘 property 소유지, 재산 solar panel 태양 전지판 install 설치하다 spot 장소 maple 단풍나무 garage 차고 go with ~에 딸려 오다 fit 맞다

47

What are the speakers discussing?
(A) A satellite television subscription
(B) A solar panel installation
(C) A security system upgrade
(D) An electric-car charging station

화자들은 무엇에 대해 논의하고 있는가?
(A) 위성 텔레비전 가입
(B) 태양 전지판 설치
(C) 보안 시스템 업그레이드
(D) 전기차 충전소

어휘 subscription 가입, 구독

해설 전체 내용 관련 – 대화의 주제
남자가 첫 대사에서 집 주변을 둘러보았고 태양 전지판을 설치하기에 좋은 조건(I've walked around your property, and I think your home's a good candidate for solar panels)이라고 하면서 다음 달에 설치할 수 있을 것(I can probably install them next month)이라고 하자 여자가 집 주변에 나무가 너무 많지 않은지(But aren't there too many trees around my house?) 물으며 태양 전지판 설치에 대한 대화를 이어 가고 있으므로 정답은 (B)이다.

48

What will the woman ask her neighbors about?
(A) Caring for some indoor plants
(B) Borrowing some garden tools
(C) Using a parking space
(D) Cutting some tree branches

여자는 이웃에게 무엇에 대해 물어볼 것인가?
(A) 실내 식물 보살피기
(B) 정원 도구 빌리기
(C) 주차 공간 이용하기
(D) 나뭇가지 몇 개 자르기

어휘 care for ~을 보살피다, ~을 좋아하다

해설 세부 사항 관련 - 여자가 이웃에게 물어볼 것

남자가 두 번째 대사에서 단풍나무 가지를 자르는 것(if you cut just a few of the branches off that maple tree)에 대해 언급하자 여자가 이웃 소유지에 있는 것이어서 자르는 게 괜찮은지 확인하는 게 좋겠다(That tree's actually on my neighbors' property, so I'd better make sure it's OK)며 나중에 물어보겠다(I'll ask them later)고 말하고 있으므로 정답은 (D)이다.

> **Paraphrasing** 대화의 cut just a few of the branches off that maple tree
> → 정답의 Cutting some tree branches

49

What will the man most likely do next?
(A) Move a vehicle
(B) Recharge a battery
(C) Check the size of a space
(D) Write down a price estimate

남자는 다음에 무엇을 할 것 같은가?
(A) 차량 이동
(B) 배터리 재충전
(C) 공간 크기 확인
(D) 가격 견적서 작성

어휘 vehicle 차량   estimate 견적(서)

해설 세부 사항 관련 - 남자가 다음에 할 일

여자가 마지막 대사에서 남자에게 차고가 작아서 패널에 딸려 오는 10킬로와트짜리 배터리의 크기가 걱정된다(my garage is pretty small, so I'm concerned about the size of the ten-kilowatt battery that goes with the panels)면서 맞을지 확인하기 위해 차고를 봐 줄 것(Can you look in there to make sure it'll fit?)을 요청하는 것으로 보아 남자가 차고의 크기를 살펴볼 것임을 알 수 있다. 따라서 정답은 (C)이다.

> **Paraphrasing** 대화의 look in → 정답의 Check

50-52 3인 대화

> M-Au ⁵⁰Astrid and Ulrike, do you have a few
> minutes before the lunch crowd arrives?

W-Am Sure, Mr. Smith. ⁵⁰Is this about our new menu?

M-Au No, not that. ⁵¹The refrigerator near the chef's station wasn't closed properly last night.

W-Am Oh no—I think that was me. I put the leftover salad in there.

W-Br And I should have checked to make sure it was shut before closing the restaurant.

M-Au It's OK, but ⁵²a repair person's coming to see if there's something that can be done to make it easier to close securely. I have to go to the bank, so ⁵²could you let him in when he arrives and help him out?

남 아스트리드와 울리케, 점심 손님들이 몰려오기 전에 잠깐 시간이 있나요?

여1 물론이죠, 스미스 씨. 신메뉴에 대한 건가요?

남 아니요, 그건 아니고요. 주방장 작업대 근처의 냉장고가 어젯밤에 제대로 닫히지 않았어요.

여1 이런. 아무래도 저였던 것 같아요. 제가 거기에 남은 샐러드를 넣었어요.

여2 그리고 제가 식당 마감하기 전에 문이 닫혀 있는지 확인해야 했어요.

남 괜찮아요, 하지만 좀 더 쉽게 문이 잘 닫히게 하려면 무엇을 할 수 있는지 알아보기 위해 수리 기사가 올 예정입니다. 저는 은행에 가야 해서, 그가 도착하면 들여보내 주고 좀 도와주겠어요?

어휘 refrigerator 냉장고   station (작업, 담당) 장소   properly 제대로   leftover 남은 음식   shut 닫다   repair person 수리공   securely 확실히, 단단히

50

Where do the speakers most likely work?
(A) At a supermarket
(B) At a restaurant
(C) At a hardware store
(D) At a manufacturing plant

화자들은 어디에서 일하는 것 같은가?
(A) 슈퍼마켓
(B) 식당
(C) 철물점
(D) 제조 공장

해설 전체 내용 관련 - 화자들의 근무지

남자가 첫 대사에서 다른 화자들의 이름을 부르며 점심 손님들이 오기 전에 시간이 있는지(Astrid and Ulrike, do you have a few minutes before the lunch crowd arrives?) 묻자 첫 번째 여자가 신메뉴에 대한 것인지(Is this about our new menu?) 되묻고 있으므로 화자들은 음식점에서 일하고 있음을 알 수 있다. 따라서 정답은 (B)이다.

51

What problem does the man mention?
(A) The door of an appliance was left open.
(B) The sign outside the business is broken.
(C) A power cord cannot be located.
(D) A training session was not provided.

남자는 어떤 문제를 언급하는가?
(A) 가전제품의 문이 열려 있었다.
(B) 업체 밖에 있는 간판이 깨졌다.
(C) 전원 코드를 찾을 수 없다.
(D) 교육 세션이 제공되지 않았다.

어휘 appliance 가전제품 locate (정확한 위치를) 찾아내다

해설 세부 사항 관련 - 남자가 언급하는 문제
남자가 두 번째 대사에서 냉장고가 어젯밤에 제대로 닫히지 않았다(The refrigerator near the chef's station wasn't closed properly last night)고 말하고 있으므로 정답은 (A)이다.

Paraphrasing	대화의 The refrigerator ~ wasn't closed properly → 정답의 The door of an appliance was left open

52

What does the man ask the women to do?
(A) Clean a work area
(B) Reschedule some shifts
(C) Assist a repair person
(D) Make a telephone call

남자는 여자들에게 무엇을 해 달라고 요청하는가?
(A) 작업장 청소하기
(B) 교대 근무 일정 다시 잡기
(C) 수리공 도와주기
(D) 전화 걸기

어휘 shift 교대 근무 assist 돕다

해설 세부 사항 관련 - 남자의 요청 사항
남자가 마지막 대사에서 좀 더 쉽게 문이 잘 닫히게 하려면 무엇을 할 수 있는지 알아보기 위해 수리 기사가 올 예정(a repair person's coming to see ~ to close securely)이라면서 그가 도착하면 들여보내 주고 좀 도와주라(could you let him in when he arrives and help him out?)는 요청을 하고 있으므로 정답은 (C)이다.

Paraphrasing	대화의 help him out → 정답의 Assist a repair person

53-55

W-Br	Hi, Adem. ⁵³During one part of our market research team meeting tomorrow, we'll need to share some information about recent consumer trends. ⁵⁴Could you create some attractive slides with this information?

M-Cn	Fabrice is exceptionally good with graphics.
W-Br	Oh, in that case, let me ask him.
M-Cn	But, as promised, I have started looking closely at what our competitors are doing to attract clients. So ⁵⁵after lunch today, I can share some ideas with you about how we might incorporate those strategies in our own work.
W-Br	Great. I definitely want to hear more about that!

여	안녕하세요, 아뎀. 내일 우리 시장 조사 팀의 회의 중 일부에서 최근 소비자 동향에 대한 몇 가지 정보를 공유해야 할 거예요. 이 내용으로 눈길을 끌 만한 슬라이드를 만들어 줄 수 있나요?
남	패브리스가 그래픽에 정말 재주가 뛰어나요.
여	아, 그렇다면 그에게 물어볼게요.
남	하지만 약속대로, 저는 고객 유치를 위해 경쟁업체들이 무엇을 하고 있는지 자세히 살펴보기 시작했어요. 그래서 오늘 점심 식사 후에 이러한 전략을 우리 업무에 어떻게 포함시킬 수 있는지에 대한 몇 가지 아이디어를 공유할 수 있어요.
여	좋아요. 관련 내용을 꼭 더 듣고 싶습니다!

어휘	market research 시장 조사 share 공유하다 trend 동향, 경향 attractive 눈길을 끄는, 멋진 exceptionally 정말, 유난히 good with ~에 재주가 있는 as promised 약속대로 closely 자세히, 면밀히 competitor 경쟁자 attract 끌어들이다 incorporate 포함하다, 통합하다 strategy 전략

53

What field do the speakers work in?
(A) Market research
(B) Art restoration
(C) Entertainment
(D) Publishing

화자들은 어떤 분야에서 일하는가?
(A) 시장 조사
(B) 미술품 복원
(C) 연예
(D) 출판

어휘 restoration 복원[복구]

해설 전체 내용 관련 - 화자들의 근무 분야
여자가 첫 대사에서 우리 시장 조사 팀의 회의 중 최근 소비자 동향에 대한 정보를 공유해야 한다(During one part of our market research team meeting tomorrow, we'll need to share some information about recent consumer trends)고 한 것으로 보아 정답은 (A)이다.

54

Why does the man say, "Fabrice is exceptionally good with graphics"?

(A) To express surprise

(B) To recommend a promotion

(C) To confirm that training is unnecessary

(D) To decline a request

남자는 왜 "패브리스가 그래픽에 정말 재주가 뛰어나요"라고 말하는가?

(A) 놀람을 표현하기 위해

(B) 승진을 추천하기 위해

(C) 교육이 불필요하다는 점을 확인하기 위해

(D) 요청을 거절하기 위해

어휘 promotion 승진 decline 거절하다

해설 화자의 의도 파악 – 패브리스가 그래픽에 정말 재주가 뛰어나다는
말의 의도

앞에서 여자가 남자에게 이 내용으로 눈길을 끌 만한 슬라이드를 만들어
줄 수 있는지(Could you create some attractive slides with this
information?) 묻자 남자가 인용문을 언급한 것으로 보아, 슬라이드를 잘
만들 수 있는 다른 사람을 추천하여 여자의 요청을 거절하려는 의도로 한
말임을 알 수 있다. 따라서 정답은 (D)이다.

55

What does the man plan to do after lunch?

(A) Submit a report

(B) Pack for a trip

(C) Share some ideas

(D) Read through an agenda

남자는 점심 식사 후에 무엇을 할 계획인가?

(A) 보고서 제출하기

(B) 여행을 위해 짐 싸기

(C) 아이디어 공유하기

(D) 의제 읽기

어휘 read through ~을 꼼꼼히 읽다 agenda 의제, 안건

해설 세부 사항 관련 – 남자가 점심 식사 후에 하려는 계획

남자가 두 번째 대사에서 점심 식사 후에 전략을 업무에 포함시킬 수 있
는 방법에 대한 아이디어를 공유할 수 있다(after lunch today, I can
share some ideas ~ those strategies in our own work)고 말하고
있으므로 정답은 (C)이다.

56-58 3인 대화

W-Am It's almost eleven o'clock. **56I'm worried
that we'll fall behind schedule.** We need to
have the drywall installed in this house by
tomorrow.

M-Au Don't worry. The delivery truck just pulled
up in front a few minutes ago.

W-Am OK, that's a relief. Let's head outside.

M-Cn **57Hi—I'm Gregor.** Apologies for the delay.
**57Traffic was an absolute nightmare on
Route 37 North.** Where should I unload the
materials?

M-Au **58You'll need to maneuver your truck over
to the back entrance.**

M-Cn **58That won't be a problem. Could one of
you guide me in?**

W-Am **58Sure, I'll do it.** It's a tight spot, so just
keep me in sight in your rearview mirror.

여 거의 11시입니다. **일정을 맞추지 못할까 봐 걱정되네요.**
내일까지 이 집에 석고 보드를 설치해야 해요.

남1 걱정하지 마세요. 배달 트럭이 조금 전에 막 요 앞에
도착했어요.

여 좋아요, 마음이 놓이네요. 밖으로 나가죠.

남2 **안녕하세요, 그레고르입니다.** 지연에 대해 사과드려요.
37번 북쪽 국도에서 교통 상황이 정말 끔찍했어요. 자재는
어디에 내려야 할까요?

남1 **트럭을 후문으로 몰고 가야 할 거예요.**

남2 **문제없어요. 한 분이 저를 안내해 주시겠어요?**

여 **물론이죠, 제가 하겠습니다.** 좁은 지점이니 백미러로 저를
계속 보면서 잘 따라오세요.

어휘 fall behind schedule 일정을 못 맞추다, 예정보다
늦어지다 drywall 석고 보드 install 설치하다 pull up
(차를) 세우다 relief 안도, 안심 apology 사과
nightmare 끔찍한 일, 악몽 unload 내리다 material
자재 maneuver (능숙하게 조금씩) 움직이다, 이동시키다
entrance 출입문 tight spot (운전, 주차 시) 좁은 지점
keep ~ in sight ~을 계속 지켜보다 rearview mirror
백미러

56

What is the woman concerned about?

(A) Having enough workers for a project

(B) Staying within budget

(C) Passing an inspection

(D) Completing work on time

여자는 무엇을 걱정하는가?

(A) 프로젝트를 위한 충분한 인력 확보하기

(B) 예산 내로 유지하기

(C) 검사 통과하기

(D) 제시간에 작업 완료하기

어휘 budget 예산 inspection 검사 on time 제시간에, 제때에

해설 세부 사항 관련 – 여자의 우려 사항

여자가 첫 대사에서 일정을 맞추지 못할까 봐 걱정된다(I'm worried that
we'll fall behind schedule)고 말하고 있으므로 정답은 (D)이다.

57

What does Gregor say about Route 37 North?
(A) Its toll prices have increased.
(B) It was closed for repairs.
(C) Traffic was really heavy.
(D) Oversized vehicles are not permitted.

그레고르는 37번 북쪽 국도에 대해 무엇이라고 말하는가?
(A) 통행료 가격이 상승했다.
(B) 보수를 위해 폐쇄되었다.
(C) 교통 체증이 정말 심했다.
(D) 대형 차량은 허용되지 않는다.

어휘 toll 통행료 oversized 대형의 permit 허용하다

해설 세부 사항 관련 – 그레고르가 37번 북쪽 국도에 대해 말하는 것
두 번째 남자가 첫 번째 대사에서 자신을 그레고르(Hi—I'm Gregor)라고 소개하고 37번 북쪽 국도의 교통 상황이 끔찍했다(Traffic was an absolute nightmare on Route 37 North)고 말하고 있으므로 정답은 (C)이다.

Paraphrasing	대화의 an absolute nightmare → 정답의 really heavy

58

What does the woman say she will do?
(A) Sign an invoice
(B) Open a garage door
(C) Guide a truck
(D) Contact a homeowner

여자는 무엇을 할 것이라고 말하는가?
(A) 송장에 서명하기
(B) 차고 문 열기
(C) 트럭 안내하기
(D) 집주인에게 연락하기

어휘 invoice 송장 garage 차고

해설 세부 사항 관련 – 여자가 할 것이라고 말하는 일
첫 번째 남자가 두 번째 대사에서 트럭을 후문으로 몰고 가야 한다(You'll need to maneuver your truck over to the back entrance)고 하자 두 번째 남자가 문제없다(That won't be a problem)며 둘 중 한 명이 안내해 줄 수 있는지(Could one of you guide me in?) 물었고 여자가 자신이 하겠다(Sure, I'll do it)고 대답하고 있으므로 정답은 (C)이다.

Paraphrasing	대화의 guide me in → 정답의 Guide a truck

59-61

W-Br	Hi. [59]**I'm here for the two o'clock weight lifting class, but there's no one in the studio.**
M-Au	[60]**That class was canceled.** The trainer injured her ankle, and she'll be out for

at least a week. [60]**I thought I sent out an e-mail to all of her students this morning.**

W-Br	Oh. I signed up only yesterday.
M-Au	I see. I'm sorry about that—e-mail lists usually take 24 hours to update. Now— [61]**we're offering several other classes this afternoon. Look at this chart. Would you like to try one of these?**

여	안녕하세요. 두 시에 하는 웨이트 리프팅 수업을 위해 왔는데, 연습실에 아무도 없네요.
남	그 수업은 취소되었어요. 트레이너가 발목을 다쳐서 적어도 일주일 동안은 쉴 거예요. 오늘 아침에 학생 모두에게 이메일을 보냈다고 생각했는데요.
여	오. 전 어제서야 등록했어요.
남	그렇군요. 죄송해요. 이메일 목록은 일반적으로 업데이트하는 데 24시간이 걸려요. 오늘 오후에는 다른 수업도 여러 가지 제공하고 있어요. 이 표를 보세요. 이 중 하나를 들어 보시겠어요?

어휘 weight lifting 웨이트 리프팅, 역도 studio 연습실, 강습실 injure 상처를 입히다 ankle 발목 sign up 등록하다, 회원 가입하다

59

Where is the conversation most likely taking place?
(A) At a medical clinic
(B) At a fitness center
(C) At a sporting goods store
(D) At a pottery studio

대화는 어디에서 이루어지고 있는 것 같은가?
(A) 병원
(B) 피트니스 센터
(C) 스포츠용품점
(D) 도자기 작업실

해설 전체 내용 관련 – 대화의 장소
여자가 첫 대사에서 웨이트 리프팅 수업을 위해 왔는데, 연습실에 아무도 없다(I'm here for the two o'clock weight lifting class, but there's no one in the studio)고 말하고 있다. 웨이트 리프팅 수업이 있다는 점으로 보아 장소는 피트니스 센터일 가능성이 높으므로 정답은 (B)이다.

60

Why does the woman say, "I signed up only yesterday"?
(A) To explain why she was not notified
(B) To confirm that she made a payment
(C) To request some needed materials
(D) To justify some class absences

여자는 왜 "전 어제서야 등록했어요"라고 말하는가?

(A) 알림을 받지 못한 이유를 설명하기 위해
(B) 지불을 했다는 것을 확인하기 위해
(C) 필요한 자료를 요청하기 위해
(D) 수업의 결석을 정당화하기 위해

어휘 notify 알리다   request 요청하다   material 자료, 재료   justify 정당화하다   absence 결석

해설 화자의 의도 파악 – 어제서야 등록했다는 말의 의도
앞에서 남자가 수업은 취소되었다(That class was canceled)고 했고 오늘 아침 학생 모두에게 이메일을 보냈다고 생각했다(I thought I sent out an e-mail to all of her students this morning)고 한 말에 여자가 어제서야 등록했다는 인용문으로 응답한 것으로 보아, 아침에 취소를 공지하는 이메일을 받지 못한 이유를 나타내기 위해 한 말임을 알 수 있다. 따라서 정답은 (A)이다.

61

What does the man most likely show to the woman?
(A) A price list
(B) A floor plan
(C) An invoice
(D) A schedule

남자는 여자에게 무엇을 보여 주는 것 같은가?
(A) 가격표
(B) 평면도
(C) 송장
(D) 시간표

해설 세부 사항 관련 – 남자가 여자에게 보여 주는 것
남자가 마지막 대사에서 오늘 오후에 다른 수업도 여러 가지 제공한다(we're offering several other classes this afternoon)고 했고 이 표를 보라(Look at this chart)며 이 중 하나를 들어 보겠는지(Would you like to try one of these?) 묻고 있는 것으로 보아, 남자는 여자에게 수업 시간표를 보여 주고 있음을 알 수 있다. 따라서 정답은 (D)이다.

> **Paraphrasing** 대화의 chart → 정답의 schedule

62-64 대화 + 매장 배치도

W-Am **⁶²Welcome to Maddox Automotive Supplies.** Can I help you find something?

M-Cn Yes. **⁶³I want to buy a new set of winter tires for my car. Where can I find them?**

W-Am **⁶³Winter tires are near the back of the store, in the section farthest from the entrance.**

M-Cn Great. Thank you.

W-Am Of course. Also, in case you're interested, **⁶⁴here's our December flyer.** It has a list of all the items that are currently being sold at a reduced price.

여 매독스 자동차용품에 오신 것을 환영합니다. 찾으시는 것을 도와드릴까요?

남 네. 제 차에 사용할 겨울용 타이어 세트를 새로 구입하려고요. 어디에 있나요?

여 겨울용 타이어는 입구에서 가장 먼 구역인 상점 뒤쪽 근처에 있어요.

남 네. 감사합니다.

여 별말씀을요, 그리고 혹시 관심이 있으실까 봐 여기 12월 전단지를 드려요. 현재 할인된 가격으로 판매되고 있는 모든 제품의 목록이 나와 있어요.

어휘   automotive 자동차의   farthest 가장 먼   flyer 전단지

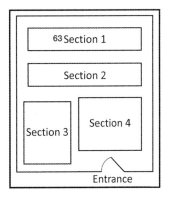

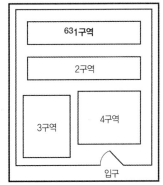

62

Where does the conversation take place?
(A) In a supermarket
(B) In an appliance store
(C) In an automotive store
(D) In a department store

대화는 어디에서 이루어지는가?
(A) 슈퍼마켓
(B) 가전제품 매장
(C) 자동차용품 매장
(D) 백화점

해설 전체 내용 관련 – 대화의 장소
여자가 첫 대사에서 매독스 자동차용품에 오신 것을 환영한다(Welcome to Maddox Automotive Supplies)고 말하고 있으므로 대화가 이루어지고 있는 장소는 자동차 관련 제품을 다루는 곳임을 알 수 있다. 따라서 정답은 (C)이다.

63

Look at the graphic. Where will the man find a product?

(A) In Section 1
(B) In Section 2
(C) In Section 3
(D) In Section 4

시각 정보에 의하면, 남자는 어디에서 제품을 찾을 것인가?

(A) 1구역
(B) 2구역
(C) 3구역
(D) 4구역

해설 시각 정보 연계 – 남자가 제품을 찾을 수 있는 곳

남자가 첫 대사에서 겨울용 타이어 세트를 구입하고자 한다(I want to buy a new set of winter tires for my car)면서 어디에 있는지(Where can I find them?) 묻자 여자가 입구에서 가장 먼 구역인 상점 뒤쪽에 있다(Winter tires are near the back of the store, in the section farthest from the entrance)고 대답하고 있고, 매장 배치도에 따르면 입구에서 가장 먼 상점 뒤쪽은 1구역이라고 나와 있으므로 정답은 (A)이다.

64

What does the woman hand to the man?

(A) A catalog
(B) A flyer
(C) A floor map
(D) A receipt

여자는 남자에게 무엇을 건네주는가?

(A) 카탈로그
(B) 전단지
(C) 평면도
(D) 영수증

해설 세부 사항 관련 – 여자가 남자에게 건네주는 것

여자가 마지막 대사에서 여기 12월 전단지를 드린다(here's our December flyer)고 말하고 있으므로 정답은 (B)이다.

65-67 대화 + 목록

M-Au	Thanks for helping me with this service event. ^{65}**I'm so glad we'll finally have a reading area in our community center.**
W-Am	Yes, it'll be a great addition, and ^{65}**this old storage space is perfect for it.**
M-Au	^{66}**I made a list of things to do this morning and assigned everyone a task.** Here it is.
W-Am	OK. ^{66}**I'll start clearing off these wooden shelves to make room for books.**
M-Au	Oh, ^{67}**a community member donated a sofa yesterday.** It'll look good in our new reading room.

남	서비스 행사에 도움을 주어 감사해요. **마침내 우리 지역 문화 센터에 독서 공간이 생겨서 정말 기뻐요.**
여	네, 큰 보탬이 될 거예요. 그리고 **이 오래된 창고가 그 공간으로 완벽하네요.**
남	전 오늘 아침에 할 일에 대한 목록을 작성해서 모두에게 업무를 나눠 줬어요. 여기 있어요.
여	알았어요. **책을 위한 공간 마련을 위해 이 나무 책장들을 치우는 것부터 시작해야겠어요.**
남	아, **문화 센터 회원 한 분이 어제 소파를 기증하셨어요.** 새 열람실에 잘 어울릴 거예요.

어휘	community center 지역 문화 센터, 복지관　storage 저장, 보관　assign (업무를) 배정하다, 할당하다　clear off 치우다　wooden 목재의　room 공간　donate 기부하다　reading room 열람실, 독서실

Morning Tasks

1. Organize books	Sarai
2. Wash windows	Astrid
3. Paint chairs	Camille
66 4. Clear shelves	Eun-Mi
5. Mop floor	Abdel

오전 업무

1. 책 정리하기	사라이
2. 창문 닦기	아스트리드
3. 의자 페인트칠하기	카밀
4. 66책장 치우기	은미
5. 바닥 걸레질하기	압델

65

Where are the speakers?

(A) At a bookstore
(B) At a community center
(C) At an art studio
(D) At a warehouse

화자들은 어디에 있는가?

(A) 서점
(B) 지역 문화 센터
(C) 미술 작업실
(D) 창고

남자가 첫 대사에서 지역 문화 센터에 독서 공간이 생겨서 기쁘다(I'm so glad we'll finally have a reading area in our community center)고 하자 여자가 이 창고가 그 공간으로 완벽하다(this old storage space is perfect for it)고 말하고 있으므로 화자들은 지역 문화 센터에서 대화를 하고 있음을 알 수 있다. 따라서 정답은 (B)이다.

66

Look at the graphic. Who most likely is the woman?

(A) Sarai
(B) Astrid
(C) Camille
(D) Eun-Mi

시각 정보에 의하면, 여자는 누구인 것 같은가?

(A) 사라이
(B) 아스트리드
(C) 카밀
(D) 은미

해설 시각 정보 연계 – 여자의 이름

남자가 두 번째 대사에서 오늘 아침에 할 일에 대한 목록을 작성해서 모두에게 업무를 나눠 줬다(I made a list of things to do this morning and assigned everyone a task)고 하자 여자가 이 나무 책장들을 치우는 것부터 시작하겠다(I'll start clearing off these wooden shelves to make room for books)고 말하고 있고, 목록에 따르면 책장 치우기 일은 은미에게 할당된 것으로 나와 있으므로 정답은 (D)이다.

67

According to the man, what happened yesterday?

(A) Furniture was donated.
(B) Cleaning supplies were delivered.
(C) Signs were ordered.
(D) Books were purchased.

남자에 따르면, 어제 무슨 일이 있었는가?

(A) 가구가 기증되었다.
(B) 청소용품이 배달되었다.
(C) 표지판이 주문되었다.
(D) 책이 구입되었다.

어휘 cleaning supply 청소용품 purchase 구입하다

해설 세부 사항 관련 – 남자가 말하는 어제 있었던 일

남자가 마지막 대사에서 문화 센터 회원 한 분이 어제 소파를 기증했다(a community member donated a sofa yesterday)고 말하고 있으므로 정답은 (A)이다.

Paraphrasing	대화의 donated a sofa
	→ 정답의 Furniture was donated

68-70 대화 + 케이크 메뉴

W-Br Hi. **68My company is having a holiday party today**, and I'd like to buy a cake. What do you have available?

M-Cn **69We have a cake menu with some different options. Here's what we're offering today.**

W-Br Let's see. A lot of my coworkers like fruit, and this one fits my budget. So **69I'll take this one with the strawberries on top.**

M-Cn Great, **70I'll package that up for you right away. Would you like me to write a custom message on it?** There's no extra charge.

W-Br No, thank you. Just package it as is.

여 안녕하세요. **오늘 회사에서 휴일 파티가 있을 예정이라** 케이크를 사려고요. 어떤 것이 있나요?

남 **다양한 옵션이 있는 케이크 메뉴가 있어요. 여기 오늘 저희가 제공하는 것들이에요.**

여 좀 볼까요. 동료들 중 많은 이들이 과일을 좋아하고, 이것이 제 예산에 맞네요. 그러면 **딸기를 위에 얹은 이것으로 할게요.**

남 좋아요. **바로 포장해 드릴게요. 맞춤 메시지를 작성해 드릴까요?** 추가 요금은 없습니다.

여 아니요, 괜찮아요. 그냥 그대로 포장해 주세요.

어휘 coworker 동료 fit 맞다 budget 예산 package 포장하다 custom 맞춤의, 주문 제작한 as is (있는) 그대로

Today's Cakes

69 Strawberry Shortcake $20.00	Chocolate Sponge Cake $22.00
Red Velvet Cupcakes $17.00	Coffee Butter Cake $25.00

오늘의 케이크

69 딸기 쇼트케이크 20달러	초콜릿 스펀지 케이크 22달러
레드 벨벳 컵케이크 17달러	커피 버터 케이크 25달러

TEST 8

68

What event does the woman mention?

(A) A client luncheon
(B) A store opening
(C) A holiday party
(D) A retirement celebration

여자는 어떤 행사를 언급하는가?

(A) 고객 오찬
(B) 매장 개업
(C) 휴일 파티
(D) 은퇴 축하

해설 세부 사항 관련 – 여자가 언급하는 행사

여자가 첫 대사에서 오늘 회사에서 휴일 파티를 가질 예정(My company is having a holiday party today)이라고 말하고 있으므로 정답은 (C)이다.

69

Look at the graphic. How much will the woman pay for the cake?

(A) $20.00
(B) $22.00
(C) $17.00
(D) $25.00

시각 정보에 의하면, 여자는 케이크 값으로 얼마를 지불할 것인가?

(A) 20달러
(B) 22달러
(C) 17달러
(D) 25달러

해설 시각 정보 연계 – 여자가 케이크 값으로 지불할 금액

남자가 첫 대사에서 다양한 옵션이 있는 케이크 메뉴가 있다(We have a cake menu with some different options)며 여기 오늘 제공하는 것들이 있다(Here's what we're offering today)고 하자 여자가 딸기를 위에 얹은 것으로 하겠다(I'll take this one with the strawberries on top)고 말하고 있고, 케이크 메뉴에 따르면 딸기를 위에 얹은 케이크는 20달러이므로 정답은 (A)이다.

70

What does the man offer to do?

(A) Reduce a price
(B) Supply plastic utensils
(C) Provide free delivery
(D) Customize an item

남자는 무엇을 해 주겠다고 제안하는가?

(A) 가격 인하
(B) 플라스틱 주방 도구 공급
(C) 무료 배송 제공
(D) 제품 맞춤 제작

어휘 utensil (주방) 도구, 식기 customize 맞춤[주문] 제작하다

해설 세부 사항 관련 – 남자의 제안 사항

남자가 두 번째 대사에서 포장을 해주겠다(I'll package that up for you

right away)면서 맞춤 메시지 작성을 원하는지(Would you like me to write a custom message on it?) 묻는 것으로 보아 정답은 (D)이다.

Paraphrasing	대화의 write a custom message → 정답의 Customize an item

PART 4

71-73 팟캐스트

M-Au Hello, listeners, and welcome to my podcast! **71With me today is the national chess champion, Olga Popova.** Just last month, Olga successfully defended her title for the second time. So, **72the fact that she is just twenty-one years old is especially impressive.** She's still the youngest national champion ever. **73Olga recently signed a lucrative deal to promote her favorite energy drink. I'll start our discussion today by asking her to tell us a little more about that.**

안녕하세요, 청취자 여러분, 제 팟캐스트에 오신 것을 환영합니다! **전국 체스 챔피언인 올가 포포바가 오늘 저와 함께합니다.** 바로 지난달에 올가는 두 번째로 타이틀 방어에 성공했습니다. 그래서 **그녀의 나이가 겨우 스물한 살이라는 사실이 특히나 인상적입니다.** 그녀는 아직 역대 전국 챔피언 중에서 가장 어린 나이입니다. **올가는 최근 자신이 가장 좋아하는 에너지 드링크를 홍보하기 위해 수익성 높은 계약에 사인했습니다. 이에 대해 좀 더 이야기해 달라고 요청하는 것으로 오늘 토론을 시작하겠습니다.**

어휘 defend 방어하다, 지키다 impressive 인상적인 lucrative 수익성이 좋은 deal 계약 promote 홍보하다

71

Who is Olga Popova?

(A) A video game designer
(B) A chess player
(C) A swimmer
(D) An actor

올가 포포바는 누구인가?

(A) 비디오 게임 디자이너
(B) 체스 선수
(C) 수영 선수
(D) 배우

해설 전체 내용 관련 – 올가 포포바의 직업

화자가 초반부에 전국 체스 챔피언인 올가 포포바가 오늘 함께하겠다(With me today is the national chess champion, Olga Popova)고 알리고 있으므로 정답은 (B)이다.

Paraphrasing	담화의 national chess champion → 정답의 chess player

72

What does the speaker say is especially impressive about Olga Popova?

(A) Her young age
(B) Her communication skills
(C) Her educational background
(D) Her volunteer activities

화자는 올가 포포바에 대해 특히 인상적인 점이 무엇이라고 말하는가?

(A) 어린 나이
(B) 의사소통 능력
(C) 학력
(D) 봉사 활동

해설 세부 사항 관련 – 화자가 올가 포포바에 대해 인상적이라고 말하는 것

화자가 중반부에 그녀의 나이가 겨우 스물한 살이라는 사실이 특히나 인상적(the fact that she is just twenty-one years old is especially impressive)이라고 말하고 있으므로 정답은 (A)이다.

> Paraphrasing   담화의 she is just twenty-one years old
> → 정답의 Her young age

73

What will be discussed next?

(A) Training strategies
(B) A sponsorship agreement
(C) Equipment recommendations
(D) A recent trip

다음에 무엇이 논의될 것인가?

(A) 훈련 전략
(B) 협찬 계약
(C) 장비 추천
(D) 최근 여행

어휘 sponsorship (재정적) 협찬[후원]   agreement 계약, 합의서

해설 세부 사항 관련 – 다음에 논의할 사항

화자가 후반부에 올가는 최근 에너지 드링크 홍보를 위한 수익성 높은 계약에 사인했다(Olga recently signed a lucrative deal to promote her favorite energy drink)며 이에 대해 이야기해 달라는 요청으로 토론을 시작하겠다(I'll start our discussion today by asking her to tell us a little more about that)고 말하고 있으므로 정답은 (B)이다.

> Paraphrasing   담화의 lucrative deal to promote her favorite energy drink
> → 정답의 sponsorship agreement

74-76 담화

W-Am Thanks for stopping by our booth to learn more about career opportunities at Mosconi Accounting. We've been in business for over three decades. **74One of the things I most appreciate about working for this company is that employees are allowed to make their own work schedules. 75We're looking for job candidates with five or more years of experience. 76If you think you're a strong candidate, please sign up for an interview** on one of the tablets on the table in front of you.

모스코니 어카운팅의 채용 기회를 알아보려고 저희 부스에 들러 주셔서 감사합니다. 저희는 30년 넘게 사업을 이어 오고 있습니다. **이 회사에서 일하는 것에 대해 제가 가장 높이 평가하는 것 중 하나는 직원들이 자신의 근무 일정을 스스로 정할 수 있다는 것입니다. 우리는 5년 이상의 경력을 가진 지원자를 찾고 있습니다. 유력한 후보라고 생각하신다면, 앞 탁자에 있는 태블릿에서 면담을 신청하세요.**

어휘 stop by ~에 들르다   accounting 회계   appreciate 높이 평가하다, 진가를 알아보다   candidate 지원자, 후보자   sign up for ~을 신청하다

74

What does the speaker appreciate about the company?

(A) It offers paid vacations.
(B) It offers promotion opportunities.
(C) It offers career development workshops.
(D) It offers flexible work hours.

화자는 회사에 대해 무엇을 높이 평가하는가?

(A) 유급 휴가를 제공한다.
(B) 승진 기회를 제공한다.
(C) 경력 개발 워크숍을 제공한다.
(D) 탄력적 근로 시간제를 제공한다.

어휘 paid vacation 유급 휴가   promotion 승진   flexible 탄력적인, 유연한

해설 세부 사항 관련 – 화자가 회사에 대해 높이 평가하는 점

화자가 초반부에 이 회사에 대해 높이 평가하는 것은 직원들이 근무 일정을 스스로 정할 수 있다는 것(One of the things I most appreciate about working for this company is that employees are allowed to make their own work schedules)이라고 말하고 있으므로 정답은 (D)이다.

> Paraphrasing   담화의 make their own work schedules
> → 정답의 offers flexible work hours

75

What qualification does the speaker mention?

(A) Five years of experience
(B) Attention to detail
(C) Interpersonal skills
(D) Professional certification

화자는 어떤 자격을 언급하는가?

(A) 5년의 경력
(B) 꼼꼼함
(C) 대인 관계 능력
(D) 전문 자격증

TEST 8

어휘 attention to detail 꼼꼼함, 세부적인 사항에 대한 주의
interpersonal 대인 관계의 certification 자격(증)

해설 세부 사항 관련 – 화자가 언급하는 자격

화자가 우리는 중반부에 5년 이상의 경력을 가진 지원자를 찾고 있다 (We're looking for job candidates with five or more years of experience)고 말하고 있으므로 정답은 (A)이다.

76

What does the speaker encourage the listeners to do?
(A) Leave their business cards
(B) Pick up a brochure
(C) Sign up for an interview
(D) Submit questions

화자는 청자들에게 무엇을 하라고 권하는가?
(A) 명함 남기기
(B) 안내 책자 가져가기
(C) 면담 신청하기
(D) 질문서 제출하기

어휘 business card 명함 submit 제출하다

해설 세부 사항 관련 – 화자의 권장 사항

화자가 후반부에 유력한 후보라고 생각한다면, 면담을 신청하라(If you think you're a strong candidate, please sign up for an interview)고 권하고 있으므로 정답은 (C)이다.

77-79 안내 방송

M-Au ⁷⁷**Ladies and gentlemen, the play will begin soon.** ⁷⁸**Please note that Arnaud Clement will not appear in tonight's performance. The role of Mr. Bertrand will be played by his understudy, Olivier Lambert. We apologize for this last-minute change.** There will be a twenty-minute intermission between the first and second acts. Refreshments will be available in the lobby at that time. Now, ⁷⁹**please take a moment to silence your mobile phones and any other electronic devices.** We hope that you enjoy tonight's performance!

신사 숙녀 여러분, 연극이 곧 시작됩니다. 아르노 클레멘트는 오늘 밤 공연에 출연하지 않는다는 점을 참고해 주세요. 그의 대역 배우인 올리비에 램버트가 버트랜드 씨 역을 연기할 것입니다. 마지막 순간에 변경이 있게 되어 사과드립니다. 1막과 2막 사이에 20분의 휴식 시간이 있을 것입니다. 그 시간에 로비에서 다과가 제공됩니다. 이제 **잠시 시간을 내어 휴대폰과 기타 전자 기기를 무음으로 설정해 주세요.** 오늘 밤의 공연을 즐기시기 바랍니다!

어휘 play 연극 appear 출연하다 understudy 대역 (배우) last-minute 마지막 순간의, 막판의 intermission 중간 휴식 시간 act (연극의) 막 refreshment 다과 silence 무음으로 설정하다, 조용하게 만들다 electronic device 전자 기기

77

Where is the announcement taking place?
(A) At a theater
(B) At an amusement park
(C) At a convention center
(D) At an art gallery

안내 방송은 어디에서 이루어지고 있는가?
(A) 극장
(B) 놀이공원
(C) 컨벤션 센터
(D) 미술관

해설 전체 내용 관련 – 안내 방송의 장소

화자가 도입부에 신사 숙녀 여러분 연극이 곧 시작됩니다(Ladies and gentlemen, the play will begin soon)라고 말하고 있으므로 정답은 (A)이다.

78

Why does the speaker apologize?
(A) There will be a long wait time.
(B) Some supplies have run out.
(C) An entrance is under construction.
(D) A replacement has been made.

화자는 왜 사과하는가?
(A) 대기 시간이 길 것이다.
(B) 물품이 소진되었다.
(C) 입구가 공사 중이다.
(D) 교체가 있었다.

어휘 run out 소진되다 entrance 입구 under construction 공사 중인 make a replacement 교체하다

해설 세부 사항 관련 – 화자가 사과하는 이유

화자가 초반부에 아르노 클레멘트는 오늘 밤에 출연하지 않는다 (Please note that Arnaud Clement will not appear in tonight's performance)고 했고 그의 대역 배우인 올리비에 램버트가 버트랜드 씨 역을 연기할 것(The role of Mr. Bertrand will be played by his understudy, Olivier Lambert)이라면서 마지막 순간에 변경이 있어 사과드린다(We apologize for this last-minute change)고 말하고 있으므로 정답은 (D)이다.

> Paraphrasing 담화의 The role of Mr. Bertrand will be played by his understudy
> → 정답의 A replacement has been made

79

What does the speaker remind the listeners to do?
(A) Pick up their parking vouchers
(B) Silence their electronic devices
(C) Purchase souvenir merchandise
(D) Download a program

화자는 청자들에게 무엇을 하라고 상기시키는가?

(A) 주차권 가져가기

(B) 전자 기기 무음으로 설정하기

(C) 기념상품 구매하기

(D) 프로그램 다운로드하기

어휘 parking voucher 주차권   souvenir 기념품

해설 세부 사항 관련 – 화자가 청자들에게 상기시키는 것

화자가 후반부에 휴대폰과 기타 전자 기기를 무음으로 설정해 달라 (please take a moment to silence your mobile phones and any other electronic devices)고 말하고 있으므로 정답은 (B)이다.

80-82 전화 메시지

W-Br Hi, Babatunde. **80The storm last night brought down some branches onto Trent Avenue, and no cars can get through.** **81There's debris from the storm on some other roadways as well, but that's the main route into the city center.** Make sure to take a bucket truck and a few additional service people with you. Oh, and **82remember that we have a meeting with a roadway maintenance director at three o'clock.** She wants to discuss some tasks for an upcoming repaving project.

안녕하세요, 바바툰데. 어젯밤 폭풍으로 트렌트 가에 나뭇가지들이 떨어져 있어서 차가 지나갈 수 없습니다. 다른 도로에도 폭풍으로 인한 잔해가 있기는 하지만 그곳이 도심으로 가는 주요 경로입니다. 반드시 버킷 트럭과 몇 명의 추가 인력을 데리고 가세요. 아, 그리고 3시에 도로 정비 국장과 회의가 있다는 것을 기억하세요. 그녀는 곧 있을 도로 재포장 공사를 위한 몇 가지 작업에 대해 논의하고 싶어 합니다.

어휘 bring down 떨어뜨리다   get through 통과하다   debris 잔해, 쓰레기   roadway 도로, 차도   as well ~도, 또한   route 경로, 길   maintenance 정비, 유지 보수   upcoming 곧 있을, 다가올   repave (도로를) 다시 포장하다

80

According to the speaker, why is Trent Avenue closed?

(A) It is blocked by fallen branches.

(B) A traffic light has stopped working.

(C) A parade is scheduled.

(D) A water pipe has burst.

화자에 따르면, 트렌트 가는 왜 봉쇄가 되었는가?

(A) 떨어진 나뭇가지들로 막혀 있다.

(B) 신호등이 작동을 멈추었다.

(C) 퍼레이드가 예정되어 있다.

(D) 수도관이 파열되었다.

어휘 block 막다   burst 파열하다, 터지다

해설 세부 사항 관련 – 트렌트 가가 봉쇄된 이유

화자가 초반부에 폭풍으로 트렌트 가에 나뭇가지들이 떨어져 있어서

차가 지나갈 수 없다(The storm last night brought down some branches onto Trent Avenue, and no cars can get through)고 말하고 있으므로 정답은 (A)이다.

Paraphrasing	담화의 brought down some branches
	→ 정답의 fallen branches
	담화의 no cars can get through
	→ 정답의 It is blocked

81

What does the speaker imply when she says, "that's the main route into the city center"?

(A) She will take a different route.

(B) She will work from home.

(C) Funding will be made available soon.

(D) A task should be given priority.

화자가 "그곳이 도심으로 가는 주요 경로입니다"라고 말할 때 무엇을 의미하는가?

(A) 그녀는 다른 경로를 택할 것이다.

(B) 그녀는 재택근무를 할 것이다.

(C) 자금이 곧 제공될 것이다.

(D) 작업에 우선순위가 주어져야 한다.

어휘 funding 자금, 자금 제공   be made available 제공되다, 사용 가능하다   priority 우선(순위), 우위

해설 화자의 의도 파악 – 그곳이 도심으로 가는 주요 경로이다는 말의 의도

앞에서 다른 도로에도 폭풍으로 인한 잔해가 있기는 하지만(There's debris from the storm on some other roadways as well, but)이라고 말한 뒤 인용문을 언급한 것으로 보아, 다른 도로보다 먼저 가서 작업을 해야 함을 상기시키려는 의도로 한 말임을 알 수 있다. 따라서 정답은 (D)이다.

82

According to the speaker, what is scheduled for three o'clock?

(A) A sales presentation

(B) An analysis of survey results

(C) A job interview

(D) A meeting with a supervisor

화자에 따르면, 무엇이 3시에 예정되어 있는가?

(A) 판매 프레젠테이션

(B) 설문 조사 결과 분석

(C) 취업 면접

(D) 관리자와의 회의

어휘 analysis 분석

해설 세부 사항 관련 – 화자가 말하는 3시에 예정되어 있는 일

화자가 후반부에 3시에 도로 정비 국장과 회의가 있다는 것을 기억하라(remember that we have a meeting with a roadway maintenance director at three o'clock)고 청자에서 상기시키고 있으므로 정답은 (D)이다.

TEST 8

83-85 설명

W-Am **83As lifeguards here at the pool, you'll each begin your shift by checking the pool's chemical balance. 84This task is important because it ensures our pool equipment stays in good condition and doesn't corrode.** Here's how it's done: take a test strip from this box, then hold the strip in the water, like this, for about five seconds. The color will tell you whether the pH level is within acceptable range. A blue color on this strip indicates that the water is OK. Now **85I'll show you where we store the chemicals in case you need them later.**

이곳 수영장의 인명 구조원으로서 여러분 각자는 수영장의 화학적 균형 상태를 확인하는 것으로 근무를 시작하게 됩니다. 이 작업은 수영장 장비를 양호한 상태로 유지하고 부식되지 않도록 하기 때문에 중요합니다. 방법은 다음과 같습니다. 이 상자에서 검사지를 꺼낸 다음, 이런 식으로 잡고 5초 동안 물에 담급니다. 색깔로 pH 수치가 허용 가능한 범위 내에 있는지를 알 수 있습니다. 이 검사지가 파란색을 띠면 물이 정상이라는 의미입니다. 자, 나중에 여러분들도 필요할 경우를 대비하여 화학용품을 보관하는 곳을 알려 드리겠습니다.

어휘 lifeguard 인명 구조원 shift (교대) 근무 chemical 화학의; 화학용품[물질] balance 균형 (상태) ensure 반드시 ~하게 하다 equipment 장비 in good condition 상태가 좋은 corrode 부식하다 test strip 검사지 acceptable 허용할 수 있는 in case ~할 경우를 대비하여

83

Where are the instructions being given?
(A) In a laboratory
(B) At a swimming pool
(C) At a national park
(D) At a sporting goods store

설명은 어디에서 주어지고 있는가?
(A) 실험실
(B) 수영장
(C) 국립 공원
(D) 스포츠용품점

해설 전체 내용 관련 - 담화의 장소
화자가 도입부에 이곳 수영장의 인명 구조원으로서 여러분은 수영장의 화학적 균형 상태를 확인하는 것으로 근무를 시작한다(As lifeguards here at the pool, you'll each begin your shift by checking the pool's chemical balance)고 말하고 있으므로 정답은 (B)이다.

84

According to the speaker, why is a task important?
(A) It prevents wasting chemicals.
(B) It promotes visitor satisfaction.
(C) It keeps equipment in good condition.
(D) It ensures accurate inventory records.

화자에 따르면, 작업은 왜 중요한가?
(A) 화학 물질의 낭비를 방지한다.
(B) 방문자 만족을 촉진한다.
(C) 장비를 양호한 상태로 유지한다.
(D) 정확한 재고 기록을 보장한다.

어휘 waste 낭비하다 accurate 정확한 inventory 재고

해설 세부 사항 관련 - 화자가 말하는 작업이 중요한 이유
화자가 중반부에 작업은 수영장 장비를 양호한 상태로 유지하고 부식되지 않도록 하기 때문에 중요하다(This task is important because it ensures our pool equipment stays in good condition and doesn't corrode)고 말하고 있으므로 정답은 (C)이다.

85

What will the listeners do next?
(A) Watch a training video
(B) See where some supplies are stored
(C) Learn how to operate a machine
(D) Review a list of safety regulations

청자들은 다음에 무엇을 할 것인가?
(A) 교육 비디오 시청
(B) 물품 보관 장소 확인
(C) 기계 작동 방법 학습
(D) 안전 규정 목록 검토

어휘 operate 가동[작동]하다 safety regulation 안전 규정

해설 세부 사항 관련 - 청자들이 다음에 할 일
화자가 마지막에 필요할 경우를 대비하여 화학용품의 보관 장소를 알려 주겠다(I'll show you where we store the chemicals in case you need them later)고 한 것으로 보아 정답은 (B)이다.

86-88 팟캐스트

M-Cn Thank you, Fritz, for having me on your podcast to introduce my new movie. **86I decided to direct this film because it's an inspiring story. 87People will get to learn about the bravery and survival strategies needed for an expedition to** a place with extremely cold conditions. The Ice Fall's expedition of 1901 took place back in a time without the sort of equipment and instruments we have today. [88]Is the film 100 percent accurate? Well, we have no way of knowing everything that happened. But we did use information from diaries kept by the Ice Fall's crew.

프리츠, 저의 새 영화를 소개할 수 있게 팟캐스트에 초대해 주셔서 감사합니다. 저는 이 영화가 감동적인 이야기여서 감독하기로 결정했습니다. 사람들은 극도로 추운 곳으로 원정을 갈 때 필요한 용기와 생존 전략에 대해 배우게 될 것입니다. 1901년 아이스폴 원정은 오늘날의 장비와 도구가 아직 없었던 시대에 진행되었습니다. 영화가 100% 정확할까요? 음, 일어났던 일의 모든 것을 알 수 있는 방법은 없습니다. 하지만 우리는 아이스폴의 선원이 작성한 일지의 정보를 활용했습니다.

어휘 direct 감독하다 inspiring 감동을 주는, 영감을 주는 bravery 용기 strategy 전략 expedition 원정, 탐험 instrument 도구, 기구 accurate 정확한 diary 일지, 일기 crew 선원, 승무원

86

Who is the speaker?
(A) A filmmaker
(B) An actor
(C) A costume designer
(D) A sound engineer

화자는 누구인가?
(A) 영화감독
(B) 배우
(C) 의상 디자이너
(D) 음향 기사

해설 전체 내용 관련 – 화자의 직업
화자가 초반부에 이야기가 감동적이라 영화를 감독하기로 결정했다(I decided to direct this film because it's an inspiring story)고 밝히고 있으므로 정답은 (A)이다.

87

What is the movie about?
(A) A historical expedition
(B) An important invention
(C) An athletic competition
(D) A medical discovery

영화는 무엇에 관한 것인가?
(A) 역사적 원정
(B) 중요한 발명
(C) 운동 경기
(D) 의학적 발견

해설 세부 사항 관련 – 영화의 주제
화자가 중반부에 사람들은 극도로 추운 곳으로 원정을 갈 때 필요한 용

기와 생존 전략에 대해 배우게 될 것(People will get to learn ~ cold conditions)이라면서 1901년 아이스폴 원정은 오늘날의 장비와 도구가 아직 없었던 시대에 진행되었다(The Ice Fall's expedition of 1901 ~ instruments we have today)고 영화에 대해 소개하고 있으므로 실제 과거에 있었던 원정에 대한 영화라는 것을 알 수 있다. 따라서 정답은 (A)이다.

88

What does the speaker mean when he says, "we have no way of knowing everything that happened"?
(A) A criticism is unfair.
(B) A story is not entirely factual.
(C) A movie reviewer is mistaken.
(D) More research is necessary.

화자가 "일어났던 일의 모든 것을 알 수 있는 방법은 없습니다"라고 말할 때 무엇을 의미하는가?
(A) 비판은 부당하다.
(B) 이야기가 전적으로 사실인 것은 아니다.
(C) 영화 평론가가 잘못 알고 있다.
(D) 연구가 더 필요하다.

어휘 criticism 비판 unfair 부당한 entirely 전체적으로 factual 사실에 기반을 둔 mistaken 잘못 알고 있는, 오해한

해설 화자의 의도 파악 – 일어났던 모든 것을 알 수 있는 방법은 없다는 말의 의도
앞에서 영화가 100% 정확할지(Is the film 100 percent accurate?) 물어보고 난 뒤 인용문에서 모든 것을 알 수는 없다고 언급한 것으로 보아, 영화에 나오는 이야기가 전부 사실에 기반을 둔 것이 아닌, 허구도 있다는 것을 알리려고 한 말임을 알 수 있다. 따라서 정답은 (B)이다.

89-91 연설

W-Am As the mayor of our city, [89]I'd like to thank you for joining us to celebrate the first day of construction for the Garfield Bridge. In less than two years, the ground we're all standing on right now will be the entrance to the south end of the bridge, linking the communities on both sides of the river. Not only will the bridge be functional—it'll also be attractive. [90]Asako Tamura, who designed the famous Molina Bridge, was our principal architect. Now, [91]I'd like to invite Ms. Tamura to be the first person to sign the ceremonial shovel, which will be used to initiate construction.

우리 시의 시장으로서 **가필드 대교를 건설하는 첫날을 축하하기 위해 함께해 주시는 여러분들께 감사드립니다.** 지금 우리 모두가 서 있는 이 땅은 2년 이내에 강을 마주하고 있는 두 지역 사회를 연결하는 다리의 남단 입구가 될 것입니다. 다리는 실용적일 뿐만 아니라 멋진 모습으로 건축될 것입니다. **유명한 몰리나 대교를 설계한 아사코 타무라는 우리**

의 수석 건축가였습니다. 이제 타무라 씨에게 공사를 시작하는 데 사용될 시공식 삽에 맨 첫 번째로 서명하는 인사가 되어 달라고 요청하겠습니다.

어휘 mayor 시장 ground 땅, 지면 entrance 입구 link 연결하다 functional 실용적인, 기능상의 attractive 멋진, 매력적인 principal 수석의; 주요한 architect 건축가 invite 요청하다 ceremonial 의식의 shovel 삽 initiate (사업을) 시작하다, 착수하다

89

What event is being held?
(A) A community fund-raiser
(B) A retirement party
(C) An anniversary celebration
(D) A project launch ceremony

어떤 행사가 열리고 있는가?
(A) 지역 사회 기금 조성
(B) 퇴직 파티
(C) 기념일 축하
(D) 프로젝트 착수식

해설 전체 내용 관련 – 개최되고 있는 행사
화자가 도입부에 가필드 대교의 건설 첫날을 축하하기 위해 함께해 주어 고맙다(I'd like to thank you for joining us to celebrate the first day of construction for the Garfield Bridge)고 말하고 있으므로 정답은 (D)이다.

Paraphrasing	담화의 celebrate the first day of construction → 정답의 A project launch ceremony

90

Who is Asako Tamura?
(A) A news reporter
(B) A professional athlete
(C) An architect
(D) A professor

아사코 타무라는 누구인가?
(A) 뉴스 기자
(B) 프로 운동선수
(C) 건축가
(D) 교수

해설 세부 사항 관련 – 아사코 타무라의 직업
화자가 중반부에 몰리나 대교를 설계한 아사코 타무라는 수석 건축가였다 (Asako Tamura, who designed the famous Molina Bridge, was our principal architect)고 알려 주고 있으므로 정답은 (C)이다.

91

What does the speaker invite Asako Tamura to do?
(A) Sign her name
(B) Give a speech
(C) Take some photographs
(D) Answer some questions

화자는 아사코 타무라에게 무엇을 해 달라고 요청하는가?
(A) 서명하기
(B) 연설하기
(C) 사진 찍기
(D) 질의응답하기

해설 세부 사항 관련 – 화자가 아사코 타무라에게 요청하는 일
화자가 마지막에 타무라 씨에게 시공식 삽에 첫 번째로 서명하는 인사가 되어 달라고 요청하겠다(I'd like to invite Ms. Tamura to be the first person to sign the ceremonial shovel, which will be used to initiate construction)고 말하고 있으므로 정답은 (A)이다.

92-94 여행 정보

M-Cn ⁹²Thanks for signing up for this guided hike in Kiftaynee State Park. Our park includes several sites of archaeological interest that have attracted a lot of attention. This afternoon's hike on Vista Trail will take us through areas where our early ancestors lived and farmed long ago. ⁹³I know that some of you expressed interest in the Claremont Trail. That's quite a long hike, and remember, our park closes at four. If you'd like to go on that hike on a future date, then please arrive during the morning. Also, ⁹⁴for those of you who think you'll be back often, consider buying a yearly pass. It'll be cheaper than paying for each visit.

키프타이니 주립 공원의 가이드 인솔 산행을 신청해 주셔서 감사합니다. 우리 공원은 많은 이목을 끌어 온 고고학적으로 관심받는 여러 장소를 포함하고 있습니다. 오늘 오후 비스타 트레일에서의 산행은 초기 선조들이 오래전에 살며 농사를 지었던 지역으로 우리를 안내할 것입니다. 여러분 중 몇 분이 클레어몬트 트레일에 관심을 보였다는 것을 알고 있습니다. 그곳은 꽤 긴 산행인데요, 기억할 것이 있습니다. 공원은 4시에 문을 닫습니다. 다음에 그 산행 코스를 가고 싶다면 아침에 와 주시기 바랍니다. 또한 자주 방문할 생각이 있으신 분들은 연간 이용권 구매를 고려해 보세요. 방문할 때마다 비용을 지불하는 것보다 저렴합니다.

어휘 guided 가이드가 안내하는 hike 산행[등산], 도보 여행 archaeological 고고학적인 attract attention 이목을 끌다 trail 루트, (등산) 코스 ancestor 선조, 조상 express 표현하다 yearly 연간의 pass 이용권

92

What does the speaker point out about Kiftaynee State Park?
(A) It is the largest in the region.
(B) It has some unusual wildlife.
(C) It is maintained entirely by volunteers.
(D) It has unique archaeological sites.

화자는 키프타이니 주립 공원에 관해 무엇이라고 언급하는가?
(A) 지역에서 가장 크다.
(B) 특이한 야생 동물이 있다.
(C) 전적으로 자원봉사자들에 의해 유지된다.
(D) 특별한 고고학 유적지가 있다.

어휘 point out 언급하다, 가리키다 region 지방, 지역 unusual 특이한, 드문 maintain 유지하다 unique 특별한, 독특한

해설 세부 사항 관련 – 화자가 키프타이니 주립 공원에 관해 언급하는 것
화자가 도입부에 키프타이니 주립 공원의 산행 신청에 감사하다(Thanks for signing up for this guided hike in Kiftaynee State Park)며 공원은 많은 이목을 끌어 온 고고학적으로 관심받는 여러 장소를 포함하고 있다(Our park includes several sites of archaeological interest that have attracted a lot of attention)고 말하고 있으므로 정답은 (D)이다.

> Paraphrasing 담화의 sites of archaeological interest that have attracted a lot of attention
> → 정답의 unique archaeological sites

93

Why does the speaker say, "our park closes at four"?
(A) To encourage a faster hiking pace
(B) To announce a change in park hours
(C) To indicate why a trail is not an option
(D) To emphasize that camping is not permitted

화자는 왜 "공원은 4시에 문을 닫습니다"라고 말하는가?
(A) 더 빠른 산행 속도를 권장하기 위해
(B) 공원 운영 시간 변경을 알리기 위해
(C) 등산 코스가 선택 사항이 아닌 이유를 나타내기 위해
(D) 캠핑이 허용되지 않음을 강조하기 위해

어휘 pace (걸음, 달리기의) 속도 emphasize 강조하다 permit 허가하다

해설 화자의 의도 파악 – 공원은 4시에 문을 닫는다는 말의 의도
앞에서 클레어몬트 트레일에 관심을 보인 사람들이 있다(I know that some of you expressed interest in the Claremont Trail)면서 그곳은 꽤 긴 산행이고 기억할 것이 있다(That's quite a long hike, and remember)고 말한 뒤 인용문을 언급하고 있으므로, 클레어몬트 코스에 걸리는 시간은 공원이 문을 닫는 시간을 초과할 수 있기 때문에 갈 수 없음을 알리려는 의도로 한 말임을 알 수 있다. 따라서 정답은 (C)이다.

94

What does the speaker encourage the listeners to buy?
(A) A park map
(B) Some hiking poles
(C) An annual pass
(D) A bird-watching guide

화자는 청자들에게 무엇을 구입하라고 권하는가?
(A) 공원 지도
(B) 등산용 스틱
(C) 연간 이용권
(D) 조류 관찰 가이드

해설 세부 사항 관련 – 화자가 청자들에게 구입하라고 권하는 것
화자가 후반부에 자주 방문할 예정이라면 연간 이용권 구매를 고려해 보라(for those of you who think you'll be back often, consider buying a yearly pass)며 방문할 때마다 비용을 지불하는 것보다 저렴하다(It'll be cheaper than paying for each visit)고 권하고 있으므로 정답은 (C)이다.

> Paraphrasing 담화의 yearly → 정답의 annual

95-97 회의 발췌 + 그래프

W-Br ⁹⁵**I've been going through all our bills and identifying where our business can cut costs.** We can certainly be smarter about some purchases, and we can also work to keep our electricity bill down. ⁹⁶**It's never exceeded 300 euros a month before, but it did once this year.** I was surprised to see that. I think the biggest savings, however, will come from approaching our long-term suppliers about lowering their prices. ⁹⁷**I'll spend some time this afternoon investigating what other suppliers charge.** If I find better prices, we'll have more negotiating power.

저는 모든 청구서를 살펴보았고 우리 업체가 어디에서 비용을 절감할 수 있는지를 확인해 봤습니다. 어떤 구매는 확실히 더 똑똑하게 할 수 있으며 또한 전기 요금을 낮추기 위한 노력도 할 수 있습니다. **전에는 한 달에 300유로를 넘은 적이 없었는데 올해는 한 번 넘었어요.** 그것을 보고 무척 놀랐습니다. 그러나 가장 큰 비용 절감은 우리의 오랜 납품 업체와 가격 인하에 대해 이야기해 보는 것에서부터 시작될 수 있습니다. **오늘 오후에는 다른 공급업체는 얼마를 청구하는지 조사하는 데 시간을 들여야겠어요.** 더 나은 가격을 찾으면 협상에 힘이 될 것입니다.

어휘 go through ~을 살펴보다, ~을 조사하다 bill 청구서, 고지서 identify 확인하다, 찾다 exceed 넘다, 초과하다 saving 비용 절감, 절약 approach ~와 교섭을 가지다, ~와 접촉하다 supplier 납품[공급]업체 lower ~을 내리다 investigate 조사하다 negotiate 협상하다, 교섭하다

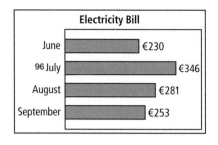

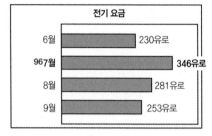

95

What is the speaker mainly discussing?
(A) When to collect data
(B) Reasons for a miscalculation
(C) Ways to reduce expenses
(D) How to be more environmentally friendly

화자는 주로 무엇에 대해 논의하고 있는가?
(A) 데이터를 수집하는 시기
(B) 계산 착오의 이유
(C) 비용을 절감하는 방법
(D) 더 환경친화적으로 되는 방법

어휘 miscalculation 계산 착오 expense 비용 environmentally friendly 환경친화적인

해설 전체 내용 관련 – 담화의 주제
화자가 도입부에 청구서를 살펴보았고 어디에서 비용을 절감할 수 있는지를 확인해 봤다(I've been going through all our bills and identifying where our business can cut costs)고 말하며 비용 절감을 위한 구체적인 방법과 관련된 이야기를 이어 가고 있으므로 정답은 (C)이다.

> **Paraphrasing** 담화의 cut costs → 정답의 reduce expenses

96

Look at the graphic. Which month does the speaker refer to?
(A) June
(B) July
(C) August
(D) September

시각 정보에 의하면, 화자는 어느 달을 언급하는가?
(A) 6월
(B) 7월
(C) 8월
(D) 9월

해설 시각 정보 연계 – 화자가 언급하는 달
화자가 중반부에 전에는 한 달에 300유로를 넘은 적이 없었는데 올해는 한 번 넘었다(It's never exceeded 300 euros a month before, but it did once this year)고 말하고 있고, 그래프에 따르면 전기 요금이 300유로를 넘은 달은 7월이므로 정답은 (B)이다.

97

What will the speaker do this afternoon?
(A) Take inventory
(B) Conduct some research
(C) Update a spreadsheet
(D) Pay a bill

화자는 오늘 오후에 무엇을 할 것인가?
(A) 재고 조사
(B) 정보 조사
(C) 스프레드시트 업데이트
(D) 청구서 지불

해설 세부 사항 관련 – 화자가 오늘 오후에 할 일
화자가 후반부에 오늘 오후에는 다른 공급업체는 얼마를 청구하는지를 조사하겠다(I'll spend some time this afternoon investigating what other suppliers charge)고 말하고 있으므로 정답은 (B)이다.

> **Paraphrasing** 담화의 investigating
> → 정답의 Conduct some research

98-100 설명 + 조리 시간표

W-Am Good morning! Thank you for visiting our booth at the trade show. **98Today, I'm going to demonstrate how to use the Gregerson Quickblast to steam your vegetables to perfection.** Let's start with some fresh asparagus. **99For this recipe, you'll need asparagus spears, a tablespoon of butter, a pinch of salt, and water.** Bring the water, butter, and salt to a boil. **99Place the vegetables in the top half of the device.** Now, set the timer for the recommended cook time. While we wait, **100please take a coupon for a twenty percent discount on the Quickblast at any local store.**

좋은 아침입니다! 무역 박람회에서 저희 부스를 방문해 주셔서 감사합니다. **오늘은 야채를 완벽하게 삶기 위한 그레거슨 퀵블래스트 사용법을 시연할 거예요.** 신선한 아스파라거스로 시작해 봅시다. **이 조리법을 위해 아스파라거스 줄기, 버터 한 테이블스푼, 소금 한 꼬집, 그리고 물이 필요합니다.** 물, 버터, 소금을 끓입니다. **기기의 상단 절반에 야채를 놓으세요.** 이제 타이머를 권장 조리 시간에 맞게 설정하십시오. 기다리는 동안 **지역 매장 어느 곳에서도 사용할 수 있는 퀵블래스트 20 퍼센트 할인 쿠폰을 받아 가세요.**

어휘 trade show 무역 박람회 demonstrate 시연하다
perfection 완벽 spear (식물의) 어린줄기[가지] pinch 꼬집(기)
bring ~ to a boil 끓게 하다 device 기기, 장치 set 설정하다

Food	Cook Time
Brussels sprouts	4 minutes
Broccoli	5 minutes
99Asparagus	6 minutes
Carrots	7 minutes

식품	조리 시간
방울다다기양배추	4분
브로콜리	5분
99 아스파라거스	6분
당근	7분

98

What type of product is the speaker demonstrating?

(A) A toaster oven
(B) An electric grill
(C) An air fryer
(D) A food steamer

화자는 어떤 종류의 제품을 시연하고 있는가?

(A) 토스터 오븐
(B) 전기 그릴
(C) 에어프라이어
(D) 찜통

해설 전체 내용 관련 – 화자가 시연하는 제품

화자가 초반부에 오늘은 야채를 완벽하게 삶기 위한 그레거슨 퀵블래스트 사용법을 시연할 것(Today, I'm going to demonstrate how to use the Gregerson Quickblast to steam your vegetables to perfection)이라고 말하고 있으므로 정답은 (D)이다.

99

Look at the graphic. How long will the ingredient be cooked?

(A) 4 minutes
(B) 5 minutes
(C) 6 minutes
(D) 7 minutes

시각 정보에 의하면, 식재료는 얼마나 오래 조리될 것인가?

(A) 4분
(B) 5분
(C) 6분
(D) 7분

해설 시각 정보 연계 – 식재료가 조리되는 시간

화자가 중반부에 이 조리법에는 아스파라거스 줄기, 버터, 소금, 물이 필요하다(For this recipe, you'll need asparagus spears, a

tablespoon of butter, a pinch of salt, and water)고 한 후, 기기에 야채를 놓고(Place the vegetables in the top half of the device), 타이머를 권장 조리 시간에 맞게 설정하라(Now, set the timer for the recommended cook time)고 말하고 있고, 조리 시간표에 따르면 아스파라거스는 조리 시간이 6분이므로 정답은 (C)이다.

100

What does the speaker offer the listeners?

(A) A discount coupon
(B) A free sample
(C) An extended warranty
(D) A recipe book

화자는 청자들에게 무엇을 제공하는가?

(A) 할인 쿠폰
(B) 무료 시식
(C) 보증 연장
(D) 요리책

해설 세부 사항 관련 – 화자가 청자들에게 제공하는 것

화자가 마지막에 지역 매장 어디에서도 사용할 수 있는 퀵블래스트 20 퍼센트 할인 쿠폰을 받아 가라(please take a coupon for a twenty percent discount on the Quickblast at any local store)고 말하고 있으므로 정답은 (A)이다.

Paraphrasing	담화의 coupon for a twenty percent discount → 정답의 discount coupon

1 (D)	2 (B)	3 (C)	4 (C)	5 (C)
6 (D)	7 (A)	8 (C)	9 (B)	10 (C)
11 (C)	12 (C)	13 (B)	14 (A)	15 (B)
16 (A)	17 (A)	18 (A)	19 (B)	20 (A)
21 (B)	22 (C)	23 (A)	24 (A)	25 (B)
26 (C)	27 (A)	28 (A)	29 (C)	30 (A)
31 (B)	32 (B)	33 (D)	34 (B)	35 (A)
36 (C)	37 (B)	38 (A)	39 (C)	40 (D)
41 (D)	42 (C)	43 (D)	44 (B)	45 (A)
46 (D)	47 (B)	48 (A)	49 (D)	50 (D)
51 (C)	52 (C)	53 (B)	54 (C)	55 (C)
56 (D)	57 (C)	58 (A)	59 (A)	60 (A)
61 (D)	62 (B)	63 (C)	64 (A)	65 (B)
66 (C)	67 (D)	68 (B)	69 (C)	70 (C)
71 (D)	72 (B)	73 (A)	74 (A)	75 (B)
76 (D)	77 (B)	78 (C)	79 (C)	80 (D)
81 (B)	82 (A)	83 (C)	84 (B)	85 (D)
86 (D)	87 (C)	88 (A)	89 (D)	90 (C)
91 (D)	92 (A)	93 (B)	94 (A)	95 (B)
96 (B)	97 (A)	98 (C)	99 (A)	100 (C)

PART 1

1 M-Cn

(A) She's stepping off a curb.
(B) She's walking down a hallway.
(C) She's waiting in line for a bus.
(D) She's wearing a backpack.

(A) 여자가 연석에서 내려서고 있다.
(B) 여자가 복도를 따라 걷고 있다.
(C) 여자가 버스를 타려고 줄을 서서 기다리고 있다.
(D) 여자가 배낭을 메고 있다.

어휘 step off ～에서 내리다 curb 도로 경계석, 연석 hallway 복도

해설 1인 등장 사진 – 사람의 동작/상태 묘사
(A) 사진에 없는 명사를 이용한 오답. 사진에 연석(a curb)의 모습이 보이지 않으므로 오답.
(B) 사진에 없는 명사를 이용한 오답. 사진에 복도(a hallway)의 모습이 보이지 않으므로 오답.
(C) 동사 오답. 여자가 버스를 타려고 줄을 서서 기다리고 있는(is waiting in line for a bus) 모습이 아니므로 오답.
(D) 정답. 여자가 배낭을 메고 있는(is wearing a backpack) 모습이므로 정답.

2 W-Br

(A) Some clothing has fallen off a counter.
(B) Clothes are on display on a rack.
(C) The man is putting an item into a cart.
(D) The man is folding jackets in a store.

(A) 옷가지가 판매대에서 떨어져 있다.
(B) 옷들이 옷걸이에 진열되어 있다.
(C) 남자가 물건을 카트에 넣고 있다.
(D) 남자가 가게에서 재킷들을 개고 있다.

어휘 counter 계산대, 판매대 rack (물건을 거는) ～걸이, 선반 fold 개다, 접다

해설 혼합 사진 – 사람/사물/풍경 혼합 묘사
(A) 사진에 없는 명사를 이용한 오답. 사진에 판매대(a counter)의 모습이 보이지 않으므로 오답.
(B) 정답. 옷들(Clothes)이 옷걸이에 진열되어 있는(are on display on a rack) 모습이므로 정답.
(C) 동사 오답. 남자가 물건을 카트에 넣고 있는(is putting an item into a cart) 모습이 아니므로 오답.
(D) 동사 오답. 남자가 가게에서 재킷들을 개고 있는(is folding jackets in a store) 모습이 아니므로 오답.

3 M-Cn

(A) One of the people is putting on sunglasses.
(B) One of the people is climbing some stairs.
(C) One of the people is posing for a photograph.
(D) One of the people is opening a gate.

(A) 사람들 중 한 명이 선글라스를 쓰고 있다.
(B) 사람들 중 한 명이 계단을 오르고 있다.
(C) 사람들 중 한 명이 사진을 찍기 위해 포즈를 취하고 있다.
(D) 사람들 중 한 명이 문을 열고 있다.

어휘 stair 계단 pose 포즈[자세]를 취하다

해설 2인 이상 등장 사진 – 사람의 동작/상태 묘사
(A) 동사 오답. 사람들 중 한 명(One of the people)이 선글라스를 쓰고 있는(is putting on some sunglasses) 모습이 아니므로 오답. 참고로 putting on은 무언가를 착용하는 동작을 가리키는 말로 이미 착용 중인 상태를 나타내는 wearing과 혼동하지 않도록 주의한다.
(B) 동사 오답. 사람들 중 한 명(One of the people)이 계단을 오르고 있는(is climbing some stairs) 모습이 아니므로 오답.

(C) 정답. 사람들 중 한 명(One of the people)이 사진을 찍기 위해 포즈를 취하고 있는(is posing for a photograph) 모습이므로 정답.

(D) 동사 오답. 사람들 중 한 명(One of the people)이 문을 열고 있는(is opening a gate) 모습이 아니므로 오답.

4 M-Au

(A) A floor is covered with boxes.
(B) A sign is leaning against a wall.
(C) Some pillows are organized on shelves.
(D) Some lamps have been placed on the floor.

(A) 바닥이 상자들로 덮여 있다.
(B) 간판이 벽에 기대어 있다.
(C) 베개들이 선반에 정리되어 있다.
(D) 램프들이 바닥에 놓여 있다.

어휘 sign 간판, 표지판   lean 기대다   pillow 베개   organize 정리하다   shelf 선반   place 놓다, 배치하다

해설 사물/풍경 사진 – 사물 묘사
(A) 사진에 없는 명사를 이용한 오답. 사진에 상자들(boxes)의 모습이 보이지 않으므로 오답.
(B) 사진에 없는 명사를 이용한 오답. 사진에 간판(A sign)의 모습이 보이지 않으므로 오답.
(C) 정답. 베개들(Some pillows)이 선반에 정리되어 있는(are organized on shelves) 모습이므로 정답.
(D) 동사 오답. 램프들(Some lamps)이 바닥에 놓여 있는(have been placed on the floor) 모습이 아니므로 오답.

5 W-Am

(A) She's lifting a bag of groceries.
(B) She's talking on a mobile phone.
(C) She's standing on a stepladder.
(D) She's reaching for a light switch.

(A) 여자가 식료품 가방을 들어 올리고 있다.
(B) 여자가 휴대폰으로 통화하고 있다.
(C) 여자가 발판 사다리 위에 서 있다.
(D) 여자가 전등 스위치에 손을 뻗고 있다.

어휘 groceries 식료품   stepladder 발판 사다리   reach for ~을 향해 손을 뻗다

해설 1인 등장 사진 – 사람의 동작/상태 묘사
(A) 동사 오답. 여자가 식료품 가방을 들어 올리고 있는(is lifting a bag of groceries) 모습이 아니므로 오답.
(B) 동사 오답. 여자가 휴대폰으로 통화하고 있는(is talking on a mobile phone) 모습이 아니므로 오답.
(C) 정답. 여자가 발판 사다리 위에 서 있는(is standing on a stepladder) 모습이므로 정답.
(D) 사진에 없는 명사를 이용한 오답. 사진에 전등 스위치(a light switch)의 모습이 보이지 않으므로 오답.

6 M-Cn

(A) He's planting some bushes.
(B) He's weeding a flower bed.
(C) He's installing a door.
(D) He's holding a hammer.

(A) 남자가 관목을 심고 있다.
(B) 남자가 화단의 잡초를 뽑고 있다.
(C) 남자가 문을 설치하고 있다.
(D) 남자가 망치를 들고 있다.

어휘 plant 심다   bush 관목, 덤불   weed 잡초를 뽑다   flower bed 화단, 꽃밭   install 설치하다

해설 1인 등장 사진 – 사람의 동작/상태 묘사
(A) 동사 오답. 남자가 관목을 심고 있는(is planting some bushes) 모습이 아니므로 오답.
(B) 동사 오답. 남자가 화단의 잡초를 뽑고 있는(is weeding a flower bed) 모습이 아니므로 오답.
(C) 동사 오답. 남자가 문을 설치하고 있는(is installing a door) 모습이 아니므로 오답.
(D) 정답. 남자가 망치를 들고 있는(is holding a hammer) 모습이므로 정답.

PART 2

7

W-Am   Will the bank be open over the holiday weekend?

M-Cn   (A) Yes, as far as I know.
         (B) Yesterday evening.
         (C) I didn't realize that.

은행이 주말 연휴에 문을 열까요?
(A) 네, 제가 아는 한 그래요.
(B) 어제저녁이요.
(C) 그것을 깨닫지 못했어요.

어휘 holiday weekend 공휴일이 낀 주말   as far as ~하는 한
     realize 깨닫다

해설 주말 연휴 동안의 개점 여부를 확인하는 조동사(Will) 의문문

(A) 정답. 은행이 주말 연휴에 문을 열지를 묻는 질문에 네(Yes)라고 대답
한 뒤, 자신이 아는 한 그렇다며 긍정 답변과 일관된 내용을 덧붙이고
있으므로 정답.

(B) 유사 발음 오답. 질문의 holiday와 부분적으로 발음이 유사한
Yesterday를 이용한 오답.

(C) 질문과 상관없는 오답.

8

M-Au Why did we hire so many people?

W-Am (A) A high-rise building.
(B) I don't have much more.
(C) Because we have several new major
contracts.

그렇게 많은 사람들을 왜 고용했나요?
(A) 고층 빌딩이요.
(B) 더 이상은 없어요.
(C) 주요한 계약이 새롭게 몇 건 생겼기 때문이에요.

어휘 high-rise 고층의   contract 계약(서)

해설 많은 사람들을 고용한 이유를 묻는 Why 의문문

(A) 유사 발음 오답. 질문의 hire와 부분적으로 발음이 유사한 high를 이
용한 오답.

(B) 연상 단어 오답. 질문의 many에서 연상 가능한 much를 이용한 오
답.

(C) 정답. 많은 사람들을 고용한 이유를 묻는 질문에 주요한 계약이 새롭
게 몇 건 생겼기 때문이라고 이유를 제시하고 있으므로 정답.

9

M-Cn You have the presentation slides ready to go,
right?

M-Au (A) It's a fantastic gift.
(B) No, I'm still working on them.
(C) I went there yesterday.

프레젠테이션 슬라이드를 시작할 준비가 되었죠?
(A) 환상적인 선물입니다.
(B) 아니요, 아직 작업 중이에요.
(C) 어제 거기에 갔었어요.

어휘 fantastic 환상적인

해설 프레젠테이션 슬라이드를 시작할 준비가 되었는지 확인하는 부가
의문문

(A) 연상 단어 오답. 질문의 presentation을 present(선물)로 착각했을
때 연상 가능한 gift를 이용한 오답.

(B) 정답. 프레젠테이션 슬라이드를 시작할 준비가 되었는지 여부를 확인
하는 질문에 아니요(No)라고 대답한 뒤, 아직 작업 중이라며 부정 답
변과 일관된 내용을 덧붙이고 있으므로 정답.

(C) 파생어 오답. 질문의 go와 파생어 관계인 went를 이용한 오답.

10

M-Cn How long is the flight to London?

W-Br (A) Just those three.
(B) More often than not.
(C) Less than four hours.

런던까지 비행기로 얼마나 걸리나요?
(A) 그 세 가지만요.
(B) 자주요.
(C) 4시간도 안 걸려요.

어휘 flight 비행, 항공편   more often than not 자주, 대개

해설 비행기로 런던까지 가는 데 걸리는 시간을 묻는 How long 의문문

(A) 연상 단어 오답. 질문의 How long에서 연상 가능한 three를 이용한
오답.

(B) 질문과 상관없는 오답.

(C) 정답. 비행기로 런던까지 가는 데 걸리는 시간을 묻는 질문에 4시간도
안 걸린다고 알려 주고 있으므로 정답.

11

M-Au Who won the employee-of-the-month award in
January?

W-Br (A) That project was completed last month.
(B) You are a highly valued employee.
(C) Someone from Human Resources.

1월에는 누가 이달의 사원 상을 받았나요?
(A) 그 프로젝트는 지난달에 완료되었어요.
(B) 당신은 매우 소중한 직원입니다.
(C) 인사부 직원이요.

어휘 award 상   valued 소중한, 가치 있는

해설 이달의 사원 수상자를 묻는 Who 의문문

(A) 단어 반복 오답. 질문의 month를 반복 이용한 오답.

(B) 단어 반복 오답. 질문의 employee를 반복 이용한 오답.

(C) 정답. 1월에 이달의 사원 상을 받은 사람이 누구인지 묻는 질문에 인
사부 직원이라고 응답하고 있으므로 정답.

12

M-Cn Did we get enough volunteers for the music
festival?

W-Am (A) Did you volunteer last year?
(B) At the hotel on Central Boulevard.
(C) Yes, some of my friends even agreed to
participate.

음악 축제를 위한 자원봉사자를 충분히 확보했나요?
(A) 작년에 자원봉사를 했나요?
(B) 센트럴 대로에 있는 호텔에서요.
(C) 네, 제 친구들도 참여하기로 했어요.

어휘 volunteer 자원봉사자; 자원봉사로 하다   participate 참가하다

해설 자원봉사자의 충분한 확보 여부를 묻는 조동사(Did) 의문문

(A) 단어 반복 오답. 질문의 명사 volunteers(자원봉사자들)를 동사
volunteer(자원봉사로 하다)로 반복 이용한 오답.

(B) 질문과 상관없는 오답. Where 의문문에 대한 응답이므로 오답.

(C) 정답. 음악 축제를 위한 자원봉사자를 충분히 확보했는지 묻는 질문에 네(Yes)라고 대답한 뒤, 자신의 친구들도 참여한다며 긍정 답변과 일관된 부연 설명을 덧붙이고 있으므로 정답.

13

M-Au Will the product be sold locally or nationwide?

W-Am (A) By October twenty-seventh.
(B) Locally, to begin with.
(C) No, I'm staying home.

제품을 지역에서 판매할 건가요, 아니면 전국에서 판매할 건가요?
(A) 10월 27일까지요.
(B) 우선은 지역에서요.
(C) 아니요, 집에 있을 겁니다.

어휘 locally 지역적으로   nationwide 전국적으로   to begin with 우선

해설 제품의 판매 범위를 묻는 선택 의문문

(A) 질문과 상관없는 오답. When 의문문에 대한 응답이므로 오답.

(B) 정답. 지역과 전국 중 제품을 판매할 범위를 묻는 질문에 우선은 지역이라며 둘 중 하나를 선택해 응답하고 있으므로 정답.

(C) Yes/No 불가 오답. 제품의 판매 범위 두 가지 중 하나를 선택하도록 요구하는 선택 의문문에 Yes/No 응답은 불가능하므로 오답.

14

W-Br Would you please put the new ink cartridge into the printer?

M-Au (A) Sure, that should be easy.
(B) It's in today's paper.
(C) I don't have a shopping cart.

새 잉크 카트리지를 프린터에 넣어 주시겠어요?
(A) 그럼요, 어렵지 않겠어요.
(B) 오늘 신문에 있어요.
(C) 쇼핑 카트가 없어요.

해설 부탁/요청의 의문문

(A) 정답. 새 잉크 카트리지를 프린터에 넣어 달라는 요청에 그럼요(Sure)라고 수락한 뒤, 어렵지 않겠다며 긍정 답변과 일관된 내용을 덧붙이고 있으므로 정답.

(B) 연상 단어 오답. 질문의 printer에서 연상 가능한 paper를 이용한 오답.

(C) 유사 발음 오답. 질문의 cartridge와 부분적으로 발음이 유사한 cart를 이용한 오답.

15

W-Br I'll need to replace the belt on the tractor.

M-Cn (A) Will they be there tomorrow, too?
(B) Yes, that's what the technician recommended.
(C) Everyone agreed to that meeting time.

저는 트랙터의 벨트를 교체해야 할 거예요.
(A) 그들이 내일도 거기에 있을까요?
(B) 네, 기사가 추천한 것도 바로 그거예요.
(C) 모두가 그 회의 시간에 동의했어요.

어휘 replace 교체하다, 대신하다   technician 기사, 기술자

해설 정보 전달의 평서문

(A) 평서문과 상관없는 오답. 질문에 3인칭 복수대명사 they로 지칭할 사람이나 사물이 언급되지 않았으므로 오답.

(B) 정답. 트랙터의 벨트를 교체해야 한다는 평서문에 네(Yes)라고 대답한 뒤, 기사가 추천한 것도 바로 그것이라며 긍정 답변과 일관된 내용으로 호응하고 있으므로 정답.

(C) 평서문과 상관없는 오답.

16

M-Au How did the project discussion go this morning?

W-Br (A) Fine, but we still need to finalize some details.
(B) So we met in the library.
(C) Sure, I could spend five minutes on the assignment.

오늘 아침 프로젝트에 대한 논의는 어떻게 진행되었나요?
(A) 좋았어요, 하지만 아직 몇 가지 세부 사항을 마무리 지어야 해요.
(B) 그래서 우리는 도서관에서 만났어요.
(C) 물론이죠, 그 일에 5분을 할애할 수 있어요.

어휘 finalize 마무리 짓다, 완결하다   detail 세부 사항   assignment 할당된 일, 과제

해설 논의가 어떻게 진행되었는지를 묻는 How 의문문

(A) 정답. 오늘 아침 프로젝트에 대한 논의는 어떻게 진행되었는지 묻는 질문에 좋았다(Fine)고 대답한 뒤, 하지만 아직 몇 가지 세부 사항을 마무리 지어야 한다고 부연 설명을 덧붙이고 있으므로 정답.

(B) 연상 단어 오답. 질문의 discussion에서 연상 가능한 met을 이용한 오답.

(C) Yes/No 불가 오답. How 의문문에는 Yes/No 응답이 불가능한데, Sure도 일종의 Yes 응답이라고 볼 수 있으므로 오답.

17

W-Br Which of these contracts should be renewed this month?

M-Au (A) All client information is in this folder.
(B) On the fifth floor.
(C) My library book is overdue.

이번 달에 갱신해야 하는 것이 어느 계약서인가요?
(A) 모든 고객 정보는 이 폴더에 있어요.
(B) 5층에요.
(C) 제 도서관 책 기한이 지났어요.

어휘 contract 계약(서)   renew 갱신하다   overdue 기한이 지난

해설 갱신해야 하는 계약서를 묻는 Which 의문문
(A) 정답. 이번 달에 갱신해야 하는 계약서를 묻는 질문에 모든 고객 정보는 이 폴더에 있다며 자료의 위치를 우회적으로 알려 주고 있으므로 정답.
(B) 질문과 상관없는 오답. Where 의문문에 대한 응답이므로 오답.
(C) 연상 단어 오답. 질문의 renewed에서 연상 가능한 overdue를 이용한 오답.

18

M-Cn Did the workers mop the floors again today?

W-Am (A) Yes, they used special cloths.
(B) Sure, if you think they'll fit.
(C) The notice on the door.

직원들이 오늘도 바닥을 대걸레로 닦았습니까?
(A) 네, 특수 천을 사용했어요.
(B) 물론이죠, 그들이 맞을 거라고 생각하시면요.
(C) 문에 붙은 안내문이요.

어휘 cloth 천, 옷감 fit 맞다 notice 안내문, 공고문

해설 바닥을 대걸레로 닦았는지 여부를 확인하는 조동사(Did) 의문문
(A) 정답. 직원들이 오늘도 바닥을 대걸레로 닦았는지 묻는 질문에 네(Yes)라고 대답한 뒤, 특수 천을 사용했다고 긍정 답변과 일관된 부연 설명을 덧붙이고 있으므로 정답.
(B) 연상 단어 오답. 질문의 workers에서 연상 가능한 대명사 they를 이용한 오답.
(C) 유사 발음 오답. 질문의 floors와 부분적으로 발음이 유사한 door를 이용한 오답.

19

W-Br Make sure you sign up for the seminar next week.

M-Au (A) A famous presenter.
(B) I attended last week's session.
(C) I'll need you to sign for the package.

다음 주 세미나에 반드시 등록하세요.
(A) 유명한 발표자예요.
(B) 지난주 세션에 참석했어요.
(C) 소포에 서명해 주셔야 합니다.

어휘 sign up for ~에 등록하다 attend 참석하다

해설 제안/권유의 평서문
(A) 연상 단어 오답. 평서문의 seminar에서 연상 가능한 presenter를 이용한 오답.
(B) 정답. 다음 주 세미나에 등록할 것을 제안하는 평서문에 지난주 세션에 참석했다는 이유를 들어 우회적으로 거절하고 있으므로 정답.
(C) 단어 반복 오답. 평서문의 sign과 for를 반복 이용한 오답.

20

M-Au Why don't we pick up some lunch from the cafeteria?

W-Am (A) I already ate.
(B) On the corner of First and Maple Streets.
(C) The new manager.

구내식당에서 점심을 사 오는 게 어떨까요?
(A) 저는 이미 먹었어요.
(B) 1번가와 메이플 가가 만나는 모퉁이에요.
(C) 새 매니저입니다.

해설 제안/권유의 의문문
(A) 정답. 구내식당에서 점심을 사 오자는 제안에 이미 먹었다는 이유를 들어 우회적으로 거절하고 있으므로 정답.
(B) 질문과 상관없는 오답. Where 의문문에 대한 응답이므로 오답.
(C) 연상 단어 오답. 질문의 cafeteria에서 연상 가능한 manager를 이용한 오답.

21

M-Cn Please put in a request for Mona to get access to the database.

W-Br (A) Yes, I like that type of computer.
(B) The IT specialist is out of the office this week.
(C) The conference room upstairs.

모나가 데이터베이스에 접속할 수 있도록 요청해 주십시오.
(A) 네, 그런 종류의 컴퓨터를 좋아해요.
(B) IT 전문가가 이번 주에는 사무실에 없어요.
(C) 위층 회의실입니다.

어휘 request 요청 specialist 전문가 conference room 회의실 upstairs 위층[2층]에

해설 부탁/요청의 평서문
(A) 연상 단어 오답. 평서문의 database에서 연상 가능한 computer를 이용한 오답.
(B) 정답. 모나가 데이터베이스에 접속할 수 있도록 요청해 달라는 요청에 IT 전문가가 이번 주에는 사무실에 없다며 요청에 응할 수 없음을 우회적으로 나타내고 있으므로 정답.
(C) 평서문과 상관없는 오답. Where 의문문에 대한 응답이므로 오답.

22

M-Au Call me when your flight arrives so I can come get you.

W-Am (A) He's at gate seventeen.
(B) A direct flight from Tokyo.
(C) Kavi's picking me up.

비행기가 도착하면 제가 데리러 갈 수 있게 전화 주세요.
(A) 그는 17번 게이트에 있어요.
(B) 도쿄발 직항 편입니다.
(C) 카비가 데리러 올 거예요.

어휘 direct flight 직항 편

해설 부탁/요청의 평서문

(A) 연상 단어 오답. 평서문의 flight에서 연상 가능한 gate를 이용한 오답.

(B) 단어 반복 오답. 평서문의 flight를 반복 이용한 오답.

(C) 정답. 비행기가 도착하면 데리러 갈 수 있게 전화해 달라는 요청에 카비가 데리러 올 것이라며 우회적으로 거절하고 있으므로 정답.

23

W-Br　Where will the workshop take place?

M-Cn　(A) It's still in the planning stages.
　　　(B) All day Friday.
　　　(C) No, I don't usually shop there.

워크숍은 어디에서 진행될 건가요?

(A) 아직 기획 단계입니다.
(B) 금요일 종일이요.
(C) 아니요, 저는 보통 그곳에서 쇼핑하지 않아요.

어휘 take place 개최되다, 일어나다　planning 기획, 계획 (세우기)
　　 stage 단계

해설 워크숍이 진행될 장소를 묻는 Where 의문문

(A) 정답. 워크숍이 진행될 장소를 묻는 질문에 아직 기획 단계라며 대답해 줄 수 없다는 것을 우회적으로 표현하고 있으므로 정답.

(B) 질문과 상관없는 오답. When 또는 How long 의문문에 대한 응답이므로 오답.

(C) Yes/No 불가 오답. Where 의문문에는 Yes/No 응답이 불가능하므로 오답.

24

M-Cn　Would you like to be seated indoors or on the patio?

W-Br　(A) It's very hot today.
　　　(B) I read that book.
　　　(C) I'm looking for pumpkin seeds.

실내에 앉으시겠습니까, 아니면 테라스에 앉으시겠습니까?

(A) 오늘은 너무 더워요.
(B) 그 책은 읽었어요.
(C) 호박씨를 찾고 있어요.

어휘 seat 앉히다　indoors 실내에　patio 파티오(집 뒤쪽에 만드는
　　 테라스)　seed 씨앗

해설 착석할 장소를 묻는 선택 의문문

(A) 정답. 실내와 테라스 중 앉을 장소를 묻는 질문에 오늘은 너무 덥다며 실내에 앉겠다는 것을 우회적으로 표현하고 있으므로 정답.

(B) 질문과 상관없는 오답.

(C) 유사 발음 오답. 질문의 seated와 부분적으로 발음이 유사한 seeds를 이용한 오답.

25

W-Am　When would you like to see the doctor for your next checkup?

M-Cn　(A) She checks her e-mail daily.
　　　(B) I'll be out of town until April.
　　　(C) It's next to the waiting room.

다음 건강 검진을 위해 언제 병원에 오시겠습니까?

(A) 그녀는 매일 이메일을 확인해요.
(B) 4월까지 이곳에 없을 거예요.
(C) 대기실 옆에 있어요.

어휘 checkup 건강 검진

해설 병원 방문 시기를 묻는 When 의문문

(A) 유사 발음 오답. 질문의 checkup과 부분적으로 발음이 유사한 checks를 이용한 오답.

(B) 정답. 다음 건강 검진을 위해 언제 병원에 올 것인지를 묻는 질문에 4월까지 이곳에 없을 것이라며 4월 이후가 될 것임을 간접적으로 알려 주고 있으므로 정답.

(C) 단어 반복 오답. 질문의 next를 반복 이용한 오답.

26

W-Br　Does Ms. Shimizu usually come to the office on Mondays or Tuesdays?

M-Au　(A) By public transportation.
　　　(B) Meeting room seven.
　　　(C) Ask her assistant.

시미즈 씨는 보통 사무실에 월요일에 오나요, 아니면 화요일에 오나요?

(A) 대중교통을 이용해요.
(B) 7번 회의실입니다.
(C) 그녀의 비서에게 물어보세요.

어휘 public transportation 대중교통　assistant 조수, 보조원

해설 시미즈 씨가 사무실에 오는 요일을 묻는 선택 의문문

(A) 연상 단어 오답. 질문의 come에서 연상 가능한 By public transportation을 이용한 오답.

(B) 연상 단어 오답. 질문의 office에서 연상 가능한 Meeting room을 이용한 오답.

(C) 정답. 월요일과 화요일 중 시미즈 씨가 사무실에 오는 요일을 묻는 질문에 그녀의 비서에게 물어보라고 알려 주며 자신은 답변해 줄 수 없다는 것을 우회적으로 표현하고 있으므로 정답.

27

W-Am　Where can I move the file cabinet?

W-Br　(A) Hector's office is empty.
　　　(B) I think that file cabinet's over there.
　　　(C) Some folders and papers.

파일 캐비닛을 어디로 옮길 수 있나요?

(A) 헥터의 사무실이 비어 있어요.
(B) 파일 캐비닛이 저쪽에 있는 것 같아요.
(C) 폴더와 서류입니다.

해설 캐비닛을 옮길 장소를 묻는 Where 의문문

(A) 정답. 파일 캐비닛을 옮길 장소를 묻는 질문에 헥터의 사무실이 비어 있다며 캐비닛을 옮길 장소를 간접적으로 제안하고 있으므로 정답.
(B) 단어 반복 오답. 질문의 file cabinet을 반복 이용한 오답.
(C) 연상 단어 오답. 질문의 file에서 연상 가능한 folders와 papers를 이용한 오답.

28

M-Au　When will Dr. Gao give her speech?

W-Am　(A) The conference schedule hasn't been finalized.
　　　 (B) I like the view from your office.
　　　 (C) Attached in her e-mail.

가오 박사님은 언제 연설을 합니까?
(A) 학회 일정이 아직 확정되지 않았어요.
(B) 당신 사무실에서 보이는 전망이 마음에 들어요.
(C) 그녀의 이메일에 첨부되어 있어요.

어휘 conference 학회, 회의　view 전망　attached 첨부된

해설 가오 박사의 연설 시점을 묻는 When 의문문

(A) 정답. 가오 박사가 연설하는 시점을 묻는 질문에 회의 일정이 확정되지 않았다며 일정이 정해질 때까지 알 수 없다는 것을 우회적으로 응답하고 있으므로 정답.
(B) 질문과 상관없는 오답.
(C) 단어 반복 오답. 질문의 her를 반복 이용한 오답.

29

M-Cn　The catering service is calling to ask about the fund-raising dinner.

W-Br　(A) There should be some in the refrigerator.
　　　 (B) Yes, over 12,000 dollars.
　　　 (C) I wasn't involved in the planning.

음식 공급업체에서 기금 모금 만찬에 대해 문의 전화가 왔습니다.
(A) 냉장고에 조금 있을 거예요.
(B) 네, 12,000달러가 넘습니다.
(C) 저는 기획에 참여하지 않았어요.

어휘 catering 음식 공급　fund-raising 모금 활동, 자금 조달　refrigerator 냉장고　be involved in ~에 참여[관여]하다

해설 정보 전달의 평서문

(A) 연상 단어 오답. 평서문의 catering과 dinner에서 연상 가능한 refrigerator를 이용한 오답.
(B) 연상 단어 오답. 평서문의 fund-raising에서 연상 가능한 12,000 dollars를 이용한 오답.
(C) 정답. 음식 공급업체에서 기금 모금 만찬에 대해 문의 전화가 왔다는 평서문에 자신은 기획에 참여하지 않았다며 문의 사항에 대해 아무 정보도 제공할 수 없다는 것을 우회적으로 응답하고 있으므로 정답.

30

W-Br　Our team will be taking a lunch break soon.

M-Cn　(A) OK, I'll see if there's an empty conference room.
　　　 (B) Remember to return it.
　　　 (C) No, we took the stairs.

우리 팀은 곧 점심시간을 가질 거예요.
(A) 알겠어요, 제가 빈 회의실이 있는지 알아볼게요.
(B) 잊지 말고 반납하세요.
(C) 아니요, 우리는 계단을 이용했어요.

어휘 return 반납하다　stairs 계단

해설 정보 전달의 평서문

(A) 정답. 우리 팀이 곧 점심시간을 가질 것이라는 평서문에 알겠다(OK)고 대답한 뒤, 빈 회의실이 있는지 알아보겠다며 점심 식사 공간을 찾아 주겠다는 의사를 표현하고 있으므로 정답.
(B) 평서문과 상관없는 오답.
(C) 파생어 오답. 평서문의 taking과 파생어 관계인 took을 이용한 오답.

31

W-Am　Which door should I go through to leave the warehouse?

M-Cn　(A) He left early yesterday.
　　　 (B) The key card you were issued works for any exit.
　　　 (C) An unusually large order.

창고를 나가려면 어느 문으로 가야 합니까?
(A) 그는 어제 일찍 떠났어요.
(B) 발급받은 키 카드는 모든 출구에서 작동해요.
(C) 평소와 달리 큰 주문입니다.

어휘 warehouse 창고　issue 발급하다　exit 출구　unusually 평소와 달리, 대단히

해설 창고를 나가는 문을 묻는 Which 의문문

(A) 파생어 오답. 질문의 leave와 파생어 관계인 left를 이용한 오답.
(B) 정답. 창고를 나가려면 어느 문으로 가야 하는지 묻는 질문에 발급받은 키 카드는 모든 출구에서 작동한다며 모든 문을 이용할 수 있다는 것을 우회적으로 표현하고 있으므로 정답.
(C) 연상 단어 오답. 질문의 warehouse에서 연상 가능한 order를 이용한 오답.

PART 3

32-34

W-Am　Hi, Fritz. Thanks for coming in early today. **[32]We have very important guests holding a meeting at nine in the hotel's main conference room. [33]One of the projectors won't switch on. Could you take a look at it?**

M-Au **³³Not a problem. I'll also check the other equipment and computers in the room and run some diagnostic tests.**

W-Am Thank you. Oh, and **³⁴let me give you the key.** The room is locked right now.

여 안녕하세요, 프리츠. 오늘 이렇게 일찍 와 주어서 감사해요. **우리는 9시에 호텔의 주 회의실에서 회의를 개최할 매우 중요한 손님이 있어요. 프로젝터 하나가 켜지지 않아요. 한번 살펴봐 줄래요?**

남 그럼요. 회의실에 있는 다른 장비와 컴퓨터도 확인하고 진단 테스트를 실행하겠습니다.

여 감사해요. 아, 그리고 여기 **열쇠를 드릴게요.** 회의실은 지금 잠겨 있거든요.

어휘 equipment 장비, 용품 diagnostic 진단의

32

Where do the speakers most likely work?
(A) At a bank
(B) At a hotel
(C) At an electronics store
(D) At a medical clinic

화자들은 어디에서 일하는 것 같은가?
(A) 은행
(B) 호텔
(C) 전자 제품 매장
(D) 병원

해설 전체 내용 관련 – 화자들의 근무지
여자가 첫 대사에서 남자에게 우리는 호텔의 주 회의실에서 회의를 개최할 매우 중요한 손님이 있다(We have very important guests holding a meeting at nine in the hotel's main conference room)고 말하는 것으로 보아 정답은 (B)이다.

33

What most likely is the man's job?
(A) Receptionist
(B) Security guard
(C) Cleaning staff member
(D) Computer technician

남자의 직업은 무엇인 것 같은가?
(A) 접수 담당자
(B) 경비원
(C) 청소 직원
(D) 컴퓨터 기사

해설 전체 내용 관련 – 남자의 직업
여자가 첫 대사에서 프로젝터 하나가 켜지지 않는다(One of the projectors won't switch on)면서 살펴봐 줄지(Could you take a look at it?) 묻자, 뒤이어 남자가 그러겠다(Not a problem)며 다른 장비와 컴퓨터도 확인하고 진단 테스트를 실행하겠다(I'll also check the

---

other equipment and computers in the room and run some diagnostic tests)고 말하는 것으로 보아 남자는 컴퓨터와 주변 기기를 다루는 기술자임을 알 수 있다. 따라서 정답은 (D)이다.

34

What will the woman give the man?
(A) A schedule
(B) A key
(C) A manual
(D) A cup of coffee

여자는 남자에게 무엇을 줄 것인가?
(A) 일정표
(B) 열쇠
(C) 설명서
(D) 커피 한 잔

해설 세부 사항 관련 – 여자가 남자에게 줄 것
여자가 마지막 대사에서 남자에게 열쇠를 주겠다(let me give you the key)고 말하고 있으므로 정답은 (B)이다.

35-37

W-Br **³⁵Thanks for calling Lyleton Tree Service. This is Lauren. How may I help you today?**

M-Au Hi. **³⁶I'm calling because one of the large oak trees on my property has died. I'd like to have it cut down before it causes any damage.**

W-Br OK, I can definitely help you with that. **³⁷First I'll need your address,** so I can schedule a time for one of our specialists to go out and evaluate the situation.

여 **라일톤 수목 서비스에 전화 주셔서 감사합니다. 저는 로렌입니다. 어떻게 도와드릴까요?**

남 안녕하세요. **제 소유지에 있는 큰 떡갈나무 하나가 죽어서 전화했습니다. 피해가 생기기 전에 자르고 싶습니다.**

여 알겠습니다, 당연히 도와드릴 수 있지요. **먼저 고객님의 주소가 필요합니다.** 전문가 한 명이 나가서 상황을 평가할 시간 예약을 할 수 있도록요.

어휘 oak 떡갈나무 property 소유지, 부지 cause 야기하다, 초래하다 specialist 전문가 evaluate 평가하다

35

Who most likely is the woman?
(A) A receptionist
(B) A florist
(C) A repair technician
(D) A woodworker

TEST 9

여자는 누구인 것 같은가?

(A) 접수 담당자
(B) 플로리스트
(C) 수리 기사
(D) 목수

해설 전체 내용 관련 – 여자의 직업

여자가 첫 대사에서 라일톤 수목 서비스에 전화해 주어 고맙다(Thanks for calling Lyleton Tree Service)면서 자신은 로렌(This is Lauren)이라고 소개하며 어떻게 도와줄지(How may I help you today?) 묻는 것으로 보아 여자는 업체에서 안내를 담당하고 있음을 알 수 있다. 따라서 정답은 (A)이다.

36

Why is the man calling?
(A) To clarify a process
(B) To ask about a delivery
(C) To request a service
(D) To complain about an invoice

남자는 왜 전화를 하고 있는가?
(A) 과정을 명확히 하기 위해
(B) 배송에 대해 문의하기 위해
(C) 서비스를 요청하기 위해
(D) 송장에 대한 불만을 제기하기 위해

어휘 clarify 분명하게 하다   request 요청하다   invoice 송장

해설 전체 내용 관련 – 남자가 전화하는 목적

남자가 첫 대사에서 자신의 소유지에 있는 떡갈나무가 죽어서 전화를 했다(I'm calling because one of the large oak trees on my property has died)고 했고, 피해가 생기기 전에 자르고 싶다(I'd like to have it cut down before it causes any damage)고 말하고 있으므로 남자는 나무를 잘라 달라는 요청을 위해 전화하고 있다는 것을 알 수 있다. 따라서 정답은 (C)이다.

37

What does the woman ask the man for?
(A) A photograph
(B) An address
(C) A telephone number
(D) A passcode

여자는 남자에게 무엇을 요청하는가?
(A) 사진
(B) 주소
(C) 전화번호
(D) 비밀번호

해설 세부 사항 관련 – 여자의 요청 사항

여자가 마지막 대사에서 남자에게 먼저 고객의 주소가 필요하다(First I'll need your address)라고 말하고 있으므로 정답은 (B)이다.

38-40

M-Au **38, 39I love this men's dress shirt! Do you have it in the next larger size?**

W-Am All we have left is the one you are holding. But **39our warehouse has any size you'd need. Would you like me to have it sent to your home?**

M-Au Actually, I prefer to try shirts on. Sometimes the fit's not exact.

W-Am You can always mail it back and get a refund.

M-Au Unfortunately, I need the shirt for a business trip tomorrow.

W-Am OK. Let me check. You are in luck! **40Our Shipleysburg store has your size. It's not far from here.**

남 이 남성용 와이셔츠가 정말 마음에 들어요! 한 치수 큰 것이 있나요?

여 지금 남아 있는 것은 손님이 들고 있는 것뿐입니다. 하지만 **저희 의류 창고에는 필요하신 모든 치수가 다 있습니다. 댁으로 보내 드릴까요?**

남 사실 셔츠를 입어 보길 원해요. 잘 맞지 않는 경우가 있어서요.

여 언제든지 우편으로 반송하고 환불받으실 수 있어요.

남 안타깝게도 내일 출장을 갈 때 입을 셔츠가 필요해요.

여 알겠습니다. 확인해 보겠습니다. 운이 좋으시네요! **쉬플리스부르크 매장에 손님이 원하는 치수가 있어요. 여기서 멀지 않습니다.**

어휘 dress shirt 와이셔츠   warehouse 창고   fit (옷의) 맞음새   exact 정확한   get a refund 환불을 받다

38

What does the man ask the woman about?
(A) A shirt size
(B) A shirt price
(C) A warehouse location
(D) Store hours

남자는 여자에게 무엇에 대해 물어보는가?
(A) 셔츠 치수
(B) 셔츠 가격
(C) 창고 위치
(D) 영업시간

해설 세부 사항 관련 – 남자의 문의 사항

남자가 첫 대사에서 와이셔츠가 마음에 든다(I love this men's dress shirt!)며 한 치수 큰 것이 있는지(Do you have it in the next larger size?) 묻고 있으므로 정답은 (A)이다.

39

What does the woman offer to do?
(A) Unlock a fitting room
(B) Look for a different color shirt
(C) Send a shirt to the man's home
(D) Put a shirt back on a shelf

여자는 무엇을 해 주겠다고 제안하는가?
(A) 탈의실 열기
(B) 다른 색상의 셔츠 찾기
(C) 남자의 집으로 셔츠 보내기
(D) 셔츠를 선반에 다시 놓기

어휘 fitting room 탈의실 shelf 선반

해설 세부 사항 관련 – 여자의 제안 사항
남자가 첫 대사에서 와이셔츠가 마음에 든다(I love this men's dress shirt!)며 한 치수 큰 것이 있는지(Do you have it in the next larger size?) 묻자, 여자가 첫 대사에서 의류 창고에 필요한 모든 치수가 다 있다(our warehouse has any size you'd need)고 한 후, 집으로 보내 줄지(Would you like me to have it sent to your home?) 묻고 있는 것으로 보아 여자는 상품의 배송을 제안하고 있다는 것을 알 수 있다. 따라서 정답은 (C)이다.

> Paraphrasing 대화의 have it sent to your home
> → 정답의 Send a shirt to the man's home

40

What will the man most likely do?
(A) Contact a manufacturer
(B) Come back tomorrow
(C) Look through a catalog
(D) Visit a different store

남자는 무엇을 할 것 같은가?
(A) 제조사에 연락하기
(B) 내일 다시 방문하기
(C) 카탈로그 살펴보기
(D) 다른 매장 방문하기

어휘 manufacturer 제조업체

해설 세부 사항 관련 – 남자가 할 일
여자가 마지막 대사에서 쉬플리스부르크 매장에 손님이 원하는 치수가 있다(Our Shipleysburg store has your size)면서 여기서 멀지 않다(It's not far from here)며 남자에게 다른 매장의 정보를 제공하고 있는 것으로 보아 정답은 (D)이다.

> Paraphrasing 대화의 Our Shipleysburg store
> → 정답의 a different store

41-43 3인 대화

M-Cn **41This art gallery's packed.** Do you think it's always like this?

M-Au I don't know, but **41there's my friend Sofia, who owns the place.** We can ask her.

W-Br Well, look who it is! Thanks for visiting!

M-Au What a beautiful space this is! I'm so glad I'm finally getting to see it. **42We were just wondering if it's always busy like this**.

W-Br Well, you know, it looks full because the space is so small. But yes, this is normal for us.

M-Au Sofia, this is Aaron. He's a colleague of mine.

M-Cn Pleased to meet you, Sofia.

W-Br Nice to meet you, too. Here, **43let me show you both some new prints we just hung up. Follow me.**

남1 미술관이 사람들로 혼잡하네요. 항상 이런 것 같나요?

남2 저는 모르겠지만, **이곳 주인인 제 친구 소피아가 저기 있네요.** 그 친구에게 물어보면 돼요.

여 어, 이게 누구인가요! 방문해 줘서 고마워요!

남2 이곳은 정말 아름다워요! 드디어 와 볼 수 있어서 정말 기뻐요. **우리는 항상 이렇게 붐비는지 궁금해하고 있었어요.**

여 글쎄요, 아시다시피 공간이 너무 좁아서 붐비는 것처럼 보이지요. 하지만 네, 이 정도는 우리에게 일상이죠.

남2 소피아, 이분은 아론이에요. 제 직장 동료예요.

남1 만나서 반갑습니다, 소피아.

여 저도 만나서 반갑습니다. 여기, **방금 전시한 새로운 판화를 두 분에게 보여 드리겠습니다. 저를 따라오세요.**

어휘 packed 혼잡한 colleague 동료 print 판화
hang up 걸다

41

Who is Sofia?
(A) A teacher
(B) An artist
(C) A real estate agent
(D) A gallery owner

소피아는 누구인가?
(A) 교사
(B) 화가
(C) 부동산 중개인
(D) 미술관 주인

해설 전체 내용 관련 – 소피아의 직업
첫 번째 남자가 첫 대사에서 미술관이 사람들로 붐빈다(This art gallery's packed)고 말하는 것으로 보아 미술관에서 이루어지는 대화임을 알 수 있고, 뒤이어 두 번째 남자가 이곳 주인인 자신의 친구 소피아가 저기 있다(there's my friend Sofia, who owns the place)고 말하고 있으므로 정답은 (D)이다.

42

What are the men curious about?
(A) The creator of some artwork
(B) The lighting in a room
(C) The number of people at an event
(D) How long a business has been open

남자들은 무엇에 대해 궁금해하는가?
(A) 미술 작품의 창작자
(B) 방의 조명
(C) 행사에 참석한 인원수
(D) 사업체를 운영한 기간

어휘 artwork 미술품 lighting 조명

해설 세부 사항 관련 – 남자들이 궁금해하는 것
두 번째 남자가 두 번째 대사에서 항상 이렇게 붐비는지 궁금해하고 있었다(We were just wondering if it's always busy like this)고 말하고 있으므로 정답은 (C)이다.

43

What will the speakers most likely do next?
(A) Purchase a painting
(B) Eat a meal together
(C) Review some floor plans
(D) Look at some artwork

화자들은 다음에 무엇을 할 것 같은가?
(A) 그림 구입하기
(B) 함께 식사하기
(C) 평면도 검토하기
(D) 미술품 감상하기

어휘 purchase 구입하다 review 검토하다 floor plan 평면도

해설 세부 사항 관련 – 화자들이 다음에 할 일
여자가 마지막 대사에서 방금 전시한 새로운 판화를 두 분에게 보여 주겠다(let me show you both some new prints we just hung up)며 따라오라(Follow me)고 말하고 있으므로 정답은 (D)이다.

Paraphrasing 대화의 prints → 정답의 artwork

44-46

M-Au Amina, **⁴⁴how are plans progressing for our mobile phone release?**

W-Br **⁴⁴Good— ⁴⁴,⁴⁵right now, I'm working with our marketing firm to develop the advertising campaign.** There are some really great ideas for commercials and print ads.

M-Au That's great. **⁴⁶I'm really concerned about the growing amount of competition for this type of product.** A lot of our competitors will also be putting out new phones around the same time, so it's important that ours stands out in the market.

남 아미나, 우리 휴대폰 출시 계획은 어떻게 진행되고 있나요?

여 잘되고 있어요. 지금은 광고 캠페인을 개발하기 위해 마케팅 회사와 협력하고 있어요. 광고 방송과 인쇄 광고물에 대한 정말 좋은 아이디어가 몇 가지 있어요.

남 아주 좋아요. 이런 유형의 제품에 대한 경쟁이 치열해지고 있어서 정말 걱정돼요. 많은 경쟁사들도 비슷한 시기에 새 휴대폰을 출시할 것이므로 시장에서 우리 제품이 두각을 나타내도록 하는 것이 중요해요.

어휘 progress 진행되다 release 출시, 발표 commercial 광고 (방송) competition 경쟁 stand out 두각을 나타내다, 눈에 띄다

44

What kind of product are the speakers discussing?
(A) A laptop
(B) A mobile phone
(C) A fitness tracker
(D) A navigation device

화자들은 어떤 종류의 제품에 대해 논의하고 있는가?
(A) 노트북
(B) 휴대폰
(C) 운동 추적기
(D) 내비게이션 장치

해설 전체 내용 관련 – 대화의 주제
남자가 첫 대사에서 휴대폰 출시 계획은 어떻게 진행되고 있는지(how are plans progressing for our mobile phone release?) 묻자 여자가 잘되고 있다(Good)고 대답한 뒤, 지금은 광고 캠페인을 개발하기 위해 마케팅 회사와 협력하고 있다(right now, I'm working ~ to develop the advertising campaign)며 휴대폰 출시에 대한 대화를 이어 가고 있으므로 정답은 (B)이다.

45

What does the woman say she is currently working on?
(A) A marketing campaign
(B) A transportation contract
(C) A fee negotiation
(D) A design feature

여자는 현재 무엇을 작업하고 있다고 말하는가?
(A) 마케팅 캠페인
(B) 운송 계약
(C) 수수료 협상
(D) 디자인

해설 세부 사항 관련 – 여자가 작업하고 있다고 말하는 것
여자가 첫 대사에서 지금은 광고 캠페인을 개발하기 위해 마케팅 회사와 협력하고 있다(right now, I'm working with our marketing firm to develop the advertising campaign)고 했으므로 정답은 (A)이다.

46

What is the man concerned about?
(A) Staff shortages
(B) Supply chain disruptions
(C) Budget constraints
(D) Increased competition

남자는 무엇을 걱정하는가?
(A) 직원 부족
(B) 공급망 중단
(C) 예산 제한
(D) 경쟁 증가

어휘 shortage 부족 disruption 중단 constraint 제한, 제약

해설 세부 사항 관련 – 남자의 우려 사항

남자가 두 번째 대사에서 이런 유형의 제품에 대한 경쟁이 치열해서 걱정(I'm really concerned about the growing amount of competition for this type of product)이라고 우려를 표현하고 있으므로 정답은 (D)이다.

Paraphrasing	대화의 growing amount of competition → 정답의 Increased competition

47-49

M-Cn	Luisa, how did your presentation at the food chemistry conference go?
W-Br	Very well, thanks. **47, 48I'm hoping the presentation increases my chances of receiving the Innovation Award this year.**
M-Cn	That would be fantastic!
W-Br	Of course, some of the numbers in my presentation came from you. **48The statistics you gave me really improved it.**
M-Cn	I'm glad those numbers were helpful. By the way, **49did you see the e-mail saying that recordings of presentations should be uploaded to our server?**
W-Br	**49Thanks for reminding me.** I'll take care of that this afternoon.

남	루이사, 식품 화학 학회에서의 발표는 어떻게 되었나요?
여	아주 잘했어요, 감사합니다. **그 발표를 통해 올해 혁신상을 받을 가능성이 높아졌으면 합니다.**
남	그러면 정말 멋질 것입니다!
여	물론, **발표의 일부 수치는 당신이 제공한 것입니다.** 제공해 주신 통계 자료 덕분에 발표를 크게 향상시킬 수 있었습니다.
남	수치들이 도움이 되었다니 기쁩니다. 그나저나, **발표 녹화 파일을 서버에 업로드해야 한다는 이메일을 보셨나요?**
여	**다시 알려 주셔서 감사해요.** 오늘 오후에 처리하겠습니다.

어휘 food chemistry 식품 화학 innovation 혁신 statistics 통계 (자료) improve 향상시키다 remind 상기시키다

47

What does the woman hope to do this year?
(A) Earn a promotion
(B) Win an award
(C) Give a presentation
(D) Move to a different city

여자는 올해 무엇을 하기를 희망하는가?
(A) 승진하기
(B) 수상하기
(C) 발표하기
(D) 다른 도시로 이사하기

어휘 earn 받다, 획득하다 promotion 승진, 진급

해설 세부 사항 관련 – 여자의 올해 희망 사항

여자가 첫 대사에서 발표를 통해 올해 혁신상을 받을 가능성이 높아졌으면 한다(I'm hoping the presentation increases my chances of receiving the Innovation Award this year)고 말하고 있으므로 정답은 (B)이다.

Paraphrasing	대화의 receiving the Innovation Award → 정답의 Win an award

48

What does the woman mean when she says, "some of the numbers in my presentation came from you"?
(A) She is grateful for the man's help.
(B) She thinks someone else got credit by mistake.
(C) The man should check the accuracy of some numbers.
(D) The man should also give a presentation.

여자가 "발표의 일부 수치는 당신이 제공한 것입니다"라고 말할 때 무엇을 의미하는가?
(A) 남자의 도움에 고마워한다.
(B) 다른 사람이 실수로 인정을 받았다고 생각한다.
(C) 남자는 일부 수치의 정확성을 확인해야 한다.
(D) 남자도 발표를 해야 한다.

어휘 grateful 고마워하는 credit 인정, 신용 accuracy 정확성

해설 화자의 의도 파악 – 발표의 일부 수치는 당신이 제공한 것이라는 말의 의도

앞에서 여자가 발표를 통해 올해 혁신상을 받을 가능성이 높아졌으면 한다(I'm hoping the presentation increases my chances of receiving the Innovation Award this year)고 말한 뒤 인용문을 언급했고, 뒤이어 제공해 준 통계 자료 덕분에 발표를 크게 향상시킬 수 있었다(The statistics you gave me really improved it)며 통계 자료가 발표에 기여한 점을 이야기하고 있다. 따라서 인용문은 남자가 통계 자료를 제공해 준 것에 대해 고마움을 표현하려는 의도로 한 말이므로 정답은 (A)이다.

49

What does the man remind the woman about?
(A) A team meeting has been canceled.
(B) A product will be released soon.
(C) A report will not be distributed.
(D) A task needs to be done.

남자는 여자에게 무엇을 상기시키는가?
(A) 팀 회의가 취소되었다.
(B) 제품이 곧 출시될 예정이다.
(C) 보고서는 배포되지 않을 것이다.
(D) 업무를 완료해야 한다.

어휘 release 출시하다 distribute 배포하다, 나누어 주다

해설 세부 사항 관련 – 남자가 여자에게 상기시키는 것
남자가 세 번째 대사에서 발표 녹화 파일을 서버에 업로드해야 한다는 이메일을 보았는지(did you see the e-mail saying that recordings of presentations should be uploaded to our server?) 묻자 여자가 다시 알려 주어 감사하다(Thanks for reminding me)고 대답하고 있으므로 남자는 여자에게 해야 할 일을 상기시키고 있음을 알 수 있다. 따라서 정답은 (D)이다.

Paraphrasing	대화의 recordings of presentations should be uploaded → 정답의 A task needs to be done

50-52

M-Au	Eniola, we have a problem. ⁵⁰**We got a notice from the city saying the water will be shut off tomorrow from six A.M. till noon due to construction on the street.**
W-Am	Oh, no! ⁵¹**Then we won't be able to open for breakfast. Hopefully we'll be able to serve lunch and dinner though.**
M-Au	Yes, we'll need to let the servers know. ⁵²**I'll call everyone who's scheduled to work the morning shift** and let them know that they don't need to come in.

남	에니올라, 문제가 생겼어요. 도로 공사로 인해 내일 오전 6시부터 정오까지 수도가 차단될 것이라고 시에서 통지를 받았어요.
여	오, 이런! 그러면 아침 식사 손님들은 받을 수 없겠어요. 그래도 점심과 저녁 식사는 제공할 수 있으면 좋겠네요.
남	네, 서빙 직원들에게 알려야 해요. **오전 근무로 예정된 직원 모두에게 전화를 걸어 출근할 필요가 없다고 알리겠습니다.**

어휘	notice 공고문 construction 공사, 건설 serve (음식을) 제공하다 server 서빙 직원, 종업원 shift (교대) 근무

50

What does the man say will happen tomorrow?
(A) New equipment will be installed.
(B) An inspection will take place.
(C) A delivery will be late.
(D) The water will be shut off.

남자는 내일 무슨 일이 일어날 것이라고 말하는가?
(A) 새로운 장비가 설치될 것이다.
(B) 검사가 진행될 것이다.
(C) 배달이 늦어질 것이다.
(D) 물이 차단될 것이다.

어휘 equipment 장비 install 설치하다 inspection 점검, 검사 take place 일어나다, 발생하다

해설 세부 사항 관련 – 남자가 내일 일어날 것이라고 말하는 일
남자가 첫 대사에서 도로 공사로 내일 수도가 차단될 것이라고 시에서 통지를 받았다(We got a notice from the city saying the water will be shut off tomorrow from six A.M. till noon due to construction on the street)고 말하고 있으므로 정답은 (D)이다.

51

Where do the speakers most likely work?
(A) At a factory
(B) At a grocery store
(C) At a restaurant
(D) At a shipping company

화자들은 어디에서 근무하는 것 같은가?
(A) 공장
(B) 식료품점
(C) 식당
(D) 운송 회사

해설 전체 내용 관련 – 화자들의 근무지
여자가 첫 대사에서 아침 식사 손님들은 받을 수 없겠다(Then we won't be able to open for breakfast)면서 그래도 점심과 저녁 식사는 제공할 수 있기를 바란다(Hopefully we'll be able to serve lunch and dinner though)고 말하는 것으로 보아 정답은 (C)이다.

52

What does the man say he will do?
(A) Conduct an interview
(B) Reschedule a training session
(C) Contact staff members
(D) Clean some filters

남자는 무엇을 할 것이라고 말하는가?
(A) 면접 실시하기
(B) 교육 시간 일정 변경하기
(C) 직원에게 연락하기
(D) 필터 청소하기

어휘 conduct 실시하다 training session 교육 세션

해설 세부 사항 관련 – 남자가 할 것이라고 말하는 일

남자가 마지막 대사에서 오전 근무로 예정된 직원 모두에게 전화를 걸겠다 (I'll call everyone who's scheduled to work the morning shift)고 말하고 있으므로 정답은 (C)이다.

Paraphrasing	대화의 call everyone who's scheduled to work the morning shift → 정답의 Contact staff members

53-55 3인 대화

M-Cn	All right, Marion. ⁵³**The new health-care software is all set up on your computer now.** You've done the training already, so it should be straightforward.
W-Am	Great. I hear a lot of health-care providers are switching to this same software.
M-Cn	Yes—⁵⁴**this platform's becoming popular because patients can access all their medical records from different providers through one central system rather than having separate profiles for each office.**
W-Br	⁵⁵**Sorry to interrupt.**
M-Cn	⁵⁵**No problem, Francesca.** I've just finished up here. ⁵⁵**What do you need?**
W-Br	⁵⁵**These forms need to be signed before the courier arrives at ten A.M.**

남	좋아요, 마리온. **이제 새 의료 서비스 소프트웨어가 컴퓨터에 모두 설치되었어요.** 이미 교육을 받았으니 간단할 거예요.
여1	좋아요. 많은 의료 서비스업체가 이것과 같은 소프트웨어로 전환하고 있다고 들었어요.
남	맞아요. **이 플랫폼은 각 의료 기관에서 별도 자료를 보유하기보다는 환자들이 하나의 중앙 시스템을 통해 여러 의료 서비스업체가 제공한 모든 의료 기록에 접근할 수 있기 때문에 인기를 얻고 있어요.**
여2	중간에 끼어들어서 죄송합니다.
남	괜찮아요, 프란체스카. 여기는 방금 마무리되었어요. **필요한 것이 무엇인가요?**
여2	택배 기사가 오전 10시에 도착하기 전에 이 양식에 서명하셔야 합니다.

어휘	health-care 의료 서비스의 straightforward 간단한 switch 전환하다 patient 환자 access 접근하다 medical record 의료[진료] 기록 separate 각각의 interrupt 끼어들다, 방해하다 courier 택배 기사[회사]

53

What did the man just do?
(A) He purchased a computer.
(B) He installed some software.
(C) He returned from a doctor's appointment.
(D) He created a training video.

남자는 방금 무엇을 했는가?
(A) 컴퓨터를 구입했다.
(B) 소프트웨어를 설치했다.
(C) 의사 진료를 받고 돌아왔다.
(D) 교육 비디오를 만들었다.

해설 세부 사항 관련 – 남자가 방금 한 일

남자가 첫 대사에서 이제 새 의료 서비스 소프트웨어가 컴퓨터에 모두 설치되었다(The new health-care software is all set up on your computer now)고 말하고 있으므로 정답은 (B)이다.

Paraphrasing	대화의 is all set up → 정답의 installed

54

According to the man, why has a product become popular?
(A) It is less expensive than similar products.
(B) It is energy efficient.
(C) It provides easy access to information.
(D) It has 24-hour customer support.

남자에 따르면, 제품은 왜 인기를 얻었는가?
(A) 유사 제품보다 저렴하다.
(B) 에너지 효율성이 높다.
(C) 정보에 쉽게 접근할 수 있다.
(D) 24시간 고객 지원을 제공한다.

어휘 energy efficient 에너지 효율적인 customer support 고객 지원

해설 세부 사항 관련 – 남자가 말하는 제품이 인기 있는 이유

남자가 두 번째 대사에서 이 플랫폼은 각 의료 기관에서 별도 자료를 보유하기보다는 환자들이 하나의 중앙 시스템을 통해 여러 의료 서비스업체가 제공한 모든 의료 기록에 접근할 수 있기 때문에 인기를 얻고 있다 (this platform's becoming popular because patients can access all their medical records from different providers through one central system rather than having separate profiles for each office)고 말하고 있으므로 제품의 편리한 접근성이 인기의 이유임을 알 수 있다. 따라서 정답은 (C)이다.

55

Why does Francesca interrupt the conversation?
(A) She needs assistance.
(B) She is taking lunch orders.
(C) Some forms require a signature.
(D) A client has arrived.

프란체스카는 왜 대화에 끼어드는가?
(A) 도움이 필요하다.
(B) 점심 주문을 받고 있다.
(C) 일부 양식에 서명이 필요하다.
(D) 고객이 도착했다.

어휘 assistance 도움 require 필요하다, 요구하다 signature 서명

두 번째 여자가 첫 대사에서 끼어들어서 죄송하다(Sorry to interrupt)고 하자 남자가 괜찮아요, 프란체스카(No problem, Francesca)라고 말하고 있으므로 두 번째 여자가 프란체스카임을 알 수 있고, 뒤이어 남자가 필요한 것이 무엇인지(What do you need?) 묻자 두 번째 여자가 택배 기사가 오전 10시에 도착하기 전에 이 양식에 서명해야 한다(These forms need to be signed before the courier arrives at ten A.M.)고 말하고 있으므로 정답은 (C)이다.

Paraphrasing 대화의 need to be signed
→ 정답의 require a signature

56-58

W-Br	Hi, Gregor. ⁵⁶**Have you had time to review the plan for maintenance on the Springville train line? Remember, we're voting on it during tomorrow's city council meeting.**
M-Au	I have. And I have some reservations.
W-Br	Oh? What are they?
M-Au	Well, ⁵⁷**shutting down that train line for six full weeks in the summer will not be popular with residents. I think I'm going to object to the plan. How about you?**
W-Br	Well, summer is the region's busiest season.
M-Au	I think we should investigate weekend-only maintenance.
W-Br	Good idea. ⁵⁸**I'll write up a list of our concerns to discuss at the meeting.**

여	안녕하세요, 그레고르. **스프링빌 기차 노선의 유지 보수 계획을 검토할 시간이 있었나요? 우리가 내일 시 의회 회의에서 그것에 대해 투표할 계획인 것을 잊지 마세요.**
남	검토했어요. 그리고 몇 가지 의구심이 들었습니다.
여	오? 무엇인가요?
남	음, **여름에 6주 내내 기차 노선을 폐쇄하는 것은 주민들에게 인기가 없을 것입니다. 저는 계획에 반대할 것 같아요. 어떻게 생각하세요?**
여	음, **여름은 이 지역에서 가장 성수기죠.**
남	주말에만 실시하는 보수를 검토해 보아야 할 것 같습니다.
여	좋은 생각이네요. **회의에서 논의할 우려 사항을 목록으로 작성할게요.**

어휘	maintenance 유지 보수 vote 투표하다 city council 시 의회 reservation 의구심 resident 주민 object 반대하다 investigate 검토하다

56

Who most likely are the speakers?
(A) News reporters
(B) Construction workers
(C) Travel agents
(D) City officials

화자들은 누구인 것 같은가?
(A) 신문 기자
(B) 건설 노동자
(C) 여행사 직원
(D) 시 공무원

해설 전체 내용 관련 - 화자들의 직업

여자가 첫 대사에서 남자에게 스프링빌 기차 노선의 유지 보수 계획을 검토할 시간이 있었는지(Have you had time to review the plan for maintenance on the Springville train line?) 물어보면서 우리가 내일 시 의회 회의에서 그것에 대해 투표할 계획인 것을 잊지 말라(Remember, we're voting on it during tomorrow's city council meeting)고 말하는 것으로 보아 화자들은 시 관계자임을 알 수 있다. 따라서 정답은 (D)이다.

57

Why does the woman say, "summer is the region's busiest season"?
(A) To express surprise
(B) To explain a price increase
(C) To agree with an opinion
(D) To request assistance with a project

여자는 왜 "여름은 이 지역에서 가장 성수기죠"라고 말하는가?
(A) 놀람을 표현하려고
(B) 가격 인상을 설명하려고
(C) 의견에 동의하려고
(D) 프로젝트 지원을 요청하려고

어휘 express 표현하다 opinion 의견 request 요청하다

해설 화자의 의도 파악 - 여름은 이 지역에서 가장 성수기라는 말의 의도

앞에서 남자가 여름에 6주 내내 기차 노선을 폐쇄하는 것은 주민들에게 인기가 없을 것(shutting down that train line for six full weeks in the summer will not be popular with residents)이라면서 계획을 반대할 것 같다(I think I'm going to object to the plan)고 말한 뒤, 어떻게 생각하는지(How about you?) 묻자 여자가 인용문을 언급한 것으로 보아, 주민들에게 인기가 없을 것이라는 남자의 의견에 동조하려는 의도로 한 말임을 알 수 있다. 따라서 정답은 (C)이다.

58

What does the woman offer to do?
(A) Make a list
(B) Confirm a meeting time
(C) Inspect some equipment
(D) Adjust a budget

여자는 무엇을 하겠다고 제안하는가?

(A) 목록 만들기
(B) 회의 시간 확정하기
(C) 장비 점검하기
(D) 예산 조정하기

어휘 confirm 확정하다 inspect 점검하다 adjust 조정하다 budget 예산

해설 세부 사항 관련 – 여자의 제안 사항

여자가 마지막 대사에서 회의에서 논의할 우려 사항을 목록으로 작성하겠다(I'll write up a list of our concerns to discuss at the meeting)고 말하고 있으므로 정답은 (A)이다.

59-61

M-Cn	Hi. **59,60I am having trouble submitting my monthly car payment online.** The system keeps telling me that my user name and password are incorrect, but I'm sure I entered them correctly.
W-Am	Thank you for your call, Mr. Ibrahim. **60I apologize, but we're having a problem with our payment network this morning.**
M-Cn	**61My car payment is due today. Will I have to pay extra or be penalized in some way?**
W-Am	**61No, we're guaranteeing that this will not happen to our valued customers.**

남	안녕하세요. **이번 달 자동차 할부금을 온라인상에서 납부하는 데 문제가 있어요.** 시스템상에서 사용자 이름과 비밀번호가 틀렸다고 계속 나오는데, 제대로 입력했다고 확신해요.
여	전화 주셔서 감사합니다, 이브라힘 씨. **죄송하지만, 오늘 아침 결제 네트워크에 문제가 발생했습니다.**
남	**자동차 할부금 납부가 오늘까지예요.** 추가 비용을 지불하거나 어떤 식이든 불이익을 받게 되는 건가요?
여	아니요, 저희는 소중한 고객에게 그런 일이 발생하지 않을 것임을 보장합니다.

어휘 submit 제출하다 payment 대금 incorrect 틀린 penalize 불리하게 하다 guarantee 보장하다 valued 소중한, 중요한

59

What is the man making a payment for?

(A) An automobile
(B) A house
(C) A credit card
(D) A medical bill

남자는 무엇에 대해 돈을 지불할 예정인가?

(A) 자동차
(B) 집
(C) 신용 카드
(D) 의료비 청구서

해설 세부 사항 관련 – 남자가 지불할 예정인 대상

남자가 첫 대사에서 이번 달 자동차 할부금을 온라인상에서 납부하는 데 문제가 있다(I am having trouble submitting my monthly car payment online)고 말하는 것으로 보아 정답은 (A)이다.

> **Paraphrasing** 대화의 car → 정답의 automobile

60

What problem does the woman describe?

(A) An online system is not working.
(B) There are not enough customer service agents.
(C) A manager is not available.
(D) A password needs to be updated.

여자는 어떤 문제를 설명하는가?

(A) 온라인 시스템이 제대로 작동하지 않는다.
(B) 고객 서비스 담당자가 충분하지 않다.
(C) 매니저가 자리에 없다.
(D) 비밀번호를 업데이트해야 한다.

해설 세부 사항 관련 – 여자가 설명하는 문제

남자가 첫 대사에서 이번 달 자동차 할부금을 온라인상에서 납부하는 데 문제가 있다(I am having trouble submitting my monthly car payment online)고 하자 여자가 죄송하지만 오늘 아침 결제 네트워크에 문제가 발생했다(I apologize, but we're having a problem with our payment network this morning)고 말하고 있으므로 여자는 온라인 네트워크의 오작동을 이야기하고 있다는 것을 알 수 있다. 따라서 정답은 (A)이다.

> **Paraphrasing** 대화의 having a problem with our payment network
> → 정답의 An online system is not working

61

What does the woman promise the man?

(A) He will be able to pay later in the day.
(B) He will receive a refund.
(C) He will not have to wait a long time.
(D) He will not be charged a late fee.

여자는 남자에게 무엇을 약속하는가?

(A) 오후에 지불할 수 있을 것이다.
(B) 환불을 받을 것이다.
(C) 오래 기다릴 필요가 없을 것이다.
(D) 연체료가 부과되지 않을 것이다.

어휘 refund 환불 charge 청구하다 late fee 연체료

해설 세부 사항 관련 – 여자가 남자에게 약속하는 것

남자가 두 번째 대사에서 자동차 할부금 납부가 오늘까지(My car payment is due today)라며 추가 비용을 지불하거나 어떤 식이든 불이

익을 받게 되는지(Will I have to pay extra or be penalized in some way?) 묻자 여자가 소중한 고객에게 그런 일이 발생하지 않을 것임을 보장한다(No, we're guaranteeing that this will not happen to our valued customers)고 대답하고 있으므로 정답은 (D)이다.

> **Paraphrasing** 대화의 pay extra
> → 정답의 be charged a late fee

62-64 대화 + 일정표

M-Au	Hello. ⁶²You've reached Graham and Associates.
W-Am	Hi. ⁶²I'd like to meet with someone about managing my accounts and preparing my taxes. Would I be able to speak to an associate sometime next week?
M-Au	Of course! ⁶³Marcel Breton is accepting new clients. Are you available the fifteenth?
W-Am	Hmm. ⁶³No, I'm not. Would the sixteenth work?
M-Au	⁶³Yes, I believe so. We have a staff meeting until eleven A.M., but Marcel has some availability afterwards.
W-Am	That works! ⁶⁴Can I have his e-mail address in case I need to contact him beforehand?

남	안녕하세요. 그레이엄과 어소시에이츠입니다.
여	안녕하세요. 계좌 관리 및 세금 준비와 관련하여 면담을 하고 싶습니다. 다음 주에 직원과 이야기할 수 있습니까?
남	물론이죠! 마르셀 브르통이 신규 고객을 담당하고 있습니다. 15일에 시간이 되십니까?
여	흠. 아니요. 16일은 가능할까요?
남	네, 그럴 것입니다. 오전 11시까지 직원 회의가 있지만 마르셀은 그 후에 시간이 됩니다.
여	저도 시간이 됩니다! 미리 연락해야 하는 경우를 대비하여 그의 이메일 주소를 알 수 있을까요?

어휘 account 계좌 associate 동료 beforehand 사전에

Marcel Breton's Schedule

Monday March 14	Ms. Smith (10–11 A.M.) Training (1–3 P.M.)
Tuesday March 15	Restaurant client (9–10 A.M.)
63 Wednesday March 16	Staff meeting (9–11 A.M.)
Thursday March 17	Vacation

마르셀 브르통의 일정

3월 14일 월요일	스미스 씨 (오전 10–11시) 교육 (오후 1–3시)
3월 15일 화요일	식당 고객 (오전 9–10시)
63 3월 16일 수요일	**직원 회의 (오전 9–11시)**
3월 17일 목요일	휴가

62

Where does the man work?
(A) At an advertising agency
(B) At an accounting firm
(C) At a publishing company
(D) At a real estate agency

남자는 어디에서 일하는가?
(A) 광고 대행사
(B) 회계 법인
(C) 출판사
(D) 부동산 중개소

해설 전체 내용 관련 – 남자의 근무지

남자가 첫 대사에서 그레이엄과 어소시에이츠(You've reached Graham and Associates)라고 전화를 받고 있고, 여자가 계좌 관리 및 세금 준비와 관련하여 면담을 하고 싶다(I'd like to meet with someone about managing my accounts and preparing my taxes)며 다음 주에 직원과 이야기할 수 있는지(Would I be able to speak to an associate sometime next week?) 묻는 것으로 보아 남자는 세금과 관련된 일을 담당하는 업체에서 근무하고 있다는 것을 알 수 있다. 따라서 정답은 (B)이다.

63

Look at the graphic. Which day will the woman meet with Marcel Breton?
(A) On Monday
(B) On Tuesday
(C) On Wednesday
(D) On Thursday

시각 정보에 의하면, 여자는 무슨 요일에 마르셀 브르통을 만날 것인가?
(A) 월요일
(B) 화요일
(C) 수요일
(D) 목요일

해설 시각 정보 연계 – 여자가 마르셀 브르통을 만날 요일

남자가 두 번째 대사에서 마르셀 브르통이 신규 고객을 담당하고 있다(Marcel Breton is accepting new clients)면서 15일에 시간이 되는지(Are you available the fifteenth?) 묻자 여자가 안 된다(No, I'm not)며 16일은 가능할지(Would the sixteenth work?) 물었고, 다시 남자가 그럴 것(Yes, I believe so)이라고 대답하고 있다. 일정표에 따르면 16일은 수요일이므로 정답은 (C)이다.

64

What does the woman ask for?

(A) An e-mail address
(B) A receipt
(C) A cost estimate
(D) A résumé

여자는 무엇을 요청하는가?

(A) 이메일 주소
(B) 영수증
(C) 견적서
(D) 이력서

해설 세부 사항 관련 – 여자의 요청 사항

여자가 마지막 대사에서 미리 연락해야 하는 경우를 대비하여 그의 이메일 주소를 알 수 있을지(Can I have his e-mail address in case I need to contact him beforehand?) 묻고 있으므로 정답은 (A)이다.

65-67 대화 + 그림

M-Au	Hi. ⁶⁵I'd like to order fifty custom sweatshirts with my company's logo on them.
W-Br	⁶⁵Great. We can put it anywhere you like, such as on the sleeve, on the back, or right in front.
M-Au	⁶⁶Could you put the logo in the bottom corner, near the waist?
W-Br	Yes, we can. ⁶⁷For fifty sweatshirts, it takes around three weeks for embroidery and two weeks for printing.
M-Au	Actually, ⁶⁷I was hoping to have them next week. Would it be possible to pay for expedited service?
W-Br	Yes, we do offer rush service. Could you come in on Thursday to approve a mock-up?

남	안녕하세요. 운동복 상의 50벌을 회사 로고를 넣어 맞춤으로 주문하고 싶습니다.
여	좋습니다. 로고는 소매, 등판, 정면 중앙 등 원하는 곳에 넣을 수 있습니다.
남	허리 근처 하단 한편에 로고를 넣을 수 있을까요?
여	네, 할 수 있습니다. 운동복 상의 50벌의 경우, 자수 작업은 3주 그리고 인쇄 작업은 2주가 소요됩니다.
남	실은 다음 주에 배송받기를 바랐는데요. 추가 요금을 내고 속달 서비스로 할 수 있습니까?
여	네, 속달 서비스를 제공합니다. 견본을 승인하기 위해 목요일에 오실 수 있을까요?

| 어휘 | custom 맞춤의 sweatshirt 운동복 상의 sleeve 소매 waist 허리 embroidery 자수, 자수법 expedite 신속히 처리하다 mock-up 견본, 모형 |

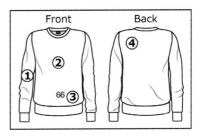

Front   Back

정면   등판

65

What type of business does the woman work for?

(A) A fashion design company
(B) A custom clothing store
(C) A sporting equipment shop
(D) A secondhand clothing store

여자는 어떤 업종에서 일하는가?

(A) 패션 디자인 회사
(B) 맞춤 제작 의류점
(C) 스포츠 용품점
(D) 중고 옷 가게

어휘 secondhand 중고의

해설 전체 내용 관련 – 여자의 근무 업종

남자가 첫 대사에서 운동복 상의 50벌을 회사 로고를 넣어 맞춤으로 주문하고 싶다(I'd like to order fifty custom sweatshirts with my company's logo on them)고 특정 요구 사항을 포함하여 주문을 하자 여자가 좋다(Great)며 로고는 소매, 등판, 정면 중앙 등 원하는 곳에 넣을 수 있다(We can put it anywhere you like, such as on the sleeve, on the back, or right in front)고 답하는 것으로 보아 여자는 의류 주문 제작 업체에 종사하고 있다는 것을 알 수 있다. 따라서 정답은 (B)이다.

66

Look at the graphic. Where does the man want a logo to appear?

(A) Location 1
(B) Location 2
(C) Location 3
(D) Location 4

시각 정보에 의하면, 남자는 로고가 어디에 들어가기를 원하는가?

(A) 1번 위치
(B) 2번 위치
(C) 3번 위치
(D) 4번 위치

해설 시각 정보 연계 – 남자가 로고가 들어가기를 원하는 위치

남자가 두 번째 대사에서 허리 근처 하단 한편에 로고를 넣을 수 있을지

(Could you put the logo in the bottom corner, near the waist?) 묻고 있고, 그림에 의하면 허리 근처 하단은 3번이라고 표기되어 있으므로 정답은 (C)이다.

67

What is the man willing to pay extra for?
(A) High-quality material
(B) An unusual color
(C) A variety of sizes
(D) A rush order

남자는 무엇에 대해 추가 비용을 지불하려 하는가?
(A) 고품질 소재
(B) 특이한 색상
(C) 다양한 크기
(D) 속달 주문

해설 세부 사항 관련 – 남자가 추가 비용을 지불하려는 것
여자가 두 번째 대사에서 운동복 상의 50벌의 경우, 자수 작업은 3주 그리고 인쇄 작업은 2주가 걸린다(For fifty sweatshirts, it takes around three weeks for embroidery and two weeks for printing)고 하자 남자가 다음 주에 배송을 받기를 바랐다(I was hoping to have them next week)면서 추가 요금을 내고 속달 서비스로 할 수 있을지(Would it be possible to pay for expedited service?) 묻고 있으므로 정답은 (D)이다.

Paraphrasing	대화의 expedited service → 정답의 rush order

68-70 대화 + 노래 목록

W-Am ⁶⁸**Are you excited about our upcoming performance at the harvest festival this weekend?**

M-Cn ⁶⁸**Yes, after all the rehearsing we've done, I think our band is ready to put on a good show.**

W-Am Right. ⁶⁹**Although I'm slightly concerned about our new drummer, since he doesn't have much stage experience.** He might be nervous when he does his drum solo.

M-Cn You have a point. ⁷⁰**The solo is in the Brandon Toprak song. We could replace that one with the other song we've been practicing together, "City Daydreams."** Let's ask him about it.

여	이번 주말 추수 축제에서 선보일 우리 공연으로 들떠 있나요?
남	네, 리허설을 모두 마치고 우리 밴드는 좋은 무대를 선보일 만반의 준비가 된 것 같아요.
여	맞아요. **새로 합류한 드러머가 무대 경험이 많지 않아서 조금 걱정이 되기는 하지만요.** 드럼 솔로를 할 때 긴장할 수도 있어요.

남	일리가 있어요. **솔로는 브랜든 토프락의 노래에 있어요. 함께 연습하고 있는 다른 곡인 "도시 백일몽"으로 교체할 수 있어요.** 그에게 한번 물어보죠.

어휘	upcoming 다가오는, 곧 있을 harvest 추수[수확] rehearse 리허설을 하다 nervous 긴장하는 have a point 일리가 있다

Song	Songwriter
"Roses on a Hill"	Marta Ruiz
"Time Again Blues"	Oliver Hughes
⁷⁰"Lake Charon"	Brandon Toprak
"Ice at Dawn"	Zaina Feras

노래	작곡가
"언덕 위의 장미"	마르타 루이즈
"타임 어게인 블루스"	올리버 휴즈
⁷⁰**"카론 호수"**	**브랜든 토프락**
"새벽의 얼음"	자이나 페라스

68

Who most likely are the speakers?
(A) Stage managers
(B) Musicians
(C) Radio show hosts
(D) Recording executives

화자들은 누구인 것 같은가?
(A) 무대 감독
(B) 음악가
(C) 라디오 쇼 진행자
(D) 음반 회사 간부

해설 전체 내용 관련 – 화자들의 직업
여자가 첫 대사에서 이번 주말 추수 축제에서 선보일 우리 공연으로 들떠 있는지(Are you excited about our upcoming performance at the harvest festival this weekend?) 묻자 남자가 리허설을 모두 마치고 우리 밴드는 좋은 무대를 선보일 만반의 준비가 된 것 같다(Yes, after all the rehearsing we've done, I think our band is ready to put on a good show)고 대답하고 있으므로 정답은 (B)이다.

69

What is the woman concerned about?
(A) A sound equipment failure
(B) Some song lyrics
(C) A band member's inexperience
(D) A rehearsal space conflict

여자는 무엇을 걱정하는가?
(A) 음향 기기 고장
(B) 노래 가사
(C) 밴드 멤버의 미숙함
(D) 리허설 공간 사용의 겹침

어휘 failure 고장 lyrics 노래 가사 inexperience 미숙, 경험 부족
conflict 겹침, 갈등

해설 세부 사항 관련 – 여자의 우려 사항

여자가 두 번째 대사에서 새로 합류한 드러머가 무대 경험이 많지 않아서
걱정(Although I'm slightly concerned about our new drummer,
since he doesn't have much stage experience)이라고 우려를 표현
하고 있으므로 정답은 (C)이다.

> **Paraphrasing** 대화의 our new drummer
> → 정답의 A band member
> 대화의 doesn't have much stage
> experience → 정답의 inexperience

70

Look at the graphic. Which song does the man
suggest replacing?
(A) "Roses on a Hill"
(B) "Time Again Blues"
(C) "Lake Charon"
(D) "Ice at Dawn"

시각 정보에 의하면, 남자는 어떤 노래를 교체하기를 제안하는가?
(A) "언덕 위의 장미"
(B) "타임 어게인 블루스"
(C) "카론 호수"
(D) "새벽의 얼음"

해설 시각 정보 연계 – 남자가 교체를 제안하는 노래

남자가 마지막 대사에서 솔로는 브랜든 토프락의 노래에 있다(The solo
is in the Brandon Toprak song)며 함께 연습하고 있는 다른 곡인 "도
시 백일몽"으로 교체할 수 있다(We could replace that one with the
other song we've been practicing together, "City Daydreams")고
말하고 있고, 노래 목록에 따르면 브랜든 토프락의 노래는 "카론 호수"로
나와 있으므로 정답은 (C)이다.

PART 4

71-73 전화 메시지

> W-Br Hello, this is Kelly from Flower Power
> Florist. **71You ordered 30 vases of zinnias for
> the tables at your restaurant.** You mentioned
> they were for a special event next week at the
> restaurant. **72I'm sorry, but there's a shortage of
> zinnias right now**. Unfortunately, the growers
> didn't produce enough this season. I could put
> together 30 vases of roses instead. Those are
> usually more expensive, but I can provide them to
> you for the same price as the zinnias. **73Please let
> me know if roses would be acceptable.** I'll be at
> the shop until five o'clock today.

안녕하세요, 플라워 파워 꽃집의 켈리입니다. **식당 테이블에 놓기 위
해 백일홍 화병 30개를 주문하셨습니다.** 다음 주 식당에서 열리는 특
별 행사를 위한 것이라고 하셨어요. **죄송하지만, 지금 백일홍이 부족
합니다.** 안타깝게도, 재배자들이 이번 계절에는 충분히 생산하지 않았
네요. 대신 장미 화병으로 30개를 채울 수 있습니다. 보통은 장미가 더
비싸지만 백일홍과 같은 가격으로 제공해 드릴 수 있어요. **장미로 받으
셔도 괜찮은지 알려 주세요.** 저는 오늘 5시까지 가게에 있을 거예요.

어휘 florist 꽃집, 꽃집 주인 vase 꽃병 zinnia 백일홍
shortage 부족 grower 재배자 instead 대신에 acceptable
받아들일 수 있는

71

Who most likely is the listener?
(A) A school secretary
(B) A farmer
(C) A delivery driver
(D) A restaurant manager

청자는 누구인 것 같은가?
(A) 학교 행정 직원
(B) 농부
(C) 배달 기사
(D) 식당 매니저

해설 전체 내용 관련 – 청자의 직업

화자가 초반부에 청자에게 식당 테이블에 놓기 위해 백일홍 화병 30개를
주문했다(You ordered 30 vases of zinnias for the tables at your
restaurant)고 말하고 있으므로 청자는 식당 주인이나 직원이라는 것을
알 수 있다. 따라서 정답은 (D)이다.

72

What problem does the speaker mention?
(A) An employee is on vacation.
(B) An item is not available.
(C) The cost of an item has changed.
(D) An order was processed incorrectly.

화자는 어떤 문제를 언급하는가?
(A) 직원이 휴가 중이다.
(B) 제품이 제공되지 않는다.
(C) 제품의 가격이 변경되었다.
(D) 주문이 잘못 처리되었다.

어휘 process 처리하다 incorrectly 잘못, 부정확하게

해설 세부 사항 관련 – 화자가 언급하는 문제

화자가 중반부에 죄송하지만, 지금 백일홍이 부족하다(I'm sorry, but
there's a shortage of zinnias right now)고 말하고 있으므로 특정 꽃
을 제공할 수 없음을 알 수 있다. 따라서 정답은 (B)이다.

> **Paraphrasing** 담화의 there's a shortage of zinnias
> → 정답의 An item is not available

TEST 9 (세로 탭)

73

What does the speaker ask the listener to do?

(A) Confirm a flower choice
(B) Approve a new delivery time
(C) Submit a receipt
(D) Call a different store

화자는 청자에게 무엇을 해 달라고 요청하는가?

(A) 꽃 선택 확인하기
(B) 새로운 배송 시간 승인하기
(C) 영수증 제출하기
(D) 다른 매장에 전화하기

어휘 confirm 확인하다 approve 승인하다 submit 제출하다
　　receipt 영수증

해설 세부 사항 관련 – 화자의 요청 사항

화자가 후반부에 장미로 받아도 괜찮은지 알려 달라(Please let me know if roses would be acceptable)고 요청하고 있으므로 정답은 (A)이다.

74-76 광고

W-Am Today's radio program is sponsored by Prospective. **74Do you have trouble finding the perfect job candidate for your business? Let Prospective handle it.** We'll check their qualifications, request references, and run background checks—so you don't have to. **75And beginning this year, Prospective now offers daily updates on each job listing you post.** Have candidate suggestions sent right to your inbox. **76To try a free fourteen-day trial of Prospective, fill out our online survey about your business at www.prospective.com.**

오늘의 라디오 프로그램은 프로스펙티브에서 후원합니다. **귀사에 완벽한 입사 지원자를 찾는 데 어려움이 있으십니까? 프로스펙티브에 맡겨 주세요.** 우리가 자격을 확인하고 추천서를 요청하며, 배경 조사를 진행할 것이므로 여러분이 직접 하실 필요가 없습니다. **그리고 올해부터 프로스펙티브는 이제 여러분이 게시하는 각 구인 목록에 대한 일일 업데이트를 제공합니다.** 추천 후보를 여러분의 편지함으로 바로 받아 보십시오. **프로스펙티브의 14일 무료 체험판을 사용해 보시려면 www.prospective.com에서 귀사에 대한 온라인 설문 조사를 작성해 주십시오.**

어휘 sponsor 후원하다 prospective 예비의, 유망한 have trouble ~ing ~하는 데 어려움을 겪다 candidate 지원자, 후보자 handle 다루다 qualification 자격, 자질 reference 추천서 background 배경 inbox 받은 편지함 trial 시험(판) fill out 작성하다

74

What service does Prospective provide?

(A) Employee recruiting
(B) Technology support
(C) Digital marketing
(D) Customized printing

프로스펙티브는 어떤 서비스를 제공하는가?

(A) 직원 채용
(B) 기술 지원
(C) 디지털 마케팅
(D) 주문 제작 인쇄

해설 세부 사항 관련 – 프로스펙티브가 제공하는 서비스

화자가 초반부에 여러분의 회사에 완벽한 입사 지원자를 찾는 데 어려움이 있는지(Do you have trouble finding the perfect job candidate for your business?) 물어보면서 프로스펙티브에 맡겨 달라(Let Prospective handle it)고 말하는 것으로 보아 정답은 (A)이다.

> Paraphrasing 담화의 finding the perfect job candidate
> → 정답의 Employee recruiting

75

What recent improvement did Prospective make?

(A) It matches competitor prices.
(B) It sends updates regularly.
(C) It offers personalized consultations.
(D) It provides international service.

프로스펙티브는 최근에 무엇을 개선했는가?

(A) 경쟁사 가격과 같도록 맞추었다.
(B) 정기적으로 업데이트를 보낸다.
(C) 맞춤형 상담을 제공한다.
(D) 국제 서비스를 제공한다.

어휘 competitor 경쟁사[경쟁업체] personalized 개인의 필요에 맞춘

해설 세부 사항 관련 – 프로스펙티브가 최근에 개선한 것

화자가 중반부에 올해부터 프로스펙티브는 여러분이 게시하는 각 구인 목록에 대한 일일 업데이트를 제공한다(And beginning this year, Prospective now offers daily updates on each job listing you post)고 말하고 있으므로 정답은 (B)이다.

> Paraphrasing 담화의 offers daily updates
> → 정답의 sends updates regularly

76

How can the listeners try Prospective for free?

(A) By entering a contest
(B) By calling a radio station
(C) By visiting a business
(D) By completing a survey

청자들은 어떻게 프로스펙티브를 무료로 이용해 볼 수 있는가?
(A) 대회에 참가해서
(B) 라디오 방송국에 전화를 걸어서
(C) 업체에 방문해서
(D) 설문 조사를 작성해서

어휘 enter 참가하다 contest 대회 complete 작성하다

해설 세부 사항 관련 – 프로스펙티브를 무료로 이용해 볼 수 있는 방법
화자가 마지막에 프로스펙티브의 14일 무료 체험판을 사용해 보려면 www.prospective.com에서 온라인 설문 조사를 작성하라(To try a free fourteen-day trial of Prospective, fill out our online survey about your business at www.prospective.com)고 알려 주고 있으므로 정답은 (D)이다.

> **Paraphrasing** 담화의 fill out → 정답의 completing

77-79 전화 메시지

> W-Br Hi, Rawad. **⁷⁷It's Kriti Hazarika from Somerville Realty.** I'm following up about the Maple Road space you expressed interest in renting as a location for your antique store. It's a great spot, **⁷⁸but I just learned from the owner that the old electrical wiring needs to be replaced.** **⁷⁹I know you're eager to get your store up and running. The owner will need to apply for a permit for the work, though,** and the process normally takes a long time. Let me know what you want to do.

> 안녕하세요, 라와드. **서머빌 부동산의 크리티 하자리카입니다.** 고객님이 골동품 가게 위치로 임대에 관심을 표하신 메이플 로 자리에 대해 더 알아보고 있는 중이에요. 좋은 자리인데, **주인으로부터 노후된 전기 배선을 교체해야 한다는 것을 방금 알게 되었어요. 가게를 운영하려는 의욕이 높다는 것을 압니다. 그러나 주인이 해당 작업에 대한 허가를 신청해야 하고** 그 절차는 보통 시간이 오래 걸려요. 어떻게 하시기를 원하는지 알려 주세요.

> 어휘 realty 부동산 follow up 더 알아보다 antique 골동품의 wiring 배선 eager 열렬한, 열심인 up and running (제대로) 운영되는 permit 허가(증)

77

Who most likely is the speaker?
(A) A property inspector
(B) A real estate agent
(C) An electrician
(D) An architect

화자는 누구인 것 같은가?
(A) 부동산 감정 평가사
(B) 부동산 중개인
(C) 전기 기사
(D) 건축가

해설 전체 내용 관련 – 화자의 직업
화자가 초반부에 자신을 서머빌 부동산의 크리티 하자리카(It's Kriti Hazarika from Somerville Realty)라고 소개하고 있으므로 정답은 (B)이다.

78

What is the problem with a property?
(A) A roof is leaking.
(B) A wall needs to be reinforced.
(C) Some wiring needs to be updated.
(D) Some windows need to be replaced.

부동산에 어떤 문제가 있는가?
(A) 지붕이 새고 있다.
(B) 벽을 보강해야 한다.
(C) 배선을 새것으로 바꾸어야 한다.
(D) 창문을 교체해야 한다.

어휘 leak 새다 reinforce 강화하다, 보강하다

해설 세부 사항 관련 – 부동산의 문제점
화자가 중반부에 주인으로부터 노후된 전기 배선을 교체해야 한다는 것을 방금 알게 되었다(but I just learned from the owner that the old electrical wiring needs to be replaced)며 상황을 알려 주고 있으므로 정답은 (C)이다.

> **Paraphrasing** 담화의 be replaced → 정답의 be updated

79

What does the speaker imply when she says, "the process normally takes a long time"?
(A) This case may be an exception.
(B) Hiring more workers is advisable.
(C) A store opening may be delayed.
(D) The listener should submit a form soon.

화자가 "그 절차는 보통 시간이 오래 걸려요"라고 말할 때 무엇을 의미하는가?
(A) 이 경우는 예외일 수 있다.
(B) 직원을 더 고용하는 것이 바람직하다.
(C) 가게 개업이 지연될 수 있다.
(D) 청자는 곧 양식을 제출해야 한다.

어휘 exception 예외 advisable 바람직한, 권할 만한 submit 제출하다

해설 화자의 의도 파악 – 그 절차는 보통 시간이 오래 걸린다는 말의 의도
앞에서 가게를 운영하려는 의욕이 높다는 것을 안다(I know you're eager to get your store up and running)면서 그러나 주인이 해당 작업에 대한 허가를 신청해야 한다(The owner will need to apply for a permit for the work, though)고 상황을 설명한 뒤 인용문을 언급하고 있는 것으로 보아, 가게 운영을 시작하는 것이 늦어질 수 있다는 것을 알리려고 한 말임을 알 수 있다. 따라서 정답은 (C)이다.

M-Au Welcome, everyone. I'm Brian Cho, your instructor. **80Over the next five weeks, I'll teach you everything you need to know about commercial truck driving.** We'll go over how to keep electronic logbooks, since **81companies have recently started requiring drivers to record their shift hours electronically—something that wasn't done in the past.** By the end of this course, you'll be ready to earn your commercial driver's license and start your new career. Fortunately, **82this is a great time to enter the profession, because the compensation is very attractive.** Many companies are even offering signing bonuses of ten thousand dollars or more to new drivers.

모두 환영합니다. 저는 강사 브라이언 조입니다. **앞으로 5주 동안, 상업용 트럭 운전에 대해 알아야 할 모든 것을 알려 드리겠습니다.** 최근 **회사에서 운전자에게 교대 시간을 컴퓨터상에 기록하도록 요구하기 시작했기에** 전자 운행 일지를 기록하는 방법에 대해 살펴보겠습니다. **이전에는 이루어지지 않았던 것이죠.** 이 과정을 마치면 상업용 운전면허를 취득하고 새로운 경력을 시작할 준비가 될 것입니다. 다행히도, **보수가 아주 매력적이기 때문에 이 직종에 뛰어들기에 좋은 시기입니다.** 많은 회사들은 심지어 신규 운전자에게 만 달러 혹은 그 이상의 계약 보너스를 제공하고 있습니다.

어휘 instructor 강사 commercial 상업의 go over 살펴보다, 검토하다 logbook 일지 electronically 컴퓨터로, 전자적으로 earn 얻다, 벌다 profession 직업, 직종 compensation 보수, 보상 attractive 매력적인 signing bonus (계약 체결 시 선지급하는) 계약 보너스

80

What type of work are the listeners training for?
(A) Construction
(B) Real estate
(C) Manufacturing
(D) Truck driving

청자들은 어떤 종류의 일을 위해 교육받고 있는가?
(A) 건설
(B) 부동산
(C) 제조
(D) 트럭 운전

해설 전체 내용 관련 – 청자들이 교육받는 일
화자가 초반부에 앞으로 5주 동안, 상업용 트럭 운전에 대해 알아야 할 모든 것을 알려 주겠다(Over the next five weeks, I'll teach you everything you need to know about commercial truck driving)며 교육 내용을 소개하고 있으므로 정답은 (D)이다.

81

What recent change does the speaker mention?
(A) Inspections are taking place more frequently.
(B) Information must be entered electronically.
(C) A training course has been shortened.
(D) Membership fees have decreased.

화자는 어떤 최근 변화를 언급하는가?
(A) 검사가 더 자주 이루어지고 있다.
(B) 정보를 컴퓨터상에 입력해야 한다.
(C) 교육 과정이 단축되었다.
(D) 회비가 인하되었다.

어휘 inspection 검사 shorten 짧게 하다, 단축하다

해설 세부 사항 관련 – 화자가 최근 변화로 언급하는 것
화자가 중반부에 최근 회사에서 운전자에게 교대 시간을 컴퓨터상에 기록하도록 요구하기 시작했고 이전에는 없었던 것(companies have recently started requiring drivers to record their shift hours electronically—something that wasn't done in the past)이라고 말하는 것으로 보아 정답은 (B)이다.

82

According to the speaker, why is it a good time to enter a profession?
(A) Pay is high.
(B) Schedules are flexible.
(C) Certification requirements are not strict.
(D) Technological innovations are expected.

화자에 따르면, 왜 직종에 들어가기 좋은 시기인가?
(A) 보수가 높다.
(B) 일정이 유동적이다.
(C) 자격 취득 요건이 엄격하지 않다.
(D) 기술 혁신이 기대된다.

어휘 flexible 유동적인 certification 자격증 requirement 필요, 요건 strict 엄격한 innovation 혁신, 쇄신

해설 세부 사항 관련 – 직종에 들어가기 좋은 시기인 이유
화자가 후반부에 보수가 아주 매력적이기 때문에 이 직종에 뛰어들기에 좋은 시기(this is a great time to enter the profession, because the compensation is very attractive)라고 했으므로 정답은 (A)이다.

> **Paraphrasing** 담화의 the compensation is very attractive
> → 정답의 Pay is high

M-Cn **83Today, reporters at Channel 7 News witnessed a historic opening ceremony here on the shores of Chesapeake Bay.** For the past several years, construction has been ongoing on a new bridge spanning the bay. **84Earlier this year,** transportation officials shared the good news **that the construction was progressing faster than expected.** And as of today, traffic is moving across the new bridge at a steady pace, two months sooner than planned! **⁸⁵I interviewed some local delivery drivers**, and as you can imagine, they are happy to see the construction barricades come down early!

오늘 채널 세븐 뉴스의 기자들은 이곳 체서피크만 해안에서 열린 역사적인 개통식을 목격했습니다. 지난 몇 년 동안, 만을 가로지르는 신축 교량 공사가 진행되었습니다. **올해 초 교통부 관계자들은 건설이 예상보다 빠르게 진행되고 있다는 희소식을 전해 주었습니다.** 그리고 오늘부로 예정보다 2개월 빨리 차량들이 새 교량을 가로질러 일정한 속도로 통행하고 있습니다! **제가 지역 배달 기사 몇 명을 인터뷰했는데요**, 예상대로, 건설 바리케이드가 일찍 철거되는 것을 보고 기뻐하고 있습니다!

어휘 witness 목격하다 historic 역사적인 shore 해안 bay 만 ongoing 진행 중인 span 걸치다, 걸쳐 이어지다 progress 진행되다 steady 일정한 barricade 바리케이드, 장애물

83

What event is the speaker reporting on?
(A) A holiday parade
(B) A speech by the city mayor
(C) An opening ceremony
(D) A building demolition

화자는 어떤 행사에 대해 보도하고 있는가?
(A) 휴일 퍼레이드
(B) 시장의 연설
(C) 개통식
(D) 건물 철거

해설 전체 내용 관련 – 보도의 주제
화자가 도입부에 오늘 채널 세븐 뉴스의 기자들은 이곳 체서피크만 해안에서 열린 개통식을 목격했다(Today, reporters at Channel 7 News witnessed a historic opening ceremony here on the shores of Chesapeake Bay)고 말하고 있으므로 정답은 (C)이다.

84

What news did officials share earlier in the year?
(A) Traffic was lighter than projected.
(B) Work was being done faster than expected.
(C) Additional workers would be hired.
(D) A project budget was being revised.

관계자들은 올해 초 어떤 소식을 전했는가?
(A) 교통량이 예상보다 적었다.
(B) 작업이 예상보다 빠르게 진행되고 있었다.
(C) 작업자를 추가로 고용할 것이다.
(D) 프로젝트 예산이 수정되고 있었다.

어휘 project 예측하다; 프로젝트 revise 변경[수정]하다

해설 세부 사항 관련 – 관계자들이 올해 초에 전한 소식
화자가 중반부에 올해 초 교통부 관계자들은 건설이 예상보다 빠르게 진행되고 있다는 희소식을 전해 주었다(Earlier this year, transportation officials shared the good news that the construction was progressing faster than expected)고 말하고 있으므로 정답은 (B)이다.

> **Paraphrasing** 담화의 the construction was progressing
> → 정답의 Work was being done

85

Who did the speaker interview?
(A) Some construction engineers
(B) A local store owner
(C) A government official
(D) Some delivery drivers

화자는 누구를 인터뷰했는가?
(A) 건설 엔지니어
(B) 지역 상점 주인
(C) 공무원
(D) 배달 기사

해설 세부 사항 관련 – 화자가 인터뷰한 대상
화자가 후반부에 지역 배달 기사 몇 명을 인터뷰했다(I interviewed some local delivery drivers)고 말하고 있으므로 정답은 (D)이다.

86-88 전화 메시지

M-Au Hi, Ife. This is Hiroki Tamura. As you may know, **⁸⁶I'm managing the company's project to develop a mobile application for Restorff Bank.** The project is already under way and has gone well so far. However, **⁸⁷yesterday I was informed by upper leadership that the client requested we have the product ready for launch a month earlier than anticipated.** Leadership wants us to make every effort to meet this request. **⁸⁸We can't hope to accomplish it with my current small team of software developers, though,** and I know you usually do excellent work. Please get back to me when you have a chance.

안녕하세요, 이페. 히로키 타무라입니다. 아시겠지만, **저는 지금 레스토프 은행을 위한 모바일 앱을 개발하는 회사 프로젝트를 주관하고 있어요.** 이 프로젝트는 이미 진행 중이며 지금까지 순조롭게 진행되고 있어요. 그런데 **어제 상위 경영진으로부터 고객이 예정보다 한 달 빨리 제품 출시를 요청했다고 들었어요.** 경영진은 우리가 이 요청을 충족하기 위해 총력을 기울여 주기를 원합니다. **현재 소프트웨어 개발 팀에 있는 적은 인원만으로는 작업 완수를 기대할 수 없는데,** 당신이 보통 일을 잘한다는 것을 알고 있어요. 기회가 되면 제게 연락 주세요.

어휘 under way 진행 중인 inform 알리다, 통지하다 launch
출시, 개시 anticipate 예상하다 accomplish 완수하다

86

What industry does the speaker most likely work in?
(A) Finance
(B) Advertising
(C) Architecture
(D) Technology

화자는 어떤 업계에서 일하는 것 같은가?
(A) 금융
(B) 광고
(C) 건축
(D) 기술

해설 전체 내용 관련 – 화자의 근무 업계
화자가 초반부에 레스토프 은행을 위한 모바일 앱을 개발하는 회사 프
로젝트를 주관하고 있다(I'm managing the company's project to
develop a mobile application for Restorff Bank)고 말하고 있으므
로 화자는 소프트웨어 개발 업체에서 일하고 있다는 것을 알 수 있다. 따라
서 정답은 (D)이다.

87

What did the speaker learn yesterday?
(A) He will be promoted to a management position.
(B) The funding for a project has increased.
(C) A client asked for work to be completed early.
(D) A client complained about a company's service.

화자는 어제 무엇을 알게 되었는가?
(A) 그는 관리직으로 승진할 것이다.
(B) 프로젝트를 위한 자금이 증가했다.
(C) 고객이 작업을 조기 완료해 줄 것을 요청했다.
(D) 고객이 회사의 서비스에 대해 불만을 제기했다.

어휘 promote 승진시키다 management 관리 funding 자금 (제공)

해설 세부 사항 관련 – 화자가 어제 알게 된 사실
화자가 중반부에 어제 상위 경영진으로부터 고객이 예정보다 한 달 빨
리 제품 출시를 요청했다고 들었다(yesterday I was informed ~ that
the client requested we have the product ready for launch a
month earlier than anticipated)고 말하고 있으므로 정답은 (C)이다.

Paraphrasing 담화의 ready for launch a month earlier
→ 정답의 completed early

88

What does the speaker imply when he says, "you
usually do excellent work"?
(A) He wants the listener to work on his team.
(B) He is surprised that the listener made an error.
(C) The listener is likely to receive a raise.
(D) The listener should replace him as project
manager.

화자가 "당신이 보통 일을 잘한다"라고 말할 때 무엇을 의미하는가?
(A) 청자가 그의 팀에서 일하기를 원한다.
(B) 청자가 실수한 것에 놀랐다.
(C) 청자가 임금 인상을 받을 것 같다.
(D) 청자가 프로젝트 매니저로서 그를 대체해야 한다.

어휘 make an error 실수하다 raise 임금 인상 replace 대체하다

해설 화자의 의도 파악 – 당신이 보통 일을 잘한다는 말의 의도
앞에서 현재 소프트웨어 개발 팀에 있는 적은 인원만으로는 작업 완수를
기대할 수 없다(We can't hope to accomplish it with my current
small team of software developers, though)고 말한 뒤 인용문을 언
급한 것으로 보아, 청자의 도움을 받아 부족한 작업 인력의 공백을 메우려
는 의도로 한 말임을 알 수 있다. 따라서 정답은 (A)이다.

89-91 회의 발췌

M-Cn Hi, everyone. **89I have exciting news. Our
company has officially decided to expand into
France. 90What that means for us here in the Data
Analytics Department is that we have a lot of work
to do to understand French consumers.** In order
to sell our cook-at-home meal kits, we need to
analyze the data we've collected about how people
in France shop now and what they buy. **91I'll start
uploading the files to our shared drive**, and then
we can begin!

안녕하세요, 여러분. 흥미로운 소식이 있습니다. 우리 회사가 프랑스
로 확장한다는 결정을 공식화했습니다. 이것이 여기 데이터 분석 부서
에 있는 우리에게 의미하는 바는 프랑스 소비자를 이해하기 위해 해야
할 일이 많다는 것입니다. 집에서 요리하는 밀키트를 판매하려면 프랑
스 사람들이 현재 어떻게 쇼핑하고 무엇을 구매하는지 수집한 데이터
를 분석해야 합니다. 파일을 공유 드라이브에 업로드할 테니 이제 시
작하면 됩니다!

어휘 officially 공식적으로 expand 확장되다 analytics 분석,
분석 정보 analyze 분석하다 shared drive 공유 드라이브

89

What news does the speaker report?
(A) The company is planning to expand.
(B) The company exceeded its sales target.
(C) New computers will be distributed.
(D) A business trip has been organized.

화자는 어떤 소식을 전하는가?
(A) 회사가 확장할 계획이다.
(B) 회사가 판매 목표를 초과 달성했다.
(C) 새 컴퓨터를 제공할 것이다.
(D) 출장이 계획되었다.

어휘 exceed 초과하다 distribute 제공하다, 나누어 주다 organize
계획하다

화자가 초반부에 흥미로운 소식이 있다(I have exciting news)면서 우리 회사가 프랑스로 확장한다는 결정을 공식화했다(Our company has officially decided to expand into France)고 알리고 있으므로 정답은 (A)이다.

Paraphrasing	담화의 has officially decided to expand → 정답의 is planning to expand

90

What department do the listeners work in?
(A) Quality Control
(B) Human Resources
(C) Data Analytics
(D) Customer Service

청자들은 어느 부서에서 일하는가?
(A) 품질 관리
(B) 인사부
(C) 데이터 분석
(D) 고객 서비스

해설 전체 내용 관련 – 청자들의 근무 부서

화자가 중반부에 이것이 여기 데이터 분석 부서에 있는 우리에게 의미하는 바는 프랑스 소비자를 이해하기 위해 해야 할 일이 많다는 것(What that means for us here in the Data Analytics Department is ~ French consumers)이라고 말하고 있으므로 정답은 (C)이다.

91

What does the speaker say he will do?
(A) Order some supplies
(B) E-mail an agenda
(C) Fix some software
(D) Upload some files

화자는 무엇을 할 것이라고 말하는가?
(A) 비품 주문하기
(B) 이메일로 안건 보내기
(C) 소프트웨어 고치기
(D) 파일 업로드하기

어휘 agenda 안건 fix 고치다, 수리하다

해설 세부 사항 관련 – 화자가 할 것이라고 말하는 일

화자가 마지막에 파일을 공유 드라이브에 업로드할 것(I'll start uploading the files to our shared drive)이라고 말하고 있으므로 정답은 (D)이다.

92-94 보도

W-Am Thanks for tuning in to KELW, Springfield's news radio station. In sports, ⁹²**the hometown Blues are under new ownership. Abalora Investment Group finalized the purchase of the baseball team this past week. ⁹³A Springfield native himself, the investment group's founder, Patrick Abalora, is passionate about building community in the Springfield area**. When contacted for a comment, ⁹⁴**Abalora said he aims to bring the franchise its first-ever championship. While that's welcome news to Blues fans who have remained loyal through many disappointing seasons, it's worth noting that we've been told that before.

스프링필드의 뉴스 라디오 방송국 KELW를 청취해 주셔서 감사합니다. 스포츠 뉴스로, 우리 지역 팀인 블루스가 새로운 주인을 맞았습니다. 아발로라 투자 그룹이 지난주에 야구단 인수를 마무리했습니다. 스프링필드 출신인 투자 그룹의 설립자 패트릭 아발로라는 스프링필드 지역에 공동체를 구축하는 데 열정적입니다. 소감을 위해 연락했을 때, 아발로라는 팀이 역대 첫 우승을 가져올 것을 목표로 한다고 말했습니다. 많은 실망스러운 시즌을 겪으면서도 의리를 지킨 블루스 팬들에게는 반가운 소식이지만, 주목할 점은 우리는 이전에도 그런 말을 들었다는 것입니다.

어휘 tune in to (채널을) ~에 맞추다 ownership 소유(권) investment 투자 finalize 마무리 짓다 founder 창립자, 설립자 passionate 열정적인 franchise 프로 스포츠 리그 소속 팀 remain 계속 ~이다 loyal 의리를 지키는, 충성스러운 disappointing 실망스러운 note 주목하다

92

What is being reported on?
(A) The purchase of a baseball team
(B) The signing of a baseball player
(C) The construction of a baseball stadium
(D) The retirement of a baseball coach

무엇에 대해 보도되고 있는가?
(A) 야구단 인수
(B) 야구 선수의 계약
(C) 야구장 건설
(D) 야구 코치의 은퇴

어휘 construction 건설, 건축 retirement 은퇴

해설 전체 내용 관련 – 보도의 주제

화자가 초반부에 우리 지역 팀인 블루스가 새로운 주인을 맞게 된다(the hometown Blues are under new ownership)고 한 뒤 아발로라 투자 그룹이 지난주에 야구단 인수를 마무리했다(Abalora Investment Group finalized the purchase of the baseball team this past week)며 구단의 인수와 관련된 이야기를 이어 가고 있으므로 정답은 (A)이다.

93

What does the speaker say Mr. Abalora is passionate about?

(A) Job creation
(B) Community building
(C) Local news reporting
(D) Innovative thinking

화자는 아발로라 씨가 무엇에 대해 열정적이라고 말하는가?

(A) 일자리 창출
(B) 공동체 구축
(C) 지역 뉴스 보도
(D) 혁신적인 사고

해설 세부 사항 관련 – 화자가 아발로라 씨가 열정을 보이는 일이라고 말하는 것

화자가 중반부에 스프링필드 출신인 투자 그룹의 설립자 패트릭 아발로라는 스프링필드 지역에 공동체를 구축하는 데 열정적(A Springfield native himself, the investment group's founder, Patrick Abalora, is passionate about building community in the Springfield area)이라고 말하고 있으므로 정답은 (B)이다.

94

Why does the speaker say, "we've been told that before"?

(A) To express doubt
(B) To support a decision
(C) To correct a colleague
(D) To reinforce an instruction

화자는 왜 "우리는 이전에도 그런 말을 들었다"고 말하는가?

(A) 의구심을 표현하기 위해
(B) 결정을 뒷받침하기 위해
(C) 동료를 바로잡기 위해
(D) 지시를 강화하기 위해

어휘 doubt 의구심 correct 바로잡다 colleague 동료 reinforce 강화하다 instruction 지시, 설명

해설 화자의 의도 파악 – 이전에도 그런 말을 들었다는 말의 의도
앞에서 아발로라는 팀의 역대 첫 우승을 목표로 한다고 말했다(Abalora said he aims ~ its first-ever championship)고 했고, 많은 실망스러운 시즌을 겪으면서도 의리를 지킨 블루스 팬들에게는 반가운 소식이지만 주목할 것이 있다(While that's welcome news to Blues fans ~ it's worth noting that)고 한 뒤 인용문을 언급한 것으로 보아, 우승을 목표로 했던 말들이 지켜진 적이 없기에 이번에도 크게 다를 바가 없을 것이라는 의도를 표현하기 위해 한 말임을 알 수 있다. 따라서 정답은 (A)이다.

95-97 담화 + 원그래프

> **W-Br** Good morning, everyone. My name is Yuri Hirata, and it's my pleasure to welcome you to the Kolee manufacturing plant. **95I always enjoy giving tours to our own sales staff. 96I hope you'll let our customers know what you learn here today about** the high quality of the products manufactured by Kolee. **97Right now we're looking at the area on the factory floor where our newest product is being assembled. You can see on your handouts that these represent only fifteen percent of our sales,** but we hope that they will become our largest seller—even larger than our weight lifting benches.

안녕하세요, 여러분. 저는 유리 히라타입니다. 콜리 제조 공장에서 여러분을 맞이하게 되어 기쁩니다. 저는 우리 영업 사원들에게 투어를 시켜 주는 것이 항상 즐겁습니다. 콜리에서 제조한 고품질 제품에 대해 오늘 여기에서 알게 된 내용을 고객들에게 잘 알려 주시기 바랍니다. 지금 우리는 최신 제품이 조립되고 있는 작업 현장 구역을 살펴보고 있습니다. 유인물을 보면 이 제품들이 판매량의 15퍼센트에 불과한 것으로 나와 있지만, 웨이트 리프팅 벤치보다도 더 잘 팔리는, 즉 우리 회사에서 제일 잘 팔리는 제품이 되기를 희망합니다.

어휘 manufacturing 제조(업)의 plant 공장 quality 품질 factory floor (공장의) 작업 현장 assemble 조립하다 handout 인쇄물, 유인물 weight lifting 웨이트 리프팅, 역도

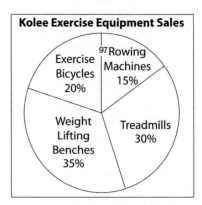

Kolee Exercise Equipment Sales

- Exercise Bicycles 20%
- 97Rowing Machines 15%
- Treadmills 30%
- Weight Lifting Benches 35%

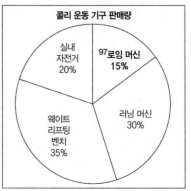

콜리 운동 기구 판매량

- 실내 자전거 20%
- 97로잉 머신 15%
- 러닝 머신 30%
- 웨이트 리프팅 벤치 35%

95

Who are the listeners?

(A) Investors
(B) Sales staff
(C) Fitness trainers
(D) Manufacturing executives

청자들은 누구인가?
(A) 투자자
(B) 영업 사원
(C) 피트니스 트레이너
(D) 제조업 임원

해설 전체 내용 관련 – 청자들의 직업

화자가 초반부에 우리 영업 사원들에게 투어를 시켜 주는 것이 항상 즐겁다(I always enjoy giving tours to our own sales staff)고 말하고 있으므로 청자가 영업 사원들임을 알 수 있다. 따라서 정답은 (B)이다.

96

What does the speaker hope will happen?
(A) The assembly process will be completed more efficiently.
(B) Customers will be told about Kolee's high-quality products.
(C) Customers will use exercise bicycles rather than treadmills.
(D) Kolee's manufacturing will be done at a different plant.

화자는 무슨 일이 일어나기를 바라는가?
(A) 조립 과정이 보다 효율적으로 완료될 것이다.
(B) 고객들이 콜리의 고품질 제품에 대해 들을 것이다.
(C) 고객들이 러닝 머신보다는 실내 자전거를 이용할 것이다.
(D) 콜리 제품의 제조는 다른 공장에서 이루어질 것이다.

어휘 assembly 조립 efficiently 효율적으로

해설 세부 사항 관련 – 화자가 일어나기를 바라는 일

화자가 중반부에 콜리에서 제조한 고품질 제품에 대해 오늘 여기에서 알게 된 내용을 고객들에게 잘 알려 주기를 바란다(I hope you'll let our customers know what you learn here today about the high quality of the products manufactured by Kolee)고 말하는 것으로 보아 정답은 (B)이다.

> **Paraphrasing** 담화의 the high quality of the products manufactured by Kolee
> → 정답의 Kolee's high-quality products

97

Look at the graphic. What type of exercise equipment does the speaker say is new for the company?
(A) Rowing machines
(B) Exercise bicycles
(C) Treadmills
(D) Weight lifting benches

시각 정보에 의하면, 화자는 어떤 종류의 운동 기구가 회사의 신제품이라고 말하는가?
(A) 로잉 머신
(B) 실내 자전거
(C) 러닝 머신
(D) 웨이트 리프팅 벤치

해설 시각 정보 연계 – 화자가 회사의 신제품이라고 말하는 것

화자가 후반부에 지금 우리는 최신 제품이 조립되고 있는 작업 현장 구역을 살펴보고 있다(Right now we're looking at the area on the factory floor where our newest product is being assembled)며 유인물을 보면 이 제품들이 판매량의 15퍼센트에 불과한 것으로 나와 있다(You can see on your handouts that these represent only fifteen percent of our sales)고 말하고 있고, 원그래프에 따르면 판매량이 15퍼센트인 것은 로잉 머신이므로 정답은 (A)이다.

98-100 녹음 메시지 + 직원 안내

W-Am Thanks for calling the education office at the Metropolitan Museum of Science. **98We're pleased to announce several new learning modules specifically for teenagers interested in computer coding.** You can find these new modules on our Web site, under the Activities tab. **99Please note that the registration deadline for this summer's science camps has been extended to March fifteenth.** Sign up now to reserve a space. You can find more information online. And finally, **100if you're a teacher arranging a class trip to the museum, please press seven after the tone and you'll be connected to our school liaison.**

메트로폴리탄 과학 박물관의 교육 사무실에 전화 주셔서 감사합니다. **컴퓨터 코딩에 관심이 있는 청소년을 위해 특별히 몇 가지 새로운 학습 모듈을 발표하게 된 것을 기쁘게 생각합니다.** 웹사이트의 활동 탭에서 이 새로운 모듈을 찾아보실 있습니다. **이번 여름 과학 캠프의 등록 마감일이 3월 15일까지 연장된 것을 유념해 주십시오.** 지금 등록하여 자리를 예약하세요. 온라인에서 더 많은 정보를 찾아보실 수 있습니다. 그리고 마지막으로, **박물관으로 학급 견학을 계획하는 선생님이시라면 신호음이 울린 후 7번을 누르세요. 그러면 학교 연락 담당자에게 바로 연결될 것입니다.**

어휘 module 모듈, 교과목 단위 specifically 특별히 registration 등록 extend 연장하다 reserve 예약하다 arrange 마련하다, 주선하다 liaison 연락 담당자, 연락

Education Office Staff Directory	
Online Activities	Sabine Klein
Camp Director	Ji-Soo Jeong
100School Liaison	Carmen Ruiz
Adult Education	Brian Hughes

교육 사무실 직원 안내	
온라인 활동	사빈 클라인
캠프 책임자	지수 정
100학교 연락 담당자	**카르멘 루이즈**
성인 교육	브라이언 휴즈

TEST 9 **259**

98

What is the speaker pleased to announce?

(A) A special exhibit
(B) A new education director
(C) Learning activities for teens
(D) Discounted museum tickets

화자는 무엇을 발표하게 되어 기뻐하는가?

(A) 특별 전시
(B) 신임 교육 이사
(C) 청소년을 위한 학습 활동
(D) 박물관 입장권 할인

해설 세부 사항 관련 – 화자가 발표하게 되어 기뻐하는 것

화자가 초반부에 컴퓨터 코딩에 관심이 있는 청소년을 위해 특별히 몇 가지 새로운 학습 모듈을 발표하게 되어 기쁘다(We're pleased to announce several new learning modules specifically for teenagers interested in computer coding)고 말하고 있으므로 정답은 (C)이다.

> **Paraphrasing** 담화의 modules specifically for teenagers → 정답의 activities for teens

99

What does the speaker say about science camps?

(A) A registration deadline has changed.
(B) No more spaces are available.
(C) A payment plan has been added.
(D) Some classes will be held in a different location.

화자는 과학 캠프에 대해 무엇이라고 말하는가?

(A) 등록 마감일이 변경되었다.
(B) 더 이상 자리가 없다.
(C) 지불 방법이 추가되었다.
(D) 일부 수업은 다른 장소에서 진행될 것이다.

해설 세부 사항 관련 – 화자가 과학 캠프에 대해 말하는 것

화자가 중반부에 이번 여름 과학 캠프의 등록 마감일이 3월 15일까지 연장된 것을 유념해 달라(Please note that the registration deadline for this summer's science camps has been extended to March fifteenth)고 말하고 있으므로 정답은 (A)이다.

> **Paraphrasing** 담화의 been extended → 정답의 changed

100

Look at the graphic. Who can the listeners speak to by pressing seven?

(A) Sabine Klein
(B) Ji-Soo Jeong
(C) Carmen Ruiz
(D) Brian Hughes

시각 정보에 의하면, 청자들은 7번을 눌러 누구와 통화할 수 있는가?

(A) 사빈 클라인
(B) 지수 정
(C) 카르멘 루이즈
(D) 브라이언 휴즈

해설 시각 정보 연계 – 청자들이 7번을 눌러 통화할 수 있는 대상

화자가 마지막에 박물관 견학을 계획하고 있는 선생님이라면 신호음이 울린 후 7번을 누르고, 그러면 학교 연락 담당자에게 연결될 것(if you're a teacher arranging a class trip to the museum, please press seven after the tone and you'll be connected to our school liaison)이라고 말하고 있고, 직원 안내에 따르면 학교 연락 담당자는 카르멘 루이즈이므로 정답은 (C)이다.

기출 TEST 10

1 (B)	**2** (C)	**3** (D)	**4** (D)	**5** (D)
6 (B)	**7** (B)	**8** (C)	**9** (B)	**10** (C)
11 (A)	**12** (A)	**13** (C)	**14** (C)	**15** (A)
16 (C)	**17** (B)	**18** (A)	**19** (A)	**20** (C)
21 (C)	**22** (C)	**23** (B)	**24** (C)	**25** (B)
26 (C)	**27** (C)	**28** (B)	**29** (C)	**30** (B)
31 (C)	**32** (B)	**33** (C)	**34** (D)	**35** (A)
36 (C)	**37** (B)	**38** (A)	**39** (D)	**40** (D)
41 (D)	**42** (C)	**43** (B)	**44** (D)	**45** (D)
46 (A)	**47** (A)	**48** (B)	**49** (C)	**50** (A)
51 (D)	**52** (C)	**53** (C)	**54** (B)	**55** (D)
56 (C)	**57** (C)	**58** (B)	**59** (D)	**60** (A)
61 (B)	**62** (C)	**63** (A)	**64** (D)	**65** (D)
66 (B)	**67** (C)	**68** (D)	**69** (A)	**70** (B)
71 (D)	**72** (C)	**73** (A)	**74** (A)	**75** (C)
76 (A)	**77** (B)	**78** (D)	**79** (C)	**80** (D)
81 (C)	**82** (B)	**83** (A)	**84** (C)	**85** (C)
86 (A)	**87** (C)	**88** (B)	**89** (A)	**90** (A)
91 (B)	**92** (A)	**93** (C)	**94** (A)	**95** (D)
96 (C)	**97** (C)	**98** (B)	**99** (B)	**100** (A)

PART 1

1 M-Au

(A) The man is climbing a ladder.
(B) The man is wearing a backpack.
(C) The man is lounging in a shaded area.
(D) The man is picking up a rock.

(A) 남자가 사다리를 오르고 있다.
(B) 남자가 배낭을 메고 있다.
(C) 남자가 그늘진 곳에서 편하게 앉아 있다.
(D) 남자가 돌을 줍고 있다.

어휘 ladder 사다리   lounge 편하게[비스듬하게] 앉다

해설 1인 등장 사진 – 사람의 동작/상태 묘사

(A) 사진에 없는 명사를 이용한 오답. 사진에 사다리(a ladder)의 모습이 보이지 않으므로 오답.
(B) 정답. 남자가 배낭을 메고 있는(is wearing a backpack) 모습이므로 정답.
(C) 동사 오답. 남자가 그늘진 곳에서 편하게 앉아 있는(is lounging in a shaded area) 모습이 아니므로 오답.

(D) 동사 오답. 남자가 돌을 줍고 있는(is picking up a rock) 모습이 아니므로 오답.

2 M-Cn

(A) The man is cutting down a tree.
(B) The man is fixing a machine.
(C) The man is measuring a board.
(D) The man is raking some leaves.

(A) 남자가 나무를 베고 있다.
(B) 남자가 기계를 고치고 있다.
(C) 남자가 판자 치수를 재고 있다.
(D) 남자가 나뭇잎을 긁어모으고 있다.

어휘 fix 고치다   measure 치수를 재다   rake 갈퀴로 긁어모으다

해설 1인 등장 사진 – 사람의 동작/상태 묘사

(A) 동사 오답. 남자가 나무를 베고 있는(is cutting down a tree) 모습이 아니므로 오답.
(B) 동사 오답. 남자가 기계를 고치고 있는(is fixing a machine) 모습이 아니므로 오답.
(C) 정답. 남자가 판자 치수를 재고 있는(is measuring a board) 모습이므로 정답.
(D) 동사 오답. 남자가 나뭇잎을 긁어모으고 있는(is raking some leaves) 모습이 아니므로 오답.

3 W-Am

(A) One of the women is writing on some paper.
(B) One of the women is closing a binder.
(C) They're looking at some photographs.
(D) They're seated across from one another.

(A) 여자들 중 한 명이 종이 위에 글을 쓰고 있다.
(B) 여자들 중 한 명이 바인더를 닫고 있다.
(C) 사람들이 사진을 보고 있다.
(D) 사람들이 서로 마주보고 앉아 있다.

어휘 be seated 앉다   across from ~의 바로 맞은편에

해설 2인 이상 등장 사진 – 사람의 동작/상태 묘사

(A) 동사 오답. 여자들 중 한 명(One of the women)이 종이 위에 글을 쓰고 있는(is writing on some paper) 모습이 아니므로 오답.

(B) 동사 오답. 여자들 중 한 명(One of the women)이 바인더를 닫고 있는(is closing a binder) 모습이 아니므로 오답.

(C) 사진에 없는 명사를 이용한 오답. 사진에 사진들(photographs)이 보이지 않으므로 오답.

(D) 정답. 사람들이 서로 마주보고 앉아 있는(are seated across from one another) 모습이므로 정답.

4 W-Br

(A) Workers are exiting from the back of a van.
(B) Some trees have fallen across a road.
(C) A man is watering some potted plants.
(D) Some people are seated outdoors.

(A) 작업자들이 승합차 뒤에서 나오고 있다.
(B) 나무들이 길을 가로질러 쓰러졌다.
(C) 남자가 화분에 심은 나무에 물을 주고 있다.
(D) **사람들이 야외에 앉아 있다.**

어휘 potted 화분에 심은

해설 혼합 사진 – 사람/사물/풍경 혼합 묘사

(A) 동사 오답. 작업자들(Workers)이 승합차 뒤에서 나오고 있는(are exiting from the back of a van) 모습이 아니므로 오답.

(B) 동사 오답. 나무들(Some trees)이 길을 가로질러 쓰러져 있는(have fallen across a road) 모습이 아니므로 오답.

(C) 동사 오답. 남자가 화분에 심은 나무에 물을 주고 있는(is watering some potted plants) 모습이 아니므로 오답.

(D) 정답. 사람들이 야외에 앉아 있는(are seated outdoors) 모습이므로 정답.

5 M-Cn

(A) The woman is adjusting her watch strap.
(B) The woman is setting up a display of paintings.
(C) A brick wall is being measured.
(D) Some chairs are facing a television screen.

(A) 여자가 시곗줄을 조절하고 있다.
(B) 여자가 그림을 전시하고 있다.
(C) 벽돌담이 측정되고 있다.
(D) **의자들이 텔레비전 화면을 향해 있다.**

어휘 adjust 조절하다　strap 끈, 줄　set up 설치하다　measure 측정하다　face 향하다

해설 혼합 사진 – 사람/사물/풍경 혼합 묘사

(A) 동사 오답. 여자가 시곗줄을 조절하고 있는(is adjusting her watch strap) 모습이 아니므로 오답.

(B) 동사 오답. 여자가 그림을 전시하고 있는(is setting up a display of paintings) 모습이 아니므로 오답.

(C) 동사 오답. 벽돌담(A brick wall)이 측정되고 있는(is being measured) 모습이 아니므로 오답.

(D) 정답. 의자들(Some chairs)이 텔레비전 화면을 향해 있는(are facing a television screen) 모습이므로 정답.

6 W-Am

(A) Some vehicles are lined up at an intersection.
(B) Some vehicles are parked in front of a fence.
(C) Some large stones are blocking access to a park.
(D) Some branches are piled beside a truck.

(A) 차량들이 교차로에 늘어서 있다.
(B) **차량들이 울타리 앞에 주차되어 있다.**
(C) 큰 돌들이 공원 접근을 막고 있다.
(D) 나뭇가지들이 트럭 옆에 쌓여 있다.

어휘 vehicle 차량　intersection 교차로　access 접근　pile 쌓다

해설 사물/풍경 사진 – 사물 묘사

(A) 사진에 없는 명사를 이용한 오답. 사진에 교차로(an intersection)의 모습이 보이지 않으므로 오답.

(B) 정답. 차량들(Some vehicles)이 울타리 앞에 주차되어 있는(are parked in front of a fence) 모습이므로 정답.

(C) 사진에 없는 명사를 이용한 오답. 사진에 큰 돌들(Some large stones)의 모습이 보이지 않으므로 오답.

(D) 동사 오답. 나뭇가지들(Some branches)이 트럭 옆에 쌓여 있는(are piled beside a truck) 모습이 아니므로 오답.

PART 2

7

M-Au　Which theater did you go to?

W-Am　(A) No, it wasn't.
　　　 (B) The one on Oak Ridge Road.
　　　 (C) At six o'clock.

어느 극장에 가셨나요?
(A) 아니요, 그렇지 않았어요.
(B) 오크 리지 로에 있는 거요.
(C) 6시예요.

해설 방문했던 극장을 묻는 Which 의문문

(A) Yes/No 불가 오답. Which 의문문에는 Yes/No 응답이 불가능하므로 오답.

(B) 정답. 어느 극장에 갔는지를 묻는 질문에 오크 리지 로에 있는 것이라고 알려 주고 있으므로 정답.

(C) 질문과 상관없는 오답. When 의문문에 대한 응답이므로 오답.

8

W-Am What's the last day to complete the survey?

W-Br (A) The customer service number.
　　　(B) We have a new supplier.
　　　(C) Wednesday.

설문 조사를 완료하는 마지막 날이 언제죠?
(A) 고객 서비스 번호입니다.
(B) 새 공급업체가 생겼어요.
(C) 수요일이에요.

어휘 complete 완료하다 survey 설문 조사 supplier 공급[납품]업체

해설 완료하는 날을 묻는 What 의문문
(A) 연상 단어 오답. 질문의 survey에서 연상 가능한 customer를 이용한 오답.
(B) 질문과 상관없는 오답.
(C) 정답. 설문 조사를 완료하는 날이 언제인지 묻는 질문에 요일로 응답하고 있으므로 정답.

9

M-Cn When are you planning to move out of your apartment?

W-Br (A) Move it to the right, please.
　　　(B) At the end of next month.
　　　(C) Here's the floor plan.

언제 아파트에서 이사하실 계획인가요?
(A) 오른쪽으로 옮겨 주세요.
(B) 다음 달 말예요.
(C) 여기 평면도 받으세요.

해설 이사 시점을 묻는 When 의문문
(A) 단어 반복 오답. 질문의 move를 반복 이용한 오답.
(B) 정답. 이사가 언제인지를 묻는 질문에 다음 달 말이라고 구체적인 시점으로 응답하고 있으므로 정답.
(C) 파생어 오답. 질문의 planning과 파생어 관계인 plan을 이용한 오답.

10

M-Au When does the show begin?

W-Am (A) Yes, I showed her already.
　　　(B) In the third row.
　　　(C) It starts in an hour.

쇼는 언제 시작하나요?
(A) 네, 제가 그녀에게 벌써 보여 줬어요.
(B) 세 번째 줄예요.
(C) 한 시간 뒤에 시작해요.

어휘 row 줄

해설 쇼의 시작 시점을 묻는 When 의문문
(A) Yes/No 불가 오답. When 의문문에는 Yes/No 응답이 불가능하므로 오답.
(B) 연상 단어 오답. 질문의 show에서 연상 가능한 the third row를 이용한 오답.
(C) 정답. 쇼가 시작하는 시점을 묻는 질문에 한 시간 뒤라고 알려 주고 있으므로 정답.

11

M-Cn Who will be leading the new team?

W-Br (A) Thomas has been selected.
　　　(B) The news release.
　　　(C) A brand-new screen.

누가 새 팀을 이끌게 되나요?
(A) 토마스가 발탁됐어요.
(B) 보도 자료예요.
(C) 신제품 화면이에요.

어휘 news release 보도 자료 brand-new 신제품의, 신형의

해설 새 팀을 이끌 사람을 묻는 Who 의문문
(A) 정답. 새 팀을 이끌 사람이 누구인지 묻는 질문에 토마스라고 답하고 있으므로 정답.
(B) 유사 발음 오답. 질문의 new와 부분적으로 발음이 유사한 news를 이용한 오답.
(C) 단어 반복 오답. 질문의 new를 반복 이용한 오답.

12

W-Br Why was your flight delayed?

M-Au (A) Because there was bad weather.
　　　(B) We can reschedule the electrician's visit.
　　　(C) At the municipal airport.

왜 비행기가 연착됐죠?
(A) 날씨가 안 좋았기 때문이에요.
(B) 우리는 전기 기사의 방문 일정을 바꿀 수 있어요.
(C) 시립 공항에서요.

어휘 reschedule 일정을 바꾸다 electrician 전기 기사 municipal 시의, 시립의

해설 비행기가 연착된 이유를 묻는 Why 의문문
(A) 정답. 비행기가 연착된 이유를 묻는 질문에 날씨가 안 좋았기 때문이라고 이유를 제시하고 있으므로 정답.
(B) 연상 단어 오답. 질문의 delayed에서 연상 가능한 reschedule을 이용한 오답.
(C) 연상 단어 오답. 질문의 flight에서 연상 가능한 airport를 이용한 오답.

TEST 10

13

M-Au Where are you planning to open your next store?

M-Cn (A) Next January.
(B) Yes, in the floor plans.
(C) Near the city center.

다음 매장은 어디에 여실 계획인가요?
(A) 내년 1월이에요.
(B) 네, 평면도에 있어요.
(C) 도심 근처에요.

해설 매장을 열기로 계획한 장소를 묻는 Where 의문문
(A) 단어 반복 오답. 질문의 next를 반복 이용한 오답.
(B) Yes/No 불가 오답. Where 의문문에는 Yes/No 응답이 불가능하므로 오답.
(C) 정답. 다음 매장을 열기로 계획한 장소를 묻는 질문에 도심 근처라고 알려 주고 있으므로 정답.

14

M-Cn Who designed the uniforms?

W-Br (A) You can sign in here.
(B) Yes, we wear them for work.
(C) A company in Chicago.

누가 유니폼을 디자인했나요?
(A) 여기에 서명하고 들어가시면 됩니다.
(B) 네, 일할 때 입어요.
(C) 시카고에 있는 어떤 회사예요.

해설 유니폼을 디자인한 사람을 묻는 Who 의문문
(A) 유사 발음 오답. 질문의 designed와 부분적으로 발음이 유사한 sign을 이용한 오답.
(B) Yes/No 불가 오답. Who 의문문에는 Yes/No 응답이 불가능하므로 오답.
(C) 정답. 유니폼을 디자인한 사람을 묻는 질문에 시카고에 있는 어떤 회사라고 응답하고 있으므로 정답.

15

W-Br I recommend the vegetarian dinner special.

M-Au (A) OK, I'll have that.
(B) Two bags of limes.
(C) Right by the elevator.

채식 특선 정찬을 추천합니다.
(A) 네, 그걸로 할게요.
(B) 라임 두 봉지요.
(C) 엘리베이터 바로 옆이에요.

어휘 vegetarian 채식의

해설 제안/권유의 평서문
(A) 정답. 채식 특선 정찬을 추천한다고 권유하는 평서문에 네(OK)라고 대답한 뒤, 그걸로 하겠다며 긍정 답변과 일관된 내용으로 호응하고 있으므로 정답.

(B) 연상 단어 오답. 평서문의 dinner에서 연상 가능한 limes를 이용한 오답.
(C) 평서문과 상관없는 오답. Where 의문문에 대한 응답이므로 오답.

16

M-Au How will we get this order filled in time?

W-Am (A) Would you like soup or salad?
(B) Maria goes there, too.
(C) We'll have to work extra hours.

어떻게 하면 이번 주문을 제때 납품할 수 있을까요?
(A) 수프를 드릴까요, 샐러드를 드릴까요?
(B) 마리아도 거기에 가요.
(C) 우리는 잔업을 해야 할 거예요.

어휘 fill an order (주문이 들어온 제품을) 납품하다   work extra hours 잔업을 하다

해설 주문을 제때 납품할 수 있는 방법을 묻는 How 의문문
(A) 연상 단어 오답. 질문의 order에서 연상 가능한 soup와 salad를 이용한 오답.
(B) 질문과 상관없는 오답. Who 의문문에 대한 응답이므로 오답.
(C) 정답. 이번 주문을 제때에 납품할 수 있는 방법을 묻는 질문에 잔업을 해야 할 것이라는 방법을 제안하고 있으므로 정답.

17

W-Am Do you have the gate code, or should I look it up?

M-Cn (A) It was recently painted.
(B) I have the number.
(C) A two-year lease.

출입문 비밀번호를 알고 있나요, 아니면 제가 찾아볼까요?
(A) 최근에 칠했어요.
(B) 저한테 번호가 있어요.
(C) 2년 임대예요.

어휘 recently 최근에

해설 비밀번호를 알고 있는지 여부를 묻는 선택 의문문
(A) 질문과 상관없는 오답.
(B) 정답. 출입문의 비밀번호를 알고 있는지 아니면 찾아봐야 하는지 묻는 선택 의문문에 자신에게 번호가 있다며 하나를 선택해 응답하고 있으므로 정답.
(C) 질문과 상관없는 오답.

18

W-Br Should we visit the warehouse this week or next week?

M-Au (A) I'll be at corporate headquarters next week.
(B) Wow, that's a lot of space!
(C) A visitor's pass.

창고를 이번 주에 방문해야 할까요, 아니면 다음 주에 방문해야 할까요?

(A) 다음 주에 저는 본사에 있을 거예요.
(B) 와, 공간이 무척 넓네요!
(C) 방문자 출입증이요.

어휘 warehouse 창고 headquarters 본사, 본부

해설 창고 방문 시점을 묻는 선택 의문문

(A) 정답. 창고 방문 시점을 묻는 선택 의문문에서 다음 주에는 본사에 있을 것이라며 창고는 이번 주에 방문하자는 의사를 우회적으로 표현하고 있으므로 정답.
(B) 연상 단어 오답. 질문의 warehouse에서 연상 가능한 a lot of space를 이용한 오답.
(C) 파생어 오답. 질문의 visit과 파생어 관계인 visitor를 이용한 오답.

19

W-Am　Don't you want to come to the employee luncheon?

M-Cn　(A) Yes, I'm looking forward to it.
　　　(B) The largest conference room.
　　　(C) A variety of sandwiches.

직원 오찬에 오고 싶지 않으세요?

(A) 네, 기대하고 있어요.
(B) 가장 큰 회의실이에요.
(C) 다양한 샌드위치예요.

어휘 look forward to ~을 기대하다 a variety of 다양한

해설 오찬에 오고 싶은지 여부를 확인하는 부정 의문문

(A) 정답. 직원 오찬에 오고 싶은지 여부를 확인하는 질문에 네(Yes)라고 대답한 뒤, 기대하고 있다고 덧붙이고 있으므로 정답.
(B) 연상 단어 오답. 질문의 employee에서 연상 가능한 conference room을 이용한 오답.
(C) 연상 단어 오답. 질문의 luncheon에서 연상 가능한 sandwiches를 이용한 오답.

20

M-Cn　Could you recommend a local hair salon?

W-Am　(A) I'll need your receipt to process the refund.
　　　(B) Yes, the weather's supposed to be nice all week.
　　　(C) There's a good stylist on Fourteenth Street.

동네 미용실을 추천해 주시겠어요?

(A) 환불 처리를 위해 영수증이 필요합니다.
(B) 네, 이번 주 내내 날씨가 좋을 거예요.
(C) 14번가에 괜찮은 스타일리스트가 있어요.

어휘 receipt 영수증 process 처리하다 refund 환불 be supposed to ~하기로 되어 있다

해설 부탁/요청의 의문문

(A) 질문과 상관없는 오답.
(B) 질문과 상관없는 오답.

(C) 정답. 동네 미용실을 추천해 달라는 요청에 14번가에 괜찮은 스타일리스트가 있다고 알려 주고 있으므로 정답.

21

W-Am　I have some documents here for you to sign.

M-Au　(A) It's at four tomorrow.
　　　(B) I like the design too.
　　　(C) All right, let me take a look.

여기 서명하실 서류들이 있어요.

(A) 내일 4시예요.
(B) 디자인도 마음에 들어요.
(C) 알겠어요, 한번 볼게요.

해설 정보 전달의 평서문

(A) 유사 발음 오답. 평서문의 for와 발음이 동일한 four를 이용한 오답.
(B) 유사 발음 오답. 평서문의 sign과 부분적으로 발음이 유사한 design을 이용한 오답.
(C) 정답. 서명할 서류가 여기 있다는 평서문에 알겠다(All right)고 대답한 뒤, 한번 보겠다며 긍정 답변과 일관된 내용을 덧붙였으므로 정답.

22

M-Au　Are you planning to dine in, or would you like to take your food with you?

W-Br　(A) Yes, it was delicious.
　　　(B) Just a little late.
　　　(C) I should probably get back to the office.

안에서 드실 건가요, 아니면 음식을 포장해서 가실 건가요?

(A) 네, 맛있었어요.
(B) 조금 늦었어요.
(C) 아마 사무실로 돌아가야 할 것 같아요.

해설 음식을 어디에서 먹을지 묻는 선택 의문문

(A) Yes/No 불가 오답. 음식을 어디에서 먹을지 묻는 선택 의문문에 Yes/No 응답은 불가능하므로 오답.
(B) 연상 단어 오답. 질문의 food에서 연상 가능한 Just a little을 이용한 오답.
(C) 정답. 음식을 안에서 먹을지 포장해서 갈 것인지 묻는 선택 의문문에서 사무실로 돌아가야 할 것 같다며 포장해서 갈 것이라는 의사를 우회적으로 표현하고 있으므로 정답.

23

W-Br　Is this carpet the right size for the room?

M-Au　(A) I'll turn it off when I'm finished.
　　　(B) I measured it three times.
　　　(C) The warehouse is on River Street.

이 카펫이 방에 맞는 크기인가요?

(A) 마치면 제가 끌게요.
(B) 제가 치수를 세 번 쟀어요.
(C) 창고는 리버 가에 있어요.

어휘 turn off 끄다 measure 치수를 재다, 측정하다

해설 카펫이 방에 맞는 크기인지 묻는 Be동사 의문문
(A) 연상 단어 오답. 질문의 room에서 연상 가능한 turn it off를 이용한 오답.
(B) 정답. 카펫이 방에 맞는 크기인지 묻는 질문에 본인이 치수를 세 번 쟀다며 방에 맞는 크기라는 것을 우회적으로 확인해 주고 있으므로 정답.
(C) 질문과 상관없는 오답. Where 의문문에 대한 응답이므로 오답.

24

W-Am You're aware that it's been six months since we've done inventory, aren't you?

M-Au (A) Can you introduce me to Victoria?
(B) That bottle goes on the top shelf.
(C) Yes, we're doing it once a year now.

우리가 재고 조사를 한 지 6개월이 지났는데 알고 있죠?
(A) 저를 빅토리아에게 소개해 주시겠어요?
(B) 그 병은 맨 위 선반이에요.
(C) 네, 지금은 1년에 한 번씩 하고 있어요.

어휘 aware 알고 있는 inventory 재고 (조사)

해설 재고 조사를 한 지 6개월이 지난 사실을 알고 있는지 확인하는 부가 의문문
(A) 유사 발음 오답. 질문의 inventory와 부분적으로 발음이 유사한 Victoria를 이용한 오답.
(B) 연상 단어 오답. 질문의 inventory에서 연상 가능한 shelf를 이용한 오답.
(C) 정답. 재고 조사를 한 지 6개월이 지난 사실을 알고 있는지 확인하는 질문에 네(Yes)라고 대답한 뒤, 지금은 1년에 한 번씩 하고 있다며 추가 정보를 제공하고 있으므로 정답.

25

M-Cn I need to know who's attending the exposition.

W-Br (A) Try turning the valve to the left.
(B) Registrations aren't due until Friday.
(C) There are samples at booth 215.

누가 박람회에 참석하는지 제가 알아야 해요.
(A) 밸브를 왼쪽으로 돌려 보세요.
(B) 등록은 금요일에야 마감이에요.
(C) 215번 부스에 견본이 있어요.

어휘 attend 참석하다 exposition 박람회 registration 등록 due 마감인

해설 부탁/요청의 평서문
(A) 평서문과 상관없는 오답.
(B) 정답. 누가 박람회에 참석하는지 알아야 한다는 평서문에 대해 등록은 금요일에야 마감이라며 그때가 되어야 알 수 있음을 우회적으로 알리고 있으므로 정답.
(C) 연상 단어 오답. 평서문의 exposition에서 연상 가능한 booth를 이용한 오답.

26

M-Au This computer is becoming quite slow.

W-Br (A) Please slow down.
(B) A computer company.
(C) Here, you can use mine.

이 컴퓨터는 꽤 느려지고 있어요.
(A) 속도를 줄여 주세요.
(B) 컴퓨터 회사예요.
(C) 여기, 제 거 쓰세요.

해설 정보 전달의 평서문
(A) 단어 반복 오답. 평서문의 slow를 반복 이용한 오답.
(B) 단어 반복 오답. 평서문의 computer를 반복 이용한 오답.
(C) 정답. 컴퓨터가 꽤 느려지고 있다는 정보를 알려 주는 평서문에 자신의 것을 쓰라며 대안을 제시하고 있으므로 정답.

27

W-Br Do you know if these towels are 100 percent cotton?

M-Au (A) These T-shirts should be folded for display.
(B) Production increased by 80 percent.
(C) There should be a label stitched on the edge.

이 수건들이 면 100%인지 아시나요?
(A) 진열을 위해 이 티셔츠들을 개야 해요.
(B) 생산량이 80% 늘었어요.
(C) 가장자리에 박음질된 라벨이 있을 텐데요.

어휘 increase 늘다 stitch 바느질하다, 꿰매다

해설 수건이 면 100%인지 여부를 묻는 조동사(Do) 의문문
(A) 단어 반복 오답. 질문의 these를 반복 이용한 오답.
(B) 단어 반복 오답. 질문의 percent를 반복 이용한 오답.
(C) 정답. 수건이 면 100%인지 여부를 묻는 질문에 가장자리에 박음질된 라벨이 있을 것이라며 직접 확인하라는 뜻을 우회적으로 전달하고 있으므로 정답.

28

M-Cn Shouldn't you send these manuscripts to your editor?

W-Am (A) Four hundred pages.
(B) I already e-mailed them to her.
(C) I should've brought my umbrella.

이 원고들을 편집자에게 보내야 하지 않나요?
(A) 400페이지예요.
(B) 벌써 그녀에게 이메일로 보냈어요.
(C) 우산을 갖고 올 걸 그랬네요.

어휘 manuscript 원고 editor 편집자

해설 원고를 편집자에게 보내야 하는지 여부를 확인하는 부정 의문문
(A) 연상 단어 오답. 질문의 manuscripts에서 연상 가능한 Four hundred pages를 이용한 오답.

(B) 정답. 원고를 편집자에게 보내야 하지 않느냐는 질문에 벌써 이메일로 보냈다고 응답하고 있으므로 정답.

(C) 단어 반복 오답. 질문의 Should를 반복 이용한 오답.

29

M-Cn I don't think Mr. Chen is back from his business trip yet.

W-Br (A) Yes, the waiting room is upstairs.
(B) I thought check-out time was at noon.
(C) I saw him just yesterday at the supermarket.

첸 씨는 아직 출장에서 돌아오지 않은 것 같네요.
(A) 네, 대기실은 위층에 있어요.
(B) 체크아웃 시간이 정오인 줄 알았어요.
(C) 제가 바로 어제 그를 슈퍼마켓에서 봤는데요.

해설 정보 전달의 평서문
(A) 유사 발음 오답. 평서문의 yet과 부분적으로 발음이 유사한 Yes를 이용한 오답.
(B) 연상 단어 오답. 평서문의 trip에서 연상 가능한 check-out을 이용한 오답.
(C) 정답. 첸 씨가 아직 출장에서 돌아오지 않은 것 같다는 의견을 제시한 평서문에 바로 어제 슈퍼마켓에서 보았다며 첸 씨가 출장에서 돌아왔음을 우회적으로 알리고 있으므로 정답.

30

W-Am Where is Barbara's office?

M-Au (A) Some office supplies, please.
(B) Oh, the sales team moved downstairs.
(C) A recent city election.

바바라의 사무실은 어딘가요?
(A) 사무용품 좀 주세요.
(B) 아, 영업팀은 아래층으로 옮겼어요.
(C) 최근 시 선거예요.

어휘 office supplies 사무용품 recent 최근의 election 선거

해설 사무실의 위치를 묻는 Where 의문문
(A) 단어 반복 오답. 질문의 office를 반복 이용한 오답.
(B) 정답. 바바라의 사무실 위치를 묻는 질문에 영업팀은 아래층으로 옮겼다며 사무실이 아래층에 있음을 우회적으로 말하고 있으므로 정답.
(C) 연상 단어 오답. 질문의 office에서 연상 가능한 city를 이용한 오답.

31

W-Am The stage entrance to the theater was moved to Fourteenth Street, wasn't it?

M-Cn (A) Oh, I really like that director's work.
(B) Sure, I can hand out the programs.
(C) I know they did some renovations recently.

극장 무대 입구가 14번가로 이동됐죠?
(A) 아, 저 감독의 작품이 정말 마음에 들어요.
(B) 그럼요, 제가 진행표를 나눠 줄 수 있어요.
(C) 제가 알기로는 최근에 보수 공사를 했어요.

어휘 entrance 입구 hand out 나눠 주다 program (연극 등의) 진행표 renovation 보수, 수리

해설 무대 입구가 14번가로 이동됐는지 여부를 확인하는 부가 의문문
(A) 연상 단어 오답. 질문의 stage와 theater에서 연상 가능한 director를 이용한 오답.
(B) 연상 단어 오답. 질문의 stage와 theater에서 연상 가능한 programs를 이용한 오답.
(C) 정답. 극장 무대 입구가 14번가로 이동됐는지를 묻는 질문에 자신이 알기로는 최근에 보수 공사를 했다며 이동됐음을 우회적으로 확인해 주고 있으므로 정답.

PART 3

32-34

W-Br Richard, [32]**we haven't received the shipment of roses yet.**

M-Au Oh no! [32]**We need them for the floral arrangements that we're supposed to create for the Korkle Hotel.**

W-Br I know. We'll have to come up with an alternative solution.

M-Au Right. [33]**I'll find another source for the flowers.** Can you start the arrangements with what we have?

W-Br Yes, of course. But, [34]**I will need to leave early today to go to the doctor.** Maria will cover the end of my shift.

여 리처드, 우리는 아직 장미 배송을 받지 못했어요.
남 이런! **코클 호텔을 위해 만들어야 하는 꽃꽂이에 장미가 필요한데요.**
여 알아요. 다른 해결책을 생각해 내야 해요.
남 그래요. **제가 꽃을 공급할 다른 업체를 알아볼게요.** 우리한테 있는 것으로 꽃꽂이를 시작할래요?
여 네, 물론이죠. 하지만 **제가 병원에 가야 해서 오늘 일찍 퇴근해야 해요.** 제 마지막 근무 시간은 마리아가 대신할 거예요.

어휘 shipment 배송(품) floral arrangement 꽃꽂이 be supposed to ~해야 한다 come up with 생각해 내다 alternative 다른, 대체하는 solution 해결(책) shift (교대) 근무

32

Who most likely are the speakers?
(A) Chefs
(B) Florists
(C) Bank tellers
(D) Fashion designers

화자들은 누구인 것 같은가?
(A) 요리사
(B) 플로리스트
(C) 은행원
(D) 패션 디자이너

해설 전체 내용 관련 – 화자들의 직업

여자가 첫 대사에서 남자에게 아직 장미 배송을 받지 못했다(we haven't received the shipment of roses yet)고 하자 남자가 난처해 하며 코클 호텔을 위해 만들어야 하는 꽃꽂이에 장미가 필요하다(We need them for the floral arrangements that we're supposed to create for the Korkle Hotel)라고 한 것으로 보아 정답은 (B)이다.

33

What does the man say he will do?
(A) Send a payment
(B) Arrange a meeting
(C) Find another supplier
(D) Review a checklist

남자는 무엇을 할 것이라고 말하는가?
(A) 대금 보내기
(B) 회의 준비하기
(C) 다른 공급업체 찾기
(D) 점검 목록 검토하기

어휘 supplier 공급[납품]업체

해설 세부 사항 관련 – 남자가 다음에 할 것이라고 말하는 일

남자가 두 번째 대사에서 꽃을 공급할 다른 업체를 알아보겠다(I'll find another source for the flowers)고 했으므로 정답은 (C)이다.

Paraphrasing 대화의 another source for the flowers
→ 정답의 another supplier

34

Why does the woman say she will need to leave early?
(A) She is going on vacation.
(B) She is having her car repaired.
(C) She has a family event.
(D) She has a medical appointment.

여자는 왜 일찍 퇴근해야 한다고 말하는가?
(A) 휴가를 갈 것이다.
(B) 차 수리를 맡긴 상태다.
(C) 가족 행사가 있다.
(D) 진료 예약이 있다.

어휘 repair 수리하다 medical appointment 진료 예약

해설 세부 사항 관련 – 여자가 일찍 퇴근해야 하는 이유

여자가 마지막 대사에서 자신은 병원에 가야 해서 오늘 일찍 퇴근해야 한다(I will need to leave early today to go to the doctor)고 했으므로 정답은 (D)이다.

Paraphrasing 대화의 go to the doctor
→ 정답의 has a medical appointment

35-37

M-Cn	Hello. This is James Davis. ³⁵**I'm calling about my appointment with Dr. Kapoor.**
W-Am	Right. ³⁵**I have you down for a regular checkup at ten thirty.**
M-Cn	Well, ³⁶**it looks like I'm going to be about twenty minutes late.** I'm stuck in some slow traffic on the Highland Bridge.
W-Am	OK. I'll let the doctor know. And remember, ³⁷**we've moved to a larger office in the medical building.** We're on the second floor now.

남	안녕하세요. 제임스 데이비스입니다. **카푸어 박사와 예약 건 때문에 전화드렸습니다.**
여	네. **10시 30분 정기 검진 명단에 올라와 있네요.**
남	저, **20분 정도 늦을 것 같아요.** 하이랜드 브리지에서 교통 체증에 갇혀 있어요.
여	알겠습니다. 의사 선생님께 얘기할게요. 그리고 기억하세요, **저희는 의료 건물에 있는 더 큰 사무실로 옮겼어요.** 지금은 2층에 있습니다.

어휘	appointment 예약 checkup 건강 검진 be stuck in traffic 교통 체증에 갇히다

35

Who most likely is the woman?
(A) A receptionist
(B) A security guard
(C) A laboratory assistant
(D) A cashier

여자는 누구일 것 같은가?
(A) 접수원
(B) 경비원
(C) 실험실 조수
(D) 출납원

해설 전체 내용 관련 – 여자의 직업

남자가 첫 대사에서 카푸어 박사와 예약 건 때문에 전화했다(I'm calling about my appointment with Dr. Kapoor)고 하자 여자가 10시 30분 정기 검진 명단에 올라와 있다(I have you down for a regular checkup at ten thirty)고 대답한 것으로 보아 병원의 접수원임을 알 수 있다. 따라서 정답은 (A)이다.

36

What problem does the man report?
(A) He has lost his identification card.
(B) Some mail was not delivered.
(C) He is going to arrive late.
(D) Some equipment is broken.

남자는 어떤 문제를 알리는가?
(A) 신분증을 잃어버렸다.
(B) 우편물이 배달되지 않았다.
(C) 늦게 도착할 것이다.
(D) 장비가 고장 났다.

어휘 identification card 신분증   equipment 장비

해설 세부 사항 관련 – 남자가 알리는 문제
남자가 두 번째 대사에서 20분 정도 늦을 것 같다(it looks like I'm going to be about twenty minutes late)고 알리고 있으므로 정답은 (C)이다.

> **Paraphrasing** 대화의 be about twenty minutes late
> → 정답의 arrive late

37

What does the woman remind the man about?
(A) A payment option
(B) A change in location
(C) Some required paperwork
(D) An online directory

여자는 남자에게 무엇에 관해 일깨우는가?
(A) 지불 방식
(B) 위치 변경
(C) 필요한 서류 작업
(D) 온라인 목록

해설 세부 사항 관련 – 여자가 남자에게 일깨우는 것
여자가 마지막 대사에서 의료 건물에 있는 더 큰 사무실로 옮겼다(we've moved to a larger office in the medical building)고 했으므로 정답은 (B)이다.

> **Paraphrasing** 대화의 moved to a larger office
> → 정답의 A change in location

38-40

W-Br	Riccardo, **³⁸the actor we were interested in for our film's leading role just called. She received another offer, so she doesn't think she'll be taking the part.**
M-Au	Her audition was fantastic. **³⁸I wouldn't want to replace her. What's the number of her agent? ³⁹Maybe I can offer her more money for the role.**
W-Br	I can get that number for you. By the way, **⁴⁰don't forget to look over the hotel options that have been selected for our filming dates.** The assistant needs to finalize those arrangements today.
여	리카르도, 영화 주연으로 우리가 관심 두던 배우가 방금 전화했어요. 다른 데서 제안을 받아서 그 역할을 못 맡을 것 같다네요.
남	오디션이 굉장했는데요. 다른 사람으로 대체하고 싶지 않네요. 에이전트 번호가 어떻게 되죠? 어쩌면 그 역할에 대해 돈을 더 주겠다고 제안할 수도 있고요.
여	제가 번호를 드릴게요. 그건 그렇고, 잊지 마시고 촬영 날짜에 선정된 호텔 선택 사항을 살펴보세요. 조수가 오늘 준비를 마무리해야 하거든요.

어휘 film 영화; 촬영하다 leading role 주연 replace 대체하다 finalize 마무리하다 arrangement 준비

38

What are the speakers mainly discussing?
(A) Hiring an actor
(B) Recreating a scene
(C) Replacing some cameras
(D) Purchasing some costumes

화자들은 주로 무엇에 대해 논의하고 있는가?
(A) 배우 채용
(B) 장면 재촬영
(C) 카메라 교체
(D) 의상 구매

해설 전체 내용 관련 – 대화의 주제
여자가 첫 대사에서 영화 주연으로 자신들이 관심 두던 배우가 전화를 했다(the actor we were interested in for our film's leading role just called)며 다른 데서 제안을 받아서 역할을 못 맡을 것 같다(She received another offer, so she doesn't think she'll be taking the part)고 배우가 말했다고 하자 남자가 다른 사람으로 대체하고 싶지 않다(I wouldn't want to replace her)면서 에이전트 번호가 어떻게 되는지(What's the number of her agent?)를 물으며 배우 채용에 대한 대화를 이어 가고 있으므로 정답은 (A)이다.

39

How does the man intend to resolve a problem?
(A) By changing a start date
(B) By doing some research
(C) By revising a film script
(D) By negotiating a salary

남자는 문제를 어떻게 해결할 계획인가?
(A) 시작 날짜를 변경해서
(B) 조사를 해서
(C) 영화 대본을 수정해서
(D) 급여를 협상해서

해설 세부 사항 관련 – 남자가 계획하는 해결 방안

중반부에 남자가 어쩌면 그 역할에 대해 돈을 더 주겠다고 제안할 수도 있다(Maybe I can offer her more money for the role)고 했으므로 정답은 (D)이다.

> **Paraphrasing** 대화의 offer her more money for the role
> → 정답의 negotiating a salary

40

What does the woman ask the man to look at?
(A) A catering contract
(B) Some flight arrangements
(C) An employment law
(D) Some lodging possibilities

여자는 남자에게 무엇을 살펴보라고 요청하는가?
(A) 음식 공급 계약서
(B) 항공편 준비
(C) 고용법
(D) 숙박 가능한 곳

어휘 catering 음식 공급[조달] lodging 숙소

해설 세부 사항 관련 – 여자가 남자에게 살펴보라고 요청하는 것

여자가 마지막 대사에서 잊지 말고 촬영 날짜에 선정된 호텔 선택 사항을 살펴보라(don't forget to look over the hotel options that have been selected for our filming dates)고 요청하고 있으므로 정답은 (D)이다.

> **Paraphrasing** 대화의 the hotel options
> → 정답의 lodging possibilities

41-43

M-Au	Hello, ⁴¹**I'm John Miller, the director of the city's Environmental Department.** May I speak with Barbara Anderson from Horizons Landscape Architecture firm?
W-Br	Speaking! How can I help you?
M-Au	⁴²**I'm pleased to inform you that your firm is being given the annual environmental sustainability award.**
W-Br	I'm so glad to hear that! ⁴³**In all our projects we're careful to use only native plants that don't require much watering.**
M-Au	⁴³**And that's been effective in helping conserve water throughout the region.**
남	안녕하세요, **저는 시 환경국장 존 밀러입니다.** 호라이즌스 조경 회사의 바바라 앤더슨과 통화할 수 있을까요?
여	전데요! 무엇을 도와드릴까요?

남	매년 수여하는 환경 지속성 상을 귀사가 받게 됐다는 소식을 알려 드리게 되어 기쁩니다.
여	정말 기쁜 소식이네요! 저희는 모든 프로젝트에서 급수가 많이 필요 없는 토종 식물만을 사용하도록 신경 쓰고 있어요.
남	바로 그 점이 지역 전체에서 물을 절약하는 데 효과가 있었어요.

어휘 landscape architecture 조경(술) sustainability 지속성 effective 효과가 있는 conserve 절약하다

41

Who is the man?
(A) A farmer
(B) A banker
(C) A restaurant owner
(D) A city official

남자는 누구인가?
(A) 농부
(B) 은행가
(C) 식당 주인
(D) 시 공무원

어휘 official 공무원, 간부

해설 전체 내용 관련 – 남자의 직업

남자가 첫 대사에서 자신을 시 환경국장(I'm John Miller, the director of the city's Environmental Department)이라고 소개하고 있으므로 정답은 (D)이다.

> **Paraphrasing** 대화의 the director of the city's Environmental Department
> → 정답의 A city official

42

Why does the man call the woman?
(A) To ask her to volunteer
(B) To hire her as a consultant
(C) To inform her about an award
(D) To collect some data

남자는 왜 여자에게 전화하는가?
(A) 그녀에게 자원봉사를 요청하기 위해
(B) 그녀를 컨설턴트로 고용하기 위해
(C) 상에 관한 소식을 전하기 위해
(D) 데이터를 수집하기 위해

해설 세부 사항 관련 – 남자가 전화하는 목적

남자가 두 번째 대사에서 매년 수여하는 환경 지속성 상을 여자의 회사가 받게 됐다는 소식을 알려 주게 되어 기쁘다(I'm pleased to inform you that your firm is being given ~ award)고 했으므로 정답은 (C)이다.

43

What strategy does the woman's company use?
(A) It keeps inventory low.
(B) It plants native species.
(C) It reduces paper waste.
(D) It maintains strong customer relations.

여자의 회사는 어떤 전략을 사용하는가?
(A) 재고를 적게 둔다.
(B) 토종을 심는다.
(C) 종이 낭비를 줄인다.
(D) 고객과 끈끈한 관계를 유지한다.

어휘 inventory 재고 reduce 줄이다 maintain 유지하다

해설 세부 사항 관련 – 여자의 회사가 사용하는 전략

여자가 두 번째 대사에서 자신들은 모든 프로젝트에서 급수가 많이 필요 없는 토종 식물만을 사용하도록 신경 쓰고 있다(In all our projects we're careful to use only native plants that don't require much watering)고 하자 남자가 바로 그 점이 지역 전체에서 물을 절약하는 데 효과가 있었다(And that's been effective in helping conserve water throughout the region)고 했으므로 토종 식물만 이용한 것이 전략임을 알 수 있다. 따라서 정답은 (B)이다.

> Paraphrasing 대화의 use only native plants
> → 정답의 plants native species

44-46

W-Br	Pierre, I checked the weather report, and **⁴⁴there's going to be continuous heavy rain throughout the week.**
M-Cn	Oh, no—**⁴⁴that'll cause problems for the employee picnic.** We rented a tent as light shelter from the afternoon sun, but now it sounds like everything's going to be drenched.
W-Br	Well, **⁴⁴we could move the event indoors.**
M-Cn	True. **⁴⁵And that wouldn't affect any of our team-building games we planned for the staff.**
W-Br	Exactly. OK, **⁴⁶so I guess booking the largest conference room is my next step.**

여	피에르, 일기 예보를 확인해 봤는데 **이번 주 내내 폭우가 계속 내린다네요.**
남	안 되는데. **그러면 직원 야유회에 문제가 생길 거예요.** 오후 햇살을 피할 시설로 텐트를 빌렸는데, 죄다 흠뻑 젖겠네요.
여	음, **행사를 실내로 옮기면 되죠.**
남	맞아요. **그렇게 하면 우리가 직원들을 위해 기획한 단합 게임에는 영향이 없겠어요.**
여	그럼요. 자, **그렇다면 제가 다음 할 일은 가장 큰 회의실을 예약하는 것 같군요.**

어휘 continuous 계속되는 shelter 대피소 drench 흠뻑 적시다 affect 영향을 미치다

44

What is causing a change in the speakers' plans?
(A) A scheduling conflict
(B) A last-minute business trip
(C) Budget reductions
(D) Upcoming weather conditions

화자들의 계획이 변경되는 원인은 무엇인가?
(A) 일정 겹침
(B) 막바지에 결정된 출장
(C) 예산 축소
(D) 다가오는 기상 상태

어휘 scheduling conflict 일정 겹침 budget 예산 reduction 축소, 절감 upcoming 다가오는, 곧 있을

해설 세부 사항 관련 – 계획의 변경 원인

여자가 첫 번째 대사에서 이번 주 내내 폭우가 계속 내린다(there's going to be continuous heavy rain throughout the week)고 하자 남자가 그러면 직원 야유회에 문제가 생길 것(that'll cause problems for the employee picnic)이라고 했고, 다시 여자가 행사를 실내로 옮기면 된다(we could move the event indoors)고 했으므로 폭우로 계획이 변경될 것임을 알 수 있다. 따라서 정답은 (D)이다.

> Paraphrasing 대화의 continuous heavy rain
> → 정답의 weather conditions

45

Which group is an event intended for?
(A) City officials
(B) Valued customers
(C) Potential investors
(D) Company employees

어떤 단체를 위해 마련된 행사인가?
(A) 시 공무원들
(B) 중요한 고객들
(C) 잠재적 투자자들
(D) 회사 직원들

어휘 potential 잠재적인, 가능성이 있는

해설 세부 사항 관련 – 행사의 대상이 되는 단체

남자가 두 번째 대사에서 그렇게 하면 자신들이 직원들을 위해 기획한 단합 게임에는 영향이 없겠다(And that wouldn't affect any of our team-building games we planned for the staff)고 했으므로 정답은 (D)이다.

46

What will the woman do next?
(A) Make a room reservation
(B) Compose an e-mail
(C) Book a music group
(D) Request a refund

여자는 다음에 무엇을 할 것인가?
(A) 방 예약
(B) 이메일 작성
(C) 음악 그룹 예약
(D) 환불 요청

해설 세부 사항 관련 – 여자가 다음에 할 일

여자가 마지막 대사에서 그렇다면 자신이 다음에 할 일은 가장 큰 회의실을 예약하는 것(so I guess booking the largest conference room is my next step)이라고 했으므로 정답은 (A)이다.

> **Paraphrasing** 대화의 booking the largest conference room → 정답의 Make a room reservation

47-49

W-Br	So Felipe, **⁴⁷it's been about three weeks since you injured your ankle playing basketball. How's it feeling?**
M-Cn	Hi, **⁴⁷Dr. Smith. It feels great! ⁴⁸My coach and I are wondering if I'll be able to play in the championship game in two weeks?** What's your professional opinion? Do you think my ankle will be healed by then?
W-Br	Hmm—Things look like they're healing, but **⁴⁹you'll need to be evaluated again before game time. Could you come back some time next week?**
여	펠리페, 농구하다가 발목을 다친 지 3주 정도 됐네요. 어때요?
남	안녕하세요, 스미스 박사님. 좋아요! 코치님과 전 2주 뒤에 있을 챔피언 결정전에 제가 출전할 수 있을지 궁금해요. 박사님의 전문적 소견은 어떠세요? 그때쯤이면 발목이 나을까요?
여	흠, 회복되고 있는 것 같기는 한데, **경기 시간 전에 다시 한 번 진단을 받아야 해요. 다음 주에 한번 오시겠어요?**
어휘	injure 부상을 입다 ankle 발목 evaluate 진단하다

47

What field does the woman most likely work in?
(A) Health care
(B) Finance
(C) Hospitality
(D) Transportation

여자는 어떤 분야에서 일하는 것 같은가?
(A) 의료
(B) 금융
(C) 접객업
(D) 교통

어휘 hospitality (주로 숙박업 등의) 접객

해설 전체 내용 관련 – 여자의 근무 분야

여자가 첫 대사에서 남자에게 농구하다가 발목을 다친 지 3주 정도 됐다(it's been about three weeks since you injured your ankle playing basketball)면서 어떤지(How's it feeling?) 묻자 남자가 스미스 박사님(Dr. Smith)이라고 부르며 좋다(It feels great!)고 대답한 것으로 보아 여자가 의료계 종사자임을 알 수 있다. 따라서 정답은 (A)이다.

48

What most likely is the man's job?
(A) Data analyst
(B) Athlete
(C) Journalist
(D) Delivery driver

남자의 직업은 무엇인 것 같은가?
(A) 데이터 분석가
(B) 운동선수
(C) 기자
(D) 배송 기사

해설 전체 내용 관련 – 남자의 직업

남자가 첫 번째 대사에서 코치와 자신은 2주 뒤에 있을 챔피언 결정전에 출전할 수 있을지 궁금하다(My coach and I are wondering if I'll be able to play in the championship game in two weeks?)고 묻고 있으므로 정답은 (B)이다.

49

What does the woman say is necessary?
(A) A revised report
(B) A bill payment
(C) A return visit
(D) A confidentiality agreement

여자는 무엇이 필요하다고 말하는가?
(A) 수정된 보고서
(B) 청구 대금 납부
(C) 재방문
(D) 비밀 유지 서약서

어휘 confidentiality 기밀성, 비밀성

해설 세부 사항 관련 – 여자가 필요하다고 말하는 것

여자가 마지막 대사에서 경기 시간 전에 다시 한 번 진단을 받아야 한다(you'll need to be evaluated again before game time)며 다음 주에 한번 오라고(Could you come back some time next week?) 요청하고 있으므로 정답은 (C)이다.

> **Paraphrasing** 대화의 come back → 정답의 A return visit

50-52

M-Au	Hello, my name's Alonso Fontana. ⁵⁰**I'd like to order a chocolate cake with strawberry sauce for an office party next Tuesday. My manager is turning 40 years old!**
W-Br	OK. Will you need candles too?
M-Au	No, we already have those.
W-Br	That'll be twenty dollars. ⁵¹**For an extra five dollars, we can deliver the cake. Would you be interested in that?**
M-Au	Well, our budget is limited.
W-Br	I understand. OK, we'll have it ready on Tuesday morning.
M-Au	Oh, also, ⁵²**I have a colleague who is allergic to nuts. That won't be a problem, will it?**
W-Br	No—we don't make any desserts with nut products in them.

남	안녕하세요, 제 이름은 알론소 폰타나예요. **다음 주 화요일 사무실 파티용으로 딸기 소스를 뿌린 초콜릿 케이크를 주문하고 싶어요. 부장님이 마흔이 되신답니다!**
여	네. 초도 필요하세요?
남	아니요, 초는 이미 있어요.
여	20달러입니다. **5달러를 더 내시면 저희가 케이크를 배달해 드려요. 관심 있으세요?**
남	어, 예산이 한정돼 있어서요.
여	이해합니다. 좋아요, 화요일 아침에 준비해 놓겠습니다.
남	아, 그리고 **견과류 알레르기가 있는 동료가 있어요. 문제가 되진 않겠죠?**
여	그럼요—저희는 견과류 제품이 들어간 디저트는 만들지 않습니다.

어휘 colleague 동료 allergic 알레르기가 있는

50

What is being celebrated next Tuesday?
(A) A birthday
(B) A retirement
(C) A work promotion
(D) A grand opening

다음 주 화요일에 무엇이 기념될 것인가?
(A) 생일
(B) 은퇴
(C) 승진
(D) 개업

해설 세부 사항 관련 – 다음 주 화요일에 기념되는 것
남자가 첫 대사에서 다음 주 화요일 사무실 파티용으로 딸기 소스를 뿌린 초콜릿 케이크를 주문하고 싶다(I'd like to order a chocolate cake with strawberry sauce for an office party next Tuesday)면서 부장님이 마흔이 된다(My manager is turning 40 years old)고 한 것으로 보아 정답은 (A)이다.

51

Why does the man say, "our budget is limited"?
(A) To request more funding
(B) To question a decision
(C) To complain about a price
(D) To decline an offer

남자는 왜 "예산이 한정돼 있어서요"라고 말하는가?
(A) 자금을 더 요청하려고
(B) 결정에 의문을 제기하려고
(C) 가격에 불만을 제기하려고
(D) 제안을 거절하려고

어휘 decline 거절하다

해설 화자의 의도 파악 – 예산이 한정돼 있다는 말의 의도
앞에서 여자가 5달러를 더 내면 케이크를 배달해 준다(For an extra five dollars, we can deliver the cake)면서, 관심 있는지(Would you be interested in that?) 묻는 말에 대한 답으로 인용문을 언급했으므로 여자의 제안을 거절하려는 의도로 볼 수 있다. 따라서 정답은 (D)이다.

52

What does the man ask the woman about?
(A) Some decorations
(B) Some ingredients
(C) A pickup location
(D) The time a store opens

남자는 여자에게 무엇에 관해 물어보는가?
(A) 장식
(B) 재료
(C) 픽업 위치
(D) 매장 여는 시간

어휘 ingredient 재료, 성분

해설 세부 사항 관련 – 남자가 여자에게 묻는 것
남자가 마지막 대사에서 견과류 알레르기가 있는 동료가 있다(I have a colleague who is allergic to nuts)며 문제가 된 않겠는지(That won't be a problem, will it?) 묻고 있으므로 정답은 (B)이다.

> **Paraphrasing** 대화의 nuts → 정답의 Some ingredients

53-55

M-Au	Noriko, we just received a call from the Croyden Company.
W-Am	Great. We've been trying to get their business. ⁵³**Did they place an order?**
M-Au	Yes, ⁵⁴**a rush request.** ^{53,54}**They want**

three thousand full-color brochures and booklets printed by Friday.

W-Am Four of our people are on vacation.

M-Au We really need to do this. ⁵⁵**What about increasing the rate we pay for overtime, just for this job?** That would motivate staff to work some extra hours.

남	노리코, 크로이든 사에서 방금 전화가 왔어요.
여	잘됐네요. 그곳과 거래하려고 애썼잖아요. **그쪽에서 주문했나요?**
남	네, 급한 요청이에요. 금요일까지 전면 컬러 안내서와 소책자 3,000부를 인쇄해 달라네요.
여	우리 직원 네 명이 휴가 중이에요.
남	이 건은 꼭 해야 해요. **이번 일에만 초과 근무 수당을 인상하는 건 어떨까요?** 그러면 직원들이 잔업할 의욕이 생길 거예요.

어휘	increase 인상하다 motivate 동기를 부여하다

53

Where do the speakers most likely work?
(A) At a bank
(B) At an advertising firm
(C) At an employment agency
(D) At a printing company

화자들은 어디에서 일하는 것 같은가?
(A) 은행
(B) 광고 회사
(C) 직업 소개소
(D) 인쇄 회사

해설 전체 내용 관련 – 화자들의 근무지

여자가 첫 번째 대사에서 그쪽에서 주문했는지(Did they place an order?) 묻자 남자가 금요일까지 전면 컬러 안내서와 소책자 3,000부를 인쇄해 달라고 했다(They want three thousand full-color brochures and booklets printed by Friday)고 대답한 것으로 보아 정답은 (D)이다.

54

Why does the woman say, "Four of our people are on vacation"?
(A) To apologize for an error
(B) To express concern about an order
(C) To suggest that a meeting be canceled
(D) To explain a company policy

여자는 왜 "우리 직원 네 명이 휴가 중이에요"라고 말하는가?
(A) 실수에 대해 사과하려고
(B) 주문에 대해 우려를 표시하려고
(C) 회의 취소를 제안하려고
(D) 회사 정책을 설명하려고

해설 화자의 의도 파악 – 직원 네 명이 휴가 중이라는 말의 의도

앞에서 남자가 급한 요청(a rush request)이라며 금요일까지 전면 컬러 안내서와 소책자 3,000부를 인쇄해 달라고 했다(They want three thousand full-color brochures and booklets printed by Friday)고 하자 자신들 직원 네 명이 휴가 중이라고 말한 것으로 보아 직원이 모두 있지도 않은데 일 처리를 제시간에 할 수 있을지 걱정을 드러내는 의도로 볼 수 있다. 따라서 정답은 (B)이다.

55

What does the man suggest offering to motivate employees?
(A) Increased time off
(B) Free meals
(C) Renovated work spaces
(D) Extra pay

남자는 직원들에게 동기를 부여하기 위해 무엇을 제안하는가?
(A) 늘어난 휴식 시간
(B) 무료 식사
(C) 개조된 작업 공간
(D) 추가 급여

해설 세부 사항 관련 – 동기 부여를 위한 남자의 제안 사항

남자가 마지막 대사에서 이번 일에만 초과 근무 수당을 인상하는 건 어떨지(What about increasing the rate we pay for overtime, just for this job?) 묻고 있으므로 정답은 (D)이다.

> **Paraphrasing** 대화의 increasing the rate we pay
> → 정답의 Extra pay

56-58 3인 대화

M-Au So, ⁵⁶**we started this initiative with the aim of increasing energy efficiency in the office. Jerome, you're leading the project. How's it going?**

M-Cn We're making progress. More efficient lighting has been installed throughout the building. And we've significantly reduced paper usage, so we're running the printers less often.

W-Br Yes, ⁵⁷**everyone seems motivated by the monthly challenge,** especially after the accounting department won gift certificates last month.

M-Au ⁵⁷**It's great that employees are responding positively to the contest.**

M-Cn Now that we've tackled some easier changes, for the next phase I think we should consider overhauling the building's heating system.

W-Br Good idea. **⁵⁸I'm going to hire a contractor to help with that.** I'll get some bids from different companies.

남1 자, 우리는 사무실의 에너지 효율을 높이겠다는 목적으로 이 계획을 시작했죠. 제롬, 프로젝트를 이끌고 있죠. 어떻게 되어 가고 있나요?

남2 진전이 있습니다. 건물 전체에 효율성이 더 높은 조명이 설치됐어요. 그리고 종이 사용량을 크게 줄여서 프린터를 덜 사용하고 있어요.

여 네, 특히 지난달 경리부에서 상품권을 획득한 후로는 **모두가 월별 도전에 의욕적으로 임하는 것 같아요.**

남1 **경쟁에 직원들 반응이 긍정적이라니 잘됐어요.**

남2 이제 쉬운 변화 몇 가지는 처리했으니 다음 단계로 건물의 난방 시스템 정비를 고려해야 할 것 같습니다.

여 좋은 생각이에요. **제가 그 일을 도와줄 계약 업체를 고용하려고 해요.** 여러 회사에서 입찰을 받을 거예요.

어휘 initiative (변화를 추구하기 위한) 계획 efficiency 효율 make progress 진전을 보이다 significantly 크게 gift certificate 상품권 positively 긍정적으로 tackle 처리하다 overhaul 정비하다 bid 입찰

56

What is the main topic of the conversation?
(A) A leadership reorganization plan
(B) An office relocation project
(C) An energy efficiency initiative
(D) An employee retirement plan

대화의 주제는 무엇인가?
(A) 지도부 개편안
(B) 사무실 이전 프로젝트
(C) 에너지 효율 계획
(D) 직원 은퇴 계획

어휘 reorganization 개편 relocation 이전

해설 전체 내용 관련 – 대화의 주제
첫 번째 남자가 첫 대사에서 자신들은 사무실의 에너지 효율을 높이겠다는 목적으로 이 계획을 시작했다(we started this initiative with the aim of increasing energy efficiency in the office)고 했고, 프로젝트를 이끌고 있는 두 번째 남자(Jerome, you're leading the project)에게 어떻게 되어 가고 있는지(How's it going?) 물으며 에너지 효율 계획에 대한 이야기를 이어 가고 있으므로 정답은 (C)이다.

57

According to the woman, what are employees responding positively to?
(A) An office relocation
(B) A revised vacation policy
(C) A monthly contest
(D) An employee survey

여자에 따르면, 직원들은 무엇에 긍정적으로 반응하고 있는가?
(A) 사무실 이전
(B) 개정된 휴가 정책
(C) 월별 경쟁
(D) 직원 설문 조사

해설 세부 사항 관련 – 여자가 말하는 직원들이 긍정적으로 반응하는 것
여자가 첫 번째 대사에서 모두가 월별 도전에 의욕적으로 임하는 것 같다(everyone seems motivated by the monthly challenge)고 했고, 첫 번째 남자가 경쟁에 직원들 반응이 긍정적이라니 잘됐다(It's great that employees are responding positively to the contest)고 한 것으로 보아 정답은 (C)이다.

> Paraphrasing 대화의 the monthly challenge
> → 정답의 A monthly contest

58

What does the woman plan to do?
(A) Lease some equipment
(B) Hire a contractor
(C) Pause item production
(D) Research some competitors

여자는 무엇을 하려고 계획하는가?
(A) 장비 임대
(B) 계약 업체 고용
(C) 품목 생산 중지
(D) 경쟁 업체 조사

어휘 competitor 경쟁 업체

해설 세부 사항 관련 – 여자의 계획
여자가 마지막 대사에서 자신이 그 일을 도와줄 계약 업체를 고용하려고 한다(I'm going to hire a contractor to help with that)는 계획을 밝히고 있으므로 정답은 (B)이다.

59-61 3인 대화

M-Cn ⁵⁹Thanks to both of you for coming out this morning. I've purchased the land on the other side of the river to expand my vegetable crops, and I'd like to build a bridge to drive my tractor across the water.

W-Am That's definitely the type of building project we do. ⁵⁹,⁶⁰We'll start today by measuring the span of the river and the height and slope of the riverbank. ⁶⁰Right, Adriana?

W-Br ⁶⁰Right. Now, do you have a specific location in mind? If not, we can make that decision ourselves. ⁶¹That area by the oak tree looks nice and flat. Let's walk over there.

남	오늘 아침에 나와 주신 두 분 모두 고마워요. 제가 채소 수확량을 늘리려고 강 건너편 땅을 샀는데, 트랙터를 몰고 물을 건널 수 있도록 다리를 짓고 싶어요.
여1	저희가 하는 건설 프로젝트가 바로 그런 유형입니다. **오늘은 강의 폭, 그리고 강둑의 높이와 경사부터 먼저 측정하겠습니다. 그렇죠, 아드리아나?**
여2	**맞아요.** 자, 생각해 두신 특정한 위치가 있나요? 없으면, 저희가 직접 결정할 수 있습니다. **참나무 옆에 있는 장소가 평평하고 좋아 보이네요.** 저쪽으로 걸어가요.

어휘	purchase 사다 expand 늘리다 crop 수확량 span 폭 slope 경사 specific 특정한 decision 결정

59

Where is the conversation most likely taking place?
(A) At a zoo
(B) At a beach
(C) At a park
(D) At a farm

대화는 어디에서 이루어지고 있는 것 같은가?
(A) 동물원
(B) 해변
(C) 공원
(D) 농장

해설 전체 내용 관련 – 대화의 장소
남자가 첫 대사에서 오늘 아침에 나와 주신 두 분 모두 고맙다(Thanks to both of you for coming out this morning)고 했고, 자신이 채소 수확량을 늘리려고 강 건너편 땅을 샀는데, 트랙터를 몰고 물을 건널 수 있도록 다리를 짓고 싶다(I've purchased the land on the other side of the river to expand my vegetable crops, and I'd like to build a bridge to drive my tractor across the water)고 하자 첫 번째 여자가 오늘은 강의 폭, 그리고 강둑의 높이와 경사부터 먼저 측정하겠다(We'll start today by measuring the span of the river and the height and slope of the riverbank)고 한 것으로 보아 화자들이 공사를 위한 준비로 농장에 나와 있음을 알 수 있다. 따라서 정답은 (D)이다.

60

What are the women going to do today?
(A) Take some measurements
(B) Pour some concrete
(C) Calculate a price estimate
(D) Clear some trees

여자들은 오늘 무엇을 할 것인가?
(A) 측정
(B) 콘크리트 타설
(C) 가격 견적 계산
(D) 나무 베기

어휘 price estimate 가격 견적

해설 세부 사항 관련 – 여자들이 오늘 할 일
첫 번째 여자가 첫 번째 대사에서 오늘은 강의 폭, 그리고 강둑의 높이와 경사부터 먼저 측정하겠다(We'll start today by measuring the span

of the river and the height and slope of the riverbank)고 한 후, 두 번째 여자에게 확인(Right, Adriana?)을 하자 두 번째 여자가 맞다(Right)고 호응하고 있으므로 정답은 (A)이다.

Paraphrasing	대화의 measuring the span of the river and the height and slope of the riverbank → 정답의 Take some measurements

61

What does Adriana point out about some land?
(A) It is dry.
(B) It is flat.
(C) It is sandy.
(D) It is surrounded by a fence.

아드리아나는 땅에 대해 무엇이라고 언급하는가?
(A) 건조하다.
(B) 평평하다.
(C) 모래투성이다.
(D) 울타리로 둘러싸여 있다.

해설 세부 사항 관련 – 아드리아나가 땅에 대해 언급하는 것
첫 번째 여자가 두 번째 여자인 아드리아나에게 작업에 대해 확인을 하자 참나무 옆에 있는 장소가 평평하고 좋아 보인다(That area by the oak tree looks nice and flat)는 점을 언급하고 있으므로 정답은 (B)이다.

62-64 대화 + 출발 정보

M-Cn	Hi. **62I wanted to check the status of my flight—I'm supposed to be in Chicago to deliver a lecture tonight.**
W-Br	Could I please see your boarding pass?
M-Cn	Sure, it's right here.
W-Br	Thank you. **63Unfortunately your flight is delayed by an hour due to a late connecting flight.**
M-Cn	OK, that's fine. I was just worried it might be canceled.
W-Br	To make up for the delay, **64the airline's offering all passengers on the flight a free meal voucher for any restaurant in the food court.**
M-Cn	**64Oh, that's a nice surprise!**

남	안녕하세요. **제 항공편 상태를 확인하고 싶어요. 오늘 밤 시카고에서 강의를 해야 하거든요.**
여	탑승권 좀 보여 주시겠어요?
남	네, 여기 있습니다.
여	감사합니다. **아쉽게도 연결 항공편이 늦어지는 바람에 고객님 비행기가 한 시간 지연됩니다.**

남	네, 괜찮습니다. 취소될까 봐 그게 걱정이었어요.
여	지연에 대한 보상으로 항공사에서 탑승객 전원에게 푸드 코트에 있는 어떤 식당이든 이용할 수 있는 무료 식사권을 제공하고 있습니다.
남	오, 뜻밖에 좋은 소식이네요!

| 어휘 | status 상태 boarding pass 탑승권 due to ~ 때문에
connecting flight 연결 항공편 make up for 보상하다 |

Flight	Status
63Flight 105	Delayed
Flight 451	On time
Flight 57	Canceled
Flight 23	Boarding

항공편	상태
63105편	지연
451편	정시
57편	취소
23편	탑승

62

Why is the man traveling?
(A) To view a property
(B) To participate in an interview
(C) To give a talk
(D) To visit family

남자는 왜 여행하는가?
(A) 부동산을 보려고
(B) 인터뷰에 참여하려고
(C) 강연하려고
(D) 가족을 방문하려고

어휘 property 부동산

해설 세부 사항 관련 – 남자가 여행하는 이유
남자가 첫 대사에서 자신의 항공편 상태를 확인하고 싶다(I wanted to check the status of my flight)면서 오늘 밤 시카고에서 강의를 해야 한다(I'm supposed to be in Chicago to deliver a lecture tonight)고 했으므로 정답은 (C)이다.

| Paraphrasing | 대화의 deliver a lecture → 정답의 give a talk |

63

Look at the graphic. Which flight did the man book?
(A) Flight 105
(B) Flight 451
(C) Flight 57
(D) Flight 23

시각 정보에 의하면, 남자는 어느 비행기를 예약했는가?
(A) 105편
(B) 451편
(C) 57편
(D) 23편

해설 시각 정보 연계 – 남자가 예약한 비행기
여자가 두 번째 대사에서 아쉽게도 연결 항공편이 늦어지는 바람에 남자의 비행기가 한 시간 지연된다(Unfortunately your flight is delayed by an hour due to a late connecting flight)고 했고, 출발 정보에 지연 상태의 비행기는 105편으로 나와 있으므로 정답은 (A)이다.

64

Why is the man surprised?
(A) A refund will be issued.
(B) A departure gate has changed.
(C) A meal will not be served on a flight.
(D) A voucher will be provided.

남자는 왜 놀라는가?
(A) 환불해 줄 예정이다.
(B) 출발 게이트가 변경되었다.
(C) 기내식이 제공되지 않을 것이다.
(D) 바우처가 제공될 것이다.

해설 세부 사항 관련 – 남자가 놀라는 이유
여자가 마지막 대사에서 항공사가 탑승객 전원에게 푸드 코트에 있는 어떤 식당이든 이용할 수 있는 무료 식사권을 제공하고 있다(the airline's offering all passengers on the flight a free meal voucher for any restaurant in the food court)고 알리자 남자가 뜻밖에 좋은 소식(Oh, that's a nice surprise!)이라고 놀람을 표현하고 있으므로 정답은 (D)이다.

| Paraphrasing | 대화의 offering all passengers on the flight a free meal voucher
→ 정답의 A voucher will be provided |

65-67 대화 + 막대그래프

W-Br	Mark, as you know, 65**sales of our pet food aren't as good as we'd hoped. I want to change our advertising strategy.** Do you have a breakdown of advertising costs for different types of media?
M-Au	Sure. This graph shows how many dollars we'll have to spend to reach 1,000 people.
W-Br	Social media seems like the obvious choice, but that's how we've been advertising. We can cheaply advertise to a lot of people that way, but they aren't buying.

M-Au	Exactly. **[66]I think we're better off spending sixteen dollars per thousand people.** It's pricier, but research shows that those people are more likely to buy the product.
W-Br	**[66]OK. [67]Please ask Paul to start drafting a new ad.**

여	마크, 알다시피 **반려동물 사료 판매가 우리가 기대했던 것만큼 좋지 않아요. 광고 전략을 바꿨으면 해요.** 다양한 유형의 미디어에 대한 광고 비용을 분석한 내역을 가지고 있나요?
남	그럼요. 이 그래프는 우리가 천 명에게 노출되려면 돈을 얼마나 써야 하는지 보여 줍니다.
여	소셜 미디어는 확실한 선택지 같지만, 우리가 광고해 온 방식이 바로 그거잖아요. 그 방식으로 많은 사람을 대상으로 저렴하게 광고할 수 있지만, 사람들이 사지를 않아요.
남	말씀대로예요. **제 생각에는 천 명당 16달러를 쓰는 편이 더 나은 듯해요.** 더 비싸긴 해도, 연구에 따르면 그 사람들이 제품을 살 가능성이 더 높다고 하네요.
여	**좋아요. 폴에게 새 광고 시안에 착수하라고 요청하세요.**

어휘	breakdown (분석을 통한) 내역, 명세 obvious 확실한 better off (형편이) 더 나은 be likely to ~할 것 같다

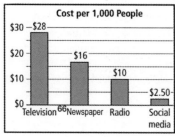

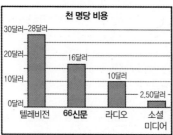

65

Why does the woman want to change an advertising strategy?
(A) A competitor has revised a prototype.
(B) Some costs are too high.
(C) A project was delayed.
(D) A product is not selling well.

여자는 왜 광고 전략을 바꾸고 싶어하는가?
(A) 경쟁사가 시제품을 수정했다.
(B) 비용이 너무 비싸다.
(C) 프로젝트가 지연되었다.
(D) 제품이 잘 팔리지 않는다.

278

어휘 prototype 시제품

해설 세부 사항 관련 – 여자가 광고 전략을 바꾸려는 이유

여자가 첫 대사에서 반려동물 사료 판매가 자신들이 기대했던 것만큼 좋지 않다(sales of our pet food aren't as good as we'd hoped)면서 광고 전략을 바꿨으면 한다(I want to change our advertising strategy)고 했으므로 정답은 (D)이다.

Paraphrasing	대화의 sales of our pet food aren't as good as we'd hoped → 정답의 A product is not selling well

66

Look at the graphic. What type of media do the speakers decide to use for advertising?
(A) Television
(B) Newspaper
(C) Radio
(D) Social media

시각 정보에 의하면, 화자들은 광고에 어떤 종류의 미디어를 사용하기로 결정하는가?
(A) 텔레비전
(B) 신문
(C) 라디오
(D) 소셜 미디어

해설 시각 정보 연계 – 광고에 사용할 미디어

남자가 마지막 대사에서 자신의 생각에는 천 명당 16달러를 쓰는 편이 더 나은 듯하다(I think we're better off spending sixteen dollars per thousand people)고 제안하자 여자가 좋다(OK)고 동의했다. 따라서 천 명당 16달러를 쓰기로 결정했다는 것을 알 수 있는데, 막대그래프에 천 명당 16달러를 쓰는 미디어는 신문으로 나와 있으므로 정답은 (B)이다.

67

What will the man most likely do?
(A) Hire an extra employee
(B) Conduct a customer survey
(C) Prepare a slideshow
(D) Contact a colleague

남자는 무엇을 할 것 같은가?
(A) 추가 직원 채용
(B) 고객 설문 조사 실시
(C) 슬라이드 쇼 준비
(D) 동료에게 연락

해설 세부 사항 관련 – 남자가 할 일

여자가 마지막 대사에서 남자에게 폴에게 새 광고 시안에 착수하라고 요청하라(Please ask Paul to start drafting a new ad)고 부탁하고 있으므로 정답은 (D)이다.

Paraphrasing	대화의 ask Paul → 정답의 Contact a colleague

W-Am **68It's great how much tourism has increased in our city this year. So many visitors to the area are coming in to ask us about things to do here!**

M-Au Absolutely. **69Ever since that cooking show premiered on television last year, tourists are asking us where to find local restaurants featured on the show.** The food map we're making of the downtown area will be really popular.

W-Am Yes, and it's almost ready to go to the printer. But—I noticed an error. **70The place at the corner of Second and Fielding Streets has moved to a bigger location north of the city.**

M-Au Oh, too bad. **70OK, I'll take it off.**

여 올해 우리 시 관광객이 얼마나 늘었는지 엄청나요. 이 지역에 오는 수많은 방문객들이 우리한테 와서 여기에서 할 수 있는 일들이 뭔지 묻고 있어요!

남 물론이죠. 지난해 그 요리 프로그램이 텔레비전에 처음 방영된 이후로, 관광객들이 그 프로그램에 나온 지역 식당이 어디에 있는지 우리에게 묻고 있어요. 우리가 만들고 있는 중심가 음식 지도는 정말 인기가 많을 거예요.

여 네, 게다가 인쇄업체에 넘길 준비가 거의 다 됐어요. 그런데 제가 오류를 발견했어요. 2번가와 필딩 가 모퉁이에 있는 음식점은 도시 북쪽에 있는 더 큰 장소로 옮겼어요.

남 저런. 알겠어요, 그건 제가 지울게요.

어휘 premiere 처음 방영하다, 초연하다 take off 지우다

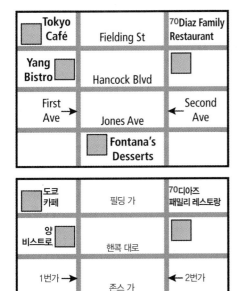

Tokyo Café	Fielding St	70Diaz Family Restaurant
Yang Bistro	Hancock Blvd	
First Ave →	Jones Ave	← Second Ave
	Fontana's Desserts	

도쿄 카페	필딩 가	70디아즈 패밀리 레스토랑
양 비스트로	핸콕 대로	
1번가 →	존스 가	← 2번가
	폰타나스 디저트	

68

Where do the speakers most likely work?

(A) At a television studio
(B) At a cooking school
(C) At a train station
(D) At a tourism office

화자들은 어디에서 일하는 것 같은가?

(A) 텔레비전 스튜디오
(B) 요리 학교
(C) 기차역
(D) 관광청

해설 전체 내용 관련 – 화자들의 근무지

여자가 첫 대사에서 남자에게 올해 자신들의 시 관광객이 엄청 늘었다(It's great how much tourism has increased in our city this year)며 이 지역에 오는 수많은 방문객들이 자신들한테 와서 이곳에서 할 수 있는 일들이 무엇인지 묻고 있다(So many visitors to the area are coming in to ask us about things to do here!)고 한 것으로 보아 정답은 (D)이다.

69

According to the man, what happened last year?

(A) A television show premiered.
(B) An advertising campaign was launched.
(C) A community garden was started.
(D) A local festival was canceled.

남자에 따르면, 지난해에 무슨 일이 있었는가?

(A) 텔레비전 쇼가 처음 방영되었다.
(B) 광고 캠페인이 시작되었다.
(C) 마을 텃밭이 시작되었다.
(D) 지역 축제가 취소되었다.

해설 세부 사항 관련 – 지난해에 있었던 일

남자가 첫 번째 대사에서 지난해 그 요리 프로그램이 텔레비전에 처음 방영된 이후로, 관광객들이 그 프로그램에 나온 지역 식당이 어디에 있는지 자신들에게 묻고 있다(Ever since that cooking show premiered on television last year, tourists are asking us where to find local restaurants featured on the show)고 했으므로 정답은 (A)이다.

> **Paraphrasing** 대화의 that cooking show
> → 정답의 A television show

70

Look at the graphic. Which business will be removed from the map?

(A) Tokyo Café
(B) Diaz Family Restaurant
(C) Yang Bistro
(D) Fontana's Desserts

TEST 10

시각 정보에 의하면, 어떤 업체가 지도에서 삭제될 것인가?

(A) 도쿄 카페
(B) 디아즈 패밀리 레스토랑
(C) 양 비스트로
(D) 폰타나스 디저트

해설 시각 정보 연계 – 지도에서 삭제될 업체

여자가 마지막 대사에서 2번가와 필딩 가 모퉁이에 있는 음식점은 도시 북쪽에 있는 더 큰 장소로 옮겼다(The place at the corner of Second and Fielding Streets has moved to a bigger location north of the city)고 하자 남자가 그건 자신이 지우겠다(OK, I'll take it off)고 했고, 지도에 2번가와 필딩 가 모퉁이에 있는 음식점은 디아즈 패밀리 레스토랑으로 나와 있으므로 정답은 (B)이다.

PART 4

71-73 관광 정보

W-Am **71Welcome, everyone, to Watanabe Nature Park**. I'm happy you all joined us for our morning hiking tour. **72I recommend stopping at the top of the mountain for bird-watching**. We may even be able to see some hawks or eagles flying overhead. You can return to the Visitor Center at your own pace, but **73please be back by twelve noon so we can all have lunch together at the picnic tables**.

여러분, 와타나베 자연공원에 잘 오셨습니다. 여러분 모두 아침 하이킹 투어에 함께해 주셔서 기쁩니다. **새 관찰을 위해 산 정상에서 멈추시기를 권합니다**. 어쩌면 머리 위로 날아가는 매나 독수리를 볼 수 있을지도 모르거든요. 각자 속도에 맞춰 방문자 안내소로 돌아가시면 됩니다만, **피크닉 테이블에서 점심을 다 같이 먹을 수 있도록 정오 12시까지는 돌아오세요.**

어휘 be able to ~할 수 있다 pace 속도

71

Where does the tour take place?

(A) At an art museum
(B) At an amusement park
(C) At a zoo
(D) At a nature park

투어는 어디에서 이루어지는가?

(A) 미술관
(B) 놀이공원
(C) 동물원
(D) 자연공원

해설 전체 내용 관련 – 투어 장소

화자가 초반부에 여러분, 와타나베 자연공원에 잘 오셨습니다(Welcome, everyone, to Watanabe Nature Park)라고 환영 인사를 했으므로 정답은 (D)이다.

72

What activity does the speaker recommend?

(A) Renting a bicycle
(B) Taking photographs
(C) Watching birds
(D) Buying souvenirs

화자는 어떤 활동을 권하는가?

(A) 자전거 대여
(B) 사진 찍기
(C) 새 관찰
(D) 기념품 구입

어휘 souvenir 기념품

해설 세부 사항 관련 – 화자가 권하는 활동

화자가 중반부에 새 관찰을 위해 산 정상에서 멈추기를 권한다(I recommend ~ for bird-watching)고 했으므로 정답은 (C)이다.

> Paraphrasing 담화의 bird-watching
> → 정답의 Watching birds

73

Why should the listeners meet the speaker at noon?

(A) To eat lunch
(B) To return some equipment
(C) To take a group photo
(D) To see a performance

청자들은 왜 정오에 화자를 만나야 하는가?

(A) 점심을 먹기 위해
(B) 장비를 반환하기 위해
(C) 단체 사진을 찍기 위해
(D) 공연을 보기 위해

어휘 equipment 장비 performance 공연

해설 세부 사항 관련 – 청자들이 정오에 화자를 만나야 하는 이유

화자가 마지막에 피크닉 테이블에서 점심을 다 같이 먹을 수 있도록 정오 12시까지는 돌아오라(please be back by twelve noon so we can all have lunch together at the picnic tables)고 요청했으므로 정답은 (A)이다.

> Paraphrasing 담화의 have lunch → 정답의 eat lunch

74-76 전화 메시지

M-Cn Hi, Ms. Wang. **74It's Richard, your real estate agent. 75I'm supposed to take pictures of your house today for your online listing, but I can't get in. I know we usually keep the key in a special place by the front door,** but we did have a cleaning crew come yesterday. I have the number of the company, so I'll call them after this. While I wait to gain access to the house, **76I'll start taking photos** of the exterior. I'll send them to you. Please decide which ones you want to use for your listing.

안녕하세요, 왕 선생님. 부동산 중개인 리처드입니다. 온라인에 올리는 용도로 오늘 선생님 댁 사진을 찍어야 하는데 들어갈 수가 없네요. 우리가 보통 열쇠를 현관 옆 특별한 곳에 보관하는 건 알지만, 어제 저희가 청소팀을 불렀네요. 저한테 회사 번호가 있으니까 바로 전화해 보겠습니다. 댁에 들어가기까지 기다리는 동안, 외부 사진부터 찍겠습니다. 사진을 보내 드릴게요. 올리는 데 쓸 사진을 결정해 주세요.

어휘 real estate agent 부동산 중개인   list 목록에 올리다

74

Who is the speaker?

(A) A real estate agent
(B) A construction worker
(C) An interior decorator
(D) A building inspector

화자는 누구인가?

(A) 부동산 중개인
(B) 건설 작업자
(C) 실내 장식가
(D) 건물 점검원

해설 전체 내용 관련 – 화자의 직업

화자가 초반부에 부동산 중개인 리처드(It's Richard, your real estate agent)라고 자신을 소개하고 있으므로 정답은 (A)이다.

75

Why does the speaker say, "we did have a cleaning crew come yesterday"?

(A) To emphasize an accomplishment
(B) To disagree with a decision
(C) To suggest an explanation
(D) To complain about a cost

화자는 왜 "어제 저희가 청소팀을 불렀네요"라고 말하는가?

(A) 성과를 강조하려고
(B) 결정에 반대하려고
(C) 설명하려고
(D) 비용에 대해 불평하려고

어휘 emphasize 강조하다   accomplishment 성과

해설 화자의 의도 파악 – 어제 저희가 청소팀을 불렀다는 말의 의도

앞에서 온라인에 올리는 용도로 오늘 청자의 집 사진을 찍어야 하는데 들어갈 수가 없다(I'm supposed to take pictures of your house today for your online listing, but I can't get in)며, 자신들이 보통 열쇠를 현관 옆 특별한 곳에 보관하는 건 안다(I know we usually keep the key in a special place by the front door)고 말한 후, 인용문을 언급했으므로 열쇠가 있어야 할 장소에 없는 이유를 설명하려는 의도로 한 말임을 알 수 있다. 따라서 정답은 (C)이다.

76

What does the speaker tell the listener to do?

(A) Choose some photos
(B) Check a schedule
(C) Submit a payment
(D) Apply for a permit

화자는 청자에게 무엇을 하라고 말하는가?

(A) 사진 선택
(B) 일정 확인
(C) 대금 납부
(D) 허가증 신청

어휘 permit 허가(증)

해설 세부 사항 관련 – 화자가 청자에게 하라고 말하는 것

화자가 마지막에 외부 사진부터 찍겠다(I'll start taking photos of the exterior)고 했고, 사진을 보내주겠다(I'll send them to you)면서 올리는 데 쓸 사진을 결정해 달라(Please decide which ones you want to use for your listing)고 요청했으므로 정답은 (A)이다.

> **Paraphrasing** 담화의 decide which ones
> → 정답의 Choose some photos

77-79 담화

W-Am OK, everyone. As you know, [77]**the music festival is starting in two hours, and we still have a lot to do before then.** [78]**The food vendors should be arriving soon. I'll have Maria direct them to their proper locations.** I'm going to help the musicians with their equipment and sound tests. [79]**In case of rain, remember, our plan is to hold the event indoors, in the building over there.** But, really, we haven't had a day this nice in a while.

자, 여러분. 알다시피 2시간 뒤면 음악제가 시작되는데 그 전에 아직 할 일이 산더미예요. 식품 판매상들이 곧 도착할 겁니다. 마리아에게 적절한 장소로 안내하라고 하겠습니다. 저는 음악가들이 장비와 음향을 테스트하는 일을 도울게요. 명심하세요. 비가 올 경우에는 실내에서 행사를 진행할 계획입니다. 저기 있는 건물이에요. 하지만 정말이지 한동안 날씨가 이렇게 좋았던 적이 없었네요.

어휘 vendor 판매상, 노점상   proper 적절한

77

What are the listeners preparing for?

(A) A sports competition
(B) A music festival
(C) A company picnic
(D) A harvest fair

청자들은 무엇을 준비하고 있는가?

(A) 스포츠 대회
(B) 음악제
(C) 회사 야유회
(D) 추수제

어휘 competition 대회 fair 축제

해설 세부 사항 관련 – 청자들이 준비하는 것

화자가 초반부에 2시간 뒤면 음악제가 시작되는데 그 전에 아직 할 일이 산더미(the music festival is starting in two hours, and we still have a lot to do before then)라고 청자들에게 말하고 있는 것으로 보아 정답은 (B)이다.

78

What will Maria be responsible for?
(A) Setting out extra chairs
(B) Collecting event tickets
(C) Putting up some decorations
(D) Showing vendors where they need to be

마리아는 무엇을 책임질 것인가?
(A) 여분의 의자 놓기
(B) 행사 티켓 징수하기
(C) 장식 걸기
(D) 판매상에게 있어야 할 위치 안내하기

해설 세부 사항 관련 – 마리아가 책임질 것

화자가 중반부에 식품 판매상들이 곧 도착할 것(The food vendors should be arriving soon)이라며 마리아에게 적절한 장소로 안내하라고 하겠다(I'll have Maria direct them to their proper locations)고 마리아가 할 일을 알리고 있으므로 정답은 (D)이다.

> Paraphrasing 담화의 direct them to their proper locations → 정답의 Showing vendors where they need to be

79

What does the speaker mean when she says, "we haven't had a day this nice in a while"?
(A) Some tests may not be necessary.
(B) She is excited about an outing with friends.
(C) An event will probably not need to be moved.
(D) The weather has been unusually cold recently.

화자가 "한동안 날씨가 이렇게 좋았던 적이 없었네요"라고 말할 때 무엇을 의미하는가?
(A) 테스트가 필요 없을 수도 있다.
(B) 친구들과의 야유회에 들떴다.
(C) 아마 행사를 옮기지 않아도 될 것이다.
(D) 최근에 날씨가 유난히 추웠다.

어휘 outing 야유회, (당일) 여행

해설 화자의 의도 파악 – 한동안 날씨가 이렇게 좋았던 적이 없었다는 말의 의도

앞에서 비가 올 경우에는 실내에서 행사를 진행할 계획(In case of rain, remember, our plan is to hold the event indoors)이며, 저기 있는 건물에서(in the building over there)라고 말한 후 인용문을 언급했으므로 장소를 바꾸지 않아도 될 것임을 알리려는 의도임을 알 수 있다. 따라서 정답은 (C)이다.

80-82 연설

M-Au **80On behalf of Travers International, I'd like to thank the news reporters who've joined me this afternoon, as I announce our latest global initiative.** Travers is conscious of the impact our ships and tankers have on the environment. **81,82As a leader in the ocean shipping industry, we're promising to reduce our waste emissions by twenty percent in the next five years. 82This will significantly decrease the amount of carbon released into the oceans. I'm very proud of this initiative.** I believe it will impact the environment in a positive way.

트래버스 인터내셔널을 대표해 오늘 오후 당사의 최근 글로벌 계획을 발표하는 자리에 함께해 주신 기자 여러분께 감사드립니다. 트래버스는 선박과 유조선이 환경에 미치는 영향을 인식하고 있습니다. **해운업계 선두 주자로서 당사는 향후 5년 안에 폐기물 배출을 20%까지 줄일 것을 약속합니다. 이것으로 바다로 방출되는 탄소량은 현저히 줄어들 것입니다. 저는 이번 계획에 자부심을 느낍니다.** 이것이 환경에 긍정적인 방향으로 영향을 미치리라 믿습니다.

어휘 on behalf of ~을 대표하여 initiative (변화를 추구하기 위한) 계획 conscious 인식하는 impact 영향; 영향을 미치다 tanker 유조선 reduce 줄이다 emission 배출 significantly 현저히 decrease 줄이다 carbon 탄소 release 배출하다 positive 긍정적인

80

Where does the speech most likely take place?
(A) At a wellness fair
(B) At an employee luncheon
(C) At a training seminar
(D) At a press conference

연설은 어디에서 이루어지는 것 같은가?
(A) 건강 박람회
(B) 직원 오찬
(C) 연수 세미나
(D) 기자 회견

해설 전체 내용 관련 – 담화의 장소

화자가 초반부에 트래버스 인터내셔널을 대표해 오늘 오후 회사의 최근 글로벌 계획을 발표하는 자리에 함께해 준 기자들에게 감사한다(On behalf of Travers International, I'd like to thank the news reporters who've joined me this afternoon, as I announce our latest global initiative)고 했으므로 담화가 이루어지고 있는 장소는 기자 회견장임을 알 수 있다. 따라서 정답은 (D)이다.

81

What industry does the speaker work in?
(A) Fishing
(B) Tourism
(C) Shipping
(D) Health care

화자는 어떤 업계에서 일하는가?
(A) 어업
(B) 관광업
(C) 해운업
(D) 의료업

해설 전체 내용 관련 – 화자의 근무 업계

화자가 중반부에 해운업계 선두 주자로서 자신들은 향후 5년 안에 폐기물 배출을 20%까지 줄일 것을 약속한다(As a leader in the ocean shipping industry, we're promising ~ in the next five years)고 했으므로 정답은 (C)이다.

82

What does the speaker say he is proud of?
(A) A hiring process
(B) An environmental initiative
(C) Funding innovative research
(D) Supporting local businesses

화자는 무엇에 자부심을 느낀다고 말하는가?
(A) 채용 절차
(B) 환경 계획
(C) 혁신 연구 자금 지원
(D) 지역 업체 지원

해설 세부 사항 관련 – 화자가 자부심을 느낀다고 말하는 것

화자가 중반부에 해운업계 선두 주자로서 자신들은 향후 5년 안에 폐기물 배출을 20%까지 줄일 것을 약속한다(As a leader in the ocean shipping industry, we're promising to reduce our waste emissions by twenty percent in the next five years)고 했고, 이것으로 바다로 방출되는 탄소량은 현저히 줄어들 것(This will significantly decrease the amount of carbon released into the oceans)이라며 이번 계획에 자부심을 느낀다(I'm very proud of this initiative)고 했으므로 정답은 (B)이다.

> **Paraphrasing** 담화의 this initiative
> → 정답의 An environmental initiative

83-85 전화 메시지

> W-Am Good afternoon. **[83]I'm calling from Blue Tern Press to ask if you'd be willing to write an introduction for a new edition of the eighteenth-century novel *Hillsbrook Hall*.** As you know, **[84]another version of the manuscript—handwritten and edited by the author—was recently discovered.** We'd like to print a new edition of *Hillsbrook Hall* based on the newly discovered

> manuscript. As an expert in eighteenth-century literature, we'd like you to write the introduction. **[85]If you're interested, call me back as soon as possible to talk about a contract for this project.**

> 안녕하세요. 블루 턴 프레스입니다. 18세기 소설 〈힐스브룩 홀〉 신판의 서문을 쓰실 의향이 있는지 여쭤보려고 전화드렸습니다. 아시겠지만, 저자가 손으로 쓰고 편집한 또 다른 원고가 최근 발견되었습니다. 저희가 새로 발견된 원고를 바탕으로 〈힐스브룩 홀〉 신판을 출간하려고 합니다. 18세기 문학 전문가로서 선생님이 서문을 써 주셨으면 합니다. 생각이 있으시면 가능한 한 빨리 전화 주셔서 이 프로젝트 계약에 대해 이야기를 나눴으면 합니다.

> **어휘** edition (간행물의) 판 manuscript 원고 edit 편집하다 expert 전문가 literature 문학

83

What industry does the speaker most likely work in?
(A) Publishing
(B) Advertising
(C) Film
(D) Hospitality

화자는 어떤 업계에서 일하는 것 같은가?
(A) 출판
(B) 광고
(C) 영화
(D) 접객

해설 전체 내용 관련 – 화자의 근무 업계

화자가 초반부에 18세기 소설 〈힐스브룩 홀〉 신판의 서문을 쓸 의향이 있는지 물어보려고 블루 턴 프레스에서 전화했다(I'm calling from Blue Tern Press to ask if you'd be willing to write an introduction for a new edition of the eighteenth-century novel *Hillsbrook Hall*)고 한 것으로 보아 정답은 (A)이다.

84

What does the speaker say recently happened?
(A) A book was made into a film.
(B) A new executive was hired.
(C) A manuscript was found.
(D) An anniversary celebration was held.

화자는 최근에 무슨 일이 있었다고 말하는가?
(A) 책이 영화로 제작되었다.
(B) 새로운 임원이 채용되었다.
(C) 원고가 발견되었다.
(D) 기념일 축하 행사가 열렸다.

어휘 executive 임원 anniversary 기념일

해설 세부 사항 관련 – 화자가 최근에 일어났다고 말하는 것

화자가 중반부에 저자가 손으로 쓰고 편집한 또 다른 원고가 최근 발견되었다(another version of the manuscript—handwritten and edited by the author—was recently discovered)고 했으므로 정답은 (C)이다.

85

Why does the speaker want the listener to call her back?
(A) To finalize a design
(B) To confirm a guest list
(C) To discuss a contract
(D) To develop a timeline

화자는 왜 청자가 자신에게 다시 전화하기를 원하는가?
(A) 디자인을 마무리하려고
(B) 손님 목록을 확정하려고
(C) 계약에 관해 논의하려고
(D) 일정을 짜려고

해설 세부 사항 관련 – 청자가 전화하기를 바라는 이유

화자가 마지막에 생각이 있으면 가능한 한 빨리 전화해 줘서 이 프로젝트 계약에 대해 이야기를 나눴으면 한다(If you're interested, call me back as soon as possible to talk about a contract for this project)고 한 것으로 보아 정답은 (C)이다.

86-88 회의 발췌

M-Au Good afternoon, everyone. I've recently announced I'm stepping down as board secretary for Winfield Paper Company, and as you know, Ji-Min Choi will be taking over my role. To make the transition easier, **86I'm making a list of what the secretary role entails.** This will also allow me to document the changes that we've wanted to make to this role. For example, **87remember in October the board discussed storing meeting minutes in a secure, online location?** I'm including that information. **88After I leave, I'll be available to assist Ji-Min with any questions that may come up.**

안녕하세요, 여러분. 최근에 제가 윈필드 페이퍼 컴퍼니 이사회 비서직에서 물러난다고 발표했죠. 아시겠지만 최지민 씨가 제 역할을 맡게 됩니다. 인수인계가 더 수월하도록 **제가 비서 역할에 필요한 업무들을 목록으로 만들고 있습니다.** 이렇게 하면 우리가 이 역할에서 바꾸기를 원했던 사항들도 기록할 수 있을 겁니다. 예를 들어, **10월에 이사회에서 회의록을 안전한 온라인 장소에 저장하는 문제에 대해 논의했는데, 기억하세요?** 제가 그 정보도 포함시키고 있습니다. **제가 떠난 후 궁금한 게 생기면 제가 지민 씨를 도울 수 있을 겁니다.**

어휘 step down 물러나다 transition 인수인계 entail 필요하다 minute 의사록 secure 안전한

86

What is the speaker currently working on?
(A) Listing some job duties
(B) Correcting errors in a report
(C) Updating an equipment manual
(D) Designing a new company logo

화자는 현재 어떤 일을 하고 있는가?
(A) 직무 목록 작성
(B) 보고서 오류 수정
(C) 장비 설명서 업데이트
(D) 새 회사 로고 디자인

해설 세부 사항 관련 – 화자가 현재 하고 있는 일

화자가 중반부에 자신이 비서 역할에 필요한 업무들을 목록으로 만들고 있다(I'm making a list of what the secretary role entails)고 했으므로 정답은 (A)이다.

87

What did the board talk about in October?
(A) Purchasing some software
(B) Changing a meeting time
(C) Keeping some documents online
(D) Opening a new branch location

이사회는 10월에 무엇에 관해 논의했는가?
(A) 소프트웨어 구입
(B) 회의 시간 변경
(C) 문서 온라인 보관
(D) 신규 지사 개점

해설 세부 사항 관련 – 이사회가 10월에 논의한 것

화자가 후반부에 10월에 이사회에서 회의록을 안전한 온라인 장소에 저장하는 문제에 대해 논의한 것을 기억하는지(remember in October the board discussed storing meeting minutes in a secure, online location?) 묻고 있으므로 정답은 (C)이다.

88

What will the speaker be available to do?
(A) Issue a press release
(B) Assist a colleague
(C) Create a progress report
(D) Revise a client contract

화자는 무엇을 할 수 있을 것인가?
(A) 보도 자료 배포
(B) 동료 지원
(C) 경과 보고서 작성
(D) 고객 계약서 수정

어휘 press release 보도 자료   colleague 동료   progress report 경과 보고서

해설 세부 사항 관련 – 화자가 할 수 있는 것

화자가 마지막에 자신이 떠난 후 궁금한 게 생기면 자신이 지민 씨를 도울 수 있을 것(After I leave, I'll be available to assist Ji-Min with any questions that may come up)이라고 했으므로 정답은 (B)이다.

> **Paraphrasing** 담화의 assist Ji-Min
> → 정답의 Assist a colleague

89-91 담화

M-Cn Hello! **89If you're watching this online video, then you've recently purchased Karoo, a state-of-the-art software program that manages different collections of data.** **90Karoo increases the efficiency of how companies share information— both internally with staff and externally with clients.** In this video, I'll walk you through the steps to setting up the program. **91Before getting started, I suggest reopening this video on a device other than the one where you're installing the program.** That way, you can use the chat function on this Web site to contact a live agent if you need to.

안녕하세요! **여러분이 이 온라인 동영상을 보고 계신다면, 다양한 데이터 수집을 관리하는 최첨단 소프트웨어 프로그램인 카루를 최근에 구입하셨을 겁니다.** **카루는 기업이 내부로는 직원과, 외부로는 고객과 정보를 공유하는 방식의 효율성을 높입니다.** 이 동영상에서는 제가 여러분께 프로그램 설정 단계를 안내해 드리겠습니다. **시작하기 전에 프로그램을 설치할 장치가 아닌 다른 장치에서 이 동영상을 다시 여시기 바랍니다.** 이렇게 하면 이 웹사이트의 채팅 기능을 사용해 필요할 경우 실시간 응대 직원과 연락할 수 있습니다.

어휘 state-of-the-art 최첨단의   efficiency 효율   internally 내부에   externally 외부에   device 장치   function 기능

89

What did the listener buy?
(A) A software program
(B) A tablet computer
(C) An advertising service
(D) A video camera

청자는 무엇을 샀는가?
(A) 소프트웨어 프로그램
(B) 태블릿 컴퓨터
(C) 광고 서비스
(D) 비디오카메라

해설 세부 사항 관련 – 청자가 산 것

화자가 초반부에 청자들이 이 온라인 동영상을 보고 있다면, 다양한 데이터 수집을 관리하는 최첨단 소프트웨어 프로그램인 카루를 최근에 구입했

을 것(If you're watching this online video, then you've recently purchased Karoo, a state-of-the-art software program that manages different collections of data)이라고 했으므로 정답은 (A)이다.

90

According to the speaker, how will the product improve a business?
(A) It will make sharing information easier.
(B) It will ensure security.
(C) It will help attract more clients.
(D) It will collect customer data.

화자에 따르면, 제품이 기업을 어떻게 개선할 것인가?
(A) 정보를 더 쉽게 공유할 수 있게 한다.
(B) 보안을 보장한다.
(C) 고객을 더 많이 유치하는 데 도움이 된다.
(D) 고객 데이터를 수집한다.

어휘 ensure 보장하다

해설 세부 사항 관련 – 제품이 기업을 개선하는 방법

화자가 중반부에 카루는 기업이 내부로는 직원과, 외부로는 고객과 정보를 공유하는 방식의 효율성을 높인다(Karoo increases the efficiency of how companies share information—both internally with staff and externally with clients)고 했으므로 정보 공유가 더 수월해짐을 알 수 있다. 따라서 정답은 (A)이다.

> **Paraphrasing** 담화의 increases the efficiency of how companies share information
> → 정답의 make sharing information easier

91

What does the speaker recommend?
(A) Writing down a serial number
(B) Using a second device
(C) Restarting a machine
(D) Conducting a quality test

화자는 무엇을 권하는가?
(A) 일련번호 기록
(B) 두 번째 장치 사용
(C) 기계 재가동
(D) 품질 검사 시행

해설 세부 사항 관련 – 화자의 권고 사항

화자가 후반부에 시작하기 전에 프로그램을 설치할 장치가 아닌 다른 장치에서 이 동영상을 다시 열기 바란다(Before getting started, I suggest reopening this video on a device other than the one where you're installing the program)고 권하고 있으므로 정답은 (B)이다.

> **Paraphrasing** 담화의 reopening this video on a device other than the one → 정답의 Using a second device

> M-Au **⁹²I think going into the new year, we should focus more of our budget on late-night programming. Local news ends at eleven o'clock, and we could follow that with a 90-minute talk show.** Viewers these days are staying up much later in search of something funny to watch. We just need a great host, and advertisers will be fighting for this time slot. ⁹³**It's usually a real challenge to find new talent,** but a comedy club just opened up in the arts district. Now, changing topics, I'd like to share some good news. ⁹⁴**A few of you have been chosen to receive the director's award for outstanding leadership. Please stand when I call your names.**

새해로 접어들면서 심야 프로그램에 예산을 더 집중해야 할 것 같습니다. 지역 뉴스는 11시에 끝나니까 이어서 90분짜리 토크 쇼를 해도 되고요. 요즘 시청자들은 재미있는 볼거리를 찾으려고 훨씬 늦게까지 깨어 있죠. 우리한테 훌륭한 진행자만 있으면 돼요. 그러면 광고주들이 서로 이 시간대를 얻으려고 다툴 겁니다. 대개 새로운 인재를 찾는 것은 정말 어려운 일이지만, 예술 지구에 코미디 클럽이 막 문을 열었답니다. 이제 화제를 바꿔, 좋은 소식을 나누고 싶습니다. 여러분 중 몇 사람이 탁월한 리더십으로 간부상 수상자로 선정되었습니다. 제가 호명하면 일어서 주세요.

어휘 stay late 늦게까지 깨어 있다 time slot 시간대 talent 인재 outstanding 탁월한

92

Where does the speaker most likely work?
(A) At a television station
(B) At a publishing company
(C) At an advertising agency
(D) At a tour company

화자는 어디에서 일하는 것 같은가?
(A) 텔레비전 방송국
(B) 출판사
(C) 광고 대행사
(D) 여행사

해설 전체 내용 관련 – 화자의 근무지

화자가 초반부에 새해로 접어들면서 심야 프로그램에 예산을 더 집중해야 할 것 같다(I think going into the new year, we should focus more of our budget on late-night programming)며 지역 뉴스는 11시에 끝나니까 이어서 90분짜리 토크 쇼를 해도 된다(Local news ends at eleven o'clock, and we could follow that with a 90-minute talk show)고 한 것으로 보아 정답은 (A)이다.

93

Why does the speaker say, "a comedy club just opened up in the arts district"?
(A) To express surprise about a timeline
(B) To complain about a location
(C) To suggest a solution to a problem
(D) To apologize for a mistake

화자는 왜 "예술 지구에 코미디 클럽이 막 문을 열었답니다"라고 말하는가?
(A) 일정에 대해 놀라움을 표현하려고
(B) 장소에 대해 불평하려고
(C) 문제에 대한 해결책을 제안하려고
(D) 실수에 대해 사과하려고

해설 화자의 의도 파악 – 예술 지구에 코미디 클럽이 막 문을 열었다는 말의 의도

앞에서 청자가 대개 새로운 인재를 찾는 것은 정말 어려운 일(It's usually a real challenge to find new talent)이라고 말한 뒤, 인용문을 언급한 것으로 보아 인재를 코미디 클럽에서 찾을 수도 있으니 인재 찾는 문제에 대한 해결 방안을 제시하려는 의도로 볼 수 있다. 따라서 정답은 (C)이다.

94

What will the speaker do next?
(A) Announce award winners
(B) Distribute invitations
(C) Play a video
(D) Ask for volunteers

화자는 다음에 무엇을 할 것인가?
(A) 수상자 발표
(B) 초대장 배포
(C) 동영상 재생
(D) 지원자 요청

어휘 distribute 배포하다

해설 세부 사항 관련 – 화자가 다음에 할 일

화자가 마지막에 여러분 중 몇 사람이 탁월한 리더십으로 간부상 수상자로 선정되었다(A few of you have been chosen to receive the director's award for outstanding leadership)며 화자가 호명하면 일어서 달라(Please stand when I call your names)고 한 것으로 보아 정답은 (A)이다.

> **Paraphrasing** 담화의 call your names
> → 정답의 Announce award winners

W-Am Do you like trying new things? Then Samantha's new snack delivery service is for you. **95Each month, our team assembles a variety of snacks from different parts of the world and delivers them to your door.** Best of all, **96starting in January, we're packaging our snacks in cooled containers.** This refrigerated shipping allows us to offer a bigger selection of foods. Just go to the Web site and choose how many months you'd like to sign up for. Right now, we're offering a special promotion. To qualify, **97just subscribe for at least three months, and you'll receive an extra box for free!**

새로운 것을 즐겨 시도하시나요? 그렇다면 사만다의 새로운 간식 배송 서비스가 여러분을 위해 있습니다. **매달 저희 팀은 세계 각지에서 온 다양한 간식들을 모아 문 앞까지 배달합니다.** 무엇보다도 **1월부터 간식을 냉각 용기에 포장할 것입니다.** 냉장 배송으로 저희는 더욱 다양하게 구비된 음식을 제공할 수 있습니다. 웹사이트로 가서 몇 개월 동안 구독할지 선택하세요. 지금 특별 판촉을 진행하고 있습니다. 자격을 얻으려면 **최소 3개월만 구독하세요. 추가로 한 상자를 무료로 받습니다!**

어휘 assemble 모으다 refrigerate 냉장하다 promotion 판촉 subscribe for (서비스를) 구독하다

Subscription Options

| 1 month $10.00 | 2 months $18.00 |
| 973 months $25.00 | 6 months $45.00 |

구독 옵션

| 1개월 10달러 | 2개월 18달러 |
| 973개월 25달러 | 6개월 45달러 |

95
What is being advertised for monthly delivery?
(A) Office supplies
(B) Potted plants
(C) Best-selling books
(D) International snacks

무엇이 월간 배송으로 광고되고 있는가?
(A) 사무용품
(B) 화분
(C) 베스트셀러 도서
(D) 해외 간식

해설 전체 내용 관련 – 월간 배송으로 광고되고 있는 것
화자가 초반부에 매달 자신의 팀은 세계 각지에서 온 다양한 간식들을 모아 문 앞까지 배달한다(Each month, our team assembles a variety of snacks from different parts of the world and delivers them to your door)고 했으므로 정답은 (D)이다.

> **Paraphrasing** 담화의 snacks from different parts of the world → 정답의 International snacks

96
What does the speaker say will be available in January?
(A) Weekend delivery
(B) Free gift wrapping
(C) Refrigerated shipping
(D) Online tracking

화자는 1월에 무엇을 이용할 수 있을 것이라고 말하는가?
(A) 주말 배송
(B) 무료 선물 포장
(C) 냉장 배송
(D) 온라인 추적

해설 세부 사항 관련 – 화자가 1월에 이용 가능하다고 말하는 것
화자가 중반부에 1월부터 간식을 냉각 용기에 포장할 것(starting in January, we're packaging our snacks in cooled containers)이라고 했으므로 정답은 (C)이다.

97
Look at the graphic. What is the smallest subscription amount needed to receive an extra box?
(A) $10.00
(B) $18.00
(C) $25.00
(D) $45.00

시각 정보에 의하면, 추가로 한 상자를 받는 데 필요한 최소 구독 금액은 얼마인가?
(A) 10달러
(B) 18달러
(C) 25달러
(D) 45달러

해설 시각 정보 연계 – 추가로 한 상자를 받는 데 필요한 최소 구독 금액
화자가 마지막에 최소 3개월만 구독하면 추가로 한 상자를 무료로 받는다(just subscribe for at least three months, and you'll receive an extra box for free)고 제안하므로 구독 옵션에서 3개월 구독을 찾으면 정답은 (C)이다.

M-Au **98Thanks for joining this online workshop on making candles. Today, we'll focus on scented candles.** As always, please write questions in the chat box, and we'll answer them as we go. Good news—99**we've just enabled automatic captioning, so if you'd like to use this new feature, please click the "Captions" button on the screen.** Finally, 100**if you'd like to see more content like this, please consider subscribing to our Web site for five dollars a month.** We release exclusive video content each week for our subscribers. Let's get started with the first step—choosing a color.

초 만들기 온라인 워크숍에 함께해 주셔서 감사합니다. 오늘은 향초에 중점을 두고 진행하겠습니다. 늘 그렇듯이 채팅창에 질문을 적으시면 진행하면서 답변하겠습니다. 반가운 소식입니다. 조금 전 자동 자막이 가능하도록 만들었으니 이 새 기능을 사용하시려면 화면의 '자막' 버튼을 클릭하세요. 마지막으로 이런 콘텐츠를 더 보고 싶으시면 한 달 5달러에 저희 웹사이트 구독을 고려해 보세요. 구독자를 위해 매주 독점 동영상 콘텐츠를 공개합니다. 첫 번째 단계, 색상 선택부터 시작합시다.

어휘 scented 향이 있는 exclusive 독점의 subscriber 구독자

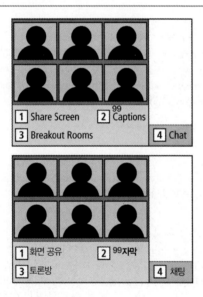

98

What is the topic of the workshop?
(A) Arranging flowers
(B) Making candles
(C) Painting pictures
(D) Decorating cakes

워크숍의 주제는 무엇인가?
(A) 꽃꽂이
(B) 초 만들기
(C) 그림 그리기
(D) 케이크 장식하기

해설 전체 내용 관련 – 워크숍의 주제
화자가 초반부에 초 만들기 온라인 워크숍에 함께해 주어 고맙다(Thanks for joining this online workshop on making candles)고 했고, 오늘은 향초에 중점을 두고 진행하겠다(Today, we'll focus on scented candles)고 했으므로 정답은 (B)이다.

99

Look at the graphic. Which button represents a new feature of the software program?
(A) Button 1
(B) Button 2
(C) Button 3
(D) Button 4

시각 정보에 의하면, 어떤 버튼이 소프트웨어 프로그램의 새로운 기능을 표시하는가?
(A) 버튼 1
(B) 버튼 2
(C) 버튼 3
(D) 버튼 4

해설 시각 정보 연계 – 소프트웨어 프로그램의 새로운 기능을 표시하는 버튼
화자가 중반부에 조금 전 자동 자막이 가능하도록 만들었으므로 이 새 기능을 사용하려면 화면의 '자막' 버튼을 클릭하라(we've just enabled automatic captioning, so if you'd like to use this new feature, please click the "Captions" button on the screen)고 했고, 컴퓨터 화면에 자막은 2번 버튼으로 나와 있으므로 정답은 (B)이다.

100

What does the speaker say is a benefit of subscribing?
(A) Additional video content
(B) Individual instruction
(C) Discounted supplies
(D) Networking opportunities

화자는 구독 혜택이 무엇이라고 말하는가?
(A) 추가 동영상 콘텐츠
(B) 개인별 강의
(C) 할인 비품
(D) 인적 네트워크 형성 기회

어휘 individual 개인별의 opportunity 기회

해설 세부 사항 관련 – 화자가 구독 혜택이라고 말하는 것
화자가 후반부에 이런 콘텐츠를 더 보고 싶으면 한 달 5달러에 자신의 웹사이트 구독을 고려해 보라(if you'd like to see more content like this, please consider subscribing to our Web site for five dollars a month)고 한 것으로 보아 정답은 (A)이다.

Paraphrasing 담화의 more content like this
→ 정답의 Additional video content